THE NEW
AMERICAN
COMMENTARY

An Exegetical and Theological
Exposition of Holy Scripture

THE NEW
AMERICAN
COMMENTARY

Volume
11

JOB

Robert L. Alden

BROADMAN
&HOLMAN
PUBLISHERS

Nashville, Tennessee

© Copyright 1993 • Broadman & Holman Publishers
All rights reserved
ISBN: 978-08054-0110-0
Dewey Decimal Classification: 222
Subject Heading: BIBLE. O.T. JOB
Printed in the United States of America
12 11 10 09 08 07 10 9 8 7 6 5 4 3

To the Students of Denver Seminary

who for twenty-five years listened
to me teach Job and honed my
understanding of the book with their
countless helpful observations

Editors' Preface

God's Word does not change. God's world, however, changes in every generation. These changes, in addition to new findings by scholars and a new variety of challenges to the gospel message, call for the church in each generation to interpret and apply God's Word for God's people. Thus, THE NEW AMERICAN COMMENTARY is introduced to bridge the twentieth and twenty-first centuries. This new series has been designed primarily to enable pastors, teachers, and students to read the Bible with clarity and proclaim it with power.

In one sense THE NEW AMERICAN COMMENTARY is not new, for it represents the continuation of a heritage rich in biblical and theological exposition. The title of this forty-volume set points to the continuity of this series with an important commentary project published at the end of the nineteenth century called AN AMERICAN COMMENTARY, edited by Alvah Hovey. The older series included, among other significant contributions, the outstanding volume on Matthew by John A. Broadus, from whom the publisher of the new series, Broadman & Holman Publishers, partly derives its name. The former series was authored and edited by scholars committed to the infallibility of Scripture, making it a solid foundation for the present project. In line with this heritage, all NAC authors affirm the divine inspiration, inerrancy, complete truthfulness, and full authority of the Bible. The perspective of the NAC is unapologetically confessional and rooted in the evangelical tradition.

Since a commentary is a fundamental tool for the expositor or teacher who seeks to interpret and apply Scripture in the church or classroom, the NAC focuses on communicating the theological structure and content of each biblical book. The writers seek to illuminate both the historical meaning and contemporary significance of Holy Scripture.

In its attempt to make a unique contribution to the Christian community, the NAC focuses on two concerns. First, the commentary emphasizes how each section of a book fits together so that the reader becomes aware of the theological unity of each book and of Scripture as a whole. The writers, however, remain aware of the Bible's inherently rich variety. Second, the NAC is produced with the conviction that the Bible primarily belongs to the church. We believe that scholarship and the academy provide an indispensable foundation for biblical understanding and the service of Christ, but the editors and authors of this series have attempted to communicate the findings of their research in a manner that will build up the whole body of Christ. Thus, the commentary concentrates on theological exegesis, while providing practical, applicable exposition.

THE NEW AMERICAN COMMENTARY's theological focus enables the reader to see the parts as well as the whole of Scripture. The biblical books vary in content, context, literary type, and style. In addition to this rich variety, the editors and authors recognize that the doctrinal emphasis and use of the biblical books differs in various places, contexts, and cultures among God's people. These factors, as well as other concerns, have led the editors to give freedom to the writers to wrestle with the issues raised by the scholarly community surrounding each book and to determine the appropriate shape and length of the introductory materials. Moreover, each writer has developed the structure of the commentary in a way best suited for expounding the basic structure and the meaning of the biblical books for our day. Generally, discussions relating to contemporary scholarship and technical points of grammar and syntax appear in the footnotes and not in the text of the commentary. This format allows pastors and interested laypersons, scholars and teachers, and serious college and seminary students to profit from the commentary at various levels. This approach has been employed because we believe that all Christians have the privilege and responsibility to read and seek to understand the Bible for themselves.

Consistent with the desire to produce a readable, up-to-date commentary, the editors selected the *New International Version* as the standard translation for the commentary series. The selection was made primarily because of the NIV's faithfulness to the original languages and its beautiful and readable style. The authors, however, have been given the liberty to differ at places from the NIV as they develop their own translations from the Greek and Hebrew texts.

The NAC reflects the vision and leadership of those who provide oversight for Broadman & Holman Publishers, who in 1987 called for a new commentary series that would evidence a commitment to the inerrancy of Scripture and a faithfulness to the classic Christian tradition. While the commentary adopts an "American" name, it should be noted some writers represent countries outside the United States, giving the commentary an international perspective. The diverse group of writers includes scholars, teachers, and administrators from almost twenty different colleges and seminaries, as well as pastors, missionaries, and a layperson.

The editors and writers hope that THE NEW AMERICAN COMMENTARY will be helpful and instructive for pastors and teachers, scholars and students, for men and women in the churches who study and teach God's Word in various settings. We trust that for editors, authors, and readers alike, the commentary will be used to build up the church, encourage obedience, and bring renewal to God's people. Above all, we pray that the NAC will bring glory and honor to our Lord who has graciously redeemed us and faithfully revealed himself to us in his Holy Word.

SOLI DEO GLORIA
The Editors

Author's Preface

Experience has shown that few people read commentaries from beginning to end. Most often they use them as reference books. When they encounter a problem text or discover that English translations differ widely on the rendering of a given verse, they turn to that point in the commentary for some illumination. Sometimes when studying through a book they use the commentary on a more regular basis.

Many commentaries on the poetical books of the Old Testament deal with large blocks of material rather than with individual verses. In this volume every verse receives a separate paragraph, in which I have tried to answer questions that I imagine inquirers might ask. Where there are marked differences in English Bibles, I endeavor to explain the basis for those differences and to give a reason why one is preferred over another. I make many observations about rare words, the infrequency of their occurrence, and the tentative nature of their translation. I caution the reader against dogmatism in those matters where uncertainty shrouds the interpretation. On more than a few occasions I have had to confess considerable dissatisfaction with even the best of options. On other occasions two readings appear equally sensible, responsible, supportable, and felicitous even though their meanings are quite different.

While every verse is addressed, not every word receives treatment. Nor do I cite or consider every observation, even by the major commentaries. The number of stones to be turned is endless. Rabbit tracks can lead far afield. Just consider the number of journal articles devoted to individual words, or the one volume of nearly three hundred pages covering only chaps. 29–31,[1] or the two-volume commentary by Word, which, when complete, will contain nearly a million words,[2] or the 159 sermons of John Calvin on this book. Every commentator must be highly selective and on each verse make a few decisions about what to include and dozens of decisions about what to exclude. Undoubtedly some major contributions and insights of others have been excluded, while some extraneous or trivial comments are included. For scratching where the readers did not itch or not

---

[1] A. R. Ceresko, *Job 29-31 in the Light of Northwest Semitic* (Rome: Biblical Institute Press, 1980).

[2] D. J. A. Clines, *Job 1-20*, WBC, 17 (Dallas: Word, 1989).

scratching where they did, I can only ask for patience, forgiveness, and understanding.

Apart from the prologue, epilogue, and brief introductions to the speakers, Job is poetry, and as such enjoys the capabilities and suffers under the limitations of that genre. It means that the second line of a verse often repeats with different words the thought of the first line. It means that the author was limited to three or four major words per line; if more words are necessary to make his thought complete the translators supply them, thus masking the crispness and cryptic nature of the original. Poetry always uses a larger vocabulary than prose for the simple reason that the common words do not carry the shades of meanings that the author wants. The net result is fewer words but rarer words. For stylistic reasons the syntax is often irregular and sometimes quite convoluted. So, given the lack of articles, pronouns, and particles, or, on the contrary, lines cluttered with these words, translating demands creativity, artistry, and what the Germans call *sprachegefühl*, "a feel for the language."

Most commentaries on Job go immediately to the question of Job's suffering and the problem of evil. They do not wrestle with the particulars of the text. But just as a building is made of many bricks, so the Book of Job is the sum total of all its words and verses. We commentary writers must not examine the individual details to the extent that we fail to see the whole, but too many see only the whole while ignoring the beauty, minor messages, and challenge of understanding the distinctive parts.

Of those relatively few commentaries that focus on the particulars of the text and struggle to determine the meaning of phrases that do not flow easily, some have a high view of the original Hebrew text, while others are quick to emend or assume there is an error. This commentary takes a high view of the Masoretic Text, that is, the one published by the Bible Society in Stuttgart.

For over a thousand years people have been trying to improve their understanding of the text of the Bible. The Jewish scholars who invented the vowel system and "pointed" the consonants so they could be pronounced by those less familiar with Hebrew were among the first to struggle with the difficulties of Job. These Masoretes themselves had a system of footnotes they called "readings" (*Qere*), which were corrections of the "writing" (*Kethib*), often amounting merely to spelling variants but sometimes affecting the meaning quite radically (as in 13:15).

To these very old and semiofficial "corrections" the editors of the Hebrew Bible have added a few more. During the heyday of German critical scholarship, some verses were completely rewritten; and editors rearranged speeches, stanzas, and individual verses, sometimes eliminating words, verses, and even stanzas. Job was almost unrecognizable.[3]

Happily that day is past as more and more scholars seek to make sense of text as it stands, on the assumption that neither the original author nor any subsequent editor or copyist would intentionally introduce confusion or nonsense. There is more respect currently for the old maxim that the difficult reading is preferred, knowing that those transmitting the text tried to facilitate rather than complicate matters.

I am grateful to Denver Seminary in several ways. I thank my colleagues and the board of trustees at the Seminary for granting a sabbatical leave to complete this project. In addition and in a general way I acknowledge my debt to a generation of students and others in Sunday School classes and assorted contexts who have plodded with me through Job. Every question they asked and every observation they made has contributed to the sharpening of my focus on Job. I want them to come to appreciate the book as a part of God's inspired Word, something worthy of study in and of itself, a piece of literature from antiquity that still describes in elegant pictures and lofty words a dimension of God's truth that often gets lost in contemporary Christianity.

As I often pray when I invoke God's blessing before starting a class, I thank God for the unnamed scribes, rabbis, monks, and priests who copied and recopied the Bible; for the clerics and scholars who made the first translations into Aramaic, Syriac, Greek, and Latin; for those who preserved in handwritten form and later in print, often at the risk of their lives, copies of God's Word; for those patient compilers of dictionaries, lexicons, and concordances; for archaeologists and epigraphers who have dug in the dust of the Middle East and labored over fragments of clay tablets; and for the countless brilliant minds who have focused their attention on this part of the Old Testament and written articles, monographs, commentaries, sermons, and lessons on Job. Ultimately I thank God for the Holy Spirit, who inspired the biblical author and who has superintended the transmission of the text from centuries before Christ to now, nearly two millennia later, and for his promise and presence to lead into all truth those who diligently seek it (John 16:13).

—Robert L. Alden

---

[3] In English an example of the extreme rearrangement of the text is M. Buttenwieser, *The Book of Job* (New York: Macmillan, 1922). For a more recent reconstruction see M. P. Reddy, "The Book of Job—A Reconstruction," *ZAW* 90 (1978): 59-94.

Abbreviations

Bible Books

Gen	Isa	Luke
Exod	Jer	John
Lev	Lam	Acts
Num	Ezek	Rom
Deut	Dan	1,2 Cor
Josh	Hos	Gal
Judg	Joel	Eph
Ruth	Amos	Phil
1,2 Sam	Obad	Col
1,2 Kgs	Jonah	1,2 Thess
1,2 Chr	Mic	1,2 Tim
Ezra	Nah	Titus
Neh	Hab	Phlm
Esth	Zeph	Heb
Job	Hag	Jas
Ps (pl. Pss)	Zech	1,2, Pet
Prov	Mal	1,2,3 John
Eccl	Matt	Jude
Song	Mark	Rev

Commonly Used Sources

AB	Anchor Bible
ABD	*Anchor Bible Dictionary*
AEL	*Ancient Egyptian Literature,* M. Lichtheim
AJSL	*American Journal of Semitic Languages and Literatures*
AnBib	*Analecta Biblica*
ANET	*Ancient Near Eastern Texts,* ed. J. B. Pritchard
AOAT	Alter Orient und Altes Testament
AOTS	*Archaeology and Old Testament Study,* ed. D. W. Thomas
ATD	Das Alte Testament Deutsch
BARev	*Biblical Archaeology Review*
BASOR	*Bulletin of the American Schools of Oriental Research*

BBR	*Bulletin of Biblical Research*
BDB	F. Brown, S. R. Driver, and C. A. Briggs, *Hebrew and English Lexicon of the Old Testament*
BHK	R. Kittel, *Biblia hebraica*
BHS	*Biblia hebraica stuttgartensia*
Bib	*Biblica*
BKAT	Biblischer Kommentar: Altes Testament
BSac	*Bibliotheca Sacra*
BSC	Bible Study Commentary
BT	*Bible Translator*
BurH	*Buried History*
BZAW	Beihefte zur ZAW
CAH	*Cambridge Ancient History*
CB	Cambridge Bible for Schools and Colleges
CBC	Cambridge Bible Commentary
CBQ	*Catholic Biblical Quarterly*
CHAL	*Concise Hebrew and Aramaic Lexicon,* ed. W. L. Holladay
CTR	*Criswell Theological Review*
DD	*Dor le Dor*
DNTT	*Dictionary of New Testament Theology*
DOTT	*Documents from Old Testament Times,* ed. D. W. Thomas
EBC	Expositor's Bible Commentary
Ebib	*Etudes bibliques*
EvQ	*Evangelical Quarterly*
FB	Forschung zur Bibel
FOTL	Forms of Old Testament Literature
GBH	*Grammar of Biblical Hebrew,* P. Joüon, T. Muraoka
GKC	*Gesenius' Hebrew Grammar,* ed. E. Kautzsch, trans. A. E. Cowley
HAT	Handbuch zum Alten Testament
HDR	Harvard Dissertations in Religion
Her	Hermeneia
HKAT	Handkommentar zum Alten Testament
HSM	Harvard Semitic Monographs
HT	Helps for Translators
HUCA	*Hebrew Union College Annual*
IB	*Interpreter's Bible*
IBC	Interpretation: A Bible Commentary for Teaching and Preaching

IBHS	B. H. Waltke and M. O'Connor, *Introduction to Biblical Hebrew Syntax*
ICC	International Critical Commentary
IDB	*Interpreter's Dictionary of the Bible*, ed. G. A. Buttrick et al.
IDBSupp	*IDB* Supplementary Volume
IEJ	*Israel Exploration Journal*
IES	Israel Exploration Society
ISBE	*International Standard Bible Encyclopedia*, rev. ed. G. W. Bromiley
ITC	International Theological Commentary
JAOS	*Journal of the American Oriental Society*
JBL	*Journal of Biblical Literature*
JEA	*Journal of Egyptian Archaeology*
JETS	*Journal of the Evangelical Theological Society*
JNES	*Journal of Near Eastern Studies*
JSOR	*Journal of the Society for Oriental Research*
JSOT	*Journal for the Study of the Old Testament*
JSOTSup	JSOT—Supplement Series
JSS	*Journal of Semitic Studies*
JTS	*Journal of Theological Studies*
JTSNS	*Journal of Theological Studies, New Series*
KAT	Kommentar zum Alten Testament
KB	Koehler and W. Baumgartner, *Lexicon in Veteris Testamenti libros*
LCC	Library of Christian Classics
LLAVT	*Lexicon Linguae Aramaicae Veteris Testamenti*
LXX	Septuagint
NICOT	New International Commentary on the Old Testament
NJPS	New Jewish Publication Society Version
OTL	Old Testament Library
Or	*Orientalia*
PCB	*Peake's Commentary on the Bible*, ed. M. Black and H. H. Rowley
POTT	*Peoples of Old Testament Times*, ed. D. J. Wiseman
RB	*Revue biblique*
RevExp	*Review and Expositor*
RSR	Recherches de science religieuse
SBLD	Society of Biblical Literature Dissertation Series
SBT	Studies in Biblical Theology
SR	*Studies in Religion/Sciences religieuses*

Contents

Job

INTRODUCTION
1. Structure
2. Date
3. Authorship
4. Geography and Culture
5. Canonicity
6. Translations
7. Literary Style
8. Theology
9. Purpose

INTRODUCTION

Many scholars draw parallels between the Book of Job and certain literary works of the ancient Near East, from Egypt to Mesopotamia. And even though there may have been many parallels and imitations since Job, the book stands alone both in the Bible and in the world of literature. Nowhere else is the struggle of an innocent sufferer to understand the surrounding tragedy so long, so intense, and so penetrating. Between Job and his four "friends," the problem of Job's misery received attention from every possible angle. Yet there was no resolution, no answer, no solution until God spoke at the end of the book. His was the last word in all senses of the word "last."

1. Structure

The structure of the Book of Job as it appears in the received text is obvious and provokes only minimal disagreement. Virtually all outlines of the book agree in general, and a glance at the "Contents" page will give the broadest indication of the structure. Detailed outlines are at the beginning of each chapter.

The book has a prose prologue of two chapters and a prose epilogue of less than one chapter. The rest of the book consists of speeches by Job's three friends interspersed with speeches of response from Job himself, four speeches by a fourth defender of tradition, and then two speeches by Yahweh with brief responses by Job.

In the prose prologue all the major players except Elihu appear. First there is Job, the dominant character in the book, with his enormous wealth, his impeccable piety, and his happy family. Next is Yahweh, the Lord, who sits in his heavenly counsel chambers with his angels reporting to him. The Satan[1] is a major character in the prologue, but he does not appear again in the book. He was the one who inflicted on Job material losses, the death of his children, and the wretched skin disease that landed him on the ash heap, ignored by friends and scorned by the local rabble. Job's wife makes a brief appearance in chap. 2 but, like the Satan, is not heard from again, not even in the epilogue. At the very end of the prologue Job's three friends—Eliphaz the Temanite, Bildad the Shuhite, and Zophar the Naamathite—appear on the scene, ostensibly to comfort Job. In fact, they accuse, irritate, and antagonize him.

Chapter 3, Job's curse on his day of birth, is a kind of buffer between the prologue and the debate section. It is not clear to whom Job spoke those words, but the jussive verbs of the first part suggest they were addressed to God. As 2:13 makes clear, this chapter contains the only words spoken by anyone during the first week that Job's friends were by his side.

If complete, the large central debate cycle would have three speeches from Eliphaz, three from Bildad, three from Zophar, and nine from Job (4:1–27:23). The pattern holds until chap. 27, where the expected third speech of Zophar is lacking. The structure within the speeches is not regular, but the speeches follow recurring themes and some generalized pat-

---

[1] In Job the name of the adversary always has the definite article, and so I use it throughout. It means "the accuser" or "the adversary." Outside Job the term שָׂטָן occurs as a reference to this supernatural arch enemy of God and his people in 1 Chr 21:1 (without the article) and Zech 3:1-2 (with the article). It is used of adversaries other than the Evil One in Num 22:22 (the angel sent to oppose Balaam); 1 Sam 29:4; 1Kgs 5:4[18]; 11:14,23,25; Ps 109:6 (without the article). The LXX uses either σαταν or ἐπίβουλος in Samuel and Kings, διάβολος in Chronicles, Zechariah, Psalms, and Job (διαβολος is also used in Esth 7:4; 8:1 for צָר, "distress," and צֹרֵר, "enemy"). In the NT this opponent of God and his people is also known generally as either σαταν or διαβολος (see Matt 4:10-11; Rev 12:9; 20:2). There σαταν only rarely occurs without the article. See the article "Satan, Beelzebul, Devil, Exorcism," in *DNTT* (Grand Rapids: Zondervan, 1978), 3:468-77.

terns. The overarching message of the three friends is that suffering is the consequence of sin. The complementary assumption is that prosperity is the reward of right living. Arguing back from these premises in view of Job's plight, the friends could only agree that Job must be a sinner and in need of repentance. This diagnosis led them to the certain conclusion (in their thinking) that Job's sin must be secret, since no one could pinpoint any transgression. It also led them to charge Job with compounding his guilt by asserting and avowing his innocence.

To support their position, the friends repeatedly rebuked Job, reasoned with him from a world full of examples, challenged him to repent, and often grew angry and frustrated in the face of his obstinacy. The advice they gave would have been fitting in many cases, but it was wrong in Job's case.

In the course of his speeches Job turned to God in complaint or petition. These responses are most common in the first cycle and least common in the third.[2]

Major debate about the organization of the book centers on chaps. 3–27, where several schemes have been proposed to identify Zophar's speech mixed in with words attributed to Job (see the commentary at those points). The easiest solution, and one that respects the canonical shape of the book, is to understand that Zophar simply had nothing to say. So Job "continued his discourse" (27:1) for another chapter. The "wisdom chapter" (chap. 28) serves as chap. 3 did, to isolate the debate cycle from the rest of the book.[3] Whether to credit it to Job, the author of Job, or someone else is inconsequential at this point. Chapters 29–31, which happen to be riddled with translation problems, are all spoken by Job and form three easily distinguished entities. Chapter 29, which also begins with the formula "Job continued his discourse," speaks of "the months gone by," the good old days of prosperity and happiness. The companion chap. 30 describes the "now" of Job's current situation with all its mocking (v. 9), misery, and mourning (v. 31).

Once past the six verses of prose introducing him (32:1-6), Elihu is the sole speaker until the end of chap. 39, his words having ended with

---

[2] See D. Patrick, "Job's Address of God," *ZAW* 91 (1979): 268-82.

[3] E. B. Smick ("Job," EBC, vol. 4 [Grand Rapids: Zondervan, 1988], 848) sees chap. 28 as the center of the book, flanked by the dialogue-dispute in three cycles (chaps. 4–27) and three monologues (Job, chaps. 29–31; Elihu, chaps. 32–37; God, chaps. 38–42). Outside those chapters are Job's opening lament (chap. 3) and his closing contrition (40:3-5; 42:1-6). Outermost of all, as everyone agrees, are the prose prologue and prose epilogue. In broad outline this reflects C. Westermann, *The Structure of the Book of Job,* trans. C. A. Muenchow (Philadelphia: Fortress, 1981), 6.

chap. 31. At least the first three of his speeches follow a pattern. Initially he would state Job's position, usually with approximate quotations. Then he would attempt to refute those arguments with reasons that sound very much like the other three friends. Finally he would urge Job to repent of sin, which, of course, the man from Uz did not do (although he did repent of his foolish words; cf. 42:6). When Elihu grew weary of failing to elicit repentance from Job, he joined the others in their silence; and all human voices stopped. "Then the LORD answered Job out of the storm" (38:1).

It is difficult to see much progress through the speeches of the five men whose words constitute the majority of the book. Some of Job's most bitter and angry words appear toward the beginning. Similarly, those few glimmers of hope that we Christians love to claim reach their climax and conclusion at 19:25. Rarely is there anything that approximates a happy aspiration from that point to the end of Job's speaking at 31:40. The first speech of Eliphaz begins rather politely, as does the first of Elihu, a courtesy that does not last long. The cruelty and venom of the friends is sprinkled randomly through their speeches. While their arguments may have become refined, their level of frustration grew to counteract anything positive. Therefore the two parties, Job on the one hand and his friends on the other, grew polarized to the point where no one had anything left to say.

The Lord delivered two speeches, each of which has two parts. The first speech (chaps. 38–39) consists of rhetorical questions and statements about the inanimate created order (38:2-38) and about a series of mostly wild animals (38:39–39:30). The second speech contains mainly questions and observations about two particularly strong, untamable creatures, the "behemoth" and the "leviathan." With the majority of modern commentators I understand these to be the hippopotamus and the crocodile.

After each of Yahweh's speeches Job made brief statements of repentance. The second statement was slightly longer and contained the actual word "repent" (42:6).

The prose epilogue, much shorter than the prologue, wraps up the story, giving what the author determined were the essential details. The three friends (excluding Elihu) were condemned but were acquitted after offering sacrifices and after Job's intercessory prayer. Job was then given double his former wealth, complete with another set of ten children, whose children and grandchildren buried him at a ripe old age. Interestingly, his daughters are named, but his sons are not (42:13-15).

Smaller, significant structural elements are within the speeches, chapters, stanzas, and individual verses. The commentary points out a number of chiastically arranged verses, a delightful twist often lost in translation. Many of the pericopes (self-contained preachable snippits) and some chapters are chiastic[4] or enclosed (inclusio) with key words, some of which are rare enough for us to believe that the author intended to use them that way.[5]

Throughout the commentary are many cross-references, primarily within Job. These are noted to underscore the unity of the work and to bolster the view that one author ultimately was responsible for the whole. These cross-references indicate unique phrases and unusual words that also contribute to the inner cohesion of the book and show that the speakers were listening, if only with one ear, to one another.

As long as we do not demand that this ancient Oriental poetry conform to modern Western standards of organization and logic, there is much to see, learn, and appreciate about the way the Book of Job was put together. Examination of structure is necessary, but we must be careful not to go beyond the evidence of the text.

2. Date

The Book of Job contains few indications of its date; and since there are no irrefutable clues, proposals have ranged over many centuries from before the time of Moses to the period between the testaments. There are no references to datable people, and the scattered geographical names provide little or no help on this matter. From the point of religious orthodoxy, no view is ruled out because nothing in this book or elsewhere in the Bible demands a specific date for Job.

The question is at least twofold: When did the events of the story take place, and when was the book written? The second question is complicated by the possibility that the book went through a transition from oral to written form and that the written form then underwent editorial revision.

The man Job, whom I take to have been an actual, historical person, is described as a wealthy man from the East (1:1-3). Presuppositions deter-

---

[4] One example is D. J. Clark's *a b c a c b a* arrangement of 28:1-11 ("In Search of Wisdom: Notes on Job 28," *BT* 33 (1982): 401-5). See also E. C. Webster, "Strophic Patterns in Job 3–28," *JSOT* 26 (1983): 33-60, and "Strophic Patterns in Job 29–42," *JSOT* 30 (1984): 95-109. Generally ignored is E. W. Bullinger, *The Companion Bible* (1899; reprint, Grand Rapids: Zondervan, 1964), the forerunner of much that today goes under the name of rhetorical criticism.

[5] Many more are noted in N. C. Habel, *The Book of Job,* OTL (Philadelphia: Westminster, 1985), including one for the whole Book of Job (p. 54).

mine whether one believes Job really lived or was simply the subject of a legend like Paul Bunyan or Hans Brinker. Unless clearly indicated otherwise, I assume that the Bible speaks of real people and places. Nothing in the text suggests that Job was a mythical, imaginary, or fictitious figure. True, there is a seeming artificiality about the numbers of his cattle (1:3; 42:12) and a certain standardization in the way the tragedies were reported (1:13-19), but this does not impinge on the historicity of the account. Everything said about him is well within the realm of possibility. He did not do superhuman feats nor possess any magical power. Except for his extraordinary wealth and exceptional piety, he was like countless others past and present.

The facts about him, which are mainly in the first two chapters, suggest that he lived around the time of the patriarchs. His wealth was measured in cattle rather than in the precious metals of the time of Solomon. He reflected no knowledge of organized religion, Mosaic, Levitical, or otherwise. Like the patriarchs he was a priest to his own household (1:5). The only other explanation for this absence of anything from the Pentateuch in Job is that he lived outside the promised land and beyond the influence of the law of Moses.[6] Probably both explanations are correct; that is, Job was very early *and* he lived in a region well outside Canaan.

Most discussion of the date of Job focuses on the composition of the book. Here there is a wide range of opinion. Some study the question of language and note that Job uses many Aramaic words and some Arabic ones. Since Aramaic grew in popularity toward the end of the Old Testament period, it is natural to assume the book was written late.[7] Recently, however, more Aramaic inscriptions from the second millennium B.C. have come to light; the use of Aramaic may actually point to the great age of the book rather than to its lateness. Since most Arabic comes from the Islamic period and its antiquity is largely shrouded in silence, arguments based on it are suspect.[8]

After Job, Psalms is the book most cross-referenced in this study. Beyond that, one can find in Job rare words, analogous constructions, and phrases that also occur in books from Genesis to Malachi. Simply because of the nature of the material, many of these features reflect the wis-

---

[6] Contrary to ancient tradition and the modern majority, D. Wolfers argues that Job was an Israelite ("Is Job after All Jewish?" *DD* 14 [1985]: 39-44).

[7] E. Dhorme, *A Commentary on the Book of Job,* trans. H. Knight from 1926 French ed. (London: Nelson, 1967), clxxvii-ix. R. Gordis, *The Book of God and Man* (Chicago: University Press, 1965), 161-63.

[8] One commentary replete with Arabic is F. Delitzsch, *The Book of Job,* 2 vols., trans. F. Bolton (Grand Rapids: Eerdmans, 1949).

dom books; and because of the size and vocabulary of Isaiah, many reflect that eighth-century prophet.

On the other side of the ledger are observations connecting the language of Job with Ugaritic, whose mid-second millennium B.C. date argues in favor of an early Job.[9] In much of this discussion we must remember that the Old Testament is the largest piece of literature to emerge from the ancient Near East. All the Ugaritic epics together do not match the volume of Job alone.[10] All the Hebrew inscriptional evidence from the Old Testament period fills only a few pages. Since the clues are few, we must eschew dogmatism on this matter of date.

The subject matter is another basis for making a judgment on the date of Job. This too can be very slippery. Some scholars would connect the trials of Job with the trials of the nation during the exile.[11] Others point to the scattered allusions to resurrection and life after death, believing that this was a late development. Some note that the word *Satan* is not mentioned in the early books of the Old Testament. Still others maintain that the highly refined discussion of the problem of suffering must reflect a later period when thinking profound thoughts and wrestling with erudite issues were more common.[12] The idea should be resisted that ancient peoples were primitive and therefore incapable of thinking of or discussing the subtle issues that fill the pages of Job.

In sum, the door must be left open until some ancient text surfaces or

---

[9] Though M. Pope espouses a date in the seventh century B.C., he notes that one could "argue that Job should be dated in the middle of the second millennium B.C. on the basis of its parallel attitude toward afterlife with the Aqhat epic" (AB, XL). See also A. Ceresko, *Job 29–31 in the Light of Northwest Semitic* (Rome: Biblical Institute Press, 1980), 195-97; W. L. Michel, *Job in the Light of Northwest Semitic,* vol. 1 (Rome: Pontifical Biblical Institute, 1987).

[10] For more discussion on ancient Near Eastern parallels see H. P. Müller, "Keilschriftliche Parallelen zum biblischen Hiobbuch. Möglichkeit und Grenze des Vergleichs," *Or* 47 (1978): 360-75; M. Pope, AB, LVI-LXXI. For a different analysis see R. L. Harris, "The Book of Job and Its Doctrine of God," *Grace Journal* 13 (1972): 6-8 (also in *Presbyterion* 7 [1981]).

[11] M. Jastrow, *The Book of Job* (Philadelphia: Lippincott, 1920), 34-36; S. Terrien "Job," *IB,* vol. 3 (Nashville: Abingdon, 1956), 890. B. D. Napier wrote, "The work as a whole unmistakably reflects Israel's own corporate catastrophic experience of the bitter sixth century" (*Song of the Vineyard* [New York: Harper, 1962], 335). Reasons for rejecting this view are found in J. J. M. Roberts, "Job and the Israelite Religious Tradition," *ZAW* 89 (1977): 107-14.

[12] See, however, the wrestling with the problem of suffering in such ancient Near Eastern works as "The Protests of the Eloquent Peasant" (*ANET,* 407-10); "Suicide" (405-7); "The Instruction of Amenemhet" (418-19); "The Dialogue of Pessimism" (600-601); and "The Babylonian Theodicy" (601-4).

some authentic reference to these people or this book comes to light. Like many of the psalms that elude positive dating, Job the man and Job the book are timeless. This timelessness makes Job easy to preach and apply to the countless sufferers whose situations mirror Job's. Rather than fret or fabricate a specific date, we should reckon the book as God's gift to everyone who suffers and knows not why. Job can be anyone, and Yahweh can be everyone's God.

3. Authorship

Hand in hand with the question of date goes the question of authorship. Again Scripture does not supply the answer; the book is anonymous, and we must not presume to know more than we are told. Unlike the Epistle to the Hebrews, there are not even any candidates.

The connection between the events of Job's life that form the background for this book and the text as we know it is an area of vigorous speculation. The likely antiquity of the events also makes it likely that there was some time when the story was only oral. From a simple telling of the story in prose there developed a poetic shape, which made it easier to remember and more enjoyable to tell and to hear. Whoever the poet was, the writing was guided by God's Spirit to record the account essentially as we have it. Unlike writers of many of the biblical books (e.g., Rom 1:1), the author declined to include his name.[13]

Whether the first draft was also the last draft is unknown. Likewise, no one knows whether or not the book grew, as many say, from the kernel of the prose prologue and epilogue to the forty-two chapters it now has. It is commonly argued that the Elihu chapters are the most recent and that the large debate section (chaps. 4–27) is most central because Job did not respond to Elihu and he is not mentioned in the epilogue. Even if the book developed in stages, a remarkable homogeneity witnesses to a single hand producing the whole.[14]

---

[13] The words of B. K. Waltke regarding Gen 1–11 ("Oral Tradition," in *A Tribute to Gleason Archer*, ed. W. C. Kaiser, Jr. and R. F. Youngblood [Chicago: Moody, 1986], 31) apply equally here: "It is difficult to verify or refute the claim that oral tradition lies behind the patriarchal narratives referring to events before the invention of writing. Whatever be the types and extent of sources that our omniscient narrator may have used and the manner in which he may have used them, the important point is that God's inspired spokesman told the sacred stories in his own way. For this reason there is no reason to doubt their historicity or to be uncertain about his meaning."

[14] M. Tsevat delineates three basic views on the composition of the book. (1) The author of the poetic parts used an old story. (2) One author wrote both the prose and poetry. (3) A later editor provided the narrative frame for the poetic sections ("The Meaning of the Book of Job," *HUCA* [1966]: 73).

Questions and theories about the literary history of a Bible book can be unsettling for those of us who believe in the inspiration of Scripture. It is easy to imagine Paul writing a single, short New Testament letter in much the form that we find it in the Bible. It is more difficult to conceive the Holy Spirit superintending a book's development over many years, perhaps even centuries. Nevertheless, there is nothing in the biblical doctrine of inspiration to disallow a book's being written over an extended period of time (the Book of Psalms is an obvious example). If the composition occurred in this manner, we can be sure that at each point the Holy Spirit was active but particularly so as the text was inscripturated and the words fixed in place. The finished product is just as God determined it to be.

So we freely say, "Eliphaz replied," or "Job answered," or "the LORD said," knowing full well that God's Spirit moved on some unknown poet to pen the words that followed.

4. Geography and Culture

At each place in the text where a place name appears, the commentary includes comments and speculation (1:1; 2:11; 32:2; etc.); but, as is typical of the wisdom literature, there are few geographical indicators.

"The land of Uz," as best we can guess, was in the area of northern Saudi Arabia or southern Jordan, which, since the time of the patriarchs has been called Edom. The names of Job's friends and their homes also point to locales in the desert country east and south of the Dead Sea.

Throughout the book are occasional references to farming, rivers, and hills, none of which would disallow the high desert of the Edomite plateau. The thunder and lightning storms as well as the unwelcome east wind are characteristic of that area. Even the hail, ice, and snow mentioned several times are known to occur there. The fourteen references to "tent" (*ʾōhēl*), though not conclusive, point in the direction of seminomadic peoples. "House" (*bēt*) occurs more often (twenty-five times) but is also more likely to be a general word for "home." Yet when the "house" of the oldest brother collapsed on the children, killing them all, it seems more likely to have been a building than a tent.

From time to time the scene seems urban with references to gates, walls, and near neighbors. Job could have been a pastoral-nomad who regularly attached himself to some city, remembering that most cities in the Bible would be counted towns or villages by our modern definitions. Since these details are not central to the story, they were not included in the written version of Job's story.

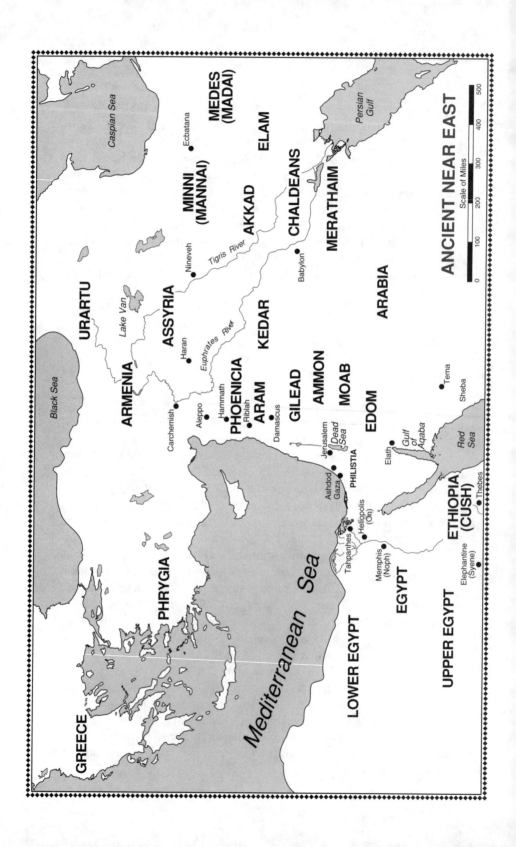

There are enough references to the activities of cattlemen and farmers for us to believe the speeches reflect authentic experience with such matters. There are allusions to hunting, trapping, mining, and other open country activities, as well as to almsgiving, commerce, and urban crime.

The only scene in the book that defies an easy interpretation is the heavenly council (1:6; 2:1). For this information the author could appeal to no human authority. Like other heavenly scenes reported in the Bible, it must have come by revelation (1 Kgs 22:19-22; Isa 6:1; Dan 7:9). Also, like the others, it raises more questions than it answers. The only satisfactory explanation is that we are given only what we need to know, not what we want to know.

5. Canonicity

In most English Bibles, Job heads what are called the poetical books (Job to Song of Songs). This follows the Greek Codex Vaticanus, which put Job after the historical books. A variety of arrangements can be found with Job after Deuteronomy (the Syriac Peshitta and Codex Sinaiticus), before Proverbs (*Baba Bathra* 14b, MT), or after Proverbs (NJPS). In the standard Hebrew Bible it is grouped with the eleven "writings" (Psalms; Job; Proverbs; Daniel; Ezra-Nehemiah; Chronicles; and the five little scrolls: Canticles; Ruth; Lamentations; Ecclesiastes; Esther). As a wisdom book it has affinities with the wisdom psalms (e.g., 1; 19; 37; 73; 119), Proverbs, and Ecclesiastes. As a lament it connects with the lament psalms (e.g., 6; 7; 22; 35; 90; 137) and Lamentations. As a story about a patriarch it has links to Genesis (chaps. 12–35). As elevated literature it compares to Isaiah, especially chaps. 40–66.

The man Job is mentioned once in the New Testament (Jas 5:11), and there is one certain quotation (5:13 in 1 Cor 3:19) introduced by a formula that indicates that Job was canonical Scripture in the first century A.D.

Despite Job's near blasphemy and his doubts about divine justice, the book's canonicity was never questioned. Even more remarkable is that though Job was most likely a non-Israelite, still this book about him was accorded a solid place among Hebrew sacred writings, perhaps because of its traditional association with Moses (*Baba Bathra* 14b and the Peshitta). Among the Qumran scrolls, only books of the Pentateuch and Job are written in the so-called Paleo-Hebrew script, an archaizing invention probably intended to distinguish these as the oldest compositions. They have in common the tradition of Mosaic authorship.[15]

6. Translations

Job was translated into Aramaic in the second century B.C., and fragments of it have been found in the caves by the Dead Sea.[16] About the same time, it appeared in Greek, although copies in that language only date to the fourth century of our era. The Septuagint is about four hundred lines shorter than the Masoretic Text.[17] Other ancient versions available to us are Syriac, Ethiopic, Latin, and Arabic.

The English versions, so frequently mentioned in this commentary, require a few words of explanation. Because readers of this commentary probably have access to most of these, it is worthwhile to note something of their history and background.

The *King James Version* (KJV), or *Authorized Version*, though not the first translation in the English language, until recently has been the most widely used. The KJV is known for its literary quality, although some consider this a weakness rather than a strength. A revision called the *New King James Version* (NKJV) was completed in 1982.

The *English Revised Version* (RV) appeared in 1881 to correct paraphrasing tendencies of the KJV and to provide a more literal translation.

An American offspring of the RV, the *American Standard Version* (ASV) came out in 1901. The two major differences between it and the RV are the use of "Jehovah" for the divine name and the Americanizing of words and spellings uniquely British. A revision of the ASV called the *New American Standard Bible* (NASB) appeared in 1971. While many verses were modernized, it has most of the strengths and weaknesses of the 1901 edition, including wooden, Hebraic-sounding phrases.

James Moffatt, a Scotsman, finished his new translation in 1922. It is a fine translation with many refreshing turns of phrase and is in many respects the precursor to the paraphrased and dynamic equivalent translations that appeared in the seventies.[18]

Another forerunner of the modern translations is *The Complete Bible:*

---

[15] K. A. Mathews, "The Background of the Paleo-Hebrew Texts at Qumran," *The Word of the Lord Shall Go Forth* (Philadelphia: ASOR, 1983), 555.

[16] M. Sokoloff, *The Targum to Job from Qumran Cave XI* (Ramat-Gan: Bar-Ilan University, 1974).

[17] The commentary occasionally mentions verses the LXX lacks. For further study on this question see H. Heater, Jr., *A Septuagint Translation Technique in the Book of Job* (Washington: Catholic Biblical Association, 1982).

[18] It is still in print (San Francisco: Harper).

An American Translation (AT). J. M. P. Smith and others produced the Old Testament, E. J. Goodspeed produced the New Testament, and the University of Chicago published it in 1939. Smith translated Job.

The *Revised Standard Version* was completed in 1952 and was the first translation to use the Dead Sea Scrolls. As the name indicates, this was a revision of the KJV. Sponsored by the National Council of Churches, this committee effort was widely received and became the official translation in those denominations belonging to the NCC. Compared with most Bibles that appeared a generation later, the RSV is quite conservative and literal.[19]

The first conservative reaction to the RSV was *The Berkeley Version,* now known as *The Modern Language Bible* (MLB). Largely the work of G. Verkuyl of Berkeley, California, this version appeared in 1959.[20]

The *Anchor Bible* (AB) is still not complete, but *Job with Introduction, Translation, and Notes* by M. H. Pope appeared in 1965 (herein often referred to simply as "Pope"). The translation is fresh and crisp. Pope is a Ugaritic specialist and brings to bear many of the new insights that the discovery of that language and literature has provided.

La Bible de Jerusalem, produced by French Catholics in 1961, appeared as *The Jerusalem Bible* (JB) in 1966. Job was translated from the French by the renowned J. R. R. Tolkien. This version is now available in a new edition, which is not cited in this commentary. The JB is a reliable translation, but it leans heavily on Greek and Latin and often takes unwarranted liberties with the text.

The Catholic counterpart to the KJV is the Douay-Rheims (1610). The *New American Bible* (NAB) was completed in 1970 to replace it. It has received much wider acceptance among Catholics and others than the JB because it is slightly more conservative.

Also in 1970 several denominations in Great Britain cooperated to produce the *New English Bible* (NEB). The heavy hand of the Arabist G. R. Driver is often evident. This, added to a low view of the Hebrew text ("full of errors of every kind," xiii), produced a Bible that has not received wide acceptance outside its sponsoring circles. A new edition called *The Revised English Bible* (REB) appeared in 1989 with some of the more bizarre renderings restored to their traditional sense (e.g., Judg 1:14).

William F. Beck died before he finished the Old Testament of *An*

---

[19] For a history of translations to this point, see F. F. Bruce, *The English Bible* (New York: Oxford University Press, 1961).

[20] It is still in print (Peabody, Mass.: Hendrickson).

American Translation (AAT), but it was completed by Elmer Smick and published in 1976. In some places the translation is very wooden; in others, quite free; but it was done with great respect for the original.

When *Good News for Modern Man* (New Testament) was finished (1966), work immediately began on the *Good News Bible* (GNB) or *Today's English Version,* which appeared in 1976. This project of the American Bible Society epitomizes the dynamic equivalence theory of translation, that is, a translation of the ideas and intentions (reader impact) rather than the words of the text. *The Living Bible* is a paraphrase, which this commentary does not cite because it is essentially a rewriting of the ASV and not a translation.

The *New International Version* (NIV) was completed in 1978, and a slightly revised edition appeared in 1983.[21] This translation, which is the basis of this commentary, is the most widely read English Bible today. Only the KJV remains higher in aggregate sales. Translated by those with a high view of the text, it represents a compromise between reliability and readability, between literary and literal.

In 1982 the third part of the Jewish Publication Society's translation, *The Writings* or *Kethubim* (NJPS) appeared. It replaced for Jews the old JPS, finally completed in 1917, which sounded much like the KJV or Douay.

In addition to the introduction of the REB, 1989 saw a revision of the RSV called the *New Revised Standard Version* (NRSV). Though there are countless minor changes from the 1952 edition, one major difference is the use of gender-neutral language.

Two translations aimed at children or others first learning to read English, the *International Children's Version* (ICV) and the *New Century Version* (NCV) appeared in 1986 and 1991, respectively. The ICV should be understood by anyone with a fourth grade education. The NCV is for those with a sixth grade education.[22]

Translations not consulted for this work are Phillips, *New World, Amplified,* and the *Reader's Digest Bible.*[23]

---

[21] For an excellent history of English versions through 1979 with complete bibliography, see J. P. Lewis, *The English Bible from KJV to NIV* (Grand Rapids: Baker, 1981).

[22] The NIV is supposedly readable by seventh graders (see J. R. Kohlenberger III, *Words about the Word* [Grand Rapids: Zondervan, 1987], 92).

[23] These and others are included by S. Kubo and W. F. Specht, *So Many Versions* (Grand Rapids: Zondervan, 1983).

7. Literary Style

The Book of Job begins with two chapters of prose and concludes with one more. The intervening thirty-nine chapters are all poetry, except for brief introductions to the speakers. The editors of the NIV and most modern versions indicate these features by having the prose go from margin to margin and wrap from one line to the next. An exception is 1:21, where a double couplet is imbedded in the prose. The poetry, on the other hand, is scanned or set up in lines, usually pairs, so that the reader can more readily grasp the fact that the paired sentences or clauses are approximately the same in length and complement one another in sense.

The prologue and epilogue are narratives. The historical Job and the heavenly background for the trials are described in chap. 1 with little editorial comment. The second chapter likewise describes the second council, the second test, and the brief dialogue between Job and his wife and introduces the three friends in a matter-of-fact manner.

The epilogue, which is not all of chap. 42 but only 42:7-17, is similarly unimpassioned. All the characters of the prologue, except for the Satan and Job's wife, reappear in the end, if we assume the ten new children to have replaced the ten dead ones. The grammar of all the prose is simple, the syntax uncomplicated, and the vocabulary chosen from well-known words. Absent are any metaphors, explanatory clauses, and obscure word pictures. The book begins directly with "there lived a man," and it ends simply with "so he died."

A simplistic approach to Job sees the poetry as a monolith of disputation between Job and his friends. Even a casual examination of the text, however, reveals that there are several types of literature contained in chaps. 3–41. A closer look at the poetry yields rich and fascinating dividends because it is a treasure trove of word pictures, metaphors, similes, tightly reasoned logic, prayers, irony,[24] insults, insinuations, protestations, exaggerations, fabrications, and interrogations. No single genre describes it all, even though some would say complaint, or lament,[25] or lawsuit[26] is prominent.

---

[24] W. J. A. Power, "A Study of Irony in the Book of Job" (Ph.D. diss., University of Toronto, 1961); E. M. Good, *Irony in the Old Testament* (Philadelphia: Westminster, 1965), 196-240.

[25] C. Westermann, *Handbook to the Old Testament,* trans. & ed. R. H. Boyd (Minneapolis: Augsburg, 1967), 226-33; *Job,* 2.

[26] S. H. Scholnick, "Lawsuit Drama in the Book of Job" (Ph.D. diss., Brandeis University, 1975), vi, 103-4; "Poetry in the Courtroom: Job 38–41," in *Directions in Hebrew Poetry* (Sheffield: JSOT, 1987), 185-204; H. Richter, *Studien zu Hiob, Der Aufbau des Hiobbuches dargestellt an den Gattungen des Rechtslebens* (Berlin: Evangelische Verlagsanstalt, 1959).

The Book of Job is like a handmade Oriental rug, the intricate design of which captures our attention as we compare the similarities and differences throughout the whole. Just when we think we see a pattern emerging, some irregularity, the artistry of the author, appears, making our explanation or theory less convincing. The Book of Job has fascinated some scholars for their entire lives.[27]

In general, poetry is harder to read and understand than prose. This is true in all languages. The rules of writing are relaxed for poets, so they are allowed incomplete sentences, run-on sentences, sentences with no verbs or helping particles, or other things we deem essential to sense. Poets seem largely to ignore verb tenses or moods, often omit pronoun suffixes, leave antecedents unclear, and rearrange the normal verb-subject-object order of a Hebrew sentence to suit their mood, rhythm, or emphasis. Many of these irregularities are for metric reasons, that is, to make the line come out right.

Some thoughts can be said in two words, but others require four or more. Since most Hebrew poetic lines have three major words, often line *b* in a couplet contains a ballast word, which adds little but makes the line correspond in length to the first line. Similarly, the poet's thought may demand more than the typical three words, and in those cases we sense that something is missing that our logic demands. When counting words, only the triliteral roots of verbs and nouns matter. Prepositions (independent or prefixed), pronouns (independent or suffixed), and particles of entreaty, the sign of the interrogative, the negative, and conjunctions generally do not contribute to the ideal sum of three. Exceptions abound, however, which indicates that the poet(s) did not feel obligated to abide by the rigorous rules we would like to press upon them.

Typically the vocabulary of poetry is larger than that of prose. In this regard Job is the most difficult book of the Bible. After Isaiah, which has twice as many words, Job has the largest number of hapax legomena (words found only once in the Bible) of any book in the Bible; and words that occur only a handful of times elsewhere in the Old Testament are found throughout the book.[28] Some of the words are pure hapaxes; that is, they have no cognates, alternate spellings, or similarities to any other Hebrew words.

As the commentary indicates, many are known from Aramaic or later Hebrew, a helpful but not absolutely trustworthy way to determine their

---

[27] E.g., S. Terrien and R. Gordis.
[28] F. E. Greenspahn, *Hapax Legomena in Biblical Hebrew* (Chico, Cal.: Scholars Press, 1984), 199.

meaning. A few times Arabic is useful, but such solutions seem to pose numerous questions and doubts. If connections to Arabic are too late (A.D. 650 or later), some think that connections to Ugaritic are too early (ca. 1500 B.C.).

In recent years the study of Hebrew poetry and parallelism specifically has undergone a resurgence. Simple categories of synonymous, antithetical, and synthetic parallels have been augmented, defined, and refined.[29] Nevertheless the predominant pattern in Job is what has been called the synonymous parallel. The terms couplet, pair, and bicolon appear in the commentary to describe these verses. Three-line units also appear, called tricola. The lines themselves are occasionally called cola, or stichs.

While exceptions are easy to find, the second line of most pairs repeats the substance of the first. This is a great help in figuring out difficult constructions or in determining the meaning of unknown words. Sometimes, however, it works to the contrary; we expect or demand that line *b* echo line *a* when, in fact, it does not. A conservative approach to the text will let the irregularity stand. Those who presume to correct the Hebrew will add, delete, or emend words to make the verse fit some predetermined pattern.[30]

Many verses are chiastically arranged, and sometimes stanzas and chapters follow this pattern. The commentary notes some of these.[31] Less common are examples of alliteration and assonance, which together produce rhyme. One author found fifty-two examples of paronomasia (puns).[32]

Cadence, beat, or meter are not as regular as we find in English poetry, but there is a certain flow to Hebrew poetry that is perhaps better described as rhythm.[33] Whereas meter is a very predictable method of

---

[29] F. M. Cross and D. N. Freedman, *Studies in Ancient Yahwistic Poetry* (Missoula, Mont.: Scholars Press, 1975); S. A. Geller, *Parallelism in Early Biblical Poetry* (Missoula, Mont.: Scholars Press, 1979); M. O'Connor, *Hebrew Verse Structure* (Winona Lake, Ind.: Eisenbrauns, 1980); J. L. Kugel, *The Idea of Biblical Poetry: Parallelism and Its History* (New Haven: Yale University Press, 1981); R. Alter, *The Art of Biblical Poetry* (New York: Basic Books, 1985); A. Berlin, *The Dynamics of Biblical Parallelism* (Bloomington: Indiana University Press, 1985); E. R. Follis, ed., *Directions in Biblical Hebrew Poetry* (Sheffield: JSOT, 1987); D. L. Petersen and K. H. Richards, *Interpreting Hebrew Poetry* (Minneapolis: Augsburg, 1992).

[30] Rather than saying "we delete," the NEB has the frequent footnote "Heb. *adds*."

[31] See N. C. Habel, *Job,* 46.

[32] I. M. Casanowicz, *Paranomasia in the Old Testament* (Boston: Norwood, 1894), 91-93.

[33] Peterson and Richards, *Hebrew Poetry,* 44-45. Rhythmic patterns involve four elements: (1) regularity (poetic lines of similar length); (2) variation (lines within a bicolon could contain a different number of syllables); (3) grouping (how lines are placed together to form a unit); (4) hierarchy ("external parallelism, namely, correspondences between various bicola").

studying and analyzing poetry, it is not so easily done in Hebrew poetry. Rather, meter might be seen as a part of the rhythm of Old Testament poetic texts. By referring to rhythm, it is understood that the poetry in the Old Testament is not confined to a system of meter. In fact, "Most classical Hebrew poetry, however, such as that found in the Book of Job, is made up of combinations of diverse rhythmic patterns."[34] In Job, therefore, each verse or section must be read on its own to distinguish its poetic composition. In most English translations of the Bible, the NIV included, Hebrew poetry has been translated into good English poetry rather than trying to reflect the rhythmic patterns of the Hebrew. The ASV is a slight exception and comes closer to capturing the nuance of the Hebrew, but it reads like broken English and may not help the reader catch the meaning of poetic texts as well as modern translations.

8. Theology

Job is not only an Old Testament book, but it also reflects an early and uncomplicated theology. All the players in the book believe in the one true God, not just as one of many gods or as an impersonal supreme force. While the author believed in Yahweh, the characters are identified only as theists. The covenant name of the God of the Israel, Yahweh, the Lord, does not appear in the poetic dialogues (except at 12:9, which probably is either a quotation from a proverb or a scribal error).[35]

The speakers used more generic names for God; *ʾēl* (about fifty times), *ʾĕlôah* (about forty times), and *ʾĕlôhîm* (four times) all translate as "God"; *šadday* (about thirty times) is "Almighty." This indicates that the speakers lived before or beyond the influence of the religion of Israel, in the patriarchal period (Exod 6:3), or in an area outside "the promised land." There is no hint of polytheism; in fact, there are strong suggestions against it. The occasional reference to stars, planets, death, the sea, and mythical monsters, which other cultures deified, does not constitute belief in them or assent to their supernatural power or personality.[36]

Of the attributes of God, the ones that stand out in the Book of Job are sovereignty, omnipotence, omniscience, and justice. Less prominent are mercy, love, and goodness. Until the Lord appeared out of the whirlwind,

---

[34] Ibid., 46.

[35] C. D. Isbell ("Initial ʾalef-yod Interchange and Selected Biblical Passages," *JNES* 37 [1978]: 228) thinks that אהיה in 12:4a should be read as יהוה.

[36] For more support see J. N. Oswalt, "The Myth of the Dragon and Old Testament Faith," *EvQ* 49 (1977): 163-72.

Job complained that God was apathetic, blind to injustice, hidden, and unresponsive. For the four counselors certainly the justice of God was most prominent in their theology, with sovereignty nearly as important. Since Job said so little after God spoke to him, it is hard to know what his new view of God was; certainly it would have acknowledged God's power, faithfulness, generosity, and mercy. That God spoke to Job at all was the ultimate honor for Job and by itself would have rectified most of his misconceptions.

Relative to anthropology, all speakers believed in the solidarity and fallenness of the race. Sin was not incurable but pardonable, and people were redeemable through repentance and atonement. Sinners received their just desserts in the form of tragedy, misery, illness, and eventual death. Good behavior, submission to God, resistance to evil, and humility all bore the fruits of God's blessing in the form of large families, good health, abundant material goods, a worthy reputation, and long life. Except in the prologue and epilogue, little is said about sacrifice, atonement, or anything suggesting organized religion. Salvation comes from God but is dependent on the human response of faith, obedience, and "fear," a general term that encompasses the first two and extends to reverence, worship, and service to others. Virtually all the evangelistic messages are on the lips of the friends, who had as their mission the conversion of Job, but Job did not need to repent and be saved. He needed a better understanding of the Savior/Creator, which he obtained through his agony and his encounter with God.[37]

Considerable debate surrounds the question of afterlife in Job. The passages of despair that look forward only to the grave (e.g., 7:9,21; 10:21-22; 14:10-12,20; 16:22; 17:13-16) outnumber the glimmers of hope by about ten to one, but they betray Job's attitude more than his considered opinion. Some say the book offers no hope of life after death at all, but that requires severe manipulation of the obvious intent of a few of the most potent passages touching the subject (e.g., 14:13-17; 19:23-27). Although certainly not as clear as we might prefer, the doctrine of resurrection can be found in the book.

More of the matters theologians deal with are absent than present. There are no references to divinely inspired and inscripturated revelation (although cf. 23:11-12), no allusions to the plurality of the Godhead, little about the many facets of soteriology (e.g., election, adoption, sanctification), and no ecclesiology or eschatology. What the book does focus on, however, it does in detail and with high drama. It ruminates, cogi-

---

[37] Tsevat calls this "education by overwhelming" ("Meaning of Job," 93).

tates, and deliberates at great length on the character of God and the problem of a good man's unexplained suffering.

9. Purpose

Since, as Paul wrote to Timothy, "all Scripture is God-breathed and is useful for teaching, rebuking, correcting and training in righteousness," it is incumbent on us to determine the purpose and value of Job.[38] Two purposes overlap each other, one corrective and instructive and the other therapeutic.

Deuteronomy, Proverbs, and isolated passages throughout the Old Testament clearly teach that you get what you deserve, you reap what you sow, and you succeed or fail on the basis of your behavior.[39] Sin will be punished, and trust and obedience will be rewarded. Not only is this simple policy taught, but it is amply illustrated from Genesis (Cain) to Malachi (3:9-12).

The patriarch from Uz, however, did not fit that pattern. He was a righteous man who suffered as if he were guilty of great wickedness. Neither he nor his friends could explain his condition because their watertight systems allowed for no exceptions. In the words of S. Lasine, they had a "worm's-eye view of justice."[40] His friends reasoned that Job must have committed some terrible sin known only to God. Perhaps he had broken some of the laws that God had built into the created order. In the commentary this is called dynamistic retribution. But Job reasoned that God was not paying him any attention, and the system of justice had gone awry as a result of his neglect. One purpose of the book, like the lament psalms and Ecclesiastes, was to address this matter of exceptions to the general principle of just rewards.

Although the Book of Job is not a comprehensive explanation of human suffering, it has always caused its readers to ask why suffering occurs. Scripture gives many reasons, but it is difficult (often impossible) even for us who have the complete biblical revelation to understand specific experiences of sorrow and trouble.[41] When is the suffering of be-

---

[38] For a broad review of treatments of Job from the pre-Christian *Testament of Job* to Robert Frost, see N. Glatzer, *The Dimensions of Job* (New York: Schocken, 1969), 12-48.

[39] W. Brueggemann discusses this issue at length in his two articles, "A Shape for Old Testament Theology, I: Structure Legitimation," *CBQ* 47 (1985): 28-46, and "A Shape for Old Testament Theology, II: Embrace of Pain," *CBQ* 47 (1985): 395-415.

[40] S. Lasine, "Bird's Eye and Worm's Eye Views of Justice in the Book of Job," *JSOT* 42 (1988): 29-53.

[41] For a more thorough discussion of this issue, see R. L. Alden, "Evil and Suffering," in *Holman Bible Handbook,* ed. D. S. Dockery (Nashville: Holman, 1992), 312.

lievers God's discipline for misbehavior (Ps 39:11; Jer 30:11; Heb 12:5-11; Rev 3:19), and when is it training for their spiritual maturity (Rom 5:3-5; 2 Cor 1:3-9; 2 Tim 2:3; 4:5-8; Jas 1:2-4) and an opportunity to glorify God by their faith (1 Thess 1:6-10; 2 Thess 1:4-5; Heb 11:37-12:1)? The condition of the man born blind, for example, was not caused by his sin or that of his parents but so that God might be glorified in his healing (John 9:2-3).[42]

What the believer does know, as the Book of Job teaches, is that we serve a personal God who is intimately aware of each person and his or her needs and concerns. Furthermore, the Lord has not only a cosmic plan but an individual purpose he is wisely, justly, and lovingly pursuing in each believer's life. Finally, our God is powerful enough to accomplish his will on earth as well as in heaven. Thus, the other purpose of Job is to give comfort to believers of all ages who find themselves in Job's situation of suffering.

Many Christians would like to blame the devil for all manner of unpleasantness from minor occasions of bad luck to the most severe of human tragedies—loss of wealth, children, health, and honor. But the message of Job is that nothing happens to us that is not ultimately controlled by the knowledge, love, wisdom, and power of our God of all comfort (2 Cor 1:3).

Like Job, we need to learn that we live and die by grace and that all of life must be lived by faith—faith that God is good and is completely aware of everything that crosses our path. We must believe that he knows all about us and "that in all things God works for the good of those who love him, and who have been called according to his purpose" (Rom 8:28). "What cannot be comprehended through reason must be embraced in love."[43] The Book of Job prods us to ask ourselves: Do I believe in God? Do I reverently and obediently fear him? With all my heart, soul, mind, and strength, do I love God?

---

[42] In this connection F. I. Andersen reminds us: "Men seek an explanation of suffering in cause and effect. They look backwards for a connection between prior sin and present suffering. The Bible looks forward in hope and seeks explanations, not so much in origins as in goals" (*Job*, TOTC [Downers Grove: InterVarsity, 1976], 68).

[43] R. Gordis, "The Temptation of Job—Tradition Versus Experience in Religion," in *The Dimensions of Job* (New York: Schocken, 1969), 85. Reprinted from *Judaism*, IV (1955).

--------- *OUTLINE OF THE BOOK* ---------

---

[44] Many of these titles for the speeches have been suggested by those in the NKJV (Nashville: Nelson, 1982).

I. PROLOGUE (1:1–2:13)
  1. Background (1:1-5)
    (1) Job's Place (1:1a)
    (2) Job's Piety (1:1b)
    (3) Job's Posterity (1:2)
    (4) Job's Prosperity (1:3)
    (5) Job's Regular Custom (1:4-5)
  2. Test of Wealth (1:6-22)
    (1) The Satan (1:6-10)
    (2) Challenge (1:11-12)
    (3) Misfortunes (1:13-19)
      Theft (1:13-15)
      Fire (1:16)
      Theft (1:17)
      Storm (1:18-19)
    (4) Job's Response (1:20-22)
  3. Test of Health (2:1-10)
    (1) The Satan (2:1-5)
    (2) Disease (2:6-8)
    (3) Job's Wife (2:9-10)
  4. Job's Three Friends (2:11-13)

I. PROLOGUE (1:1–2:13)

The prologue is absolutely essential to the Book of Job. In it the writer introduces the readers to the main character, Job of Uz. With just a few strokes of the pen he sketches the heavenly council, the challenge from the Accuser, and Job's loss of his wealth, his children, and his health.

The prologue, like the epilogue, is in prose, but it is a lofty prose that almost shades into poetry. Rare words; unusual word order; and the use of special numbers, repetition, and parallelism mark the prose as of a different character than, for example, Genesis.

In the prologue the readers are informed of something that Job never learned, that is, that he was a test case. We know that he was innocent. God knows that he was innocent. The Satan knows that he was innocent. The friends who came to counsel him were sure he was not innocent. Job was quite certain of his innocence, but even sane people begin to question their sanity when faced with excruciating losses and prolonged illness. Happily for God and Job and us, Job survived; he passed the test and established himself as a great hero of faith.

1. Background (1:1-5)

In these opening five verses the necessary facts about Job appear—his locale, his wealth, his children, and, most important of all, his godliness.

(1) Job's Place (1:1a)

[1]In the land of Uz there lived a man whose name was Job.

1:1 Unlike most Hebrew sentences, which begin with the verb, this one begins with the noun "a man."[1] Such deviations from the usual order of verb-subject-object are often for emphasis. Could it be that the humanity, the finitude, the frailty of the major character is the point of the text in making "a man" the first word?[2] "Lived" translates a simple verb "to be," literally, "A man was in the land of Uz."[3]

The location of the land of Uz is uncertain. Uz is the name of three Old Testament characters: (1) the son of Aram and grandson of Shem (Gen 10:22 = 1 Chr 1:17); (2) Abraham's nephew, the son of Nahor and Milcah and brother of Buz (Gen 22:21); and (3) an Edomite, one of the sons of Dishan the Horite, who lived in Seir (Gen 36:28 = 1 Chr 1:42).[4] The last of these most likely gave his name to the land of Uz.[5]

Jeremiah 25:20 mentions the "kings of Uz" among those forced to

---

[1] For a detailed discussion of the word order, see M. Weiss, *The Story of Job's Beginning* (Jerusalem: Magnes, 1983), 17-20.

[2] שׁיא is one of the two most common words for "man," the other being אָדָם. Both are equally represented in this book. Generally אָדָם refers to man as opposed to animals and sometimes means "humankind." שׁיא refers to man as opposed to woman and can mean "husband." That, however, is not the point in either of its two occurrences in this opening verse. The point is that a specific man is in view. This is clear not just from this word but also from the fact that the man's name occurs later in the verse.

[3] S. Meier notes several connections between Adam and Job. Both were blameless, unique, lived in an ideal world, controlled many animals, and were tested by God ("Job I-II: A Reflection of Genesis I-III," *VT* 39 [1989]: 183-93).

[4] M. Görg believes the biblical name should be connected to the Egyptian ʿ3d, "land on the edge of the desert at the border of the regularly watered region" ("Ijob aus dem Lande ʿUs\Ein Beitrag zur 'theologischen Geographie,'" Biblische Notizen 12 [1980]: 7-12).

[5] Uz may mean "counsel," but that too is uncertain. The "z" is a שׂ and not a ז, so it is not the root in the names Uzza or Uzziah.

drink the cup of the Lord's wrath. Separate in that list are Edom, Moab, and Ammon (v. 21). Lamentations 4:21 has Uz parallel with Edom.[6]

Wadi Sirhan, a depression about two hundred miles long running from northwest (near Zarqa) to southeast (near Jawf) is the most likely candidate for the land of Uz. It is the catchment for the waters that run off Jebel Druz and is capable of supporting large herds of livestock such as Job had. Today it lies mainly in the northernmost part of Saudi Arabia. It was close enough to Edom to be occasionally linked with it, yet it was also within striking distance for Chaldean raiders (1:17).

Outside this book the name Job occurs only in Ezek 14:14,20, where the hero is listed with two other worthies, Noah and Daniel. Efforts to link this otherwise unknown name with the root 'āyab, "enemy," are futile. All but one of the more than 250 occurrences of "enemy" are qal participles. Three of them are in Job but never in such a way that one might connect it with the name Job (13:24; 27:7; 33:10).

(2) Job's Piety (1:1b)

This man was blameless and upright; he feared God and shunned evil.

Verse 1b contains two adjectives that readers often question. Job was "blameless" ("perfect," KJV) and "upright." The first of these (tām) will occur six more times in Job. Because the English word "perfect" has overtones of sinless perfection, it is best to avoid it in translation. A glance at two places where tām appears illustrates its range of meanings.[7] The word never describes God although it does characterize his work (Deut 32:4), his way (2 Sam 22:31 = Ps 18:30[31]), and his law (Ps 19:7[8]). Jesus urged his followers to "be perfect, . . . as your heavenly Father is perfect" (Matt 5:48).[8]

Perfection, integrity, or blamelessness referred to the absence of certain observable sinful acts. Job, his friends, and the author of the book were thinking of honesty, marital fidelity, just treatment of servants, generosity to the poor, and the avoidance of idolatry. Job denied wrongdoing

---

[6] In both these places the LXX lacks the name Uz. The Vulgate has *Hus* in Lamentations and *Ausitidis* in Jeremiah, which is what the LXX has at Job 1:1. While supporting an Edomite Uz, G. Schmitt traces alternate traditions for its location ("Die Heimat Hiobs," *Zeitschrift des deutschen Palastina-Vereins* 101 [1985], 56-63).

[7] תֵּם describes Jacob in Gen 25:27 (NIV "quiet"), the girl of Song of Songs, "my flawless one" (5:2) or "my perfect one" (6:9), and "the innocent" in Ps 64:4[v. 5, Heb.].

[8] Matthew 5:48 has τέλειος, whereas the LXX has ἀληθινός in Job 1:1. Matthew 5:48 comes closest to Lev 19:2, "Be holy because I, the LORD your God, am holy."

in all these areas in chap. 31, his long self-maledictory oath. Neither Job
nor his friends was thinking of perfection in the theological New Testament sense. If Job were perfect in that sense, then he would not have had
to repent as he did at the end of the book (42:6).

"Upright," *yāšār,* is more common than *tām* but is essentially equal to
it and serves as ballast to give the line adequate weight. "Upright" most
frequently occurs in Psalms and Proverbs. The verb form is in the well-
known Prov 3:6, "In all your ways acknowledge him, and he will make
your paths *yāšār.*"

As if to elaborate on what "blameless and upright" meant, the remain-
der of the verse declares in two short sentences that Job "feared God" and
"shunned evil." "Fear" in Hebrew has a wider range of meaning than it
does in English, including fright and scare, but it also encompasses reverence and awe. The picture here is not of a man cowering before an offended deity but of a devout man who respects God and obeys his laws.

The predominant words for God throughout the poetical parts of Job
are *ʾēl* and *ʾĕlôah.* Here, however, the word is the more common *ʾĕlōhîm,*
which, though frequent in the prologue, occurs only a few times in the
rest of the book. Yahweh (*yhwh*),[9] the name of the God of Israel, will
come up a few times in the opening and closing chapters of the book but
only once in the debate cycles (12:9). That is the name in the common
phrase "the fear of the LORD" (e.g., Job 28:28; Prov 1:7).

"Shunned" or "turned from" represents the other side of the coin from
"feared God." The first phrase was positive; the second is negative. Good
people turn *to* God and *away from* evil. The good life involves not only
the doing of right but also the avoidance of wrong. Again, "evil" was defined as mainly overt acts such as those Eliphaz listed in 22:6-9—ruthless
and cruel demanding of collateral and conscious neglect of the weary and
hungry, the widow and orphan. In 29:12-17 Job countered these charges
and added more good deeds to his list, all of which reflect his fear of God
and his shunning of evil.

(3) Job's Posterity (1:2)

[2]He had seven sons and three daughters.

1:2 Literally this says, "Seven sons and three daughters were born to
him."[10] Seven and three are special numbers in the Bible. Seven days

---

[9] The NIV translates the name as "the LORD," following the long-standing tradition κυ-
ριος ("Lord"). The ASV (1901) rendered the Hebrew the popular "Jehovah."
[10] The verb is not "had," as in the NIV, but the niphal of ילד.

make a week. Abraham offered seven lambs to Abimelech (Gen 21:28). Jacob served seven years for each of Laban's daughters (Gen 29:18-30). Joseph dreamed of seven ears of corn and seven cattle (Gen 41), and so on. The number seven represents perfection or completeness. Three is only slightly less common. Noah had three sons (Gen 6:10). Abraham entertained three heavenly visitors (Gen 18:2). Three also was prominent in Joseph's dreams (Gen 40:10,12-13,16,18-19). Jochebed hid Moses for three months (Exod 2:2). The sum of seven and three is ten, another special number. Ten was the lowest number Abraham bargained for as he pleaded for Sodom to be spared (Gen 18:32). Eliezer took ten camels to buy a bride for Isaac (Gen 24:10). Joseph's ten brothers who went to Egypt returned with ten donkeys loaded with food (Gen 42:3; 45:23), and so on.

It is unwise to try to make any of these numbers symbolize anything such as Pentecost (the Feast of Weeks), the Trinity, or the Decalogue. But the numbers point to the highly stylized nature of the prologue of the book. These same numbers are in the next verse. Later there appears the author's preference for the number four. While there is no reason not to believe that Job did, in fact, have exactly seven sons and three daughters, it can also be said that he had the ideal family, with ideal numbers of children of each gender. When God restored Job's fortunes in the last chapter, Job once more had seven sons and three daughters (42:13).

(4) Job's Prosperity (1:3)

³and he owned seven thousand sheep, three thousand camels, five hundred yoke of oxen and five hundred donkeys, and had a large number of servants. He was the greatest man among all the people of the East.

1:3 Not only did Job have the ideal number of children, but his holdings in livestock also came in ideal numbers. The first category refers to small livestock—sheep and goats—perhaps a mixture but more likely sheep only. The "very wealthy" Nabal had only a thousand goats and three thousand sheep (1 Sam 25:2). Yet during Asa's reform the priests sacrificed seven thousand sheep (2 Chr 15:11). Solomon offered 120,000 sheep and goats at the dedication of the temple (1 Kgs 8:63 = 2 Chr 7:5). "Mesha king of Moab raised sheep, and he had to supply the king of Israel with a hundred thousand lambs and with the wool of a hundred thousand rams" (2 Kgs 3:5). Much earlier the Reubenites captured from the Hagrites' 250,000 sheep (1 Chr 5:21). Measured against these numbers, Job was very wealthy, but his holdings did not compare to those of a whole tribe or to the holdings of all Israel at a later date.

While the measurement of wealth by livestock points to the antiquity of Job, the references to camels was thought at one time to point in the opposite direction. The debate, however, over when the camel was domesticated has subsided.[11] "Camel" occurs seventeen times in Gen 24 alone. Camels were more the animals of the desert than they were of the settled Israelites. There is no indication that the Israelites had camels during their wilderness wanderings. Most references to them are in connection with desert dwellers who depended on them. Furthermore, the camel was, according to Lev 11:4 and Deut 14:7, an unclean animal. This is one more reason to believe that the man Job was earlier than Moses (or at least outside the pale of Israelite influence).

The list continues with "five hundred yoke of oxen and five hundred donkeys." "Yoke" means "pair"; therefore Job had a thousand oxen. "Yoke" also suggests that they were harnessed and used for plowing. That, in turn, indicates that Job was not purely nomadic but must have farmed the land (cf. v. 14).

Hebrew has separate words for male and female donkeys, not just masculine and feminine forms of the same word. They are like our archaic English terms jack and jenny. The word here in Job 1:3 is the female, but there must have been some males to perpetuate the herd, even though the females were perhaps preferred.[12]

"A large number of servants" concludes the inventory. The translation "servants" is certain, but this spelling, 'ăbuddâ, occurs only here and in Gen 26:14.[13]

The short second half of the verse simply summarizes the prowess of Job by telling the reader that "he was the greatest man among all the people of the East." "East," which can also mean "wisdom," depends on the standpoint of the writer. More than likely the writer was an Israelite living west of the Jordan River. The east, then, can mean virtually any place from Damascus to Arabia and as far east as Persia.[14]

---

[11] Cf. A. E. Day and R. K. Harrison, "Camel," *ISBE* 1:583-84.

[12] Only Zech 9:9 has both words in the same verse.

[13] It is a fem. sing. word, but that is no reason to believe that it refers only to female servants. It is a collective. On collective singulars, see the discussion in *IBHS* § 7.1–7.4.3.

[14] The designation certainly does not preclude placing Job and the land of Uz about fifty miles east of modern Amman, Jordan. Judges 6:3,33; 7:12; 8:10, and a few scattered places in the prophets speak of the people of the east. In Judges it means Midianites who were more to the southeast than to the east. In Ezek 25:4 the people of the east are those who would possess the Ammonites, so a place more directly east of Israel is indicated. Jeremiah 49:28 has them parallel with Kedar, a desert tribe located somewhere east or southeast of Palestine.

The picture in the first three verses of Job is of a godly, wealthy, fulfilled man. He was the ideal candidate for the tests soon to follow. He would lose the children of v. 2 and the possessions of v. 3. But would he also lose the godliness and righteousness of v. 1?

(5) Job's Regular Custom (1:4-5)

⁴His sons used to take turns holding feasts in their homes, and they would invite their three sisters to eat and drink with them. ⁵When a period of feasting had run its course, Job would send and have them purified. Early in the morning he would sacrifice a burnt offering for each of them, thinking, "Perhaps my children have sinned and cursed God in their hearts." This was Job's regular custom.

The next two verses elaborate on and illustrate Job's routine of piety. The idiomatic nature of the Hebrew in v. 4 makes anything close to a literal translation unintelligible. The gist in the NIV seems normal enough, but one cannot be certain of the precise meaning of the literal phrase "the house of each his day." Not that it is important, but the text does not say how often the brothers hosted their sisters. Was it on their birthdays? Were they established feast days? Were these parties every day of the week since there were seven brothers? Why did not the sisters invite the brothers to their homes? Were any or all of these children married? Were all the children at all the parties or just one brother at a time with his three sisters? Did Job attend all these affairs? How close to one another did these family members live?

Though lacking details, the text does describe a big, happy family. They not only got along with each other but enjoyed each other's company. It was a truly convivial clan.

1:4 Three pairs of hendiadys[15] make the verse wordy. Literally it says, "His sons *went,* and they *made.*" "They *sent,* and they *called* to their three sisters to *eat* and to *drink* with them." The root for "drink" (*šth*) occurs twice in the verse, in the noun "feast" and the infinitive "to drink."

1:5 It is not clear how long it took for the feast days to run their course. Certainly Job did not offer these sacrifices after each feast but perhaps after every seventh feast. This seems to be the basic meaning of the relatively unusual verb *nqp,* "to go around."

Job would summon his children and "purify" or "sanctify" them. It simply may have been a prayer of absolution or some ceremony in con-

---

[15] This is a form of expression that uses two words of the same part of speech to express one idea, e.g., "answered and said."

junction with the sacrificing that the next clause describes. It was Job's way of reminding his children to do what they were doing in moderation, a gentle, parental nudge in the direction of holy living.

The Hebrew speaks of the sacrifices in the plural, and the NIV translates the "all of them" distributively as "each of them." The presence of the word "number," *mispar,* suggests one animal for each child. Certainly it appears that the sacrifices are for the usual purpose of covering sin rather than a cultic slaying for food.

Job was not certain his children had committed sins for which a sacrificial animal was necessary, but he wanted to make sure; hence the "perhaps" in the words he spoke to himself. *Better to err,* he thought, *on that side than on the other.* After all, who can know what his children may have said "in their hearts"?

"Curse" is the translation of the common *brk* that ordinarily means "bless." The context makes clear that *brk* is intended here as a euphemism. Such a diametrically opposite meaning occurs again at 1:11; 2:5,9.[16]

"This was Job's regular custom" concludes v. 5. One of the arguments for the antiquity of the man Job is that he was a priest to his own family. Like Abraham, he was not dependent on another to make sacrifices. Job was a patriarch in the sense that he was the head of his clan. He also was a patriarch in that he offered sacrifices for himself and for others. He knew nothing of the Levites or the laws of Moses. The story took place in very ancient times.

2. Test of Wealth (1:6-22)

The rest of chap. 1 describes the first of two tests to which Job was put, the test of wealth, that is, the loss of his children, servants, and possessions. In this test the Satan, who first appeared in v. 6, gained permission from the Lord to take everything from Job except his health.

Out of the conversation with the Lord, the Satan presented Job with a challenge. He claimed that Job was only good toward God because God had been good toward him. To prove that such was not the case, the Lord allowed the accuser to take away all that supposedly was the reason for Job's piety.

The second half of this section catalogs those losses. Did Job pass the

---

[16] Used in this polar sense בֵּרֵךְ occurs also in 1 Kgs 21:10,13; Ps 10:3. E. Tov (*Textual Criticism of the Hebrew Bible* [Minneapolis: Fortress, 1992], 272) explains that it could be either a scribal change or a euphemism used by the original author.

test? Was God right, or was the Satan right? Verse 22 is the answer.

(1) The Satan (1:6-10)

[6]One day the angels came to present themselves before the LORD, and Satan also came with them. [7]The LORD said to Satan, "Where have you come from?"

Satan answered the LORD, "From roaming through the earth and going back and forth in it."

[8]Then the LORD said to Satan, "Have you considered my servant Job? There is no one on earth like him; he is blameless and upright, a man who fears God and shuns evil."

[9]Does Job fear God for nothing?" Satan replied. [10]"Have you not put a hedge around him and his household and everything he has? You have blessed the work of his hands, so that his flocks and herds are spread throughout the land.

The scene described in these verses is difficult to understand. Scholars have raised several questions: Who is the Satan?[17] Where did he come from? Is this the devil found elsewhere in the Bible? Why does the definite article precede the name? Does that mean it is a common noun and not a name? How can he have such easy and direct access to the Lord? When did Satan fall from heaven? Who are the other angels? Why does the Lord stoop to answer the Satan? Can Satan still access and challenge God like this concerning one of us?

1:6 The "sons of God" are both plural and inferior to God. The words appear again in 2:1; 38:7; cf. Gen 6:2,4; Ps 89:6[7].[18] Apparently God has a council or cabinet (see 1 Kgs 22:19; Jer 23:18,22; and Ps 89:5-7[6-8]). These "holy ones" (Ps 89:5,7[6,8]) serve as messengers to do God's bidding. Not every one of them is good because 1 Kgs 22:20-23 speaks of a "spirit" willing to be a "lying spirit in the mouths of all his [i.e., Ahab's] prophets." The Satan was among them or perhaps even their leader.

The Satan (or the Accuser) represented those who opposed God and his good people. In Job the Satan assumed his classical pose of charging a good man with evil (Rev 12:10). The boundaries of operation that God allowed him are uncertain. At times his power seems not only supernatural but also a threat to God's sovereign and beneficent control of the world. At other times the Satan seems like a vain, weak, and hopeless antagonist

---

[17] See special essay in N. Tur-Sinai, *The Book of Job,* rev. ed. (Jerusalem: Kiryat-Sefer, 1967), 38-45.

[18] "Sons of God" in Ps 89:6[7] is בְּנֵי אֵלִים while Job has the standard spelling of "God," אֱלֹהִים.

against the omnipotent God of the universe. One of the loose threads left hanging at the end of the Book of Job is the resultant embarrassment of the Satan. His charge was not true. Job did not curse God when he lost everything.

This is the first appearance of God's covenant name, Yahweh (sometimes written YHWH since the Masoretes did not pronounce the name), or, as most versions have it, "the LORD." In this book its thirty-two occurrences are confined to chaps. 1–2; 12:9; 38:1; 40:1,3,6; and chap. 42.

1:7 A dialogue between the Lord and the Satan fills vv. 7-12. Mainly it is a question-and-answer session. At first the Lord asks the questions (vv. 7-8), and the Satan answers. In vv. 9-10 the Satan asks the questions. The Lord does not exactly answer the questions but simply grants the accuser a limited amount of freedom to persecute Job. The dialogue ends with the Satan leaving the presence of the Lord.

The first question God asked was, "Where have you come from?" It cannot be that the omniscient God lacks information that only the Satan can provide. Nor is it an exclamation as if the Satan's presence among the sons of God were something that startled the Lord. It is simply the Lord's way of starting the conversation.

Two verbs, "answered and said," a hendiadys, introduce the response. The answer is indirect, "Nowhere in particular and everywhere in general," to paraphrase his response. However lofty or poetic the language even of the prose prologue, this answer does speak to the supernatural character of the Satan. He had ready access to all spheres. His answer also has a ring of sarcasm to it. He avoided a direct answer but retorted with one that really provided no information.

1:8 One might presume that the conversation was much longer than the few verses devoted to it here. The author, however, was interested in getting to the point, which was Job and how Job came to be the focus of the book that bears his name. As if out of nowhere, the Lord raised the subject of his servant Job's good behavior.

The idiom in Hebrew is literally, "Have you set your heart on?" The heart is not only one of the seats of emotion in Hebrew psychology; but it is also one of the locations of thinking, reasoning, or planning.

Without waiting for an answer, the Lord elaborated on Job. Job was unique on the earth or in the world. While no one is exactly like another person, this does sound like hyperbole, a perfectly legitimate literary device. The latter part of the description of Job is identical to part of v. 1. English speakers might wonder about God speaking of himself in the third person. This is so common in the Old Testament, not only of God but of all writers, that it should not come as a surprise or be an occasion to stumble. The text does not say that Job was the most blameless and upright of men. His uniqueness may have been that few men were of his economic stature and also righteous. It was a small company to which he belonged. If the three friends are indicative of that company, then Job clearly stood above them.

1:9 As in v. 7b the Satan answered the Lord's question with a question of his own, a typical Semitic way of speaking. Three of the four words of his question in Hebrew are repeated from the Lord's words. "For nothing," *ḥinnām*, was his contribution and, indirectly, his accusation. The Lord used this, the Satan's word, in his answer in 2:3. The Satan here asked if Job feared God "for no reason." In 2:3 God accused the Satan of being behind Job's sufferings "for no reason."

While there is a certain insidiousness about this charge, it is a worthy question. There were people in the New Testament who followed Jesus because of the benefits he gave them, not because they wished to be his disciples. And today there are those who attach themselves to the church for the advantages that come their way. It is a question all believers might ask themselves, Would I fear God even if there were no blessings here and now and greater ones promised for the hereafter?

The question cuts to the heart of genuine faith. The issue is whether God deserves to be worshiped because of the greatness of his character or must "buy" his worship with gifts and promises of blessing. The serpent raised a similar issue when he accused God of being less than good and honest (Gen 3:12-15).

1:10 The Satan's questions continue into v. 10. The negative interrogative, *hălōʾ*, could do double duty and introduce the second half of v. 10 as well as the first. Then it would read, "Have you not blessed the work of his hands?" Consequently there would be a total of three questions in the Satan's response.

The first charge or question is that God had put a hedge[19] around Job, his house(hold), and all he owned. Using a biform of this rare verb, Job would later complain that God had "hedged" him in with troubles (3:23).

"The work of his hands," as in Ps 90:17, is a way of saying everything he put his hands to, or his life's work. Job was a success regardless of how success was measured.

"Flocks and herds" in the NIV translates the same word that was missing in the translation of v. 3, "his possessions." "Land," *ʾ ereṣ*, translates

---

[19] "Hedge" is שׂוּךְ, a root that occurs elsewhere only in 10:11 and Hos 2:6[8]. A biform, spelled with a ס, is in Job 3:23; 38:8. The related noun סֻכָּה is known from Sukkoth, the Feast of Booths or Tabernacles.

the same word that was "earth" in v. 8. The word does not mean the planet
or globe, though there are places where *'ereṣ* can have that connotation.

(2) Challenge (1:11-12)

**¹¹But stretch out your hand and strike everything he has, and he will sure-
ly curse you to your face.
¹²The LORD said to Satan, "Very well, then, everything he has is in your
hands, but on the man himself do not lay a finger."**

What follows is no surprise. The Satan challenged the Lord to with-
draw that blessing that the Satan believed was the reason for Job's piety.
He dared the Lord to stretch out his hand and strike everything Job had.

1:11 The opening word, "But," translates an adversative particle,
'ûlām, that is stronger than the simple *waw*.[20] "Curse" is again the polar
meaning of *brk* as in v. 5 (cf. 2:5,9; 1 Kgs 21:10,13). Happily it turned out
that Job did not curse God to his face. The worst he would do was question the justice of God (9:24), which is quite different from cursing.

1:12 Verse 12 is interestingly and intriguingly tied with v. 11. First,
the expression "everything he has" appears for the third time (vv.
10,11,12). Second, the Satan had asked God to stretch out his hand
against Job. God did not do that but permitted the Satan to stretch out his
hand against all that Job had, but not against Job himself. Third, the words
for "face" in v. 11 and "presence" in v. 12 are the same. We may ask
whether the author was intentionally playing with these and other repeated words.

Verse 10 lists three categories: "him," "his household," and "everything
he has." In this verse the Satan receives permission to afflict only the last
two. The affliction of Job's body would be the substance of the second test
(2:7).

God granted the accuser only limited power over his servant. This
agrees with other places in the Bible where the devil is restricted or confined by the greater authority of God himself.[21]

---

[20] Ten of the nineteen OT occurrences are in Job.

[21] First Chronicles 21:1 has the Satan inciting David, while 2 Sam 24:1 says that the
Lord incited David to take a census (cf. 2 Sam 24:16). Satan was to do the apostle's bid-
ding in 1 Cor 5:5. In the end Christ will destroy the devil (Heb 2:14; Rev 12:9; 20:2,10).
Cf. R. Dillard, "David's Census: Perspectives on 2 Samuel 24 and 1 Chronicles 21," in
Through Christ's Word (Phillipsburg, N.J.: Presbyterian and Reformed, 1985), 94-107, and
M. Tate, "Satan in the Old Testament," *RevExp* 89 (1992): 461-75.

(3) Misfortunes (1:13-19)

[13]One day when Job's sons and daughters were feasting and drinking wine at the oldest brother's house, [14]a messenger came to Job and said, "The oxen were plowing and the donkeys were grazing nearby, [15]and the Sabeans attacked and carried them off. They put the servants to the sword, and I am the only one who has escaped to tell you!"

[16]While he was still speaking, another messenger came and said, "The fire of God fell from the sky and burned up the sheep and the servants, and I am the only one who has escaped to tell you!"

[17]While he was still speaking, another messenger came and said, "The Chaldeans formed three raiding parties and swept down on your camels and carried them off. They put the servants to the sword and I am the only one who has escaped to tell you!"

[18]While he was still speaking, yet another messenger came and said, "Your sons and daughters were feasting and drinking wine at the oldest brother's house, [19]when suddenly a mighty wind swept in from the desert and struck the four corners of the house. It collapsed on them and they are dead, and I am the only one who has escaped to tell you!"

These verses catalogue the catastrophes that befell Job as a direct result of the Lord permitting the Satan to touch all that he had. There are four catastrophes: (1) theft of oxen and donkeys (1:13-15), (2) fire (1:16), (3) theft of camels (1:17), and (4) the storm that killed his children (1:18-19). Certain features of the reports are repeated, and it is this stylized nature of the prologue that points to an author concerned with poetic structure. Four times the refrain is exactly the same, "I am the only one who has escaped to tell you." There is no reason to disbelieve that these tragedies happened. But we must allow the inspired author to structure his report in a way that the impact on the readers is even greater than a prosaic chronicle.[22]

THEFT (1:13-15). It is now evident why a point was made earlier in the chapter of Job's children feasting in each other's homes. Those celebrations figured in the first and fourth of the calamities.

1:13 Like v. 6, v. 13 begins with "One day."[23] The text gives no indication how long after the Satan's challenge this took place, but one can imagine that he began immediately to exercise his right to afflict Job.

The children were eating and drinking wine. "Wine" is not in v. 4. One

---

[22] *BHS* has vv. 16-19 set up as poetry.

[23] While technically there are two independent clauses in v. 13, the NIV makes the entire verse a clause dependent on v. 14. Literally rendered v. 13 begins: "There was the day. His sons and daughters."

should not assume that they were drunk. This was not a judgment against them but a test for Job. On the other hand, v. 5 describes Job's offering a sacrifice for them just in case they had sinned and cursed God in their hearts. That would more easily have happened if they were not sober.

It was the turn of the firstborn son to host the feast when this fateful day arrived. Maybe he was the wealthiest and could throw the biggest banquet; or perhaps this was the beginning of a new cycle of feasts, and they made the rounds in order, from the home of the oldest to the youngest. As the firstborn he was in line to inherit a double share of his father's wealth (cf. Deut 21:17). Perhaps he already had received it[24] and was thereby the prime target of these desert marauders.

1:14 A *mal'āk,* messenger (elsewhere "angel" 4:18; 33:23), reported to Job the background of the first disaster. The oxen (of v. 3) were plowing, and the donkeys (also from v. 3) were grazing beside them.[25] Living on the edge the desert as he did, this indicates some time in the fall when the first rains had fallen and softened the soil so that it could be plowed. Otherwise there are few indicators in this book to tell the time of these events.

Because of the stylized nature of this and the following reports, it is unwise to press the details. Were all five hundred yoke of oxen plowing or just a few of them? Such a task would require many servants, as many as five hundred, to control that many teams. It is best not to dwell on the uncertainties of the particulars but stand at the right distance to view the entire series of events in perspective.

1:15 The Sabeans were nomadic marauders descended from Sheba, a grandson of Abraham (Gen 25:3). Eventually they settled in the southernmost part of the Arabian peninsula.[26] Sheba became a wealthy nation by

---

[24] The lost son of Luke 15:12 received his share of the estate before his father died.

[25] Once again these were female donkeys or she-asses, the same as were doubled for Job in 42:12. He must also have had some males to service this herd.

[26] The Hebrew text has Sabean in the singular, and the verb agrees. It is a collective and properly read as plural. Other Shebas are the son of Cush, the Hamite (Gen 10:7; 1 Chr 1:9), and the son of Joktan, a descendant of Shem (Gen 10:28; 1 Chr 1:22). It is possible that these two and the one of Gen 25:3 are the same person or tribe since all are connected with Arabia. Those of Gen 10:7; 25:3 both have Dedan as a brother. The Sheba of Gen 10:28 is the son of Joktan while the one of Gen 25:3 is the son of Jokshan, a difference of one letter in Hebrew. A queen from Sheba came to Solomon (1 Kgs 10:1) probably, among other things, to work out a trade agreement. Located at modern Yemen and probably controlling the Bab al Mandab at the southern end of the Red Sea, her nation exercised considerable control over the trade routes between India to the east and Africa to the west. It is in that connection that the prophets mention the Sabeans or the people of Sheba (Isa 60:6; Jer 6:20; Ezek 27:22; 38:13; Joel 3:8[4:8]. Cf. Ps 72:10,15; Job 6:19).

the time of Solomon. That the Sabeans were pirates points to a time earlier than that of the famous Queen of Sheba (1 Kgs 10; 2 Chr 9). From Marib, the capital of Sheba, to where we think Job lived was over a thousand miles.

The idyllic scene of plowing oxen, grazing donkeys, and busy servants was rudely interrupted by these invaders who stole the animals and slaughtered the workers (lit. "young men," *nĕʿārîm*). Only the reporting messenger escaped with his life. His report is replete with emphatic elements.[27] There are two words for "only" or "alone" (*raq* and *lĕbadî*) and an extra independent first person pronoun (*ʾănî*). Fully and literally it would read: "And I have escaped! Only me! I alone to tell you!"

FIRE (1:16).   The four catastrophes are linked together by the opening words of the second, third, and fourth of them: "While he was still speaking, another came and said."[28]

1:16   This time the "fire of God fell from the sky" or "heavens." Verse 3 indicated that Job had seven thousand sheep. It must have been quite a lightning bolt to have burned up the sheep and "eaten"[29] the young men. It probably caused a fire. It was the "fire of the LORD" that struck the grumbling Israelites in the wilderness (Num 11:1). It also kindled Elijah's sacrifice on Mount Carmel (1 Kgs 18:38) and struck the first two groups of fifty men that King Ahaziah sent to Elijah (2 Kgs 1:10,12,14). The expression "fire of God" may be the equivalent of "a great fire" or "fire from the sky," that is, lightening,[30] but it should not be taken to imply that the Satan had some kind of control over God since these are the words of the messenger.

The messenger's concluding words are identical to those in v. 15, an indication of the author's penchant for order and repetition. The verb "attacked" in v. 15 is the same verb (*nāpal*) translated "fell" in vv. 16,20. The verb "carried off" in v. 15 (*lāqaḥ*) occurs again in v. 17.

THEFT (1:17).   **1:17**   The third catastrophe corresponds to the first in that it came from other human beings, whereas the second and fourth were weather related.

The first and last phrases of this verse are identical to the corresponding phrases in v. 16. The middle phrase describes the third catastrophe.

---

[27] The verb "escaped" has a paragogic ה, which indicates a certain urgency to the action.

[28] Messenger" is not in Hebrew; it has simply "this" and "this," which is idiomatic for "this" and "another."

[29] In Hebrew there is a verb for each victim. The fire burned (בער) the sheep and ate (אכל) the servants.

[30] R. Gordis, *The Book of God and Man* (Chicago: University Press, 1965),16.

Instead of Sabeans it was Chaldeans[31] who attacked. They would have come from the northeast since they were Mesopotamians. The mention of three bands may be an extraneous detail, or it may show some organization on the part of the raiders. Camels, no doubt, were harder to corral than sheep.

STORM (1:18-19).   For the fourth and last catastrophe the author offered more detail. This is also the only episode in this first stage of testing that employs the particle *hinnēh,* "behold," suggesting this is the climactic episode. While the number of Job's children did not compare with the numbers of lost livestock, there is no comparing the grief that arises from losing children.

1:18   Again the opening line is the same as vv. 16-17.[32] That and the mention of Job's children feasting (cf. v. 13) has a way of tying these four tragedies together. Such details point to a brief period. All these misfortunes befell Job within the time of one feast.

1:19   The first and third calamities were from human enemies. The second and fourth were from natural causes (although all four calamities were caused by the Satan, according to Job 1–2). In v. 16 it was the "fire of God," and here it is a "mighty wind." The wind came across the desert, indicating the sirocco, a hot sandy wind that blows predominately at the beginning and the end of summer.[33]

The wind struck the four corners of the house, which in turn fell on the "youths," killing them. This last word for the children is the same one that has been translated "servants" in the preceding verses. Undoubtedly here it refers to Job's children and not the servants. Again the author's reiteration of stock words gives unity to this section. It is also interesting to notice that in this *fourth* episode the author referred to the *four* corners of the house, and in the epilogue (42:16) Job is said to have lived to see "his children and their children to the *fourth* generation," thus suggesting full restoration.

This loss was the most tragic of all for Job, since these children were

---

[31] While Chaldeans are best known from later OT history as the core of the neo-Babylonian Empire, in the early period they were nomads whose base was in southern Mesopotamia. The only early OT references apart from here are to Ur of the Chaldeans in Gen 11:28,31; 15:7. The Hebrew word כַּשְׂדִּים is related to the Akkadian *kašdu,* but there are no records of them from the second millennium B.C.

[32] Except that the opening word is עַד rather than עֹד. See J. Barr, "Hebrew עַד especially at Job i.18 and Neh. vii.3," *JSS* 27 (1982): 177-88.

[33] The Hebrew words are simply "mighty wind" (רוּחַ גְּדוֹלָה), not one of the specialized terms for storm or whirlwind (סוּפָה or סְעָרָה). The effects suggest a tornado, but the choice of words seems to indicate an extraordinarily strong east wind.

his own flesh and blood. Through shrewd maneuvering he might have been able to restore his fortunes in livestock and servants, but children are a special gift from God (Ps 127:3). A similar loss befell Horatio Spafford when his four children perished at sea, an event that prompted him to pen the hymn "It Is Well with My Soul." That, in fact, will be the tenor of Job's response.

(4) Job's Response (1:20-22)

²⁰**At this, Job got up and tore his robe and shaved his head. Then he fell to the ground in worship ²¹and said:**
    Naked I came from my mother's womb,
        and naked I will depart.
    The LORD gave and the LORD has taken away;
        may the name of the LORD be praised."
²²**In all this, Job did not sin by charging God with wrongdoing.**

Job's response to these tragedies is one of the high points of the book. It beautifully illustrates his piety that the first verse mentioned. One could wish that God's children always responded in such a way to the vicissitudes of life. Unfortunately our tendency is to bless God in fair weather and grumble or even curse in foul.

1:20 Five of the nine Hebrew words in this verse are verbs, and Job is the subject of all of them: He got up, he tore, he shaved, he fell, and he worshiped. The rising and falling at the beginning and end of the series creates poetic balance, a merismus.[34]

The tearing of clothing and the shaving of the head were standard ancient Near Eastern demonstrations of grief.[35] Only the wearing of sackcloth is absent here as a typical expression of anguish, but that will appear in 16:15. The garment he tore was his robe, *mĕ'îlô*, an outer garment worn by people of rank such as the high priest, Saul, Jonathan, David, and Job's three friends (2:12).

The tearing and the shaving are the expected reactions to the tragedies that suddenly and recently came to Job. The falling to the ground and

---

[34] Merismus is a figure of speech in which totality is described by words with opposite meanings such as *night* and *day*. See W. G. E. Watson, *Classical Hebrew Poetry* (Sheffield: JSOT, 1986), 31, 321-24.

[35] Other instances of tearing of clothes are in Gen 37:29,34; 44:13; Num 14:6; Josh 7:6; 2 Sam 1:11; 13:19,31; 2 Kgs 5:7; 6:30; 19:1; Ezra 9:3; Isa 36:22; 37:1; Jer 41:5; and elsewhere. For shaving the head or beard see Isa 15:2; Jer 7:29; 16:6; 41:5; Ezek 27:31; Mic 1:16. Only the Jeremiah and Micah passages use the same verb for shave, גזז, that Job has. Usually גזז means "to shear sheep."

worshiping are what separate him from others.[36] He did not shake his fist
skyward and scream, "Why me, Lord?" but bowed to the ground in humble acknowledgment of and capitulation to God's sovereign will.

1:21 The well-balanced poem that Job speaks in his grief is a model
of submissive piety and obedient surrender to a God whose ways are not
our ways and whose thoughts are not our thoughts (Isa 55:8). From a
structural point of view, the word "naked" ties the two halves of the first
line together. Then there is a merismus (see comments on 1:20) created by
the contrasting verbs, "came" and "depart." Another merismus is in the
second line with the antithesis of the verbs "give" and "take away."

The NIV "depart" is literally "return" (*šûb*). But one ought not read too
much into his statement that he would return to his mother's womb or try
to solve the problem by understanding her to be mother earth. This is poetry. It is simply his way of saying that he was born with nothing, and he
will die with nothing. Whatever we accumulate during our lifetimes must
be surrendered at death. Shrouds have no pockets.

"The LORD" occurs three times in the second line. He has given, he has
taken away, and his name is worthy of praise.[37]

1:22 Antecedent to "this" are the calamities of vv. 13-19. Any one of
those events might have caused lesser men to lose faith, abandon hope, or
even charge God with neglect or deliberate evil. The "sin" that Job did not
commit was to accuse God of "wrongdoing."[38] He did indirectly acknowledge that God had sent these troubles, but he did not at this point
question God's justice, love, wisdom, or sovereignty. It is a rare and commendable posture that the hero from Uz assumed, one that should characterize all God's children whatever turns life might take.

Thus the chapter ends with "the greatest man among all the people of
the East" destitute, childless, and broken. In the space of less than a page
and in a brief span of time, he went from being the greatest to being the
least of men. We the readers know something that Job did not, and so we
cannot enter into his sorrow. Like God, we know the end from the beginning. We know all about the fact that Job had been chosen as a test case.
Because of his godliness God selected him for this trial. Job was unaware
that his troubles were a great honor. Would Job remain faithful? Will we?

---

[36] "Worship" is יִשְׁתָּחוּ, a *histaphal* (*IBHS* § 21.2.3d) that expresses repeated, reflexive,
or reciprocal action, in this case repeated bowing or falling both prostrate and supine.

[37] "Praise" is בָּרַךְ, elsewhere "bless," the term that has been translated with its opposite meaning in vv. 5,11.

[38] "Wrongdoing" is תִּפְלָה, a fem. noun that occurs elsewhere only in Job 24:12; Jer
23:13, where it is translated "repulsive." A masc. form of it translated "worthless" is in Job
6:6; Lam 2:14.

3. Test of Health (2:1-10)

A number of similarities exist between this chapter and the preceding one. Verses 1-3a are nearly identical to 1:6-8. Job 1:12 corresponds with 2:6, and 1:22 corresponds with 2:10c. In these ten verses Job's testing intensifies. Up to this point he has lost his possessions and his children. Now he would lose his health, which the Satan hoped would break his will and prompt him to curse his God. These two tests together produce yet other losses that we will note in the course of the debate cycle: honor, respect, standing in the community, friendships, and even the support of his wife and brothers (12:4; 16:10; 19:13-19; 30:1,9-10).

(1) The Satan (2:1-5)

¹On another day the angels came to present themselves before the LORD, and Satan also came with them to present himself before him. ²And the LORD said to Satan, "Where have you come from?"

Satan answered the LORD, "From roaming through the earth and going back and forth in it."

³Then the LORD said to Satan, "Have you considered my servant Job? There is no one on earth like him; he is blameless and upright, a man who fears God and shuns evil. And he still maintains his integrity, though you incited me against him to ruin him without any reason."

⁴"Skin for skin!" Satan replied. "A man will give all he has for his own life. ⁵But stretch out your hand and strike his flesh and bones, and he will surely curse you to your face."

With several phrases identical to 1:6-8, the second conversation between the Lord and the Satan is described. The upshot was that the Lord gave permission to the accuser to test Job even further, to afflict his physical well-being.

2:1 Though the NIV has "another day" at the beginning of the verse, the only difference in the Hebrew between this verse and 1:6 is the addition of the repetitive phrase at the end, "to present himself before him." The same questions that went unanswered in chap. 1 linger here.

The duplication of the phraseology from chap. 1 points up once more the tight structure and repetitive style of the author. While we may think such reiteration is unimaginative writing, it is a feature quite typical of ancient Near Eastern literature.[39]

---

[39] Just one example is the Ugaritic Legend of Keret. In a detailed dream Keret is instructed how to besiege the neighboring city and ask its king for his daughter's hand. Upon waking, Keret follows the instructions to the letter. The result is many lines of text that exactly echo the instruction (*ANET*, 144-45).

2:2 Except for different interrogative particles, 2:2 and 1:7 are identical.[40]

2:3 The first half of 2:3 is identical to 1:8. "Integrity" is from the same root as "blameless."[41] In other words, despite the losses he incurred, Job still did not tarnish his perfect record. "Incite" is the same action the Satan used when he prompted David to take a census (1 Chr 21:1). "Ruin" is the more common *bl'*, often "swallow" as in Job 7:19 or Jonah 1:17[2:1].[42]

"Without cause" is an adverb the author used in 1:9. There the Satan asked whether Job feared God "for nothing." Here it is "for nothing" that the Satan incited Yahweh to destroy Job. God and good people do not do things "for nothing"; Satan does.

2:4 Apart from Exodus and Leviticus, which have much to say about rams' skins and infectious skin diseases, Job has the most references to "skin" of any Old Testament book. The repeated use of it here may hint at the nature of the disease that was soon to strike Job. The expression does not occur elsewhere but is reminiscent of "eye for an eye and tooth for a tooth" (Exod 21:24; Lev 24:20; Deut 19:21). The Satan wagered that Job would willingly surrender everything he owned to save his life.[43] But what did Job have left to give? Did the Satan hope that Job would give up even his faith in God and his spotless record of piety? As the adversary of godliness and godly people, that is Satan's purpose in all temptation.

2:5 The first five words of this verse are identical with 1:11, again showing the author's fondness for order, regularity, and repetition. Undoubtedly the conversation between Yahweh and the Satan was much longer than this brief report indicates.

Instead of striking "everything he has," the tempter told God to strike his bone and his flesh. That is another merismus (see comment at 1:20), since the body consists of hard parts (bones) and soft parts (flesh). The word for "bone" sometimes refers to the essence or innermost parts of something. The Satan wished Job to be diseased totally, thoroughly

---

[40] In 1:7 it is מֵאַיִן, "from where?" In 2:2 it is אֵי מִזֶּה, "where from this?" The former occurs two other places in Job (28:12,10) and sixteen times altogether in the OT. This interrogative particle never appears without the prefixed מִן. The latter occurs six other places in Job and forty times altogether in the OT. A slight difference also is the verb "from roaming" is spelled with a full *šureq* in 1:7 (מִשּׁוּט) and with a *kibbutz* in 2:2 (מִשֻּׁט).

[41] "Blameless" is תָּם, and "integrity" is תֻּמָּה, which will appear again in 2:9; 27:5; and 31:6. Elsewhere in the OT it is only in Prov 11:3.

[42] The more literal "swallow" is limited to the *qal* stem. Its meaning in the intensive stems and often in the *qal* is "destroy." In this passage it is *piel*.

[43] Hebrew נֶפֶשׁ, often "breath/soul/neck/throat."

racked with pain, and plagued in every physical dimension. Later Elihu said, "His flesh wastes away to nothing, and his bones, once hidden, now stick out" (33:21).

The last five words are identical with the last five of 1:11. Job passed the first test, that of losing his wealth and family. Will he pass the second one, the loss of his health?

(2) Disease (2:6-8)

⁶The LORD said to Satan, "Very well, then, he is in your hands; but you must spare his life."

⁷So Satan went out from the presence of the LORD and afflicted Job with painful sores from the soles of his feet to the top of his head. ⁸Then Job took a piece of broken pottery and scraped himself with it as he sat among the ashes.

Finally the Satan reduced Job financially, family-wise, and physically, as low as he could. Job lost everything except his life, and the worth of living it he questions seriously in chap. 3.

2:6 The verse begins as 1:12 does. In chap. 1 God hands over to the Satan everything that belongs to Job. Now he hands over Job himself. The adversary was allowed to afflict Job's flesh and bones, but not to take his life. Killing Job would prove nothing and benefit neither God nor the Satan.

2:7 The opening of v. 7 is almost the same as the close of 1:12.[44] It is the last we hear of the Satan in the book. The Satan told God to strike (*ngʿ*) Job, but in this verse it is the Satan who strikes (*nkh*) him. He afflicted him with "painful sores[45] from the soles of his feet to the top of his head."[46] This is another merismus (see on 1:20); Job was totally covered with these eruptions on his skin.

It is uncertain just what disease Job had. Guesses range from melanoma to leprosy and assorted less serious itches. In 7:5 he complained, "My

---

[44] Job 1:12 has מֵעַם, while 2:7 has מֵאֵת. Both are compound prepositions, "from" (מִן) plus "with" (עַם or אֵת).

[45] Hebrew שְׁחִין. The same word describes the sixth plague on the Egyptians (Exod 9:9-11; Deut 28:27,35). Leviticus 13 has it four times in connection with the legislation on skin infections. It is also what afflicted King Hezekiah (2 Kgs 20:7; Isa 38:21). Here is the only occurrence in Job. While Hezekiah seems to have had a single boil, the Egyptians, their animals, and Job were covered with them. Deuteronomy 28:35 even has the same expression as in Job, "from the soles of your feet to the top of your head."

[46] "The top of his head" is קָדְקֹד, a reduplicated noun derived from קדד, "bow down." Cf. גֻּלְגֹּלֶת, "head, skull," a reduplicated noun derived from גלל, "to roll, be round," hence "Golgotha."

body is clothed with worms and scabs, my skin is broken and festering." In 30:30 he moaned, "My skin grows black and peels; my body burns with fever." Weight loss and a generally repulsive appearance were among the unpleasant side effects (2:12; 19:19-20). Perhaps for fear of catching what he had, friends and relatives distanced themselves from him (19:13-14).

2:8 Job took a potsherd, or a piece of a broken clay pot, to scratch or scrape himself.[47] Pots and potsherds illustrate commonness (Prov 26:23), insignificance (Isa 30:14; Lam 4:2), and fragility (Jer 19:1,10). Unlike the verbs "took" and "scraped," which are indicative, "sat" in line *b* is a participle that suggests a more or less permanent situation. One might translate, "He was a dweller among the ashes." "Ashes" are one more characteristic element associated with mourning (2 Sam 13:19; Esth 4:1,3; Dan 9:3; Jonah 3:6). "Ashes" would be the last word Job utters in this book (42:6).

(3) Job's Wife (2:9-10)

⁹His wife said to him, "Are you still holding on to your integrity? Curse God and die!"
¹⁰He replied, "You are talking like a foolish woman. Shall we accept good from God, and not trouble?"
In all this, Job did not sin in what he said.

2:9 For the first and only time Job's wife spoke. Job mentioned her in the course of his complaint (19:17) and in his self-maledictory oath (31:10). Was she the mother of the ten children who had died? Did she mother the second set of seven sons and three daughters at the end of the book? One must remember that though she was not physically afflicted, she also suffered the loss of children and wealth. Now it appears that she would lose her husband. Let us not be too hard on her.[48]

No interrogative particle marks her first sentence, but it surely makes better sense if it is a question. Apart from the change in the pronoun ("he" to "you"), the Hebrew words are the same as in 2:3.

---

[47] "Scrape" is a hapax legomenon; but cognates in Aramaic, Syriac, Phoenician, and Arabic help establish the translation. גרד is in the *hithpael* stem, which suggests reflexive, repeated, or back-and-forth action.

[48] In the Aramaic Targum, Job's wife is named Dinah, alluding to the episode in Gen 34. In the pseudepigraphical Testament of Job she is called Sitis, a corruption of the LXX translation of Uz. The LXX adds five verses of material at this point. They are an elaboration of her speech. For a translation see J. E. Hartley, *The Book of Job*, NICOT (Grand Rapids: Eerdmans, 1988), 83, n. 7.

Indeed Job did maintain his integrity throughout the ordeal. As late as 27:5-6, Job's last speech in the debate cycle, he claimed: "I will not deny my integrity. I will maintain my righteousness and never let go of it."

Job's wife's advice was brief and final, "Curse[49] God and die." Both verbs are imperatives. She believed as the counselors did that there is a direct and immediate connection between sin and punishment. To curse God is tantamount to committing suicide.[50] She suggested that he do something to effect his own death. The legislation of Lev 24:10-16 requires the community to stone to death anyone guilty of cursing God, but it is not likely that Job's wife was reflecting these laws.

2:10 The middle part of this verse is another of those classic, quotable insights from the mouth of Job. It is preceded, however, by his abrupt and insulting rebuke to his wife. More literally it reads, "You speak like the speaking of one of the foolish women."[51] It is impossible to say what "foolish women" he had in mind.

The central phrase is fulsome, repetitive, and arranged so that "good" and "trouble"[52] are in the prominent positions. It reads in Hebrew word order: "The good shall we accept from God, and the trouble shall we not accept?" No interrogative particle begins either phrase, but it carries more force if translated that way. It is a rhetorical question to which Job did not expect an answer.

This is a hard lesson for some believers to learn, especially if they feel they have been promised health and wealth or have (mis)understood that God's wonderful plan for their lives involves only pleasantness and not trouble. Believers on this side of the cross have many more examples from both the Bible and church history of God's people who have suffered. Job was much more in the dark. Yet out of that darkness his strong

---

[49] "Curse" is again, as in 1:5,11, ברך in the polar sense. Ordinarily it means "bless." See M. Rotenberg, "Did Job's Wife Use a Euphemism?" *Lešonēnu* 52 (1987-88): 176-77 (Hebrew).

[50] The verb מות, "die," is not a reflexive, i.e., *hithpael*, but a simple *qal* imperative— "drop dead!"

[51] Of the several words for "fool" in Hebrew, this root, נבל, carries with it the overtones of being morally corrupt, dishonorable, insensitive, and irreverent. The immoral dimension is illustrated by its use in Judg 19:23-24; 20:6,10. The irreverent side appears in Ps 14:1 = 53:1[2]). It is the name of Abigail's foolish first husband, Nabal (1 Sam 25:25). "Foolishness" is in Gen 34:7, so the Talmud had Dinah married to Job (*Baba Bathra* 15b; similarly The Testament of Job 1:6, although she is there his second wife, the mother of the ten children of chap. 42 [*Old Testament Pseudepigrapha*, vol. 1, ed. J. H. Charlesworth [Garden City: Doubleday, 1983], 829-68]).

[52] "Good" is the normal טוב, but "trouble" is רע, often translated "evil." Job 42:11 and Isa 45:7 present a similar problem: How can God be responsible for evil?

belief in the sovereignty of God shone forth all the more brilliantly. Somehow he already knew that the clay does not ask the potter, "What are you making?" (Isa 45:9). Job acted as though he had read 2 Cor 4:17, "For our light and momentary troubles are achieving for us an eternal glory that far outweighs them all."

4. Job's Three Friends (2:11-13)

[11]When Job's three friends, Eliphaz the Temanite, Bildad the Shuhite and Zophar the Naamathite, heard about all the troubles that had come upon him, they set out from their homes and met together by agreement to go and sympathize with him and comfort him. [12]When they saw him from a distance, they could hardly recognize him; they began to weep aloud, and they tore their robes and sprinkled dust on their heads. [13]Then they sat on the ground with him for seven days and seven nights. No one said a word to him, because they saw how great his suffering was.

The last paragraph of the prose prologue introduces the readers to Job's three friends. They started as friends, but before the debates were over, Job used less-than-friendly words to describe them. Throughout this commentary these three will be called "friends" because that is the word in the text at this point. Though not an ideal term, it certainly is better than "comforters" (cf. 16:2). These three probably were wealthy sheiks like Job. They had the time to talk for what may have been several months with their suffering comrade. Nothing is told about their families or stations in life. They seem to have come from a distance, yet they apparently spoke the same language and drew their illustrations and observations from the same common pool of experiences that Job had.

2:11 This long and somewhat complicated sentence has been rearranged in the NIV so that the names of the principal characters appear earlier than they do in the Hebrew text. First we read that three friends of Job heard of all the trouble[53] that had befallen him. The text does not provide the source of the information or the agency by which they heard. It is not important to the story.

To read "three of Job's friends" is better than "Job's three friends." Let us hope that he had more, but only three came for this extended visit. The question arises whether the number three is of any consequence. Did three actually come, or did the author write the book in such a way that Job's many visitors are reduced to three in number? The fact that their names

---

[53] רַע, "trouble," as in the preceding note and in v. 10.

and tribes are in the text argues for the factuality of the report.

Eliphaz came from Teman. Genesis 36:4 records a son born to Esau and Adah named Eliphaz. In turn, Teman was born to Eliphaz (Gen 36:11). Teman came to be the name of a prominent city in the area of Edom southeast of the Dead Sea.[54] If the identification of this and Job's location is correct, it meant for Eliphaz a journey of over a hundred miles.

Bildad came from Shuah. The name "Bildad" does not occur elsewhere in the Bible.[55] "Shuah" is the name of a son of Abraham by his wife or concubine Keturah (Gen 25:2; 1 Chr 1:32). Otherwise that name is unknown.

Zophar came from Naamath. His name also is unique to the Book of Job,[56] and the place he came from also is unknown. Etymologically it means "pleasant," an appropriate name for a city or area. As with Job's name and home, we have little information about families or places of residence.

These three "met together by appointment"[57] to do three things: to go, to sympathize, and to comfort. The first of these is an abundantly common verb. The second is less common, but the meaning is well established from this and other contexts. The third appears over a hundred times in the Old Testament, yet it has the quite different meanings of "repent" and "comfort."[58] The latter meaning is appropriate here. The friends came to comfort but found themselves at the end having to repent (42:7-9).

2:12 The verb "they lifted up" occurs twice in this verse. The three "lifted up their eyes," and "they lifted up their voices." Both are Hebrew idioms usually paraphrased in modern English translations. In the desert one can see for great distances because no trees, mountains, or buildings are in the way. Even from a distance when persons are recognizable, they did not recognize Job. He was much thinner. His skin was black. He was not wearing his usual finery. And he was not at the city gate where he customarily sat but on the ash heap. The sight of their friend prompted them

---

[54] Jeremiah 49:7 and Obad 8,9 connect Teman with wisdom. The prophets included Teman when they announced judgment against Edom (see Jer 49:20; Ezek 25:13; Amos 1:12; Obad 9). As a common noun תֵּימָן means "south," a fem. form of יָמִין, "right/south." The modern Tawilan, three miles east of Petra, Jordan, is a good candidate for the ancient Teman.

[55] Two elements of Bildad's name, בַּל and דֹד, can mean "lord" and "beloved/love" (cf. Eldad in Num 11:26-27, which can mean "god" and "beloved/love").

[56] *BDB* lists five roots with widely differing meanings, all spelled with the letters of Zophar's name, צֹפַר: "return," "twitter," "braid," "fingernail," and "billy goat"!

[57] A *niphal* of יָעַד, "appoint/meet."

[58] It is *piel* that always means "comfort." When it is niphal, it often has the meaning "repent." Job 42:6 has occasioned considerable discussion because of this problem.

to "weep aloud," or more literally, "They lifted up their voices and they wept." Nowhere in the book did Job weep for himself; perhaps he was beyond that point in his grief.

"They tore their robes" just as Job had done in 1:20. "And they sprinkled dust on their heads heavenward."[59] Though not as common as ashes, dust is another sign of mourning (Josh 7:6; 2 Sam 1:2; Ezek 27:30; Mic 1:10).[60] The NIV does not represent the "heavenward," but the NASB, for example, has "toward the sky" (cf. the NRSV's "in the air"). The addition does provide a detail to this overt, even ostentatious, display of anguish. One must assume that this grief on their part was genuine even if it is markedly different from our own customs.

2:13 Sitting on the ground was yet another way of showing humility and sorrow (Isa 3:26; 47:1; Lam 2:10; Jonah 3:6). Notice that they sat "with him," entering into his grief in this demonstrable way. The "seven days and seven nights" correspond to other examples of week-long periods of mourning mentioned in Gen 50:10; 1 Sam 31:13; and Ezek 3:15. "Seven" may be an imprecise number for something more than a day but less than a month, although it could have been a literal week.

The sight of Job's excessive suffering left the friends silent. Good counselors know that sometimes the best thing they can do is simply listen. Just the presence of a sympathetic person can provide comfort altogether apart from any spoken words. This probably was the finest demonstration of love these three could have shown. If they had simply returned home without saying anything, their reputations would be much different. After listening to each give his first speech, Job wished they might resort to their original treatment of him and suggested that silence would better prove their wisdom (13:5).

So ends the prologue of the book. The stage has been set. We, the readers, have been informed of basic facts that the major characters do not know. All the players (except Elihu) have been introduced. It is time for the contest of wills and words to begin. Let the curtain be lifted for the next scene.

---

[59] "Over their heads" rather than "on their heads" is argued by C. Houtman, "Zu Hiob 2:12," *ZAW* 90 (1978): 269-72.

[60] In 42:6 "dust" (עָפָר) and "ashes" (אֵפֶר) appear together (cf. Gen 18:27).

II. JOB'S CURSE (3:1-26)
1. Introduction (3:1-2)
2. Curse on His Birth (3:3-10)
3. Longing for Death (3:11-19)
   (1) Hatred of Life (3:20-23)
   (2) Concluding Moan (3:24-26)

II. JOB'S CURSE (3:1-26)

1. Introduction (3:1-2)

¹After this, Job opened his mouth and cursed the day of his birth. ²He said:

The third chapter of Job must be one of the most depressing chapters in the Bible.[1] While some might be as depressed as Job was and use these verses to give vent to their feelings, few sermons are made from this chapter, few verses are claimed as promises, and few are remembered for the warmth of their sentiment. It is the lowest of several low points in the book and seems to counter the high faith of 1:21 and 2:10.[2]

3:1 The antecedent of "this" refers to all the events of the first two chapters but in particular to the tragedies of lost wealth, lost children, and lost health.[3] The NIV translation is literal and straightforward except that "birth" does not appear in Hebrew.[4] Nevertheless the translation is

---

[1] Only Jer 20:14-18 compares to it.

[2] R. D. Moore points out that the four motifs of 1:21 are all reversed in chap. 3: womb, tomb, deity, and theocentricity. The recurrence of these themes supports the unity of the book ("The Integrity of Job," *CBQ* 45 [1983]: 17-31).

[3] In answer to the question of why such a depressing chapter, D. Clines writes: "His anxiety is not because of his skin disease nor even because he fears he may soon be dead, but rather because he is experiencing a shaking of the foundations of cosmic moral order. He is disoriented by the anomie of his experience and longs for Sheol as a place where order reigns, the order, indeed, of inactivity and effacement of earthly relationships, to be sure, but an order where the conflicts of the absurd have been swallowed up by a pacific meaninglessness" (*Job 1-20*, WBC 17 [Dallas: Word, 1989], 105).

[4] Cf. KJV, RV, ASV, etc.

fully justified in light of v. 3, which does include "birth."

The term translated "curse" is one of the two common roots to express this idea.[5] Etymologically the root means to "be light" or in this case to "treat lightly/view with contempt/spurn." In the Hebrew way of thinking the opposite is "honor," which has behind it the notion of "weight/worth."

3:2 The two verbs of this brief compound sentence are treated as a hendiadys and are coalesced into one. As a result of this, Job 3:2 is the shortest verse in the NIV Bible.[6]

2. Curse on His Birth (3:3-10)

> [3]"May the day of my birth perish,
>   and the night it was said, 'A boy is born!'
> [4]That day—may it turn to darkness;
>   may God above not care about it;
>   may no light shine upon it.
> [5]May darkness and deep shadow claim it once more;
>   may a cloud settle over it;
>   may blackness overwhelm its light.
> [6]That night—may thick darkness seize it;
>   may it not be included among the days of the year
>   nor be entered in any of the months.
> [7]May that night be barren;
>   may no shout of joy be heard in it.
> [8]May those who curse days curse that day,
>   those who are ready to rouse Leviathan.
> [9]May its morning stars become dark;
>   may it wait for daylight in vain
>   and not see the first rays of dawn,
> [10]for it did not shut the doors of the womb on me
>   to hide trouble from my eyes.

Jussive or wish-form verbs dominate this first large section of chap. 3. Many of the lines begin with the word "may," the English way of rendering this kind of third person imperative. While the entire chapter is titled "Job's curse," the essence of the curse is in these eight verses.

3:3 The two lines that constitute this verse function as a synopsis of

---

[5] The AB has "damn the day I was born."

[6] John 11:35 is the shortest verse in the KJV. First Thessalonians 5:16 is the shortest verse in the Greek NT. First Chronicles 1:25 is the shortest verse in the Hebrew OT. In Hebrew Job 6:1; 9:1; 12:1; 16:1; 19:1; 21:1; 23:1; 26:1 are the same as 3:2.

what will follow—curses on the day and the night of Job's birth. Verses 4-6 condemn the day and vv. 6-9 the night. The first of many commands in this section opens v. 3. "Perish" is from the root *'ābad*, which is known from Rev 9:11, where Abaddon appears, "the angel of the Abyss." The name means "destroyer." The verb does double duty, carrying over to the second line, where "night" is the subject. The noun "birth" translates, in fact, a passive verb, "I was birthed." And the verb "birthed" is usually translated "conceived" as in 15:35.[7] Most conceptions occur at night. So in this verse Job cursed not only the day he emerged from his mother's womb but the night nine months earlier when the spark of his life was kindled in his parents' marriage bed. As in other places in this book (10:10-11) and elsewhere in the Bible (Ps 139:16; Jer 1:5), Job believed that his personhood went back to his conception, not merely to his birth.[8]

3:4 This tricolon contains three prohibitions. The first and third have to do with light and darkness while the middle line wishes that God himself might abandon that day. This is the first appearance of the divine name *'ĕlôah*[9]—the common term for the deity in Job. It is very infrequent elsewhere in the Old Testament.

3:5 The poet continues to pile up synonyms for "darkness," adding in this verse "deep darkness," "cloud," and "blackness."[10] The "deep darkness" is not a combination of noun and adjective but the term that is well known from Ps 23:4, "shadow of death." The term *ṣalmāwet* seems to be a combination of "shadow" (*ṣal*) and "death" (*māwet*). "Darkness" and "death" go together just as "light" and "life" do in 3:16,20. This term will appear again in 10:21-22; 12:22; 16:16; 24:17; 28:3; 34:22; 38:17, this last being the only place where the NIV renders it "shadow of death." Job uses this word more than all the other Old Testament books together. Behind the first verb, "claim," lies the common root *g'l*, "redeem."

3:6 In vv. 6-7 Job curses the night. One more synonym for "dark-

---

[7] The word probably comes from הָרַר, not הָרָה.

[8] "Boy," גֶּבֶר, usually is "man," in fact, more than that, a "soldier/hero/he-man." It is a favorite term of this author with fifteen of the sixty-six occurrences in the Bible and appears in such well-known places as 38:3; 40:7.

[9] This is considered a singular of the common אֱלֹהִים, a form that occurs in Job only six times. אֱלוֹהַּ, on the other hand, appears in Job forty-one times and only sixteen times elsewhere in the OT.

[10] כִּמְרִירֵי is a hapax. If, as M. Pope suggests, it is from the root מרר plus the preposition כְּ, then it should read "like the bitterness of." See M. Pope, *Job*, AB (Garden City: Doubleday, 1973), 29; cf. Deut 32:24.

ness," 'ōpel, appears for the first time. It too is a favorite word in Job, with six of the nine Old Testament occurrences.[11] Job wished that he had never been born. But putting it poetically, he wanted the day eliminated from the calendar. Just as no February 30 exists in our calendar, so he wanted his day scratched from the record. "Days" and "months" are simply the A and B words in this typical synonymous parallel.

3:7 While "barren" is a rare word,[12] there is little question of its meaning. Again Job wished that on that night no babies had been born and especially that he had not been born. While ordinarily it is women who are barren and not nights, the reader should have no trouble making this association of ideas. Usually a "shout of joy" such as "A boy is born!" (v. 3) accompanied such an event. In light of where Job now found himself and in the grief of his loss and bewilderment, such a happy note would have been inappropriate.

3:8 "Curse" translates two different words. The participle "those who curse" is the more common and refers to professional cursers like Balaam (Num 22:5-6). A cursed day would be the opposite of a blessed day. It is a day you wish had never happened, a day you rue and would like to eliminate from history. Two plays on words are present: "Those who curse" is 'ōrĕrê, and "to arouse" is 'ōrēr. "Day" is yôm, and "sea," of which Leviathan is the mythological monster, is yām. Although yām is not the way the Masoretes pointed the text, some read it as "sea" or "sea monster."[13] As a monotheist Job did not deify the sea or believe in the existence of a sea god, any more than a modern preacher who cites a nursery rhyme believes in the existence of those fictional characters.[14]

3:9 Although literal translations help to understand the Hebrew word order and picturesque terms, they are not always understood. In the RV 3:9 reads: "Let the stars of the twilight thereof be dark; let it look for light, but have none; neither let it behold the eyelids of the morning."[15]

---

[11] Others are in 10:22 (twice); 23:17; 28:3; 30:26; Pss 11:2; 91:6; Isa 29:18.

[12] גַלְמוּד appears again only in Job 15:34 speaking of the company of the godless, in Job 30:3 translated as "haggard," and in Isa 49:21, where it is parallel to שְׁכוּל, another rare word that means "barren/bereaved."

[13] The NEB has "the monster of the deep," the NRSV has "the Sea," and the REB has "sea monster." In Ugaritic ym can be either the "sea" or "Yam," the god of the sea.

[14] For an evangelical perspective on the use of mythology in Job, see E. Smick, "Mythology and the Book of Job," *JETS* 13 (1970): 101-8, and "Another Look at the Mythological Elements in the Book of Job," *WTJ* 40 (1978): 213-28. M. Pope follows H. Gunkel and reads "sea" for "day." They assume that Job was a polytheist and espoused all the current mythology.

[15] Even the KJV paraphrased this last expression into "the dawning of the day."

The NIV indicates the subjects of the first line are the "morning stars," which are any of the planets that shine before the rising sun—Venus, Jupiter, Mars, Mercury, or Saturn. The middle phrase is straightforward, but the last contains the curious expression "eyelids of the morning."[16] As one's eyelids typically open slowly in the morning, so the morning itself slowly opens each new day.

3:10 Verse 10 provides the reason for all the imprecations of the preceding seven verses. The day of Job's birth should be cursed because it allowed him to be born. Again in typical, picturesque, Semitic metaphors the poet blamed that day because "it did not shut the doors of the womb." Job was permitted to escape the confines of his prenatal habitat. He emerged to life, but it was a life of trouble. In his condition he seems to have forgotten the good old days when the Lord gave abundantly. Now his eyes focused only on "trouble," a term that is elsewhere translated "evil" (4:8), "hardship" (5:6), and "misery" (7:3).

3. Longing for Death (3:11-19)

> [11]"Why did I not perish at birth,
>   and die as I came from the womb?
> [12]Why were there knees to receive me
>   and breasts that I might be nursed?
> [13]For now I would be lying down in peace;
>   I would be asleep and at rest
> [14]with kings and counselors of the earth,
>   who built for themselves places now lying in ruins,
> [15]with rulers who had gold,
>   who filled their houses with silver.
> [16]Or why was I not hidden in the ground like a stillborn child,
>   like an infant who never saw the light of day?
> [17]There the wicked cease from turmoil,
>   and there the weary are at rest.
> [18]Captives also enjoy their ease;
>   they no longer hear the slave driver's shout.
> [19]The small and the great are there,
>   and the slave is freed from his master.

In this section Job wished that he were dead. The outcome is the same as the preceding section, but here the tone is one of longing rather than cursing. If he had died at birth, he imagined that he would have had an

---

[16] This reduplicated form עַפְעַפִּים may be related to Aramaic עֲפִי, "leaf."

elegant burial or at least would have been free of the present grief as a slave is only and ultimately free at death.

3:11 For this rhetorical question Job found no answer. Even at the end of the book when Yahweh spoke, the answer was not like anything Job expected. In this question are wrapped up all the questions of all sufferers throughout the ages. "Why me?" or "My God, why have you forsaken me?" (Ps 22:1) has been on the lips of all those who believe in God but cannot comprehend his ways. If he had never been born, Job thought, he would not have been in the present predicament.

3:12 The questions continue and in graphic terms describe the first sensations of a newborn baby. It is from between the "knees" of the mother that the child passes, and it is to her nursing breasts that he is moved.[17] If, for some reason, Job had never been received by those knees or nursed at those breasts, he would not have survived but would have been a stillborn infant (as v. 16).

3:13 The initial *kî,* "for," might be better translated "indeed." Then follow four verbs that we put into a subjunctive mode although Hebrew, unlike Greek and English, is incapable of such precision. "I would lie down; I would be quiet; I would be asleep; I would be at rest." To the once-noble man from Uz—weary with grief, spent from scratching his sores, and completely befuddled with why God should allow these tragedies to happen to a "blameless and upright" man—such alternatives were welcome indeed.

3:14 The sentence begun in v. 13 continues through v. 15. Job hoped and imagined his final resting place in the luxurious and opulent tombs of royalty and nobility.[18] Majestic tombs are often neglected by subsequent generations who do not share the same reverence for the deceased as those who erected them originally. Job may have been a desert sheik, but not a "king." He referred to "counselors" in 12:17 and perhaps included himself in their number.

3:15 Most likely Job fantasized about the elegant burial he would have had if he had died before the present circumstances struck him. With his accumulated wealth he too could have been compared to those "rulers who had gold" and "who filled their houses with silver." These "rulers," or "chief men" as they are translated in 29:9, "refrained from

---

[17] "Knees" does not refer to the mother's lap on which a slightly older child might sit but to the actual details of the human birthing process. Note, however, the use of "knees" in connection with birth in Gen 30:3 and in connection with nursing in Isa 66:12.

[18] "Places now lying in ruins," חֳרָבוֹת, is difficult. Without any manuscript support, some have emended it to similar Hebrew words such as אַרְמְנוֹת ("fortresses"), הֵיכָלוֹת ("palaces"), רְחֹבוֹת ("plazas"), and חֲרָמוֹת (mausolea"). See Pope, *Job,* 31-32.

speaking" in deference to the more honor-worthy Job.

3:16 Retreating from the imaginary picture of a sumptuous mausoleum, Job reflected again on the benefits of death at birth, the theme that began this section. "Stillborn child," *nēpel*, a word occurring elsewhere only in Ps 58:8[9] and Eccl 6:3, is related to the common verb root *npl*, "fall." "In the ground" is not in the Hebrew but is logical. "Of day" similarly is not in Hebrew but helps to balance the length of the lines.

3:17 This and the next two verses list more categories of those who are happier dead than alive: the wicked, the weary, the captives, and the slaves. It is first "the wicked" who enjoy an end to their "trouble/rage/ turmoil/agitation." While it could refer to the trouble that the wicked cause others, it refers more likely to the unhappy and fear-filled lives that the wicked lead. "Weary" translates a redundant expression, "wearied of strength," a combination of two well-established words that never appear elsewhere joined like this. Occasionally, one hears tired or troubled Christians say that they are going to sleep for the first century they are in heaven. Job, too, anticipated an afterlife where toil would cease.

3:18 In the next category of beneficiaries are the "captives" who also "enjoy their ease."[19] Job then added the little detail of their no longer hearing the slave driver bark his orders. The same word for "slave drivers" appears in Exod 3:7 as the taskmasters the Egyptians put over the Israelites. The third stanza of "I'll Fly Away" has similar sentiments.

3:19 The section ends with a merismus (see explanation at 1:20), "the small and the great," and a repetition of the idea of v. 18, freedom for the slave. Job had been great; now he was small. Regardless, death levels all. "All corpses look alike," and "Shrouds have no pockets," the rabbis said.[20] "Death is the destiny of every man," said Qoheleth (Eccl 7:2). On this depressing note the section ends, but Job had not yet finished his bitter and biting lament.

(1) Hatred of Life (3:20-23)

> [20]"Why is light given to those in misery,
>   and life to the bitter of soul,
> [21]to those who long for death that does not come,
>   who search for it more than for hidden treasure,
> [22]who are filled with gladness

---

[19] This root, שׁאן, occurs five times as a verb and always in the *piel:* Prov 1:33; Jer 30:10; 46:27; 48:11. It is used ten times as an adjective including Job 12:5.

[20] *Leo Rosten's Treasury of Jewish Quotations* (New York: McGraw-Hill, 1972), 173, 370.

      and rejoice when they reach the grave?
[23]**Why is life given to a man**
      whose way is hidden,
      whom God has hedged in?

From a grammatical viewpoint, these four verses make up a single question. The repetition of the interrogative "why" in v. 23 is not in Hebrew but is supplied to keep the sentence from becoming inordinately long in English. While it is a question, it is a rhetorical one. By this means Job expressed his abhorrence of life and again displayed his longing for death, some of the benefits of which he stated in the previous section.

3:20 As noted earlier, light and life are poetic parallels, just as are darkness and death in vv. 3-10 (cf. v. 16b). The "misery" of this verse is from the same root translated "trouble" in v. 10. The combination "bitter of soul" is also in 1 Sam 1:10; 22:2; 2 Sam 17:8; Prov 31:6; and similar expressions are in Job 7:11; 10:1; 21:25.

3:21 "Those who long" translates a participle that continues the sentence begun in v. 20, but "search" is a finite verb, thus making the last phrase an independent clause. The same is true of the second half of v. 22. The sense is not affected. It cannot be denied that Job wished he were dead. There is a fine line, however, between such a wish and a plan to commit suicide. Job never contemplated the latter although his wife had virtually suggested it (2:9). Certainly suicide was known in ancient times, and there are at least six examples of it in the Bible.[21]

3:22 The NIV has paraphrased an unusual Hebrew expression: "Those who rejoice upwards joy."[22] Job and his contemporaries probably understood little about the afterlife. The common expectation of persons in the ancient Near East was of a situation very much like that which they saw, felt, and heard inside a tomb: darkness, insects, and absolute quiet. They expected no activity, conversation, conviviality, or pleasure, just a long, drowsy, morbid eternity. Only someone whose life was full of misery would long for such an existence. Only divine promises assure us of a better future.

3:23 The Hebrew line begins simply, "To a man whose way is hidden." The verse is not a tricolon but a typical bicolon. The phrase "why is

---

[21] Samson (Judg 16:30), Saul and his armor bearer (1 Sam 31:4-5), Ahithophel (2 Sam 17:23), Zimri (1 Kgs 16:18), and Judas (Matt 27:5). See R. K. Harrison, "Suicide," *ISBE* 4:652-53.

[22] Hosea 9:1 has an almost identical phrase, גִּיל, rather than אֱלֵי גִיל. The RSV translates here "which rejoice exceedingly" and in Hosea "for joy."

life given?" has been added from v. 20. "Light" could have been supplied rather than "life." Job sensed that he had lost the way. The road he ought to take was obscured. He felt that life took a wrong turn, but he did not know where. He only knew that it led him into the misery of loss and ill health. In the second line he indirectly charged that God "has hedged" him in. This picture of hostile forces surrounding him appears in more elaborate form in 19:6,8,12. It is ironic that the Satan charged God with putting a "hedge" around Job to protect him.[23] Putting these two passages together, we learn that hedges can make one feel safe and protected or fearful and threatened. In both instances it was God who put the hedge around Job.

(2) Concluding Moan (3:24-26)

> [24]For sighing comes to me instead of food;
>   my groans pour out like water.
> [25]What I feared has come upon me;
>   what I dreaded has happened to me.
> [26]I have no peace, no quietness;
>   I have no rest, but only turmoil."

Job's concluding lament is depressing to the extreme. First he compared his grief to food and drink. Then he confessed that the things he feared the most had materialized. Finally he summarized his lot as the loss of three good things in exchange for the possession of one bad thing—turmoil.

3:24 Both v. 24 and v. 25 begin with the mild causal conjunction that might better be read as an emphatic particle, "surely/indeed," or with no word at all.[24] Although the metaphor is mixed, the point of the complaint is clear. The terms speak of a loss of appetite, a side effect that Job and Elihu would note later in the book (6:7; 33:20). Such a reaction is understandable.

3:25 A cognate accusative begins this verse, "The fear I feared." "Dreaded" translates a word that occurs twice in Job (9:28) and only five places elsewhere.[25] There is no record of Job's fear, but all parents worry about their children. Imagine the intensity of the sorrow at the loss of ten

---

[23] The verb in 1:9 is שׂוּךְ, which occurs elsewhere only in Hos 2:6[8] and Job 10:11, while here is סוּךְ or סָכַךְ, a more common verb.

[24] Cf. NJPS, Beck, NEB, REV, NCB, and others.

[25] It is built on the same root, יגֹר, as the "Magor-Missabib" of Jer 20:3.

children all in one catastrophe. People also fear disease. How much must this have been the case when medicine was primitive and the workings of the body even more of a mystery than they are today.

3:26 Three negatives on three verbs make up the first three quarters of v. 26. The first good thing Job lacked was not *šālôm* ("peace") but a similar word, *šālâ,* which also means "peace" (12:6). Instead of these irenic conditions, Job found that only "turmoil" came his way. In death even the wicked appear to be free from turmoil, but in life turmoil was the righteous Job's constant companion. It is easy to understand how such pain could have caused Job to lose sight of the pleasantness that had once filled his life so that now he longed to forfeit life for peace and rest.

III. THE DEBATE BETWEEN JOB AND HIS THREE FRIENDS
    (4:1–27:23)
    1. Eliphaz: Job Has Sinned, and God Is Chastening Him[1]
      (4:1–5:27)
      (1) Rebuke (4:1-6)
      (2) Reasoning (4:7-11)
      (3) Revelation (4:12-16)
      (4) More Reasoning (4:17–5:7)
          Divine Morality and Human Mortality (4:17-21)
          Human Proclivity to Folly and Trouble (5:1-7)
      (5) Recommendations (5:8-27)
          Appeal to the God of Justice (5:8-16)
          The Lessons and Rewards of Suffering (5:17-26)
          His Concluding Charge (5:27)
    2. Job: My Complaint Is Just, but I Lack Comfort (6:1–7:21)
      (1) Anguish (6:1-7)
      (2) Request for Death (6:8-10)
      (3) Hopelessness (6:11-13)
      (4) Disappointment with His Friends (6:14-23)
      (5) Request for Advice (6:24-27)
      (6) Plea for Understanding (6:28-30)
      (7) Query about Life (7:1-6)
      (8) Address to God (7:7-21)
          Life Is Brief (7:7-10)
          Life Is Not Worth Living (7:11-16)
          Why Does God Bother with People? (7:17-21)

III. THE DEBATE BETWEEN JOB AND HIS THREE FRIENDS (4:1–27:23)

1. Eliphaz: Job Has Sinned, and God Is Chastening Him (4:1–5:27)

---

[1] Many of these titles for the speeches have been suggested by those in the NKJV (Nashville: Nelson, 1982).

The three friends who were introduced at the close of chap. 2 have not said a word for a week; now they begin to speak. This central and largest section in the book fills more than half the volume with its twenty-four chapters. Each of the three friends spoke, and each time Job responded. This cycle goes around three times with Eliphaz speaking three times, Bildad speaking three times, but Zophar speaking only twice. Job had eight or nine speeches (depending on whether chaps. 26–27 are separate speeches, as I believe).

Some generalizations characterize the speeches. They will be mentioned in the course of the commentary, but among them is the fact that the speeches grow shorter. Bildad's third speech in chap. 25 is especially brief. The speeches grow in intensity. Both the friends and Job became less courteous and more critical of one another. All of the speakers, and notably Elihu, who appears later in the book, anticipated the theophany or the speeches of Yahweh by making observations about God's evident power in creation and his apparent sovereignty over the world. Usually the friends' speeches include rebuke and advice. Usually Job turned to God in petition or complaint. The friends never prayed.

The overall thrust of the friends' speeches is that the wicked suffer and the righteous are rewarded; thus, since Job was suffering, he must have sinned. He needed only to confess that sin, and God would restore his former fortunes. Job regularly countered that generalization and wished that he had an explanation for his suffering from his accusers but, even more, from God. His inability to get an explanation made him more frustrated and angry, aggravating his desire for death. Interspersed through his speeches, however, are occasional glimmers of hope—hope in a redeemer, hope in a resurrection, hope for ultimate vindication.

(1) Rebuke (4:1-6)

¹Then Eliphaz the Temanite replied:
²"If someone ventures a word with you, will you be impatient?
  But who can keep from speaking?
³Think how you have instructed many,
  how you have strengthened feeble hands.
⁴Your words have supported those who stumbled;
  you have strengthened faltering knees.
⁵But now trouble comes to you; and you are discouraged;
  it strikes you and you are dismayed.
⁶Should not your piety be your confidence
  and your blameless ways your hope?

Two of the features just noted are evident in this opening segment of Eliphaz's first speech: rebuke and a good measure of courtesy. His speech seems almost apologetic, and one can almost picture his nervousness. After all, he and the other two had been sitting in silence with Job for seven days and seven nights. It is understandable that the first words would be gentle and cautious.[2]

4:1 The first verse in this chapter and in every chapter where there is a change of speaker is a prose introduction. Rather than make a separate point in the outline for such brief preludes, they are included in the first section.[3] In each instance the sentence has two verbs: "answered" and "said." The NIV understands them as a hendiadys and always reads simply "replied."[4]

4:2 Eliphaz was the essence of tenderness and sympathy as he spoke his first words to Job. Actually he asked two questions: the first was a request that Job hardly could deny, and the second was a rhetorical question expecting the answer "No one." None of the vocabulary is difficult, but it is noteworthy that "speaking," *millâ*, occurs thirty-four times in Job and only four times elsewhere. It is one of the arguments to support the view that one author was responsible for the whole book. It usually is translated "word" as in 4:4.

4:3 The particle *hinnēh* ("think how") is hard to translate into English with any consistency. The archaic "behold" of KJV, RV, RSV, NASB, and others simply does not communicate. Sometimes an exclamation mark at the end of a sentence represents this term, which usually appears at the beginning of a sentence. "Think how" introduces the premise of an argument, which comes in vv. 5-6. Eliphaz was preparing Job for the very thing he intended to do, that is, "instruct/rebuke/straighten out," by reminding Job that Job himself had done this many times before. In 29:7-10,21-23 Job would list, among other good deeds, that he was a town elder whose counsel was received, esteemed, and acted upon. Chapter 29 also records what would fit into the category of strengthening "feeble hands" (29:12-13,15-16).

4:4 The two lines of this verse merely parallel the second line of v. 3. Although we have reason to believe from chap. 29 and elsewhere that Job's support and strengthening of others involved more than words,

---

[2] Assessing the three speakers, R. Gordis says: "Undoubtedly Eliphaz, the most dignified and urbane of the Friends, is the profoundest spirit among them; his intense religious convictions have not robbed him of sympathy for the distraught and suffering Job" (*The Book of God and Man: A Study of Job* [Chicago: University Press, 1965], 77).

[3] The six-verse introduction of Elihu in 32:1-6 is an exception to this rule.

[4] A minor but significant variation appears at 27:1, which will be discussed there.

there is no record that his three friends offered anything more than words. Would not true friends offer material assistance? Would they not share of their flocks to begin a new herd? Would they not contribute to the rebuilding of his houses and barns? Now Job had "stumbled." He had the "feeble hands" and the "faltering knees." It was their turn to strengthen and support him.

4:5 "Trouble" has been supplied by the translators as the subject for the verb "comes," which otherwise has no named subject. The result of trouble coming is discouragement and dismay. The former of these two verbs (*l'h*) is translated in v. 2 "be impatient," but elsewhere it means "be weary." The latter verb (*bāhal* in *niphal*) is "unmanned" in the NEB and "unnerved" in the NJPS. Job undoubtedly experienced all these conditions and more in view of his losses and his inability to understand the ways of God with him.

4:6 Eliphaz's introductory paragraph concludes with a question consisting of two clauses, as is typical of most verses in the poetical portions of the Bible. The expected answer to this rhetorical question is yes. It seemed to Eliphaz that Job's piety and "blameless ways" should now be expressed appropriately as confidence and hope. One would expect Job to have reflected on his religious faith and on his good record. That, however, was precisely the problem. His "piety" and "hope"[5] was that God was good and did good things for those whose ways were "blameless" (a term God himself used in 1:8 to describe Job to the Satan).[6]

(2) Reasoning (4:7-11)

> [7]"Consider now: Who, being innocent, have ever perished?
>   Where were the upright ever destroyed?
> [8]As I have observed, those who plow evil
>   and those who sow trouble reap it.
> [9]At the breath of God they are destroyed;
>   at the blast of his anger they perish.
> [10]The lions may roar and growl,
>   yet the teeth of the great lions are broken.
> [11]The lion perishes for lack of prey,
>   and the cubs of the lioness are scattered.

---

[5] "Hope" is also a favorite word in Job with thirteen of its thirty-two OT occurrences: 4:6; 5:16; 6:8; 7:6; 8:13; 11:18,20; 14:7,19; 17:15 (2x); 19:10; 27:8.

[6] The word order of the second line in the Heb. text is unusual, "Your hope and perfect your ways." חָם is singular while דְרָכֶיךָ is plural. A. C. M. Blommerde said, "The *waw* in *wetōm* is emphatic *waw* as recognized already by F. Delitzsch, by Koenig and Dhorme" (*Northwest Semitic Grammar and Job* [Rome: Pontifical Biblical Institute, 1969], 40).

For the first of many times the standard argument of the friends appears: there are certain rules by which the universe operates. These rules dictate that good comes to those who are righteous and bad comes to those who are wicked. Working backwards from effect to cause, it means that if people suffer, it is because they have sinned; and if they are blessed, it is because they have trusted and obeyed.

4:7 For the third time in seven verses Eliphaz resorted to the rhetorical question to state his case. The expected answers to both questions in this verse are no one and no where. Eliphaz seemed to know of no innocent person who suffered, and he apparently had never witnessed the upright destroyed. He had no place in his theology to put Job except among the guilty and the godless. Despite all he knew of Job's piety and good works, Eliphaz could not account for Job's suffering except to view it as punishment for sin. Neither he nor his friends had a category for the righteous sufferer. None of them had read about the man born blind in John 9:1-3 or of God's purpose in pruning fruitful vines in John 15:2.

4:8 Nowhere else in this book did the friends state better their standard view of divine justice than in this verse. Theirs was the theology of Prov 22:8, "He who sows wickedness reaps trouble."[7] As a general rule this is true. But Job and numbers of others in the Bible, most notably Jesus Christ, were exceptions to this rule. Eliphaz might be dealt with more gently because he introduced this maxim with the words "As I have observed." Right before his eyes, however, was an exception. Throughout his three speeches he found it easier to condemn Job than to adjust his view of retributive justice.

4:9 Two different words for "wind/breath/blast/spirit" begin the two halves of v. 9. The second, *rûaḥ,* was used in 1:19 to describe the desert storm that collapsed the house where Job's children were partying. This is one of several cruel allusions that the friends made to the deaths of those seven sons and three daughters (cf. 8:4; 18:19; 27:14).

4:10 Five synonyms for "lion" appear in vv. 10-11, another evidence of the rich vocabulary the poet-author of Job possessed.[8] Strictly speaking there is but one verb in v. 10. The first line is literally, "A roar of a lion, a growl/voice of a [another kind of] lion." The point is that even lions, the king of beasts, will suffer. While the verse does not say how the teeth were broken,[9] this proverblike saying illustrates that the strong and

---

[7] Cf. Hos 10:12-13; Gal 6:7-8.

[8] For a brief elaboration on this variety of lions, see J. Hartley, *Job*, NICOT (Grand Rapids: Eerdmans, 1988), 108. For more detail see R. K. Harrison, *ISBE* 3:141-42.

[9] "Broken" translates נתע, a hapax legomenon. Since often צ becomes ע in Aramaic, it may be the more common נתץ, meaning "break/destroy." See BDB, 683.

oppressive ultimately receive their due.

4:11 Continuing the illustration of v. 10, Eliphaz told how these lions die of starvation and their cubs (another allusion to Job's "children"?) are orphaned. In Job's case he was the one made childless rather than made parentless, as in the case of these young lions.

(3) Revelation (4:12-16)

> [12]"A word was secretly brought to me,
>		my ears caught a whisper of it.
> [13]Amid disquieting dreams in the night,
>		when deep sleep falls on men,
> [14]fear and trembling seized me
>		and made all my bones shake.
> [15]A spirit glided past my face,
>		and the hair on my body stood on end.
> [16]It stopped,
>		but I could not tell what it was.
>	A form stood before my eyes,
>		and I heard a hushed voice:

Having appealed to reason or tradition, Eliphaz tried a new tack. One cannot be certain whether Eliphaz really had the vision he described here or whether he fabricated it for the purpose of bolstering his presentation to Job.[10] It is hard to argue with people who claim to have special revelation. Such people cannot be easily dissuaded of their convictions, even though it is obvious that the dream or vision often corroborates what they otherwise believe or want to do.

4:12 Eliphaz claimed that he had received a secret word. The verb "was secretly brought" is from the root *gnb,* "to steal/gain by stealth."[11] The other unusual word in this verse is "whisper." In this form it occurs only here and in 26:14.[12] At this point the information came only orally. In v. 16 Eliphaz adds the visual dimension.

---

[10] Elihu in 33:14-16 may have had this report of Eliphaz in mind. In any case, he, along with most ancient people, believed in the authenticity and authority of dreams.

[11] The only other occasions for the *pual* of this moderately common root are Gen 40:15; Exod 22:7[6]). Jeremiah 23:30 uses it in the *piel* to speak of false "prophets who steal from one another words supposedly from me." This use comes closest to the sense in Job 4:12.

[12] A fem. form, שׁממה, is in Exod 32:25 translated in the NIV "laughingstock." The KJV's "little" in the two Job passages is confirmed by the later Hebrew of Sir 10:10; 18:32 and medieval Hebrew, i.e., Kimḥi and Rashi. See Gordis's discussion in *Job,* 48, and Dhorme, *Job,* 48.

4:13 Three of the six words in this verse are rare.[13] Despite this specialized vocabulary there is no question about the meaning of the verse. It is true that dreams can sometimes be very disturbing.

4:14 As if to impress Job further with the intensity and legitimacy of the vision, he described the physical effects it had on him. "Fear [or better "shaking"] and trembling" seized him and, literally, "many"[14] of his bones shook. The first and last words of the verse are both from the root *phd*, a subtle inclusio.

4:15 The dreamer from Teman continued to detail the picture of his eerie vision. Lacking the word "goose pimples," Eliphaz described the same phenomenon with the rare word "stood on end," a term that occurs elsewhere only in Ps 119:120.[15] It is not certain whether the "spirit" should be understood as a divine spirit or whether we should read "breeze/wind" with the GNB and NJPS. "Spirit" is preferable because "it" in v. 16 is parallel to "a form" in the next verse, and the wind is not spoken of (in Hebrew).

4:16 This three-line verse develops the spiritual revelation that Eliphaz claimed to have had. Whatever it was, it "stopped" or "stood still." Eliphaz did not or could not[16] understand what he was seeing. The term *mar'eh*, "what it was," is sometimes translated "vision" (Ezek 8:4; 11:24; Dan 8:16; 9:23). The noun *dĕmāmâ* ("hushed") is used in just two other places including the well-known "still" small voice of 1 Kgs 19:12. Eliphaz heard something superhuman in a quiet voice. Job definitely would hear Yahweh speak out of the whirlwind at the end of the book.

(4) More Reasoning (4:17–5:7)

> [17]'Can a mortal be more righteous than God?
>   Can a man be more pure than his Maker?
> [18]If God places no trust in his servants,
>   if he charges his angels with error,
> [19]how much more those who live in houses of clay,
>   whose foundations are in the dust,

---

[13] "Disquieting" appears elsewhere in the Bible only in 20:2. Four of the nine occurrences of this spelling for "dreams" are in Job (7:14; 20:8; 33:15). "Deep sleep" is only six other places, including Job 33:15.

[14] Cf. the NASB margin, "the multitude of."

[15] A noun from this verb is in Jer 51:27 referring to a kind of locust ("Bristling locust," BDB, 702. M. Pope has, "The hair of my body bristled" (*Job*, AB [Garden City: Doubleday, 1965]).

[16] There is no verb such as יכל in the text, but it is legitimate to translate the verb in the sense the NIV does.

who are crushed more readily than a moth!
²⁰Between dawn and dusk they are broken to pieces;
    unnoticed, they perish forever.
²¹Are not the cords of their tent pulled up,
    so that they die without wisdom?'

¹"Call if you will, but who will answer you?
    To which of the holy ones will you turn?
²Resentment kills a fool,
    and envy slays the simple.
³I myself have seen a fool taking root,
    but suddenly his house was cursed.
⁴His children are far from safety,
    crushed in court without a defender.
⁵The hungry consume his harvest,
    taking it even from among thorns,
    and the thirsty pant after his wealth.
⁶For hardship does not spring from the soil,
    nor does trouble sprout from the ground.
⁷Yet man is born to trouble
    as surely as sparks fly upward.

Presumably what follows the description of the apparition is its accompanying message. Just how many verses constitute the message of the Spirit (single quotation marks) is debatable, but certainly vv. 17-21 are defendable.[17] The entire section closing chap. 4 and beginning chap. 5 is another appeal to Job's reason.

DIVINE MORALITY AND HUMAN MORTALITY (4:17-21).   The vision or spirit gave no new information. Not surprisingly it agreed with what Eliphaz and his friends said throughout the debate cycle. For that reason Eliphaz's testimony is not entirely trustworthy. The essence of the message is that humankind is inherently displeasing to God and very frail and transitory.

4:17   Yet once more Eliphaz used rhetorical questions (cf. vv. 2,6-7,21). Again the anticipated answers are in the negative. No man (*'ĕnôš*) can be more righteous than God,[18] and no man (*geber*) can be more pure than the Creator. Job echoed these words in 9:2, one of the few places where the hero of the book quoted his friends. Here and the next two verses are Old Testament expressions that "all have sinned and fall short" of God's demands (Pss 14:3; 53:3[4]; Rom 3:10-11,23).

---

[17] Note the NIV footnote that some interpreters end the quotation after v. 17.

[18] As in v. 16, the verbs are translated as potential imperfects (can, may, should).

4:18   Verse 18 is the first half or protasis of a conditional sentence. The apodosis is v. 19, although it is not a typical result clause. The "servants" must be understood in the sense of superhuman servants in light of the parallel "angels." Verses such as this support the popular notion that angels are good, but a serious study of *malʾāk* and *ággelos* through the Bible indicates that not all are confirmed in goodness. Even in those who are on God's side, he does not place his faith (*ʾāman*).[19] A verse similar to this appears in Eliphaz's second speech (15:15).

4:19   Verse 18 spoke of "angels"; v. 19, of mortals. The "houses of clay" and "foundations" of "dust" refer to the fragile and transient bodies we occupy, not to bricks and cement. This "dust" was what God used in Gen 2:7 to make the first man, and it is what the Redeemer will stand on in the end (Job 19:25). From the picture of an earthly dwelling, Eliphaz moved to illustrate with a moth the brevity of the life.[20]

4:20   Still thinking of the shortness of life for moth and man, Eliphaz noted that it is only a matter of a day before they are "broken to pieces."[21] "Unnoticed" translates the elliptical expression "with none placing," meaning "with none taking it to heart." As no one counts dead moths, so people are soon forgotten.

4:21   In this last verse of the speech connected to the vision, Eliphaz introduces a new metaphor, that of a dismantled tent.[22] Again it is a negative rhetorical question expecting a positive answer: yes, their tent cords are pulled up, and they do die without wisdom. A human life is too brief to understand the ways of God. The most aged of us are immature, unenlightened, and ignorant of the ways of God. It is a depressing note but not unlike others that sound from the mouths of the other two friends as well as from Job.

One feature that makes this dismal assessment of human worth and knowledge different from, for example, 8:22; 18:21; 36:12 is that this

---

[19] The word "error," תָּהֳלָה, is a hapax unless it is a mistake for תִּפְלָה, which occurs in Job 24:12; Jer 23:13. I find attractive Ehrlich's suggestion to allow the negative particle of the first stich to do double duty and repoint the word in question as תְּהִלָּה, "praise/glory." The second half of v. 18 would then read, "And to his angels he ascribes no glory." See Blommerde, *Northwest Semitic and Job,* 41-42. Could this be behind Paul's use of δόξης in Rom 3:23?

[20] Job has three of the seven occurrences of עָשׁ, "moth," in the OT (cf. 13:28; 27:18). J. A. Rimbach, however, would read the מִבְּקֶר at the beginning of v. 20 at the end of v. 19, thus replacing "moth" with "their maker," עֹשָׂם (" 'Crushed before the Moth' [Job 4:19]," *JBL* 100 [1981]: 244-46).

[21] *Hophal* of כתת.

[22] Instead of "the cord of their tent," the KJV has "their excellency," an interpretation based on the Aramaic Targum, Latin Vulgate, and Syriac.

one speaks despairingly of all people, not just the wicked.

HUMAN PROCLIVITY TO FOLLY AND TROUBLE (5:1-7). Eliphaz continued to strengthen his view that the wicked suffer with this section that
speaks of the miserable end that comes to fools. The trouble they generate eventuates in hunger, hardship, danger, and death.

5:1 Eliphaz challenged Job to call, presumably to an angel or one of
the "holy ones." Such a challenge is hypothetical, but it makes the point
that Job would find no help because in Eliphaz's eyes he was an unrepentant sinner and hence a fool. To this rhetorical question as well the answer is negative: no one will answer you, and there is no holy one to
whom you can turn, implying that angels are not prepared to help fools.

5:2 More than half a dozen Hebrew words translate as "fool/folly."[23]
Two are in this verse, and there are only shades of difference between
them. The first "fool" is one who "despises wisdom and discipline" (Prov
1:7), whose way is "right in his own eyes" (Prov 12:15, KJV), and who
became a fool because of his rebellious ways and iniquities (Ps 107:17).
This variety "spurns his father's instruction" (Prov 15:5) and repeats his
folly "as a dog returns to its vomit" (Prov 26:11). The second kind, "the
simple," is a more pardonable sort of fool.[24] He is immature, impressionable, gullible, and lacks discernment; however, there is hope for him.

The two agents of death, "resentment" and "envy," admit a variety of
interpretations, with many turning the second in the direction of "anger."
The NAB has "impatience" and "indignation." The NASB has "vexation"
and "anger." Job has evidenced none of these tendencies so far, but he
will in the chapters that lie ahead. Perhaps Eliphaz noticed them in Job
though they are unrecorded at this point in the book.

5:3 Once more Eliphaz appealed to his experience gained from a
lifetime of watching fools go wrong and pay dearly for their folly.[25]
"Taking root" normally is a good thing (but contrast Ps 37:35). Often the
well established are uprooted quickly. Zophar said it even better in 20:5:
"The mirth of the wicked is brief, the joy of the godless lasts but a moment."

---

[23] W. T. Dayton, "Folly" in *ZPEB* 2:581.

[24] פֹּתֶי is a *qal* active participle. Finite forms occur in Job 31:9,27. The noun פֶּתִי appears almost exclusively in Proverbs.

[25] "I cursed" is the way some translations read the verb (e.g., KJV, RV, RSV, NASB).
אֶקּוֹב may be from קבב II (so BDB, 866) or נקב (so Wigram, *The Englishman's Hebrew and Chaldee Concordance to the Old Testament* [London: Bagster, 1890], 837). For
more discussion and alternatives see D. Clines, *Job*, WBC 17 (Dallas: Word, 1989), 115.
"House" is not the usual בַּיִת but נָוֶה, a term that means "habitation" in general whether of
animals or humans. It is in 5:24 translated "property" and in 18:15 "dwelling."

5:4 If it were not for the second line that says this fool's "children are crushed in court without a defender," one would think Eliphaz was pointing at Job's children, who were "far from safety." It still is possible to read it that way since "court" is also "gate," and "defender" could be rendered "rescuer/savior."[26] As it stands, however, the verse addresses a forensic situation with "safety" referring to the protection of the law.

5:5 The wording, vocabulary, and pointing of the Hebrew words in v. 5 are difficult; but the overall sense of the verse is clear: others will consume the goods of the fool. The first of the three lines is clearest and says essentially that. The second line with its "thorns" is more enigmatic.[27] The usual explanation is that farmers protected their piles of grain with fences or hedges made from tangled briars. Marauders would sometimes steal despite these defensive measures. "Thirsty" in the third line is the major problem. The word *ṣammîm* means "trap/snare" in its only other occurrence (18:9), but most assume *ṣmm* is an alternate or defective spelling of *ṣm'* ("thirsty").

5:6 Eliphaz said that the land is neutral; it is not a part of the morality or immorality of the race. One cannot blame the earth for "hardship" and "trouble." The curse on the ground following the sin of Adam and Eve comes to mind in this connection (Gen 3:17-19). It was not the ground's fault. It was the first couple's fault. What trouble people have they bring on themselves.

5:7 A well-known proverblike verse concludes Eliphaz's long section on reasoning. This was his way of saying what David said in Ps 51:5[7], "Surely I was sinful at birth." As naturally and normally "as sparks fly upward," so do people find themselves in trouble—trouble with one another and trouble with God.[28]

(5) Recommendations (5:8-27)

[8]"But if it were I, I would appeal to God;
    I would lay my cause before him.
[9]He performs wonders that cannot be fathomed

---

[26] AAT has for v. 4, "His children, far from help, are crushed in the gate, and with nobody to rescue them."

[27] צן occurs only here and Prov 22:5.

[28] "Sparks" is literally "the children of Resheph," the god of fire, fever, and pestilence. In none of the six occurrences of the term in the OT can one assume the speaker believed in such a deity. It is comparable to our use of Saint Elmo's fire to speak of static electricity just before a lightning strike. Pope, who is sympathetic to the mythological background of Job and Song of Songs, makes much of this in his commentary (*Job,* AB). Cf. R. L. Harris, *TWOT,* 2223.

and miracles that cannot be counted.
¹⁰He bestows rain on the earth;
   he sends water upon the countryside.
¹¹The lowly he sets on high,
   and those who mourn are lifted to safety.
¹²He thwarts the plans of the crafty,
   so that their hands achieve no success.
¹³He catches the wise in their craftiness,
   and the schemes of the wily are swept away.
¹⁴Darkness comes upon them in the daytime;
   at noon they grope as in the night.
¹⁵He saves the needy from the sword in their mouth;
   he saves them from the clutches of the powerful.
¹⁶So the poor have hope,
   and injustice shuts its mouth.

¹⁷"Blessed is the man whom God corrects;
   so do not despise the discipline of the Almighty.
¹⁸For he wounds, but he also binds up;
   he injures, but his hands also heal.
¹⁹From six calamities he will rescue you;
   in seven no harm will befall you.
²⁰In famine he will ransom you from death,
   and in battle from the stroke of the sword.
²¹You will be protected from the lash of the tongue,
   and need not fear when destruction comes.
²²You will laugh at destruction and famine,
   and need not fear the beasts of the earth.
²³For you will have a covenant with the stones of the field,
   and the wild animals will be at peace with you.
²⁴You will know that your tent is secure;
   you will take stock of your property and find nothing missing.
²⁵You will know that your children will be many,
   and your descendants like the grass of the earth.
²⁶You will come to the grave in full vigor,
   like sheaves gathered in season.

²⁷"We have examined this, and it is true.
   So hear it and apply it to yourself."

This long division begins and ends with advice (vv. 8,27) and has one imperative in the middle (v. 17b). In between are smaller sections devoted to the power and justice of God, especially as he administers that justice to offenders and blesses those who heed his discipline. They are themes that will appear repeatedly in the following chapters and from the lips of all four friends.

APPEAL TO THE GOD OF JUSTICE (5:8-16). These nine verses stress three features of God's governance of the universe: his sovereign control over the weather and the fortunes of humankind, his apprehension and punishment of wrongdoers, and his deliverance of the needy and oppressed.

5:8 Our idiom is, "If I were you." But the Hebrew way of saying the same thing is, "If it were I."[29] Eliphaz suggested two things. First, Job should "appeal" (lit. "seek") to God. Second, Job should lay his cause before God. Bildad suggested the same thing in 8:5. Job wanted nothing more and nothing less (23:3-8). Eventually Job would contend with God (chaps. 29–31) and God would answer (chaps. 38–41).

5:9 Each speaker in the book anticipates the theophany of chaps. 38–41. Here Eliphaz spoke of God's "wonders" and "miracles." Job discoursed on God moving mountains, giving orders to the sun, stretching out the heavens, and treading on the sea (9:5-8).[30] Bildad closed the three friends' speeches with a brief monologue on God's dominion of the heights of heaven (25:2). Zophar reflected on the fathomless mysteries of God (11:7-9). Elihu, more than any of the others, addressed these topics. His last chapter and a half are essentially an introduction to the manifestation of God in the storm (36:22–37:23).

5:10 For people in dry places and for all engaged in agriculture, weather is very important and rain especially so. Often in the Old Testament the absence or presence of rain in drought or flood played an important role. From the deluge of Genesis (chaps. 6–9) to the drizzle of Ezra (10:9), rain had been a factor in the weal and woe of ancient Israel. Rain was and is capricious (cf. Amos 4:7), and to this day the predicting of it is uncertain. It remains one dimension of the created order that God reserves to himself. While eclipses, equinoxes, solstices, and some comets are highly predictable, the weather is markedly inconstant.[31]

5:11 From the realm of the created order Eliphaz moved to the sphere of human fortunes. Grammatically v. 11 is a continuation of v. 10 because "he sets" translates an infinitive, "to lift." The giving or withholding of rain serves the purposes of his justice (cf. 37:13). As Joshua

---

[29] אוּלָם is a strong adversative conjunction translated elsewhere as "nevertheless" (Gen 48:19; Num 14:21), "yet as surely as" (1 Sam 20:3), and "otherwise" (1 Sam 25:34). Whether or not intentional, it is curious that eight of the nine words in v. 8 begin with א: אוּלָם אֲנִי אֶדְרֹשׁ אֶל־אֵל וְאֶל־אֱלֹהִים אָשִׂים דִּבְרָתִי.

[30] Job speaks the identical words of this verse in 9:10.

[31] "Countryside," חוּצוֹת, is more literally "outside." For this term in 18:17 the NIV has "land" and in 31:32 "street."

was aided by the hail (Josh 10:11) and Ahab was punished with drought (1 Kgs 17:1), so in less dramatic and unrecorded ways God honors the humble and saves those who walk through the valley of the shadow of death.[32] This sentiment and its counterpart, "pride goes before destruction" (Prov 16:18), are found in both Testaments (Jas 4:6; 1 Pet 5:5).

5:12 Here Eliphaz again reached the point of this two-chapter speech to Job. Job had been "thwarted" by God, and all his success had been undone by divine justice. Indirectly Eliphaz indicted Job here and in the next few verses.

5:13 Repeating the same ideas as in the preceding verse, Eliphaz or the author of the book presented this timeless truth in a format unique from a poetic standpoint. The NIV follows the word order of the Hebrew exactly. Note the chiastic structure:

A   He catches
  B   the wise
    C   in their craftiness[33]
    C'   and the schemes of
  B'   the wily
A'   are swept away.

This is the only certain quotation from Job in the New Testament (with the possible exception of Job 41:11 in Rom 11:35), quoted in 1 Cor 3:19.[34]

5:14 A progression marks vv. 12-14. First, God thwarts the wicked (v. 12). Then he apprehends them (v. 13). And now he punishes them (v. 14). The sentences are structured the same with "they" the subject of both verbs. The first line is literally, "They come upon darkness in the daytime."[35] In a world without electricity, night and darkness had a frightening dimension that we moderns rarely experience. The New Tes-

---

[32] "Those who mourn" translates קֹדְרִים, from the root קדר, "dark/black."

[33] Both עֹרֶם, "craftiness," and נִפְתָּל, "the wily," occur but five times each according to T. Armstrong, D. Busby, and C. Carr, *A Reader's Hebrew-English Lexicon of the Old Testament* (Grand Rapids: Zondervan, 1989), 483. Minor orthographic variations will add several more to each count so that the meaning is well established.

[34] Paul's argument there is that the world's wisdom is of no value for salvation. It is better to be counted by the world a fool than to miss the wisdom of God for the sake of intellectual pride.

[35] This verse too is chiastic in Hebrew:
A   By day
  B   they come upon
    C   darkness
    C'   as in the night
  B'   they grope
A'   at noon.

tament frequently associates darkness with judgment (Matt 8:12; 22:13; 25:30; 2 Pet 2:17; Jude 6,13; Rev 16:10).

5:15 Eliphaz again looked at the positive side of divine justice, the defense and deliverance of the needy and oppressed. "The sword of their mouth" is an interesting expression in light of the more common Hebrew idiom "the mouth/lip of the sword." If Eliphaz was still speaking of a court scene rather than a literal battle situation, the arrangement is fitting (cf. 4:10; 5:4). The accusations and charges of the wicked against the righteous are the "swords" from which God saves the them.[36]

5:16 The word "mouth" links vv. 15-16. The swordlike mouth that accused the poor and needy is now shut in light of the justice of God. The downtrodden, abused, and powerless now have hope.[37]

THE LESSONS AND REWARDS OF SUFFERING (5:17-26). This section takes a different tack from the usual thrust of the friends' case. Rather than focusing on suffering as punishment, Eliphaz posited the possibility that trouble is therapeutic and remedial and that God had Job's good in mind and not only his justice.

5:17 "Blessed" is *'ašrê*, the same word that opens the Psalter (1:1). The person whom God makes the effort to "correct"[38] should be considered blessed. It is easier said than done. For the first of thirty-one times *šadday,* "the Almighty," appears. This is the second most common word for God in the book. This fact may point to scenes that took place outside Israel where God's name was not known or to a time before that special name was revealed (Exod 6:3). The best explanation of its origin is in the Akkadian word *šadu* and the Ugaritic word *td,* both "mountain," hence, El Shaddai means "God of the mountains" (cf. 1 Kgs 20:23; Judg 5:5; Neh 9:13; Ps 68:8[9],17[18]).[39] The imperative "do not despise" occurs in the middle of this speech.

5:18 Eliphaz had a high view of God. He was not a dualist who saw the bad coming from some evil deity and the good coming from God. Everything came from God's hand, both the wounding and the healing.[40]

---

[36] The NIV has translated the verb "save" twice, a common device in synonymous parallelism. It keeps the Hebrew line in balance with three major words each half.

[37] For "hope" see footnote at 4:6 that lists the many places in Job where this significant word appears.

[38] Job has more than a fourth of the OT's sixty occurrences of יכח, "reprove/rebuke/correct/judge."

[39] The LXX translated this name as παντοκράτορος, and the Vulgate sometimes as *Omnipotens,* and that is the basis of the English "Almighty" (V. Hamilton, *TWOT* 2:907, 2333).

[40] Three of the four verbs of this verse appear in Isa 30:26: רפא / מחץ / חבש.

5:19 Eliphaz used an x + 1 formula to illustrate the "calamities" from which God would rescue his faithful ones.[41] "Seven," the culminating number, indicates perfection or completion and appears here to underscore the fact that God will save us from all troubles. The seven dangers appear in the following verses: death by famine and battle sword (v. 20), tongue and destruction (v. 21), destruction (again), famine (a different word from the one in v. 20), and beasts (v. 22).

5:20 The catalog of calamities begins with famine and death and adds to it "the hands of a sword." "By sword" is the Old Testament's way of speaking of a violent death, usually in battle. A soldier might be killed by javelin, arrow, fire, or missile; but "sword" covers all those categories. It is the opposite of a peaceful death at the end of a long life (v. 20).

5:21 Next Job would be "hidden/protected" from the damage a whiplike tongue might inflict. Gossip, false accusation, and other imprudent and dangerous uses of the tongue receive strong condemnation throughout the Bible (Exod 20:16; Prov 11:13; 16:28; 2 Cor 12:20; Jas 3:6). Freedom from fear of "destruction/devastation/ruin" is the second element in v. 21 and links this to the next verse.

5:22 The opposite of fearing is laughing, and that would be the response to "destruction and famine"[42] from those healed and rescued by their God. For those living on the border between the desert and the sown land, these two threats were frequent and real. Destruction could come from thieving bands of Sabeans or Chaldeans. Famine could have come as the result of a year of sparse rains.

5:23 Eliphaz suggested in this beautiful verse that if you are obedient to God, not only will he bless Job but Job will also live in an irenic world of mutual respect with even the animate and inanimate creation. This ecological covenant will be with the "stones of the field" and will result in living at peace with the "animals of the field," the Old Testament's word for "wild animals" as opposed to domestic ones. When God spoke from the whirlwind at the end of the book, it was clear that he had such a covenant with them. They were his pets, his flocks, and his herds. The scene anticipates the beatific and peaceable kingdom Isaiah foresaw where "the wolf will live with the lamb, the leopard will lie down with the goat, the calf and the lion and the yearling together, and a little child

---

[41] See W. M. W. Roth, "The Numerical Sequences x/x+1 in the Old Testament," *VT* 12 (1962): 300-311.

[42] In v. 20 "famine" translates the common word רָעָב, and in v. 22 it translates כָּפָן, a noun occurring elsewhere only in Job 30:3. A verb with these same radicals is in Ezek 17:7, "sent out" (roots for water).

will lead them" (Isa 11:6-9).

5:24 If vv. 24-26 anticipate the end of Job's life, then Eliphaz's words ironically were true but for a different reason in the case of Job. Less pleasant is the possibility that Eliphaz was reflecting on Job's losses again when he referred to property and children. "Secure" is *šālôm,* the same root as "peace" in v. 23. "Property" probably refers to "cattle" because elsewhere the term means "pasture" (2 Sam 7:8; Isa 65:10; Jer 23:3; Ezek 25:5). "Tent" need not be taken literally; it could as well mean "house."[43]

5:25 The opening words are the same as v. 24, only here Job's certainty would be of his human family, not merely his flocks, herds, and buildings. Big families were considered a token of God's favor; the Old Testament encouraged the bearing of many children (Gen 13:16; 22:17; Pss 127:4-5; 128:3). Their numbers would be like blades of grass, innumerable.[44]

5:26 Even the death of the blessed ones is timely and proper. Before the present tragedies came upon him, this was the way Job thought he would die. He had hoped to die in his own house with his "days as numerous as the grains of sand" (28:18). At this point in the book, little did Eliphaz or Job realize the accuracy of this verse. Job lived after this trial, most likely "in full vigor,"[45] for 140 (more?) years, double (or triple) the full life span of Ps 90:10 (cf. Gen 15:15). "Like sheaves gathered in season," some people die at precisely the right time.

His Concluding Charge (5:27). Eliphaz ended his first and longest speech with a testimony to his own convictions and with two imperatives to Job.

5:27 Because Eliphaz used the plural, he must have been speaking for his two companions as well. At the mouth of these three witnesses (Deut 19:15) he believed it was so; and so should Job. The advice was "hear" and "know for yourself" (cf. the opening words of vv. 24-25). So ends the first of eight speeches by these three friends. They were resolute at the beginning and were not dissuaded at the end from their belief that they were right and Job was wrong.

---

[43] אֹהֶל and בַּיִת are poetic parallels in 1 Kgs 12:16. In fact, אֹהֶל is found a second time in that verse and translated "home" in the NIV and others.

[44] Neither word for "children" in the verse is the usual בָּנִים; the first is זֶרַע, "seed," and the second is the reduplicated צֶאֱצָאִים, a derivative of יָצָא, "go forth." Only Job (four times) and Isaiah (seven times) used it.

[45] This rare word, כֶּלַח, occurs only here and in 30:2. For a lengthy discussion and references see Pope, *Job,* 46-47.

2. Job: My Complaint Is Just, but I Lack Comfort (6:1–7:21)

Now it was Job's turn to speak. Unfortunately this, like most of the speeches, is a monologue. The participants did not usually converse in the sense of dialogue. Each had his own agenda and seemed to turn a deaf ear when his opponent spoke.[46] In this two-chapter response Job introduces some of the themes that characterize his speeches throughout the book: depression, disappointment, and desire for death.

(1) Anguish (6:1-7)

[1]Then Job replied:
[2]"If only my anguish could be weighed
  and all my misery be placed on the scales!
[3]It would surely outweigh the sand of the seas—
  no wonder my words have been impetuous.
[4]The arrows of the Almighty are in me,
  my spirit drinks in their poison;
  God's terrors are marshaled against me.
[5]Does a wild donkey bray when it has grass;
  or an ox bellow when it has fodder?
[6]Is tasteless food eaten without salt,
  or is there flavor in the white of an egg?
[7]I refuse to touch it;
  such food makes me ill.

The title of this section comes from the subject of the first clause, "anguish." First protesting that his misery was heavy, Job went on to justify his complaint by comparing himself to hungry farm animals or to one given food too insipid to ingest.

6:1 This standard introduction will be repeated in 9:1; 12:1; 16:1; 19:1; 21:1; 23:1; 26:1.

6:2 The desiderative particle *lû*, "If only/"O that," opens the speech. Job wished that his "anguish" and "misery"[47] might be measured.[48]

6:3 The weighing would show that his anguish was unbearably

---

[46] N. Klaus argues to the contrary, that they did listen and reflect what each other said ("Between Job and His Friends," *Beth Mikra* 31 [1985/86]: 152-68; "Joban Parallels—To Job," *Beth Mikra* 32 [1986/87]: 45-56 [Hebrew]).

[47] "My misery" translates the *qere* וְהַוָּתִי from הַוָּה rather than the *kethib* הַיָּתִי (lit., "I was"). Cf. 6:30; 30:13; Ps 5:10; Isa 47:11; etc.

[48] "Weigh" is emphatic because of the infinitive absolute preceding the finite verb שָׁקֹל, the root of "shekel."

heavy. The crux of the sentence is the term "impetuous." Unlike the KJV, which took it from the root *lûaʿ* ("swallow"), most modern versions understand *lāʿû* differently and translate it in a variety of interpretations: "rash" (AT, RSV, NASB, NKJV), "wild" (JB, NEB), "recklessly" (NJPS), "careless" (NCV), "frenzied" (REB).

6:4 Job believed that God was punishing him, though he did not here or anywhere speculate what the offense might have been. To his credit his monotheism demanded that from God alone come all things, good and bad. With militaristic terminology he described affliction as poison arrows (cf. 16:12-14). The third line of this tricolon compares the assaults on his person to "God's terrors"[49] arrayed against him.

6:5 Verses 5-6 are interrogatives. Several rare words put the translation of individual phrases in question, but the overall sense is undisputed. The answer to the queries in v. 6 is no. Donkeys do not bray[50] and oxen do not bellow[51] when they are satisfied with food.[52] But Job was not satisfied with what God had dished out to him.

6:6 Unfortunately this oft-quoted verse is riddled with uncertainties. Fortunately no major doctrinal issues are at stake. The certain words are "Is . . . eaten without salt, or is there taste." From the known are derived guesses for the unknown. The "tasteless food" is a hapax. The "egg" is another hapax. And the "white" occurs elsewhere only at 1 Sam 21:13[14], "saliva" (NASB, NIV), "spit" (GNB, NCV). The "white of an egg" goes back to the Aramaic Targum and the KJV. The AT and RSV have "slime of the purslane." The JB has "mallow juice" (cf. NRSV, REB). The AB has "slimy cream cheese." The point of the verse is that Job felt he had been served a tasteless and even repulsive diet by God.

6:7 Figuratively speaking, Job found the meal that God served so unpalatable that he refused it altogether. The motif of food that began in v. 4 concludes here with Job's total rejection of the menu. To partake of it made Job sick,[53] but he had no choice.

(2) Request for Death (6:8-10)

8Oh, that I might have my request,
that God would grant what I hope for,

---

[49] A rare word, בְּעוּתִים, that occurs only here and Ps 88:16[17]. The meaning is established by the sixteen occurrences of the cognate verb בָּעַת, "fear."

[50] "Bray," נָהַק, appears only here and in 30:7 in the OT.

[51] "Bellow," גָּעָה, occurs only here and in 1 Sam 6:12.

[52] "Fodder," בְּלִיל, is found elsewhere only at 24:6 and Isa 30:24.

[53] "Sick," דְּוַי, is a rare word, occurring only here and in Ps 41:3[4].

⁹**that God would be willing to crush me,**
  to let loose his hand and cut me off!
¹⁰**Then I would still have this consolation—**
  my joy in unrelenting pain—
  that I had not denied the words of the Holy One.

Through all of chap. 3 Job wished that he were dead.[54] Here in his first speech he picked up that theme once more. He seemed to fear that he might blaspheme God if he continued to live. An early death would preclude that possibility.

6:8   A different formula from the one in v. 2 opens this verse (cf. 19:23). Literally the idiom is, "Who will give?"[55] Thus the verb *nātan*, "give/grant," appears twice. What that "request" and "hope" were is the subject of the next verse.

6:9   Like Moses (Num 11:15) and Elijah (1 Kgs 19:4), Job wished to die. Both the verbs "crush" and cut off"[56] are metaphors for death and do not refer to any particular method.

6:10   The translation of the first and third lines of v. 10 are relatively certain; the middle one, not so. Taking only the first and third, the sense is that Job would have been happy to die in the knowledge that he had kept the faith. Sometimes the extremes of pain prompt people to curse God. Two rare words confound the second line: "my joy" and "pain." The latter is made certain by cognates, but there are two different directions taken by translations of the first Hebrew word of that line. The KJV has, "I would harden myself in sorrow." The RV and others through the NRSV have, "I would exult." The NJPS has, "I writhed."[57]

(3) Hopelessness (6:11-13)

¹¹**"What strength do I have, that I should still hope?**
  What prospects, that I should be patient?
¹²**Do I have the strength of stone?**
  Is my flesh bronze?
¹³**Do I have any power to help myself,**

---

[54] Suicide was not a possibility he considered. See W. Riggans, "A Note on Job 6:8-10, Suicide and Death Wishes," *DD* 15 (1987): 173-76.

[55] Job has nine of the twenty-four occurrences of this idiom: 6:8; 13:5; 14:13; 19:23; 23:3; 29:2; 31:31,35 from the mouth of Job and 11:5 from Zophar.

[56] Some (e.g., Pope) have pointed out that this term describes what a weaver does with the thrum (Isa 38:10).

[57] "The verb is סלד. See Clines, *Job*, 159; W. Riggans, "Job 6:8-10," *ET* 99 (1987): 45-46.

now that success has been driven from me?

The hopelessness Job articulated in these three verses is in the rhetorical question format. The answers to each of the five questions Job understood to be no or none.

6:11   The NIV translates the Hebrew straightforwardly, although there is a way of taking the last phrase less metaphorically. Literally it reads "that I should prolong my soul/breath." A modern paraphrase is, "Why go on living?" AAT has something similar with its "prolong my life."[58]

6:12   Of course, Job's strength was not as strong as stone or his flesh as tough as bronze. It is interesting that these analogies are also applied to the behemoth (40:18) and the leviathan (41:24[16]),[59] another support for the view that one hand is responsible for the entire book.

6:13   Though this is a difficult verse, the NIV has the correct sense, that is, that Job considered himself helpless and hopeless. "Success" is the most obscure word but is generally agreed upon by the majority of translators.[60] With bitter sarcasm Job shot back at the friends with words similar to the end of their speeches: "How you have helped the powerless!" (26:2).

(4) Disappointment with His Friends (6:14-23)

¹⁴"A despairing man should have the devotion of his friends,
      even though he forsakes the fear of the Almighty.
¹⁵But my brothers are as undependable as intermittent streams,
      as the streams that overflow
¹⁶when darkened by thawing ice
      and swollen with melting snow,
¹⁷but that cease to flow in the dry season,
      and in the heat vanish from their channels.
¹⁸Caravans turn aside from their routes;
      they go up into the wasteland and perish.
¹⁹The caravans of Tema look for water,
      the traveling merchants of Sheba look in hope.
²⁰They are distressed, because they had been confident;

---

[58] But cf. Hartley (135, n. 8zz), who reminds us that this is the opposite of "shorten the spirit/breath," which means "be impatient" as in 21:4.

[59] Job 6:12 is the only place "bronze" (נְחוּשׁ) is not a fem. noun.

[60] Of the six occurrences of "success" in Job, the KJV has five different translations. The NASB has "deliverance," arrived at by emending תֻּשִׁיָּה to תְּשׁוּעָה. The NRSV has "resource"; the NEB, "aid"; and the NAB, "advice," following the traditional "wisdom" of the KJV and others.

they arrive there, only to be disappointed.
²¹Now you too have proved to be of no help;
you see something dreadful and are afraid.
²²Have I ever said, 'Give something on my behalf,
pay a ransom for me from your wealth,
²³deliver me from the hand of the enemy,
ransom me from the clutches of the ruthless'?

In this section Job compares his friends to desert streams that swell with water after a storm but dry up in the heat of summer. He presses the illustration by imagining further the disappointment and tragic results of caravans that perish because they do not find life-sustaining water. Job's disappointment with his friends is analogous. Though in the past he never needed their aid, he does now; but they respond with empty hands.

6:14 The crux of v. 14 is the first word. The NIV reads it from the verb *mss*, "melt/despair." Others prefer to emend it to *m's*, "refuse/reject" (so RSV, MLB, JB).[61] These versions also turn the sentence around so that it becomes the friends who "forsake the fear of the Almighty." "Devotion" is *ḥesed*, a multifaceted word encompassing "loyalty," "love," "faithfulness," "piety," "mercy," and "promise keeping." "Fear" in both its verb and noun forms also goes well beyond the semantic sphere of "fear" in English and includes "reverence," "devotion," and even "religion."

6:15 Here begins a three-verse description of an intermittent desert stream, what in Hebrew is a *nāḥāl,* in Arabic a *wadi,* in Spanish an *arroyo,* and in southwestern American a "gulch," "gully," or "wash." In the springtime or after a rain, such streams are deceiving. They seem abundant, but they soon will fail (1 Kgs 17:7; Jer 15:18; Amos 5:24).

If Job meant "brothers" sincerely, he was very generous. More likely he was being cynical. In v. 14 he called them "friends," but that term has greater breadth and need not carry with it any sense of commitment.

6:16 Some uncertainty attends v. 16, especially the second half. "Thawing" represents no Hebrew word, but ice must melt in order to flow down and "darken" an otherwise dry stream bed. The three words that constitute the second half would be literally translated "upon it/it is hidden/snow." The preposition has an unusual spelling. And some, including the NIV, assume the verb's root is *ʿrm,* used once in this sense at Exod 15:8, rather than *ʿlm.*[62]

---

[61] Also Hartley, *Job,* 136, n. 1.

[62] Alliteration may be behind the choice of עָלֵימוֹ יִתְעַלָּם. For a fuller discussion of this problem see Clines, *Job,* 160; A. Fitzgerald, "The Interchange of L, N, and R in Biblical Hebrew," *JBL* 97 (1978): 483.

6:17 The NIV paraphrases here because there is no way to produce a smooth and literal translation. The Hebrew word represented by "dry" (*zrb*) occurs only here, its meaning derived from this one context. "Channels" is the common word for "places."[63] Like those streams, these friends failed, so to speak, when the heat was on. As a seasonal stream is undependable, so Eliphaz and his comrades had no help to give when Job needed it most.

6:18 Though *'ōraḥ* usually means "road," it must be elliptical for "those who travel roads," hence "caravans" in vv. 18-19. "Turn aside" is a rare word too, occurring in this stem only here and in Ruth 3:8. "Wasteland" is *tōhû*, which occurs in Gen 1:2 as "formless." Job used it twice more (12:24; 26:7). In Deut 32:10 it is parallel to "desert." The caravans perished because the water they expected to find had dried up. Similarly the help Job expected to receive from his friends also dried up.

6:19 Drawing out the picture even further, Job provided another pair of lines to describe these hypothetical caravans. They were from Tema and Sheba. Tema is the modern Teima at the junction of the roads from Damascus to Mecca and from the Persian Gulf to Aqaba[64] (it has no connection with Teman, the home of Eliphaz). Sheba approximates modern Yemen in the south of the Arabian peninsula. It is the same place from which the Sabeans of 1:15 came. The caravans "looked" and "hoped"[65] for refreshment and camaraderie at the caravansary.[66]

6:20 Both the first and last verbs are synonyms, "distressed" and "disappointed." Their basic meaning is "embarrassed," but their semantic spheres easily embrace the notion of "confounded/mortified/abashed" as well as the two the NIV has chosen. Job spelled out this picture of frustration and consternation in order to illustrate how he felt toward his unhelpful and disappointing friends.

6:21 The cryptic Hebrew of the first half of v. 21 is even more stinging: "Indeed, now you are nothing."[67] They were afraid when they saw "something dreadful" (a "terror"), another hapax whose meaning is quite certain from cognate verbal and nominal forms. In the second half the

---

[63] A word for "channel," אָפֵק, was in v. 15 but left untranslated.

[64] See D. Dorsey, "Tema," in *ISBE* 4:758.

[65] There is no "water" in Hebrew unless the לָמוֹ, "for them," i.e., "for the streams," at the end of the verse is changed to לְמֵימ.

[66] That is, in Eastern countries, an inn surrounding a court where caravans resided at night.

[67] This follows the *kethib* לֹא. The *qere* לוֹ would yield, "Indeed, now you are his" (i.e., God's). The RSV, NRSV ("Such you have now become to me"), MLB, NEB follow the LXX (ἀτὰρ δὲ καὶ ὑμεῖς ἐπέβητέ μοι ἀνελεημόνως, "But you also came to me without pity") and read לִי "to me," but such a choice parries the thrust.

poet may have been playing with the similar sounds of *tirʾû*, "you see,"
and *tîrāʾû*, "you are afraid."

6:22 In vv. 22-23 Job, using a rhetorical question, reminded his
friends that he had never before asked them for help. The interrogative
particle that opens v. 22 applies to the quotation that extends to the end
of this section. The expected answer is no, meaning that Job was not in-
debted to them in any way. In particular he never asked them for a "ransom."[68] The RSV and many others have "bribe" at this point, which may
be a better choice since a different and more widely established word for
"ransom" occurs in the next verse.

6:23 Continuing the question, Job asked if he had ever called upon
them to save him from an enemy or to buy off his captors. He had asked
for nothing tangible. All he hoped for from them was loyalty and mercy
(v. 14), but he had received none.

(5) Request for Advice (6:24-27)

> [24]"Teach me, and I will be quiet;
>   show me where I have been wrong.
> [25]How painful are honest words?
>   But what do your arguments prove?
> [26]Do you mean to correct what I say,
>   and treat the words of a despairing man as wind?
> [27]You would even cast lots for the fatherless
>   and barter away your friend.

Although only Eliphaz had spoken up to this point, Job used plural
imperatives. Apparently he understood that the words of Eliphaz reflected
the thoughts of all three. He requested them to address his situation, not
merely argue with him about whether or not he had sinned. Job already
had found their counsel unproductive and meanspirited.

6:24 None of the friends had pointed to any sin that Job committed.
In his third speech Eliphaz charged Job with demanding unreasonable security deposits, withholding food and water from the weary and hungry,
and neglecting the widows and fatherless (22:6-9). In the long, self-
imprecatory oath of chap. 31, Job declared that he was innocent of those
and similar crimes. "I have been wrong" translates *šgh,* a verb referring
to inadvertent sin, or sins of omission. The NIV translates "sins uninten-

---

[68] "Pay a ransom," שׁחד, as a verb occurs only here and in Ezek 16:33; but the noun,
usually translated "bribe/gift," is used in the OT twenty-one times including Job 15:34. The
more common verb for "ransom," פדה, is in v. 23.

tionally" in Lev 4:13 and "go astray" in Job 19:4. Certain that he had committed no crimes, Job invited them to point out to him even any minor shortcomings.

6:25 Not all translate the first verb as "are painful" or the like. Some read just the opposite: "fair" (JB), "agreeable" (NAB).[69] A case can be made for either. Job wished for "honest words" but did not think he had heard any from his friends. Such words could be considered sweet and welcome to those who love truth, or they could be "painful" and unwelcome to those in error.

6:26 The root of "argue/prove" that is twice in the Hebrew of the preceding line opens this verse as an infinitive, "to correct." "Do you think you can disprove my words?" is the gist of the first line. They did try, treating his words as untrue. In 8:2 Bildad said, "Your words are a blustering wind." In 15:2 Eliphaz charged Job with answering "with empty notions" (literally "windy knowledge") and filling "his belly with the hot east wind."

6:27 The cruelest elements of the friends' speeches are yet to come in the book, but even at this early stage Job reminded them of their heartlessness. The "lots" are not in the text (as indicated by the italics in the RV, ASV, NASB) but are understood just as they were in Josh 23:4. Because the first line is about merchandizing people, the verb in the second line, *krh,* is taken in its secondary meaning, "barter," rather than in its first, "dig" (KJV).[70]

(6) Plea for Understanding (6:28-30)

> 28"But now be so kind as to look at me.
>   Would I lie to your face?
> 29Relent, do not be unjust;
>   reconsider, for my integrity is at stake.
> 30Is there any wickedness on my lips?
>   Can my mouth not discern malice?

Job softened the tone of his criticism between v. 27 and v. 28. Whether he noticed on their faces the agony of rebuke or whether he caught himself being unduly bitter we do not know. It is a pleasant shift.

6:28 Two requests are in the first half of the verse: "be willing" and

---

[69] One manuscript has נמלצו rather than נמרצו. The former is four times in the OT including this passage and Job 16:3. The latter is once, Ps 119:103. See Clines, *Job,* 161; W. E. Barnes, "Job vi 25: מֶרֶץ, *JTS* 29 (1927-30): 291-92.

[70] The meaning "dig," however, is not impossible. Cf. Pss 35:7; 119:85; Jer 18:20,22.

"face me." False accusers have a problem facing their victims, and that reluctance on the friends' part to look Job in the eye may have been behind this entreaty. "Face" as a noun is in the second half. Job denied that he would lie to their faces. The particle *ʾim* is an asseverative that could be translated "surely" or as a rhetorical question. The MLB, AB, and NAB chose the former; the NEB, NIV, REB chose the latter.

6:29 "Relent" and "reconsider" translate the same verb that begins each half of v. 29.[71] They had charged Job with evil; here he asked them not to be evil or unjust. "Integrity" is *ṣedeq,* the standard word for "right." One's reputation for righteousness was crucial to one's standing in the community. To attack it was tantamount to bearing false witness against a neighbor.

6:30 In a tone that sounds pleading, Job asked his friends whether he had said[72] anything wicked, the same word translated "unjust" in v. 29. When people disagree so diametrically, at least one party must be wrong. Job did not see anything wrong in himself and asked his friends to point it out. "Malice" is the same word translated "misery" in v. 2.[73] Together they form an inclusio, marking off this chapter as a literary unit. At the conclusion of the first half of his first response, Job saw a deadlock. By strong innuendo Eliphaz explained his suffering based on God's strict laws of retribution. Job, on the other hand, maintained his integrity, something he would do to the end.

(7) Query about Life (7:1-6)

> [1]"Does not man have hard service on earth?
>   Are not his days like those of a hired man?
> [2]Like a slave longing for the evening shadows,
>   or a hired man waiting eagerly for his wages,
> [3]so I have been allotted months of futility,
>   and nights of misery have been assigned to me.
> [4]When I lie down I think, 'How long before I get up?'

---

[71] The Masoretes read שֻׁבוּ for the impossible שֶׁבִּי, thus making it agree with the opening word.

[72] The word חֵךְ, translated "mouth," is actually "palate," the seat of taste (*CHAL*; see Ps 119:103). It also occurs parallel to "tongue" in 20:12-13 and as a possible emendation in Ps 22:16 (see E. Tov, *Textual Criticism of the Hebrew Bible* [Minneapolis: Fortress, 1992], 360).

[73] The exact thrust of הַוּוֹת is uncertain. The NIV's "malice," KJV's "perverse things," and NAB's "falsehood" were chosen to be synonyms for עַוְלָה, while others have taken it in the sense it has in v. 2, "calamity" (RSV, NASB). The NJPS "evil" is a happy compromise.

 The night drags on, and I toss till dawn.
[5]**My body is clothed with worms and scabs,**
 my skin is broken and festering.

[6]**"My days are swifter than a weaver's shuttle,**
 and they come to an end without hope.

Only v. 1 is a question. Nevertheless Job ruminates through these six verses on his seemingly endless hard lot in life. Like the long working days of a slave or hours of a sleepless night, his life in his disease-racked body drags on. Verse 6 is herein grouped with the opening section, contra NIV but in agreement with Knox,[74] NASB, Hartley,[75] and others.

7:1 Life is hard, and working days are long. This is the point of the two questions that open this section. The only unusual word is "hard service" because *ṣbʾ* normally means "war/warfare/army" as a noun. The KJV and others have "warfare." "Service" in English includes the meaning "military service," so it is easy to see why the word could be parallel to the working days of a hired man (cf. Isa 40:2).[76]

7:2 "Hired man" occurs again in v. 2 and is parallel to "slave." The verbs in the two halves, "longing" and "waiting," are parallel also. But whereas the hired man can anticipate payment (perhaps daily; cf. Lev 19:13) for labor, the slave only wishes for shade.[77] "Evening" is not in the text. During the hot season any shady spot provides welcome relief, especially in the heat of the day.

7:3 The sentence begun in v. 2 is completed in v. 3. Job grumbled that his lot was "months of futility"[78] and "nights of misery." The term "misery" occurs five times before this in Job (3:10; 4:8; 5:6,7,26). This reference to "months" provides one of the few clues to the time frame of Job's ordeal. About all one can say is that the trial lasted more than one month and probably less than a year, otherwise "year" would have been in a verse such as this.[79]

---

[74] *The Holy Bible*, trans. R. Knox (New York: Sheed & Ward, 1950).

[75] Hartley, *Job,* 142-43.

[76] "Hard service" appeared as early as 1922 in Moffatt.

[77] "Wages" translates פֹּעַל, a word that normally means "work/deed" but by legitimate extension can mean "pay for work." Leviticus 19:13 and Isa 62:11 use it this way. In fact, the Isaiah passage has both פֹּעַל and שָׂכִיר as here.

[78] "Futility" translates שָׁוְא. The word is used of anything morally or (as here) materially worthless (*TWOT*, 908). What the reader knows, of course, is that the suffering is not worthless at all but has a definite divine purpose.

[79] "Rabbi Akiba deduced from this word that Job's affliction lasted one year (*M. Eduy* 2:10), while *The Testament of Job* (5:19) assigns seven years of suffering to him" (R. Gordis, *The Book of Job* [New York: Jewish Theological Seminary, 1978], 79).

7:4   In Hebrew v. 4 is long, yet it is not a tricolon.[80] "Night" is the
common word for "evening," and "dawn" is a term that refers to the
quasidarkness, whether in the evening or in the morning. Clearly the end
of the night is indicated here. Literally Job said he was "full of tossings"
(a hapax built from the root *ndd,* "flee/stray").[81] Insomnia aggravated
Job's anxiety and pain.

7:5   In gruesome and graphic explicitness Job described his physical
affliction. "Worms" is more frequent in Job than anywhere else with five
of its seven occurrences (cf. 17:14; 21:26; 24:20; Isa 14:11). "Scabs" is a
guess for the unpronounceable *"gyyš* of dust."[82] The last phrase is nearly
as difficult. "Skin" is clearly in parallel with "flesh/body," but the translation of the verbs in this context is uncertain.[83]

7:6   It seems contradictory—the nights drag on, yet the days[84] pass
quickly. Most people feel that their lives pass quickly, but sometimes
those who have accomplished the least feel it the most. There are for
them few milestones and no noteworthy accomplishments to mark the
passing years. Job felt that his life was swiftly fleeting and that there was
no goal, no hope toward which to press.

Only the phrase "weaver's shuttle" is uncertain. The same phrase is in
9:25 except that the comparison is to "a runner." The only other occurrence of the noun *ʾāreg* is in Judg 16:14, where its translation is equally
uncertain; but the corresponding verb is used fourteen times and with little question means "weave."[85] The noun *tîqwâ,* "hope," also means
"thread/rope" (Josh 2:18,21), a play on words recognized long ago by
Rabbi Ibn Ezra. Job could see his life racing to a monotonous end like a
weaver's supply of thread (the NEB translates "and come to an end as the
thread runs out").

(8) Address to God (7:7-21)

> [7]Remember, O God, that my life is but a breath;
>   my eyes will never see happiness again.

---

[80] With NIV I agree that the Masoretes misplaced the *ʾatnaḥ* two words beyond the
middle and that the verse should be scanned as it is in our translation.

[81] Targum has נדת שנתא, "flight of sleep."

[82] For alternates and speculations from others, see Clines, *Job,* 163.

[83] Something like "cracks and oozes" seems close. Cf. NAB, REB. This assumes the
root is מאס II, which according to BDB occurs elsewhere only at Ps 58:7[8].

[84] The word "days" in the opening and closing verses of this section form an inclusio
supporting the stanza division I have presented.

[85] N. H. Tur-Sinai tried to make a case for "smoke" (*The Book of Job* [Jerusalem: Kiry-
at- Sefer, 1967], 137-38). The LXX has λαλιᾶς, "[mere] talk."

[8]The eye that now sees me will see me no longer;
   you will look for me, but I will be no more.
[9]As a cloud vanishes and is gone,
   so he who goes down to the grave does not return.
[10]He will never come to his house again;
   his place will know him no more.

[11]"Therefore I will not keep silent;
   I will speak out in the anguish of my spirit,
   I will complain in the bitterness of my soul.
[12]Am I the sea, or the monster of the deep,
   that you put me under guard?
[13]When I think my bed will comfort me
   and my couch will ease my complaint,
[14]even then you frighten me with dreams
   and terrify me with visions,
[15]so that I prefer strangling and death,
   rather than this body of mine.
[16]I despise my life; I would not live forever.
   Let me alone; my days have no meaning.

[17]"What is man that you make so much of him,
   that you give him so much attention,
[18]that you examine him every morning
   and test him every moment?
[19]Will you never look away from me,
   or let me alone even for an instant?
[20]If I sinned, what have I done to you,
   O watcher of men?
Why have you made me your target?
Have I become a burden to you?
[21]Why do you not pardon my offenses
   and forgive my sins?
For I will soon lie down in the dust;
   you will search for me, but I will be no more."

Job usually addressed God somewhere in the course of his speeches, and here is the point where he did so in the first speech. Complaint characterizes his addresses to God more than do prayers in the usual sense of that word. In this discourse he complained that his life was brief, that it was not worth living, and that it was unworthy of God to bother with people.

LIFE IS BRIEF (7:7-10). Included in vv. 7-10 are the first of several statements to the effect that death ends all. Job evidenced a pardonable ambivalence on this issue. Through the commentary both his pessimistic and his optimistic observations on this question will be underscored. Unhappily the negative statements outnumber the positive ones.

7:7 The vocative "O God" is not in Hebrew here or anywhere else in this chapter, but there is little doubt to whom Job addressed the words of this and the following verses (cf. vv. 14,17-21). "Breath" is *rûaḥ,* elsewhere rendered "spirit/wind," a frequent word in this book. It makes little difference whether Job was saying that he was one breath away from death or that life is like the passing wind. In either case it represents his depression and expectation of death.

7:8 "Eye" appears in both lines of this verse in Hebrew, linking it with v. 7. The second line begins (literally), "Your eyes (are) on me." "The eye that now sees me" refers to Job's human acquaintances. The next line says, in effect, that he would soon be even beyond the reach of God (cf. v. 20). Verse 21 ends with the same word(s).[86] Job apparently believed at this point that the grave would literally hide him from the eye of God and man.[87] The LXX lacks v. 8,[88] but there is no adequate reason for deleting it. As Andersen has pointed out, Job desperately wanted to see God (19:27), but he knew that God must be the initiator (14:15) and that he must act before Job's death or it would be too late.[89]

7:9 Disbelief in the resurrection could hardly be affirmed more bluntly that it is here. "Grave" is *šě'ôl,* the place of the dead, thought to be very much like the inside of the caves where corpses or skeletons were placed—a cave full of maggots, darkness, stale air, and silence and lacking any sign of life. Both the righteous and the wicked went there.

7:10 Job believed that he would never return home and even if he did his old surroundings would disown him (cf. 8:18). The idea of never returning surfaces again in 10:21 and 16:22. In Akkadian literature "the land of no return" is a euphemism for the grave.[90]

LIFE IS NOT WORTH LIVING (7:11-16). Job returned to the death wish theme that has been only slightly below the surface in so much of

---

[86] Despite the similarity between 7:8a and 20:9a, they have only one word in common, "eye."

[87] Blommerde reads אַבְנֶ֫נִּי as a denominative *piel* and translates "annihilate me" (*Northwest Semitic Grammar,* 109).

[88] For elaboration on this see E. Dhorme, *A Commentary on the Book of Job,* trans. H. Knight (London: Nelson, 1967), 102.

[89] F. I. Andersen, *Job,* TOTC (Downers Grove: InterVarsity, 1976), 135-36. Andersen translates the לֹא as assertative and offers for the whole verse, "(Your) eye(s) will gaze for me: your eyes will look for me; but I won't be there." He also says here that the importance of 14:15 "for the whole book of Job cannot possibly be exaggerated."

[90] See, e.g., "The Descent of Ishtar to the Nether World," *ANET,* 106-9, lines 1, 12, 41.

what he has said already in this chapter. He preferred death to constant divine surveillance and the terror of nightmares.

7:11 Three first person verbs distinguish the three lines of v. 11. The first is made emphatic by the particle *gam* and by the independent personal pronoun. Three different features are in the three lines as well: "mouth" (the first line literally has, "I will not restrain my mouth"), "spirit," and "soul." There are enough places where the relatively rare *śîḥ* means more than the usual "meditate/muse" to justify the translation "complain" here (cf. Ps 142:2[3] and all the nominal references in Job 7:13; 9:27; 10:1; 21:4; 23:2).

7:12 As in 3:8 Job again alluded to characters in popular mythology. "The sea," *yām,* was personalized and deified by second millennium B.C. Canaanites at Ugarit. The terms "monster of the deep" (Heb. *tannîn*), Leviathan (Ugaritic *Lotan;* cf. 3:8; Ps 74:13-14; Isa 27:1), and Rahab (9:13; 26:12; Isa 51:9) were also mythological sea deities. According to the Ugaritic myth, Yam was the boisterous opponent whom Baal captured. Job protested that he was not such an unruly foe that he needed constant guarding.[91]

7:13 The NIV and KJV are almost identical, which means there is little that modern scholarship has produced to change the translation of this verse. Actually v. 13 is the first half of a long sentence that ends only with v. 16. Job grumbled that even bedtime provided him no deliverance from divine oppression. Sick people often do not sleep well.

7:14 The four Hebrew words of v. 14 form a simple, clear chiasmus:

A   Then you scare me
 B   with dreams
 B'   and with visions
A'   You terrify me.

Job possibly was alluding to Eliphaz's vision (4:12-16), which was a frightening experience. Or he may have been reliving the tragedies that recently had come upon him.

7:15 The NIV scansion of v. 15 does not reflect the balance of the Hebrew lines: "My body chooses strangling / death rather than my bones." "Strangling/hanging" occurs but once as a noun and twice as a verb (2 Sam 17:23; Nah 2:12[13]). "Bones" used metaphorically means

---

[91] There is much discussion of this question and another associated with the verb "guard" found in Pope, *Job,* 60-62; L. Grabbe, *Comparative Philology and the Text of Job,* SBLD 34 (Missoula, Mont.: Scholars Press, 1977), 55-58; E. Smick, *Job,* EBC 4 (Grand Rapids: Zondervan, 1988), 904; and "Another Look at the Mythological Elements in the Book of Job," *WTJ* 40 (1978): 235

"essence" and, by extension, "body/life/self."[92]

7:16 "My life" is supplied by the translators because the verb demands an object (cf. 9:21; 10:1). While living forever sounds good to the healthy and happy, such a prospect is much less desirable to the sick and miserable. For Job life was not worth living. His days were "meaningless" *(hebel,* a word that occurs four times in Eccl 1:2). At points like this Job and Qoheleth come close to each other in their role as foils to the standard retribution theology of Deuteronomy and Proverbs. It may suggest here that he was "nothing but skin and bones."

WHY DOES GOD BOTHER WITH PEOPLE? (7:17-21).   In asking this question, Job really asked why God bothered with him. He felt as though God were a cat and he were the mouse. Surely God had better things to do than pick on him.

7:17 Almost all detailed commentaries point out the parallel between 7:17 and Ps 8:4[5] (and to a lesser extent to Ps 144:3), but there is no agreement on the question of who quoted whom. Neither is there a problem in assuming no connection whatever.[93] The point of the psalm is that God honors us[94] by paying attention to us. The point of Job is that God makes too much of us with his incessant surveillance and unforgiving scrutiny.

7:18 The verb "examine," *pqd,* "visit" in the older versions, is also in Ps 8:4[5]. Again, the "visiting" in Ps 8 was an honor; here it is an intense aggravation. Job used the verb "test" again in 23:10, a much more positive context.

7:19 The verb "look," as others in this section, can have positive connotations (e.g., Gen 4:4) or negative, undesirable ones as here. Ordinarily it is a good thing to have God's eye on you. But Job wished that God would stop watching him because it meant to him only condemnation and grief (although this was far from true; cf. 1:8). The NIV has paraphrased the explicit picture of Job's disgust with God's espionage in the last phrase of v. 19. Most translate literally something like, "Let me alone until I swallow my spit."[95]

7:20 The length of v. 20 is bothersome to some commentators.[96] "O

---

[92] Some emend עצם to עצב and translate "my pains (Moffatt, NAB), "my sufferings" (JB), or "sufferings of mine" (AAT, REB).

[93] M. Fishbane, "The Book of Job and Inner-Biblical Discourse," *The Voice from the Whirlwind* (Nashville: Abingdon, 1992), 87-89.

[94] The less common word for "man," אֱנוֹשׁ, occurs here and in Ps 8. Job uses the word eighteen of the forty-two times in the Hebrew Bible.

[95] Job has two of the three occurrences of the noun "spit," רֹק, in the OT (cf. 30:10; Isa 50:6).

[96] See Dhorme, *Job,* for further discussion.

watcher of men" is a short line by itself, but attached to the first stich it is too long (cf. 35:6; Isa 27:3). Despite its length, the first line is cryptic, lacking a word for "if." By this question Job wanted to know what the offense was that occasioned him such intense suffering. "Target" occurs only here, but most agree it can be nothing else.[97] The NIV footnote on the second occurrence of "to you" points to a widely adopted ancient suggestion to change the original text to the more felicitous "to myself."[98]

7:21 This four-line verse could have been made into two because unlike v. 20 it has four distinct phrases, although the particles that make the first half a negative question must do double duty and apply to the second line as well. Job did not confess any sins because he could think of none that he had committed. He was willing to repent of anything, but he had no idea what the offense was. In the end of the book it will turn out that God did not condemn Job for sins in the usual sense of that word but for speaking without knowledge and questioning divine justice. We who have read the first two chapters of the book know why Job suffered, but he was not privy to that council.

The chapter ends on the note of death. Job expected to die soon, and then he would be unavailable for any court appearance or to receive any pardon or apology from God. In the view of the ancients justice demanded a historical resolution in time.

---

[97] The NEB's translation "butt" sounds odd to American ears, but the term can designate an object of ridicule or criticism.

[98] For a detailed explanation of this case of *tiqqune sopherim* and references, see Gordis, *Job*. E. Tov (*Textual Criticism of the Hebrew Bible* [Minneapolis: Fortress, 1992], 66-67) lists this as one of several passages where "the alleged original, uncorrected readings mentioned by the Masorah are known as variants from other sources." Here the Masorah is supported by the LXX, which has ἐπὶ σοί.

3. Bildad: Job Should Repent (8:1-22)
   (1) Rebuke (8:1-4)
   (2) Advice (8:5-7)
   (3) Reasoning (8:8-19)
       Learn from the Past (8:8-10)
       Learn from the Papyrus (8:11-13)
       Learn That Life Is Fragile (8:14-19)
   (4) Results (8:20-22)
4. Job: Though It Seems Hopeless, I Will Plead with God
   (9:1–10:22)
   (1) God Is Incontestably Sovereign (9:1-13)
   (2) The Innocent Have No Access to God (9:14-20)
   (3) God Seems Distant and Unconcerned (9:21-24)
   (4) Life Is Brief, and the Innocent Cannot Win (9:25-31)
   (5) Negotiation Is Impossible (9:32–10:1)
   (6) Address to God (10:2-22)
       Condemned without Charges (10:2-7)
       I Am Your Creation (10:8-12)
       God's Intolerance of All Sin (10:13-17)
       A Death Wish (10:18-22)

3. Bildad: Job Should Repent (8:1-22)

Bildad, whom we met at 2:11, now takes his turn to speak. Perhaps he was the second oldest. Of him R. Gordis said, "Bildad is a traditionalist who contributes little more to the discussion than a restatement of accepted views."[1] That assessment is based on this and his other speeches and is particularly well illustrated by 8:8, "Ask the former generations."

(1) Rebuke (8:1-4)

¹Then Bildad the Shuhite replied:
²"How long will you say such things?
    Your words are a blustering wind.
³Does God pervert justice?

---

[1] R. Gordis, *The Book of Job* (New York: Jewish Theological Seminary, 1978), 77.

> Does the Almighty pervert what is right?
> [4]When your children sinned against him,
>   he gave them over to the penalty of their sin.

Rebuke is one of the features of the friends' speeches that is rarely missing. In typical fashion Bildad began his speech on that note which must have been most unwelcome to Job. Bildad escalated the confrontational nature of the debate with this opening, unsympathetic, accusatory salvo. His impetuosity is illustrated here and at the beginning of his second speech in 18:2 with the question, "When/how long?"

8:1   See remarks at 4:1.

8:2   Like Eliphaz, Bildad started with a question, only his was less tactful and more offensive. Little did he know how much longer Job would say such things. Job did outlast his friends in this long debate. No amount of insult moved Job to change his mind on the fundamental issue, that is, whether he was suffering because of his sin. "Blustering" is somewhat of an overtranslation for *kabbîr*, "strong/mighty."

8:3   For all his lack of polish, Bildad did, in this verse, come to the heart of the issue. His two questions remarkably approximate God's questions of Job in 40:8, both verses including the widely used pair of roots, *mišpāṭ* and *ṣedeq,* "justice" and "right."[2] They also sound like Abraham's question about the destruction of Sodom in Gen 18:15: "Will not the Judge of all the earth do right [*mišpāṭ*]?"[3]

8:4   The most cruel and least tactful part of Bildad's confrontation is just a restatement of the basic theology of retribution that the three friends held to so tenaciously. Bildad's reasoning was that Job's children must have sinned in order for God to have taken their lives. There is no hint in 1:19 of any sin, and certainly they had nothing to do with the afflictions the Satan sent to Job, except in this passive way. Job had, in fact, sacrificed a burnt offering for each of his children after their parties just in case they had sinned and "cursed God in their hearts" (1:5).

(2) Advice (8:5-7)

> [5]But if you will look to God
>   and plead with the Almighty;

---

[2] As S. H. Scholnick points out, מִשְׁפָּט refers to both the application of justice and the governance of the universe ("The Meaning of *mišpāṭ* in the Book of Job," *JBL* 101 [1982]: 521-29).

[3] Of the assortment of divine names in this book, Bildad uses only שַׁדַּי and אֵל (never the medium length אֱלוֹהַ or the long אֱלֹהִים).

> ⁶**if you are pure and upright,**
> **even now he will rouse himself on your behalf**
> **and restore you to your rightful place.**
> ⁷**Your beginnings will seem humble,**
> **so prosperous will your future be.**

Another typical feature of the friends' speeches is the giving of advice. They invariably preached at Job, urging him to repent, return, renounce, or refrain from some unidentified and unidentifiable sin. The advice is good when directed to a true sinner; but like good medicine given for the wrong ailment, the results can be nil at best and disastrous at worst.

8:5 "Look" and "plead" are the two actions Bildad recommended. The former, *šāḥar,* as a noun means "morning," so several versions add some adjective such as "betimes"[4] (KJV, NEB), "diligently" (RV, MLB,), "earnestly" (NKJV, AAT), "eagerly" (Hartley). The second verb, *ḥānan,* is the root of "grace." In the reflexive stem, as here, it means to "seek grace/ implore favor." The same pair of divine names as in v. 3 recurs here.

8:6 A third condition introduces v. 6. In addition to looking and pleading, Job also had to be "pure and upright."

"Pure" is not a frequent word but is common enough in the Bible to show that usually it refers to moral purity as opposed to things physically clean or hygienic. "How can a young man keep his way pure?" the psalmist asked (Ps 119:9); "by living according to your word," he answered. "Upright" has already described Job three times (Job 1:1,8; 2:3).

In response God would do two things, Bildad promised. He would wake up,[5] and he would "make the habitation of [Job's] righteousness prosperous" (KJV, RV, ASV). This last phrase is open to different interpretations. The verb is *šlm,* from which the word "shalom" derives. The NIV is in company with the RSV with its focus on restoring Job. Others (e.g., KJV, JB, NAB, AB) make "place/habitation/estate"[6] the object of the causative verb. The result is essentially a figurative expression for what is in the NIV.

8:7 With a simple merismus (see explanation at 1:20) Bildad promised a great end to contrast with the small "beginnings"[7] of Job's life.

---

[4] "Betimes" is archaic English for "early."

[5] J. J. Stamm argues for "protect," a *qal* of עיר in place of "rouse/wake up" ("Ein ugaritisch-hebräisches Verbum und seine Ableitungen," *TZ* 35 [1979]: 5-9).

[6] נְוַת is fem. construct of the masc. noun that was in 5:3 ("house") and 5:24 ("property").

[7] "Beginnings" of v. 7 and "former" of v. 8 are from the same root, possibly linking in Bildad's mind Job's relatively recent birth and the age-old wisdom of the forefathers.

Two rare but uncontested words are in this six-word verse. "Humble" occurs in but four other places (two are in Gen 19:20), and the verb "be prosperous" is found elsewhere only four verses later and in Pss 73:12; 92:12[13]. While Job's beginnings in chap. 1 were hardly insignificant, how true this prediction about his "prosperous future" turned out to be; but his prosperity did not depend on the conditions laid down by Bildad.

(3) Reasoning (8:8-19)

8"Ask the former generations
    and find out what their fathers learned,
9for we were born only yesterday and know nothing,
    and our days on earth are but a shadow.
10Will they not instruct you and tell you?
    Will they not bring forth words from their understanding?
11Can papyrus grow tall where there is no marsh?
    Can reeds thrive without water?
12While still growing and uncut,
    they wither more quickly than grass.
13Such is the destiny of all who forget God;
    so perishes the hope of the godless.
14What he trusts in is fragile;
    what he relies on is a spider's web.
15He leans on his web, but it gives way;
    he clings to it, but it does not hold.
16He is like a well-watered plant in the sunshine,
    spreading its shoots over the garden;
17it entwines its roots around a pile of rocks
    and looks for a place among the stones.
18But when it is torn from its spot,
    that place disowns it and says, 'I never saw you.'
19Surely its life withers away,
    and from the soil other plants grow.

Because of his appeal to the "former generations" and the "fathers," Bildad is labeled the traditionalist. The second two subsections draw on illustrations from nature: the papyrus that quickly withers, the frailty of a spider's web, and the brief legacy of uprooted plants.

LEARN FROM THE PAST (8:8-10). Bildad never explicitly said what Job should learn from history, but presumably it was the lessons that fill the rest of the chapter. Of course, Bildad would cite only those that supported his position, which he put succinctly in v. 20.

8:8 The verse is straightforwardly translated in the NIV.[8] What Bildad and the others offered is well-established, long-held wisdom. In large measure Job's instructors were correct, and numerous places elsewhere in both Testaments support them. It was their inflexibility and closed-mindedness that so bothered Job and annoys us as we read the prologue.

8:9 In contrast to the patriarchs, Bildad and his generation just arrived on the scene. "Born" is not in Hebrew, but "we are of yesterday" (with most other translations) is awkward English. Comparisons of life's brief span to a shadow are made elsewhere (1 Chr 29:15; Pss 102:11[12]; 144:4; Eccl 6:12; 8:13). While former generations have passed away, their accumulated wisdom remains, and to that old wisdom Bildad made his appeal.

8:10 The negative interrogative particle does triple duty, making each of the three verbs a question expecting an affirmative answer. "Yes," they will instruct. "Yes," they will tell. "Yes," they will bring forth. The middle phrase is short enough that it is combined with the first, keeping this a typical two-line verse. "Understanding" is literally "heart," a seat of the intellect as well as of the emotions in ancient psychology.

LEARN FROM THE PAPYRUS (8:11-13). The first of Bildad's nature illustrations to support his point about the necessary relationship between cause and effect is from the papyrus plant.

8:11 Several rare words are in this verse, but most translations differ only in choice of synonyms and not in substantial matters of interpretation. "Papyrus" appears only three others times, at least two of them in connection with the Nile (Exod 2:3; Isa 18:2). It does not mean that the scene took place in a swampy area but only that the author had this and other words from far away in his vocabulary.[9] Bildad's point in citing this proverb was that certain conditions must prevail in order for specific results to follow.

8:12 A second lesson from these swamp grasses is that they are short-lived. They seem to die in midlife and for no cause. On this point too Bildad was subtly making an application to Job.[10]

---

[8] Several minor variations in spelling such as the absence of quiescent א in רישׁיון and the final *mem* on "fathers" are discussed by A. C. M. Blommerde, *Northwest Semitic Grammar and Job, Biblica et Orientalia 22* (Rome: Pontifical Biblical Institute, 1969), 50-51. See also E. Tov, *Textual Criticism of the Hebrew Bible* (Minneapolis: Fortress, 1992), 255.

[9] The verb "grow tall" is also rare, but cognate nouns and adjectives that mean "proud" support the translation here. "Marsh," too, only appears once more in Job (40:21) and once elsewhere (Ezek 47:11). "Reed(s)" appears only here and in Gen 41:2,18.

[10] Additional unusual but not uncertain words mark v. 12. "Growing" appears only here and in Song 6:11. But the Aramaic אב in Dan 4:12[9],14[11],21[18] is identical. "Cut" appears once more in Job, once in Deuteronomy, and twice in Ezekiel.

8:13 Without naming Job or making the association specific, Bildad said that those who forget God will likewise perish. The NIV followed the Greek in reading "destiny/end/fate" (AB, NAB, NEB, NJPS) instead of "paths"[11] (KJV, RSV, NASB, NRSV). Indirectly he called Job "godless," which is by others translated "hypocrite" (KJV), "irreligious" (AT), "impious" (AB).[12]

LEARN THAT LIFE IS FRAGILE (8:14-19). This section contains two illustrations, the fragile spider's web and the well-watered but uprooted plant. There is no concluding application, for example, in v. 13; but vv. 20-22 provide a conclusion to the whole speech.

8:14 This verse makes vivid the condition of the godless, but several key words are rare and of uncertain translation. "Spider" occurs only here and in Isa 59:5, so the "house of the spider" comes out "web." This relatively certain picture helps construct the first line. The line is literally, "What is fragile his trust," but "trust" (*kesel,* occurring only six times) can also be "stupidity" or "loins." The verb occurs only here. The terseness of the NEB and REB is commendable, "His confidence is gossamer."[13]

8:15 By contrast all the words of v. 15 are known, and their meanings are well established. The "web" once more translates *bêt,* referring to the house of the spider. While it holds a spider, it cannot hold a human being. Leaning on or clinging to it is futile, even as the hope of the ungodly is surely vain.

8:16 Bildad left the illustration about the spider's web and pictured in this and the following three verses a healthy plant soon to be uprooted. Metaphorically the wicked are a *rāṭōb,* "a well-watered plant," a definition based almost entirely on this context and 24:8, its only other occurrence. Perhaps, by analogy, the shoots represent the offspring of this evil man (cf. Ps 128:3).

8:17 The plant seems to survive even under difficult circumstances. To avoid those difficult circumstances some have offered to turn the "rock pile," *gal,* into a "spring," that is, "pile of water" or "garden," *gan,* on the analogy of Song 4:12, where an even more troublesome problem with *gal* appears.[14] Jastrow,[15] Pope, Hartley, and Clines among the com-

---

[11] The LXX has ἔσχατα, a meaning arrived at by simple metathesis: אַחֲרִית for the MT אָרְחוֹת. Cf. אַחֲרִית in v. 7. On metathesis see Tov, *Textual Criticism,* 250-51.

[12] Nothing seems to be gained by the NEB and REB in reading תִּקְוָה as "thread" rather than "hope."

[13] For more alternatives and emendations see N. Tur-Sinai, *The Book of Job,* rev. ed. (Jerusalem: Kiryat-Sefer, 1967); E. Dhorme, *A Commentary of the Book of Job* (London: 1967), and D. Clines, *Job 1–20,* WBC 17 (Dallas: Word, 1989).

[14] See Clines, *Job 1–20,* for options and support of these views, which he rejects.

[15] M. Jastrow, Jr., *The Book of Job* (Philadelphia: Lippincott, 1920), 225.

mentators and GNB, NASB, AAT, and NJPS among the versions adopt the emendation of "see" to "grasp/seize."[16] It makes an easier reading than the expanded "looks for a place."

8:18 The demise of the plant comes "when it is torn from its spot." The verb *bālaʿ* specifically means "swallow,"[17] but generally and metaphorically it means "destroy." The next verb has an even wider range of meanings that include "lie/deny/fail." What the "place" (a subject supplied by the translators) does is lie about the former existence of the plant by saying, "I never saw you." It may be that the "place" has a short memory just as people do. Proverbs 10:7b says, "The name of the wicked will rot." We readers must remember that Bildad was not simply giving lessons in botany but preaching at Job. In 19:14-17 Job complained that he was a forgotten man.

8:19 The NIV footnote points to the problem of translating the first line of v. 19. The word *māśôś* means "joy" in its sixteen other occurrences, but that meaning does not fit well here. The LXX has *katastrophe*. Driver said Bildad used it ironically.[18] Jastrow said it was sarcasm.[19] Tur-Sinai emended it to mean "renew."[20] Dhorme by an ingenious route arrived at "rotting."[21] Gordis has "goes on its way."[22] "Withers away" (NEB, NIV) comes by reading the Hebrew letter *samek* for *śín*, a well-attested exchange.[23] Bildad's message to Job was that he would soon be gone, and someone else would own his wealth, occupy his house, and replace him at the city gate. Such pessimism is reminiscent of Eccl 1:3-4.

(4) Results (8:20-22)

> [20]"Surely God does not reject a blameless man
>   or strengthen the hands of evildoers.
> [21]He will yet fill your mouth with laughter
>   and your lips with shouts of joy.
> [22]Your enemies will be clothed in shame,

---

[16] This means instead of יהוה the text reads יהו, short for יהוא. See Gordis, *Job,* and Clines, *Job 1–20.*

[17] The AB uses "swallow." Cf. NASB margin.

[18] S. R. Driver, *The Book of Job* (Oxford: Clarendon, 1908), 22. Although "mirth" represents a different Heb. word, 20:5 supports the traditional translation.

[19] Jastrow, *Job,* 225.

[20] Tur-Sinai, *Job,* 152-53.

[21] Dhorme, *Job,* 123-24. The JB adopted this suggestion.

[22] Gordis, *Job,* 93.

[23] מסס, "melt," can easily embrace the notion "wither." Cf. its use in Ps 112:10, "waste away"; Deut 20:8, "faint."

and the tents of the wicked will be no more."

Bildad brought his speech to an end with a lesson designed inescapably for Job. Each use of "your" is in the masculine singular. Bildad may have hoped that Job would heed his advice, but he probably thought his predictions about Job's future bliss were very remote. Little did he realize that, in fact, Job would again rejoice and that among his enemies "clothed with shame" would be Eliphaz and his two friends (42:7).

8:20 "Blameless" is the adjective God used to describe Job (1:8; 2:3). We readers know that God had not "rejected" Job but that he had allowed him to be a test case for the Satan. Ultimately Job had the extreme honor of being addressed by God himself and privileged to a magnificent display of divine power. Job, in speeches yet to come, provided many examples of "evildoers" whose hands appeared to be strong. There were and are exceptions to the neat theology of retribution that most people then and now subscribe to. The good sometimes die young. The wicked sometimes get away with murder.

8:21 This happy prediction of a blissful future for the repentant is straightforward and without competing interpretations. From the standpoint of poetic parallelism it presents a well-balanced pair of synonymous lines. The verb "fill"[24] of the first stich carries over, unrepeated, to the second line.[25] "Laughter" is the verb behind the name Isaac (Gen 17:17-19).[26]

8:22 Throughout the Old Testament we notice a certain joy at the downfall of enemies, what the Germans call *schadenfreuden*. Proverbs 24:17 admonishes, "Do not gloat when your enemy falls; when he stumbles, do not let your heart rejoice." Nevertheless, that sentiment, even in the very words of this verse, "clothed with shame," occurs in Pss 35:26; 109:29; 132:18. There the expression occurs in prayers based on the Davidic covenant, expressing "desire that the treaty curses come into effect, thereby delivering the king from the unwarranted crisis and at the same time vindicating God as the Lord and King of Israel."[27] Here it is from

---

[24] "Fill" is spelled מלה rather than the usual מלא. Some manuscripts and editions have the latter.

[25] The two nouns of the second stich contain the same number of stressed syllables as the verb and two nouns of the first stich.

[26] Isaac is usually spelled יצחק, but in three places it is ישחק, reflecting more closely the verb in the verse under discussion. The five sibilants in the Hebrew alphabet occasionally interchange, another illustration of which is found in v. 19.

[27] P. C. Craigie, *Psalms 1–50*, WBC (Waco: Word, 1983), 288, commenting on Ps 35:26.

the mouth of Bildad, an ancient Edomite whose theology is not affirmed by Scripture.

Chapters 7–8 end with the same word, translated "will be no more," which may be an indication that the opponents caught an occasional word from one another, although, in large measure, the four spoke in monologues rather than dialogue. Job thought he would perish without vindication just like the wicked, even though he was, in fact, "blameless." Bildad thought Job would perish because he was among the wicked. Both were wrong.

4. Job: Though It Seems Hopeless, I Will Plead with God (9:1–10:22)

Job's second speech in the debate cycle is almost three times as long as Bildad's. But his speeches, like the friends' speeches, grow generally shorter as the conversations progress. In this speech chap. 9 seems to be a reply to Bildad, although there are few connections and no direct quotations. Job touched on some of the same themes as before but introduced some new ones, which themselves will become old and worn before the book is finished. Chapter 10 is almost entirely an address to God, a feature that regularly distinguishes Job's speeches from the others' speeches.

(1) God Is Incontestably Sovereign (9:1-13)

¹Then Job replied:
²"Indeed, I know that this is true.
    But how can a mortal be righteous before God?
³Though one wished to dispute with him,
    he could not answer him one time out of a thousand.
⁴His wisdom is profound, his power is vast.
    Who has resisted him and come out unscathed?
⁵He moves mountains without their knowing it
    and overturns them in his anger.
⁶He shakes the earth from its place
    and makes its pillars tremble.
⁷He speaks to the sun and it does not shine;
    he seals off the light of the stars.
⁸He alone stretches out the heavens
    and treads on the waves of the sea.
⁹He is the Maker of the Bear and Orion,
    the Pleiades and the constellations of the south.
¹⁰He performs wonders that cannot be fathomed,
    miracles that cannot be counted.

¹¹**When he passes me, I cannot see him;**
   when he goes by, I cannot perceive him.
¹²**If he snatches away, who can stop him?**
   Who can say to him, 'What are you doing?'
¹³**God does not restrain his anger;**
   even the cohorts of Rahab cowered at his feet.

Here is the first extended discourse on the greatness of God. All the speakers and especially Elihu spoke similar words. Many of the specifics will actually be part of God's speeches in chaps. 38–39. As F. I. Andersen argues, "Job and his friends are in basic agreement about the character of God." Their disagreement comes in explaining his dealings with Job.[28]

9:1   See remarks at 6:1.

9:2   Job's response to Bildad was limited to the first line of this verse, "Indeed, I know that this is true." But Job also knew that other things were true that Bildad had not included. Job knew of exceptions to the friends' generalizations.

Job's question of Bildad and of anyone who would listen is stated in the second half of v. 2. Eliphaz had asked a similar question in 4:17.[29] They would have answered in terms of good behavior, but Job knew himself to be one of those righteous mortals apparently not considered "righteous before God."

9:3   Job's phrasing of his frustration with the divine silence will take many forms. God cannot be found. God will not respond. God always wins any argument. God plays all the roles in the courtroom: accuser, witness, bailiff, jury, and judge. Elsewhere in this chapter Job used such terminology in vv. 14-16,19-21,24,32 and in chap. 10:2,14-15,17.[30] At least at this point Job had no lawyer, no advocate, no defender, and no hope. Even on the remote chance that a mortal could argue with the deity, his hope of any satisfaction would be less than one tenth of a percent. His expected inability to answer God's questions is proven correct in chaps. 38–41.

---

[28] F. I. Andersen, *Job,* TOTC (Downers Grove: InterVarsity, 1976), 143-44.

[29] Smick thinks that Eliphaz and Job were using "righteous" in different but legitimate ways. "Eliphaz's righteousness was based on ontological superiority while Job was thinking of juridical vindication, that is, innocence" (*Job,* EBC 4:910).

[30] "Dispute" is רִיב, one of many words connected with the law courts that have prompted some to posit this as the predominant theme of the book. Cf. N. Habel, *The Book of Job,* OTL (Philadelphia: Westminster, 1985); S. Lasine, "Job and His Friends in the Modern World," in *The Voice from the Whirlwind* (Nashville: Abingdon, 1992), 144-55.

9:4 The first line is terse in Hebrew, so all versions must supply words to make the four words of the original into a sensible translation. They are simply, "Wise of heart and mighty of strength." Just as the theophany is anticipated by many of the speeches, so the wisdom chapter (chap. 28) also has its antecedents in the earlier part of the book (11:6; 12:13). "Come out unscathed" is somewhat paraphrastic for the simple imperfect of *šlm*, "prosper/be at peace/complete." The NJPS brings out the force better with "come out whole." The answer this question expects is no one. Just as the plant of 8:19 "withered/melted," so does any mortal who has a confrontation with the Almighty.

9:5 In this hymn Job made several commendable statements about God's majesty and power, but the point is not so much to give God glory as to paint a backdrop for his own feeling of hopelessness and helplessness. God may be great; but to Job he was removed, unconcerned, unreachable, and incomprehensible. Job had earthquakes in mind and assumed that the accompanying noise and shaking was an evidence of God's wrath.

9:6 The description of the earthquake continues. The verbs that begin vv. 4-7 are all participles and might be rendered, "He is the one who." But in the second stich of v. 6 the "pillars/foundations" are the subject of the reflexive verb "tremble" (cf. 26:7,11).[31]

9:7 The commentaries and translations are divided on whether the verb should be "rise" or "shine." In most of the eighteen places where it occurs, the definitions could be interchanged. "Shine" fits better here, where the line parallels one that speaks of sealing "off the light of the stars." The unusual word for "sun" occurs in but one other place (Judg 14:18), but its meaning is not debated.[32] Job was referring to eclipses and overcast days and cloudy nights.

9:8 Continuing his description of God's control of and activity in the natural sphere, Job alluded to creation. This brief hymn sounds like the longer hymn on the creation in Ps 104. All these references to the world around—sun, stars, sea, heaven, and earth—attest to Job's monotheism. Unlike the neighbors of ancient Israel who attributed each of these domains to separate deities, Job and all the Bible's authors believed that God "alone" was responsible for their creation and regulation.[33]

---

[31] The verb פלץ occurs only once, but a half dozen derived nouns establish the meaning as "tremble."

[32] חֶרֶס is also a place name, "Heres," in Judg 8:13.

[33] M. Pope presents these as references to Ugaritic and Babylonian myths. Verse 8b he translates "Trod of the back of Sea," assuming it is a veiled allusion to Baal's victory over the sea-god Yamm (*Job,* AB [Garden City: Doubleday, 1973], 68, 70). The GNB, NEB, REB translate as "back of the sea monster."

9:9 Four astral constellations are also God's making.[34] Some question surrounds these four terms. "Pleiades" is most certain. "Orion" translates a word that ordinarily means "fool" and is fairly certain. These star patterns and Ursa Major ("big bear," also known as the Big Dipper) probably were known to peoples of the ancient Near East. On the translation of the first there is more diversity. The KJV's "Arcturus" is wrong. The NEB's and REB's "Aldebaran," the brightest star of the Hyades, is a possibility, but "the Bear" has the most supporters. The least certain is the fourth, "the chambers of the south" (KJV, RV, ASV, RSV, etc.). "It could refer to the very bright section of the sky from Argus to Centauri that would have been visible on the southern horizon in Israel. It could also refer to the zodiac.[35] The first three are in 38:31 (cf. Amos 5:8).

9:10 Eliphaz spoke these identical words in 5:9.[36] "Wonders" more literally is "great things" as the NIV translates it in 37:5; Ps 71:19; and elsewhere. The Hebrew "there is no fathoming" has been rendered as a potential imperfect with the inclusion of "cannot"; so, too, in the second line with "cannot be counted" for the more literal "there is no number." "Fathom/search," *ḥeqer,* is a favorite word in Job with seven of its twelve occurrences. The word *niplā'ôt,* "miracles," translates one of the three standard words for this concept, the others being *'ōtôt,* "signs," and *ḥeqer,* "wonders."[37]

9:11 The attribution of praise ends with this verse, and Job began to describe the negative side of this mighty, wonder-working Creator-Sovereign. All powerful, all knowing, and all present as God may be, Job found him invisible, intangible, and evasive. Job was frustrated, knowing that God was at work, but he could not see or understand him. Like a magician practicing sleight of hand and tricks that the audience does not understand, God's ways went right past Job without his comprehending them. Eliphaz used the verb "goes by" (*yaḥălōp*) when he described the "spirit that glided past my face" (4:15). Job 23:8-9 expands on the theme of the hiddenness of God.

9:12 The verb "snatches away" occurs only here,[38] but there is little

---

[34] For discussion and diagrams of these constellations see W. D. Reyburn, *A Handbook on the Book of Job* (New York: UBS, 1992), 781-83.

[35] J. M. Everts, "Astronomy," *ISBE* 1:347. Tur-Sinai, 158-61.

[36] Unfortunately, the KJV, RSV, NASB, and others do not translate 5:9; 9:9 the same.

[37] The root פלא, the one here in this fem. plural *niphal* participle, is more often in this form than as a finite verb. The same root is in Isa 6:6[5], "And he will be called *Wonderful Counselor.*"

[38] A noun formed on this root, חתף, appears in Prov 23:28; and there the NIV translates "bandit." The similar root חטף is in Judg 21:21; Ps 10:9 (2x), where the meaning is "catch." Gordis says it is not necessary to emend the original (*Job*, 105).

question about its meaning. The point Job made is that God does what he pleases, even when it borders on what Job would call illegal. It is possible that he had the loss of his goods and children in mind when he virtually called God a bandit. Just as the Danites took Micah's Levite and idols over his protests and told him in so many words to be quiet (Judg 18:18-26), so Job felt it achieved nothing to question God.

9:13 All bad things that happened to the world or to people were viewed as expressions of God's anger (v. 5). In this regard Job shared the common view that God always punishes evil even though the wrong cannot be identified. His retributive justice extended even to the mythical sea monster "Rahab" and his "helpers" (KJV).[39]

(2) The Innocent Have No Access to God (9:14-20)

> 14"How then can I dispute with him?
>   How can I find words to argue with him?
> 15Though I were innocent, I could not answer him;
>   I could only plead with my Judge for mercy.
> 16Even if I summoned him and he responded,
>   I do not believe he would give me a hearing.
> 17He would crush me with a storm
>   and multiply my wounds for no reason.
> 18He would not let me regain my breath
>   but would overwhelm me with misery.
> 19If it is a matter of strength, he is mighty!
>   And if it is a matter of justice, who will summon him?
> 20Even if I were innocent, my mouth would condemn me;
>   if I were blameless, it would pronounce me guilty.

The first thirteen verses were about God's greatness and sovereignty. Beginning with v. 14 Job complained how those features of God's *modus operandi* affected him. Thus from here to the end of the chapter first person pronouns dominate. The reader knows that Job was innocent. Job was quite sure of his innocence. Yet he felt he was getting less than a fair trial, that he was the victim of a legal system that need not rest on principles he perceived as fair. He was in a contest with a far superior power.

9:14 A pair of particles begins v. 14, which, when put together like

---

[39] "Rahab" means "proud/boisterous," and the name sometimes refers to Egypt, specifically the Nile and even more specifically the crocodile of the Nile. It is not the same name as the harlot of Jericho. She is רחב, and the name is here רהב. See J. B. Payne, *TWOT* 2:834-35. Cf. Job 26:12; Ps 89:10[11]; Isa 30:7; 51:9.

this, means "indeed" or "how much more" (cf. 15:16; 25:6).[40] The point is that if Rahab's cohorts "cowered at his feet," what kind of chance did Job have to argue with God, much less win that argument?

9:15 The verb *ʿānâ* is in vv. 14-16. The NIV translates it "dispute" in v. 14, "answer" in v. 15, and "respond" in v. 16. In the preceding verses Job's grievance was that he could not find God. But he felt that even if he should find him, even though innocent he would still have to plead for mercy, something an uncondemned defendant ought not have to do.[41] Some debate surrounds "my Judge." The RV has "my adversary," the RSV has "my accuser," and Hartley has "my opponent-at-law."[42] In any case God was to Job both the prosecutor and the judge. In most of the complaint psalms the plaintiff demanded justice and insisted that God exonerate the righteous. Only rarely was there a plea for mercy.

9:16 Frustrated by his effort to press his case in a divine court, Job anticipated further failure. Summoning God seemed out of the question. His response seemed even more remote. So Job concluded with doubt that God would "give him a hearing," a satisfying way to translate the verb that means "ear" (cf. "hear" and "ear" in English). Bildad had urged Job to "plead" with God, but Job considered that a hopeless effort.[43]

9:17 Job believed that he might even be punished for taking his case to court. He was persuaded that God would crush[44] him without trial or jury, "with a storm" as he had done not so long ago.[45] It was "a mighty wind" that took the lives of Job's ten children (1:19), but it turned out in fact to be "with a storm" that God addressed Job in 38:1; 40:6. The multiplying of "wounds for no reason" probably refers to Job's skin disease (cf. 2:3).

---

[40] They are אַף כִּי, not one of the usual interrogative pronouns. The "can" in both lines is a translation of the verbs as potential imperfects.

[41] Andersen (*Job,* 146-47) suggests that the "not" of v. 15 should be understood to apply to v. 15b as well. Otherwise Job was following Bildad's advice to plead for mercy (8:5). Job's point, then, would be, "'I won't appeal to my judge for clemency (for it is vindication I am insisting on, not mercy).'"

[42] The reading "my opponent" takes מְשֹׁפְטִי as an unusual *poel* (or *polel*) participle. Blommerde points it לְמִשְׁפָּטוֹ and translates "to his justice," assuming the suffix is third person. "My Judge" reads an enclitic *mem* on the preposition and divides it as שֹׁפְטִי לְמוֹ. See the technical commentaries, e.g., Clines, for the history of this question.

[43] Andersen suggests understanding the לֹא as assertative, "certainly," rather than "not." Thus, "It is not misgivings about God's fairness that cause Job's anxiety. It is the fearful consequences of such direct exposure to the divine presence that fill him with terror (verse 34)" (*Job,* 147-48).

[44] The verb translated "crush" is שׁוּף and occurs elsewhere only at Gen 3:15; Ps 139:11, where the NIV has "hide."

[45] "Storm" is spelled שְׂעָרָה with a שׂ rather than a ס as is the case in 38:1; 40:6,28; other places. Only Nah 1:3 spells it as here.

9:18 Job both reflected on and anticipated the dreadful treatment he was to receive from the hand of God. Out of breath and filled with "misery/bitternesses" (*mammĕrōrîm*), all he expected was more of the same. "Regain my breath" (*rûaḥ*) and "restore my soul" (*nepeš*, Ps 23:3) are very similar. The Lord who gave breath and life to his people was seen by Job as the one who denied it to him. Using a variation of the same word ("misery"), Job saw himself like Naomi, who wanted to be called "Mara/bitter" (Ruth 1:20).

9:19 Verses 19 and 20 begin with conditional clauses. Job felt that no matter what, he would be overwhelmed by God. Certainly God was stronger. Just a few verses earlier Job had cataloged some of God's cosmic activities. If it were a legal matter, Job felt that no one could issue God a summons to appear in court.[46] God is, as it were, above the law.

9:20 Job concluded this subsection with the greatest of frustration, believing that right would be turned to wrong and that he, an "innocent" and "blameless" man, would still end up "guilty" and "condemned." As in modern law he felt that anything he said could and would be held against him. Once more the word "blameless" appears, the word God himself used to describe Job in 1:8; 2:3. "Pronounce guilty" translates the infrequent root *ʿāqaš*, which in other versions is "perverse" (KJV, RSV, AB), "hypocrite" (JB), "crooked" (AAT, NJPS, REB).

(3) God Seems Distant and Unconcerned (9:21-24)

> [21]"Although I am blameless,
>   I have no concern for myself;
>   I despise my own life.
> [22]It is all the same; that is why I say,
>   'He destroys both the blameless and the wicked.'
> [23]When a scourge brings sudden death,
>   he mocks the despair of the innocent.
> [24]When a land falls into the hands of the wicked,
>   he blindfolds its judges.
>   If it is not he, then who is it?

Job took a slightly different tack at v. 21. The focus is less on Job and more on God's administration or failure to administrate the world. Job

---

[46] The suffix on the verb "summon" is first person, "me." The LXX has third person, "him." Blommerde lists thirty-two places in Job where the suffix *-y* or *-i* is third person as it occasionally is in Ugaritic and regularly in Phoenician (*Northwest Semitic Grammar and Job*, 8, and bibliographic references there).

was more angry and bitter in this section than any other place in the book. At v. 24 in particular he came closer than anywhere else to charging God with injustice. He walked, as it were, very close to the precipice but stepped back to safer ground and thus avoided catastrophe. Just as Job voiced doubts about God's justice with rhetorical questions, so in 40:6 God demanded of Job: "Would you discredit my justice? Would you condemn me to justify yourself?" Both cases are less-than-direct accusations. They observe the polite Semitic rules and social graces.

9:21 Instead of the usual two lines with three main words in each, this verse consists of three lines with two words each. The "I am blameless" is identical to the phrase in v. 20b. The next phrase is open to alternative translations and interpretations. Literally it reads, "I do not know my soul." It may mean that Job could not be sure about himself.[47] There may have been hidden sin that occasioned his suffering (Pss 19:12[13]; 139:23-24). The direction the NIV took finds support in the last line, which cannot be read any other way.

9:22 "Innocent/blameless" and "wicked" are words laced through this portion of Job's complaint (vv. 20-24). The two are opposites, but not to God, fretted Job (cf. Matt 5:45). They are one and the same. Both meet destruction or "come to an end." That God destroys the wicked would be affirmed by Job's friends, but that he treats the godless and the godly alike is what separated Job's position from theirs (cf. Mal 3:18).

9:23 Two rare words beset v. 23, but the overall meaning is not affected by their uncertainty. "Scourge," *šôṭ,* is usually "whip"; but here and in at least two other places it must be understood metaphorically as referring to the tragedies of chap. 1. "Despair" is a hapax but derived from *mss,* "to melt," a root that Job used in 6:14, translated "despairing." "Mock" will be used four more times in Job (11:3; 21:3; 22:19; 34:7), but the sense here is best paralleled by Pss 2:4; 59:8[9]. The point is that death comes to all regardless of their guilt or innocence.[48] God is said to "mock" in that he does not come to deliver the innocent from disaster.

9:24 There is general agreement on the meaning of v. 24. "Blind-

---

[47] S. M. Paul suggests it means "out of my mind" ("An Unrecognized Medical Idiom in Canticles 6,12 and Job 9,21," *Bib* 59 [1978]: 545-47).

[48] According to Clines: "It is not primarily the justice of God that is on trial in this speech, but his sympathy. While many commentators have read the whole speech as an indictment of 'cosmic injustice' or of the moral arbitrariness of God, a closer reading suggests that the nub of Job's resentment is the divine aloofness (9:4-12,16,19,32) which terrifies humans and is experienced by them as cruelty and anger (9:5b,12a,13,17-18,22-24,34-35; 10:3-17)" (*Job 1–20,* 238).

folds" is an interpretive translation for the simple "covers."[49] By this question Job virtually charged God with wrongdoing (cf. 1:22), but still it is a question and not a declarative sentence. Job almost cursed God, but not quite.

(4) Life Is Brief, and the Innocent Cannot Win (9:25-31)

> [25]"My days are swifter than a runner,
>   they fly away without a glimpse of joy.
> [26]They skim past like boats of papyrus,
>   like eagles swooping down on their prey.
> [27]If I say, 'I will forget my complaint,
>   I will change my expression, and smile,'
> [28]I still dread all my sufferings,
>   for I know you will not hold me innocent.
> [29]Since I am already found guilty,
>   why should I struggle in vain?
> [30]Even if I washed myself with soap
>   and my hands with washing soda,
> [31]you would plunge me into a slime pit
>   so that even my clothes would detest me.

Still immensely frustrated with his basic problem, that is, to know why he was suffering, Job in this section had two major complaints. His life was quickly passing with no hint of improvement. He presumed that though he were innocent, God would still hold him guilty.

9:25 In 7:6 he compared his days to a weaver's shuttle; in these verses he compares them to a runner, boats, and eagles. In 7:6 the days were hopeless; here they are joyless, literally, "They see no *ṭôb*," the general word for "good" of all kinds.

9:26 There are two words in v. 26 that occur only once: *ʾēbeh*, "papyrus," and *ṭûś*, "swooping down." "Papyrus" is widely agreed on because a similar word occurs in Akkadian and Arabic with the meaning "reed" or the like (cf. the other word for "papyrus" in 8:11 and its connection with boats in Isa 18:2). "Swooping down" may also be in Num 11:31. The root appears in Syriac and Aramaic and frequently in modern Hebrew.[50]

9:27 Not surprisingly "complaint," *śākaḥ*, is a common word in Job

---

[49] Perhaps our statue of blindfolded Lady Justice was in the minds of the translators (*The NIV Study Bible* [Grand Rapids: Zondervan, 1985], 744). But the sense is different. Job referred to disregard for justice rather than impartiality.

[50] The root in Syriac and Aramaic is spelled with ܣ rather than ܫ. Gordis notes that from this root come modern Hebrew words for "airplane," "flight," "pilot," and "airport" (*Job*, 109).

with five of its fourteen occurrences. The hardest problem with v. 27, however, is the expression in the second half, "I will forsake my face." Some (NEB, REB) read, "I will show a cheerful face" based on an Arabic cognate. Others, using a Ugaritic cognate, have "fix my face" (AB). Most understand some adjective to modify "face" and assume the text means to say, "I will forsake my sad face." AAT has "give up looking as I do."[51] "Smile" (*blg*), though occurring in only three other places, probably is within the semantic sphere of the root. The NIV has "have joy" in 10:20 and "rejoice" in Ps 39:13[14].

9:28 The verse furnishes the apodosis or result of the conditional sentence begun in v. 27. He could not just "grin and bear it" because he dreaded further suffering and because of the continuing uncertainty of his relationship with God. Job had used *ygr*, "dread," in 3:25. What he dreaded then came upon him. After the tragedies had happened, he feared their continuation or intensification because it had become apparent to him that there was no escaping the charge of guilty.

9:29 Most versions expand the first phrase, which in Hebrew is simply "I, I'm evil/wrong/guilty." The KJV has "if I be wicked." One could cryptically translate the verse: "I'm guilty. Why bother?" *Hebel*, "in vain/meaninglessness," occurred as recently at 7:16. With a shrug and a tear Job was resigned to his miserable lot in life.

9:30 Technical terms usually present uncertainties, and that is the case in v. 30. The Masoretes saw the problem with what appears to be "water of snow" in the first line (KJV, RV).[52] The translation "soap" is based largely on the word's parallel with *bōr*, "washing soda/lye" in the accompanying line (NEB, NIV, REB, NRSV). The entire illustration of vv. 30-31 is, of course, figurative. Sin does not literally dirty the hands and soil the clothes. The point Job made is that no effort on his part could make him clean in God's sight.

9:31 "Slime pit," *šaḥat*, seems exaggerated unless with Pope and others it is understood as a synonym for the underworld with its putrid quagmire of filth.[53] The usual word for "grave," *še'ôl*, does not carry with it the idea of water or slime. "Clothes" are the subject of the verb "detest," resulting in a colorful description of the putrid state of his body.

---

[51] See Clines, *Job 1–20*, 219, for discussion and documentation.

[52] The MT *qere* reads "snow water" or "maker of snow." The MT *kethib* reads "in snow." If "snow" is to be retained, it is better to read בְּמוֹ, the preposition with enclitic מ, than בְּמֵי, the preposition on "water" in construct.

[53] See Pope, *Job*, 75. *CHAL* has "pit/grave." It is used in Ezek 19:4 of a pit for trapping animals.

(5) Negotiation Is Impossible (9:32–10:1)

   [32]"He is not a man like me that I might answer him,
       that we might confront each other in court.
   [33]If only there were someone to arbitrate between us,
       to lay his hand upon us both,
   [34]someone to remove God's rod from me,
       so that his terror would frighten me no more.
   [35]Then I would speak up without fear of him,
       but as it now stands with me, I cannot.

   [1]"I loathe my very life;
       therefore I will give free rein to my complaint
       and speak out in the bitterness of my soul.

In this closing paragraph of the complaint section of Job's response to Bildad, the point is that God cannot be brought to the arbitration table. It was impossible that Job could obtain a restraining order until the case came to court or was resolved by some other means.

9:32 Job was able to "answer" his three friends because they had no power to implement their sentences against him. But contending with God was another matter, a losing proposition. "Court" translates *mišpaṭ*, a term that elsewhere is "justice" (8:3; 9:19), "[legal] case" (13:18), "judgment" (14:3), and "right" (34:4,6).[54]

9:33 The interesting word of v. 33 is "someone to arbitrate," often translated "umpire" (Moffatt, AAT, RSV, and most others). "Referee" is a choice none has made but which represents the idea because the picture in the second line is of one separating two fighters locked in a clinch, slugging ineffectively at each other. Verses 33–35 show that at the base of Job's agony and complaining was his search for reconciliation with God in the face of what seemed to him sure evidence of God's rejection (cf. Ps 22). As Hartley has said, "His sense of meaninglessness before inexplicable suffering is deepened by God's absence from his life."[55]

9:34 Job hoped that this arbiter would "remove his rod" ("God" is not in the Hebrew text), a symbol of God's wrath throughout the Old Testament (21:9; Exod 17:9; Ps 89:32; Isa 10:5; cf. 2 Sam 7:14). "Terror" and "frighten" are also words that describe Job's anxious dilemma.

9:35 "I speak" is grammatically marked as indicating a degree of urgency as in the NAB, "Would that I might speak." The last half of the

---

[54] "Court" often translates שַׁעַר, "gate," as in 5:4; Prov 22:22.
[55] Hartley, *Job,* 181.

verse is idiomatic. Literally it reads, "For/but not so I with me."[56]

10:1   This tricolon concludes the complaint section and introduces the direct appeal to God. Job has been complaining to the friends (and to his readers). He will now turn his face upward and address heaven. The middle line's unusual choice of words has prompted some emendations, but none is convincing. Thus the NIV has kept the original text, translating *ʿzb*, "forsake/leave," as "give free rein." "Bitterness of my soul" appeared also in 7:11 (cf. 3:20; 21:25).

(6) Address to God (10:2-22)

[2]I will say to God: Do not condemn me,
   but tell me what charges you have against me.
[3]Does it please you to oppress me,
   to spurn the work of your hands,
   while you smile on the schemes of the wicked?
[4]Do you have eyes of flesh?
   Do you see as a mortal sees?
[5]Are your days like those of a mortal
   or your years like those of a man,
[6]that you must search out my faults
   and probe after my sin—
[7]though you know that I am not guilty
   and that no one can rescue me from your hand?

[8]"Your hands shaped me and made me.
   Will you now turn and destroy me?
[9]Remember that you molded me like clay.
   Will you now turn me to dust again?
[10]Did you not pour me out like milk
   and curdle me like cheese,
[11]clothe me with skin and flesh
   and knit me together with bones and sinews?
[12]You gave me life and showed me kindness,
   and in your providence watched over my spirit.

[13]"But this is what you concealed in your heart,
   and I know that this was in your mind:

---

[56] Gordis takes this as a third case of *tiqqune sopherim* ("corrections of the scribes"; see 7:20, note 98) in this chapter (vv. 19,24,35) and reads with Ehrlich, "For he is not honorable, just, with me" (*Job*, 111). Clines cites additional alternatives on p. 220. The wordy paraphrase of the NEB, REB, and NRSV does not help, "For I know I am not what I am thought to be." Hartley's version of it honors the MT and commends itself, "though I am not right with myself" (*Job*, 179).

^{14}If I sinned, you would be watching me
and would not let my offense go unpunished.
^{15}If I am guilty—woe to me!
Even if I am innocent, I cannot lift my head,
for I am full of shame
and drowned in my affliction.
^{16}If I hold my head high, you stalk me like a lion
and again display your awesome power against me.
^{17}You bring new witnesses against me
and increase your anger toward me;
your forces come against me wave upon wave.

^{18}"Why then did you bring me out of the womb?
I wish I had died before any eye saw me.
^{19}If only I had never come into being,
or had been carried straight from the womb to the grave!
^{20}Are not my few days almost over?
Turn away from me so I can have a moment's joy
^{21}before I go to the place of no return,
to the land of gloom and deep shadow,
^{22}to the land of deepest night,
of deep shadow and disorder,
where even the light is like darkness."

After complaining to his friends and readers throughout chap. 9, Job turned to God and addressed his complaint to him. This is not exactly prayer but a combination of what he had said before, concluding with another death wish similar to chap. 3.

CONDEMNED WITHOUT CHARGES (10:2-7). The title for this section comes from v. 2, but the rest of the verses elaborate Job's description of a God who hounds and hassles and who seems to delight in incessant inquisition.

10:2 The first phrase is an introduction to the address to God and stands outside it. Rather than compound the page with secondary quotation marks (as NASB, NKJV), a colon separates these words from the actual quotation. "Condemn" is the verb "be evil" in the causative stem that demands the translation "treat as evil" or simply "condemn."[57] The word appears again in v. 7, "guilty," forming an inclusio to this pericope.

10:3 Verse 3 begins a series of questions that Job felt reflected legitimately how God was treating him. If Job had known Rom 8:28, he would

---

[57] The *hiphil* of רשע was in 9:20 and will appear again in 15:6; 32:3; 34:12,17,29; 40:8. Altogether Job accounts for one third of the uses of this root as a verb.

have thrown that verse into God's face because it appeared to him that God delighted in oppressing rather than in blessing. Job thought of himself as "the work of your hands" and in vv. 8-12 elaborated on the fact that he was a product of divine, mysterious craftsmanship (cf. 14:15; Ps 138:8). "Smile" is not the same word as in 9:27 but *yp*ʿ, a verb that is also in 3:4; 10:22; 37:15 and carries the notions of "shine/light/flash."[58] Job demanded to know why he, the innocent one, suffered while the wicked went unpunished. This thread weaves its way through Job's speeches from beginning (7:21) to end (21:16; 31:6).

10:4 Job hoped that God would look beyond the surface of things. Eliphaz and his two friends could not be expected to see beyond the externals; but from God, Job presumed something better, that he would look "at the heart" and not be like a man who "looks on the outward appearance" (1 Sam 16:7). God could see that he was innocent.

10:5 Human life spans are limited. Some prediluvian patriarchs lived to be nearly a thousand years old. Postdiluvians lived only a few hundred years. By the time Moses wrote Ps 90:10, the average was down to seventy, with a few die-hards making it to eighty, although Moses himself lived to 120 (Deut 31:2). The thrust of Job's query here was that God was acting as if he were human, with all the limitations of time and knowledge that go with humanness.

10:6 After the initial asseverative particle, *kî* ("that"), v. 6 is a perfect chiasmus:

A   You search
  B   out my faults
  B'   and after my sins
A'   you probe.

All the verbs and nouns are frequent and standard words with no translation problems. The only difficulty is the one Job had with a God who seemed to be acting as a human investigator who because of limitations of time employed cruel tactics to discover the truth and extract a confession.[59]

10:7 Job knew that God was aware of his innocence, but his quandary was that God was treating him as if he were guilty. The other point that this verse makes is that Job knew there was no escaping what seemed like the retributive hand of God. Job had no "rescuer," a participle from *nāṣal*, elsewhere called a "defender" (5:4; cf. 5:19). Job also

---

[58] Job accounts for four of the eight occurrences of this verb in the OT.
[59] Hartley, *Job*, 184-85.

used other terms to describe his need for someone to come to his aid: "arbitrator" (9:33), "witness," "advocate" (16:19), "intercessor," "friend" (16:20), and "redeemer" (19:25). The Christian reader of these passages cannot help but think that the one Job sought for has come to us in Jesus Christ (cf. Luke 1:74; Rom 7:24; Gal 1:4; 2 Tim 4:18; 2 Pet 2:9).

I AM YOUR CREATION (10:8-12). In these five verses Job elaborated on the idea that he was the work of God's hands (v. 3). From his conception to the onslaught of his present problems, Job thought of himself as under the special, caring oversight of God.

10:8 The certain and well-balanced lines of the preceding verses now give way to the unusual and difficult poetry more characteristic of Job. "Shaped" ('āṣab II in piel)[60] occurs elsewhere only in Jer 44:1. The second line reads literally, "Together around and you will destroy me" (see KJV, ASV, NASB and margin). The reading of the NIV, like most modern versions, follows the LXX in reading "after" for "together."[61]

10:9 This verse is a well-crafted picture of the potter who having produced a fine vessel now reduces it to its primal element. It is reminiscent of the curse on Adam in Gen 3:19, "Dust you are and to dust you will return" (cf. Job 30:19; 34:15).

10:10 Two rare words raise questions about the precision of the second line of v. 10. The word translated "curdle" (qāpaʾ) is found elsewhere only in Exod 15:8 ("congealed") and in Zeph 1:12 ("left"). "Cheese" (gĕbinnâ) occurs only once, but its meaning is established in postbiblical Hebrew, Aramaic, and Arabic. Whatever Job knew of the growth of the fetus in the womb, his imagery has suggested to some a process of growth from milklike semenal fluid within which there is a thickening into the features that mark a body, as v. 11 will delineate.[62] The verse impinges on the abortion debate because it suggests that from the point of conception Job was a person for whom God cared.

10:11 The question of v. 10 continues as does Job's description of his prenatal development. The verb "knit together," skk II, appears elsewhere in this sense only in Ps 139:13, a passage similar to this one. After the initial coagulation there develops eventually in the womb discernible "skin," "flesh," "bones," and "sinews."

---

[60] עצב II, according to BDB, not עצב I, "grieve/hurt." The noun עָצָב, "idol," is related to our word.

[61] It is another instance of confusion of daleth and resh: אַחַר for אַחַד. See Clines for alternative pointings of סכך (Job, 221).

[62] Gordis, Job, 522-23; Pope, Job, 78; Hartley, Job, 187; and Clines, Job, 248 support this explanation; but Tur-Sinai rejects it. Habel prefers to view the imagery simply as highlighting "the mystery and intimacy of God's involvement in prenatal growth" (Job, 199).

10:12 The process culminated in a life that enjoyed God's *ḥesed*, "kindness," a multifaceted word that embraces the notions of "faithfulness/love/mercy/covenant fidelity" as well. His "spirit" also enjoyed God's "providence," another rich word that others translate "solicitude" (AT), "vigilance" (Knox), "care" (RSV, GNB, NASB, NKJV), "tender care" (JB). This was Job's beatific beginning and life until the tragedies of chap. 1 struck. The miseries that began at that point are mostly what consumed his thoughts and filled his speeches.

GOD'S INTOLERANCE OF ALL SIN (10:13-17). From the relatively pleasant deliberations of vv. 8-12, Job once more degenerated into that accusing tone that characterizes so much of his addresses to God. Once more the theme of these verses is that God was against him for no known cause.

10:13 "This" refers to God's plan of oppressive watchfulness described in v. 14. Job charged God with premeditating his current crises from as far back as his birth. While it can be comforting to believe that God knows the end from the beginning, Job held God accountable for foreknowing what would befall him and for actually planning his ruin.

10:14 "Watched" in v. 12 was in a good sense. That God "watched" Job in v. 14 was an undesirable surveillance. The NIV paraphrases the second line from a straightforward "and from my guilt you would not absolve me." Somehow the "kindness" of which Job spoke in v. 12 would have no effect if he should sin.

10:15 Verse 15 is a tricolon and can be scanned that way (e.g., NAB, REB) by putting the NIV's third and fourth lines together and eliminating the extraneous words. "Guilty" is the word that began this address in v. 2 ("condemn"). The exclamation *ʾalělay*, "woe," occurs elsewhere only in Mic 7:1. Not to lift the head is a sign of shame, grief, or cowardice (Judg 8:28; Lam 2:10; Zech 1:21). Though he should have been able to lift it, Job's suffering caused him to be "full of shame" and "drowned in affliction." "Drowned" translates *rěʾēh*, which looks like "see" (KJV) or "look" (RV, RSV, etc.) but probably is an alternate spelling of the root *rwh*, "satiate/fill."[63]

10:16 Holding the head high was a sign of pride, success, and honor (Gen 40:20; 2 Kgs 25:27; Ps 27:6). "Head" is not in the Hebrew text but is understood with this verb, the nominal and adjectival forms of which mean "pride/proud." "Display your awesome power" translates the only

---

[63] The same pair of verbs as here appear in Ps 91:16: שָׂבַע and רָאָה, although the NIV translates the latter in the traditional sense there. Cf. the NEB's "enjoy the fullness of my salvation," AAT's "drink his fill of My salvation."

hithpael of *pl'*, "do wonders/marvelously." The "lion" can be understood either as predator or prey. Either God is like a lion stalking Job or God is stalking Job as a hunter would stalk a lion. Either picture could describe the way Job felt. Inevitably he would be trapped.

10:17 The first two thirds of this tricolon that closes this section is perspicuous and relatively free of difficulty.[64] God seemed to be augmenting his case against Job and compounding his anger toward him. Instead of matters getting better, they were growing worse for Job. The last line of v. 17 literally has "changes and army are with me."[65] The first word, which refers to one thing substituting for another (see KB), is rendered "shifts" in 1 Kgs 5:14. The second word occurs in Job 7:1; 14:14, where it is translated "hard service," although its more frequent meaning is "army." The two words form a hendiadys meaning that fresh and new problems and tragedies followed one another in Job's life. Certainly the account of the four disasters (1:13-19) seemed like "wave upon wave."

A DEATH WISH (10:18-22). The sentiments that close Job's response to Bildad's first speech sound much like chap. 3, his curse on the day of his birth. This section is replete with thoughts on death, disorder, and darkness.

10:18 Echoes of 3:11 sound in v. 18. In the first line Job asked God why he was ever born. The simple imperfect of the verb *gāwaʿ* is given a volative force, "I wish I had died."[66]

10:19 The same force of "wish" could have been given in translation of the verbs in v. 19 as well. Then the terse wording would read: "I wish I were as though I had not been. I wish I had gone from womb to tomb."[67] The second verb means "to be carried," first by the midwife and then by the pallbearers.

10:20 The leading ideas of this verse are all found elsewhere in Job's speeches. The notion of "few days" is in 14:1. The verb *ḥādal*, "cease," translated here "are almost over," was in 7:16 translated "let me alone."[68] That wish is expressed differently in the second line of this

---

[64] However, W. G. E. Watson would not read עֵדָי as "witnesses" but, on the basis of Ugaritic, "troops/combatants" ("The Metaphor in Job 10,17," *Bib* 63 [1982]: 255-57). Pope has "hostility" instead of "witnesses" (*Job*, 79, 81). For a defense of the traditional see L. Grabbe, *Comparative Philology and the Text of Job*, SBLD 34 (Missoula, Mont.: SBL, 1977), 63-66.

[65] These two words, חֲלִיפֹה and צָבָא also appear together in 14:14. See Dhorme, *Job*, 153-54.

[66] See GKC § 107n.

[67] Cf. the reading of Pope, "carried from womb to tomb" (*Job*). The opening כַּאֲשֶׁר, "if only," can also be rendered "as if" (cf. Zech 10:6; *GBH* § 174d).

[68] The MT *qere* takes this as an imperative וַחֲדָל, "and cease!" This would parallel the thrust of the second line. See Clines, *Job 1-20*, 222-23.

verse. Job's wish for a momentary reprieve from God's incessant badgering also was expressed in 7:19.

10:21 The two verbs of the first half of v. 21 read, "I will go and not return." A similar idea is in 7:10; 16:22. "Gloom/darkness" and "deep shadow" occur also in 3:5.[69]

10:22 Job's complaint ends with a thesaurus of terms for darkness. "Deepest night" translates two words: ʿēpâ, which is found elsewhere only in Amos 4:13, and ʾōpel, which occurs a second time at the end of the verse. "Deep shadow" (or "shadow of death"; ṣalmāwet) was in the preceding verse. "Order," šĕdārîm, is a hapax but is known in postbiblical Hebrew. With this gloomy picture of the grave Job concluded his second speech of the debate. He wondered, and so might we, if what he expected would not indeed come true.

---

[69] See the study of the OT vocabulary of death in D. L. Block, "Beyond the Grave: Ezekiel's Vision of Death and Afterlife," *BBR* 2 (1992): 113-41.

5. Zophar: Repent, Job (11:1-20)

Zophar probably was the youngest of the three friends. He was impetuous, tactless, direct, unsympathetic, but not altogether without some contribution to make to the friends' case. His speeches are the shortest; in fact, he has only two. His opening speech contains three characteristic motifs: rebuke, remarks on God's sovereign justice, and advice.

(1) Rebuke (11:1-6)

[1]Then Zophar the Naamathite replied:

[2]"Are all these words to go unanswered?

Is this talker to be vindicated?
³Will your idle talk reduce men to silence?
   Will no one rebuke you when you mock?
⁴You say to God, 'My beliefs are flawless
   and I am pure in your sight.'
⁵Oh, how I wish that God would speak,
   that he would open his lips against you
⁶and disclose to you the secrets of wisdom,
   for true wisdom has two sides.
   Know this: God has even forgotten some of your sin.

Zophar's brashness is evident immediately in the way he opened his first speech. Nevertheless, he did in these first six verses encapsulate much of what the friends said throughout the debate cycle. He cited Job's claim of innocence; and he wished that God would answer Job, which is exactly what happened in chaps. 38–41.

11:1   See comments at 4:1.

11:2   Four questions begin Zophar's frontal attack on Job, all expecting negative replies. Like the other two, he first complained about Job's many words. That is how Bildad began his first two speeches (8:2; 18:2) and how Eliphaz began his second speech (15:2). For the sixth out of sixteen times in this book, *ṣedaq* is used as a verb. Here it sounds like a passive, "be vindicated," but it is active. Literally translated the second line is, "Or is/can a man of lips [be] right?" The NJPS has, "Must a loquacious person be right?" The NCV has, "Is this talker in the right?"

11:3   These two rhetorical questions complement the two of v. 2. As in many poetic lines, the secondary elements often use rare words as they seek further to specify or make less ambiguous the more general statements of the primary lines. The vocabulary of v. 3 is not common but not unknown either. For example, "idle talk" (*bad*) appears in only five other places. "Men" is *mĕtîm,* a word that is found six times in Job and only fifteen more elsewhere. The verb "mock" (*lāʿag*) occurs only eighteen times in the Old Testament.

11:4   "To God" has been added by the translators but justifiably so; the "your" is singular, and "God" is in the next verse. Strictly speaking, Job said neither of these sentences that Zophar quoted, but he came close to maintaining the second in 10:7. "Beliefs" translates *leqaḥ,* a relatively rare noun built on a common verb that means "receive/take." The "doctrine" (KJV, RSV, AB, etc.) is what he "received" from parents, teachers, or elders. These are the words that Zophar felt obligated to refute.

11:5   According to Zophar, Job had done too much talking (v. 2), and

God had not done enough. We know how fully Zophar's wish[1] came true.

11:6   The first line continues Zophar's simple wish, while the second and third present problems to the interpreter. God did not exactly "disclose the secrets of wisdom" at the end of the book, but he did make Job realize how few of those secrets he knew. Just realizing that fact was a significant step for Job and can be for those of us who live life under God's laws.[2] The RV's rendering of the second line is unintelligible, "that it is manifold in effectual working." The two words that make up the line are both difficult. "True wisdom" (*tûšîyâ*) is found six times in Job and twelve altogether, so its meaning is well established.

"Two sides" (*kiplayim*) occurs only here; 41:13[15]; and Isa 40:2. The NAB has "twice as effective," and AAT has "wisdom is twofold."[3] Others use "manifold" (RSV) or "many sides" (NJPS). Zophar did not spell out what the "two sides" are. Perhaps he was alluding to our adage that there are two sides to every story (Prov 18:17). Some say that it has to do with the overt and covert dimensions of wisdom, the obvious and the hidden or deeper dimensions.[4] The thrust of Zophar's last line seems to be that God was punishing Job for only some of his sins and that Job should be glad that he was not getting all that he deserved. While Ezra recognized the same leniency on God's part (Ezra 9:13), the remark was inappropriate under the circumstances.

(2) Rhetorical Examination (11:7-12)

   [7]Can you fathom the mysteries of God?
      Can you probe the limits of the Almighty?
   [8]They are higher than the heavens—what can you do?
      They are deeper than the depths of the grave—what can you know?
   [9]Their measure is longer than the earth
      and wider than the sea.

   [10]"If he comes along and confines you in prison
      and convenes a court, who can oppose him?
   [11]Surely he recognizes deceitful men;
      and when he sees evil, does he not take note?

---

[1] See comments at 6:8 for "how I wish."

[2] "Secrets" (תַּעֲלֻמוֹת) is from the root עלם, meaning "hide" and from which comes עוֹלָם, "eternity." "He has also set eternity in the hearts of men; yet they cannot fathom what God has done from beginning to end" (Eccl 3:11).

[3] By adding an א and reading the initial כ as an asseverative, some arrive at פֶלֶא, "mysteries" or "wonderful" (NEB). For a creative alternative see J. J. Slotki, "Job XI 6," *VT* 35 (1985): 229-30.

[4] See E. B. Smick, "Job," EBC 4 (Grand Rapids: Zondervan, 1988), 917-18.

¹²**But a witless man can no more become wise
than a wild donkey's colt can be born a man.**

Now it is Zophar's turn to speak of God's grandeur and justice. These two themes persist through the book and come to a climax when God confronts Job in the whirlwind.

GOD'S INCOMPREHENSIBILITY (11:7-9). The "mysteries" and "limits" of God are the focus of all three verses in this subsection designed to make Job bend his knee before such an incomprehensible deity.

11:7 Again Zophar's questions clearly expect a negative reply. Both "fathom" and "probe" are *tîmṣâ*, "do/can you find." A "mystery" is something for which one must search. Usually it is used metaphorically (e.g., Ps 139:23), but sometimes it refers to a literal search (Judg 18:2). "Limits" (*taklît*) is from the root *kl*, meaning "all/completeness/end," hence "limits." Of course, Job could not carry out such a search, but there is a certain arrogance in Zophar's tone that suggests he had fathomed farther and probed deeper than Job.

11:8 The lines are only of average length in Hebrew, which outdoes English in succinctness; so the NIV uses almost three times as many words as the Hebrew. The second line is particularly wordy, translating *šĕʾôl* with "depths of the grave." Again neither Job nor anyone else could answer these questions. They were rhetorical devices to humble, even humiliate, Job further. They were torturous encumbrances to the heavy burdens that Job already carried.

11:9 Verse 8 spoke of the height and depth of God's ways (cf. Isa 55:9), and v. 9 speaks of the length and width, much as Paul did in Eph 3:18 of the love of Christ.

GOD'S INCONTROVERTIBLE JUSTICE (11:10-12). Having established that God's ways are beyond human finding out, Zophar moved to God's unopposed and indiscernible way of exacting justice.

11:10 The answer to Zophar's question is no one. Humans have no right to question or "oppose"⁵ God's dispensing of justice because our knowledge is inferior to his (vv. 7-9). If he acts in judgment,⁶ it is because he knows of sins committed (vv. 11-12).

11:11 On this verse Elihu elaborates in 34:21-25. God sees through people. He reads the thoughts and intents of the heart. "Deceitful" is

---

⁵ The verb translated "oppose" is the *hiphil* of שׁוּב as in 9:12.

⁶ R. Gordis (*The Book of Job* [New York: Jewish Theological Seminary, 1978], 122) emends the word translated "comes along" (יַחֲלֹף) to read "seizes" (יַחְטֹף; cf. NAB). A. Guillaume points out that "snatches away" (יַחְתֹּף) is in 9:12, a passage that Zophar seems to have been reflecting (*Studies in the Book of Job* [Leiden: Brill, 1968], 90).

šāwĕʾ as in 7:3 and ordinarily means "vain/useless/worthless." The translation "deceitful" is influenced by the word "evil" in line *b* and similar parallels elsewhere (31:5; Pss 12:2[3]; 26:4). The negative in the second line must either be understood as a negative rhetorical question (as NIV) or repointed as the emphatic particle *lū*.[7]

11:12 This is an enigmatic proverb. The Hebrew words behind "witless" (*nābub*) and "become wise" (*yillābēb*) are similar in sound, but both are rare words. The former in its other three contexts refers to the "hollow" altar (Exod 27:8; 38:7) or the "hollow" pillars (Jer 52:21), so here it describes a man who is hollow or empty in some sense. The verb, presumably related to the noun meaning "heart/mind" (used in v. 13),[8] occurs elsewhere only in Song 4:9. Pope, followed by Clines (and NCV), understands "colt" (*ʿayir*) as "domesticated ass." He takes the terms "wild donkey" followed by "man" (*ʾādām*) together as "wild ass of the steppe" (interpreting *ʾādām* as equivalent to *ʾădāmâ*, "ground"). The second line would then be translated "when a wild ass is born tame."[9] Clearly Zophar's point was the impossibility of a wild donkey being born either "human" or "tame."[10] Zophar seems to have implied in these verses that Job was hopelessly "deceitful," "evil," and "witless" (cf. v. 20). The following verses, however, declare that there was hope for him if he repented.

(3) Advice (11:13-20)

[13]"Yet if you devote your heart to him
    and stretch out your hands to him,
[14]if you put away the sin that is in your hand
    and allow no evil to dwell in your tent,
[15]then you will lift up your face without shame;
    you will stand firm and without fear.
[16]You will surely forget your trouble,
    recalling it only as waters gone by.
[17]Life will be brighter than noonday,
    and darkness will become like morning.
[18]You will be secure, because there is hope;
    you will look about you and take your rest in safety.

---

[7] As the footnote in *BHS* suggests.

[8] *IBHS* § 23.5b translates it as a denominative *niphal*, "to get a heart."

[9] M. Pope, *Job,* AB (Garden City: Doubleday, 1965), 83; D. Clines, *Job 1–20*, WBC (Dallas: Word, 1989), 253, 256, 266.

[10] The lines are joined by a comparative *waw* as in 5:7 (cf. Prov 25:25; 26:14; see GKC § 161a).

¹⁹**You will lie down, with no one to make you afraid,**
      and many will court your favor.
²⁰**But the eyes of the wicked will fail,**
      and escape will elude them;
      their hope will become a dying gasp."

The Naamathite structured his advice to Job in the form of conditions and results. If you do such and such, then this and that will result. The two verses of the protasis are very preachable and can serve to challenge the unregenerate in any age. The apodoses are not unlike the promises some evangelists make to their hearers—"God has a wonderful plan for your life." Good as the advice is and true as the promises of subsequent bliss are, Job was not the audience that needed to hear this. His was a different problem, not met by these strict cause-and-effect axioms.

THE PROTASIS—REPENT (11:13-14). The particle "if" begins each verse, but actually four conditions are listed in these two verses. To experience the pleasant things of vv. 15-19, one must do the unpleasant things of vv. 13-14.

11:13 An independent second person pronoun gives Zophar's phrase a tone of individuality, "If you, even you, devote." The verb is *kûn*, which has a range of meanings surrounding "establish/set/prepare." It is used with "heart" in several other cases to express the idea of loyalty to or trust in the Lord (Pss 78:8,37; 112:7; cf. 2 Chr 12:14). Stretching out the hands to God has a biblical precedent, but unfortunately only a few Christians now practice it as a sign of repentance or worship (Pss 88:9[10]; 143:6; 1 Tim 2:8). Happily the custom seems to be spreading.

11:14 The two conditions of v. 13 are positive; the third and fourth in v. 14 are negative—"put away sin" and "allow no evil." This verse is a chiasmus.

A   If sin
 B   in your hand
  C   you put away
  C'   and allow not to dwell
 B'   in your tent
A'   evil

All the words are well known, but perhaps "sin" and "evil" were chosen for the similarity of their sounds, *ʾāwen* and *ʿawlâ*. Eliphaz will give similar advice in 22:23.

THE APODOSIS—BENEFITS (11:15-20). Zophar cataloged ten benefits that would come to Job if he met the conditions of the preceding verses. While what he said was not incorrect, he failed to note that sometimes God's good people suffer. That is the mistake that characterizes all the friends' speeches and makes their basic premise flawed. In their tight system of theology there was no room for suffering that was *not* caused by sin or for bliss that was *not* based on goodness.

11:15 The NIV has "then" only at the beginning of this verse, but it could have been put at the beginning of vv. 16-19 as well.[11] "Lift up the face" means essentially the same thing as "lift up the head," a phrase found in 10:15.[12] "Shame" translates the less common *mūm*, which describes the "blemish" on a sacrificial animal in fifteen of its twenty occurrences. "Stand firm" is from a verb meaning "to pour out" as in the case of molten metal. Few commentators seem bothered by this odd use; they explain it as a comparison to metal once molten but now solidified.[13] Freedom from fear is one of the benefits of the gospel as well (1 John 4:18).

11:16 "Trouble" (*āmāl*) is the term that has been used six times already in this book to describe sin and its consequences (Job 3:10,20; 4:8; 5:6-7; 7:3). The "waters gone by" refers to the fact that rain quickly soaks into the desert soil of the Near East, and streams run only sporadically.

11:17 All translations have had recourse to some paraphrasing in order to make sense of the first line of v. 17, which literally reads, "And from noonday will arise life/world."[14] The last word, *ḥeled,* appears only four other times (all in Psalms) and may be in a variant form in Isa 38:11. By extension from the life of the world, it refers here to the life of Job. Almost as a contrast to Job's frequent contemplation of darkness (3:4-5; 10:20-21), Zophar promised that that very "darkness" (*tā'upâ*, a unique spelling of the same root found in 10:22) would "become like morning."

11:18 The "hope" Job felt had ended (7:6) Zophar now promised could be his. "Secure" and "safety" translate the twice-occurring root

---

[11] A כִּי asseverative begins vv. 15-16, which, if translated, probably should be "indeed" or "surely" rather than "because" or "for." *GBH* (§ 167s) explains it as a כִּי of affirmation, "rather frequent in the apodosis of the conditional clause."

[12] See uses in BDB, 670.

[13] The NJPS translates "when in straits" and explains in the footnote that they follow a few manuscripts that have מִצָּק instead of מֻצָק. The root would then be צוּק rather than מצק.

[14] *IBHS* (§ 14.4d) explains that "the adjective on which מִן depends is omitted and must be supplied from the context." Other examples given are Isa 10:10; 40:17; 41:24; Mic 7:4; Ps 62:10.

bṭḥ, first a verb and then a noun.

11:19 Leviticus 26:6 has a different word for "make afraid," but the promise is the same as here (cf. Ps 23:2,4; Isa 17:2; Zeph 3:13). "Court your favor/face" is from a root that means "be sick/soft" and by derivation comes the meaning "entreat."[15] The verse may reflect, as Hartley suggests, Job's complaint in 10:16 that he was a hunted man.

11:20 Verse 20 stands somewhat outside Zophar's advice to Job. Like an appendix it presents an alternative to what has gone before. Should Job not repent and turn to God, he would join the "wicked" whose "eyes will fail" and for whom there will be no "escape." "Fail" is *kālâ*, a term Job used in 7:6. For the repentant there was "hope" in v. 18, but for the wicked "their hope will become a dying gasp," or a "puff of breath" (KJV margin). In the ancient way of thinking, life was breath; and when the last breath left, then life left with it. So Jesus "gave up the ghost" (KJV), or "breathed his last" (Mark 15:37).

6. Job Defends Himself and Prays to God (12:1–14:22)

Though the response in 12:1–14:22 is longer than the other responses (this is the only three-chapter one), the issues Job raised are essentially the same. Large sections deal with exceptions to the generalized rules of retributive theology, with God's sovereignty over the world, and with complaints addressed to God because Job received no hearing and would rather die than live.

(1) Defense (12:1-3)

[1]Then Job replied:
[2]Doubtless you are the people,
   and wisdom will die with you!
[3]But I have a mind as well as you;
   I am not inferior to you.
   Who does not know all these things?

Job smarted under the recriminations of the friends and in the two opening verses of this response snapped back with sarcasm and denial.

12:1 See comments at 6:1.

12:2 The first line makes little sense without the second. Together

---

[15] חלה is one of those rare roots that occurs in all seven stems. For further discussion of its use here see Tur-Sinai, *The Book of Job*, rev. ed. (Jerusalem: Kiryat-Sefer, 1967), 201-2.

they may be paraphrased, "You are people of wisdom, and when you die, wisdom will die too."[16] It was Job's turn to be contentious.

12:3 Job defended himself with three simple statements. The first can hardly be translated differently. "Mind" ("brains," Moffatt) is *lēbāb,* "heart" (cf. 11:12-13). The second line is also in 13:2. The verb is *npl,* "fall," suggesting that their argument will not fell him as easily as they might have thought. The third line is difficult because there is no verb "know." Literally it reads, "With whom are there not like these things?" The simple way the NIV and most others put it carries the sense, making paraphrases such as the NEB's and REB's unnecessary.[17]

(2) Exceptions (12:4-12)

> [4]I have become a laughingstock to my friends,
>   though I called upon God and he answered—
>   a mere laughingstock, though righteous and blameless!
> [5]Men at ease have contempt for misfortune
>   as the fate of those whose feet are slipping.
> [6]The tents of marauders are undisturbed,
>   and those who provoke God are secure—
>   those who carry their god in their hands.
>
> [7]"But ask the animals, and they will teach you,
>   or the birds of the air, and they will tell you;
> [8]or speak to the earth, and it will teach you,
>   or let the fish of the sea inform you.
> [9]Which of all these does not know
>   that the hand of the LORD has done this?
> [10]In his hand is the life of every creature
>   and the breath of all mankind.
> [11]Does not the ear test words
>   as the tongue tastes food?
> [12]Is not wisdom found among the aged?
>   Does not long life bring understanding?

How the three counselors could have failed to see what Job pointed out in these verses is hard to understand. Surely they knew of unpunished criminals, of the greedy rich who gained their wealth through exploita-

---

[16] Gordis has "the people that count" (*Job*, 128). Pope and Hartley (*Job*, NICOT [Grand Rapids: Eerdmans, 1988]) have "the gentry." The JB, GNB, and NJPS have "the voice of the people"; the NAB, "the intelligent folk"; the REB, "the intelligent people."

[17] They have, "What gifts indeed have you that others have not?" The JB has, "And who, for that matter, has not observed as much?"

tion, and of people who literally got away with murder. Almost all of chap. 21 is an expansion of these themes. A complementary theme is that God knows about and allows this flagrant wickedness.

REWARDS DO NOT MATCH BEHAVIOR (12:4-6). **12:4** "A laughing-stock" (*śĕḥōq*) is what Job twice in this verse said his friends thought of him. Here was a man whose piety, righteousness, and blamelessness were known far and wide. The verb "called" is a participle and describes Job's former close relationship with God, who would answer when Job prayed. This is what he missed the most (Job 13:22; 23:5; 30:20-21; 31:35). But now he was regarded by all as one whose secret sins had found him out; his honor had turned to derision and his fame to shame. It is easy and tempting to take joy in the demise of the rich and famous.

12:5 Several rare words in this verse make its translation less than certain. The first Hebrew word looks like "lamp" (KJV), but dividing it into a preposition plus noun produces "for misfortune."[18] The first stich is literally, "For misfortune contempt according to the opinion/thought of one at ease." "Opinion" is *ʿaštût*, a hapax related to the verb translated "take notice" (also a hapax) in Jonah 1:6 and to the noun translated "plans" in Ps 146:4 (another hapax). The adjective "at ease" is translated "complacent" in Isa 32:9,11 and describes those whose security is false (cf. Amos 6:1; Zech 1:15; Ps 123:4).

The word *nākôn*, another hapax that begins the second half of v. 5, probably is a noun, "something that strikes," from the verb "to strike" (what apparently the NIV has read). The versions all differ on wording but seem to mean the same thing, that is, that Zophar and his friends could afford to be smug because they were rich and healthy. For them it was easy to advise and even berate Job, who lacked both health and wealth.

12:6 The first two lines of v. 6 are relatively certain, but the third has prompted a plethora of options, one of which is in the NIV footnote.[19] The sense of lines *a* and *b* certainly comports with what Job said elsewhere (e.g., 21:7-9), but line *c* is a unique statement apparently criticizing idol worshipers.

TESTIMONIES TO DIVINE SOVEREIGNTY (12:7-12). Job summoned

---

[18] פִּיד is elsewhere only in Job 30:24; 31:29; Prov 24:22.

[19] This reads "secure/in what God's hand brings them." The problem is in part because "those" of the second line is plural, but "those" of the third is singular. Furthermore, there is no "their" in the third line, just the usual poetic parallel to אֵל in the second line. The NAB, NEB, GNB, and REB omit the line. The JB has "and make a god of their two fists." Clines (*Job 1–20,* 279) rejects the NIV margin as "impossible" and translates "those whom God has in his own power" (cf. v. 10).

witnesses from the animal world as well as the general observation of people to support his contention of the preceding stanza that God is sovereignly responsible for all that happens in the world, including flagrant and unpunished crime.

Animals (12:7-9). This is neither the first nor the last time the speakers drew support for their points from the fauna and flora around them. Later God would do the same thing on a far grander scale.

12:7 "Animals" is *bĕhēmôt,* the feminine plural of "cattle" but also the "behemoth" of 40:15, one of the two especially invincible creatures in God's menagerie. The word "teach" in vv. 7-8 is also noteworthy because from the same root comes the noun *tôrâ,* commonly translated "law" but meaning "instruction/teaching."

12:8 "Speak" is more often "complain" (occurring as the noun "complaint" in 7:13; 9:27; 10:1; 21:4; 23:2). Precisely what the natural world teaches is not clear. To some these verses seem more at home in the mouths of the friends, especially since all the *you's* are singular. Gordis, followed by Clines and others, proposed that vv. 7-12 are Job's quotation of them or at least something he imagined they would have said. But Job could also have been citing this fragment of a wisdom poem to support his contention that all are subject to this sovereign yet capricious God.

12:9 A rhetorical question concludes this subsection. The obvious answer is that all animals know that God[20] is in control of the world. In a sense v. 10 is the answer to the question. The second line is repeated exactly in Isa 41:20.

Humans (12:10-12). These three verses sound like three disparate proverbs laced together here to support Job's contention that God's adjudication of the world is not so predictable as his friends have been maintaining.

12:10 This well-balanced verse reiterates the truth that God is in charge. Here Job only spoke it, but he would existentially embrace it when God spoke it to him in chaps. 38–41. Daniel said it to Nebuchadnezzar when he urged the monarch to "acknowledge that the Most High is sovereign over the kingdoms of men and gives them to anyone he wishes" (Dan 4:17,25). Paul's quotation from "some of your own poets" in Acts 17:28 is similar to this verse.

12:11 Elihu said almost exactly the same words as this verse in 34:3.

---

[20] "LORD" is the only occurrence of יהוה in the speeches of Job and his friends, another reason for believing that this is a quotation from a proverb or a hymn. Hartley suggests it was a scribal error for אֱלוֹהַּ because of the similarity of Isa 41:20b (*Job,* 209).

It must have been a current proverb in either its declarative or interrogative form. The point is that just as the tongue decides what is good or bad tasting, so the ear, a surrogate for the mind, ascertains what is true and false.[21] In other words, everyone should judge as true Job's claim that God is the Lord of the universe, the king of creation, and the ultimate determiner of human destiny.

12:12 Job's friends, especially Eliphaz (15:10) and Bildad (8:8-10), would answer yes to this question. Job would not be so sure, and Elihu said, "It is not only the old who are wise" (32:9). Therefore there may be sarcasm in this verse and perhaps the previous one as well.

(3) God's Government of the World (12:13-25)

13"To God belong wisdom and power;
    counsel and understanding are his.
14What he tears down cannot be rebuilt;
    the man he imprisons cannot be released.
15If he holds back the waters, there is drought;
    if he lets them loose, they devastate the land.
16To him belong strength and victory;
    both deceived and deceiver are his.
17He leads counselors away stripped
    and makes fools of judges.
18He takes off the shackles put on by kings
    and ties a loincloth around their waist.
19He leads priests away stripped
    and overthrows men long established.
20He silences the lips of trusted advisers
    and takes away the discernment of elders.
21He pours contempt on nobles
    and disarms the mighty.
22He reveals the deep things of darkness
    and brings deep shadows into the light.
23He makes nations great, and destroys them;
    he enlarges nations, and disperses them.
24He deprives the leaders of the earth of their reason;
    he sends them wandering through a trackless waste.
25They grope in darkness with no light;
    he makes them stagger like drunkards.

---

[21] The verb translated "taste," טעם, in its noun form can also mean "discernment/ judgment" and thus approaches the semantic sphere of "test" in English.

In the course of God's running the world, he regularly breaks the rules that people think he has made. Scattered through this long catalog of areas of his dominion are several where he does the opposite of the expected, for example, shackling kings, stripping priests, silencing advisers, and disarming the mighty. He controls the weather (v. 15) and brings some things into the dark and others into the light (v. 22). He seems to delight particularly in humbling, even humiliating, human rulers (vv. 24-25). All of this counters Eliphaz's position that God uses his wisdom and power in proper ways (5:10-16)

12:13 "Power" and three synonyms for "wisdom" are attributed to God. With this all the speakers of the book agreed. This is the point in the speech where Job anticipated the theophany of chaps. 38-41.

12:14 "What" is the object supplied to the first verb so that "it," the subject of the second verb, can have an antecedent.[22] The first line brings to mind God's instructions to Jeremiah about tearing down and building up (Jer 1:10). The second line, with its verbs "shut" and "open" ("imprison" and "release" in the NIV), points toward Rev 3:7.

12:15 The weather and the rain in particular are also within the parameters of God's rule. As sovereign he can create "drought" by withholding the rain as he did in the days of Elijah and Ahab (1 Kgs 17:1,7), or he can send too much rain so that the earth floods as it did in the days of Noah (Gen 7:11-12:20).

12:16 "Victory" is *tûšîyâ,* the definition of which encompasses "success" (5:12; 6:13), "true wisdom" (11:6), and "insight" (26:3).[23] The word is paired with "strength" much as "wisdom" (*ḥokmâ*) and "power" were paired in v. 13. "Deceived" and "deceiver" ("pervert and perverter" in AB) are a merismus representing the totality of humanity (see explanation at 1:20). Deception is everywhere, and it is all under God's control.

12:17 God, it seems, delights in undoing human doings. Not only here but elsewhere in the Bible, he exalts the humble and humiliates the proud. Since the Tower of Babel, he has come up with creative ways to dismantle human enterprises while at the same time executing his own miraculous undertakings. "Stripped" (*šôlāl*) occurs only here, in v. 19 (with the same verb), and in Mic 1:8 ("barefoot"). "Counselors" here refers to royal advisers. God can act contrary to the best of human wisdom,

---

[22] Verses 14 and 15 both begin with הֵן, explained in *GBH* § 167l as conditional.

[23] Gordis points out in his comments at 5:12 that תֻּשִׁיָּה "possesses two meanings that are related to each other, . . . (a) effective wisdom; (b) its result, i.e., success" (*Job*, 56). It is similar in sound and meaning to תְּשׁוּעָה, "salvation," but emendation is not necessary.

making foolishness of it all (cf. Isa 44:25; 1 Cor 18–19).[24]

12:18 As the NIV's footnote indicates, there is a difference of opinion on the second line. Are the synonymous lines parallel or antithetic? Most feel it is the latter even though the verses preceding and following have synonymous lines.[25] The poet appears to have been playing with words. "Shackles" and "ties" are from the same root. "Ties" and "loincloth" sound alike. The gist of the verse is not in question. God's "strength and victory" (v. 16) exceed that of counselors, judges, priests, "men long established" (v. 19), advisers, elders, nobles, and the mighty (vv. 20-21); therefore, he can remove kings or reverse their decisions.

12:19 "Priests"[26] and "men long established" are two more categories of leading citizens ordinarily deserving of honor. The latter term may refer to nobles or to a hereditary priesthood.[27] According to Job, God places no value on traditional social categories.

12:20 "Trusted advisers" is a *niphal* participle of the root *ʾāman,* "true/faith/believe." It is not, like "elders," a regular category of leaders in the Old Testament. "Silences" translates the same verb that begins v. 24, "deprives."

12:21 The first line of v. 21 is without problems, but the second is afflicted with two hapax legomena, *mĕzîaḥ,* "belt/girdle," and *ʾāpîq,* "mighty." The first has a cognate in Ps 119:19 that establishes its meaning. The second, though ordinarily meaning "stream" (6:15),[28] must be an adjective from *ʾpq,* "restrain."[29] God loosens the military girdle of the one so girded or, in plainer NIV English, "disarms the mighty."

---

[24] According to KB, "makes fools" is a *poel* of the root הלל III. BDB has it under הלל II, "praise," but it occurs enough times for us to know it is not from the same root as "praise." See Grabbe, *Comparative Philology and the Text of Job,* SBLD 34 (Missoula, Mont.: SBL, 1977), 41-43, and Gordis, *Job,* 139. Ecclesiastes 7:7 and Isa 44:25 have the same verb form as here.

[25] While most agree with the sense of the NIV, the NEB and REB have for the second line "and removes the girdle of office from their waists." Hartley has "and removes the waistband from their loins" (211). For support of this view see Blommerde, *Northwest Semitic Grammar and Job* (Rome: Pontifical Biblical Institute, 1969), 63. The NAB seeks to clarify the second line by reading "and leaves but a waistcloth to bind the king's own loins."

[26] This solitary mention of "priests" in Job does not impinge on the question of the book's date. The reference need not be to Levitical priests. Virtually all ancient religions had priests.

[27] Clines, *Job 1–20,* WBC 17 (Dallas: Word, 1989), 300-301.

[28] The NAB moves v. 21 to a place between vv. 18 and 19 and reads, "He breaks down the barriers of the streams."

[29] Aramaic has תְּקֵיף, and Akkadian has *epêqu,* both meaning "strong." See E. Dhorme, *A Commentary on the Book of Job,* trans. H. Knight (London: Nelson, 1967), 178.

12:22 As in Amos 5:8 or Dan 2:22 God lights up dark things as he has been doing ever since the creation when he said, "Let there be light" (Gen 1:3).

12:23 "Make great" (*śgʾ*) here is one of two occurrences of that verb (see 36:24).[30] "Disperses," *nḥḥ,* presents a problem because that root always has the positive connotation of "lead," whereas one expects a negative word to parallel "destroy." The NIV may have understood the meaning "lead away" (see RSV, Pope). It is also possible to emend the root to *nûaḥ* and read it as a causative form meaning "cause to rest," hence "leave/abandon."[31]

12:24 The "nations" (v. 23) and their "leaders" are all under the sovereign control of God. Like pawns on a chessboard he moves them at will. The first line has a string of genitives, "He deprives the heart of the heads of the people of the earth"[32] (cf. Dan 4). The place where he makes them wander is the *tōhû,* the "formless/waste" of Gen 1:2 (cf. 6:18; 26:7; Ps 107:40).

12:25 Job concluded his essay on God's government of the world on a depressing note, watching its leaders groping and staggering like the sightless and inebriated. The verse has a contemporary ring to it. For all the accumulated wisdom of the ages, modern rulers seem as unable to cope with their problems as did desert sheiks and tribal chiefs. In depriving leaders of their reason, does the God of all the earth have other plans?

(4) Defense and Complaint to the Friends (13:1-12)

> [1]My eyes have seen all this,
>   my ears have heard and understood it.
> [2]What you know, I also know;
>   I am not inferior to you.
> [3]But I desire to speak to the Almighty
>   and to argue my case with God.
> [4]You, however, smear me with lies;
>   you are worthless physicians, all of you!
> [5]If only you would be altogether silent!
>   For you, that would be wisdom.
> [6]Hear now my argument;

---

[30] The root occurs as an adjective in Job 36:26; 37:23. Spelled with a final ה rather than a final א, it appears four times as a verb including Job 8:7,11. שׂגא appears as a verb and adjective in the Aramaic parts of Ezra and Daniel.

[31] For support for this emendation see Gordis, *Job,* 140-41.

[32] On this Hebrew construction see *IBHS* § 9.3c.

listen to the plea of my lips.
7Will you speak wickedly on God's behalf?
   Will you speak deceitfully for him?
8Will you show him partiality?
   Will you argue the case for God?
9Would it turn out well if he examined you?
   Could you deceive him as you might deceive men?
10He would surely rebuke you
   if you secretly showed partiality.
11Would not his splendor terrify you?
   Would not the dread of him fall on you?
12Your maxims are proverbs of ashes;
   your defenses are defenses of clay.

The friends believed that they were on God's side and saw things from his perspective. Job was far from convinced. In fact, he believed that they were absolutely wrong; so he wished for God to meet with him and them. He expected to be exonerated and that they would be chagrined. That is, in fact, what happened; but much more remains to be said before the whirlwind (Job 38).

13:1 "All this" refers to the last thirteen verses of chap. 12. In fact, 12:9, which leads up to the dissertation on God's universal dominion, has a similar sentiment to 13:1. It is common knowledge, he maintained, that God does the unusual and often operates in ways directly opposite of what is expected. God seems to delight in belittling the great and leading leaders astray.

13:2 The first line is similar to that of 12:3; the second line is identical.

13:3 The verb "desire" does not occur in the Hebrew until line two, but it gives the nuance of resolve or strong desire to the verb "I will speak" in line one. This statement is one central to Job's complaint. An auxiliary to this request is that God would explain to him why he suffered. He felt quite sure that God's explanation of the matter would be different from the interpretation his friends were putting on it.

13:4 Verses 3-4 both begin with the strong adversative, *'ûlām,* rendered "but" in v. 3 and "however" in v. 4. Rather than hear their paltry explanation, Job wanted an audience with God; but unfortunately he could talk only with his three friends, who "smeared lies" on him. The NIV has defined this verb on the basis of an alternately spelled noun "whitewash" in Ezek 13:10-11,14-15 (cf. RSV, NRSV).[33] The second

---

[33] Job 13:4 has טפל while Ezekiel has תפל. Tur-Sinai (*Job,* 221-22) has "red paint" for שֶׁקֶר. Clines (*Job 1-20,* 276, 306) translates "lying soothers."

line solidifies the point of the verse. Job had no faith in their phony unguents and pompous quackery.

13:5 Before any of the three friends spoke, they were silent with grief for a week (Job 2:13). Job declared that that was their wisest course of action and the most helpful counsel (Prov 17:28).[34]

13:6 Job pleaded for them to hear him out, but in their subsequent speeches it does not appear that they gave him much heed. Both words, "argument" and "plea," are legal terms.

13:7 These next three verses consist of six rhetorical questions that Job put to his friends. In the first two Job added adverbs, "wickedly" and "deceitfully." It was enough that they presumed to speak for God, but to represent him with evil and deceit was compounding their arrogance. Job correctly believed that it was wrong to use lies and false reasoning even in the service of truth.

13:8 "Lift up his face" is the idiom translated "show him partiality" (cf. v. 10; Lev 19:15; Lam 4:16). If there were a dispute between Job and God, it was the obligation of the friends to be impartial, tempting and safe as it might be to join God's side. Job must argue his case, and God must argue his. By this question Job asked them not to take sides.

13:9 Job proposed turning the tables on his friends by asking them if they would submit to a divine inquisition, even as he had been cast into the role of defendant. Though "deceive" translates a different word from the one in 12:16, Job's point was that God could see through their flimsy case against him. Eliphaz, Bildad, and Zophar had the encouragement of one another. They confirmed each other's erroneous assessment of Job.

13:10 The verb *ykḥ*, which appears so often in the book and with a variety of meanings, occurs here twice. It means "rebuke" here, but in 22:4 it means "correct"; in 5:17 and 6:26, "chasten"; in 33:19, "present his case"; in 23:7, "argue"; in 6:25 (also 13:3; 15:3), "prove"; in 6:25 and 32:12, "defend"; in 13:15, "arbitrate"; and in 40:2, "accuse" (all NIV).[35]

A similar distribution is found in the forty-two uses of the word outside of Job. The noun form of the same root is rendered "case" in v. 3 and "argument" in v. 6. The divine verdict of 42:8 will vindicate Job be-

---

[34] "Altogether silent" translates an infinitive absolute plus imperfect, and this follows that combination of words that introduces an urgent wish (cf. 6:8; 11:5; 14:13; 19:23, etc.), "If only," or "O that." *IBHS* § 35.3.1g translates, "*Would to God* you would be silent!" *GBH* § 123j explains the infinitive as expressing perfection and translates, "I wish to God that you would be completely quiet!"

[35] Clines (*Job 1–20*, 276, 309) translates "begin (legal) proceedings against." He notes that showing partiality as a witness would be a crime.

cause God said of them, "You have not spoken of me what is right, as my servant Job has."

13:11 "Splendor" and "terrify" are both uncommon but not uncertain words. The former is from the verb *nāśā'*, "lift up," hence "that which is lifted up" or "splendor/glory."[36] Though the words of this verse do not describe Job's reaction to the theophany in chaps. 38–41, they would be appropriate. We are not told how God spoke to the friends in 42:7-9; whatever the means, it must have been a terrifying experience (cf. 31:23).

13:12 "Your maxims" (*zikrōnêkem*) is from the root meaning "remember" and might be translated "reminders."[37] One can almost picture Job grasping a handful of ashes from where he was sitting as he spoke these words and letting them sift through his fingers (2:8). Then he might have picked up a potsherd and broken it as he spoke the second line. Several commentators and translations render *gab* not as "defenses" but "replies/answers."[38] It fits better with the parallelism but rests on cognates in Aramaic and Arabic.

(5) Advice and Testimony (13:13-19)

> [13]"Keep silent and let me speak;
>   then let come to me what may.
> [14]Why do I put myself in jeopardy
>   and take my life in my hands?
> [15]Though he slay me, yet will I hope in him;
>   I will surely defend my ways to his face.
> [16]Indeed, this will turn out for my deliverance,
>   for no godless man would dare come before him!
> [17]Listen carefully to my words;
>   let your ears take in what I say.
> [18]Now that I have prepared my case,
>   I know I will be vindicated.
> [19]Can anyone bring charges against me?
>   If so, I will be silent and die.

Couched in the middle of this section is one of the high points of Job's

---

[36] Apart from seven references to "swelling" in Leviticus, it occurs six other times, including Job 31:23; 41:25[17]. Nearly a fourth of the forty-seven occurrences of "dread," פַחַד, are in Job as well.

[37] NAB, Clines, *Job 1–20*. The KJV has "remembrances"; NKJV has "platitudes."

[38] So *CHAL*. For persuasive support for this see Dhorme, *Job*, 186; Gordis, *Job*, 143; Hartley, *Job*, 218; Clines, *Job 1–20*, 282. Cf. JB, "retorts"; NJPS, "responses."

speeches. But not all agree, and v. 15 has provoked more emendations and alternate translations than almost any verse in the book. Following the NIV text rather than the footnote,[39] I understand v. 15 and this pericope to be a positive affirmation of our hero's faith. Framing the section are words directed to the friends to listen (v. 13) unless they have verifiable accusations to bring (v. 19).

13:13 For the second time in this chapter Job asked his friends to be quiet (v. 5).[40] All parties wanted the last word, but the last word would in the end be God's. "Let come to me what may" expresses Job's determination and his faith in God.[41]

13:14 "Take my life in my hands" is an idiom common to Hebrew and English, but "put myself in jeopardy" translates the idiom "put my flesh in my teeth." The NEB translates it "put my neck in the noose." The REB has "expose myself to danger" (cf. NCV).[42] The answer to Job's question is that he was convinced he was innocent. He was not afraid to meet God or be tried before him. He would rather die proclaiming his innocence than live under the assumed verdict of guilt.

13:15 The crux of the problem is the word *lōʾ* ("not") in the first line of the Masoretic Text. These same Masoretes had an alternate tradition, however, to read it *lō* ("to/for/in him"; reflected in the MT margin). The former produces a text with a sense of hopelessness on Job's part.[43] The latter makes this one of the few positive statements of faith from the lips of our hero, in line with 1:21 and 2:10.[44] John Calvin attempted to retain

---

[39] "He will surely slay me; I have no hope." This alternate translation correctly reflects that there is no word "yet" in the Hebrew. Also note that the initial הֵן can have various translations.

[40] The cohortative force of "Let me speak" accurately represents the paragogic ה on the verb and the independent personal pronoun אָנִי, "I."

[41] The expression "what may" translates the simple interrogative מָה. A similar use is found in 2 Sam 18:22. The translation "then" is only suggested by the context (see *GBH* § 115c).

[42] "Life" (נֶפֶשׁ) can mean "throat." If a translation were to keep the idiom about "flesh" and "teeth" in the first stich, perhaps the second should say something about putting the hands to the throat. Cf. Tur-Sinai, *Job*, 224-25.

[43] See NIV footnote, NRSV, JB, GNB. The attitude of hopelessness may be mitigated somewhat by translating יִקְטְלֵנִי in the first line as a modal, "He may slay me" (with Clines, *Job 1–20;* the NJPS translates the second clause similarly, "I may have no hope"), or mitigated further by translating as a conditional with הֵן, "If he were to slay me" (Hartley, *Job*). Beginning Hebrew students often practice their paradigms with the verb קטל, which occurs elsewhere only in 24:14 and Ps 139:19.

[44] So KJV, RV, MLB, NAB, Guillaume, Andersen. E. B. Smick (*Job* 4:922-23) accepts the written text but explains the sense, "Even if slain he would not wait . . . but would defend his ways before God and was sure God would vindicate him."

both the written text and the confidence of Job by turning the line into a
rhetorical question, "Shall I not hope?"[45] M. Dahood suggested that $lō'$
could be an asseverative, "surely."[46] The verb $yḥl$ ("hope") is read as
"hesitate" by the NEB,[47] "quaver" by AB, and "be quiet" by Gordis.[48] In
the end it is the context that shapes the translator's choice, and I tilt toward the traditional rendering of the KJV and NIV on the basis of vv.
15b,16a, and especially v. 18b. Andersen asserts that "this speech expresses the strongest confidence of Job in both his innocence and God's
justice."[49] Job reasoned that though God might consider him presumptuous and slay him, Job would wait in hope, trusting him to do otherwise.
The larger context of this speech (chaps. 12–14) and all of Job's responses are more negative than positive, but that is no reason to eliminate
those glimmers of hope and those flashes of faith that punctuate these
otherwise depressing chapters. The second line is relatively clear, except
the initial particle $'ak$ may be translated either as an emphatic "surely" or
a restrictive "nevertheless/but."[50] The verb $ykḥ$ ("defend") is translated
"rebuke" in v. 10.[51]

13:16 "Deliverance" translates $yĕšûâ$, elsewhere rendered "salvation" (Exod 15:2 and over sixty times in Psalms and Isaiah; it is the Hebrew equivalent of the name "Jesus"). Paul may have had this verse in
mind when he penned Phil 1:19. "Dare" is not in the Hebrew text but reflects an interpretation of the verb "come" as expressing willingness or
desire. Only those who are sure of winning their cases press their suits in
court.

13:17 For the third time in this chapter Job ordered them to listen to
him (vv. 6,13,17).[52] "What I say" translates $'aḥwātî$, which occurs only

---

[45] John Calvin, *Sermons from Job,* trans. L. Nixon (Grand Rapids: Baker, 1952), 71.

[46] M. Dahood, "Two Pauline Quotations from the Old Testament," *CBQ* 17 (1955): 24,
n. 23.

[47] The REB translates the line, "If he wishes to slay me, I have nothing to lose."

[48] Gordis, *Job,* 130, 144. Habel (*Job*) has "wait [silently]." It is also used in 6:11;
14:14; 30:26. Andersen (*Job,* TOTC [Downers Grove: InterVarsity, 1976], 166) identifies
the issue of this word's meaning as the chief problem of the verse.

[49] Andersen, *Job,* 166.

[50] The latter is the understanding of most, including KJV, NASB, NRSV, Hartley,
Clines, Gordis, and Dhorme.

[51] J. G. Janzen notes that the nominal form of this verb occurs in 9:33 (translated
"someone to arbitrate" in NIV: "There Job had longed for an umpire, a referee or adjudica-
tor, to equalize the discrepancy between the dread power of God and fearful Job (9:34). By
now Job is willing to argue his own case" (*Job,* INT [Atlanta: John Knox, 1985], 107).

[52] Only here he uses the emphatic form with an infinitive absolute. *GBH* § 123l translates "listen well, listen closely."

here.[53] There is no verb in the second line. Literally it reads "and my speaking in your ears."

13:18 Job's confidence in the rightness of his cause appears again here. Usually the verb translated "vindicated" is in a question format and comes from the friends (cf. 4:17; 11:2; 15:14; 22:3; 25:4) or is in the subjunctive (9:15,20; 10:15; 35:7), but this sentence can hardly be taken other than as declarative and indicative. To this verse Elihu will allude in 34:5 when he quotes Job (cf. 32:2; 40:8).

13:19 Job's confidence in the legitimacy of his complaint appears again in v. 19. He was persuaded that no one could "bring charges" against him. If so, he was prepared to shut up and die. He was silent when God spoke out of the whirlwind, but he did not die.[54]

(6) Address to God (13:20–14:22)

20"Only grant me these two things, O God,
   and then I will not hide from you:
21Withdraw your hand far from me,
   and stop frightening me with your terrors.
22Then summon me and I will answer,
   or let me speak, and you reply.
23How many wrongs and sins have I committed?
   Show me my offense and my sin.
24Why do you hide your face
   and consider me your enemy?
25Will you torment a windblown leaf?
   Will you chase after dry chaff?
26For you write down bitter things against me
   and make me inherit the sins of my youth.
27You fasten my feet in shackles;
   you keep close watch on all my paths
   by putting marks on the soles of my feet.

28"So man wastes away like something rotten,
   like a garment eaten by moths.

1"Man born of woman
   is of few days and full of trouble.
2He springs up like a flower and withers away;
   like a fleeting shadow, he does not endure.

---

[53] BDB understands it as an Aramaic *afel* infinitive from חוה III, "tell/declare."

[54] "Die" (גוע) is another Joban word with eight of its twenty-three occurrences and six of them from the lips of Job himself.

³Do you fix your eye on such a one?
   Will you bring him before you for judgment?
⁴Who can bring what is pure from the impure?
   No one!
⁵Man's days are determined;
   you have decreed the number of his months
   and have set limits he cannot exceed.
⁶So look away from him and let him alone,
   till he has put in his time like a hired man.

⁷"At least there is hope for a tree;
   If it is cut down, it will sprout again,
   and its new shoots will not fail.
⁸Its roots may grow old in the ground
   and its stump die in the soil,
⁹yet at the scent of water it will bud
   and put forth shoots like a plant.
¹⁰But man dies and is laid low;
   he breathes his last and is no more.
¹¹As water disappears from the sea
   or a riverbed becomes parched and dry,
¹²so man lies down and does not rise;
   till the heavens are no more, men will not awake
   or be roused from their sleep.

¹³"If only you would hide me in the grave
   and conceal me till your anger has passed!
   If only you would set me a time
   and then remember me!
¹⁴If a man dies, will he live again?
   All the days of my hard service
   I will wait for my renewal to come.
¹⁵You will call and I will answer you;
   you will long for the creature your hands have made.
¹⁶Surely then you will count my steps
   but not keep track of my sin.
¹⁷My offenses will be sealed up in a bag;
   you will cover over my sin.

¹⁸"But as a mountain erodes and crumbles
   and as a rock is moved from its place,
¹⁹as water wears away stones
   and torrents wash away the soil,
   so you destroy man's hope.
²⁰You overpower him once for all, and he is gone;
   you change his countenance and send him away.

²¹If his sons are honored, he does not know it;
if they are brought low, he does not see it.
²²He feels but the pain of his own body
and mourns only for himself."

Though the name of God does not appear anywhere in this prayer (NIV added it in 13:20), the second person pronouns are singular from here on, and that indicates a different addressee.[55] The themes that fill this chapter and a half are ones we have heard before and will hear again: desire for a hearing, rumination on the brevity of life, and despair that death ends all. As in the middle of chap. 13, however, there is a glimmer of hope in 14:13-17, which draws the Christian's attention like a gold nugget sparkling in a gravel pit.

RELENT AND EXPLAIN (13:20-28). These were Job's two basic requests of God: "Stop afflicting me, and explain why I am suffering." In this section Job had little hope of satisfaction.

13:20 An awkward Hebrew first line—"Only two things do not do with regard to me"—is altered in the NIV into a positive request by reading the negative ʾal as ʾēl, "God." Most think the two things are the parallel items of v. 21, God's hand and his terrors.[56] God had to meet these two conditions if Job were to argue his case before him. Job did not want to be hidden from God any longer (v. 24).[57] It becomes clear from the imperatives in the following verses, however, that Job had more requests: "Summon me," "let me speak," "reply" (v. 22), and "show me my offense" (v. 23). In 14:13 he would pray that God would "hide" him in the grave, but his desire there was to be hidden only from God's anger, not from God himself.

13:21 The "hand" of God in Scripture can be either blessed (e.g., Neh 2:8,18) or frightening (Ps 139:5; Heb 10:31). Clearly it was the afflicting hand of God that Job wanted removed. Both "frighten" (bʿt) and "terrors" (ʾêmâ) are favorite Joban words.[58] As elsewhere Job was referring to the tragedies of chap. 1 and the skin disease of chap. 2.

---

[55] The RSV, NEB, NASB have a system whereby humans are addressed as "you" and "your" but deity as "thou," "thee," and "thy" (complete with the archaic second person verbs, e.g., "dost" and "wilt"); the latter begin at this point.

[56] E.g., Gordis, *Job*, 145; Clines, *Job 1–20*, 316-17.

[57] Andersen (*Job,* 167) prefers a passive translation of the *niphal* סתר and notes that the same phrase occurs in Gen 4:14 with the addition here of "not."

[58] "Frighten" (בעת) is in 3:5; 7:14; 9:34; 13:11,21; 15:24; 18:11; 33:7; and only eight places elsewhere. "Terror," אֵימָה, is in 9:34; 13:21; 20:25; 33:7; 39:20; 41:14[6]; and eleven places elsewhere.

13:22   Job offered God a choice. If God would call him, he would answer. Or if Job spoke first, he expected God to respond. His frustration was that God said nothing, leaving him to stagger and rage in doubt and despair.

13:23   Four words for "sin" (one used twice[59]) dominate v. 23.[60] This request was central to Job's complaints because the friends' point that suffering implies sin was not foreign to his own thinking.[61] Somehow suffering is easier to endure if we know the reason for it. Taking it one step further, Rabbi Levi Isaac ben Meir of Berdichev said, "What I want to know is not why I suffer, but whether I suffer for Thy sake."[62]

13:24   In v. 20 Job had requested not to be hidden from God. In v. 24 he asked why God was hiding from him (cf. Ps 13:1[2]). More than that, Job sensed that God was not merely neutral but actively hunting him down, treating him as an "enemy." Similar wording is in 19:11.

13:25   Job compared himself to a "windblown leaf" (cf. Lev 26:36) and dry chaff, both worthless and useless. He implied that it was beneath God's dignity to spend effort tormenting and chasing these tokens of a life that once was.

13:26   Easier to understand than the first, the second line asserts that God kept detailed records and punished sins committed long ago, a belief alluded to in Ps 25:7. Assuming the first line must say essentially the same thing, various emendations have been made to the word *mĕrōrôt* "bitter things," but that is not necessary in light of that root's use in Hab 1:6 and Judg 18:25, where it means "savage/fierce/violent." Rather than trying to adjust the object, Clines comes to a viable solution by understanding that "write down" is parallel to "make inherit," hence, "You ordain me to suffer bitterness."

13:27   "Shackles" occurs only here and in 33:11, but it is known from Syriac and Aramaic. The first two lines are easily understood, but the third employs an idiom or reflects some practice that is unknown to us. Literally it reads, "On the roots of my feet you engrave."[63] Some, like the NIV, assume it refers to branding of the feet; and that notion fits somewhat with the first line. Clines has "take note of my footprints," an

---

[59] Along with many others elsewhere in the OT, J. S. Kselman noted the *ABCB* pattern in this list, "The *ABCB* Pattern: Further Examples," *VT* 32 (1982): 228.

[60] See K. Koch, *TDOT* 4:309-13.

[61] As pointed out in *The NIV Study Bible,* Job "does not yet understand that God has a higher purpose in his suffering" (p. 748).

[62] In *Leo Rosten's Treasury of Jewish Quotations* (New York: McGraw-Hill, 1972), 498.

[63] The verb is חָקֹּֽה תִתְחַקֶּ, which looks like a *hithpael* of חָקַק, "engrave."

idea that fits well with the second line.[64] The NJPS translation "hemming in my footsteps" is apparently idiomatic. Similarly, "you set a bound for the soles of my feet" (NRSV) makes little sense. Apart from the uncertainties of the third line, the gist of the verse is like others where Job complained of God's dogged surveillance (7:19; 10:6).

13:28 Verse 28 is detached from the preceding and almost fits better with what follows in chap. 14. It is a hinge to connect the ideas of worthlessness (v. 25) with the subject that follows, namely, the brevity of life. We and all we have decay and rot away like rusty metal, soggy wood, or mothy wool (Matt 6:19-20; Luke 12:33; Jas 5:2).

BREVITY OF LIFE (14:1-6). All the wisdom literature touches on the theme that life is brief: Job in 7:6, Bildad in 8:9, Moses in Ps 90:10, David in 1 Chr 29:15, Qoheleth in Eccl 6:12, Solomon in Prov 10:27b, Isaiah in 40:7, and James in 4:14. Without the hope that the fuller perspective of the New Testament provides, such a passage as this is dreary, dismal, and depressing.

14:1 "Man born of woman" is a poetic way of saying "everyone." Contrary to the claims of the friends (8:12-13), the situation described here applies to righteous and wicked alike. There is a kind of contrast in the next two phrases. Our "days" are too "few," and our "troubles" (cf. 3:17,26) are too many; in fact, we are "full" of them. The verb form of the noun translated "trouble" means "tremble/quake" as in an earthquake (9:6; 1 Sam 14:15). It also describes persons trembling because of inner turmoil (2 Sam 18:33; Isa 14:2; 32:10-11).

14:2 Job compared the brevity of life to a "flower," quickly springing up and soon withering away,[65] and to a "shadow" that vanishes at noon or at sunset. The figure of the dying flower is used in Jas 1:10; Pss 37:2; 90:5-6; and Isa 40:6-7. Bildad, David, and Qoheleth compared life to a shadow (Job 8:9; 1 Chr 29:15; Pss 102:11; 144:4; Eccl 6:12).

14:3 Verse 3 consists of two questions with implied answers of yes. God apparently had fixed his eye on Job and would bring him to judgment.[66] S. Cox clarifies Job's point: "Can it be right, then, that a creature

---

[64] Pope (*Job*) notes that a brand on the foot of a slave would leave telltale footprints should he or she run away—very imaginative but without support. *IBHS* § 26.2e understands the *hithpael* form of the verb as "benefactive reflexive" and translates, "You *put slave markings* [for yourself] on the soles of my feet."

[65] "Withers away" is from נמל‎, מול‎, or מלל‎, "cut off." The expected verb is נבל‎, "wither/fade," which is parallel to our verb in Ps 37:2, its only occurrence outside of Job.

[66] As the NIV footnote indicates, Greek, Latin, and Syriac read "him," while the Masoretic Text has "me." Orthographically it is a minor difference. "Me" is אתי‎, and "him" is אתו‎. Nevertheless, sense-wise Job had been speaking of himself indirectly in the third person, not the first.

so frail, so evanescent, so laden with sorrow, should be dogged with a suspicious and incessant vigilance, and called to a stern judicial account?"[67]

14:4 This short verse, a question and an answer, presents the cardinal theological doctrine of total depravity. We do not know whether Job was thinking back to Adam; but the fallenness of the race, inherited sin, and associated doctrines all relate to this simple verse (cf. 15:14; 25:4; Pss 14:1b; 51:5[7]; John 3:6; Rom 5:12). God made one original pair of parents in Eden so that none of us can boast about our parentage being any different from anyone else. Job never claimed to be sinless, only that his sin was an insufficient explanation for his suffering. In view of the sinful condition of humanity, he demanded to know why his sins deserved such treatment.

14:5 In this tricolon "days," "months," and "limits"[68] are parallel as are also "determined," "decreed," and "set." "Decreed" is not, however, in the Hebrew. The text reads, "The number of his months is with you." The verse teaches that God's sovereignty controls human life spans. Such a truth should not lead to despair but to assurance and hope. Our times are in his hands (Eccl 3:1-2a,11a).

14:6 In 7:1-2 Job compared his life to that of a slave yearning for quitting time. Here again, using the third person rather than the first, he thinly veiled his own feelings by picturing God as a glowering taskmaster ready to whip a weary worker.

FINALITY OF DEATH (14:7-17). This now-familiar theme in Job's speeches surfaces again toward the close of this long response to Zophar (because it closes the first cycle, it may be considered a response to all three friends). A happy turn of perspective and another glimmer of hope punctuate this otherwise dismal chapter. While Job expected to die, he reflected on the possibility of life after death in 14:13-15.

For All Humankind (14:7-12). Two illustrations from nature fill this pericope. People are not like trees that grow back after they are cut down. They are like the water that disappears in a dry gulch.

14:7 The sense of this comparison is obvious. Trees often come to life even though they have been felled because the root system is intact. Two key words are in this verse, "hope" and "sprout." "Hope," which occurs eleven times elsewhere in Job, more than in any other book, will re-

---

[67] S. Cox, *A Commentary on the Book of Job*, 2d ed. (London: Kegan Paul, Trench & Co., 1885), 170.

[68] "His limits" was written חֻקּוֹ, singular, "his limit"; but the Masoretes read (*qere*) as חֻקָּיו, "his limits," commonly "statutes." In the sense of "limits" cf. Job 14:13; 26:10; 38:10. It is a difference of little consequence.

appear in v. 19. Here a tree has hope; according to v. 19 God "destroys man's hope." The noun form of the verb "sprout" occurs in v. 14 translated "renewal." While the meaning is clear here, at v. 14 there is considerable disagreement.

14:8 The protasis of this two-verse sentence states that a tree may be long truncated, its stump dead and roots long buried; but life is still present despite appearances.

14:9 As the apodosis, v. 9 says that roots of felled trees can and do come to life at the "scent of water." Once more they may "bud" and "put forth shoots." Perhaps Job had in mind the olive tree that can live over a thousand years. Large parts of the tree look dead, but living and productive branches are still growing.

14:10 But a *geber* ("man") or *ʾādām* ("he") is not like a tree. They are "laid low" (*ḥālaš*, a rare root that has occasioned several emendations and alternate translations). Clines explains that it refers to "human loss of power after death as contrasted with the tree's continuing vitality after it is cut down."[69] The last word, "and is no more," has traditionally been read as an interrogative particle plus pronominal suffix, "Where is he?" The NIV alone of the standard versions reads here the negative particle with suffix.[70]

14:11 The second and shorter illustration is of water that "disappears from the sea" or a river that dries up. The oceans do not dry up, but *yām* can refer to lakes; these can dry up.[71] Two synonymous verbs describe what happens to a river in the dry season (cf. 6:15-17; Isa 19:5).

14:12 The NIV, like most translations, takes the *waw* as a comparative, "so."[72] "Till the heavens are no more" means eternally (cf. Deut

---

[69] Clines, *Job 1–20*, 329 (see also p. 284). He translates, "As man, when he dies, loses every power." The verb חלש occurs elsewhere only in Exod 17:13, "overcame," and Isa 14:12, "laid low." Noun derivatives occur in Exod 32:18, "defeat," and Joel 3:10[4:10], "weakling."

[70] KB, 35, and BDB, 32, read from אֵי, "where?" In Exod 2:20 the same form וְאַיּוֹ occurs, with the NIV translation, "And where is he?" The NIV translates the form without *waw* in 20:7, "Where is he?" See also 2 Kgs 19:13; Mic 7:10. Clines (*Job 1–20*, 329) explains that the answer intended was "in Sheol." The negative particle with suffix would normally be אֵינֶנּוּ as in Gen 5:24; 42:36, "He is no more" (cf. "I will be no more" in 7:8). Support for the NIV interpretation as a negative is in the LXX's οὐκέτι ἔστιν, in the prefix found in 1 Sam 4:21 (אִי כָבוֹד, "Ichabod"), and in Job 22:30 (אִי נָקִי, "not innocent," an interpretation that is questioned by some). M. Dahood ("The Conjunction *wn* and Negative *î* in Hebrew," *UF* 14 [1982]: 51-54) favors the NIV interpretation.

[71] Dhorme offers another worthy interpretation, that is, that the sea and the rivers will dry up before a man lives again, *Job*, 199-200. See also Hartley, *Job*, 234-35.

[72] See *GBH* § 174h.

11:21; Isa 51:6; Jer 31:35-36; Pss 72:5; 89:29,36-37; 102:25-27) "men will not awake." At this point Job spoke tentatively of the journey to the grave as one of no return (cf. 10:21; 16:22; Eccl 15:5c). As Hartley explains, "In the present world order no evidence exists that a person may return to life."[73] This, however, was not Job's last thought on the subject.

Job's Hope after Death (14:13-17). In the midst of the resignation and gloom that precedes and follows this subsection, there appears this extraordinary affirmation of hope that one day Job would experience "renewal" (v. 14), converse with God, and have his sins forgiven and forgotten.[74]

14:13 The passage begins with the wish formula we have seen elsewhere, literally "who will give," "if only," or simply "O that" (cf. Job 6:8; 11:5; 13:5; 19:23; 23:3; 29:2; 31:35). His desire was that God would let him die and enjoy the safety of the grave (again *šĕ'ôl*) until his present wrath was over.[75] The third and fourth lines could be rendered: "Then set me a time and remember me."[76]

14:14 Andersen argues that vv. 14-17 serve as the high point of Job's speech and reaffirm his faith expressed in 13:15.[77] The question of v. 14 is one question in the book where the answer is not certain. It is not a rhetorical question but really sounds as if Job were asking for information. Will people rise from the dead? Though it goes contrary to much of what Job said before and after, at this point he appeared to believe. Even trying to divest ourselves of the additional revelation of the New Testament, which Job did not have, it still sounds like Job affirmed a hope in the resurrection (see 19:27 and comments there).

"Hard service" is *ṣābā'*, usually "army/war," but cf. this use in 7:1; Isa

---

[73] Hartley, *Job*, 234.

[74] S. Cox (*Job*, 173) explains: "Brooding in awe and wonder over the fate of man, in his recoil from the very conviction to which he had felt his way, that a tree is more vital than a man, his mind springs aloft in disdain of so base a conclusion, and at least for an instant he catches a glimpse of life and immortality." If a tree should rise at the scent of water, so also should man when "touched by the Divine 'breath.'"

[75] The central question here is life after death. None of the ancillary issues arising from the NT, e.g., soul sleep or how a tribulation fits into an eschatological calendar, is addressed by these hope passages in Job. Clines' observation, however (*Job 1–20*, 330), that this passage describes "God hiding someone from God himself" and "a God beyond the God he is now experiencing" furnishes food for thought from an NT perspective. He also mentions (p. 331) a possible relationship between Job's idea of God's anger passing and such passages as Gen 8:1; Ps 30:5; Isa 54:8.

[76] Pope, *Job*, 99.

[77] Andersen, *Job*, 170.

40:2. "Renewal" (*ḥălîpātî*) is the most important word. In most of the other nine places where this noun occurs, it means "changes" of clothes (e.g., Gen 45:22), an idea that Paul used in 1 Cor 15:53-54 to describe the resurrection.[78] The verb *ḥlp* is more frequent (twenty-eight times in Hebrew and three times in the Aramaic of Daniel) and has a variety of translations usually having to do with "change/pass." Contexts supporting the sense of "renewal/new life" are 14:7 ("sprout") and 29:20 ("ever new").[79]

14:15 One of Job's complaints had been that God had avoided him and not answered him. These very verbs were Job's demands in 13:22. Later those demands would be met because God not only would "call" and Job "answer," but God also would "long for the creature" he made (see 7:8 and comments there).

14:16 Among the blessed changes would be God's counting his steps (cf. 13:27; 31:4), not like a hunter tracking the prey or a spy following a lead but like a father watching his child walk (Pss 85:13; 119:133). Job's sins would be overlooked in this new state of affairs.[80]

14:17 Two additional categories for "sin" appear here, thus encompassing all the categories for which Job might have been charged. The verse has two nice illustrations for how God would handle those sins. He would seal them up in a bag and plaster them over. The verb in the second line appeared in 13:4, "smear." The JB has "whiten," and several versions have "coat over." Job anticipated the obliteration of his sins on that great day of "renewal," and as a result he would be white as snow or wool (Isa 1:18).

ABSENCE OF HOPE (14:18-22). Unfortunately the clouds of doubt and despair closed in swiftly, and Job did not end this first cycle of speeches on the high and bright notes of the preceding stanza. Verse 18 picks up where v. 12 left off, comparing the fleeting days of mortals to eroding mountains.

---

[78] See also 10:17, where it occurs with צבא.

[79] Those predisposed to disbelieve there could be any talk of resurrection at this early period explain the passage as a whole and the word "renewal" on the analogy of its negative uses, "pass away/wither" (Isa 2:18, "disappear") and ignore the ones listed in the discussion, 14:7 in particular. Pope (*Job*) has "relief," Gordis has "release" in the sense of a soldier concluding his tour of duty (*Job*, 132, 150), and the NJPS has "replacement." Some (AB, JB, NAB, AAT, NJPS, NRSV, and Driver, *Job*, 40) blunt these affirmations by casting the verbs of v. 14 onward into a subjunctive mood, "would" (as NIV has done in v. 13 only).

[80] The REB must have taken לא as a negative affirmation (following Driver, *Job*, 40) in order to read "watching all my errant course.

14:18 This and v. 19 form a series of four analogies from nature (two pairs) to human hopelessness. In v. 18 the poet describes eroding mountains and dislodged rocks. At the foot of every cliff is the debris that once was up on the cliff. Every year more of the mountain falls away.

14:19 The second illustration is similar. "Water wears away[81] stones" and the soil suffers erosion.[82] The third line is the point of these two verses. Like wind and water, God destroys man's hope for preservation in this life (see comments on "hope" at 14:7).

14:20 The term translated "once for all" (*lāneṣaḥ*) is usually "forever," and for that reason some connect it with the second verb, "he is gone."[83] It is not certain what "change his countenance" means.[84] The GNB paraphrased it, "His face is twisted in death."

14:21 In Job's view death ended all communication with the world of the living. If a man's sons "are brought low/humiliated," it is just as well that he "does not see it." But if they "are honored,"[85] it is too bad that he "does not know it" (cf. Eccl 9:5).

14:22 "Body" and "soul" (which the NIV renders as "self") constitute the entirety of a person who suffers—physical pain and mental anguish. It is a sad and sour note for Job to end on, but the book is not over.

---

[81] This verb occurs only four times in the Bible: Exod 30:36, "grind"; 2 Sam 22:43; Ps 18:42[43], "beat." It may be onomatopoeic, שָׁחַק.

[82] Ancient farmers were well aware of erosion and went to extreme measures to conserve both the water and the soil that washed down the normally dry river beds.

[83] So Vg., *in perpetuum pertransiert;* Dhorme, *Job,* 205; MLB; and Andersen, *Job,* 173-74. The NEB's and REB's "finally" works with either verb and carries the sense well.

[84] B. Halpern, comparing this phrase in the Amarna tablets, argues for, "He contemplates treachery" ("Yhwh's Summary of Justice in Job xiv 20," *VT* 28 [1978]: 472-74). For more discussion see Hartley, *Job,* 239, n. 5.

[85] "Honored" and "brought low" constitute a merismus, one of several in Job (see 1:20). Some are pointed out in the commentary, and others are listed in J. Krasovec, "Merism-Polar Expression in Biblical Hebrew," *Bib* 64 (1983): 231-39.

7. Eliphaz Accuses Job of Folly (15:1-35)
    (1) Rebuke (15:1-13)
        Job Has Sinned by What He Said (15:1-6)
        Job Is Ignorant and Arrogant (15:7-13)
    (2) On God and Human Sinfulness (15:14-16)
    (3) Lessons from the Past (15:17-35)
        Appeal to Tradition (15:17-19)
        The Wicked Get What They Deserve (15:20-35)
            Present Woes (15:20-26)
            Future Grief (15:27-35)
8. Job Reproaches His Pitiless Friends and Prays for Relief
        (16:1–17:16)
    (1) Criticism of Friends (16:1-5)
    (2) Complaint to God (16:6-14)
    (3) Plea of Innocence (16:15-17)
    (4) Hope for Vindication (16:18-21)
    (5) Prospect of a Near and Unhappy Death (16:22–17:2)
    (6) Address to God (17:3-5)
    (7) More Complaint (17:6-8)
    (8) Innocence and Hope in Death (17:9)
    (9) More Despair (17:10-16)
        The Worthlessness of the Friends (17:10-12)
        Hope Only in Death (17:13-16)
9. Bildad: The Wicked Are Punished (18:1-21)
    (1) Criticism of Job (18:1-4)
    (2) Dynamistic Retribution on the Wicked (18:5-21)
10. Job, Despite His Friends, Looks to His Redeemer (19:1-29)
    (1) Criticism of Friends (19:1-6)
    (2) Complaint against God (19:7-20)
        The Legal Case Is Lopsided (19:7-12)
        Forsaken by Friends (19:13-20)
    (3) Plea to Friends and Family(19:21-22)
    (4) Testimony of Hope (19:23-27)
    (5) Advice to Friends (19:28-29)

7. Eliphaz Accuses Job of Folly (15:1-35)

Here begins the second round of speeches with all the participants following the same order as in the first. In Eliphaz's second speech, some of
the themes are the same (rebuke and appeal to tradition). Since Eliphaz
was the first speaker in the first round, there was no reflection on what
Job said. But in this speech he began by berating Job for what he said.

(1) Rebuke (15:1-13)

¹Then Eliphaz the Temanite replied:
²"Would a wise man answer with empty notions
    or fill his belly with the hot east wind?
³Would he argue with useless words,
    with speeches that have no value?
⁴But you even undermine piety
    and hinder devotion to God.
⁵Your sin prompts your mouth;
    you adopt the tongue of the crafty.
⁶Your own mouth condemns you, not mine;
    your own lips testify against you.
⁷"Are you the first man ever born?
    Were you brought forth before the hills?
⁸Do you listen in on God's council?
    Do you limit wisdom to yourself?
⁹What do you know that we do not know?
    What insights do you have that we do not have?
¹⁰The gray-haired and the aged are on our side,
    men even older than your father.
¹¹Are God's consolations not enough for you,
    words spoken gently to you?
¹²Why has your heart carried you away,
    and why do your eyes flash,
¹³so that you vent your rage against God
    and pour out such words from your mouth?

Rebuke is one of the elements present in almost every speech of the
friends, and as the debate goes on, the rebukes become sharper. Eliphaz
almost apologized at the beginning of his first discourse (4:2a). Here, as
in the other two, he was less courteous and more direct.

JOB HAS SINNED BY WHAT HE SAID (15:1-6). Now that Job had
spoken three times, Eliphaz had much to which he could react. And react
he did with uncivil and arrogant criticism and accusation.

15:1 See comments at 4:1.

15:2 A little of the poetic flavor is lost by obscuring the first of two parallel words for wind in this verse. The AT and RSV reflect it better, rendering the first line, "Should a wise man answer with windy knowledge?"[1] The "hot east wind" (*qādîm*) came off the desert and was particularly unwelcome in May and October.[2] Eliphaz's point of comparison seems an acceptance of Job's bait in 6:26.

15:3 The second pair of questions used no analogies but directly asked whether Job would "argue" (see comment on 13:10) his case with words that *are* not *useful* and speeches that do not *have value*. Job's words are described by two verbs, the first appearing in this form (*qal*) only in Job (22:2; 34:9; 35:3), meaning "be of use." The second is better represented, especially in Isaiah and Jeremiah as they harangued the people for going after things/gods/nations that could not "profit."[3]

15:4 What Eliphaz had in mind when he made the charges of v. 4 is not clear. Perhaps he was referring to the ways that Job challenged God, treating him more like a litigant in court than like deity in heaven. The Temanite used the word "piety/fear" in 4:6 (cf. 1:1,8; 2:3; 22:4; 28:28).

15:5 "Prompts" (*ʾālep*) is used elsewhere only in 33:33; 35:11; Prov 22:25 ("teach/learn"; cf. Matt 12:34; Jas 3:6).[4] "Crafty" (along with "piety") is another word unique to Eliphaz (cf. 5:12-13). In Proverbs the word usually means "prudent," but this context demands a pejorative tone.

15:6 Although he did not actually quote from Job's speeches, Eliphaz still declared that Job condemned himself by what he said (cf. 1:22). Job had said something very similar to this in 9:20, that God would condemn him regardless of what he said. Eliphaz presumed Job was guilty, and thus anything he said would compound his guilt.

JOB IS IGNORANT AND ARROGANT (15:7-13). Eliphaz charged Job with hubris of the worst kind because he presumed to know more than Eliphaz and his friends, more than the elders, and, by implication, more than the mind of God, and because he spoke angrily to and about God.

---

[1] The phrase in this line is דַעַת־רוּחַ. F. I. Andersen notes that to Eliphaz, Job was a "windbag" whose speeches were "an excretion of belly wind" (*Job*, TOTC [Downers Grove: InterVarsity, 1976], 175).

[2] קָדִים is not the term in 1:19 although that "mighty wind swept in from the desert." See E. Russell, "East Wind," in *ZPEB* 2:180. In Mediterranean countries it is the "sirocco," a word that comes from an Arabic term for "east."

[3] Cf. Isa 30:5-6; 44:9-10; 57:12; Jer 2:8,11; 7:8; 12:13; 16:19; 23:32. The exact phrase occurs with the negative in Prov 11:4. Eliphaz accused Job of the sin of unprofitable speech mentioned centuries later in Titus 3:9.

[4] The verb is also the first letter of the alphabet, hence the connection between learning the alphabet and reading. See M. D. Coogan, "*ʾlp. *ʾlp, 'To Be an Abecedarian,'" *JAOS* 110 (1990): 322.

15:7 Of the four main words for "man/mankind" in Job, it is significant that in this verse, which speaks of the "first man," *ʾādām* is used.[5]

15:8 Though the word "council" is not in chaps. 1–2, those scenes
come to mind in connection with Eliphaz's question. Did the author of
the book have that discussion between Yahweh and the Satan in mind? Of
course, Job was not there, but neither was Eliphaz. We were present, as
readers, and so we know that Eliphaz was fundamentally wrong in his
castigation of Job (cf. Jer 23:18). "Limit" (*gāraʿ*) was in v. 4, "hinder."
Eliphaz was denying everything we are told about Job in the opening
verses of the book (cf. 15:4).

15:9 There is an echo of 12:3 and 13:2 in this verse, except that
Eliphaz was exaggerating Job's claims to knowledge. Each party claimed
that he knew as much as the other and that what they were discussing
was common knowledge anyway.

15:10 Eliphaz, the traditionalist, appealed to the wisdom of the aged
(v. 10) and of the ages (v. 18). Three relatively rare terms describe these
venerable supporters of Eliphaz's position. The first, "gray-haired" (a
participle), appears as a verb elsewhere only in 1 Sam 12:2[6]; the second,
"aged," appears only in Job; and the third literally is "greater than your
father [with respect to] days."[7]

15:11 Since God had not spoken to Job, it is hard to identify his
"consolations." Eliphaz must have had in mind his own words from his
first speech (chaps. 4–5), especially such passages as 5:17-26. He may
have "spoken gently" in the first speech, but all the disputants grew more
caustic through these three long cycles.

15:12 An interrogative particle, *mâ*, begins each half of v. 12, which,
together with v. 13, concludes this subsection. We could answer the question: Job could not reconcile his innocence and his suffering with their
simplistic theology of retribution. He saw no reason for his misery, yet
everyone believed that it must have been caused by sin.

"Flash" (*rzm*) is a hapax but probably a variation of a better established
Aramaic and Syriac word, *rmz*.[8] It is not certain whether the eyes "flash"

---

[5] The four words are אָדָם (twenty-seven times), אִישׁ (twenty-eight times), אֱנוֹשׁ
(thirty-one times), and גֶּבֶר (fifteen times).

[6] A noun form occurs in 1 Kgs 14:4; Gen 15:15; 42:38; Deut 32:25. The participle/noun
form is five times in the Aramaic portions of Ezra (5:5,9; 6:7-8,14).

[7] See *GBH* § 127b. The root כָּבַב I is only in Job (six times as an adjective and twice
as a verb) and Isaiah (four times as a adjective).

[8] NJPS, AB, and Clines (*Job, 1–20*, WBC [Dallas: Word, 1989]) follow Tur-Sinai (*The
Book of Job* [Jerusalem: Kiryat-Sefer, 1967]) in reading something like "weakened" based
on an Aramaic cognate.

(Moffatt, RSV, NIV, etc.), "blink" (NAB), or "wink" (KJV, RV); but "flash with anger" (ICB, NCV) fits best with what follows.

15:13 "Vent your rage" is a bit strong for the literal "turn your spirit," but most translations have something like this. "Vent" is the dynamic equivalence of the Hebrew *rûaḥ,* "spirit." Even from Eliphaz's choice of words it can be said fairly that Job was angry with God.

(2) On God and Human Sinfulness (15:14-16)

> ¹⁴"What is man, that he could be pure,
>   or one born of woman, that he could be righteous?
> ¹⁵If God places no trust in his holy ones,
>   if even the heavens are not pure in his eyes,
> ¹⁶how much less man, who is vile and corrupt,
>   who drinks up evil like water!

The theme of inherent and unavoidable human sinfulness has been heard several times and will be heard again (4:17; 5:7; 9:2; 14:4; 25:4). Eliphaz's words are so eloquent it is a pity they are not more often quoted to support the doctrine of original sin. Though much about the friends was objectionable (e.g., their lack of compassion and their faulty doctrine of suffering and retribution), much of their theology was accurate and can be appropriated today if it is in harmony with the rest of Scripture (the hermeneutical principle of the analogy of Scripture).

15:14 Eliphaz's choice of words reflects Job's (7:17; 14:1,4). The speaker had a low view of native morality and showed with this rhetorical question that people simply cannot be "pure" and "righteous," especially when compared to God.

15:15 In 4:18 Eliphaz spoke of "angels" and "servants" and probably referred to the same superhumans by the term "holy ones." Humans are ruled out because of the parallel to "heavens" in the companion line. Bildad in his brief third speech quoted this passage with alterations (25:4-6).

15:16 Both adjectives "vile" and "corrupt" are strong; the first is from a root that translates "abominate/abhor" in KJV, and the second is from a rare root, *ʾlḥ,* that the KJV renders "filthy" here and in its only other occurrences (Ps 14:3 = Ps 53:3[4]). "Vile/abominable," *tʿb,* is also in Pss 14:1; 53:1[2]. "Who drinks up evil like water" is a way of saying that people sin as easily and as often as they drink water, without giving a thought to it (cf. 5:7).

(3) Lessons from the Past (15:17-35)

¹⁷"Listen to me and I will explain to you;
   let me tell you what I have seen,
¹⁸what wise men have declared,
   hiding nothing received from their fathers
¹⁹(to whom alone the land was given
   when no alien passed among them):
²⁰All his days the wicked man suffers torment,
   the ruthless through all the years stored up for him.
²¹Terrifying sounds fill his ears;
   when all seems well, marauders attack him.
²²He despairs of escaping the darkness;
   he is marked for the sword.
²³He wanders about—food for vultures;
   and knows the day of darkness is at hand.
²⁴Distress and anguish fill him with terror;
   and overwhelm him, like a king poised to attack,
²⁵because he shakes his fist at God
   and vaunts himself against the Almighty,
²⁶defiantly charging against him
   with a thick, strong shield.

²⁷"Though his face is covered with fat
   and his waist bulges with flesh,
²⁸he will inhabit ruined towns
   and houses where no one lives,
   houses crumbling to rubble.
²⁹He will no longer be rich and his wealth will not endure,
   nor will his possessions spread over the land.
³⁰He will not escape the darkness;
   a flame will wither his shoots,
   and the breath of God's mouth will carry him away.
³¹Let him not deceive himself by trusting what is worthless,
   for he will get nothing in return.
³²Before his time he will be paid in full,
   and his branches will not flourish.
³³He will be like a vine stripped of its unripe grapes,
   like an olive tree shedding its blossoms.
³⁴For the company of the godless will be barren,
   and fire will consume the tents of those who love bribes.
³⁵They conceive trouble and give birth to evil;
   their womb fashions deceit."

Eliphaz was at his best when he reasoned from the past. His strongest suit was to pile up illustrations to bolster his major tenet, that is, that the wicked suffer especially for their defiance of the deity. Not far below the surface of his description of the tormented offender was his diagnosis of Job.

APPEAL TO TRADITION (15:17-19). Like Bildad earlier, Eliphaz appealed to traditional wisdom (8:8). In his view (but not in Elihu's [32:9] or Job's [12:12]) old folks are wise folks, so an appeal to them strengthened his case.

15:17 In relating his dream in 4:12-16, Eliphaz introduced his findings as if they were those of an eyewitness. "Seen" is not the expected *rā'â* but *ḥāzâ,* often meaning "to envision/see by revelation."[9] He ordered Job to "listen," *šĕma'* (Deut 6:4), while he explained and told. "Explain" is a rare word found outside of the five Job references only once (Ps 19:2[3]).[10]

15:18 A relative pronoun, "what," begins the verse, tying it closely to the introductory words of v. 17. The word "received" was supplied by the translators, who correctly understood the prepositional phrase "from their fathers" to function as the object of the verb "hiding." Eliphaz was not speaking of hiding something "from their fathers."[11] Eliphaz's point was that this wisdom is indigenous, ancient, and above debate.

15:19 Parentheses are not indicated in the Masoretic Text, but parenthetical statements certainly do occur. Whereas the NIV places v. 19 in parentheses, the RV, RSV, NEB place both vv. 18 and 19 in parentheses; the REB and NRSV have no parentheses (although they have a dash after v. 17 and the REB has a colon after v. 19). The NIV treatment probably is the clearest. Apparently Eliphaz wanted further to underscore the antiquity of the wisdom he was about to unload on Job by noting that their ancestors were the original and unchallenged recipients of "the land/earth."

THE WICKED GET WHAT THEY DESERVE (15:20-35). The message is the same as elsewhere; only the rhetoric is different as the friends one by one presented their basic argument that it is wrongdoers who suffer, and

---

[9] So Ps 63:2[3]; Isa 1:1; 2:1; 13:1; Lam 2:14; Ezek 13:6-8; Amos 1:1; Mic 1:1; Hab 1:1; Zech 10:2. The derived nouns חֹזֶה and חִזָּיוֹן mean "seer" and "vision," respectively.

[10] See Job 15:17; 32:6,10,17; 36:2. It is used fourteen times in the Aramaic sections of Daniel (2:4,6,7,9,10,11,16,24,27, etc.). It is translated "declare" in Ps 19:2[3]. Another translation here is "instruct." See *TDOT* 4:248.

[11] The words כחדו מאבותם, "they hid from their fathers," are often divided to form כ,חדום אבותם, "their fathers hid them." Cf. the RSV, NEB, and their successors the REB and NRSV. Harder to explain is the NAB "and have not contradicted since the days of their fathers."

God's incontestable justice is behind the punishment.

Present Woes (15:20-26). Eliphaz's presentation is in two sections. This first half describes in the present tense what evil people endure. It must be noted that tenses hardly exist in Hebrew poetry and that the system of perfect and imperfect verbs has little of the precision that it does in narrative portions of the Old Testament. It is largely up to translators whether to make statements past, present, or future.

15:20 The verb translated "suffer torment" in other forms refers to a mother writhing in childbirth (cf. Job 39:1; Ps 51:5[7]; Prov 8:24-25).[12] The second line is literally "the number of years are stored up for the ruthless." The idea is that the ruthless also suffer torment for a preset period of time. Once more the author's inclination toward predestination is evident (14:5).

15:21 The first clause is verbless, so the NIV has supplied the verb "fills." The KJV supplies "is." "Terrifying sounds" is literally "the sound of terrors." The noun "terror" (*pāḥad*) and its synonyms are sprinkled all through the debates from 3:24 to 31:23 and are heard from the lips of all three friends and Job. They are dealing with serious issues, and "it is a dreadful thing to fall into the hands of the living God" (Heb 10:31). "When all seems well" translates the phrase "in peace."

15:22 From the frights occasioned by "terrifying sounds" and attacking muggers, the wicked believe there is no escape. "The sword" is a term indicating all manner of violence. "Destined" translates an unusual passive participle that suggests "the sword" is on the lookout for him.

15:23 The first line reads literally, "He wanders for the food where?" The translation "vultures" involves a slight vowel change from *'ayyēh* ("where") to *'ayyâ* ("vulture"). The older versions and a few modern ones (NASB, NJPS, NRSV) have a less grisly picture by reading, "Where is it?" in place of "vultures." The vowel change yields a better sense and follows the LXX (cf. Prov 30:17; Luke 17:37). The word *'ayyâ* also occurs in 28:7 (without repointing), but there the NIV translates it "raven."[13] In many places Job associated "darkness" with death, and that probably is what Eliphaz had in mind when he spoke the second line.[14]

---

[12] The verb is חיל / חול and is *hithpael,* which KB translates as "writhe in fear." The *hiphil* occurs in Ps 29:8, which the NIV translates "shake," and the *polel* in Ps 29:9 is translated as "twists" in the text and "gives birth" in the footnote.

[13] This particular species is elsewhere only in the lists of unclean birds in Lev 11:14; Deut 14:13. See *Fauna and Flora of the Bible* (London: UBS, 1972), 40-41.

[14] The NAB, NEB, REB, E. Dhorme (*A Commentary on the Book of Job,* trans. H. Knight [London: Nelson, 1967] and J. Hartley (*Job,* NICOT [Grand Rapids: Eerdmans, 1988) follow the LXX in making "the day of darkness" (v. 23) the subject of the verb at the beginning of v. 24, "Fill him with terror." Verse 24 is then a tricolon.

15:24   Most scholars agree on the translation of this verse, although several of the words in v. 24 are rare, the introduction of "king" is unusual, and the last word ("attack") occurs only here.[15] There is no peace for the wicked (Isa 48:22; 57:21).

15:25   Verses 25-26 give the reasons the wicked are so harassed. With a gesture of contempt and the posture of a soldier,[16] the wicked demonstrate their resistance to submission to God.

15:26   Almost all paraphrase the first line, which literally reads, "He runs at him with a neck." This "neck" is not the word translated twelve times "stiffnecked" (except Ps 75:5[6]); but most understand that sense and read "defiantly" (NIV, NJPS), "stubbornly" (RSV, AAT, NKJV, NRSV), or the like. Some of the imagery is preserved by the NASB "headlong," the NEB "head down," and the REB "head lowered." Of the three Hebrew words in the second line, only the meaning "his shields" is certain in this context, but again there is general agreement that these two verses employ military terminology in their description of the wicked's offensive tactics.

Future Grief (15:27-35).   In the closing stanza of his second speech Eliphaz predicted the assorted punishments that would befall the godless. They include homelessness, poverty, and barrenness.

15:27   In ancient times prosperity was evident in fatness, while thinness betrayed penury (cf. Prov 11:25; 13:4, where the KJV translates literally "made fat"). Naturally the wealthy wicked were obese, with fat faces and bulging waistlines.[17] The AB has for the second line "bloated his loins with blubber," but the NIV is also colorful.

15:28   Those proofs of prosperity will, according to Eliphaz, give way to impoverishment when the once opulent find themselves holing up in abandoned buildings like squatters. The three lines describe their living conditions as "ruined," "uninhabited," and "destined to become heaps of ruins" (RSV).

15:29   Two complementary negative statements make up the first half of v. 29. The second half contains a word that only occurs here (i.e., a hapax), *minlām*, which the MLB and the NIV render "his posses-

---

[15] The only cognate scholars find for כִּידוֹר is in an Arabic word *kadara,* "rush down" (as a bird of prey). See Dhorme, *Job,* 219. "Poised" (עָתַד, here *hithpael*) occurs elsewhere only as a *piel,* "get ready" in Prov 24:27. For an altogether different slant on line *b,* see Tur-Sinai (*Job,* 254), who reads, "He braceth himself like a king-hero for the fight."

[16] "Vaults" translates the *hithpael* of גָּבַר, meaning something like "act bravely/manly."

[17] "Flesh" translates פִּימָה, a hapax for which the KJV has "collops"!

sions."[18] The JB and NAB follow the LXX (*skian*) and read "shadow." The AT, RSV, and NEB follow the Vulgate (*radicem*) and read "root(s)." The NASB compares it to a similar hapax in Deut 23:25[26] and reads "grain."

15:30 Eliphaz augmented his projection of gloom and doom for the ungodly by taking the justly rewarded sinner right to the grave. "Darkness" carries that meaning (10:21-22). The third line speaks of the demise of the impious in terms Eliphaz used earlier (cf. 4:9). "Shoots," *yōnaqtô*, is from a root that means "suck/nurse," and this may be an indirect reference to Job's children.[19] The verb *yāsûr* in the first and third lines is a play on words since it has a causative sense in the last line.[20] "God" is supplied in our text for "his" in the original.[21] The simple rendering of the AB and NJPS is literal and adequate, "He will pass away by the breath of His mouth," especially since "pass away" is an English euphemism for "die."

15:31 In this verse also the author used twice a key word, *šāw'* ("worthless/nothing"). The NRSV renders it thus: "Let them not trust in emptiness, deceiving themselves; for emptiness will be their recompense." The term does not refer to false gods but usually to "lies," "false prophecies/visions," or "vain hopes." Eliphaz could have had Job's occasional statements of hope in mind (13:15; 14:13-17) as he now urged him to abandon them.

15:32 Many emend *timmālē'*, "be paid in full," to *timmāl*, "cut down/wither," following the LXX.[22] The idea of dying young as a punishment is not foreign to the Old Testament (cf. Job 22:16; Ps 55:23[24]; Eccl 7:17).

15:33 Eliphaz continued with his comparisons between plants and wicked people. Using a perfectly matched pair of parallel lines, he said they will—

shake off / like a vine / its grapes
shed / like an olive (tree) / its blossoms.

---

[18] Following R. Gordis, *The Book of Job* (New York: Jewish Theological Seminary, 1978); M. Pope, *Job*, AB (Garden City: Doubleday, 1965); KB[3]; and supported by Hartley, Clines, and others. The alternates also have their supporters among the commentaries.

[19] Technically "fire" was the agency of the second tragedy; Job's children died as a result of a "mighty wind" (1:16,19).

[20] Gordis reads the second one as a noun meaning "branch" (*Job*, 158, 165-66).

[21] Those versions (e.g., RSV, JB, NAB, NEB) that read "blossom" for "mouth" follow the LXX, ἄνθος.

[22] "Wither" or the like is in the first line in the AB, JB, NAB, NEB, GNB, NJPS, ICB, REB, NCV.

In particular "unripe grapes" are indicated here illustrating, as in the preceding verse, a premature death.

15:34 Eliphaz's reference to the loss of Job's goods and the deaths of his children is transparent. "Barren," a rare word, was Job's wish for his mother on his birthday (3:7). Strictly speaking, he and his wife were not barren but had now become childless. Without heirs, however, the results were the same, with no hope of seeing children to the third and fourth generations. "Those who love bribes" is simply "bribes" in Hebrew but implies those who live by that usually crooked system, both as givers and takers of bribes.

15:35 Eliphaz contrasted the barrenness of the wicked with the fact that they do "conceive" and "give birth" but only to "trouble," "evil," and "deceit." The two events of the first line mark the beginning and end of the nine months of prenatal development, thus constituting a merismus representing the whole period (see explanation at 1:20). So the second line is parallel, not consequential, to the first. Isaiah 59:4 is almost identical to our first line, and Ps 7:14[15] is very close. Eliphaz brought his second presentation to an end without ever directly charging Job with these sins, but the innuendoes and implications are clear.

8. Job Reproaches His Pitiless Friends and Prays for Relief (16:1–17:16)

One could grow weary of Job's litany of criticism, complaint, and despair if it were not for the rich vocabulary and fascinating word pictures he used to present his position. The same could be said for the friends. Another feature of Job's speeches that the others never express brightens the otherwise dreary landscape: his occasional exhibition of hope. Such traces of trust appear in this speech at 16:19-21 and 17:9.

(1) Criticism of Friends (16:1-5)

¹**Then Job replied:**
²**"I have heard many things like these;**
    miserable comforters are you all!
³**Will your long-winded speeches never end?**
    What ails you that you keep on arguing?
⁴**I also could speak like you,**
    if you were in my place;
I could make fine speeches against you

and shake my head at you.
⁵But my mouth would encourage you;
comfort from my lips would bring you relief.

As in chaps. 12 and 13, Job began this speech with a reminder to his friends that they had presented nothing that was not common knowledge. Furthermore, he charged them with a lack of sympathy.

16:1   See comments at 6:1.

16:2   So far Job's friends had taught him nothing, had given no usable advice, and in general had aggravated his condition rather than alleviated it. So he branded them "miserable comforters." "Miserable" translates ʿāmāl, one of the last words Eliphaz had spoken, translated "trouble" (15:35). According to 2:16 these three had come to Job "to sympathize with him and comfort him." To this point there has been none of either. The lesson is, "Helpful advice is usually brief and encouraging, not lengthy and judgmental."[23]

16:3   Eliphaz had opened his last speech by comparing Job's words to "the hot east wind." Now Job asked Eliphaz if there was any end to his "words of wind."[24] There is some debate on "ails," but most concur with the NIV and compare 6:25, where the NIV translates "painful."[25] "Keep on arguing" translates a simple imperfect, but such a continuous sense is legitimate in cases like this.[26] They could have asked the same of Job, although his ailment should have been more conspicuous.

16:4   In this doubly long verse Job imagined that if the roles were reversed, he could treat them as they were treating him. The protasis is line *b*, "If you were in my place"; the apodoses are lines *a, c, d*. The NIV chose the auxiliary verb "could" rather than "would" because Job probably would not have been as mean as the friends were, even though he had that ability. There is a note of sarcasm in the expression "make fine speeches."[27] "Shake my head" was a gesture of spiteful pleasure (Ps 22:7[8]; 109:25; Lam 2:15; Matt 27:39).

16:5   The verbs in v. 5 could also be translated with "could," like v. 4,

---

[23] E. Smick and R. Youngblood in the *NIV Study Bible*, 751.

[24] Hebrew has no negative "never," Again the AB is commendable for its succinctness: "Have windy words a limit? What moves you to prattle on?" (M. Pope, *Job*, 115.

[25] In addition to 6:25 and 16:3 the root מרץ is found only in 1 Kgs 2:8 ("bitter") and Mic 2:10 ("beyond all remedy").

[26] GKC § 107f.

[27] Differences of opinion also exist about how to read and translate this once-occurring verb, חבר. "Join" (KJV, RSV, Gordis) reflects the Heb. noun that means "fellow/companion/friend" and is the root behind the name Hebron, city of Abraham, the "friend" of God. "Make fine" (AAT, NIV, KB) comes from the Arabic *abara*. "Declaim/harangue" (NAB, NEB, Pope) is based on Ugaritic *ḥbr* (see Clines, *Job*, 369, for documentation).

rather than "would." "Comfort" translates *nîd,* which occurs only here but is related to the verb meaning "move/shake/wander."[28] Job's "trembling/ quivering" lips would prove his sincerity.

(2) Complaint to God (16:6-14)

> [6]"Yet if I speak, my pain is not relieved;
>   and if I refrain, it does not go away.
> [7]Surely, O God, you have worn me out;
>   you have devastated my entire household.
> [8]You have bound me—and it has become a witness;
>   my gauntness rises up and testifies against me.
> [9]God assails me and tears me in his anger
>   and gnashes his teeth at me;
>   my opponent fastens on me his piercing eyes.
> [10]Men open their mouths to jeer at me;
>   they strike my cheek in scorn
>   and unite together against me.
> [11]God has turned me over to evil men
>   and thrown me into the clutches of the wicked.
> [12]All was well with me, but he shattered me;
>   he seized me by the neck and crushed me.
>   He has made me his target;
> [13]   his archers surround me.
>   Without pity, he pierces my kidneys
>   and spills my gall on the ground.
> [14]Again and again he bursts upon me;
>   he rushes at me like a warrior.

Although "God" is not in the Hebrew text of vv. 7 or 9, in vv. 6-8 Job spoke to God in the second person. In vv. 9-14 he spoke of God in the third person ("God" is in the text at v. 11). Unlike other complaint sections, in this passage Job did not ask for an explanation of his suffering; here he mainly recited his woes and reviewed his troubles, all with the suggestion that they came from an unmerciful God.

16:6 "Relief" and "relieved" tie together vv. 5-6, translating two forms of the same Hebrew root. Job found that neither speaking nor remaining silent brought any lessening of his pain. About half the English versions retain the question format of the second line (KJV, RV, Moffatt, RSV, NASB), and the other half (NAB, NEB, GNB, AAT, NIV, REB)

---

[28] An alternate spelling of the noun נִידָה occurs in Lam 1:8. The verb נוּד occurs in the *hiphil* (Jer 18:16) and *hithpael* (Jer 48:27; Ps 64:9) with the meaning "shake [the head]."

have a negative statement, "It does not go away."

16:7 That God is the addressee is clear from the singular pronouns "you" and the nature of the statements. In Job's thinking God, not Eliphaz, "devastated" his "entire household" (*ʿēdâ* usually "company/congregation/assembly," as in 15:34 and eighty times in Numbers).

16:8 "Bound" (*qmṭ*) appears only here and in 22:16. The KJV has "filled with wrinkles"; some translate as either "shriveled" or "wizened," but that is based on postbiblical Hebrew. "Bound" or the like fits also at 22:16, where the NIV has "cut off." The advantage of the alternate is that it makes a good parallel with "gauntness," over which there is less question. By these statements Job said there was incontrovertible proof of his suffering. His contention elsewhere was that it was not occasioned by his sin.

16:9 Speaking now of God in the third person, Job used strong language to describe God's maltreatment. "Assails" was usually translated elsewhere in the KJV as "hate" (Gen 27:41; Ps 55:3[4]). To "gnash teeth" depicts anger as in Ps 35:16; Lam 2:16; Acts 7:54. "Opponent" (*ṣar*) is ordinarily used of personal and political enemies. To bring out the force of the last verb, which basically means "sharpen," the NIV adds the adjective "piercing" (cf. NEB, "look daggers at me").

16:10 This verse is reminiscent of some of the passages that the Evangelists used to describe the crucifixion (e.g., Ps 22:13-16; Isa 50:6; 53:3-4b,7). Though no New Testament passage ever cited him as a type of Christ, Job nevertheless belonged to that company of righteous sufferers who anticipated the one who was perfect righteousness and who suffered even death on a cross.[29]

16:11 "The evil men" and "the wicked" to whom God turned Job over might have been the Sabeans and Chaldeans of 1:14,17, but I believe Job used these strong words to describe the three friends, who came to console but ended up opposing him.[30]

16:12a,b When the book began, "all was well with" Job (1:1-3). But soon God "shattered," "seized," and "crushed"[31] the one the author called "the greatest man among all the people of the East."

16:12c,13a The NIV has correctly scanned vv. 12-13. These six lines constitute three bicola because v. 12c belongs with v. 13a. The met-

---

[29] "Unite" translates the only *hithpael* of the common verb מלא. The nominal form carries this sense in Gen 48:19; Isa 31:4.

[30] *Midrash Rabbah* on Genesis ([London: Soncino, 1977], 57:4, 506) sees the Satan as the "evil one."

[31] "Shattered" (וַיְפַרְפְּרֵנִי from פרר II) and "crushed" (וַיְפַצְפְּצֵנִי from פצץ) were chosen because of their sounds. The former occurs only four times; the latter, three.

aphor of both has to do with shooting arrows. "Target" (*maṭārâ*) has this meaning elsewhere only in 1 Sam 20:20. "Archers" (*rab*) too is rare with just one other occurrence (Jer 50:29).[32] Job felt that God had specially selected him to suffer what he did. We readers know that is true because the author gave us a glimpse into the heavenly council (1:8).

16:13b,c The idea of shooting carries into v. 13b as Job described an arrow "piercing" his "kidneys," which even these ancient people knew to be a vital organ. "Gall" translates *mĕrērâ*, a unique form of a well-established root meaning "bitter" (Ruth 1:20).

16:14 A literal translation would read, "He bursts upon me with burst in the face of burst." The NASB comes close to that with "break" and "breach." The NIV and most modern versions have chosen to be literary rather than literal and thus produced better English while sacrificing some Hebrew idioms. In the last verse of this complaint section Job compared God with a relentlessly attacking soldier.

(3) Plea of Innocence (16:15-17)

> ¹⁵"I have sewed sackcloth over my skin
>   and buried my brow in the dust.
> ¹⁶My face is red with weeping,
>   deep shadows ring my eyes;
> ¹⁷yet my hands have been free of violence
>   and my prayer is pure.

Much in the preceding verses was hyperbole. The real effects of being God's target are recounted in the next two verses, with v. 17 giving a reason for the title of this short section.

16:15 From Jacob mourning over Joseph (Gen 37:34) to the people and cattle of Nineveh (Jonah 3:8), the wearing of sackcloth signified loss and grief. While elsewhere Job applied the customary "dust and ashes" (42:6), this is his sole reference to "sackcloth" (cf. Esth 4:1; Isa 58:5; Jonah 3:6). As the older translations indicate, the word "brow" is actually "horn," the Hebrew idiom for "strength/pride."[33]

16:16 Graphically Job described himself as one looks after extended

---

[32] The LXX, Vulgate, Targum, Moffatt, AT, Knox, KB, JB, NAB, NEB, GNB all have "arrows" rather than "archers."

[33] Two hapax legomena affect the certainty of any translation. "Skin" is גִּלְדִּי, but there are Akkadian, Aramaic, and Arabic cognates to assure the meaning. "Buried" is עֹלַלְתִּי, but in this context it cannot have the usual meanings "do" or "glean," so it is understood to be a separate root (עלל II in KB) akin to one in Ugaritic, Aramaic, Syriac, and Arabic.

crying.[34] "Deep shadows" is again possibly "shadow of death" (cf. 3:1; 10:21-22), and "eyes" is elsewhere "eyelids" (cf. 3:9; 41:18[10]).

16:17 As in other places Job once more pleaded innocent (6:29; 10:7,15; 11:4; 27:5-6; 31:6; 32:1). He may have had in mind Bildad's words in 8:5-6. Toward other people he could say, "My hands have been free of violence"; toward God he could say, "My prayer is pure." Psalm 24:4a has both these qualifications for those who would enter the Jerusalem sanctuary.

(4) Hope for Vindication (16:18-21)

> [18]"O earth, do not cover my blood;
>   may my cry never be laid to rest!
> [19]Even now my witness is in heaven;
>   my advocate is on high.
> [20]My intercessor is my friend
>   as my eyes pour out tears to God;
> [21]on behalf of a man he pleads with God
>   as a man pleads for his friend.

In the midst of this, Job's fifth speech, there shines another ray of hope. Admittedly Job was inconsistent. Those who demand consistency even of a man in the throes of grief and disease explain away these positive passages that hint at resolution, divine provision, and life after death. But people can be forgiven for being more or less optimistic and even for vacillating between doubt and faith, all the more so when they are experiencing the emotional trauma of losing ten children in one catastrophe and being afflicted with a gruesome, offensive, painful, physical affliction. Let us rejoice with Job when his spirit soared, and let us weep with him when he wept.

16:18 By these somewhat cryptic words Job repeated his wish that he experience vindication before he died. To "cover blood" meant to conceal a crime (Gen 4:10; Isa 26:21). Likewise Job wanted his "cry" to be answered rather than buried.[35]

16:19 In vv. 19-20 are four terms describing the one Job hoped would

---

[34] "Is red" is the verb חֳמַרְמְרוּ, a reduplicated stem (*pealal* or *poalal*) of חמר IV (BDB), the only stem in which the verb appears. Cf. Lam 1:20; 2:11. Dhorme (*Job*, 238) explains the *qere* as plural and the *kethib* as singular. Gordis (*Job*, 177) describes them only as variations of the plural, the *kethib* being "the older third person fem. plur. of the perfect still extant in Arab. *qatala* and Aram. *qetala* but occurring only rarely in biblical Hebrew."

[35] "Laid to rest" translates the noun מָקוֹם, "a place." Most agree that it must be taken as "resting place," though there are no parallels to which to appeal.

come to his defense: "witness," "advocate," "intercessor," and "friend."
All these terms can and do apply to human beings elsewhere in the Old
Testament, but the prepositional phrases "in heaven" and "on high" push
the interpreter to think in terms of a divine redeemer. From a New Testament perspective it is a simple matter to identify this person, but for Job he
was unknown and undefined. The content of Job's faith was rudimentary.
The glass through which he looked was even darker than ours (1 Cor
13:12). In Gen 31:50 God is called a "witness" (cf. Rom 1:9; 1 Thess 2:5).
"Advocate" translates the hapax *śāhēd,* which is known from Aramaic and
appears in Gen 31:47, incorporated into the Aramaic name of Galeed, "Je-
gar Sahadutha." As Hartley explains, the best candidate for this witness/
advocate within Job's limited knowledge was God himself: "Job appeals
to God's holy integrity in stating his earnest hope that God will testify to
the truth of his claims of innocence, even though such testimony will seem
to contradict God's own actions."[36]

16:20 "Intercessor" is one who passes messages between those who
cannot meet or understand each other. It is the "interpreter" in Gen 42;23,
the "envoys" in 2 Chr 32:31, and the (angelic) "mediator" in Job 33:23.[37]

16:21 This verse defines what the "intercessor/advocate" does. He
argues the case of his friend before the bar of divine justice.[38] His task is
similar to that of the Messiah in Isa 2:4; 11:4, where the same verb appears (cf. Rom 8:34; Heb 7:25).

(5) Prospect of a Near and Unhappy Death (16:22–17:2)

> [22]"Only a few years will pass
>   before I go on the journey of no return.
> [1]My spirit is broken,
>   my days are cut short,
>   the grave awaits me.
> [2]Surely mockers surround me;
>   my eyes must dwell on their hostility.

---

[36] J. Hartley, *Job,* NICOT (Grand Rapids: Eerdmans, 1988), 246.

[37] Apart from the *hiphil* participles, as here, the root לוּץ means "mock/scorn." This
explains the NIV's alternative in the footnote. The MT does have רֵעַי (pl.) rather than
רֵעִי (sing.). Alternatively, the verse can be read, "My friends are [God's] spokesmen," interpreting for God the accusations (see Tur-Sinai, *Job,* 268). But v. 21 makes this reading
less likely.

[38] Some commentators and versions read בֵּין, "between" ("Let Him arbitrate between
a man and God as between a man and his fellow," NJPS) for בֶּן, "son [of man]" i.e., "mortal" (NAB, NEB, NJPS, REB, Gordis, *Job,* 170; Hartley, *Job,* 263).

This three-verse pericope describes Job's plunge into another slough of despair. He did not directly mention God's treatment of him but mainly pointed to his sickness and the hostility of "mockers" (friends?).

16:22   The chapter division obscures the connection of our verse with what follows.[39] The second line is almost identical to 10:21a (see comments there). As depressed as he was, Job's expectation of even "a few years" is surprising. Clues are few about Job's age when these tragedies befell him. According to 42:16, he lived 140 more years, which may indicate, on the principle that his holdings were doubled, that he was seventy at this time (cf. Ps 90:10).

17:1   Each line translates two words in Hebrew. There is no good way to divide them three and three to produce two lines. "Broken" in "spirit" is an idiom shared by both cultures and languages, Job's and ours. "Cut short" is uncertain, occurring only here; but something like that must be intended.[40] "Grave" is in the plural, "graves," referring to the "graveyard" (NJPS) or "cemetery" (AAT).[41]

17:2   By "mockers" Job probably was referring to Eliphaz, Bildad, and Zophar since twice he had used the verb form of this otherwise unused noun in 13:9 ("deceive"). So far in the book these three are the only ones who spoke anything to Job (but cf. 30:1-10). Using different words, Job elsewhere referred to their counsel as "mocking" (11:3; 12:4; 16:10; 21:3). Other servants of God who were surrounded by hostile mockers are mentioned elsewhere (e.g., Pss 22:7,12; 119:51; Jer 20:7; Matt 27:29,41).

(6) Address to God (17:3-5)

[3]"Give me, O God, the pledge you demand.
   Who else will put up security for me?
[4]You have closed their minds to understanding;
   therefore you will not let them triumph.

---

[39] Not all agree with the NIV's division. The NJPS, e.g., has a break between vv. 1 and 2. The origins of the verse and chapter divisions and numbers are obscure. The Masoretes made verse divisions and major and minor paragraph or stanza divisions, but these latter do not correspond to our chapters. The chapter numbers date to the twelfth century and the verse numbers to the sixteenth, not very long before the publication of the KJV.

[40] It looks like a *niphal* of זעך, an unknown root. The NIV and others read דעך, which also is in Job 6:17; 18:5-6; 21:17: "vanish/snuffed out/goes out." Others presumably read זעך. The NEB and REB have, "My days are numbered." The JB, eliminating "days," puts the last three words together to produce "and the gravediggers are gathering for me."

[41] There is no verb, so most versions supply "awaits" or "is ready." The MLB has the very graphic "is yawning for me!"

⁵**If a man denounces his friends for reward,**
   the eyes of his children will fail.

As in the middle of chap. 16 Job turned his eyes heavenward and
spoke to God (16:6-14), so in the midst of chap. 17 are these three verses
directed to the deity. They are a mixture of supplication and complaint.
   17:3 The interpretation of this verse is dependent on the understanding of two cultural practices, not too different from our own. "Pledge" in
the first line refers to some proof necessary to back up words. No testimony other than God's would do to persuade Job's friends that he was
sinless.
   The idiom of the second line is literally, "Who will strike hands?" that
is, agree with a handshake to vouch for Job. Both verbs occur in Prov
6:1, a passage warning against cosigning notes. Job could find no one to
endorse his innocence and by this question in v. 3b did not expect to find
anyone other than God (cf. 16:19).[42]
   17:4 Job complained that the reason no one would stand by him is
that God had "closed their minds to understanding." So it was God's
fault. The verb in the second line is troublesome, so the NIV added
"them" to provide an object for it; others make it passive, hence God
"will not be exalted."[43]
   17:5 Job quoted a proverb of unknown origin to bolster his point
against his unsupportive friends. Like many proverbs, it is cryptic and
open to several interpretations. The verse suggests that the sins of the father will harm his children.[44] This was a common thought in the ancient
Near East, but the point of the verse seems to be that friends should not
be sold for a price. Friends are a precious experience and should not be
taken advantage of.

(7) More Complaint (17:6-8)

⁶**"God has made me a byword to everyone,**

---

[42] The NIV adds "O God" on the basis of the second person pronouns in vv. 3-4.

[43] So Hartley, *Job,* 266. Clines, following the same route, has, "Therefore you will win
no honor on that account" (*Job 1–20,* 368, 373; cf. KB). This means reading תֹּרֵמֵם as a
passive *pilel* as in Ps 75:10[11]; Neh 9:5. Andersen (*Job,* 114) understands Job's point in v.
4 to be that the friends' stupidity furnishes evidence of God's rejection of their position.
Bildad responds to the charge in 18:3.

[44] The KJV's paraphrase of line *a* is, "He that speaketh flattery to *his* friends." Clines
(*Job 1–20*) follows Moffatt, who paraphrased, "Like one who bids friends to a feast and
lets his children starve!" For the entire verse the NAB has, "My lot is described as evil,"
which is arrived at by reading רָעֵים not as "friends" but "evil" and eliminating line *b*.

a man in whose face people spit.
⁷My eyes have grown dim with grief;
    my whole frame is but a shadow.
⁸Upright men are appalled at this;
    the innocent are aroused against the ungodly.

Now speaking of God in the third person, Job persisted in his complaint, blaming God for his illness and for his shabby treatment at the hands of others. In an indirect way the gloom lifted in v. 8 in preparation for one of Job's minor declarations of hope in v. 9.

17:6 Again "God" is not in the text, but the insertion is justified on the basis of the pronouns. This section is called "More Complaint" because it picks up where v. 2 left off, Job speaking of "mockers" (v. 2) who use him as a "byword" (cf. 30:9, where both those English words occur).[45] Job has indeed become a "byword" because of the expression in Jas 5:11, "the patience of Job,"[46] although that was not the sense Job had in mind. "Spit" (*tōpet*) occurs only here; and together with the following word, "in face," it has given rise to several alternative translations, though the NIV is with the majority.[47] In this respect Job intimated the archetype of righteous sufferers, Jesus (cf. 16:10; Matt 26:67).

17:7 The first figure of speech, "eyes have grown dim," is common (e.g., Gen 27:1; Deut 34:7; 1 Sam 3:2); the second is unique to this passage, although the general idea is in Job (16:8; 19:20).[48] These could be the effects of his disease, of his mental anguish, or both.

17:8 The only way to leave this verse as it is in the Hebrew Bible is to understand that Job was speaking ironically, or to put it conditionally, "Upright men should be appalled." Ordinarily one would expect good folks to respond to such injustice with dismay and righteous indignation. Instead, Job's three friends distanced themselves from Job and were "aroused" against him.[49]

---

[45] "Byword" is מְשֹׁל, an infinitival form or alternate spelling of the noun meaning "proverb/parable/taunt." Tur-Sinai understands it from the verb שׁלל, "prey" (*Job*, 276-78).

[46] "Perseverance" in the NIV.

[47] "Spit" is supported by both Arabic and Ugaritic cognates. The KJV reads, "And aforetime I was as a tabret." The RV has, "And I am become an open abhorring." Blommerde would read לפנים as "for my ancestors," i.e., "those before me" (*Northwest Semitic and Job*, 79-80). The NEB and REB emend תֹפֶת to מֹפֵת, "portent/marvel." The NJPS reads it as a proper noun, "I have become like Tophet of old." Cf. Jer 7:31.

[48] "My frame," יְצֻרָי, occurs only here but comes from the well-known verb יצר, "form/conceive."

[49] The verb in line *a* is plural, as is "upright men," but singular in line *b*, as is "innocent one." The second can be taken distributively or the singular for the group.

(8) Innocence and Hope in Death (17:9)

⁹Nevertheless, the righteous will hold to their ways,
and those with clean hands will grow stronger.

17:9 Despite the plurals throughout this verse in the NIV, the nouns and verbs in Hebrew are all singular (cf. KJV, RV, RSV, etc.). Job spoke of himself in this oblique statement of faith. Andersen said of v. 9, "There is hardly a place in the book of Job concerning which commentators are in wider disagreement than this statement."[50] But F. Delitzsch said of it: "These words of Job are like a rocket which shoots above the tragic darkness of the book, lighting it up suddenly, although only for a short time."[51] Job obviously was "holding to his way" and believed that because of his "clean hands" he would increase in strength.[52]

(9) More Despair (17:10-16)

¹⁰"But come on, all of you, try again!
I will not find a wise man among you.
¹¹My days have passed, my plans are shattered,
and so are the desires of my heart.
¹²These men turn night into day;
in the face of darkness they say, 'Light is near.'
¹³If the only home I hope for is the grave,
if I spread out my bed in darkness,
¹⁴if I say to corruption, 'You are my father,'
and to the worm, 'My mother' or 'My sister,'
¹⁵where then is my hope?
Who can see any hope for me?
¹⁶Will it go down to the gates of death?
Will we descend together into the dust?"

Job's fourth speech ends in depression as do most of them. With no connection to the positive outlook of v. 9, and while still throwing barbs at his unhelpful friends, the passage is one more of several where the hero looked forward only to death and the grave.

---

[50] Andersen, *Job,* TOTC (Downers Grove: InterVarsity, 1976), 185. Support for the position presented here comes from F. Delitzsch, *Biblical Commentary on the Book of Job,* vol. I (Grand Rapids: Eerdmans, 1949), 299-300; A. B. Davidson, *The Book of Job, The Cambridge Bible* (Cambridge: University Press, 1895), 128; Hartley, *Job,* 269-70. Some commentators simply do away with vv. 8-10.

[51] F. Delitzsch, *Job,* 300.

[52] "Strength," אֹמֶץ, a noun from a verb with the same letters, occurs only here.

THE WORTHLESSNESS OF THE FRIENDS (17:10-12).   In his friends Job found neither wisdom (v. 10) nor truth (v. 12). This resulted in shattered plans and unmet desires (v. 11).

17:10   A strong disjunctive particle opens the verse, which warrants beginning a new section here. It is as if Job offered his friends another opportunity to demonstrate their wisdom. But his pessimism about any possible change was immediately evident in the second line. In 12:2 he had insulted their wisdom with satire. This statement is just as blunt.

17:11   The verse is plagued with problems. First, it is a tricolon, but the third colon has no verb (cf. v. 1, where it presented less of a problem). Second, "plans," *zimmâ,* in its twenty-eight other occurrences means something like "wicked plans/lewd thoughts." Could it be neutral here, as Gordis says?[53] Third, "desires," *môrāšîm,* occurs only here, although a related form (*ʾărešet*) occurs in Ps 21:2[3].[54] Despite these uncertainties the gist of the verse is generally agreed on. Job saw his life fleeting fast with dreams unfulfilled and hopes dashed.

17:12   "These men" and "they say" have been added to bring out the sense. The sufferer from Uz essentially accused his friends of calling evil good and good evil and putting light for darkness and darkness for light (Isa 5:20). Perhaps he alluded to Zophar in 11:17 when he promised that "darkness will become like morning."

HOPE ONLY IN DEATH (17:13-16).   Four conditions fill vv. 13-14 (although there is only one "if" in Hebrew and only three verbs), and the result in vv. 15-16 takes the form of four rhetorical questions. The upshot of this passage and of this entire two-chapter speech is that Job expected to be buried along with his hopes.

17:13   Although in the form of a condition, the effect of v. 13 is that Job expected to die and lie in darkness. Both "spread" and "bed" are rare words, but in this context there is little doubt about their meaning.[55]

17:14   "Corruption"[56] and "worm"[57] are words that go with "death"

---

[53] Gordis, *Job,* 183.

[54] It is not from the root ירשׁ, "possessions," as in the KJV margin. Others follow the LXX's ἄρθρα and read מֵיתָר, hence the JB's "every fibre," the NEB and REB's "my heart strings," and the NJPS' "strings of my heart."

[55] "Spread," רפד, is in only two other places, 41:30[22] and Song 2:5, with a derived nominal form in Song 3:10. "Bed," יצוּע, is four times elsewhere as a noun and four times as a verb.

[56] See comments on at 9:31 for שׁחת. Elihu used this term translated "pit" in 33:18,22,24,28,30.

[57] "Worm," רמָּה, is elsewhere in Job 7:5; 21:26; 24:20; 25:6. Otherwise it is only in Exod 16:24; Isa 14:11.

and "grave" or are substitutes for them. By this grotesque analogy Job
said that these would be his most intimate relations, his closest family.

17:15 The first two questions that constitute the result clauses in this
four-verse group are arranged chiastically.

A   Where then
 B   my hope?
 B'   My hope
A'   who can see?[58]

The point of both questions is that Job had no hope.

17:16 "Gates" is *bādîm*, literally "bars" (KJV, RSV). Most, emending it to *běyadî* or the like, read "with me" (so AB, JB, NAB, NEB,
NASB, AAT), which fits well with the second line. Thus Job and his hope
"go down to the grave" and "descend together into the dust." Like all the
other responses so far (6:21b; 10:21-22; 14:20-22), Job ends with
thoughts of death. But he has not yet heard from God.

9. Bildad: The Wicked Are Punished (18:1-21)

In his second speech the Shuhite began with a plea for Job to give up
and agree with him and the others. The larger part of the speech, however, is given over to an elaboration of the theology of retribution, especially its negative dimensions. In short, the wicked are punished.

(1) Criticism of Job (18:1-4)

¹Then Bildad the Shuhite replied:
²"When will you end these speeches?
  Be sensible, and then we can talk.
³Why are we regarded as cattle
  and considered stupid in your sight?
⁴You who tear yourself to pieces in your anger,
  is the earth to be abandoned for your sake?
  Or must the rocks be moved from their place?

It is virtually standard procedure at this point in the debate to begin a
speech with strong words of criticism and/or advice. In fact, the opening
words of this speech are identical to those of Bildad's first speech (8:2;
cf. 19:2). Bildad bluntly told Job to stop and listen, respect him and his

---

[58] As pointed out at 7:8, this word for "see," רוש, is a favorite of the author of Job with
ten of the fifteen total occurrences in the OT.

comrades, and not destroy himself with anger.

18:1 See comments at 4:1.

18:2 Since Job showed no signs of running out of things to say, Bildad began to wonder if there was no end[59] to his defense. The verbs are plural, an irregularity hard to explain. Perhaps Bildad was lumping Job with all those who defended their righteousness in the face of what Bildad considered positive proof to the contrary. "Be sensible" is an insult as well as an imperative because it implies that Job had not been sensible.

18:3 Bildad may have had 17:10 in mind when he chided Job for considering him and his friends as dumb animals. "Considered stupid" is a translation of *ṭāmâ*, a hapax for which there are several alternate suggestions. The NIV and most others choose this one mainly on the basis of the parallelism.[60]

18:4 Bildad branded Job with the epithet "he who tears his soul in his anger" (literal translation). In a sense Bildad was right because Job seemed to be making no progress toward spiritual wellness and psychological wholeness as a result of his raving and raging. Bildad went on to ask him if he expected the universe to adjust itself to his reordering. The implication is that the principle of divine retribution for sin is an essential part of the cosmos. It was natural or nature's way of reconciling wrongs. Job should not assume that he was right and the rest of the world wrong.

(2) Dynamistic Retribution on the Wicked (18:5-21)

[5]"The lamp of the wicked is snuffed out;
    the flame of his fire stops burning.
[6]The light in his tent becomes dark;
    the lamp beside him goes out.
[7]The vigor of his step is weakened;
    his own schemes throw him down.
[8]His feet thrust him into a net

---

[59] "End," קִנֵּץ, is a hapax as it stands. The RV and AB translate "snares"; the ASV, RSV, and NASB, "hunt"; the NEB, "bridle." The Aramaic Job fragment from the Dead Sea Caves shows that this is an alternate spelling of קֵץ, "end." Incidentally, the first verb, the only one preserved, is singular. See M. Sokoloff, *The Targum to Job from Qumran Cave XI* (Ramat-Gan: Bar-Ilan University, 1974), 28.

[60] The KJV has "vile"; the ASV has "unclean," assuming that טָמֵה is a form of טָמֵא (cf. Lev 11:43). Similar is the Vulgate's *sorduimus*. The NAB, following Dhorme (*Job*) reads "their equals," assuming the verb is דָּמָה. "Considered stupid" assumes the Aramaic and modern Hebrew root טָמַם. See *BHS* footnote.

and he wanders into its mesh.
⁹A trap seizes him by the heel;
   a snare holds him fast.
¹⁰A noose is hidden for him on the ground;
   a trap lies in his path.
¹¹Terrors startle him on every side
   and dog his every step.
¹²Calamity is hungry for him;
   disaster is ready for him when he falls.
¹³It eats away parts of his skin;
   death's firstborn devours his limbs.
¹⁴He is torn from the security of his tent
   and marched off to the king of terrors.
¹⁵Fire resides in his tent;
   burning sulfur is scattered over his dwelling.
¹⁶His roots dry up below
   and his branches wither above.
¹⁷The memory of him perishes from the earth;
   he has no name in the land.
¹⁸He is driven from light into darkness
   and is banished from the world.
¹⁹He has no offspring or descendants among his people,
   no survivor where once he lived.
²⁰Men of the west are appalled at his fate;
   men of the east are seized with horror.
²¹Surely such is the dwelling of an evil man;
   such is the place of one who knows not God."

There is a subtle difference between divine retribution and dynamistic retribution.[61] In the former God is active in the administration of his justice and in the punishment of the offenders. In the latter a natural system of justice built into the universe takes over to enforce its laws. The law of gravity is an illustration. God is not directly involved every time something or someone falls. Rather, gravity is the outworking of laws that he incorporated into the creation. Often the friends spoke in terms of God's discipline or chastisement, but in this long section of Bildad's speech the dynamism of the created order executes justice on the evildoer.

18:5 The motif of vv. 5-6 is a light failing in darkness. Using four different words for "light" and four clauses, Bildad said the wicked will

---

[61] Cf. R. L. Hubbard ("Dynamistic and Legal Processes in Ps 7," *ZAW* 94:2 (1982): 267-80), who attributes the concept to K. Koch, "Gibt es ein Vergeltungsdogma im Alten Testament?" *ZTK* 52 (1955): 1-42.

be plunged into the cold and the dark. "Lamp" is in lines 5a and 6a. "Snuffed out/stops burning" (*dāʿak*) is in lines 5a and 6b. "Flame" (*šābîb*) occurs only here in Hebrew but appears in the Aramaic sections of Daniel (3:22; 7:9).

18:6   Elsewhere "dark" refers to death (3:5; 10:21; 17:13), so at this point Bildad probably meant that the wicked will die. The verb here and the noun in v. 18 are a kind of inclusio. Death marks the beginning and the end of this pericope.

18:7   The motif of hunting starts here as Bildad pictured the wicked as an animal weary from being chased. "Weakened" is from a root meaning "to be constricted," perhaps referring to the way a tired runner or animal takes shorter steps. In the end the wicked falls victim to "his own schemes/counsel" much like Rehoboam or Ahab (1 Kgs 12:8-17; 2 Kgs 22:30-35).

18:8   Six synonyms for "trap" are in vv. 8-10.[62] The main way to bag game was using traps of various kinds, and some of them are in this catalog. The two words in this verse, "net" and "mesh," refer to a thin covering of a pit dug for the victim to fall into.

18:9   The word "trap" is one of the most common, and "snare" is one of the rarest. Because of the verbs "seize" and "hold fast," these devices must have snapped shut on the victim's limbs or throat.

18:10   "Noose" is "rope" elsewhere, so this undoubtedly is some kind of lasso, in this case camouflaged "on the ground." The last term is found only here but is formed from a well-known verb root meaning "to take." Though translated "trap," it is not the same device as in v. 9.

18:11   Using yet another word for "terrors,"[63] Bildad continued to paint a picture of the wicked constantly harassed and unnerved[64] (15:21). "Dog" usually means "scatter," so it could mean his footsteps are scattered. The NJPS has "and send his feet flying."[65]

18:12   "Calamity" comes by emending the problem third word of the

---

[62] Though the total number of vocabulary words is small in Hebrew and in most primitive languages, whatever the speakers of that language do, they have a large vocabulary for it. For example, Hebrew has only two words for "boat," while English has over three hundred because the English live with the sea. English has only two words for "camel," while Arabic has many.

[63] בַּלָּהָה also occurs in 18:14; 24:17; 27:20; 30:15; and elsewhere only five more times. It probably is a metathesized form of בהל, meaning "trouble," mostly as a verb and a few times as a noun.

[64] "Startle," בעת, is also a favorite word in Job, which has eight of the sixteen occurrences in the OT.

[65] The REB has "so that he cannot hold back his urine."

line. It otherwise means "his strength/vigor" (KJV, RV, RSV, NEB, NASB), from *'ōnô* to *'āwen*, the reversing of two letters.[66] This adjustment makes a better synonymous parallel. The motif of trapping may still have been in Bildad's mind as he thought of the wicked as prey fallen into a pit.

18:13 Despite appearances in English the two lines are similar. The first two words of each, "eats/devours" and "parts/limbs," are identical. It is tempting to make one of the verbs passive, a move that involves no changes in the consonants, and adjust *baddê*, "parts of," to *bidway*, "by disease," involving only vowels and vowel letters. Hence, "his skin is eaten by disease."[67] "Death's firstborn" usually is understood as a reference to the disease itself, but it is common in light of Ugaritic studies to find references in the commentaries to Mot, the god of death.[68] The Baal Epic describes Mot's mouth reaching "one lip to earth and one to heaven."[69] But Isaiah reversed the figure when, in an eschatological scene, he said the Lord "will swallow up death forever" (Isa 25:8; cf. 1 Cor 15:54).

18:14 In this graphic scene the wicked are arrested and forced to march to their deaths; that is what "king of terrors" means. Death is the ultimate enemy to whom all must eventually surrender, but even that enemy will be destroyed when Christ returns (1 Cor 15:26). Bildad knew of no such hope.

18:15 The NIV has followed an emendation proposed by M. Dahood to arrive at the text they translated.[70] Otherwise the NIV footnote represents the standard Hebrew text,[71] variations of which can be seen in the KJV, ASV, AT, RSV, MLB, NASB. The scene is reminiscent of Sodom and Gomorrah (Gen 19:24) and the "fiery lake" in the last book of the Bible (Rev 21:8).

18:16 Using the merism "roots below" and "branches above," Bildad spoke of the total destruction of the wicked from the earth.[72]

---

[66] For yet more emendations and alternatives see Clines, *Job 1–20*, 405-6.

[67] See Hartley, *Job*, 277; Dhorme, *Job*, 265, who followed G. H. B. Wright, *The Book of Job* (London: Williams and Norgate, 1883).

[68] So Pope, *Job*, 135; Clines, *Job*, 403, 406, 416-18. The NRSV capitalizes and thus personifies "Death." So too the NEB here and in v. 14. The JB has all three words capitalized, "Death's First Born." AAT nicely skirts the question by reading "a fatal disease."

[69] *ANET*, 138.

[70] M. Dahood, "Some Northwest Semitic Words in Job," *Bib* 38 (1957): 312-14. To arrive at "fire," מִבְּלִי לוֹ is changed to מַבֶּל, with the לוֹ read as an emphatic *lamed* at the beginning of the next clause. The newly formed Hebrew word is cognate with Akkadian *nablu* and Ugaritic *nbl*, which mean "fire." This produces a nice parallel to "burning sulfur."

[71] It reads, "Nothing he had remains."

[72] Other examples of this figure are Amos 2:9; Mal 4:1.

18:17   For most in the ancient Near East and for most modern Jews, life after death consists of the remembrance of the deceased by their survivors and descendants. They live on only in the "memory" of their good deeds. To be forgotten was a fate worse than death (cf. Ps 34:16; Prov 10:7). Childlessness, therefore (v. 19), was a significant part of dynamistic retribution.

18:18   The motif of light and darkness (vv. 5-6) reappears here near the end of this section. More clearly than elsewhere "darkness" stands for death and annihilation.

18:19   Since one lived on in children, to die childless was considered a great misfortune and even divine punishment.[73] Stories of barrenness and only sonship reflect this major concern, from Abraham and Sarah and the other patriarchs to Manoah and his wife (Judg 13:2), from Elkanah and Hannah (1 Sam 1:2) to Hezekiah (who was granted fifteen more years of life because he apparently had not yet begotten an heir to the throne [2 Kgs 20:6 compared with 2 Kgs 21:1]), from the widow's son at Nain (Luke 7:12) to the one and only Son of God (John 3:16). Though Job had fathered ten children, he was now childless, and there is no doubt that this was in the minds of both Bildad and Job when Bildad spoke these words.

18:20   "Fate" is "day" in the sense of one's last day (cf. 1 Sam 26:10; Ps 37:13; Jer 50:27,31; Ezek 21:25[30],29[34]; Amos 6:3). "East" and "west"[74] constitute another merism meaning that all will be horrified when they see the fate of the wicked.

18:21   The "dwelling" and the "place" of the ungodly[75] is the grave, but the route by which they arrive is dreadful and disgusting. This "evil man" of Bildad's description was emaciated, scared, and ignorant of God, a forgotten man. And these were supposed to be words of comfort?

10. Job, Despite His Friends, Looks to His Redeemer (19:1-29)

Because of the "Redeemer" passage (v. 25), this is the most quoted chapter in Job. Unfortunately, that ray of hope is surrounded by themes

---

[73] Both "offspring" (נִין) and "descendants" (נֶכֶד) are rare words with both of them occurring only twice elsewhere (Gen 21:23; Isa 14:22). They are alliterated in Hebrew; note Moffatt, "son nor scion"; AT, "kith or kin"; NJPS, "seed or breed"; Tur-Sinai, *Job*, "breed nor brood"; and Hartley, *Job*, "posterity or progeny."

[74] This pair of words can mean "after" and "before" in the sense of time (so KJV, RV, NAB, NJPS). People of the ancient Near East were "oriented" with east before them and west behind them. By the same reckoning, south was right and north was left. So Ps 121:5 could read "your shade on your south side," the direction from which the sun shines.

[75] "One who knows not God" is an asyndetic relative clause. See *GBH* §129q.

more characteristic of Job—criticism of friends, complaint to God, and despair. Some downplay Job's hopelessness, while others completely ignore, water down, or argue away his hope. In an effort to be fair with Scripture, we must notice both.

(1) Criticism of Friends (19:1-6)

¹**Then Job replied:**
²**"How long will you torment me**
  and crush me with words?
³**Ten times now you have reproached me;**
  shamelessly you attack me.
⁴**If it is true that I have gone astray,**
  my error remains my concern alone.
⁵**If indeed you would exalt yourselves above me**
  and use my humiliation against me,
⁶**then know that God has wronged me**
  and drawn his net around me.

Bitterly Job accused his friends of tormenting, crushing, reproaching, and attacking him. Why, he wanted to know, did they enjoy their exaltation and his humiliation when it was God and not they who designed this turn of events?

19:1 See comments at 6:1.

19:2 At approximately the halfway point of the debate Job wondered if his three friends would ever give up or change their approach from one of accusation to one of support. It was not to be. Instead of comforting him as they had originally come to do, they tormented and crushed him by their words. The term "crush," Hartley explains, "represents the feelings of worthlessness and futility one experiences when overwhelmed by misfortune."[76] One could be very successful counseling the depressed by simply applying in reverse the principles exhibited by these three friends.

19:3 "Ten" is a round or unspecific number. It is useless to try to enumerate the insults the three friends had thrown at Job thus far. Verse 3 has three verbs in Hebrew: "you have reproached," "you are not ashamed," and "you attack."[77]

---

[76] Hartley, *Job*, 283.

[77] "Attack," הכר, is a hapax, but G. H. A. von Ewald (*Commentary on the Book of Job*, trans. J. F. Smith [London: Williams and Norgate, 1882], 203), B. Duhm (*Das Buch Hiob* [Freiburg: Mohr, 1897], 98), and most others connect it to an Arabic and Akkadian root spelled with ח rather than ה that means "oppress/ill treat."

19:4 As in 6:24, where the verb first appeared, Job allowed for the possibility that he had "gone astray," that is, trespassed inadvertently or was guilty of a sin of omission (Lev 5:18; Num 15:28). The noun "error" is from the same root.[78] By the entire sentence Job asked what business it was of theirs even if he were guilty of this, the least serious variety of sin. They could point to none, and even if they could, they should have acted redemptively, not condemningly.

19:5 There are two ways to be higher than your neighbor: by putting your neighbor down and by lifting yourself up. Job charged that his friends did both. He could well have prayed the imprecation of Ps 35:26b, "May all who exalt themselves over me be clothed with shame and disgrace," a verse that uses both key words of 19:5 (cf. Ps 38:16[17]).

19:6 The condition expressed in v. 5 has its result in v. 6. Two important words tie the concluding verse of this section to earlier statements by Bildad. "Wronged" (*ʿāwat*) occurred twice in 8:3, where Bildad asked: "Does God perfect justice? Does the Almighty pervert what is right?" He would have said no, but Job here argued that God indeed had wronged him. By the term "net" (though not one of the six traps in 18:8-10) Job connected his predicament to that which befalls the wicked, according to Bildad. Only Job did not consider himself wicked, so what Bildad regarded as dynamistic retribution Job called divine injustice.

(2) Complaint against God (19:7-20)

> [7]"Though I cry, 'I've been wronged!' I get no response;
>   though I call for help, there is no justice.
> [8]He has blocked my way so I cannot pass;
>   he has shrouded my paths in darkness.
> [9]He has stripped me of my honor
>   and removed the crown from my head.
> [10]He tears me down on every side till I am gone;
>   he uproots my hope like a tree.
> [11]His anger burns against me;
>   he counts me among his enemies.
> [12]His troops advance in force;
>   they build a siege ramp against me
>   and encamp around my tent.
>
> [13]He has alienated my brothers from me;
>   my acquaintances are completely estranged from me.

---

[78] Though מְשׁוּגָה is a hapax, it is related to the root שׁגג. In Yiddish *meshugge* means "insane."

¹⁴My kinsmen have gone away;
   my friends have forgotten me.
¹⁵My guests and my maidservants count me a stranger;
   they look upon me as an alien.
¹⁶I summon my servant, but he does not answer,
   though I beg him with my own mouth.
¹⁷My breath is offensive to my wife;
   I am loathsome to my own brothers.
¹⁸Even the little boys scorn me;
   when I appear, they ridicule me.
¹⁹All my intimate friends detest me;
   those I love have turned against me.
²⁰I am nothing but skin and bones;
   I have escaped with only the skin of my teeth.

"God" does not appear in this pericope, but he is the subject of the verbs in vv. 8-13 and the one responsible for all the social alienation Job described so pathetically in vv. 14-19. In a sense these verses are embellishments of the picture of the "net" drawn around him (v. 6). It "blocked" his way (v. 8), was "on every side" (v. 10), was "around" his tent (v. 12), and kept his kin and kith at a painful distance (vv. 14-19).

THE LEGAL CASE IS LOPSIDED (19:7-12).   Beginning with legal terminology, Job moved to other metaphors to describe how God mistreated him. God plunged him into darkness (v. 8). He uncrowned him (v. 9). He uprooted him (v. 11). He besieged him (v. 12).

19:7   The Hebrew is more pithy. For "I've been wronged!" it has the single word *ḥāmas,* translated "violence" (RSV, AB, NJPS, NASB, and most commentaries), "injustice" (NAB), or "murder" (Moffatt, AT, NAB; cf. Hab 1:2). It is the opposite of "justice," the key word of line *b* (cf. Isa 53:8-9). As in other places, Job felt ignored by an apathetic God.

19:8   Like Balaam (Num 22:24) or Jeremiah (Lam 3:7), Job felt he was at an impasse. God hedged him in (3:23), not to protect him (1:10) but to restrict and restrain him. "Darkness" with all its accompanying hardships, dangers, and fears faced the man from Uz wherever he turned. To the wandering Israelites God had been a pillar of fire (Exod 13:21), and to the psalmist he was "light" and "salvation" (Ps 27:1). Such was not Job's testimony, for now his lot was darkness and deadlock (compare these verses with Lam 3:1-18).

19:9   Like the stripped counselors and befuddled judges of 12:17, Job was "stripped" of his "honor" and divested of his "crown," a figure of speech denoting the loss of self-esteem or personal worth. Sickness and accompanying depression have a way of devaluing life and making the victim self-deprecating and even suicidal (cf. v. 2).

19:10   The contrast between "tear down" and "root up" is more English than Hebrew, but it does describe how Job felt God was dealing with him. Both statements are quite graphic. "Tear down" (*nātaṣ*) often describes the demolition of heathen altars or city walls (cf. 12:14, but the verb is *hāras*). "Uproot" (*nāsaʾ*) is a more general word for "remove," but by the analogy of a tree, it signifies something done with vigor and violence. In 14:7 Job said, "There is hope for a tree: If it is cut down, it will sprout again," but that is not so with an uprooted tree (cf. 18:16).

19:11   Though it was not really the case, Job interpreted his bad fortune as God's anger burning against him. In fact, God's anger burned against Eliphaz and his two friends, according to 42:7, because they had not spoken of God what was right. Abraham was the "friend of God" (2 Chr 20:7; Isa 41:8; Jas 2:23), but Job thought God "counted"[79] him "among his enemies." Job erred, like his three counselors, in judging God's attitude from circumstances. Certainly we who have the Scriptures should never make that mistake (cf. Rom 5:8; 8:39).

19:12   The section ends with a tristich with all three lines describing military movements. Perhaps Job compared his three friends to the "troops" who allied themselves against him. Their arguments were like "siege ramps,"[80] and their unwillingness to refrain from their accusations was like so many encampments of hostile soldiers waiting for surrender. The irony is that all this military might was directed at a mere "tent."

FORSAKEN BY FRIENDS AND FAMILY (19:13-20).   The scene Job sketched here is one of the most pathetic and pitiful in the entire book. All his friends distanced themselves from him. His servants did not obey him. Little boys scorned him. Even his wife and brothers found him offensive and loathsome.

19:13   At the beginning of this list of strained and estranged relationships, Job posited God as the source, "He has alienated" (causative of *rāḥaq*, "put far away"). "Brothers" are probably not siblings (v. 17) but fellow countrymen (cf. Pss 69:8[9]; 88:8[9]).

19:14   Two more categories of former associates severed their contacts with Job: "kinsmen" (*qārôb*, "near one/neighbor") and "friends" (or "acquaintances," from the verb "to know"). In vv. 13-15 the author employed the antonyms "far" and "near," "be strange" and "know" to de-

---

[79] The NIV at 13:24 translates "considered" for the same verb, חשׁב, but the word for "enemy" is different.

[80] Literally, "raised up a way," which R. Gordis unconvincingly takes to refer to "the paving of roads for the passage of chariots and horses" (*Job*, 201).

scribe how topsy-turvy Job's world had become.

19:15 Because v. 14 is so short (four Hebrew words) and v. 15 so long (eight Hebrew words), some translations make v. 14 into one line and v. 15 into three by moving the verb "forgotten" to v. 15 (RSV, NEB, GNB).[81] We must reckon with the fact that the author was not bound by the rules of poetry as strictly as we might wish. The point is clear however the verses are divided—those who should have known and honored Job treated him like a "stranger," *zār,* or an "alien/foreigner," *nokrî,* with all the aloofness those terms involved.

19:16 First the female servants did not recognize him, then Job's male servant was unresponsive. The master ought never have to "beg" his servant, but so great was the alienation and disrespect Job endured.

19:17 While there is no doubt about the meaning of this verse in general, some of the specifics of the translation are in question. "My breath" is *rûḥî,* which could also be "my spirit" or even "my self."[82] As it stands, Job must have had halitosis.[83] The parallel synonymous verbs in the verse occur only here.[84] The last irregularity is the expression "my own brothers," which is literally "sons of my womb." Many are satisfied simply to live with the anomaly of Job here referring to his children, while the prologue records their deaths (AB, NJPS).[85] The RV, ASV, and RSV in different ways added "mother," something the NIV and all others that read "brothers" do by implication.

19:18 In the preceding verses Job complained that his acquaintances distanced themselves or ignored him. In vv. 18-19 other categories actively offended and spurned him. "Little boys,"[86] who should have re-

---

[81] AAT, following the *BHS* scansion, moved the "guests" to v. 14. See H. H. Rowley, *Job,* NCBC (Grand Rapids: Eerdmans, 1970), 135.

[82] Some emend it to רֵיחִי, "my smell/odor" (*BHK* footnote; NJPS).

[83] From Latin *halitum,* the word in the Vulgate. D. Clines (*Job 1–20,* WBC [Dallas: Word, 1989] 448) argues vigorously against the "bad breath" interpretation and in favor of "my life."

[84] "Is offensive" is זָרָה, which looks like a form of the verb זוּר, "be strange" (cf. vv. 13,15), but most take it as a hapax, זוּר II, meaning "be loathsome" (so BDB, 266; KB has it under זוּר III, 253-54). Likewise the verb in line *b* is another hapax and a biform of a common root meaning "be gracious" in the simple stems and "entreat" in the *hithpael* (as in KJV, ASV, and in v. 16b). So it is a synonym of the first verb, "be loathsome."

[85] Several seek a middle course with "my own family"; cf. NEB, AAT, NCV, REB, NRSV. Hartley (*Job,* 289) suggests that "Job is using stereotyped language of lament without making specific adjustments to the particulars of his case."

[86] "Little boys" are עֲוִילִים, a term that occurs only three times, all in Job. In 16:11, because of its affinity to the well-established root עוּל, it is "evil men." That interpretation would do here (so KJV margin). In 21:11 it must be "children," related to an Arabic root with that meaning. See Gordis, *Job,* 202.

spected their elders, were the first to "scorn" and "ridicule"[87] Job.

19:19 "My intimate friends" is literally "men of my council"[88] (or "counsel"). Even these few with whom one would dare to share confidences had nothing to do with Job (Ps 55:12-14[13-15]). "Those I love" at the end of this list serves as a catchall to review all the categories Job listed in vv. 14-19. While he loved them, they "turned against" him.

19:20 Many options exist for both the translation and interpretation of this verse.[89] The first problem is that the verse does not seem to fit with the preceding context, which does not deal with Job's physical condition.

Second, the first line reads literally, "On my skin and on my flesh sticks my bone." But "bone" does not "stick" on "skin" and "flesh." The other way around would be more likely.[90]

Third, the occurrence of "skin" in line *a* makes the line rather long and suggests to some that it may be an error, especially since Ps 102:5[6] has literally "my bone sticks to my flesh."[91]

The fourth problem is that since "teeth" do not have "skin," what does it mean to escape with (or by) it? One possibility is that Job meant he escaped with nothing (there is no word "only" in the text).[92] Some suggest it may refer to gums (NIV margin, "only my gums"). The phrase "skin of my teeth" is now an entrenched English idiom. Elsewhere Job hinted that he was emaciated (16:8; cf. 33:21), so the best interpretation is one that assumes this verse speaks to that condition. If so, v. 20 goes better with the next section, which has "flesh" in the last line.

---

[87] "Ridicule" translates וַיְדַבְּרוּ בִי (cf. Pss 50:20; 78:19). The AB has "revile"; the JB, "ready with a jibe"; the GNB, "laugh"; Hartley, "jeer"; Buttenwieser, "insult" (*Book of Job* [New York: Macmillan, 1922], 124).

[88] So Hartley, *Job*, 287. The AT has "men of my circle." The NJPS has "my bosom friends."

[89] See Clines for a thorough review and interaction with many of them (*Job 1–20*, 430-32). He begins his comment on the verse by noting that "this famous crux is one of the most problematic verses of the whole book" (p. 450),

[90] Clines (*Job 1–20*, 450-52) notes that the verb "stick/cling/cleave" (דבק) always speaks of something weaker clinging to or depending on something stronger or more significant. He cites, among others, 29:10; 31:7; Gen 2:24; 34:3; Jer 13:11; Ezek 29:4; Ps 101:3; Ruth 1:14; 2:8,21,23; Deut 10:20; 11:22; 13:5[4]; 30:20; Josh 22:5; 23:8. He suggests the picture is of bones so weak or diseased that the body has to be supported by the flesh. He understands this metaphorically, however, of "the overpowering sense of weakness and being worn out" (cf. 6:12-13; 13:25,28; 16:7-8; 17:7). The treatment Job had received caused him to "collapse in a heap."

[91] So, e.g., Hartley, *Job,* 287. On the other hand, the NIV has not translated "my flesh."

[92] Clines (*Job 1–20*, 452) says the idea is that the escape is "not worth having."

(3) Plea to Friends (19:21-22)

> [21]"Have pity on me, my friends, have pity,
>   for the hand of God has struck me.
> [22]Why do you pursue me as God does?
>   Will you never get enough of my flesh?

Having charged his friends and relatives with neglect and even active abuse, Job now pled with them for mercy. It was bad enough that God was against him; he hoped his friends could at least be sympathetic.

19:21 The two imperatival pleas for mercy are right together at the beginning of the verse. Would the friends side with God against a fellow human being, an intimate friend, even a relative? The word for "struck" (*nāgaʿ*) is the same the Satan used in 1:11; 2:5 when he told God to "strike" Job. God handed Job over to the Satan, so strictly speaking it was not God who "struck" Job.

19:22 "Pursue" was the verb Job used in 13:25 when he compared God's pursuit of him to the "chasing after dry chaff." With the use of these two rhetorical questions, he hoped to elicit some support, discover a kinsman-redeemer, or just find anyone who would cross over to his side. In this consuming struggle he had to maintain his integrity and innocence and yet explain his suffering. Some people who think they stand with God are actually standing against him.

(4) Testimony of Hope (19:23-27)

> [23]"Oh, that my words were recorded,
>   that they were written on a scroll,
> [24]that they were inscribed with an iron tool on lead,
>   or engraved in rock forever!
> [25]I know that my Redeemer lives,
>   and that in the end he will stand upon the earth.
> [26]And after my skin has been destroyed,
>   yet in my flesh I will see God;
> [27]I myself will see him
>   with my own eyes—I, and not another.
>   How my heart yearns within me!

For many this is the high point of the book; v. 25 has been often quoted and put to music. But Andersen's words of caution must be heeded:

This passage is notoriously difficult. Much depends on the authenticity and meaning of its central affirmation, *my Redeemer lives*. Unfortunately it is followed by several lines which are so unintelligible that the range of translations offered is quite bewildering. Two extremes should be avoided. There is no need for the loud note of Job's certainty of ultimate vindication to be drowned by the static of textual difficulties. But too much of later resurrection theology should not be read back into the passage.[93]

The NIV capitalizes "Redeemer," making clear the translators' understanding that a divine person was in view.[94] Though this is a central question, it is only one of several questions that arise from these verses.[95] Regardless of details, this pericope is certainly another of Job's rays of hope in an otherwise dismal assortment of groans and grievances.

19:23 This is one of ten passages in Job where the idiom appears that reads literally "who would give," translated here and frequently elsewhere as "oh, that."[96] Job wished for a permanent record, one "written" (*kātab* in the first line) and "inscribed" (*ḥaqaq* in the second line).[97] Job feared that he would die before he was vindicated, so he wanted his testimony preserved for later generations. This is not unlike people having Bible verses engraved on their tombstones.

19:24 Verse 24 continues the sentence begun in v. 23. "Inscribed" is not in Hebrew but rather "engraved" (*ḥāṣab*).[98] Job wanted this account of his faith preserved eternally on "rock."[99] It is uncertain whether Job had in mind a writing instrument made partly of lead or filling or lining the letters in lead so that they would shine and endure.[100]

---

[93] Andersen, *Job*. The number of NIV footnotes confirms for the reader that its Committee on Bible Translation was not unanimous. E. M. Good does not even translate vv. 25b-27c (*In Turns of Tempest: A Reading of Job, with a Translation* [Stanford, Cal.: Stanford University Press, 1990], 257).

[94] But note the NIV margin, "defender." Those versions that use lowercase are KJV, RV, AB, NEB, GNB.

[95] For a nontechnical list of the pros and cons on this matter, see A. Barnes, *Job,* in *Notes on the Old Testament* (1846; reprint, Grand Rapids: Baker, 1950), I:330-34.

[96] The other places it occurs in Job are 6:8; 11:5; 13:5; 14:4,13; 23:3; 29:2; 31:31,35. *GBH* § 163d discusses the various uses of the expression.

[97] The noun form of this latter verb means "statute/decree/law," so more than "write," it means to write with permanence and authority.

[98] This is the only time out of seventeen occurrences that this root means something like "write." Ordinarily it means "hew/carve/dig."

[99] Not "a rock" or "a stone" but on something much larger, e.g., a mountain. Darius's trilingual inscription on the Behistun Rock in the Zagros Mountains of Iran comes to mind.

[100] Hartley, *Job,* 291; W. C. Kaiser, Jr., *Hard Sayings of the Old Testament* (Downers Grove: InterVarsity, 1988), 150.

19:25 Job was sure of one thing, "As for me, I know." His certainty was about his "Redeemer." The word, an active participial, is from the verb (*gāʾal*) that describes what one does to property in hock (Lev 19:29), or what a friend or close relative does for someone in slavery (Lev 19:47-48) or in debt (Lev 19:25), or for one who has been killed (Num 35:12; 2 Sam 14:11; cf. Rev 6:10; 19:2) or widowed (Ruth 2:20).[101] In the Pentateuch and historical books the word was basically commercial or legal, but in the psalms and prophets it became a theological term (e.g., Ps 19:14[15]; Isa 43:1; Jer 50:34; Mic 4:10).[102] The question is whether Job was using it in the older sense, hoping for some relative to stand up for him, or whether in the later sense that Yahweh was Israel's Redeemer. It is possible both were in his mind. Certainly he had wished for some fellow human being then and there to say a good word for him before God and his neighbors, but he also envisioned a divine Redeemer (note vv. 26-27 and see comments at 16:19 and 17:3).[103]

One can offer substitute synonyms for the words in the second half that might alter the meaning, but all the words are well known and used in Job. "In the end," for example, might be "latter/last/afterwards." "Earth" might be "dust" (but it is "earth" in 28:2; 30:6; 41:33[25]).[104] "Stand" might be "arise/be established." Each of these alternatives raises new possibilities about the meaning of the verse, but as usual the straightforward sense is best. The Redeemer would eventually appear. Though Job would die and his stone testimony would stand in silence, he anticipated a Redeemer who "lives" and acts on behalf of those in need who rely on him.

Along with the prophets, Job spoke words that we can understand best from the perspective of the New Testament. Job's understanding of God's eternal plan for the redemption of his people through the death of Christ was surely limited, but that does not diminish the veracity of the statement. For Job and for every believer before and after him there is a divine Redeemer. We know his name is Jesus, and at the last day he will stand up and defend us because he has bought us with his blood (Acts 20:28; Eph 1:7; 2:13; Col 1:20; 1 Pet 1:18-19; Rev 1:5; 5:9).

---

[101] See *TDOT* 2:350-55.

[102] Hartley (*Job,* 292) notes several passages (Ps 119:154; Prov 23:11; Jer 50:34; Lam 3:58-59) where it describes the Lord as initiating "a lawsuit to win back or redress the rights of a brother who had been wronged."

[103] Andersen opines that "verses 25-27 are so tightly knit that there should be no doubt that the *Redeemer* is God" (*Job*).

[104] Hartley, who understands Job as expecting vindication before his death, says that "the word *dust* emphasizes that God would appear at the ash heap on which Job sits (2:8) . . . the very place of his humiliation" (*Job,* 294-95).

19:26   This verse has the most problems of any in this section.[105]
"After" is another form of the word translated "in the end" in v. 25. "My
skin," even with no adjustment of vowels, can be read "I awake/arise."[106]
That option, however, would leave no subject for the verb "has been destroyed."[107] "In my flesh" ordinarily would be "from my flesh" (see NIV
footnote) or even "without my flesh" (AB). The translators, however, appealed to a less common but occasional use of the preposition (*min*)[108]
and rendered it as if from Job's viewpoint, that is, "from within," partly
because of the emphasis in v. 27 on his bodily identity. As Andersen
points out, "The references to *skin, flesh* and *eyes* make it clear that Job
expects to have this experience as a man, not just as a disembodied
shade, or in his mind's eye."[109] This is the first of three statements aver-
ring his anticipation of seeing God.[110]

19:27   The second and third verbs for "see" are in the first two lines
of this tricolon,[111] with the additional emphasis of "my eyes." "Not another" can be understood to mean either that "I and not another will see"
or "I will see God and not another."[112] The latter is more likely, that is,
"God will not be a stranger." It is a debated point whether Job expected
this experience to occur following a bodily resurrection, in a conscious
state following his death, or even before his death. Andersen's path probably is wisest. He agrees with those who, "while admitting that the pas-

---

[105] J. G. Williams feels that vv. 26-27 "have been difficult for commentators because of
theological controversies, not because of the condition of the text. Without one word, זֹאת
in v. 26a, everything else would be intelligible and grammatically correct" ("Job and the
God of Victims," in *The Voice from the Whirlwind* [Nashville: Abingdon, 1992], 217).

[106] This would be the *qal* infinitive construct with first singular pronominal suffix, literally "my waking" (though it never appears elsewhere). See the NIV footnote. The same
term meaning "my skin" also occurs in 7:5; 30:30.

[107] According to BDB, נָקַף I occurs only here (*piel*) and Isa 10:34 (*niphal*), although
both could be either *piel* or *niphal*. BDB translates here "after my skin, which they have
struck off (alluding to ravages of his disease)–this!" *Niphal*, i.e., passive, is read by the
NIV. The KJV read it *piel*, i.e., active, but had to supply "worms" for the subject. Pope
translates "is flayed" (*Job,* AB [Garden City: Doubleday, 1929).

[108] Smick notes that the idea of seeing God "apart from" flesh, i.e., in a disembodied
state, "is at best a rare concept in the OT" (EBC 4:944). The interpretation that Job would
see God "in" his flesh is made more likely by his confidence in v. 27 that he would see God
with his own eyes.

[109] Andersen, *Job,* 193.

[110] A. B. Davidson pointed out that as Job's main distress was his feeling of God's hiding his face from him, so "his redemption must come through his again beholding God in
peace" (*The Book of Job* [Cambridge: University Press, 1951], 168).

[111] The verb was חָזָה in vv. 26b,27a and רָאָה in v. 27b.

[112] "Another" is זָר, "stranger," from a root Job had used twice in this chapter (vv. 13,17).

sage falls short of a full statement of faith in personal bodily resurrection, find in it the hope of a favourable meeting with God after death as a genuine human being."[113]

The attention commentaries devote to this passage and the number of articles on all facets of it are enormous. In this relatively brief presentation the emphasis has been on the text as it exists (rather than as it can be emended) and on the most likely interpretation in consideration of the way the key words are generally used in the Old Testament and in Job in particular. Like the other passages expressing hope, it stands in sharp contrast to the surrounding gloom and doom, but that background also serves to accentuate the extraordinary character of these passages. Diamonds are displayed best on black velvet.

(5) Advice to Friends (19:28-29)

> [28]"If you say, 'How we will hound him,
>   since the root of the trouble lies in him,'
> [29]you should fear the sword yourselves;
>   for wrath will bring punishment by the sword,
>   and then you will know that there is judgment.'"

There may well have been a temporal pause here, for v. 28 represents an abrupt change of attitude and subject matter. Just a verse earlier Job was anticipating the sight of God. Now his focus turned once again on his friends, and he lashed out at them with this stern warning.

19:28 The premise of this two-verse conditional sentence is v. 28, which incorporates a quotation that is not exact but represents what Job sensed they were saying and doing. The verb translated "hound" (*rdp*) is the same as in v. 22, "pursue." In fact, the general tenor of v. 22 resumes in v. 28. One facet of their contention was that "the root of the trouble lies" in Job,[114] that is, Job himself was the source of the problem with his unacknowledged sin.

---

[113] Andersen, *Job,* 194. He goes on to clarify on the basis of 14:13ff. that "the hope of resurrection lies at the very heart of Job's faith." On the concept of resurrection in the OT see W. C. Kaiser, Jr., *Toward Rediscovering the Old Testament* (Grand Rapids: Zondervan, 1987), 141-44.

[114] The Masoretic Text has בִּי, "in me," but the LXX and Vulgate translated as if it were בוֹ, "in him," a form that a few Hebrew manuscripts have. Even if "in me" is original, it can be explained as another case of perspective. Though Job was quoting them, he referred to himself even within the quotation as "me."

19:29 The essence of Job's advice was to "fear"[115] the execution of divine justice themselves (5:20; 15:22; Lev 26:25,33; Ps 45:3[4]). The Bible strongly warns against false accusation (Exod 20:16; 23:1,7; Ps 101:5; Jer 9:3-9; 2 Tim 3:3; Titus 2:3; 2 Pet 2:10-11), and that was essentially what Bildad and his two friends were committing. The last word of the chapter is an impossible form here translated "that there is judgment." Most, like the NIV, read it as the relative pronoun (ša) plus the common noun "judge" or "judgment." Without the last letter the consonants spell one of the common names for God, "Shaddai."[116] The friends' contention had been that Job was being judged. In these verses Job warned them they should beware of judgment themselves, a warning that turned out to have substance in light of 42:7.

---

[115] Translating גּוּר III, not the common גּוּר I, "sojourn."

[116] The *kethib* is usually read as שְׁדִין; *qere* is the unknown form שְׁדוּן. KB gives the emendation שְׁ דִּין, "there is a judge." See Gordis, *Job,* 207-8. Cf. Moffatt, AAT, and NIV footnote, "Almighty"; RSV, "God"; AB, "Shaddayan."

11. Zophar's Discourse on the Fate of the Wicked (20:1-29)

Zophar's second speech follows the same broad outline as Bildad's second speech—criticism of Job and a lengthy tirade on retribution for sin. Bildad's was more dynamistic; Zophar's was more divine, that is, stressing the activity of God in the administration of justice on the wicked. Zophar seemed less able to say anything new. This, in fact, was the last time he spoke.

(1) Offense at Criticism (20:1-3)

¹**Then Zophar the Naamathite replied:**

²**"My troubled thoughts prompt me to answer**
    because I am greatly disturbed.
³**I hear a rebuke that dishonors me,**
    and my understanding inspires me to reply.

The opening of this speech is less blunt than the last few. Zophar is al-

most as polite as Eliphaz was in 4:2. He nevertheless indirectly charges
Job with insulting him, and this presumably gives him warrant to articu-
late again his cause-and-effect theory of suffering.

20:1 See comments at 4:1.

20:2 Zophar had been listening, we assume, to the dialogue in these
eight chapters. Finally his "thoughts"[1] prompted him to answer.[2] Furthermore, he was "greatly disturbed" or "pained" by what he had heard.[3]

20:3 Zophar seemed most disturbed, not by Job's affirmation of hope
but because he was "dishonored" by his warning at the close of chap. 19.
Job used the same word (*klm*) in 19:3 when he charged the friends with
"reproach." First his "thoughts," now his "understanding" moved him to
enter the discussion again.[4] With anticipation we await his wisdom.

(2) Retribution for the Wicked (20:4-29)

[4]"Surely you know how it has been from of old,
   ever since man was placed on the earth,
[5]that the mirth of the wicked is brief,
   the joy of the godless lasts but a moment.
[6]Though his pride reaches to the heavens
   and his head touches the clouds,
[7]he will perish forever, like his own dung;
   those who have seen him will say, 'Where is he?'
[8]Like a dream he flies away, no more to be found,
   banished like a vision of the night.
[9]The eye that saw him will not see him again;
   his place will look on him no more.
[10]His children must make amends to the poor;
   his own hands must give back his wealth.
[11]The youthful vigor that fills his bones
   will lie with him in the dust.

---

[1] A word that occurs only here and in 4:13, שְׂעִפִּים.

[2] An unusual *hiphil* of שׁוּב with double causative force.

[3] This verb usually has been understood as inf. con. of חוּשׁ I, "hasten" (BDB); hence
the AV rendering "and for this I make haste" (also ASV, RV, RSV, JB, NEB, REB). Most
now would derive it from חוּשׁ II, "feel (pain)" (KB[3]); hence NIV, NKJV, NCV, Pope (*Job*,
137), E. Dhorme (*Job* [London: Nelson, 1967], 289-90), Clines (*Job 1–20*), Hartley, (*Job*,
300), etc. Cf. Eccl 2:25, the only other occurrence.

[4] Verses 2-3 follow a general chiastic outline.

A   My thoughts prompt an answer
  B   I am disturbed
  B'   I am dishonored
A'   My understanding inspires a reply.

12"Though evil is sweet in his mouth
    and he hides it under his tongue,
13Though he cannot bear to let it go
    and keeps it in his mouth,
14yet his food will turn sour in his stomach;
    it will become the venom of serpents within him.
15He will spit out the riches he swallowed;
    God will make his stomach vomit them up.
16He will suck the poison of serpents;
    the fangs of an adder will kill him.
17He will not enjoy the streams,
    the rivers flowing with honey and cream.
18What he toiled for he must give back uneaten;
    he will not enjoy the profit from his trading.
19For he has oppressed the poor and left them destitute;
    he has seized houses he did not build.

20"Surely he will have no respite from his craving;
    he cannot save himself by his treasure.
21Nothing is left for him to devour;
    his prosperity will not endure.
22In the midst of his plenty, distress will overtake him;
    the full force of misery will come upon him.
23When he has filled his belly,
    God will vent his burning anger against him
    and rain down his blows upon him.
24Though he flees from an iron weapon,
    a bronze-tipped arrow pierces him.
25He pulls it out of his back,
    the gleaming point out of his liver.
 Terrors will come over him;
26 total darkness lies in wait for his treasures.
 A fire unfanned will consume him
    and devour what is left in his tent.
27The heavens will expose his guilt;
    the earth will rise up against him.
28A flood will carry off his house,
    rushing waters on the day of God's wrath.
29Such is the fate God allots the wicked,
    the heritage appointed for them by God."

This long section is subdivided into three similar subsections. As in Bildad's speech, God's name is absent from the first subsection. Not far behind the bad fortunes of the wicked stands God, who is credited with assorted gory penalties designed for those who appear temporarily to be thriving.

THE WICKED HAVE ALWAYS SUFFERED (20:4-11).   Tradition and history support Zophar's contention that the apparent good luck of evildoers is fleeting and ephemeral. Before long no sinner escapes some form of retribution that completely reverses the picture of prosperity.

20:4   In Hebrew this is a negative rhetorical question, but the effect is the same. Job should have known how the world operates since it has not changed since Adam.[5] "Was placed" (lit. "he placed") assumes God as the subject. Lacking a subject in the text, most turn to a passive construction.

20:5   The profound and eternal truth Zophar so elegantly introduced is simply a restatement of retributive justice. From a poetic point of view, this verse is a nearly perfect example of synonymous parallelism.

20:6   This verse too is noteworthy from the standpoint of structure. In Hebrew it is a perfect three-step chiasmus.

A   Though reaches
  B   to the heavens
    C   his pride[6]
    C'   and his head
  B'   to the clouds
A'   touches.

The boasts of the king of Babylon imagined in Isaiah's taunt song come to mind (Isa 14:13-14).

20:7   Zophar became crude but graphic as he compared the demise of the wicked to "dung."[7] The ten words of line *b* represent three in Hebrew, but there is hardly a more succinct way of phrasing it. The ungodly will disappear without a trace.

20:8   As elsewhere in the speeches of Job (7:10) and Bildad (8:18), attention is called to the brevity of life. Contrary to his friends, however, Job maintained that it was not always the bad who died young and the good who lived long. Psalm 90:10 also used the verb "fly away," except that in Zophar's mind it meant to disappear, not to go to heaven.

20:9   The motif of the vanishing wicked that began in v. 7 continues in this verse. The synonyms for "see/look" are both unusual, but their translation is not in doubt[8] (cf. 7:8).

---

[5] אָדָם is the name of the first man as well as a common word for "man/mankind." See the NIV footnote. The REV and NRSV, both completed since the advent of feminist sensitivities, translate "mortals."

[6] The root behind this hapax is נשׂא. "Pride" certainly is an extension of the notion "lift up/exalt/be high." The RSV has "exulting"; the NASB has "loftiness."

[7] From the widely used root גלל, "to be round," comes this word that occurs elsewhere only in 1 Kgs 14:10; Zeph 1:17.

[8] "See," שׁזף, occurs only once in the first line and is elsewhere only in 28:7; Song 1:6. The second is שׁור, which occurs nine times in Job and only five or six times elsewhere.

20:10 All the ill-gotten gain will return to those who deserve it. To the children of the wicked will fall the task of settling their father's accounts and perhaps surrendering their own inheritance to do so.

20:11 This section concludes with the wicked lying in the dust of death. The reference to "youthful vigor" means either that his life will pass quickly or he will die young.[9]

GOD WILL CERTAINLY PUNISH THE WICKED (20:12-19). There are only slight differences between the main message of this section and that of the first. God is active in v. 15, whereas he is not mentioned in vv. 4-11. Also the descriptions of the punishments are more vivid, even repulsive (vv. 14-16). Furthermore, there is a specific sin mentioned for which the evildoers earn this treatment (v. 19). Finally, all the verses except v. 19 have something to do with eating.

20:12 Verses 12-13 serve as the first half of a three-verse concessive sentence that concludes with the result in v. 14. A concessive sentence combines elements of condition and contrast.[10] The wicked savor evil and expect it to produce pure satisfaction, but in fact the opposite results. The major motif that colors all of this section begins here with the mention of "mouth" and "tongue." "Evil" at the time may seem "sweet," but as subsequent verses will point out, it turns sour and makes the partaker nauseated (cf. Prov 9:17).

20:13 "Evil" continues as the antecedent object of the three verbs in this verse: "he spares it," "he does not let it go," and "he keeps it."[11] Evil is like some delicious but deadly food.[12] Some people cannot resist food or drink they know will kill them.

20:14 What the wicked ingested will simply turn in his stomach (the verb does not mean "turn sour"). The second line elaborates what his food will turn into, that is, the "venom"[13] of a "serpent."[14]

20:15 As one expectorates something bitter, so the wicked will "spit

---

[9] "Youthful vigor," עֲלוּמָיו, occurs elsewhere only in 33:25; Ps 89:45[46]; Isa 54:4, but it is clearly related to the well-known root meaning "youth/virgin."

[10] The one אִם, "though," must be understood for all four lines of vv. 12-13. Verse 14 lacks the usual *waw* to indicate the beginning of the apodosis. On concessive clauses see *GBH* § 171. On the use or nonuse of *waw* in conditional sentences, see *GBH* § 167.

[11] See KJV, ASV, RV for this awkward but literal translation.

[12] The word for "mouth" in v. 13 is not פֶּה as in v. 12 but חֵךְ ("palate"; see 6:30).

[13] "Venom" is yet another word built on the root מרר. Cf. מַר, "bitter," in 3:20, etc.; מְרָה, "hostility," 17:2; מְרִי, "bitter," 23:2; מָרַר, "taste bitterness," 27:2; מְרֹרָה, "gall," 16:13; מְרֹרָה, "bitter things," 13:26; "poison" here in 20:14; "liver" 20:25. See D. Pardee, "*mᵉrôrat-pᵉtānîm* 'Venom' in Job 20:14," *ZAW* 91 (1979): 401-16.

[14] Verses 14,16 both have פְּתָנִים, which may be the horned viper (*Cerastes cornutus Forsk*) or cobra (*naja haje*). See KB.

out" what was swallowed. This is the first connection of "riches" with "evil," although they often go hand in hand as the rich exploit the poor; the poor steal from the rich; and cheating, fraud, and greed run rampant. Many have proven the truth of 1 Tim 6:10, "For the love of money is a root of all kinds of evil." "God" appears for the first time in Zophar's speech here as the agent to "make [the evildoer's stomach] vomit."[15]

20:16   Zophar returned to the poisonous snake theme, repeating one term from v. 14 and adding "adder."[16] "Fangs" is *lāšôn,* "tongue." There is a tradition in the Bible of connecting evil and snakes. The tradition began in the garden of Eden (Gen 3), continued with the serpents in the wilderness (Num 21:6; cf. 2 Kgs 18:4), and on to "that ancient serpent called the devil" (Rev 12:9).

20:17   The opposite of "venom" and "poison" is "honey and cream." The "cream" was milk at some stage of fermenting, perhaps buttermilk or thin yogurt. The verse has three words for "river" in a row, but in translation the last is made into a verb, "flowing."[17]

20:18   Verse 18 is difficult and the translation somewhat uncertain.[18] "What he toiled for" is the only use of this root as a noun. "His trading" appears only five more times in the Bible, and "enjoy" occurs only here. Most translations and commentaries concur with the NIV in general. The verse means that the wicked must surrender their ill-gotten gain.

20:19   For the first time a specific sin appears. The primary crime that Zophar had in mind, for which these criminals suffered, was oppression. Throughout the Old Testament are found numerous injunctions to care for the poor, be generous to widows, and exercise generosity and hospitality (Lev 19:10; Deut 15:4; Ps 72:4,12-14; Prov 31:8-9; Isa 10:1-2; Ezek 18:12; Amos 5:11, etc.). Benevolence is a mark of a God-fearing people.

THE FATE GOD ALLOTS THE WICKED (20:20-29).   The motif of eating persists through v. 23. Then the Naamathite listed an assortment of grievous tragedies that strike the wicked, concluding with the judgment that this was God's doing and the just reward for sin.

20:20   "Surely he does not know peace in his belly" is a literal rendering of the Hebrew (cf. AB). The NJPS took "belly" in the sense of "womb/offspring" when it translated, "He will not see his children tran-

---

[15] An unusual use of the common verb יָרֵשׁ ("possess/dispossess/drive out").

[16] Perhaps אֶפְעֶה is the carpet viper, *echis colorata,* common in the Jericho plain. See *Fauna and Flora of the Bible* (London: UBS, 1972), 72.

[17] They are פְּלַגָּה, a fem. of the more common פֶּלֶג; נָהָר, the most common word for "river"; and נַחַל, which often means "canyon/valley" as well as "river."

[18] See Clines (*Job,* 475) for a review of the problems and various solutions that have been offered by emending the text or appealing to unusual meanings for common words.

quil." The NAB took "belly" to mean "greed"; the NEB, "appetite." The NASB has simply "within him." Whatever the exact sense of "his belly," all agree that there is no rest for the wicked (Isa 48:22; 57:21) and that wealth cannot buy escape from punishment or death (Prov 18:11).

20:21 As the subsequent verses indicate, the ungodly suffer sudden loss. Despite his gains and prosperity, the wicked oppressor is plunged instantly into poverty and starvation. No food is left, and his "prosperity" or "good" (*tôb*) will not "endure."[19] Riches are fleeting.

20:22 A straightforward translation of the Hebrew of this verse communicates little, "In the fullnesses of his plenty[20] it will be restrictive to him; every hand of misery will come to him." The NIV's paraphrase is acceptable, describing what has been repeated many times: the demise of the wealthy, the fall of the powerful, the humiliation of the proud, the collapse of corporations, and the sudden death of those who thought they were immortal.

20:23 In this tricolon the NIV has added "God" as the subject of the verbs in the last two lines. The subject in the first line could be either God or the wicked.[21] When the wicked or God has a full "belly" (translated "craving" in v. 20), God sends burning anger and rains down "blows."[22]

20:24 One disaster after another greets the hapless wicked. Isaiah (24:18) and Amos (5:19) described the plight of the godless with similar series of misadventures. One can only imagine what the "iron weapon" is since it is a term to describe an "armory" or "warfare" in general.[23] "Bronze" arrowheads have been found throughout the ancient Near East.

20:25 The last line of v. 25 and the first line of v. 26 are parallel and should have been numbered as a separate verse. The six lines of these two verses constitute three pairs as the NIV scansion indicates.[24] On the other hand, v. 25b is very short and has no verb. Verse 25a has two verbs, "He pulls, and it comes out of his back."

"Gleaming point" translates a word that usually means "lightning" but

---

[19] From חִיל/חוּל II, which occurs elsewhere only in Ps 10:5.

[20] "Plenty" is שֶׂפֶק, a hapax. But a cognate verb is in 1 Kgs 20:10 (cf. Job 27:23; Isa 2:6). סֶפֶק is apparently an alternate spelling that appears here in some MSS and in 36:18.

[21] The LXX lacks the first line, an omission reflected in Moffatt, JB, NAB, NEB.

[22] This rare word (לְחוּם) occurs only here and Zeph 1:17, where the NIV translates "entrails." In Job 20:23 the NIV either follows the LXX ὀδυνας ("pain," which means emending בלחום to חבלים) or understands it as a form of לְחֹם, "fight/war" (cf. AT, JB, NAB, NJPS; see Grabbe, *Job,* 76-77). Others read "while he is eating" (KJV, RV, NASB), "food" (RSV, MLB, NRSV), "fire" (AB), or "flame" (AAT); also see Clines, *Job,* 477-78.

[23] The NJPS makes the arrows iron and the parallel a bow of bronze. Cf. AAT.

[24] The NAB omitted the middle line of v. 25, and the NEB omitted the third line.

occasionally describes a sword or spear (Deut 32:41; Nah 3:3; Hab 3:11). "Liver" is not the usual *kābēd* ("honorable" or "heavy" organ) but a derivative of the root *mrr,* "bitter" (see note on "venom" at 20:14).

20:26 Zophar here resumed the motif of lost "treasures" from vv. 20-22, although the Hebrew word is different from the one in v. 20. If "blows" in v. 23 should be "flame/fire" as some have it, then that would tie to the middle line of v. 26. "What is left" is the same word as in v. 21. And the theme of eating, from the middle verse of the chapter, echoes in the last two lines of v. 26.

20:27 "Heavens" and "earth" comprise a merismus (see explanation at 1:20), indicating that the guilt of the wicked will be evident to all, God in heaven and fellow humans on earth. For a culture where loss of reputation was especially serious, this threat was one of the more severe. "Expose" (from *gālâ*) also means "make naked" or "send/carry into exile" (cf. v. 28), ideas not unrelated since captives were taken away stripped. In this case the wicked person was "stripped" of respect and reward.

20:28 Taking a clue from the term "rushing waters" in the second line, the NIV and most modern versions read the unusual *yĕbûl* as "flood" rather than "increase" (KJV, NASB) or "possessions" (RSV, NRSV).[25] For desert people water was a welcome sight, but it could also be a frightening one. Memories of flash floods washing through steep canyons spoke of the destructive power of too much water. The only biblical examples of destruction by water are Noah's flood (Gen 7:22-23) and the Red Sea (Exod 14:26-28), but there are at least two Old Testament prophecies of floods (Dan 9:26; Nah 1:8; cf. also Matt 7:25).

20:29 "God" appears twice in v. 29 (though it is not in the Hebrew of v. 28). Line *a* has *ʾĕlōhîm,* and line *b* has *ʾēl* (cf. 27:13). Because the first line is so long, some delete "God" (AB, NAB, GNB), and others delete *ʾādām,* "man" (JB, AAT, NIV, REB, NRSV).[26] As Andersen observes, Zophar seems rather cold-blooded, leaving no room in his speech for repentance or mercy. He also appears to view the loss of possessions as the final tragedy rather than the loss of fellowship with God.[27] The verse not only concludes the chapter but is the conclusion of Zophar's argument and the last he will speak in the Book of Job. We will not miss him.

12. Job's Reply That the Wicked Go Unpunished (21:1-34)

Whereas Zophar filled his speech with illustrations of how the wicked

---

[25] Cf. יוּבַל, "stream," in Jer 17:8; אוּבָל or אָבָל in Dan 8:2-3,6; מַבּוּל in Gen 6:17 and twelve times elsewhere.

[26] The line reads literally, "This is the portion of a wicked man from God." Hebrew has five words in line *a* and only three in line *b.* The pronoun in the second line is singular.

[27] Andersen, *Job,* 197.

are punished, Job filled this response with illustrations of how the wicked escape unscathed. This is the nub of the question and the irreconcilable difference between the friends' view of retribution and Job's sure conviction that he was an innocent sufferer.

(1) Request for Attention (21:1-3)

¹Then Job replied:

²"Listen carefully to my words;
   let this be the consolation you give me.
³Bear with me while I speak,
   and after I have spoken, mock on.

As is typical of all the speakers, they demand attention; so at the beginning of this, Job's sixth response, he insisted that he have an opportunity for rebuttal. Until the end of v. 3 he sounded polite, but before the introduction was over, he released one ironic jab.

21:1 See comments at 6:1.

21:2 "Consolation" here and in v. 34 frames the chapter. It is the multifaceted Hebrew word *nāḥam* in an unusual noun form that is seen elsewhere only in 15:11.[28] With this word the friends came to "comfort" him in 2:11, and with it Job earlier upbraided them with the epithet "miserable comforters" (16:2). In effect, Job said that the best "comfort" they could give him was simply to listen.

21:3 "Mock on" is not only a sarcastic imperative but also Job's assessment of their advice. He considered it mockery, ridicule, or scorn, the kind of thing that is irritating even if it is not true. They, for their part, considered his attitude arrogant, insolent, and even blasphemous.

(2) Exceptions to the Rule (21:4-26)

⁴"Is my complaint directed to man?
   Why should I not be impatient?
⁵Look at me and be astonished;
   clap your hand over your mouth.
⁶When I think about this, I am terrified;
   trembling seizes my body.
⁷Why do the wicked live on,
   growing old and increasing in power?
⁸They see their children established around them,
   their offspring before their eyes.

---

[28] In Job it is fem., תַּנְחוּמוֹת; three other places it is masc., תַּנְחוּמִים.

⁹Their homes are safe and free from fear;
  the rod of God is not upon them.
¹⁰Their bulls never fail to breed;
  their cows calve and do not miscarry.
¹¹They send forth their children as a flock;
  their little ones dance about.
¹²They sing to the music of tambourine and harp;
  they make merry to the sound of the flute.
¹³They spend their years in prosperity
  and go down to the grave in peace.
¹⁴Yet they say to God, 'Leave us alone!
  We have no desire to know your ways.
¹⁵Who is the Almighty, that we should serve him?
  What would we gain by praying to him?'
¹⁶But their prosperity is not in their own hands,
  so I stand aloof from the counsel of the wicked.

¹⁷"Yet how often is the lamp of the wicked snuffed out?
  How often does calamity come upon them,
  the fate God allots in his anger?
¹⁸How often are they like straw before the wind,
  like chaff swept away by a gale?
¹⁹[It is said,] 'God stores up a man's punishment for his sons.'
  Let him repay the man himself, so that he will know it!
²⁰Let his own eyes see his destruction;
  let him drink of the wrath of the Almighty.
²¹For what does he care about the family he leaves behind
  when his allotted months come to an end?

²²"Can anyone teach knowledge to God,
  since he judges even the highest?
²³One man dies in full vigor,
  completely secure and at ease,
²⁴his body well nourished,
  his bones rich with marrow.
²⁵Another man dies in bitterness of soul,
  never having enjoyed anything good.
²⁶Side by side they lie in the dust,
  and worms cover them both.

In this major section Job vividly described the good life that the wicked enjoy. For all their ignoring God they seem to be blessed with children, cattle, long life, and happiness. All this was to counter what the friends said was the terrible lot of the evildoers. The way God treats people is more complicated than any of them understood.

THE UNCHALLENGED LIFE OF THE WICKED (21:4-16). Job asked his friends to consider the prosperity and merriment that wicked folks enjoy. Why, he asked, can those who have nothing to do with God be so blessed by him?

Introduction (21:4-6).   Before describing the lucky lot of the ungodly, Job introduced the topic by warning them that he found it scary and that they should be prepared for a surprise.

21:4   The two questions that constitute this verse seem unrelated. The answer to the first is no; Job's complaint was directed to God, not people. The second question, a negative one, anticipates a positive response. Yes, Job had every reason to be "short of spirit" or "impatient." He expected comfort from his friends but received only criticism, indictment, and rebuke. He was a good man, and yet he was suffering, something that was not supposed to happen according to the general rules of retribution. For this gross departure from the standardized view of rewards, he wanted an explanation from God but so far had gotten none.

21:5   In 17:8 Job had said that "upright men are [or should be] appalled at" the sight of a man suffering as he did. The same verb translates "astonished" here as Job again asked them to consider what he had been going through and to act with compassion rather than with censure. Out of respect for Job the elders in the gate used to "cover their mouths with their hands" (29:9), something he now asked his friends to do (cf. 13:5). In the end (40:4) Job did the same in the presence of God.

21:6   The situation Job was about to describe terrified him. He responded in the same way to the prosperity of the wicked that Bildad did to their destruction (18:20). Upon reflection it was a frightening thought to realize the wicked "live on" and "increase in power" while Job knew that he would soon die, since he felt himself growing weaker. The outcome of such a process is a world filled with wickedness and totally bereft of righteousness.

It Seems They Get Only Good (21:7-16).   Job described the beatific life of the wicked in terms of long life, many children, healthy herds, music and dancing, and a peaceful passing. That is astonishing. The description is similar to the way the friends described the blessings of the upright (cf. 5:24-25).

21:7   The section on the blessed wicked begins with a rhetorical question for which the friends would have no answer. Jeremiah asked similar questions (Jer 12:1-2), and so might we. The question points to cases in which Zophar's description of the fate of the wicked is observably false. The "mirth of the wicked" is not always "brief" (20:25).

21:8   The NIV's turning the prepositional phrase "before them" into a verb, "they see," is a neat way of handling the problem of two prepositional phrases in a row (cf. KJV "in their sight with them").[29] Some translations leave out the phrase "with them" (RSV, NEB, NJPS, NRSV); others omit "before them" or some representation of it (AB).[30] Having children was very important, and everyone hoped to live long enough to see grandchildren (Ps 127:4; Gen 45:10). Job, we must remember, had no children at this point. He was contradicting Bildad, who had asserted that the wicked would die childless (18:19).

21:9   Job had wished in 9:34 for "someone to remove God's rod." Now he said that "God's rod" is not on the wicked. Unlike the house that collapsed on his children, the "home" of the unrighteous has "safety" (*šālôm*) and not "fear" (*pāḥad*) such as came upon Job (3:25). He could point to many cases in which the wicked man was not "torn from the security of his tent" (18:14; cf. 5:24).

21:10   The good fortune of the wicked extends to their[31] cattle. Both genders succeed in their respective assignments. The bulls effectively inseminate, and the cows deliver live calves. "Breed" translates the very common verb *ʿābar*, "pass over," and is either a euphemism or a special use of this term.[32]

21:11   From v. 8 Job picked up the theme of "children." Not only do the wicked have "a flock" of children,[33] but those children appear happy.

21:12   "They sing" translates the common verb "to lift up," conveying the idea of lifting up their voices. "Tambourine/timbrel" and "harp/zither" are frequent enough to be certain, but "flute" is relatively rare and possibly some other kind of wind instrument.[34] All three classes of instruments are represented here: percussion, strings, and winds. It had been a while since Job had had reason to "make merry."

21:13   The NIV has paraphrased in v. 13, but not without precedent and warrant. "Years" are really "days," and "in peace" is, as the margin indicates, "in an instant." The point is that even in death the godless have it good. Theirs is no lingering death, no months of excruciating pain, no

---

[29] This solution is not original with the NIV; Moffatt did it in 1922.

[30] Apparently the NAB has either read עִם, "with," as עַם, "people," in order to have three synonyms in this verse—"progeny, kinsfolk, offspring," or, following Dahood and Blommerde, has read לִפְנֵהֶם, "before them," as "the ones who lived before them, i.e., ancestors" (M. Dahood, "Hebrew-Ugaritic Lexicography III," *Bib* 47 [1966]: 411; Blommerde, *Northwest Semitic Grammar and Job* [Rome: Pontifical Biblical Institute, 1969], 91).

[31] The pronouns in this verse are singular, "his bull," etc.

[32] See Gordis, *Job*, 229.

[33] For the third and last time in Job and in the OT appears this unusual word for children, עֲוִילִים.

[34] See Dhorme, *Job*, 312.

ongoing agony and protracted grief for the family. At the end of a long and fulfilled life, they die quickly and painlessly (cf. 29:18). The return to the theme of long life and prosperity for the wicked (v. 7) suggests that vv. 7-13 is a unit, and the question "Why?" applies to the whole.[35] Their response to such blessings is given in the following verses.

21:14 Those Job had been describing were not simply wicked but also godless in the true sense of that word. They did not care what God thinks and preferred him to absent himself from their lives and consciences. Though they seem to have believed in his existence, they were practical atheists. "Know" is broader than simple cognition but involves obedience, honor, and practice of the "ways" of God. Eliphaz would use the first half of this verse in 22:17.

21:15 The quotation Job framed to express their resistance to God continues through v. 15, where it takes the form of two rhetorical questions. The first question sounds like the one Pharaoh asked of Moses (Exod 5:2). The second would be its corollary. There will always be prosperous and powerful individuals who will ask these questions, but the religion of Job's friends had no answers. The two questions together seem to strike at the heart of the issue in the book. If religion were purely a matter of recompense and retribution, what would this say about the nature and character of God, his worthiness, and his beauty? Is God to be worshiped for gain? If this were the case, why would the prosperous ever submit to his will and worship and commune with him?

21:16 At the end of this section Job stepped aside from the position he had been taking and disclaimed any affiliation with those godless words he had just spoken. He believed that "their prosperity" came from God even if they did not acknowledge it. And he distanced[36] himself from the kind of "counsel" he had just put into their mouths.

THEY ESCAPE PUNISHMENT (21:17-21). Despite their defiance of the deity, the godless often seem to go through life with his blessing and without any obvious discipline or punishment. None or few of the tragedies that struck Job ever befall them. They seem immune to God's judgment and wrath.

21:17 This and the next verse are rhetorical questions, "How often?"[37] Job's answer would be, "Not very often" or "Not often enough to support Zophar's premise that the wicked are always punished." The first

---

[35] Andersen, *Job*, 199-200.

[36] The verb translated "stand aloof" is רחק, "be distant."

[37] The combination כַּמָּה means "how much?" or "how many?" (*IBHS* § 18.3d). Cf. 7:19; 13:23.

line contradicts Bildad's statement in 18:5 that "the lamp of the wicked is
snuffed out." The phrase speaks of a sudden death. But even while alive
they are seldom the victims of "calamity."[38] "The fate" of the third line
translates a root with multiple meanings, so some prefer "sorrow" (KJV,
ASV, MLB), "pains" (RSV, AB, AAT), "suffering" (NEB), "snares" (AT),
"portion" (NAB), "lot" (NJPS), "destruction" (NASB). The NIV's "fate"
(like "portion/lot") reads ḥebel in the sense of what is measured by a
"cord" (another meaning of the word is reflected in the AT's "snare").[39]

21:18 The illustrations of v. 18 are reminiscent of Ps 1:4, which says
the wicked "are like chaff that the wind blows away." Psalm 1 is in the
wisdom category, and as such it speaks in the same generalities Proverbs
does, not addressing the exceptions as Job, the lament psalms, and Ecclesiastes do. Normally the wicked are destroyed like chaff, but Job asserted
by this question that he rarely witnessed it. The figures of "wind" and
"gale" bring to mind the way Job's children died (1:19).

21:19 Verse 19a is a proverb that is out of character for Job, so even
the RV in 1885 introduced it with an italicized "Ye say" by analogy with
v. 28. Indeed, it sounds like the three friends and not like Job (cf. 5:4;
20:10).[40] The exact phrase is nowhere else in the Bible, but it reflects Jer
31:29 and Lam 5:7, which probably were based on a misunderstanding of
Exod 20:5-6 (cf. Ezek 18:2).[41] Job rejected the principle and insisted that
God "repay the man himself" rather than defer punishment to his descendants.

21:20 These two imprecations elaborate on the one in v. 19b.[42] The
defense against Job's criticism (i.e., that there were many wicked who
prospered) was that their children would pay for their sins. This, Job
thought, would be unfair and ineffective as a deterrent to evil. The translation "destruction" (with KJV) is uncertain, since the word occurs only
here and has no certain cognates.[43] The motif of drinking God's wrath is
repeated throughout Scripture (Pss 11:6; 75:8[9]; Isa 51:17,22; Jer 25:15;

---

[38] "Calamity," אֵיד, has six of its twenty-two occurrences in Job: 18:12; 21:17,30;
30:12; 31:3,23.

[39] Deuteronomy 3:3,13-14; 32:9; Josh 17:5,14; 19:9; 1 Chr 16:18; Ezek 47:13 read
חֶבֶל in that sense. The notion of "sorrow/suffering" finds support in Isa 13:8; 26:17; Jer
22:23; Hos 13:13, all referring to birth pangs.

[40] Similar non-Joban statements will occur in 27:13-23. See Andersen, *Job,* 198.

[41] See. F. B. Huey, Jr., *Jeremiah, Lamentations,* NAC (Nashville: Broadman, 1993), 279.

[42] The verbs can be either regular finite forms or jussives, as the NIV has taken them.
The alternative is given in the NIV footnote on vv. 17-20.

[43] Tur-Sinai (*Job,* [Jerusalem: Kiryat-Sefer, 1967], 329) has "cup," but he does not
emend to כּוֹסוֹ as Ehrlich did (see Dhorme, *Job,* 317, who emends to פֵּידוֹ, "his misfortune").

49:12; Ezek 23:31-34; Matt 26:39; Rev 14:10; 18:6).

21:21 One of the signs of consummate selfishness and wickedness would be not to care for the world or the family left behind. King Hezekiah evidenced it when, after Isaiah's rebuke and announcement of future exile, he said in effect, What do I care since I'll be gone when the invasion comes? (Isa 39:8). As long as the punishment did not affect the guilty but fell on the successive generations, people would sin wantonly. Ezekiel denounced that viewpoint and announced, "The soul who sins is the one who will die" (Ezek 18:4). That is not good news for sinners.

GOD'S APPARENT ARBITRARINESS (21:22-26). Job had been overstating the case as he disputed with his three friends. More on balance he would not say the evil are blessed and the righteous are cursed but that God seems not to be active in the distribution of rewards for behavior. All people, good or bad, receive similar treatment (cf. Matt 5:45). In vv. 22-23 Job described the death of a healthy man and in v. 24 that of a miserable man. Death is the great leveler.

21:22 The answer to this question must be negative. No one can teach God anything. It is a way of saying that God is all-knowing. If he "judges even the highest," meaning angels (?), surely there is no way for a mortal to contest his rulings (cf. Ps 82:1; Isa 40:13-14).

21:23 First, Job portrayed a healthy and wealthy man who dies. He was, to give a literal translation, "with unblemished bones" and "completely at ease and secure."[44]

21:24 While all agree on the overall meaning of the first line, several options exist for the word translated "his body,"[45] which is said to be literally "full of milk." In ancient times the success of the rich often was obvious in their corpulence. Extra weight was a proud token of material success. This verse thus describes one who is well fed and well heeled.

21:25 The dark side of the picture is of the man who "dies in bitterness of soul" (cf. 10:1).[46] "Enjoyed" is actually "eaten," so there is con-

---

[44] Perhaps for alliterative reasons these two words were chosen: שַׁלְאֲנַן וְשָׁלֵיו, but the first is not a hapax but a misspelling of שַׁאֲנָן, which is in several manuscripts (cf. 12:5). A. Guillaume (*Studies in the Book of Job* [Leiden: Brill, 1960], 104-5) calls it a normal form with an "intrusive *L*" common in Arabic. The second one is also in 16:12; 20:20.

[45] The KJV, RV following the Targum has "breasts." Moffatt, following BDB's "pails," has "vessels." The NJPS, NKJV have "pails." The RSV has "body" but, along with others, revocalized חָלָב, "milk," to חֵלֶב, "fat." The MLB and NASB, following the Syriac, have "sides." The AB compared it to Akkadian and Arabic cognates and offered "haunches." The JB and AAT have "thighs," and the NEB, REB, NRSV have "loins." Following Gordis (*Job,* 233), Hartley (*Job,* 317) has "testes."

[46] See comments in footnote to 20:14 on "bitter."

trast between the one whose rich diet was obvious and this one who "ate nothing good."

21:26 Job concluded the long central section of this response with the depressing observation that in death all distinctions about earthly bliss disappear. The "worms" enjoy equally the wicked and the righteous, the rich and the poor.[47]

(3) Request for Friends to Consider This (21:27-33)

> [27]"I know full well what you are thinking,
>   the schemes by which you would wrong me.
> [28]You say, 'Where now is the great man's house,
>   the tents where wicked men lived?'
> [29]Have you never questioned those who travel?
>   Have you paid no regard to their accounts—
> [30]that the evil man is spared from the day of calamity,
>   that he is delivered from the day of wrath?
> [31]Who denounces his conduct to his face?
>   Who repays him for what he has done?
> [32]He is carried to the grave,
>   and watch is kept over his tomb.
> [33]The soil in the valley is sweet to him;
>   all men follow after him,
>   and a countless throng goes before him.

Job expected his friends to counter him with illustrations of the demise of the wicked in order to champion their views. But he said that they simply had not traveled widely enough and that their observations were limited. Job contended that the wicked wealthy, even in death, enjoy a measure of luxury and respect.

21:27 Since the debate was well along, each party knew the positions of the others, so Job anticipated what Eliphaz, whose turn it was next, might say. Indeed, in 22:16-18 he took this very position, that the godless die young. The term "schemes" well reflects Job's assessment of their often-sinister opinions and reasoning.

21:28 Although these words cannot be found in the speeches of the friends, the quotation certainly encapsulates their view of theological retribution. By this rhetorical question put into their mouths, Job had them say that the "houses" and "tents" of the "great" and "wicked" are no more. Job's contention was that the opposite is true, "their homes are

---

[47] Job uses רִמָּה, "worm," five of the seven times it appears in the OT: 7:5; 17:14; 21:26; 24:20; 25:6. In 25:6 the NIV translates "maggot," saving "worm" for תֹּלֵעָה.

safe and free from fear" (v. 8).

21:29   Now Job impugned their experience or their learning. Even if they had not witnessed the injustice of which he spoke, surely they should have heard from those who traveled more widely.[48]

21:30   The "accounts" that Job cited form the substance of v. 30. Just as Eliphaz's vision in 4:12-21 supported his view, so Job's hearsay from travelers advanced his, that is, that evil people escape "the day of calamity" and "the day of wrath" (cf. 20:28).[49]

21:31   With these two questions Job implied that no one challenges the arrogant wicked or demands accountability of them for their actions. The rich can be so imperious and overbearing that none dare confront them with their sin. So they continue in their prosperous impiety, thinking that no judgment will ever come.

21:32   Instead of being carried off by some calamity, the wicked are "carried to the grave." As Gordis has noted: "The Wisdom writers were particularly exercised by the fact that after a lifetime of ill-gotten prosperity, there is no moment of truth for the evildoers even at the very end. Their true character is not revealed even then, but high-flown obsequies of praise are offered before they are taken to their graves."[50]

"Grave" is plural in Hebrew, indicating a measure of opulence. "Tomb" (*gādîš*) in its other three occurrences is translated "shocks of grain" or "sheaves," so this may refer to some kind of funerary mound (cf. KJV margin, AAT).[51]

21:33   As evil was "sweet" (according to Zophar, 20:12) to this archetypal sinner, so now the "soil of the valley is sweet to him" as well, according to the scenario Job was spelling out. Even death is an enjoyable affair to the one who had an inordinate share of joy in life. The procession consists of "a countless throng" before him and "all men" (certainly hyperbole) after him.[52]

---

[48] "Their accounts," אֹתֹתָם, usually means "signs/tokens." The strangeness of that word here prompted Hartley to adopt a secondary, almost polar, meaning of the verb נכר and translate, "Have you not denied their evidence?" (*Job*, 319).

[49] The alternate reading (KJV, RV, NASB) in the margin of the NIV turns on the verb חָשַׂךְ in *niphal* and on the very flexible preposition לְ on "day of calamity." I prefer the text over the footnote on the principle of synonymous parallelism.

[50] Gordis, *Job*, 235. He translates the first line, "He is borne in pomp to the grave" (p. 226).

[51] Cf. Tur-Sinai for a defense of the translation "shocks of grain" (*Job*, 334).

[52] The NIV footnote offers an alternative. Apparently the "all men" and the "countless throng" refer to those who precede and follow the wealthy wicked in death, not in the funeral procession.

(4) Denunciation of Friends (21:34)

[34]"So how can you console me with your nonsense?
Nothing is left of your answers but falsehood!"

21:34 Job concluded his sixth response with one of the most acidic criticisms found anywhere in the book. In no uncertain terms he judged their "comfort" (2:11) to be "nonsense" (Eccl 1:2) and their "answers" to be "falsehood." This last term could be stronger: "treachery/fraud/perfidy."[53] The possibility that Job and his friends could arrive at some understanding seems more and more remote. Eliphaz and Bildad each spoke once more, but the rift between them and Job widened before the talks broke off altogether.

---

[53] See BDB, 591; KB, 547.

13. Eliphaz: This Is Why You Suffer, Job (22:1-30)
    (1) God's Detachment from Human Behavior (22:1-3)
    (2) God's Justice (22:4-5)
    (3) Specific Accusations against Job (22:6-9)
    (4) Resultant Woes (22:10-11)
    (5) The Punishing God (22:12-18)
    (6) The Righteous React to the Sinners' Ruin (22:19-20)
    (7) Advice (22:21-24)
        Submission (22:21)
        Acceptance (22:22)
        Returning (22:23)
        Resigning (22:24-25)
    (8) Expected Benefits (22:26-30)
14. Job: Innocent but Frustrated with God's Apathy (23:1–24:25)
    (1) Longing (23:1-9)
        He Wishes He Could Find God (23:1-7)
        He Cannot Find God (23:8-9)
    (2) Job Declares His Innocence (23:10-12)
    (3) Frustration at God's Apathy (23:13–24:17)
        God's Total Control of the Case (23:13–24:1)
        The Unpunished Wicked (24:2-17)
            Their Oppression of the Poor (24:2-12)
            Killers, Adulterers, Burglars (24:13-17)
    (4) The Accursed Wicked (24:18-25)

13. Eliphaz: This Is Why You Suffer, Job (22:1-30)

There is not much new in Eliphaz's third speech. He touched on most of the themes that the friends had used. For the first time we read of specific accusations (vv. 6-9), a move that represents a further emboldening on his part and a wider rift between him and Job. Toward the end of the speech (vv. 21-30) is a fine evangelistic sermon with several well-turned phrases. While it would be applicable for many situations, Job was not the one who needed to hear it. It is another example of good medicine given to the wrong patient.

(1) God's Detachment from Human Behavior (22:1-3)

¹Then Eliphaz the Temanite replied:

²"Can a man be of benefit to God?
Can even a wise man benefit him?
³What pleasure would it give the Almighty if you were righteous?
What would he gain if your ways were blameless?

Rather than insult Job or demand that he listen, Eliphaz took a different tack at the outset of this response. And rather than describe a God who actively watches every move people make, he portrayed one who was unaffected by what they do.

22:1 See comments at 4:1.

22:2 The point of the verse is that God is not advantaged by good deeds. He is distant and detached. But how to render the Hebrew has always plagued translators and commentators. The same verb, *skn*, is in both halves and can have at least three meanings.[1] Furthermore, are the lines synonymous? Or should the "him" be "himself" in line *b* (KJV, RV, RSV, JB, NASB)?[2] Does the interrogative particle at the beginning of the verse make both lines questions, or just the first? Judging from the general pattern of parallel pairs of lines throughout Job, the NIV is best. With this general interpretation agree AB, NEB, GNB, AAT, NJPS, NRSV.

22:3 The greater certainty in translating this verse supports the choice made in v. 2. "The Almighty" has neither "pleasure" nor "profit" if Job is a good man. Note that Eliphaz moved from generic "man" (*geber*) in v. 2 to "you" (Job) in v. 3. The point the Temanite was making is that God is transcendent, far removed from this earthly scene, and indifferent toward all people including Job.

(2) God's Justice (22:4-5)

⁴"Is it for your piety that he rebukes you
and brings charges against you?
⁵Is not your wickedness great?
And not your sins endless?

---

[1] The *hiphil* is translated "submit" in v. 21, and the *niphal* is "endangered" in Eccl 10:9. The differences may be a matter of stem change only (KB) or of different roots as well (BDB). See R. Gordis (*The Book of Job* [New York: Jewish Theological Seminary, 1978], 244) for a fuller discussion.

[2] E. Kissane said that this interpretation "introduces an idea which is alien to the context and would have been expressed differently in Hebrew" (*The Book of Job* [New York: Sheed and Ward, 1946], 144).

Eliphaz took it for granted that God was rebuking Job. The only question was why. Eliphaz's answers to these three questions are exactly opposite the truth. As a matter of fact, it *was* because of Job's piety that he was chosen as a test case when the Satan posited that good people served God for personal gain. No, Job's wickedness was not great and his sins were not endless.

22:4 "Piety" translates a word derived from "fear," in the sense of "the fear of the LORD." In 1:1,8; 2:3 it says that Job "feared God." Eliphaz judged Job the most impious of men, whereas in fact he was the most pious.

22:5 In a theological sense Job was a sinner like every descendant of Adam and Eve. But in Eliphaz's sense he was not (cf. 15:4-6). In chap. 31 Job disavowed committing sins of all kinds but particularly the kind Eliphaz had in mind and which he enumerated in vv. 6-9.

(3) Specific Accusations against Job (22:6-9)

> ⁶You demanded security from your brothers for no reason;
>   you stripped men of their clothing, leaving them naked.
> ⁷You gave no water to the weary
>   and you withheld food from the hungry,
> ⁸though you were a powerful man, owning land—
>   an honored man, living on it.
> ⁹And you sent widows away empty-handed
>   and broke the strength of the fatherless.

For the first time one of the friends charged Job with specific sins, all in the area of wealth—greed and miserliness. Next to pride, sins involving the use and misuse of money are perhaps the most flagrant, especially among capitalists.

22:6 Eliphaz's first indictment was that Job unnecessarily kept the clothing of debtors as deposits on loans, even to the point of leaving them naked. Exodus 22:26[25] required that such pledged clothing be returned by sundown (cf. Deut 24:6,17; Ezek 18:12).[3]

22:7 The next sin was denying water to the weary and food to the hungry. Job denied guilt in this area in 29:12-16; 31:13,16-17,21.

---

[3] Neither Eliphaz nor Job probably had heard of this specific legislation, but laws that speak to the subsequent infringements were widespread in the ancient near east. It must be said, however, that fairness, not charity, was legislated, though some boasted of it. Cf. Keret C:vi:30-37 in *ANET*, 149; Aqhat A:v:7-8 in *ANET*, 151; Code of Hammurabi #66, 90, 96; Epilogue 59-61, 72 in *ANET*, 169, 178.

22:8 Some treat this verse as a quotation of a proverb put in Job's mouth by Eliphaz. Hence, Hartley begins the verse, "You think."[4] And Gordis has, "For you believe."[5] The point is that landowners grow arrogant and abuse their status as successful businessmen.[6]

22:9 "Widows" and "the fatherless" (not "orphans" who have neither parent) were among the most defenseless of an ancient community's citizenry. Their families lacked the one who at that time was expected to own the land, make the decisions, and support the family. They were special objects of God's care and the subject of many admonitions to charity. To abuse them was relatively easy, and for that reason there were special laws to protect them. Eliphaz charged Job with being lazy and greedy toward the widows and with outright cruelty to those without parents (i.e., orphans; cf. Deut 10:12-11:32; 1 Kgs 17:17-24).[7] The prologue and epilogue inform us, however, that Job was innocent of these charges. Eliphaz was only guessing, perhaps based on practices that were common at the time.

(4) Resultant Woes (22:10-11)

[10]That is why snares are all around you,
   why sudden peril terrifies you,
[11]why it is so dark you cannot see,
   and why a flood of water covers you.

By now it is not surprising to hear the friends connect sin and punishment. In general they were right. But the only evidence they had in Job's case is the suffering. From it they deduced that he must have sinned. In this short section Eliphaz made the connection between Job's alleged sin and his present terrible circumstances.

22:10 It was Bildad who discoursed on the variety of traps in chap. 18, but here Eliphaz picked up that theme to remind Job that he was surrounded by "snares" and terrified by "sudden peril." "Sudden" underscores the relatively recent onslaught of the troubles and the brief span of time the book probably covers.

---

[4] J. Hartley, *Job,* NICOT (Grand Rapids: Eerdmans, 1988), 324.

[5] He cites strong support for this in the Qumran Targum's opening word, ואמרת (*Job,* 246; cf. M. Sokoloff, *The Targum to Job from Qumran Cave XI* [Ramat-Gan: Bar-Ilan University, 1974], 38).

[6] Other examples of this unusual idiom for "honored," נְשׂוּא פָנִים, literally "lifted up of faces," are in 2 Kgs 5:1; Isa 3:3; 9:14.

[7] Surely Eliphaz did not think that Job literally "broke the arms of the fatherless." זְרוֹעַ, "arm," can also refer metaphorically to "strength."

22:11 Job's afflictions are here described in terms of "darkness" and "flood," two natural phenomena that were most frightening to desert dwellers (cf. 20:28). At nighttime bandits operated. In the dark one can stumble and fall. Little work can be accomplished when the sun goes down. Especially the winter and moonless nights compounded the fear. While water was always short, a torrential rain could suddenly flood a riverbed without warning. It washed out planted fields and sometimes claimed a life. It is used metaphorically here but nevertheless points to the overwhelming nature of Job's losses.

(5) The Punishing God (22:12-18)

> ¹²"Is not God in the heights of heaven?
>   And see how lofty are the highest stars!
> ¹³Yet you say, 'What does God know?
>   Does he judge through such darkness?
> ¹⁴Thick clouds veil him, so he does not see us
>   as he goes about in the vaulted heavens.'
> ¹⁵Will you keep to the old path
>   that evil men have trod?
> ¹⁶They were carried off before their time,
>   their foundations washed away by a flood.
> ¹⁷They said to God, 'Leave us alone!
>   What can the Almighty do to us?'
> ¹⁸Yet it was he who filled their houses with good things,
>   so I stand aloof from the counsel of the wicked.

It has been some time since one of the speakers touched on the theme of God's governance (12:13-25), but it was frequent earlier and will grow more so until the climax in the theophany of chaps. 38-41. This section starts with reflections on the transcendence of God, but soon it moves to the matter of divine justice exercised against the wicked.

22:12 None would dispute Eliphaz that God is "in the heights of heaven." That is the point of this rhetorical question—to prompt Job to agree with him first here and then later. The imperative "see" is a little unusual, but taken as an exclamation it is generally left unchanged.[8]

22:13 Again (assuming the case in v. 8) Eliphaz put words into Job's

---

[8] M. Jastrow (*Job* [Philadelphia: Lippincott, 1920], 276) emended it to read, "Thou seest." Kissane (*Job,* 142) moved it to the first line so as to read, "Doth not God behold." N. Habel (*Job,* OTL [Philadelphia: Westminster, 1985], 331) repointed it to רֹאֶה, the participle, and translated "He who sees." Others would delete רֹאשׁ, "highest," as dittography (S. R. Driver and G. B. Gray, *Job,* ICC [New York: Scribner, 1921], II:154).

mouth—words that cannot be found in any of Job's responses. He said Job believed that God knows nothing because he is so far away, that too much "darkness" enshrouds him for him to make a judgment. In 23:8-10 Job complained about the inaccessibility of God but still averred that God knew his every step.

22:14 Job might have agreed with Eliphaz about God veiled with "thick clouds," but he would not concede that God "does not see" (cf. Pss 18:11[12]; 97:2; and especially Jer 23:23-24).

22:15 Having ended his quoting of Job, Eliphaz now queried Job whether he would persist in his pernicious "path,"[9] assuming all along that Job was evil and rightly noting that Job had given no indication of moving toward their position on these questions.

22:16[10] A relative pronoun connects v. 16 with v. 15 and serves to modify "evil men." It is another way of Eliphaz stating that the bad die young (cf. 15:32).[11] "Flood" is really "river" and should not be associated with Noah's flood but rather with any number of sudden catastrophes God devised to punish the wicked (e.g., Sodom and Gomorrah in Gen 19:23-25 or the earth swallowing Korah and his band in Num 16:31-33; cf. Prov 29:1).

22:17 At this point Eliphaz did quote our hero correctly when he repeated what Job said the wicked tell God, "Leave us alone" (21:14).[12] Such are the words of arrogant infidels even today. Each of us may occasionally hope in those cases that Eliphaz was right and that suddenly God will hold them accountable and mete out punishment.

22:18 The first line sounds like a concession to Job's position (12:6), so Eliphaz immediately repudiated it and branded it "the counsel of the wicked," another quotation from Job (21:16b). Another view is that he was distancing himself from the statements of the wicked in v. 17.[13]

(6) The Righteous React to the Sinners' Ruin (22:19-20)

[19]"The righteous see their ruin and rejoice;
the innocent mock them, saying,

---

[9] Instead of "old" with the majority M. Pope (*Job,* AB [Garden City: Doubleday, 1973] and Beck in AAT translated "dark" from the root עלם, "be hidden" (28:21; 42:3).

[10] In the Masora at this verse is חצי הספר בפסוקים, "half the book by verses."

[11] "Carried off," קמט, occurs only here and in 16:8.

[12] Verse 17 actually begins with a participle, "the ones saying," which qualifies the third person pronouns of v. 16 (cf. *GBH* §122r). That is, the ones judged in v. 16 are those who tell God to leave them alone.

[13] *GBH* § 112k translates the perfect רָחֲקָה as an optative, "I wish it were far from me." Cf. *IBHS* § 30.5.4.

20'Surely our foes are destroyed,
   and fire devours their wealth.'

The end result of the arrogance and insolence that the wicked display
is their demise. At their demise the righteous rejoice, a feature of some
psalms (58:10[11]; 63:11[12]; 107:42) that goes counter to the warning
of Prov 24:17, "Do not gloat when your enemy falls; when he stumbles,
do not let your heart rejoice."

22:19 "Ruin" is not in the Hebrew but may be understood from the
context. Likewise, "saying" was added to introduce the quotation of
v. 20. Surely Eliphaz considered himself "righteous" and "innocent." Job
already called him a "mocker" (21:3). Eliphaz would have considered his
mocking justified, but Job viewed it as misguided cruelty.

22:20 Although there has been no mention of hostility between the
good and the wicked, such is understandable and hence the glee that
rings in this verse.[14] "Fire" may allude to the "fire of God [that] fell from
the sky and burned up the sheep and the servants" in 1:16. Eliphaz has
become more vicious.

(7) Advice (22:21-24)

21"Submit to God and be at peace with him;
   in this way prosperity will come to you.
22Accept instruction from his mouth
   and lay up his words in your heart.
23If you return to the Almighty, you will be restored:
   If you remove wickedness far from your tent
24and assign your nuggets to the dust,
   your gold of Ophir to the rocks in the ravines,
25then the Almighty will be your gold,
   the choicest silver for you.

The following four subpoints of Eliphaz's admonition to Job could
easily be turned into a sermon for today. Results from these imperatives
("submit, accept, return, assign") are all desirable outcomes ("peace,
prosperity, restoration, [spiritual] gold and silver"). Eliphaz's error,

---

[14] "Foes" is קִים, a form of קוּם unique to this passage. N. Tur-Sinai (*Job* [Jerusalem:
Kiryat-Sefer, 1967], 344-45) by a circuitous route came to "babe." Following the LXX, E.
Dhorme (*Job* [London: Nelson, 1967], 335-36) reads "their possessions." The AB, NEB,
NJPS, and Hartley (*Job*, 329) have "their substance." These make a better parallel with
"wealth" in line *b* but involve adjusting the suffix as well as the vowels. Kissane (*Job*, 142,
147) has "their greatness."

which could be ours, was preaching this fine sermon to one already saved. The message that Job needed God himself would deliver in chaps. 38–41. These verses form another high point of the book, though sadly they are inappropriately applied.

SUBMISSION (22:21). **22:21** The verb for "submit," *sākan*, was used twice in v. 2, but its different meaning here is dependent on the Vulgate's *acquiesce* and a Ugaritic cognate.[15] The KJV translation "acquaint" (likewise ASV, AT, MLB) is like the use in Ps 139:3, "You [God] are familiar with all my ways."[16] "Be at peace" translates a strange form that looks like an imperative but is read as a result.[17] The English of NIV and most others can be taken either way.[18] The message of Eliphaz is the standard wisdom fare as presented by Proverbs (e.g., 3:9-10; 8:10-11,18; 21:21; 22:4).

ACCEPTANCE (22:22). **22:22** Two additional imperatives bolster Eliphaz's formula for success.[19] Both phrases resemble verses from wisdom psalms (cf. Pss 19:14[15]; 37:31; 119:11). Both are good advice for virtually all people in all situations, but at this point Eliphaz himself needed a broader and better understanding of the ways of God.

RETURNING (22:23). **22:23** This command is in the form of a conditional clause, "If you return." The result of "returning" will be "restoration." The NIV understands vv. 23b-24 as making explicit what would be involved in returning to the Almighty. The result is given in v. 25. Like Bildad in 8:5 or the often-used invitation hymn "Softly and Tenderly," this is an offer to come home to God. But Job had never fled from God.

---

[15] W. Bishai, "Notes on *hskn* in Job 22:21," *JNES* 20 (1961): 258-59. Dhorme (*Job,* 336) explains the sense with the following עמו as "to become familiar with someone once more," thus "to be reconciled with him."

[16] The fragmentary Targum from the Dead Sea has הסתכל, a reflexive of סכל that corresponds to Hebrew שכל, "be wise" (Sokoloff, *Targum to Job,* 40).

[17] *BHS* has וּשְׁלם. Many manuscripts have וּשְׁלָם with *athnach,* which is also missing from the standard text. F. Delitzsch (*Biblical Commentary on the Book of Job, vol. 1* [Grand Rapids: Eerdmans, 1949], 441) calls it "consecutive" and compares it to the two imperatives that read like results in Prov 3:4. Pope (*Job,* AB) translated it as imperative, "submit," noting that this is the watchword and etymology of Islam. For more discussion see Dhorme, *Job,* 336-37.

[18] The NEB, REB clearly take it as result with the translation, "you will prosper." Moffatt took it as an imperative, "submit to him," and JB has "be reconciled." See *GBH* §116f. The phrase "with him" in the NIV is not in the Hebrew text. The beginning of line *b,* "in this way," reflects the Hebrew בָּהֶם, "by these things," referring either to the two actions of submission and reconciliation (so Dhorme, *Job,* 336) or to the collective actions involved in submission (*GBH* §149a).

[19] This is the only occurrence of תוֹרָה in Job, but it does not prove that Job knew about the law of Moses. Hence it is properly translated "instruction" here.

On the contrary, he desperately wished he could find him (13:22,24; 23:3). "Restored" is from the root (*bnh*), whose usual meaning is "build/ rebuild," either of buildings or family. It is an interesting choice in light of Job's eventually having seven more *bānîm*, "sons," and three more *bānôt*, "daughters" (42:13).

RESIGNING (22:24-25). The last recommendation is to abandon material wealth, something that Job hardly had to do since he had lost everything as a result of this trial.

22:24 Paranomasia undoubtedly prompted the choice of some of the words in v. 24. "Nuggets" is *bāṣer;*[20] "to the rocks" is *bĕṣûr;* "dust" is *ʿāpār;* "Ophir" is *ʾôpîr*.[21] The advice is not much different from what Jesus gave the rich young ruler (Luke 18:22).[22] On this point as well Job denied any guilt, swearing in 31:24 that he did not put his trust in gold.

22:25 Instead of material wealth, God would be his "nuggets" ("gold" in v. 25 is the same word as "nuggets" in v. 24) and "choicest silver."[23] Such an exchange would be a bargain to the repentant sinner, but few make it.

(8) Expected Benefits (22:26-30)

> [26]Surely then you will find delight in the Almighty
>   and will lift up your face to God.
> [27]You will pray to him, and he will hear you,
>   and you will fulfill your vows.
> [28]What you decide on will be done,
>   and light will shine on your ways.
> [29]When men are brought low and you say, 'Lift them up!'
>   then he will save the downcast.
> [30]He will deliver even one who is not innocent,
>   who will be delivered through the cleanness of your hands."

---

[20] Driver and Gray assume this noun that occurs only here and in v. 25 is from the verb בצר, "cut off" and go from that to "crumble" and eventually to "nuggets," II:156.

[21] "Ophir" is a metonymy for "gold." It is located in southern Arabia near the Red Sea (R. L. Omanson, "Ophir," in *ISBE* 3:607-8).

[22] The clause containing the verb "assign" (וְשִׁית) could be read as declarative (KJV, RV) or directive (GNB, ICB, NCV) rather than conditional as in NIV and most others.

[23] "Choicest" is a guess based on context. תוֹעֲפוֹת occurs only here and in Num 23:22; 24:8 (which in general support "choicest"); and Ps 95:4. Some prefer "piles/heaps," based on Ps 95:4, and assume a metathesized Arabic root. So AB, JB, GNB, AAT, Hartley, *Job,* 332; Habel, *Job,* 332; following BDB, 419, and Dhorme, *Job,* 339. L. Grabbe argues against any emendation and prefers to understand a different Arabic root, עוּף, "profit" or "double" (*Comparative Philology and the Text of Job,* SBLD 34 [Missoula, Mont.: SBL Press, 1977], 81-83. Cf. NEB, REB.

Eliphaz continued to promise bigger benefits for repentance. Some of them sound very grand but are not unlike what Jesus promised those who trust, obey, and pray (Matt 7:7-11; Mark 11:23-24).

22:26 Zophar had a similar sermonette in 11:13-19 and even used the expression "lift up your face." Lifting the face or head symbolized freedom from shame or defeat (Ps 27:6; Judg 8:28) or acceptance by a superior (Esth 2:9,17; Jer 52:31). "Delight" in the Lord (or in his law) is both a command and a promise in the psalms (37:4; 1:2; 112:1; cf. Isa 58:14; 61:10). In 27:10 Job will refer back to Eliphaz's words.

22:27 This plain promise also rings of the cut-and-dried simplicity of the wisdom literature. Job, however, could testify that he had prayed, but there was no answer. No one wants to renege on vows, and the keeping of them can be thwarted for many reasons (Eccl 5:4-5).

22:28 Eliphaz's list of assured blessings goes on. These wonderful promises are too good to be true, but it was the Temanite's habit to characterize Job a worse sinner than he was and to inflate the advantages of repentance beyond what is realistic. Zophar did the same in 11:17. Job used a similar figure of a divinely illuminated path when he described the days prior to the present troubles (29:2-3; cf. Prov 18-19).

22:29 Smick says, "This verse is notoriously difficult." His attractive solution is to drop one vowel letter and read, "He (God) will bring (you) low if you speak in pride."[24] Otherwise "brought low" is plural, and the isolated word gēwâ is an exclamatory imperative, "Lift them up."[25] "The downcast" are literally "low of eyes." Since the verb is third person, it makes sense that "he" also be the subject of the verb in line a.

22:30 Because one expects God to "deliver" the "innocent" (not the "noninnocent"), some have ignored the negative particle (LXX, Vulgate, REB, GNB[26]) or emended it to read "man" (RSV),[27] "God,"[28] or

---

[24] E. Smick, "Job," EBC 4 (Grand Rapids: Zondervan, 1988), 955. His suggestion involves understanding the final vowel of the verb הִשְׁפִּילוֹ as the result of dittography with the initial *waw* of the following word, וַתֹּאמֶר.

[25] Elsewhere גֵוָה appears only in 33:17; Jer 13:17; Dan 4:37[34] in Aramaic. Gordis says it is a contraction of גַּאֲוָה, a well-established word with twenty or so occurrences in the fem. and more than that in masc. (*Job,* 252).

[26] The GNB translates, "He will rescue you if you are innocent," making it clear that Eliphaz was referring to Job.

[27] The particle is אִי (cf. *GBH* §102j). "Man" is אִישׁ. E.g., G. Fohrer, *Das Buch Hiob* KAT (Götersloh: Mohn, 1963), 350, 352; G. Hölscher, *Das Buch Hiob,* HAT (Tübingen: Mohr-Siebeck, 1952), 56; KB³; Dhorme, *Job,* 342 (who cites the parallel אָדָם רֶשַׁע, "the wicked man" in 20:29). Gordis (*Job,* 252), who accepts the reading "not innocent," says it "is definitely not to be emended" to אִישׁ. Habel (*Job,* 333) agrees. KJV, from Ibn Ezra, reads אִי as "island." See also H. H. Rowley, Job, NCBC (Grand Rapids: Eerdmans, 1970), 158.

[28] So *BHS* footnote; KB.

"whomsoever."[29] But the text makes sense as it stands. It is the repentant guilty that God "will deliver." And that deliverance will occur through the instrumentality of "your hands." How these words must have haunted Eliphaz when God had Job pray for him and his friends (42:7-10).

14. Job: Innocent but Frustrated with God's Apathy (23:1–24:25)

Job ignored everything that Eliphaz said and launched into the themes that characterize his speeches. In this two-chapter response he again expressed his yearning for an audience with God and complained at his lack of success in that endeavor. He protested God's apparent apathy while describing in some detail all the crimes that sinners commit without incrimination. In chaps. 23–24 there is one glimmer of hope (23:10) but no discourse on the greatness of the Creator.

(1) Longing (23:1-9)

¹Then Job replied:

²"Even today my complaint is bitter;
   his hand is heavy in spite of my groaning.
³If only I knew where to find him;
   if only I could go to his dwelling!
⁴I would state my case before him
   and fill my mouth with arguments.
⁵I would find out what he would answer me,
   and consider what he would say.
⁶Would he oppose me with great power?
   No, he would not press charges against me.
⁷There an upright man could present his case before him,
   and I would be delivered forever from my judge.

⁸"But if I go to the east, he is not there;
   if I go to the west, I do not find him.
⁹When he is at work in the north, I do not see him;
   when he turns to the south, I catch no glimpse of him.

The initial area of frustration to which Job gave vent in this response was his inability to contact God. He thought that if he could find him, he might present his case and receive some explanation. But such was not to be, at least for a while.

HE WISHES HE COULD FIND GOD (23:1-7). Job believed in God, that

---

[29] So Guillaume, *Studies in Job*, 107. The NJB has "anyone who is innocent."

he existed, that he was aware of what was happening on earth, and that he would listen to a reasonable complaint from one of his followers. So his wish, elaborately stated here, was that he might connect with this one whose name he does not mention until v. 16.

23:1 See comments at 6:1.

23:2 "Bitter" and "complaint" also occurred together in Job's first response to Eliphaz (7:11). That is understandable in light of Eliphaz's caustic criticisms and indefensible indictments. As the two NIV footnotes suggest, there are problems in v. 2b. Hebrew has "my hand," which is hard to fit into any reading, so the NIV has adopted the LXX and Syriac, "his hand." The second footnote takes the usual meaning "upon" for the preposition rather than "in spite of" (RSV, NASB, NIV, NRSV). The NIV's choice of meaning for that preposition finds support in 10:7; 16:17.[30]

23:3 Like the wishes of 6:8; 11:5; 14:13; and 19:23, Job here longed to know where he might find God. The "if only" appears only at the beginning of the verse, so the second clause might read, "I would go to his dwelling."[31] Job did not have some local sanctuary in mind, but he was prepared to search the ends of the earth or even the heavens to locate God (cf. vv. 8-9).

23:4 If Job could find God, he would "state" or "spread out," as on a table, his legal "case" (*mišpāṭ*). The "arguments" with which he would fill his mouth fill the pages of this book that bears his name. Undoubtedly he would declare his innocence; he would cite example after example of ungodly people who were not suffering; he would demand an explanation for the catastrophes that fell all around him.

23:5 This verse does not add much because it states the obvious. If God answers, then Job will know. If God speaks, then Job will understand. Those four verbs express precisely what had not happened. God had not answered. Therefore Job was unaware of what God was thinking.

23:6 With the verb "oppose" (*rîb*, also "argue/bring litigation"), legal language reappears (cf. 10:2; 13:3-10). Job anticipated a friendly court and a beneficent judge because he knew himself to be innocent of known sin and very devout. Those who truly fear God are not afraid to meet him.

23:7 Of course, Job was speaking of himself when he said "upright

---

[30] See GKC § 160c, although it does not recognize the concessive use in Job 23:2b.

[31] "Dwelling" translates the unusual תְּכוּנָתוֹ, which comes from כּוּן, "establish/stand/prepare." The AB has "tribune," NAB "judgment seat," NEB "court," GNB "where he is," KJV "seat," and AAT "place."

man." He longed to "present his case" (*nôkāḥ*)[32] to God because he expected it to eventuate in his acquittal, exoneration, and "deliverance/escape." As it turns out, he never had the opportunity (or the need) to state his case at God's tribunal, but nevertheless he did win, simply because he endured the suffering and did not deny his God (Matt 10:22; 24:13; Heb 12:7).

HE CANNOT FIND GOD (23:8-9). Job's frustration with the inaccessibility of God reached a high point in these two verses. Though there is no record of Job literally making any journeys, he engaged metaphors to describe the utter impossibility of discovering God.

23:8 The first merismus is "east-west."[33] Neither in the direction of Mesopotamia or across the Mediterranean could God be found. "Find" is the same verb (*bîn*) translated "consider" in v. 5. Usually it means "understand/perceive." So the wish of v. 5 was still unfulfilled in v. 8.

23:9 The second merismus (see comment at 1:20) is "north-south." Though God appeared to be active in Syria to the north and in Arabia to the south, Job always arrived there too late to see him (cf. 9:11).

(2) Job Declares His Innocence (23:10-12)

¹⁰But he knows the way that I take;
 when he has tested me, I will come forth as gold.
¹¹My feet have closely followed his steps;
 I have kept to his way without turning aside.
¹²I have not departed from the commands of his lips;
 I have treasured the words of his mouth more than my daily bread.

Though Job was stymied in his efforts to find God, he was sure that God knew where he was. Therefore Job also was certain God knew he rejected sin and obediently walked in paths of righteousness.

23:10 This statement of faith has lent strength to believers through the ages as they passed through fires of tribulation and trial. John Rippon's "How Firm a Foundation" contains a fine commentary on Job 23:10.

When through fiery trials thy pathway shall lie,
My grace, all sufficient shall be thy supply;
The flame shall not hurt thee; I only design
Thy dross to consume, and thy gold to refine.

---

[32] See comments at 13:10 ways the root יכח is translated in the NIV of Job.

[33] In Hebrew the points of the compass are קֶדֶם, "front" for "east"; אָחוֹר, "behind" for "west"; שְׂמֹאול, "left" for "north"; יָמִין, "right" for "south."

There are three noteworthy items of faith here: (1) Job believed that God knew his situation; (2) Job believed that God was testing him; (3) Job believed that he would emerge a better man.

23:11 Job walked in God's "steps" and "way." The wisdom literature often speaks of life as a road and behavior as a way or path (e.g., Pss 1:1,6; 119:105; Prov 9:9; 10:9). We do not know how much Job understood about God's "steps" and "way" or how he had encountered God's "commands" or "the words of his mouth" (v. 12), since he was removed by both time and distance from the law of Moses. In 31:4-40 Job would delineate his understanding of the wicked path—falsehood, adultery, injustice, greed, lack of compassion, materialism, idolatry, refusing hospitality, hypocrisy, and oppression. Such a list reflects the conduct condemned in the rest of Scripture.

23:12 From the metaphor of walking on right roads, Job moved to the theme of obeying God's spoken words. "My daily bread" is the noun (*ḥōq*) that usually means "statute/decree" (cf. v. 14). It is taken by many (KJV, NASB, NIV, NJPS) in the sense "my portion [of food] appointed to me" (Gen 47:22; Prov 30:8; 31:15). Others follow the Greek and Latin versions and adjust the vowels to read "in my bosom" (RSV, AB, *BHS* footnote), sometimes paraphrased as "in my heart" (NAB, NEB, AAT; cf. 19:27; Ps 119:11).[34] Such a change commends itself since the "daily bread" translation relies on a less common meaning of the noun and introduces into the text a new idea that has no parallel.

(3) Frustration at God's Apathy (23:13–24:17)

> ¹³"But he stands alone, and who can oppose him?
>   He does whatever he pleases.
> ¹⁴He carries out his decree against me,
>   and many such plans he still has in store.
> ¹⁵That is why I am terrified before him;
>   when I think of all this, I fear him.
> ¹⁶God has made my heart faint;
>   the Almighty has terrified me.
> ¹⁷Yet I am not silenced by the darkness,
>   by the thick darkness that covers my face.

> ¹"Why does the Almighty not set times for judgment?

---

[34] The LXX reads ἐν δὲ κόλπῳ. Following this reading would mean changing מֵחֻקִּי to מְחֵקִי or בְּחֵקִי, although מִן can mean "in" as well as the usual "from/than." See Blommerde, *Northwest Semitic Grammar and Job* (Rome: Pontifical Biblical Institute, 1969), 101-2. Gordis (*Job,* 262) mentions another possibility, כְּחֻקִּי, "as my law."

Why must those who know him look in vain for such days?
²Men move boundary stones;
  they pasture flocks they have stolen.
³They drive away the orphan's donkey
  and take the widow's ox in pledge.
⁴They thrust the needy from the path
  and force all the poor of the land into hiding.
⁵Like wild donkeys in the desert,
  the poor go about their labor of foraging food;
  the wasteland provides food for their children.
⁶They gather fodder in the fields
  and glean in the vineyards of the wicked.
⁷Lacking clothes, they spend the night naked;
  they have nothing to cover themselves in the cold.
⁸They are drenched by mountain rains
  and hug the rocks for lack of shelter.
⁹The fatherless child is snatched from the breast;
  the infant of the poor is seized for a debt.
¹⁰Lacking clothes, they go about naked;
  they carry the sheaves, but still go hungry.
¹¹They crush olives among the terraces;
  they tread the winepresses, yet suffer thirst.
¹²The groans of the dying rise from the city,
  and the souls of the wounded cry out for help.
  But God charges no one with wrongdoing.

¹³"There are those who rebel against the light,
  who do not know its ways
  or stay in its paths.
¹⁴When daylight is gone, the murderer rises up
  and kills the poor and needy;
  in the night he steals forth like a thief.
¹⁵The eye of the adulterer watches for dusk;
  he thinks, 'No eye will see me,'
  and he keeps his face concealed.
¹⁶In the dark, men break into houses,
  but by day they shut themselves in;
  they want nothing to do with the light.
¹⁷For all of them, deep darkness is their morning;
  they make friends with the terrors of darkness.

GOD'S TOTAL CONTROL OF THE CASE (23:13–24:1). Not only was God inaccessible, but he acted independently and like an absolute sovereign. In the language of the KJV, "The LORD most high is terrible; he is a great King over all the earth" (Ps 47:2[3]). Job's attitude in these verses was not the confident one of vv. 10-12.

23:13 "Alone" translates a Hebrew word (*'eḥād*[35]) that usually means "one," as in Deut 6:4, "Hear, O Israel: The LORD our God, the LORD is *one.*" Although this is not an apologetic context, it does reflect Job's monotheism. "Oppose" is a stronger translation than "turn/change [his mind]" that most others have. The NJPS has "dissuade." Again, though not a didactic passage, this statement reflects the doctrine of God's immutability (Num 23:19; Mal 3:6; Jas 1:17).

23:14 The Hebrew of v. 14 is cryptic and requires expansion in English to make sense of it.[36] "His decree against me" is literally "my decree." It translates the same problematic word (*ḥuqqî*) rendered "my daily bread" in v. 12.[37] The second line is literally "and like these many with him." Job's God was an absolute monarch and decreed all things, even Job's suffering (cf. 1 Thess 3:3). This view may be discouraging, but it can be tempered by Eccl 3:11, "God makes all things beautiful in his time" (author's translation).

23:15 For the third time in the chapter Job used the verb *bîn* (vv. 5, 8) but here in the reflexive "when I think." Somehow the vigor with which Job pressed his case began to wane as the image of a real confrontation with God became more vivid. Job did become terrified when God finally spoke to him out of the whirlwind. All our hero could do was confess his unworthiness and cover his mouth (40:4). When we see God, that is what we will do as well.

23:16 "Terrified" occurs again in the following verse. As Habel says, "Job is poised between the two poles of compulsion and fear."[38] Boldness prompted by frustration alternates with fear that God will dispatch a new round of troubles his way. In v. 16 the fear dimension is in view, but it will give way to boldness in v. 17.

23:17 As in 19:8, Job felt lost in the dark. But here he insisted that it would not "silence" him.[39] The second line then elaborates on "dark-

---

[35] The preposition on בְּאֶחָד is a *beth essentia* (cf. *GBH* §133c). Pope (*Job*) emended the combination to בָּחַר, "he chooses," citing a parallel in Ps 132:13.

[36] The LXX lacks the verse altogether, and Moffatt omits it.

[37] And again the suffix is first person when third is expected. Syriac and Vulgate read third person. Blommerde, following Dahood and others, finds this another of thirty-two examples in Job of *-y* or *-i* as a suffix for the third person in Hebrew, as it is occasionally in Ugaritic and regularly in Phoenician, 8, 102. Thus the NEB translates, "What he determines, that he carries out."

[38] Habel, *Book of Job*, 351.

[39] Gordis (*Job*, 262-63) has just the opposite sense by reading כִּי לֹא as an asseverative, resulting in, "Indeed, I am destroyed by darkness."

ness" by providing a synonym, "thick darkness," a verb, "covers," and an unusual use of what is normally a preposition, "my face."[40]

24:1 Like the RSV and others, the NIV added "of judgment" to clarify the meaning of the literal "times" (cf. Ps 81:15[16]; Eccl 9:12; Ezek 21:25[30]). While the AB also translates the verb in the first line as "set," its literal meaning is "hide/store up" (cf. 15:20).[41] Job was further frustrated because God never held court. The second stich is also expanded from a literal "those who know him do not see his days." Jesus seemed to say the same in Acts 1:7, "It is not for you to know the times or dates the Father has set by his own authority." Job, of course, was not thinking of the last judgment but of any occasion when he might find the divine court in session so that he could present his case and receive a hearing.

THE UNPUNISHED WICKED (24:2-17). Job wanted God to explain why he, a righteous man, had to suffer as he did. Also he wanted an explanation of why so many wicked folks went through life unpunished. This latter theme fills chap. 24, as the variety and intensity of sins and sinners and the suffering of their victims is spelled out in some detail.[42]

Their Oppression of the Poor (24:2-12). The victims of the cruel and thieving wicked are forced to endure the most wretched of conditions—starvation, cold, and expulsion. These desperate circumstances and more are pictured in these verses in order to underscore the absence of justice and the seeming apathy of the divine judge.

24:2 The first two sins reflect the pastoral culture from which Job came. The moving[43] of "boundary stones" was forbidden in Deut 19:14; Prov 22:28; 23:10.[44] Stealing or seizing (cf. 20:19) flocks was, of course, forbidden in the law of Moses and in virtually every other law code yet

---

[40] Still the translation is not altogether certain. מִפְּנֵי ("by") in the first stich and מִפָּנָיו ("my face") in the second look suspicious. Some translations simply omit the negative particle, which casts the whole verse into a negative mood matching the surrounding context. So Moffatt, AT, RSV, MLB. Others change לֹא to לוֹ and read it as a wish. So the AB and NAB have, "Would that" and NRSV, "If only I could vanish."

[41] In 15:20 and 24:1 it is *niphal*. It occurs in 21:19; 23:12 in the *qal*. Gordis translates 24:1, "Since the times of judgment are not hidden from the Almighty, why do those who love Him never see the days of retribution?" See also Hartley, *Job,* 343; Habel, *Job,* 351.

[42] Gordis (*Job,* 531) explains that "this chapter is undoubtedly one of the most difficult in the book, with regard to its form, its content, and its relevance to the context."

[43] The usual verb for displacing a boundary marker is the *hiphil* of נסג. The form that occurs here, יַשִּׂיגוּ, is a variant spelling of that verb (cf. KB³, 1223). The verb נשׂג, "overtake," does not suit this context. The reverse occurs in Mic 2:6, where יִסַּג occurs in a context calling for the meaning "overtake."

[44] "The Instruction of Amen-em-opet" also forbids this specific crime in the sixth chapter of that work (*ANET,* 422).

discovered. It is possible that these two crimes were interconnected. By moving the boundaries while the flock grazed near the border, the thief thus brought them over to his side of the line.

24:3 This chiastically arranged verse introduces the victims of these crimes. They are the powerless members of the community, those with no men to lead their families (see comment on 22:9). Deuteronomy 24:6 forbids seizing the means of livelihood as payment for a debt. The donkey and the ox were necessities for the "orphan" ("fatherless" in 22:9; 23:9) and the "widow" (Deut 10:12-19).

24:4 Several commentators and English translations rearrange the verses of this section, but if the flow seems irregular or the logic flawed, it must be remembered who was speaking and the extreme anguish that he was suffering. This is no trial lawyer with a polished presentation but a man with a dreadful disease, on an ash heap, accused of awful crimes by healthy friends with sick arguments.[45] Only GNB and NIV make the passive verb in the second stich active. Such a move improves the parallelism, but it is less vivid than the NEB "the destitute huddle together." The ungodly "thrust" and "force" the "poor" and "needy" "from the path" and "into hiding" (cf. Prov 28:28). Habel suggests a metaphorical interpretation: "When the property and possessions of the poor are appropriated, they are compelled to leave the mainstream of society and eke out an existence in the hidden corners of their community."[46]

24:5 How to arrange this long verse into lines is the major challenge of the translator. As Rowley says, "Innumerable emendations have been proposed, but none has been generally accepted."[47] The NIV has included all the words and presented three lines fairly equal in length. The three preceding verses reported what the wicked did; now the focus is on the situation of the oppressed victims.[48] Like animals they spent their days gathering enough food to sustain life. The least productive area, the desert, was their harvest field and hunting ground.

24:6 The comparison seems to continue in this verse. Their extreme

---

[45] Moffatt and Buttenwieser have v. 9 between vv. 3 and 4. The AB has vv. 9, 21 between vv. 3 and 4. The JB has vv. 7-9 between vv. 11 and 12. The NEB and REB have the verses in the order 1,2,6,3,9,4,5,7,8,10. Fohrer (KAT, 367-68) has 1-4,9-12,22-23,5-8,13-14,16a,15,16b-18aα,20b,18aβ-21,24-25. The lack of unity in these samples indicates that the "correct" order is not abundantly obvious. Gordis (*Job*, 531) explains that the problem is the antiphonal arrangement of themes, the recognition of which makes rearrangement unnecessary.

[46] Habel, *Job*, 359.

[47] Rowley, *Job*, 163.

[48] Verse 9 again has the oppressors as the subject; therefore some move it forward.

poverty is graphically illustrated, assuming that the "fodder" they gather is for themselves rather than their animals.[49] "Gleaning" was regularly the way the poor fed themselves (cf. Lev 19:10; Ruth 2).[50]

24:7 To the discomfort of banishment and starvation, Job added the hardship created by lack of shelter and clothing. Exodus 22:27 forbad keeping an outer garment overnight for collateral (Job 22:6).

24:8 Job's picture of the poor and oppressed grows more pitiful with each verse. Now they are abandoned, starved, naked, and "drenched by mountain rains."

24:9 The Hebrew verbs here are active, the subjects understood to be the wicked. Because of the shift in subject, the NIV resorted to passive verbs so that the orphan "is snatched" and the nursing infant[51] "is seized." In v. 3 the wicked wealthy took "the widow's ox in pledge." Here they take the suckling child for the same reason.

24:10 Except for the verb, v. 10a is identical to v. 7a. Like other phrases in this description of oppression, Job echoed terms that Eliphaz used in his accusation of Job. So "take in pledge" and "naked" were in 22:6, "hungry" in 22:7, and "widows" and "fatherless" in 22:9. The second stich is parallel to the two in v. 11. In the midst of plenty they must do without.

24:11 Surrounded by grain, olives, and wine, the oppressed workers must suffer starvation and thirst. The law provided that even the animals that trod out the grain should be allowed to nibble of it (Deut 25:4). Here, human beings are forbidden to partake of the rich man's abundance for which they toil. The first line is uncertain. Of it Pope said, "The difficulties . . . are formidable and one can only guess at the meaning."[52] An NIV footnote gives a very possible alternative to "among the terraces" (lit. "between their walls") as "between the millstones."[53] The verb occurs only here but is assumed to be related to *yiṣhār*, "[olive] oil."

24:12 Job concluded his description of the abuses and exploitation

---

[49] בְּלִיל, "fodder," is elsewhere only in 6:5 and Isa 24:6. Tur-Sinai (*Job*, 362) adjusts it to בְּלִי לוֹ, "in which there is no corn." Others read the same emendation as "not his," yielding the translation, "They reap in a field not their own" (Gordis, *Job*, 254, 265-66). Dhorme (*Job*, 358) would emend it to בְּלַיְלָה, "during the night." Pope (*Job*) reads בְּלִיַּעַל "of the villain," which makes a nice parallel with "the wicked."

[50] "Glean" here is לָקַשׁ, which occurs elsewhere only as a noun in Amos 7:1 and in the cognate מַלְקוֹשׁ, "latter rain." The usual verb for "glean" is לָקַט.

[51] NIV (with all but KJV, RV, ASV, NASB, NKJV) follows the LXX (ἐκπεπτωκότα from ἐκπινω, "to drink") in revocalizing the preposition עַל as the noun עוּל, "suckling."

[52] Pope, *Job*, 177.

[53] Gordis (*Job*, 266) understands the noun שׁוּרָה, which occurs only here, to refer to rows of olive trees.

of the poor by the rich by telling of their dying groans and vain cries for help. Job reached another low point in his view of divine justice and came almost as close to blasphemy as he did in 9:22-24. It appeared to him that God was oblivious to all this evil.

Killers, Adulterers, Burglars (24:13-17). Verses 13 and 17 form the introduction and conclusion to this short list of serious offenses, crimes that parallel the sixth, seventh, and eighth commandments (Exod 20:13-15). The motif of darkness pervades this passage; all three offenses are committed at night. Verses 13-16 are all triplets.

24:13 "Light" is associated with right, just as darkness is with wrong.[54] Evil people rebel against what is right and prefer darkness to light because they do not want their deeds to be seen.

24:14 The point of the verse is clear—murderers kill innocent and weak people. But the Hebrew says they do it "at the light."[55] It could be understood as a merismus (see comment at 1:20): By day they kill; by night they are like robbers.[56]

Most commentaries and translations produce a better parallel and work around what seems inconsistent with v. 13 by reading "at twilight" (AB),[57] "at dusk" (NRSV), "before daylight" (NEB), "at dawn" (NASB, AAT),[58] "when there is no light" (NAB, reading the preposition as a negative),[59] "at evening" (NJPS).[60]

24:15 The next category of malfeasance is adultery. This variety of sinner likewise prefers the darkness (Prov 7:8-9). He "covers/conceals/disguises" the face, further to ensure anonymity. Murder and adultery, but not theft (cf. Exod 22:1-4), were capital crimes in ancient Israel (Gen 9:6; Exod 21:12; 22:2; Lev 20:10). Virtually all ancient law codes outside Israel dealt similarly with these offenses.

24:16 Verses 14-16 are framed by the word "light," just as vv. 13-17

---

[54] Gen 1:4; Job 18:5; Pss 37:6; 97:11; Prov 13:9; John 3:19-21; 2 Cor 6:14; 1 John 1:5-7.

[55] The word is לְאוֹר.

[56] The LXX lacks vv. 14c-18a. Some would move v. 14c closer to v. 16 so that all the lines about thieves are together and at the same time turn two tricola into three bicola. So Dhorme, *Job*, 363-64; Kissane, *Job*, 149; Pope, *Job*. Hartley (*Job*, 349) moves v. 16a to a position after v. 14c. N. Ararat ("'Light' Which Doesn't Cast Light in Bible Language," *Beth Mikra* 34 [1988/89]: 316-27 [Hebrew]) takes it in its polar meaning, "darkness" (cf. Ps 139:11).

[57] So Hartley, *Job*, 348.

[58] So Dhorme, *Job*, 362-63.

[59] So Driver and Gray, *Job* II:169. The NIV 2 probably is following this solution.

[60] So Gordis (*Job*, 268), who translates "at nightfall," citing the Aramaic אוּרְתָא, "evening."

are enclosed by the opposites "light" and "morning."[61] Thieves also operate under cover of darkness for obvious reasons (John 3:20).

24:17 This summary verse maintains the themes of light and darkness. In v. 16c the text reads literally, "They do not know the light." By contrast in v. 17, "They make friends with the terrors of darkness." Both words in v. 17 for "darkness" are ṣalmāwet, "shadow of death" (Ps 23:4). Like all fast-talking lawbreakers they turn things upside down and call them by opposite names, so their "morning" is "darkness" (cf. Isa 5:20; 29:16; Amos 5:7; 6:12b; Matt 6:22-23).

On this depressing note Job ended his description of the wicked, who appear to go unpunished because of an apathetic God. Some psalms reflect a corresponding attitude, and so may some of God's people today as they suffer defenselessly at the hands of others or watch tyrants misusing and victimizing the powerless.

(4) The Accursed Wicked (24:18-25)

> [18]"Yet they are foam on the surface of the water;
>   their portion of the land is cursed,
>   so that no one goes to the vineyards.
> [19]As heat and drought snatch away the melted snow,
>   so the grave snatches away those who have sinned.
> [20]The womb forgets them,
>   the worm feasts on them;
> evil men are no longer remembered
>   but are broken like a tree.
> [21]They prey on the barren and childless woman,
>   and to the widow show no kindness.
> [22]But God drags away the mighty by his power;
>   though they become established, they have no assurance of life.
> [23]He may let them rest in a feeling of security,
>   but his eyes are on their ways.
> [24]For a little while they are exalted, and then they are gone;
>   they are brought low and gathered up like all others;
>   they are cut off like heads of grain.

---

[61] The poet's play on terms for "light" and "darkness" can be diagrammed chiastically:
A   Light (v. 13a)
  B   Light (v. 14a)
    C   Night (v. 14c)
      D   Twilight (v. 15a)
    C'   Dark (v. 16a)
  B'   Light (v. 16c)
A'   Morning (v. 17b,c)

²⁵"If this is not so, who can prove me false
and reduce my words to nothing?"

Verses 18-25 do not sound like Job but rather like one of the friends. For this reason some move all or most of these eight verses to the end of chap. 27, assuming they are the missing third speech of Zophar.[62] The GNB leaves them in place but labels them Zophar. The NAB translates only two lines of vv. 18-21. Some consider it, like chap. 28, an independent poem by the author of the book.[63] The incongruity, however, between these verses and the rest of Job's speeches is not as great as is often supposed. Job does not say elsewhere that God never punishes the wicked or rewards the righteous but only that there is often no observable connection between behavior and blessing or punishment.[64] Rather than excising or moving the verses, some would read them either as imprecations or as an unannounced quotation of the friends as in 21:19 and 26:12.[65] Hartley "cautiously" prefers the former solution, explaining that "since Job wants God to execute his justice against these wicked as proof that he will act justly in his own favor, he utters a series of curses against the lawless."[66] Thus he translates most of the verbs as jussives (e.g., in v. 18, "Let their portion be accursed in the land"). The exceptions are v. 18a and vv. 24-25.[67]

As translated in the NIV, the passage exhibits a change of perspective similar to the one that occurs in Ps 73:16-20. After complaining there about the carefree arrogance of the wicked in the face of his own innocent suffering, the psalmist wrote: "When I tried to understand all this, / it was oppressive to me // till I entered the sanctuary of God; / then I understood their final destiny" (vv. 16-17). All agree that the Hebrew in this

---

[62] So S. Terrien, "Job," *IB* 3 (New York: Abingdon, 1954), 1088-89; Dhorme, *Job*, 366; Pope, *Job*; JB.

[63] So Habel, *Job*, 357-58.

[64] Andersen, *Job*, 213-14; Smick, "Job," EBC 4:960.

[65] The latter view is argued by the RSV and Gordis, *Job*, 533. The RSV begins v. 18 with the addition "You say" and continues the quote through v. 20. It has Job answering in vv. 21-25.

[66] Hartley, *Job*, 352-53. Andersen (*Job*, 214) says, "We may suspect that the whole is a string of curses, beginning with verse 18, where an imprecation, not a statement, should be read, as the grammar shows." See also NJPS. The NKJV translates vv. 18-20 with obligatory imperfects, e.g., "Their portion *should be* cursed in the earth."

[67] He apparently translates differently in v. 24 so that v. 25 will have something to connect to when it begins, "If not, who can prove that I lied" (NIV, "If this is not so, who can prove me false?"). A difficulty of many interpretations of vv. 18-24 is explaining the connection to v. 25.

section of Job is very difficult, and many parts of it cannot be translated with any certainty.[68]

24:18 Though in Hebrew there is no conjunction, with the addition of "yet" the NIV accents the change of perspective and theme from the crimes of the wicked to their destruction. "Foam" is *qal,* something "worthless/light/swift," a play on words with *tĕqullal,* "is cursed," in the second line. The NJPS has "flotsam"; the NEB translates "scum." The point is that the wicked will not endure (cf. 7:6; 9:25). Since "the land is cursed," there is no reason to go to "the vineyards"; there would be no fruit.

24:19 The translators have had to make this verse into a comparison, even though there are no comparative particles in the text. Also, the verb "snatch away" occurs only in the first line. The second line is very terse— "*šĕ'ôl* (NIV "grave") those who have sinned." Job had another illustration using "snow" in 6:15-17 (cf. 38:22). As a snowball has no chance to survive the heat, so *šĕ'ôl* will "snatch away" sinners.[69]

24:20 Each of the four lines in v. 19 is short, but each is an independent clause with its own verb present or understood. "Womb" and "worm" constitute a merismus (see explanation at 1:20). The womb is our home at the beginning of life; the worm is our companion at the end. "Feasts" translates "his sweetness," that is, "the worm" finds corpses "sweet" (cf. 7:5; Ps 49:14; Isa 66:24 quoted in Mark 9:48). The verbs are mainly singular in this section but understood as generic, hence the plural "men" and "they." The third line is literally "he is no longer remembered." The subject "evil men" in the NIV is derived from the last line, whose subject in Hebrew is "evil" (cf. KJV).

24:21 Some would move v. 21 to the preceding stanza where the crimes of the wicked are listed, but if left here it serves well to clarify the subject of the verbs and to remind that such punishment is well deserved (note especially the connection between "the barren and childless woman" and "the womb" in v. 20). The Old Testament tells the stories of disappointment and frustration that "barren and childless" women endured (Sarah, Rachel, Tamar, Hannah, Manoah's wife). These women had no heirs; widows no longer had husbands (Ps 127:3-5). On these unfortu-

---

[68] Kissane (*Job*, 160) quotes Gray's description of 'these corrupt, difficult, ambiguous and unintelligible verses." Then he adds with amazing confidence, "The text is indeed very corrupt, and the meaning in many cases obscure; nevertheless, with a few changes, the most important of which have the support of the LXX, the original can be restored with practical certainty."

[69] The KJV often translated שְׁאוֹל "hell" (though not here), but only Deut 32:22 makes any connection to fire.

nate, weaker members of the community the ungodly "preyed/fed."[70]

24:22 There are several ways to recast this and the neighboring verses, all of which have some merit.[71] Not only are the Hebrew words found in unusual contexts and their semantic spheres stretched in translation, but orthographic irregularities abound and the pronoun antecedents are not clear. A review of options is beyond the scope of this commentary, so the remarks focus on the NIV in an effort to explain how it interpreted the verse. "God" was supplied as a subject for the verb that has "the mighty" as its object and as an antecedent for "his power."[72] The very wordiness of the second line indicates an original that is less than straightforward. Literally it reads, "He will rise, and he will not believe in the lives" (with "lives" spelled with an Aramaic plural). The line seems to say that the wicked will eventually receive their due and they know it (cf. Deut 28:66).[73]

24:23 As in v. 22 the godless often get a reprieve from immediate judgment. But God's "eyes are on their ways," not in the sense of blessing but in the sense of surveillance. "God will bring every deed into judgment, including every hidden thing, whether it is good or evil" (Eccl 12:14).

24:24 The meaning of this tricolon is less debated. The wicked, "for a little while" or "a little bit," may rise, but soon they are no more (Ps 37:10). "Brought low," though a rare word, fits well here as Job moved to the imagery of harvest.[74] "Cut off" is the end of life as far as the grain is concerned,[75] and it is the end of the road for the godless.

24:25 Job concluded his response to Eliphaz with a challenge to be proven false in what he said earlier in his speech and perhaps also in this

---

[70] The NIV has understood the participle רֹעֶה to be from רעה, "to graze." Gordis (*Job,* 270) takes it as a byform of רָעַע, "to crush." Andersen (*Job,* 214) and Hartley (*Job,* 351) follow Fohrer in taking it from רעה II, "to associate with," and read it substantivally as "female companion/lady." The concluding לֹא תְלֵד of line *a,* "she does not bear," then becomes the only verb in the line, yielding "the barren lady does not bear," or (reading the verb as jussive) "let not the barren lady bear." The NIV treats this final verb phrase as a relative clause (cf. KJV) like the final חָטָאוּ in v. 19, translating as the adjective "childless." Gordis translates it as a result clause, "so that she cannot give birth."

[71] The NAB omits it, filling the line with dots to show the translators' frustration.

[72] This translation has the support of Dhorme, *Job,* 390-91; Hölscher, *Job,* 60.

[73] Eliphaz's similar words in 15:20-23 could be interpreted as supporting the idea that Job is sarcastically quoting the friends or that he is dissatisfied with either an eventual or a "piecemeal" destruction of the wicked and wants their public condemnation accompanied by the vindication of the righteous (see Smick, "Job," EBC 4:961).

[74] The root מכך is elsewhere only in Ps 106:43 and Eccl 10:18.

[75] The verb is from נמל, not מלל, "wither," as in BDB, 576.

awkward last stanza. "Prove me false" is mild for "make me a liar."[76] Strong language has been common throughout this debate. It is a pity no description of their actions or record of the look on their faces has come down to us. Far from Job's words being reduced to nothing, he has much to say and that rather soon.

---

[76] It is the *hiphil* of כזב, "to lie," in the *qal* (Ps 116:11) or the *piel* (6:28; 34:6; Pss 78:36; 89:35[36]; Prov 14:5), and "be proven a liar" in *niphal* (41:1; Prov 30:6). The noun כָּזָב, "lie," also occurs (Pss 5:6[7]; 58:3[4]).

15. Bildad: How Can We Be Righteous? (25:1-6)
    (1) God's Greatness (25:1-3)
    (2) Human Failure at Being Right (25:4-6)
16. Job's Review of Themes: Divine Sovereignty, His Own
    Innocence, and the Fate of the Wicked (26:1-14)
    (1) Insult with Irony (26:1-4)
    (2) God's Absolute Control (26:5-14)
17. Job's Ongoing Discourse (27:1-23)
    (1) Protest of Innocence (27:1-6)
    (2) Curse on Enemies (27:7-10)
    (3) Fate of the Wicked (27:11-23)
        Introduction (27:11-12)
        Terrors the Wicked Can Expect (27:13-23)

15. Bildad: How Can We Be Righteous? (25:1-6)

This is Bildad's third and last speech, and it is very short. He and the others have run out of things to say to Job. Already they have become repetitious. Zophar has no third speech, and we hear no more of any of them until 42:7.

(1) God's Greatness (25:1-3)

¹Then Bildad the Shuhite replied:

²"Dominion and awe belong to God;
he establishes order in the heights of heaven.
³Can his forces be numbered?
Upon whom does his light not rise?

Happily Bildad did not end his and the friends' portion of the book on a caustic and critical note. Instead he began with another look at the greatness of God. In this way he, like Job and his friends elsewhere, foreshadowed the revelation of God in the whirlwind (chaps. 38–41).

25:1 See comments at 4:1.

25:2 Bildad began his first two speeches with insults and irony (8:2; 18:2), much as Job did in his response (26:2-4). It is a welcome change to hear him begin with this lofty and worshipful theological statement.

God rules. He reigns. He resides in the "heights," where all is *šālôm*, "peace/order."

25:3   These two rhetorical questions underscore two divine attributes: God is powerful; he is the Lord of hosts.[1] And second, his revelation of himself is universal (cf. Ps 19:1-6[2-7]).

(2) Human Failure at Being Right (25:4-6)

> **⁴How then can a man be righteous before God?**
>   **How can one born of woman be pure?**
> **⁵If even the moon is not bright**
>   **and the stars are not pure in his eyes,**
> **⁶how much less man, who is but a maggot—**
>   **a son of man, who is only a worm!"**

Bildad turned from the perfections of God to the imperfections of humanity. In light of divine demands, "all have sinned and fall short of the glory of God" (Rom 3:23). Compared to God, the Creator, the Sovereign, the Judge, we are but maggots and worms.

25:4   With these two questions Bildad emphasized the fact of total depravity. Sin has infected the entire race. Each one inherits it from parents because all of us are "born of woman." Eliphaz asked similar questions in 4:17, and so did Job in 14:4.

25:5   Speaking cosmically and with hyperbole, Bildad faulted "the moon" and "stars," created bodies incapable of sin, with failure to please God.[2] This too is reminiscent of something Eliphaz said in 15:15-16.

25:6   Certainly people cannot be pure in God's sight because each is "a son of man" or "a descendant of Adam." Paul, speaking of our common Father, said, "The first man was of the dust of the earth. . . . As was the earthly man, so are those who are of the earth" (1 Cor 15:47-48). But Bildad spoke in terms of "maggots" and "worms" (cf. Ps 22:6[7]; Isa 14:11), an extreme depiction that seems to deny human worth and dignity as God-given (cf. 7:17-20; Gen 1:26-27; 5:1-3; Ps 8:4-5).[3] Thus he con-

---

[1] The word for "forces" is גְּדוּדִים, not the usual צְבָאוֹת.

[2] The verb "is bright" (יַאֲהִיל) is either a hapax (אהל II, "to shine" in KB[3]) or "an extreme plene spelling" (R. Gordis, *The Book of Job* [New York: Jewish Theological Seminary, 1978], 277) of יְהִ, *hiphil* imperfect from the root הלל I, "shine" (29:3; 31:26; 41:18[10]; Isa 13:10).

[3] It could be argued, of course, that Bildad's statement, like the hymn writer Isaac Watts's "for such a worm as I," is not a denial of the divine image in humankind but an affirmation of the inherent unworthiness of sinful people before a holy God and, thus, an affirmation of the greatness of God's grace (1 Cor 1:26-31; 2 Cor 4:7; Eph 2:3-5).

cluded his short speech, and "on this disgusting and hopeless note the words of Job's friends end."[4]

16. Job's Review of Themes: Divine Sovereignty, His Own Innocence, and the Fate of the Wicked (26:1-14)

After an initial retaliatory flurry of insults, Job filled the rest of chap. 26 with observations about the Creator and his creation. This is where Job's words, more than at any other point, anticipated the theophany. Such passages point to the unity of the authorship of the book, but they also raise the question of why Job needed God to impress these facts on him when he seemed to understand so well already.

(1) Insult with Irony (26:1-4)

[1]Then Job replied:

[2]"How you have helped the powerless!
How you have saved the arm that is feeble!
[3]What advice you have offered to one without wisdom!
And what great insight you have displayed!
[4]Who has helped you utter these words?
And whose spirit spoke from your mouth?

The brief and unoffensive speech of Bildad hardly warranted this bitter response from Job, but the pronouns are singular, so he most likely was addressing the Shuhite.[5] Certainly it is true that Bildad's words were not helpful and offered no new insights. Perhaps Job was hoping for something more—sympathy, comfort, support, a truly helpful perspec-

---

[4] F. I. Andersen, *Job,* TOTC (Downers Grove: InterVarsity, 1976), 215.

[5] Moffatt moved 26:2-4 to after 25:1, thus giving Bildad chaps. 25–26. The AT, AB, and JB move 26:2-4 to the end of the chapter, thus making 26:5-14 part of Bildad's speech. So too N. Habel (*The Book of Job*, OTL [Philadelphia: Westminster, 1985]), Gordis (*Job*), E. Dhorme (*A Commentary on the Book of Job* [London: Nelson, 1967]), Marshall (*The Book of Job*, AACOT [Philadelphia: American Baptist Publishing Society, 1904], 89). The GNB keeps the verses in order but puts Bildad's name at the beginning of 26:5. So too H. H. Rowley, *Job*, NCB (Grand Rapids: Eerdmans, 1976), 172. J. Hartley (*The Book of Job*, NICOT [Grand Rapids: Eerdmans, 1988], 355) attaches 27:13-23 to Bildad's short response. Buttenwieser's rearrangement of the verses from chaps 23–37 is complicated beyond belief in large measure because he eliminates or redistributes all of the Elihu verses among the other speakers. The Qumran Targum (ca. 200–150 B.C.) supports the order of the Masoretic Text (M. Sokoloff, *The Targum to Job from Qumran Cave XI* [Jerusalem: Kiryat-Sefer, 1974], 44-49).

tive, wise counsel, or affirmation. Hearing only more of what he had heard before, he even may have cut Bildad off by butting in or with the wave of a hand.

26:1   See comments at 6:1.

26:2   The four exclamations or rhetorical questions that begin this section have the effect of saying that his friend's counsel has neither "helped the powerless" nor "saved the arm that is feeble." Several times earlier Job spoke of his lack of strength, especially in the face of God's omnipotence (6:11-13; 9:19; 12:16; 24:22), so he alluded to himself in these two lines.

26:3   Likewise, none of them "displayed/made known" any "advice" or "great insight." The friends failed physically (v. 2) and intellectually (v. 3) to help their suffering comrade.

26:4   The first line is awkward. The Hebrew text has only "With whom did you utter words?" The gist of the question is like that of the second line—Whence came this information that is so lacking in profundity and so helpless in its effects? By these words Job rejected their counsel, their subtle accusations, and their neat and inflexible theology of retribution.

(2) God's Absolute Control (26:5-14)

⁵"The dead are in deep anguish,
  those beneath the waters and all that live in them.
⁶Death is naked before God;
  Destruction lies uncovered.
⁷He spreads out the northern skies over empty space;
  he suspends the earth over nothing.
⁸He wraps up the waters in his clouds,
  yet the clouds do not burst under their weight.
⁹He covers the face of the full moon,
  spreading his clouds over it.
¹⁰He marks out the horizon on the face of the waters
  for a boundary between light and darkness.
¹¹The pillars of the heavens quake,
  aghast at his rebuke.
¹²By his power he churned up the sea;
  by his wisdom he cut Rahab to pieces.
¹³By his breath the skies became fair;
  his hand pierced the gliding serpent.
¹⁴And these are but the outer fringe of his works;
  how faint the whisper we hear of him!

Who then can understand the thunder of his power?"

Abruptly Job launched into this magnificent hymn that sings of the powers God himself revealed to him at the end of the book. The focus is on cosmic evidences of divine power far beyond human control or understanding. God is the subject of most of the verbs. The elements have no will of their own. Also the verbs are in the active voice, as God is active in the administration of his cosmos. The chapter concludes with one of the loftiest and most beautiful expressions in the entire Bible: "These are but the outer fringe of his works."

26:5 The meaning of this verse is uncertain. "The dead" are rĕpā'îm, "ghosts/shades/spirits of the deceased," and they are parallel to "those beneath the waters." As Bildad just spoke of God's dominion over the heights, so now Job speaks of that rule in the depths. All who are there "writhe" in abjection before him from whom nothing is hidden.

26:6 "Death" and "Destruction" are translations of Hebrew "Sheol" and "Abaddon," as the NIV footnote indicates. The capital letters indicate the translators' ambivalence about whether these should be personified with Hebrew names or translated as common nouns (cf. 28:22; 31:12; Prov 15:11; 27:20; Ps 88:11[12]). My earlier remarks about Job's use of popular mythology, specifically about Yam and Leviathan in 3:8, Rahab in 9:13, and Mot in 18:13, also apply here. Hebrews 4:13 interprets this verse: "Nothing in all creation is hidden from God's sight. Everything is uncovered and laid bare before the eyes of him to whom we must give account."

26:7 Echoes of Gen 1 sound here, especially in the choice of tōhû, "empty space" (cf. Gen 1:2, "formless"). Some commentators remind us that pagans considered the north to be the dwelling of the gods.[6] Even if Job had that in mind, line a indicates that that sacred mountain was created by the God our hero honored. Job's assertion that the earth hangs on nothing is amazingly accurate and certainly counters the charge that the Bible's writers held that the earth stood on something else.

26:8 Another advanced meteorological observation appears next. Clouds are water, but in the language of poetry they appear as overstuffed bags. Job was intrigued, knowing how heavy water was, that it did not always and immediately fall from the clouds.

26:9 The NIV follows Ibn Ezra and those who read "full moon"

---

[6] So M. Pope, *Job*, AB (Garden City: Doubleday, 1965), 183. But J. de Savignac maintains that a more fundamental meaning of צָפוֹן is "clouds/cloudy sky" ("Le sens du terme Ṣâphôn, *UF* 16 [1984]: 273-78).

(RSV, AB, JB, NAB, NEB, GNB, NASB) rather than "throne" (KJV, ASV, AT, NJPS).[7] "Spreading" is widely agreed on although it translates an unusual verb form.[8] Again the point of the verse is that God is in complete control of celestial phenomena, uncovering "the grave" in v. 6 but covering the "moon" in v. 9.

26:10 Yet another prescientific observation contributes to the fascination of this passage. "The horizon/circle"[9] is that dividing point from the viewer's perspective between what can be seen ("light") and what cannot ("darkness"), separating the lighted world above the ground and water from the dark world under the ground or water. Technicalities aside, both here and in Gen 1 the important fact is that God is the subject of the verb. The earth and the heavens are his design and his handiwork (Ps 19:1; Prov 8:27,29; Isa 40:22).

26:11 The description of "pillars" rebuked and quaking[10] demonstrates the poet's artistic imagination (cf. 9:6; 26:7). Why would God "rebuke" heaven's pillars? Job chose these figures to describe the rumbling of the thunder (v. 14). Verses 11-12 portray a storm, while v. 13 depicts the subsequent calm. As a servant quakes at the rebuke of his master, so the heavens thunder in subjection to God's will.

26:12 The verb *rgʿ* has two opposite meanings—"divide/churn" or "calm/rest."[11] "Churn" links the verse with the preceding. "Calm" would link it to the following. The NIV's choice makes the two lines approximate parallels. Rahab was the mythical monster of the deep, supposedly responsible for tempestuous seas; however, no creature, real or imaginary, is beyond God's control. The behemoth and leviathan chapters (40–41) also make this point.

26:13 If one chose "calm" in v. 12a, a case could be made for vv. 12-13 paralleling each other thus:

---

[7] The text has כֶּסֶה. "Throne" is כִּסֵא (but with ה in 1 Kgs 10:19). "Full moon" is כֶּסֶא, which only occurs in Ps 81:3[4] (but with א in Prov 7:20). Gordis, Habel, and Hartley argue for reading "throne" rather than "moon" with the support of the ancient versions. M. Jastrow, Fohrer, and Dhorme favor "moon."

[8] For a discussion of the possible parsing of פַּרְשֵׁז see Gordis, *Job,* 279. נטה was the verb translated "spreads" in v. 7.

[9] "Horizon" is חֹק ("limit/boundary/barrier" in 14:5; Prov 8:29; Jer 5:22) and "marks out" is חָג, *qal* perf. from חוג, which occurs only here. In Prov 8:27-29 the same roots occur in opposite grammatical form, with the noun חוּג, "horizon" (22:14, "vault"; Isa 40:22, "circle") and the qal inf. const. חֻקּוֹ from חקק, "dig out/inscribe/decree."

[10] This root רפף occurs nowhere else in the OT but is known from Arabic and Syriac.

[11] "Divide" is the meaning in Job 7:5; Isa 51:15; Jer 31:35. "Rest" is the meaning in Deut 28:65; Isa 34:14; 51:4; Jer 47:6; 50:34. The commentators and English versions are divided as well. The ASV offered "stirreth up" in the text and "stilleth" in the margin.

A calm
   B Rahab
A fair
   B serpent

As it is, however, "the skies became fair" because "his hand pierced the gliding serpent."[12] He put to death the source of the oceans' agitation (cf. Mark 4:39).

26:14 Job concluded this poem with the astute observation that all these celestial and terrestrial manifestations of divine power "are but the outskirts of his ways" (ASV). We mortals do not see or appreciate what is behind these operations of the universe. When we hear God speak through wind and thunder, it is only his "whisper."[13] Job's final question is still with us, "Who could understand" if he spoke in full voice, that is, with "the thunder of his power?" With finite minds we, like Job, seek to grasp the ways of God, forgetting what he said in Isa 55:8-9.

> "My thoughts are not your thoughts,
> neither are your ways my ways," declares the LORD.
>
> As the heavens are higher than the earth,
> so are my ways higher than your ways
> and my thoughts than your thoughts.

Beginning in chap. 38 Yahweh "whispered" to Job out of the storm.

17. Job's Ongoing Discourse (27:1-23)

The introductory formula is different from any of the preceding chapters. Zophar should have replied, and it is likely that Job waited for him to do so. When he did not, Job began speaking (cf. 29:1). The features of this last speech in the debate cycle are characteristic of Job's other speeches. He protested his innocence and spoke of the fate of the wicked. Because vv. 13-23 sound more like what the friends had been saying, these verses can be understood as a quotation of them introduced by Job's term "meaningless words" at the end of v. 12.[14]

---

[12] נָחָשׁ בָּרִיחַ is also in Isa 27:1 and identified as "Leviathan." See comments at Job 3:8.

[13] Hebrew שֵׁמֶץ, a word that occurs only here and in 4:12. A fem. form, שִׁמְצָה, is in Exod 32:25 translated "laughingstock" in the NIV.

[14] Needless to say, some commentators move these verses to another place (Hartley) or assume they belong to Zophar and insert his name before v. 11. So AB, JB, GNB, Habel, Gordis, Rowley, etc. The similarity of Zophar's last words (20:29) to v. 13 support their choice, but it could also be, as F. Delitzsch pointed out, "Job now begins as Zophar concluded" (*Biblical Commentary on the Book of Job* [Grand Rapids: Eerdmans, 1949], II:72).

(1) Protest of Innocence (27:1-6)

[1]And Job continued his discourse:

[2]"As surely as God lives, who has denied me justice,
     the Almighty, who has made me taste bitterness of soul,
[3]as long as I have life within me,
     the breath of God in my nostrils,
[4]my lips will not speak wickedness,
     and my tongue will utter no deceit.
[5]I will never admit you are in the right;
     till I die, I will not deny my integrity.
[6]I will maintain my righteousness and never let go of it;
     my conscience will not reproach me as long as I live.

As in other places through the course of this debate, Job asserts his innocence (cf. 6:29-30; 9:15,20-21; 10:2; 13:23; 16:17; 19:7; 23:10-12). Since this is the last time our hero addresses his friends, there is more vehemence in his voice, and we can imagine his fists clenched tighter than ever.

27:1 In typically wordy semitic fashion this introduction literally reads, "And Job continued lifting up his parable/proverb/speech,[15] and he said." This separate introduction indicates that chap. 27 is distinct from chap. 26. Apparently there was no response from Zophar, so Job simply "continued."

27:2 Verses 2-3 introduce the oath, the essence of which is in vv. 4-6. He invoked two of the standard names for God, *ʾēl* and *šadday,* and, by way of apposition, charged him with "turning aside his legal case" and "embittering his soul." For Job, as for anyone convinced of the former charge, the latter charge followed naturally. "Bitterness" usually is the first spontaneous reaction when we draw a miserable lot in life.

27:3 The third common name for "God" is here (*ʾĕlôah*), along with two more synonyms for "soul" (*nepeš* in v. 2): "life" (*nišmâ*) and "breath" (*rûaḥ*). Job would sooner die than compromise his integrity by admitting to sins he did not commit. He would not fabricate a confession simply to placate his friends. That, in itself, would be a sin.

27:4 Job 13:7 has the same two synonyms for "wickedness" and "deceit" as we find here. But there Job charged his friends with speaking falsely, something that he here forbad himself to do. The lies he refused to tell are in the next verses. He vigorously repudiated his

---

[15] The term מָשָׁל described Balaam's "oracles" (Num 23:7, etc.), Isaiah's "taunt" (14:4), and Micah's "mournful song" (2:4); and it is the name of the Book of Proverbs.

friends' explanation for his suffering.

27:5   A strong exclamation ("far be it from me!" or "God forbid!"[16]) opens the first line. Admitting that they were right on this issue would mean denying his "integrity,"[17] an idea that repulsed Job.

27:6   Once more and with different words, Job averred his innocence. "Righteousness," *ṣdq* in its nominal, verbal, and adjectival forms, is also widespread in Job; but elsewhere in the Old Testament its sense is broader than "integrity."[18]

(2) Curse on Enemies (27:7-10)

> [7]"May my enemies be like the wicked,
>   my adversaries like the unjust!
> [8]For what hope has the godless when he is cut off,
>   when God takes away his life?
> [9]Does God listen to his cry
>   when distress comes upon him?
> [10]Will he find delight in the Almighty?
>   Will he call upon God at all times?

Verse 7 is Job's imprecation on his enemy (singular or generic), and the other three verses describe God's treatment of such wicked people. It is unclear who the enemy was, whether the most recent antagonist or all three of the friends, or perhaps all who had treated Job disrespectfully. Verses 8-10 are somewhat out of character for him since they describe bad things happening to bad people. That is what the friends usually said, not Job.

27:7   Bildad had accused Job of being "wicked" (*rāšāʿ*, 18:5,22) and "unjust" (*ʿawwāl*, 18:21), and the other two had done the same;[19] now Job prayed that Bildad (or all three friends) might be punished as the wicked deserve. Some of the trouble and trust psalms are freighted with imprecations (Pss 35:1-8,22-26; 69:22-28[23-29]; 109:6-20, especially v. 17). The curses are usually tied to the nature of the abuse the psalmist

---

[16] *IBHS* § 40.2.2c; *GBH* § 93h, § 105f, §165k.

[17] The word used here is תֻּמָּה, found elsewhere only in 2:3,9; 31:6; Prov 11:3. The root of this word is found throughout Job and might be called Job's most admirable trait. The adjective תָּם, "blameless," is in 1:1,8; 2:3; 8:20; 9:20-22, accounting for more than half the OT occurrences. The masc. noun תֹּם, "completeness/blamelessness," is in 4:6; 21:23.

[18] The two verbs "not let go" and "not reproach" are placed next to each other in the middle of the verse because they have similar sounds—לֹא אַרְפֶּהָ לֹא יֶחֱרַף.

[19] See 11:14,20; 15:16,20; 20:5,29; 22:18,23.

suffered at the hands of the ones he cursed. While not recommended procedure for Christians (Rom 12:14; 1 Cor 4:12), imprecation did serve a legal purpose and constituted a nonviolent form of retaliation.[20]

27:8 The verbs "cut off" and "take away"[21] describe the death of the "godless." That seems out of chronological order in view of unheard and unanswered prayer in the next verse, but logical or chronological considerations in composition were not necessary in making his point.

27:9 Actually, God would not "listen to his cry" if the godless were alive, much less "cut off" as v. 8 indicated. All these rhetorical questions in vv. 8-10 expect a negative answer. On the other hand, Job earlier said that wicked people had neither room nor time for God (21:14-15); so it is unlikely they would call to him unless, as is often the case, "distress comes upon him" (cf. 35:12; Isa 1:15; Mic 3:4). Trouble turns all sorts of godless people to God.

27:10 No, the ungodly find no "delight in the Almighty" (see comment at 22:26). No, they rarely call upon God, so he does not respond on those occasions of extreme distress when they do cry out.

(3) Fate of the Wicked (27:11-23)

¹¹"I will teach you about the power of God;
    the ways of the Almighty I will not conceal.
¹²You have all seen this yourselves.
    Why then this meaningless talk?

¹³"Here is the fate God allots to the wicked,
    the heritage a ruthless man receives from the Almighty:
¹⁴However many his children, their fate is the sword;
    his offspring will never have enough to eat.
¹⁵The plague will bury those who survive him
    and their widows will not weep for them.
¹⁶Though he heaps up silver like dust
    and clothes like piles of clay,
¹⁷what he lays up the righteous will wear,
    and the innocent will divide his silver.
¹⁸The house he builds is like a moth's cocoon,
    like a hut made by a watchman.

---

[20] See also M. Breneman, *Ezra, Nehemiah, Esther*, NAC (Nashville: Broadman & Holman, 1993), 194-95.

[21] There is some question about this unusual form, יֶשֶׁל, but understanding it to be from שׁלל, "take as prey," is better than שׁלה, "be quiet," as BDB, 1017. The JB follows Dhorme in reading "pray" as the verb in line *a* and "lifts up his soul to God" in line *b,* thus emending the verb in question to יִשָּׂא אֶל־אֱלוֹהַ.

¹⁹He lies down wealthy, but will do so no more;
   when he opens his eyes, all is gone.
²⁰Terrors overtake him like a flood;
   a tempest snatches him away in the night.
²¹The east wind carries him off, and he is gone;
   it sweeps him out of his place.
²²It hurls itself against him without mercy
   as he flees headlong from its power.
²³It claps its hands in derision
   and hisses him out of his place.

Since the "you" is plural, Job clearly addressed all three friends in these two verses. The problem turns on whether vv. 13-23 are Job's teaching "about the power of God" or (more likely) the "meaningless talk" he quoted from them. Because the canonical shape of the book must have made sense to its first readers and there is no compelling reason to emend the text, it is best to understand these verses as Job's.

INTRODUCTION (27:11-12). These two verses serve as an introduction to what follows in this chapter and perhaps even to chap. 28, for which there is no introduction.

27:11 Job spoke of God's "power" in his first response to Zophar (12:13) and most recently in response to Bildad (26:12,14).²² That he intended to "teach" more than simply God's power is evident by the broader parallel phrase in line b, literally, "whatever is with the Almighty."

27:12 The first line is reminiscent of 12:3c; 13:1-2a; 16:2a. Job maintained that his side of the argument was also patently obvious, that is, that the righteous sometimes suffer and the wicked often prosper. The long quotation of the friends' position is introduced and caricatured as jabbering gibberish.²³

TERRORS THE WICKED CAN EXPECT (27:13-23). As noted above, many commentators posit that this is the lost third speech of Zophar. Since it lacks the introductory formula common to all the other speeches, we are understanding it as Job's quotation of their position, which he has just labeled "meaningless talk." Several subjects in these verses reflect things the friends said to Job through the course of the dialogue.

27:13 Within this section v. 13 is another introduction. After it follows the assorted tragedies that are here called the "fate" and the "heri-

---

²² "Power" in 27:11 translates יָד, "hand." See also 10:7; 12:9-10; 27:22; 30:21.
²³ The verb is denominative from הֶבֶל ("vanity"), which is also the cognate accusative, hence literally something like "you vanity a vanity."

tage" of the "wicked" and "ruthless."

27:14 Eliphaz in 5:4, Bildad in 8:4 and 18:19, and Zophar in 20:10 all indirectly connected Job's alleged sin to the fate of his children. It was the old popular theology that children suffered for their parents' misdeeds (see comment on 21:19).

27:15 The usual word for "death" (*māwet*)[24] is read as "plague."[25] The NIV has followed the LXX and Syriac in reading the singular pronoun as a collective, translating "their widows," to avoid an allusion to polygamy; but why should wicked men not have multiple wives?[26]

27:16 Verses 16 and 17 form one sentence structured chiastically with several lexical parallels.[27] The wicked may accumulate money and clothes (v. 16), but they will eventually forfeit to the righteous/innocent both clothes and money (v. 17). The accumulation of material goods is not limited to a modern Western phenomenon.

27:17 According to Job, he who dies with the most clothes and silver does not win anything but loses all. The happy prospect for the "righteous" and "innocent" is that they will enjoy these goods left behind by those whose behavior is exactly the opposite. Proverbs 28:8 and Eccl 2:26 both address this anomaly with the same results (cf. Jas 5:1-5).

27:18 The moth's house is a cocoon, a frail and temporary shelter, and the shack a watchman sets up only for the duration of the harvest is similarly flimsy and impermanent. Both are gone with the turn of the seasons, and, by analogy, so will the elaborate dwellings of the wicked disintegrate. Bildad's illustration in 8:14-15 was "a spider's web" (cf. Luke 12:16-34).

27:19 The overall message of the verse is clear—wealth can disappear overnight. The verb translated "will do so no more" has been emended from *'sp*, "gather," to *ysp*, "add/repeat," on the basis of the LXX and because it makes better sense.[28]

27:20 Some advocate emending *kammayim*, "like a flood" (lit. "the

---

[24] Cf. the KJV, which follows the Hebrew in translating the verb as passive.

[25] So most translations. See Gordis, Hartley, and others for convincing support from extrabiblical languages.

[26] Few translations follow the Masoretic text: KJV, RV, ASV, AT, AB. The only plural in the Hebrew of this section is v. 13b, where the NIV has turned "oppressors" into "a ruthless man."

[27] "Piles" in v. 16 translates the verb יָכִין, which begins v. 17 where it is translated "lays up." The noun "clothes" in v. 16 (מַלְבּוּשׁ) is from the same root as the verb "wear" (יִלְבָּשׁ) in v. 17.

[28] The KJV and RV have "he shall not be gathered." The ASV added "to the fathers." Moffatt has, "It is the end!" The NAB has "one last time," and the NJPS has "with [his wealth] intact." Otherwise all concur with the emendation.

waters"), to a form of *yāmîm*, "days," so that line *a* has a parallel to "night" in line *b*.[29] Water and floods, however, are found elsewhere in Job as illustrations of disasters or punishment (14:19; 20:28; 22:11,16; 24:18).

27:21 As in v. 20, where the agent of destruction was "a tempest," here "the east wind" is the vehicle God uses to eliminate the wicked.[30]

27:22 The metaphor of the punishing storm that began in v. 20 continues through v. 23. The wind blows against the wicked man and his house. But the man finds there is no way to "flee" its punishing blasts.[31] Job spoke in this vein when he described the plight of the victims of oppressors in chap. 24. Now those wretched conditions will be the lot of the oppressors themselves. For those who have not made a friend of God, there is no shelter in the time of storm.

27:23 The two verbs that describe the sound of the storm were chosen for onomatopoetic and alliterative reasons. "It claps" is *yiśpōq*[32] and "hisses" is *yišrōq*.[33] Thus the wicked comes to his end, blown away by the shrieking wind, erased from the face of the earth. To these sentiments the three friends would assent, but for Job, God's moral administration of the world was not that simple.

This is the end of the debate cycle. The four contenders have not come to any resolution. Fortunately truth is not determined by popular vote. We will hear no more from the three friends, but Job has much yet to discuss, including the source of real wisdom.

---

[29] Jastrow, Dhorme, Pope, JB, NAB, and others make such a change. Dhorme (*Job*, 396-97) favors יוֹמָם (along with Pope, *Job*, 173) and translates "in broad daylight," citing the parallel in 5:14. The Qumran Targum fragment supports the Masoretic Text.

[30] The verb שָׂעַר translated "sweep" is related to the noun שְׂעָרָה translated "storm" in 9:17.

[31] "Flees headlong" translates a verb plus inf. abs. construction that uses the common verb בָּרַח, "flee." Gordis (*Job*, 296) suggests the construction depicts the wicked's "unremitting attempts to escape."

[32] This spelling occurs only here and Isa 2:6, but סָפַק is used seven times including Job 34:26,37. In Lam 2:15 סָפַק appears with שָׁרַק as here. There it has nothing to do with the wind but derisive responses to the recently vanquished city of Jerusalem.

[33] For parallels to such clapping and hissing in anger and derision, see Num 24:10; Ezek 27:36. שָׁרַק is translated "scoff" in Jer 49:17; Lam 2:15; Zeph 2:15;

IV. THE WISDOM CHAPTER (28:1-28)
1. Wisdom Cannot Be Mined (28:1-11)
2. Wisdom Cannot Be Bought (28:12-19)
3. Wisdom Cannot Be Found (28:20-22)
4. Wisdom Is with God (28:23-28)

IV. THE WISDOM CHAPTER (28:1-28)

The wisdom chapter is distinct from anything in the Book of Job. Commentators discuss whether these are Job's words or those of the author/ editor(s) of the book or some combination of those.[1] As with the rest of the book, it seems best to credit the substance of the speeches to the speakers named but believe that the Holy Spirit worked through an inspired author to turn the whole into the magnificent literary masterpiece that has come down to us.

As chap. 3 served as an interlude between the prose introduction and the debate cycle, so chap. 28 serves as an interlude between the debate cycle and the four major sections that follow. Efforts to explain why it should be elsewhere in the book and theories about its origin are speculative and diverse.

Chapter 28 is a little beyond the halfway point in the book as a whole. Job and his three friends have been unable to resolve the tension that Job's experience presents, that is, the suffering of a good man. The readers, of course, know from the first two chapters that Job is a test case that God chose to prove the Satan wrong about why people worship God. This chapter provides the readers a chance to reflect on the dilemma from the point of view of those who do not know the whole story. With its conclusion that God is the repository of all wisdom, it looks forward to the concluding chapters of the book where God makes that point repeatedly

---

[1] Note that the NIV does not have closing quotation marks at the end of chap 27. There is no introduction to chap. 28, so its translators tacitly acknowledged Job as the speaker. So too the RSV, MLB, NASB, NKJV, NRSV, ICB, NCV. See R. B. Zuck, *Job*, EvBC (Chicago: Moody, 1978), 122-23. Along with the Elihu speeches (chaps. 32–37) S. Mitchell omits this chapter from his *Into the Whirlwind: A Translation of the Book of Job* (Garden City: Doubleday, 1979).

with his many questions about the operation of the universe.

The chapter is about wisdom, a topic touched on only randomly so far. As is characteristic of the wisdom literature of the Bible and other ancient Near Eastern writings, wisdom is described as elusive and precious, something that can only be had through "the fear of the Lord" (v. 28). Job would have been a wisdom book without this chapter, but its inclusion raises the value of Job to even loftier heights.

1. Wisdom Cannot Be Mined (28:1-11)

> [1]"There is a mine for silver
>   and a place where gold is refined.
> [2]Iron is taken from the earth,
>   and copper is smelted from ore.
> [3]Man puts an end to the darkness;
>   he searches the farthest recesses
>   for ore in the blackest darkness.
> [4]Far from where people dwell he cuts a shaft,
>   in places forgotten by the foot of man;
>   far from men he dangles and sways.
> [5]The earth, from which food comes,
>   is transformed below as by fire;
> [6]sapphires come from its rocks,
>   and its dust contains nuggets of gold.
> [7]No bird of prey knows that hidden path,
>   no falcon's eye has seen it.
> [8]Proud beasts do not set foot on it,
>   and no lion prowls there.
> [9]Man's hand assaults the flinty rock
>   and lays bare the roots of the mountains.
> [10]He tunnels through the rock;
>   his eyes see all its treasures.
> [11]He searches the sources of the rivers
>   and brings hidden things to light.

The author evidenced considerable familiarity with mining methods. Poetically and graphically he portrayed the inaccessibility of precious ores and the extreme measures human beings have taken to extract them. Not much changed in the thousands of years between Job and the California gold rush of 1849 and the Colorado rush a decade later.[2] This pas-

---

[2] The definitive word on these matters is in R. J. Forbes, *Studies in Ancient Technology, VII*, (Leiden: Brill, 1966), 104-245; for Bronze Age Palestine in particular, see pp. 128-33.

sage could be a description of the challenge and the meeting of that challenge from the second millennium B.C. or the nineteenth century of our era.

28:1   The chapter opens with the simple chiastically[3] arranged statement of the two basic steps in the production of precious metals. First is the mine;[4] then there is the smelter or the refining process because only rarely are these metals found unmixed with worthless gravel or rock. "Wisdom" is not mentioned until v. 12, but at many points there is an analogy between it and mining.[5] Wisdom is precious like silver and needs refining like gold.

28:2   From the nobler elements, gold and silver, the poet moved to the more common but functional ones, iron and copper. Deuteronomy 8:9 spoke of "a land where the rocks are iron and you can dig copper out of the hills."[6] The verb is "pour/smelt" and is found only here and in 29:6.[7]

28:3   "Man" was supplied by the translators[8] for the subject of the verb here and in the following verses. Verse 3 has three words for "darkness," words that are scattered through this book but in altogether different contexts. Such repetition may have prompted the Greek translators to abridge this chapter to half the length of the Hebrew.[9] This verse begins

---

[3] Diagrammed according to the order in Hebrew, v. 1 is:

A   there is
  B   for silver
    C   a mine
    C'   a place
  B'   for gold
A'   they refine

[4] The root behind "mine" is the common verb יָצָא, "come/go out" (used in v. 11b), so מוֹצָא is the place where something "comes out," a "source" or "spring" as in 2 Kgs 2:21; Ps 107:33,35; Isa 41:18.

[5] Two of the six major words in vv. 2 and 12 are the same because "found" is from the same root, יָצָא, as "mine," and "dwell[ing]" is the same as "place," מָקוֹם.

[6] "Copper mines dating as early as the end of the fourth millennium B.C. have been found on both sides of the Arabah between the Dead Sea and the Gulf of Aqabah (Elath), notably at Timna' in Israel and at Punon (Feihán) in Jordan. The largest iron mine in Palestine is found at Mugháret el-Wardeh in the 'Ajlún Mountains of Gilead" (R. A. Coughenour, "Mine," ISBE 3:364). "The oldest silver prob. came from northern Syria (the Aramean state of Zobah in 1 Sam 14:47) and from parts of Asia Minor. Silver was known ca. 4000 B.C. in Egypt" (D. R. Bowes, "Silver," ZPEB 5:438). Gold is not found in Palestine and Syria but early on was widely known and used.

[7] KB[3] lists it as *qal* from a possible rare root צוק II, "pour/flow" but prefers to revocalize it as *hophal* יוּצָק from the more common צוק, "pour."

[8] So too the RSV and others, but the ICV, NCV, NRSV, sensitive to gender matters, supplied "miners."

[9] Missing from the LXX are vv. 3b,c,4a,5-9a,14-19,21b,22a,26b,27a.

the section on hard rock mining versus placer or surface mining. The result of digging into the ground is that light is brought into the darkness.[10]

28:4   Mines were and are often located in the most inaccessible and inhospitable places, not the places "where people dwell." Unknown, unexplored, and unmapped, they could be described as "forgotten." The most vivid scene of all is the miners swinging on ropes as they lowered themselves down vertical shafts in order to access the drifts or horizontal passageways where the exposed veins were being worked. It was a scary and dangerous business, but the rewards could be great if they struck it rich.[11]

28:5   While vegetation grows on the surface, below ground miners turned the earth upside down, meaning that they exposed the insides of mountains. Lacking explosives and pneumatic hammers, ancient miners would crack the rock by heating it with "fire." Two other explanations are that this line refers to a volcanic eruption or to the miners' torches.[12]

28:6   "Sapphires," *sappîr,* appear also in v. 16 among other jewels. Here sapphires rather than silver are coupled with "gold." The Hebrew syntax is almost nonexistent, just a list of words that translators must put together into sentences. Neither of these treasures had utilitarian value, but both had great commercial value.[13]

28:7   With v. 8 there are four varieties of wild animals who have never explored (underground) for these jewels and metals. Verse 7 lists two kinds of birds, the first an unspecified raptor[14] and the second a peregrine "falcon." These are the fowl with especially good eyesight, but even they do not discover what the ambitious miner finds.

28:8   "Lion" in the second line helps define the creatures in the first line who are called in Hebrew "sons of pride," from a word that occurs only here and 41:34[26].[15] As the falcon rules the skies, the lion rules the

---

[10] N. Habel (*The Book of Job,* OTL [Philadelphia: Westminster, 1985], 396) believes that "the terminology used to describe the darkness of the deep where miners penetrate has overtones of the underworld "(cf. 10:21-22).

[11] A quite different translation of the entire verse is offered by M. B. Dick, "Job xxviii 4: A New Translation," *VT* 29 (1979): 216-21.

[12] For more details on location, antiquity, procedures at mines, and bibliography, see E. Smick, *Job*, EBC (Grand Rapids: Zondervan, 1988), 4:976.

[13] BDB, 705 and KB³, 722 both suggest that סַפִּיר was really lapis lazuli (so the NEB text and the RSV, NIV margin), a precious stone found in ancient Afghanistan. Sapphires came from far away Ceylon (R. Bullard, "Stones, Precious," *ISBE* 4:628-29).

[14] The verb עִיט, "fly/dart," is from the same root but does not help in the identification. See G. Stratton-Porter, "Birds of Prey," *ISBE* 1:513-14.

[15] There is a curious similarity between שַׁחַץ, "pride," and שַׁחַל, "lion." This is not the English collective "pride of lions."

land. Yet no lion has ever been down a mine shaft or found wisdom.

28:9 In his effort to locate the gold vein and silver-bearing ore, the miner "assaults"[16] the "flint"[17] and "lays bare" or brings to the surface the lowest parts of the mountains. The latter verb is the same as "transformed" in v. 5b.[18]

28:10 The verb "tunnels" translates both the verb "cleave/split/ chop" and its object "rivers/channels" or "galleries" (NEB). It is a moment of special triumph for a miner to break away rock and realize he has hit pay dirt. With special joy "his eyes see all its treasures." Would that people ferreted out wisdom with equal effort and viewed its discovery as a treasure.

28:11 Two adjustments of the Hebrew text were necessary to arrive at the reading of the first line, a reading that most commentators and modern versions adopt.[19] Tailing piles spilling down from mountainside mines are the innards of the earth that miners have "brought to light." With luck they have not discarded the treasures with the trash. R. Gordis conveys the point thus: "All hidden material things man can bring to light, but not Wisdom, the light of the world."[20]

2. Wisdom Cannot Be Bought (28:12-19)

12"But where can wisdom be found?

---

[16] The verb is שׁלח "stretch out/send," and "his hand" is its object.

[17] In three of the other four places where חַלָּמִישׁ appears (Deut 8:15; 32:13; Ps 114:8), it is either in construct with or parallel to צוּר, "rock," which is understood here. צוּר is in v. 10. E. Dhorme translated "silex" (*A Commentary on the Book of Job*, trans. H. Knight [Nelson: London, 1967], 404). The NEB has "granite rock." As R. K. Harrison points out, "This substance, which is an imperfect type of quartz, is found in abundance in the limestone rocks of Syria, Palestine, and Egypt" ("Flint," ISBE 2:315).

[18] The verb is הפך, "invert/turn." The rest of the line is literally "from the root of the mountains." N. Habel (*Job*, 388) translates the line, "And overturn mountains by the roots," citing a parallel in 9:5 where God is said to overturn mountains.

[19] The verb חבשׁ, "bind," is understood as an alternate form of חפשׂ, "search" (cf. M. Pope, *Job*, AB [Garden City: Doubleday, 1965], 181; A. C. M. Blommerde, *Northwest Semitic Grammar and Job* (Rome: Pontifical Biblical Institute, 1969), 106-7). "Bind" is read by R. Gordis, *The Book of Job* (New York: Jewish Theological Seminary, 1978), 300, and Habel (*Job*, 388), who translates "dam up." And מִבְּכִי "from weeping of," is emended to מַבְּכֵי, "from sources of," which has an analogy in Ugaritic (see Pope, *Job*, 181). The latter is the preposition plus the noun נֵבֶךְ, which is only in Job 38:16. The NIV reading of this line is supported by the LXX (βάθη δὲ ποταμῶν ἀνεκάλυψεν, "the depths of the rivers he laid bare").

[20] Gordis, *Job*, 308.

> Where does understanding dwell?
> [13]Man does not comprehend its worth;
>   it cannot be found in the land of the living.
> [14]The deep says, 'It is not in me';
>   the sea says, 'It is not with me.'
> [15]It cannot be bought with the finest gold,
>   nor can its price be weighed in silver.
> [16]It cannot be bought with the gold of Ophir,
>   with precious onyx or sapphires.
> [17]Neither gold nor crystal can compare with it,
>   nor can it be had for jewels of gold.
> [18]Coral and jasper are not worthy of mention;
>   the price of wisdom is beyond rubies.
> [19]The topaz of Cush cannot compare with it;
>   it cannot be bought with pure gold.

Verse 12 serves as a hinge to connect the lengthy discourse on mining with this comparison of wisdom to wealth. It is a question, comparable to v. 20, that serves the same purpose of concluding what precedes and introducing what follows. Only the list of jewels in the high priest's breastplate compares with this passage's catalog of precious stones and metals (Exod 28:17-20; 39:10-13).

28:12   For the first time "wisdom" appears in this chapter (cf. vv. 18,20,28). The rhetorical questions imply that it cannot "be found" (cf. v. 13), and no one knows where "understanding" dwells. Verses 13-19 are all negative responses. The positive answer is in v. 23.

28:13   Neither "man" (*'ĕnôš*) nor any living creature on the earth can comprehend or find it (cf. v. 21). Some read "way" instead of "worth" on the basis of the LXX and because the surrounding verses deal with *where* rather than *why* or *how much* (but cf. vv. 15-19).[21]

28:14   As v. 13 reported that the wisdom is not found above ground, "the land of the living," so v. 14 declares that neither is it under water.[22]

28:15   Having discussed *where* wisdom is and how inaccessible it is, the poet now began to list *what* might compare to it. "Gold" and "silver" (cf. v. 1) are the first in a catalog of precious stones and metals that are unacceptable as tender for wisdom (cf. Prov 8:10; 16:16). The term *sĕgôr* is the first of four different words translated "gold" in this section

---

[21] So Dhorme, *Job,* 406; Gordis, *Job,* 308; Moffatt, AT, RSV, AB, JB, NEB, AAT.

[22] These two lines, almost identical in English, differ more in Hebrew (using different negative constructions) but serve as a good example of regular synonymous parallelism.

and probably means "solid [gold]."[23]

28:16 "Gold of Ophir" is the next element that cannot buy wisdom (see comments at 22:24 for the location of Ophir).[24] "Onyx"[25] and "sapphires"[26] are similarly worthless to barter for wisdom.

28:17 The term for "gold" in the first line is the most common one for this mineral. A different word (*pāz*) is used in line *b*. "Crystal" is "glass" in other versions, which then use "crystal" instead of "jasper" in v. 18. The word is unique to this Job passage.[27]

28:18 "Coral,"[28] "jasper,"[29] and "rubies"[30] are the jewels of v. 18, although "coral" is not a gem stone. The noun "price," *mešek,* a hapax, may be related to the verb "drag along," a system of fishing for coral.[31]

28:19 "The topaz of Cush" is the last stone, coupled with "pure gold," the same "gold" as in v. 16.[32] The phrase "it cannot be bought" is identical to v. 16. The poet has made his point: wisdom is not a commodity for sale in the gem market. Its price is not in gold or jewels but an attitude of reverence and submission, as v. 28 declares.

3. Wisdom Cannot Be Found (28:20-22)

[20]"Where then does wisdom come from?
   Where does understanding dwell?
[21]It is hidden from the eyes of every living thing,
   concealed even from the birds of the air.

---

[23] See Dhorme (*Job,* 408), who says it is from the well-known root סגר, "shut/close." The KJV has "shut up" in the margin of 1 Kgs 6:20. M. Görg argues that it means "hammered gold" based on an Egyptian cognate ("Ein Ausdruck der Goldschmiedekunst im Alten Testament," *BZ* 28 [1984]: 250-55). KB explains it as "pure gold hammered to thin foils, used for gilding." But the NIV has "pure gold" for זָהָב סָגוּר in 1 Kgs 6:20 and seven other places. "Pure gold" in v. 19 is כֶּתֶם טָהוֹר. Verse 16 has כֶּתֶם אוֹפִיר, "the gold of Ophir."

[24] "Be bought" in v. 15 was a *pual* of נתן and in vv. 16,19 a *pual* of סלה.

[25] For "onyx," "sapphire," "jasper" (which R. Bullard translates "crystal"), "rubies," and "topaz," see Bullard, *ISBE* 4:626-29. Cf. also the technical comments for all these in F. Delitzsch, *Job* (Grand Rapids: Eerdmans, 1949), II:108-10.

[26] See note at v. 16.

[27] It is זְכוֹכִית, defined in KB[3] as "ornamental glass."

[28] See A. E. Day, "Coral," *ISBE* 1:771-72. N. Tur-Sinai prefers "mother-of-pearl" or "crystal" (*The Book of Job* [Jerusalem: Kiryat-Sefer, 1967], 405-6).

[29] See S. M. Goldstein under "Glass," *ISBE* 2:475-77.

[30] Delitzsch strongly prefers "pearls" here (*Job,* II:109, n. 2). Cf. Prov 3:15; 8:11.

[31] So BDB, 604. See also Gordis, *Job,* 309.

[32] "The OT term probably designates yellow chrysolite. Chrysolite was obtained mainly from the island of Zabarqad off the Egyptian coast, called by Pliny (Nat. hist. xxxvii.9) "Topaz Island" (Pope, *Job,* 204).

²²**Destruction and Death say,**
    'Only a rumor of it has reached our ears.'

The third and shortest section in this chapter listing unprofitable routes to wisdom consists of two questions at the beginning (as in v. 12). Then there are two generalized and comprehensive categories, life and death, that have no sure knowledge of wisdom's whereabouts.

28:20 Except for a different verb in the first line, v. 21 is identical to v. 22. Like v. 12 it serves as a bridge between segments of the chapter.

28:21 Somewhat parallel to v. 13b and reminiscent of the birds of v. 8, the verse states that neither the "animals" on land nor the "birds in the sky" have access to wisdom.

28:22 In 26:6 *'ăbaddōn,* "Destruction," and *šĕ'ôl,* "grave/Death," appeared; here we have *ăbaddōn* and *māwet,* "Death." Both are personified because they "say" something. Death completes the merismus (see comment at 1:20), which "living thing" began in v. 21a. Wisdom is not with the living or the dead.

4. Wisdom Is with God (28:23-28)

²³**God understands the way to it**
    and he alone knows where it dwells,
²⁴**for he views the ends of the earth**
    and sees everything under the heavens.
²⁵**When he established the force of the wind**
    and measured out the waters,
²⁶**when he made a decree for the rain**
    and a path for the thunderstorm,
²⁷**then he looked at wisdom and appraised it;**
    he confirmed it and tested it.
²⁸**And he said to man,**
    'The fear of the Lord—that is wisdom,
    and to shun evil is understanding.'"

At last the poet provided the answer to the questions of vv. 12 and 20 and found a way when no one or nothing else could. The solution to the search for wisdom is God (v. 23) and the fear of the Lord (v. 28). Here is the treasure worth seeking with more energy and creativity than the elaborate mining procedures of vv. 3-11, the treasure whose value surpasses all the gold and gems of vv. 14-19.

28:23 The verb "understands" reflects the noun "understanding" in

vv. 12 and 20. "Know" and its noun form "knowledge" are also synonyms for wisdom.

28:24 The preceding verses have been speaking of the hiddenness and inaccessibility of wisdom by those above, on, and under the ground. So God, because he "views the ends of the earth" and "sees everything under the heavens," knows where it is (cf. Ps 33:13-14).

28:25 This verse reflects in a vague way on the creation of the world, when both wind and water were present (Gen 1:2). This and the following two verses resemble the wisdom hymn in Prov 8:22-31.

28:26 These verses also give a foretaste of the theophany that begins in chap. 38. In fact, v. 26b is the same as 38:25b (cf. Sir 40:13).[33] Rainstorms were the work of God's wisdom and power, either in blessing or in judgment (cf. 5:10; 36:27–37:18; 38:24-38; Deut 11:11-17; 28:12; 1 Sam 12:17; 1 Kgs 17:14; Ps 135:6-7; Jer 10:12-16).

28:27 Four verbs describe what God did with "wisdom," although that word is not in the Hebrew.[34] All four are well known, but the translations are highly contextual. Their usual meanings are "saw," "counted," "established," and "searched." The overall teaching of this verse and the ones immediately preceding is that the sovereign God utilized wisdom from the very beginning, the same point in Prov 8:22-29.

28:28 The "man" who had been looking for wisdom inside mountains and who would, if he could, buy it with this world's wealth[35] now hears the simple but profound truth—wisdom consists in fearing the Lord on the one hand and shunning evil on the other. "The fear of the LORD" appears at the beginning of Proverbs (1:7), at the end of Ecclesiastes (12:13), and here in the middle of Job.

---

[33] חֲזִיז, "storm-cloud" (KB) or "strong wind" (KB[3]), occurs only in these two verses of Job and in Zech 10:1 (plural there, translated "storm clouds" by NIV). קֹלוֹת is literally "voices," used of thunder in 1 Sam 12:17 and Exod 9:33 (where it also occurs with מָטָר, "rain"); Exod 19:16; 20:18. Thunder is said to be the voice of God in 1 Sam 7:10; 2 Sam 22:14. There is some disagreement whether חֲזִיז קֹלוֹת refers to the lightning, the thunder, or both. Since they occur simultaneously, BDB translates "thunderbolts" (see also Gordis, *Job,* 302). Dhorme (*Job,* 412) has "the rumble of the thunder." The JB has "thunderclaps." Tur-Sinai (*Job,* 408) has "lightning of the thunder." The RSV, NAB, AB have "thundershower"; AAT has "thunderclouds."

[34] S. L. Harris considers the creation itself the object of these four verbs ("Wisdom or Creation? A New Interpretation of Job 28:27," *VT* 33 [1983]: 419-27).

[35] Cf. Gen 3:6 and the comments in J. G. Janzen, *Job,* INT (Atlanta: John Knox, 1985), 189-91.

V. JOB: HIS PAST, HIS PRESENT, AND HIS INNOCENCE (29:1–31:40)

1. Memories of When God Blessed Him (29:1-25)
   (1) God's Watchcare and Provision (29:1-6)
   (2) His Place of Honor in the Community (29:7-17)
   (3) Anticipation of a Peaceful Death (29:18-20)
   (4) His Well-Received Counsel (29:21-25)
2. The Present Abusive Situation (30:1-31)
   (1) Abuse from Men (30:1-15)
      His Worthless Mockers (30:1-8)
      Their Hostile Deeds (30:9-15)
   (2) Abuse from God (30:16-19)
   (3) Address to God (30:20-23)
   (4) Lamentation (30:24-31)
3. His Self-malediction (31:1-40)
   (1) Introduction (31:1-4)
   (2) Disavowal of Falsehood (31:5-8)
   (3) Disavowal of Adultery (31:9-12)
   (4) Disavowal of Injustice (31:13-15)
   (5) Disavowal of Uncharitableness (31:16-23)
   (6) Disavowal of Materialism and Paganism (31:24-28)
   (7) Disavowal of Meanness and Secret Sin (31:29-34)
   (8) Conclusion (31:35-37)
   (9) Disavowal of Tenant Farmer Abuse (31:38-40)

V. JOB: HIS PAST, HIS PRESENT, AND HIS INNOCENCE (29:1–31:40)

1. Memories of When God Blessed Him (29:1-25)

Chapters 29 and 30 form a pair. In the first Job recalled the good old days when "the LORD gave" (1:21). In the second he mourned his current wretchedness, after "the LORD has taken away" (1:21). In chap. 29 he reminisced about his former estate, the esteem he enjoyed in the community, and his ministries of charity among the needy.

(1) God's Watchcare and Provision (29:1-6)

¹Job continued his discourse:
²"How I long for the months gone by,
   for the days when God watched over me,
³when his lamp shone upon my head
   and by his light I walked through darkness!
⁴Oh, for the days when I was in my prime,
   when God's intimate friendship blessed my house,
⁵when the Almighty was still with me
   and my children were around me,
⁶when my path was drenched with cream
   and the rock poured out for me streams of olive oil.

Job could have quoted Ps 16:6: "The boundary lines have fallen for me in pleasant places; / surely I have a delightful inheritance." His lot in life had been a good one, and he acknowledged that it was a gift of God and not based on his merit. He had divine light, many children, and a comfortable and prosperous life.

29:1 As in 17:1, it may be that Job waited for any response from Eliphaz, Bildad, or Zophar. Or this may be the editor's way of isolating the wisdom chapter (28) from those speeches that certainly are Job's.

29:2 Using the wish formula that we have seen before (6:8; 11:5; 14:13; 19:23), Job yearned for the bliss of yesteryear.[1] His complaint was that God either paid him no attention or hounded him relentlessly as a form of torment (7:17-20; 13:24-25; 23:2-9). This watchcare is like that of Ps 121:3-8.[2]

29:3 "Light" and blessing go hand in hand in this book and many other places in the Old Testament (22:28; 33:28; Exod 10:23; Pss 43:3; 112:4; cf. also 1 John 2:8-10). "Lamp" and "light" refer figuratively to the Lord's gentle guidance and the resultant security of knowing where we are.

29:4 "Prime" translates a word that usually means "winter" (RSV, "autumn"), but most agree that in this context it refers to that time in life when one can relax and reflect.[3] "Intimate friendship," *bĕsôd* ("in secret,"

---

[1] See *GBH* §163d.

[2] "When God watched over me" is an example of a genitival clause in construct with כִּימֵי, "as days of." See *GBH* §129p. In כִּימֵי as in כְּיַרְחֵי, "as months of," the preposition בְּ is understood (*GBH* §133h).

[3] M. H. Pope (*Job*, AB [Garden City: Doubleday, 1965], 185) suggests that as the time of harvest in Palestine, winter would suggest a time of "maturity and prosperity" rather than the current connotation of one's declining years.

cf. KJV) is not accepted by all. The JB reads "hedged around"; the NAB, "sheltered"; the NEB and AAT, "protected."[4] It is a spiritually wholesome situation to invite God to know all our secrets. Then he might let us in on some of his.

29:5   Since he mistakenly felt that now God had forsaken him, he could say that back then "the Almighty was still with" him. Likewise there was a time when his "children were around" him.

29:6   "Oil" and "cream" were his in abundance, as it were, washing his path and pouring out of the rocks.[5] These tokens of wealth comport well with the description of Job's comfortable situation in the opening verses of chap. 1. But it was now only history.

(2) His Place of Honor in the Community (29:7-17)

[7]"When I went to the gate of the city
   and took my seat in the public square,
[8]the young men saw me and stepped aside
   and the old men rose to their feet;
[9]the chief men refrained from speaking
   and covered their mouths with their hands;
[10]the voices of the nobles were hushed,
   and their tongues stuck to the roof of their mouths.
[11]Whoever heard me spoke well of me,
   and those who saw me commended me,
[12]because I rescued the poor who cried for help,
   and the fatherless who had none to assist him.
[13]The man who was dying blessed me;
   I made the widow's heart sing.
[14]I put on righteousness as my clothing;
   justice was my robe and my turban.
[15]I was eyes to the blind
   and feet to the lame.
[16]I was a father to the needy;
   I took up the case of the stranger.
[17]I broke the fangs of the wicked
   and snatched the victims from their teeth.

---

[4] These follow B. Duhm (*Das Buch Hiob* [Tübingen: Mohr, 1897], 138) and others who read בְּסֻכֹּה, inf. of סָכַך (cf. 3:23). Pope (*Job*, 207) understands it from the verb יסד, deletes אֱלוֹהַּ, and translates the preposition as a divine name, "When 'Aliy founded my family."

[5] Rock-hewn olive presses from the eighth century B.C. were found in the Yarkon basin. D. Eitam, "And Oil from a Flinty Rock," *Qadmoniot* 16 (1983): 23-27 (Hebrew).

This section has two foci: the honor Job received as a community leader and the reason for that honor, that is, his many and various deeds of charity. The hinge between these two emphases is vv. 11-12, both of which begin in Hebrew with "because/when" (*kî*). Some commentators and translators, unable to live with material not arranged according to modern Western standards, move vv. 21-25 to follow v. 10.[6] Such an adjustment puts all the verses about honor together but makes the last verses before chap. 30 less appropriate. It is best to leave the verses in the order that has come down to us.

29:7 In the first chapter Job was described as a desert sheik with huge herds of cattle. "House" in 29:4 translated what is usually "tent." But here in v. 7 he seems to have been a town dweller, with sessions at the gate. Seats at the city gate, which served as a court, were places of honor and prestige, granted only to the noblest and worthiest of the senior citizens. Job was one of them.

29:8 The merismus (see comment at 1:20) formed by "young" and "old,"[7] and supported by the verbs "stepped aside" (usually "hide") and "rose," indicates that people of all ages acknowledged Job's stature in the community and acted appropriately. The first verb is translated "were hushed" in v. 10 where it applies to the "nobles." Regardless of the distance between us and ancient Edom, respect for people of worth is a virtuous trait.

29:9 The second of three synonyms for the leading men of the community is *śarîm*, often "princes." They were quiet like the "nobles" of v. 10.[8] An expression similar to "cover the mouth with the hand" is in 21:5, where it describes something Job asked his friends to do.

29:10 There is no reason to think that these three categories of com-

---

[6] So Moffatt, AB, NAB, NEB, REB. N. Habel (*The Book of Job*, OTL [Philadelphia: Westminster, 1985], 406-7) recognizes the broad chiastic outline of the chapter and leaves it in its canonical shape (see also Smick, EBC 4:980-81):

Introduction (v. 2)
A　Past blessings (vv. 3-6)
　B　Past honor (vv. 7-10)
　　C　Past administration of justice (vv. 11-17)
A'　Expected blessing (vv. 18-20)
　B'　Past honor (vv. 21-24)
Summation (v. 25)

[7] The term for "old men," יְשִׁישִׁים, is unique to Job with all four of it occurrences in this book: 12:12; 15:10; 29:8; 32:6. See N. Tur-Sinai, *The Book of Job* (Jerusalem: Kiryat-Sefer, 1967), 211-12.

[8] "Speaking" or "words," מִלִּים is also typical in Job with thirty-four of its thirty-eight occurrences in the Hebrew OT. It is also Aramaic and occurs twenty-four times in Daniel.

munity leaders are different from each other. They are synonyms for the same group. No doubt Job was one of them; but because of his extraordinary holdings, wisdom, and piety, he was esteemed more than the rest. Sticking "tongues" was not some disease or even a literal phenomenon but yet another way of saying that their silence honored him.

29:11 With mixed metaphors the poet described what oral witnesses said and what visual witnesses spoke. Literally, "When an ear heard, it pronounced me happy, [and when] an eye saw, it commended me." "Pronounced happy/blessed" is from the same root as the first word in Psalms, and it probably was true that Job did "not walk in the counsel of the wicked or stand in the way of sinners or sit in the seat of mockers" (Ps 1:1).

29:12 The focus of the chapter now turns from *how* Job was honored to *why* he was honored. The first two categories of beneficiaries of Job's largess were the "poor" (*ʿānî*), a word Job used three times earlier as he described those violated by oppressors (24:4,9,12), and the "fatherless" (*yātôm*; cf. 24:3,9).[9] In a society with no government welfare system, it was easy for those with no families to become indigent. That is one reason the Bible so often enjoined the giving of alms.

29:13 It is not clear precisely what Job did for the "dying" and the "widow" to make them "bless" and "sing," but we can imagine it was a mixture of verbal sympathy and tangible assistance.

29:14 The last four verses of this section all have Job as the subject of the verbs. He has been the object of the verbs in vv. 11-13. The imagery of wearing attributes as one wears clothing or armor is employed elsewhere (Ps 132:9; Isa 52:1; 59:17; 61:10; Eph 6:13-17). In other texts (Judg 6:34; 1 Chr 12:18; 2 Chr 24:20) the Spirit "clothed" certain individuals.

29:15 In premodern times and even today in undeveloped areas of the world, blindness and lameness are more widespread, and opportunities to aid people so afflicted are plentiful. Though such a ministry is tedious and demanding, this noble man served as their guide and support.

29:16 In the same vein Job testified that he was "a father to the needy" and a legal "inspector/investigator"[10] for "the stranger," literally, "one I did not know."[11] "Needy" (*ʾebyôn*) is a category of those exploited

---

[9] *GBH* §160oa explains the use of לֹא here as signifying "categorical negation." Thus we might render "with absolutely no one to assist him." See also 18:17,19; 21:9; 33:9.

[10] The verb is חָקַר, "search," here in the sense of researching the particulars of a case with a view to helping the defendant who, because he has no local connections, was often disadvantaged in court. The AB, AAT, and NRSV have "championed," which is quite a bit stronger than NJPS' "looked into."

[11] This is an asyndetic relative clause. See *GBH* §129q.

by the powerful (cf. 24:4,14).

29:17 The background of this illustration is a wild animal tearing the flesh from its victim (cf. Prov 30:14; Ps 3:7[8]; 58:6[7]). The self-portrait Job painted is one of tenderness, generosity, service, justice, and bravery, an admirable assortment of attributes that all God's people would do well to own.

(3) Anticipation of a Peaceful Death (29:18-20)

[18]"I thought, 'I will die in my own house,
   my days as numerous as the grains of sand.
[19]My roots will reach to the water,
   and the dew will lie all night on my branches.
[20]My glory will remain fresh in me
   the bow ever new in my hand.'

Verse 18 is clear that Job expected to live a long life and enjoy a peaceful death. The figures of vv. 19-20 are quite foreign to modern Western ways of describing those desirable dreams.

29:18 The picture of a peaceful death is even more tender if *qēn* is translated in its usual sense of "nest" rather than "house" (cf. the standard versions). Some add one consonant, reading *ziqnî*, "my old age" (apparently the LXX and so Moffatt, AB.)[12] Elsewhere "sand" illustrates things beyond number (Gen 22:17; Josh 11:4; Judg 7:12; 1 Sam 13:5; Ps 139:18; Isa 48:19).[13]

29:19 "Roots" and "branches" form a merismus (see comment at 1:20). For a desert dweller water was all important. In the absence of rain, plants gained moisture through roots that tapped underground water and from nightly dew (Ps 1:3; Jer 17:8; Gen 27:28,39; 1 Kgs 17:1; Zech 8:12). Job had hoped to be similarly nourished and healthy.

29:20 In 19:9 Job complained that God had stripped him of his

---

[12] R. Gordis writes of this verse: "The Vss. offer a plethora of conflate double renderings, *ad hoc* translations, free paraphrases, and probably some variant readings. The LXX renders: 'My age shall grow old as the stem of a palm tree; I shall live a long time'" (*The Book of Job* [New York: Jewish Theological Seminary, 1978], 321). Gordis himself reads, instead of "like sand" for כְּחוֹל, "as the phoenix," based on the LXX's word for palm tree, φοίνικος. The MLB, NAB, AAT, NJPS, NRSV all translate, "phoenix." The JB has "palm tree." For further discussion see J. Hartley, *Job*, NICOT (Grand Rapids: Eerdmans, 1988), 392-93, n. 3; Pope, *Job*, 214-15; L. L. Grabbe, *Comparative Philology and the Text of Job*, SBLD 34 (Missoula, Mont.: Scholars Press, 1977), 98-101.

[13] Just because one's years are not elsewhere compared to "sand" is not reason enough to translate this verse otherwise, as illustrated in the previous note.

"honor/glory." Here he said how he had hoped it would be "ever fresh."[14] "The bow" represents strength and resilience and is parallel to "strong arms" in Gen 49:24 (cf. 1 Sam 2:4). Job expected to be energetic and youthful until the day of his death.

(4) His Well-Received Counsel (29:21-25)

> [21]"Men listened to me expectantly,
>   waiting in silence for my counsel.
> [22]After I had spoken, they spoke no more;
>   my words fell gently on their ears.
> [23]They waited for me as for showers
>   and drank in my words as the spring rain.
> [24]When I smiled at them, they scarcely believed it;
>   the light of my face was precious to them.
> [25]I chose the way for them and sat as their chief;
>   I dwelt as a king among his troops;
>   I was like one who comforts mourners.

As in vv. 7-10 (or v. 11) Job, in this concluding section, spoke of the honorable way people had treated him in the past.[15] His words were welcomed and heeded as he counseled with compassion and authority.

29:21 Job was so accustomed to people listening to, hoping, and waiting for his counsel that when his three friends charged him with sin, disagreed with his theology, and rebuked him for his arrogance, it was a jolt to his self-esteem as much as the tragedies of chaps. 1–2.

29:22 Like disciples at the feet of a guru or litigants waiting for the judge's verdict, people sat in silent respect for wisdom to fall from the lips of this revered sage from Uz. As the most honored elder at the city gate, which corresponds to a court of law, Job had the final word. "Fell gently" translates a word (*nāṭap*) that in other contexts speaks of dripping honey (Cant 4:11) or water (Judg 5:4), flowing wine (Joel 3:18[4:18]) or myrrh (Cant 5:13), and words of prophecy in Mic 2:6. "Ears" is not in the Hebrew.

29:23 Although the technical word for early rains is not in this verse, the first rains of autumn are undoubtedly what is referred to in line *a*. After four months of drought, such precipitation was greeted with great re-

---

[14] Hebrew כָּבוֹד also means "liver," the organ second only to the heart in importance for good health (cf. Ps 16:9). The NJPS translates "vigor." See Hartley, *Job,* 393.

[15] These are the verses that so many commentators and versions move forward to follow v. 10, but for reasons cited there in the commentary we leave the order as it is in the Masoretic Text.

joicing. The "spring rain" or the "latter rains" mark the end of the wet season and fall around Easter time. Since people knew how long it would be before they saw rain again, these last rains too were met with unusual appreciation. So were Job's words welcomed and appreciated by his hearers (cf. Deut 32:2).

29:24 Both lines could be read differently. Instead of "they scarcely believed it," one could translate "them who had no faith" (cf. ASV, RSV, NASB, NRSV). The second stich reads literally, "And the light of my face they did not make to fall." That could be paraphrased as "they encouraged me," or as Gordis has it, "They did nothing to cause me displeasure."[16] Since the context speaks of the benefit Job was to others, the NIV is preferable because it keeps the action moving outward from Job.

29:25 A tricolon concludes the chapter and this section in which Job described his former honored position in the community. In 1:3 we read that "he was the greatest man among all the people of the east," so terms like "chief/head" and "king" are not out of order. The third line does not fit well with the first two, so several have emended the Hebrew.[17] On the other hand, it certainly reflects the ministry Job had with the poor and oppressed as vv. 12-16 indicate. Thus ends Job's sketch of the days before he unwillingly and unwittingly became the subject of a test. They were grand days, but we who have read the last chapter know they will return.

2. The Present Abusive Situation (30:1-31)

"But now" at the beginning of this chapter is significant because here commences the dark side of the picture, the plight into which Job was plunged by the wager between Yahweh and the Satan in chaps. 1–2. In chap. 29 Job described how it used to be with him. In chap. 30 he described how it was now—an abrupt contrast, a total reversal of fortunes.

(1) Abuse from Men (30:1-15)

1"But now they mock me,
    men younger than I,
  whose fathers I would have disdained
    to put with my sheep dogs.

---

[16] Gordis, *Job,* 316.

[17] Pope (*Job*) has "Wherever I guided they were led." Dhorme (*Job*) is similar. Gordis (*Job,* 323-34) also reads the verb as נחה, "lead/guide," rather than נחם, "comfort," and offers "like the leader of a camel train." The LXX lacks vv. 19-20,24b-25, so M. Jastrow, Jr., and others, omit the third stich (*Job* [Philadelphia: Lippincott, 1920], 301-2).

²Of what use was the strength of their hands to me,
   since their vigor had gone from them?
³Haggard from want and hunger,
   they roamed the parched land
   in desolate wastelands at night.
⁴In the brush they gathered salt herbs,
   and their food was the root of the broom tree.
⁵They were banished from their fellow men,
   shouted at as if they were thieves.
⁶They were forced to live in the dry stream beds,
   among the rocks and in holes in the ground.
⁷They brayed among the bushes
   and huddled in the undergrowth.
⁸A base and nameless brood,
   they were driven out of the land.

⁹"And now their sons mock me in song;
   I have become a byword among them.
¹⁰They detest me and keep their distance;
   they do not hesitate to spit in my face.
¹¹Now that God has unstrung my bow and afflicted me,
   they throw off restraint in my presence.
¹²On my right the tribe attacks;
   they lay snares for my feet,
   they build their siege ramps against me.
¹³They break up my road;
   they succeed in destroying me—
   without anyone's helping them.
¹⁴They advance as through a gaping breach;
   amid the ruins they come rolling in.
¹⁵Terrors overwhelm me;
   my dignity is driven away as by the wind,
   my safety vanishes like a cloud.

The first and longest section of the chapter initially describes the "base and nameless brood" (v. 8) who were the scum of society, the outcasts of the community, and those never found in good company. Job depicted them as coarse, wild animals, motivated by instinct and totally bereft of decency. The second focus of this section is on their hostile actions toward Job. Taking advantage of his weakness, they militantly advanced and ruthlessly attacked him who had been "the greatest man among the people of the East."

HIS WORTHLESS MOCKERS (30:1-8). Job portrayed his adversaries as young, ill-bred undesirables. They were unworthy even of the basest jobs and rejected by all civilized folk.

30:1 The subjects of the sentences through v. 7 are identified here as youngsters/little ones and in v. 8 as "a base and nameless brood." It was this "brood" of "youths" that mocked Job and "whose fathers I would have disdained to put with sheep dogs." Usually "dogs" in Scripture are mentioned with great disrespect. This is one of the few places that indicates these generally unappreciated animals served any purpose at all.[18]

30:2 The hostile riffraff had no "vigor"[19] of their own, and even if they did, their "strength" would not have helped Job. It is not clear if Job was describing "dogs" or these malicious hoodlums when here and in the following verse he portrayed a sick and starving pack. Certainly by v. 5 Job was portraying men, not animals. In biblical times dogs were mostly scavengers, never pets.[20]

30:3 Scavengers are always hungry, so Job described his antagonists as haggard, wanting, and hungry.[21] Other rare words make the last line uncertain, but essentially Job depicted them there as denizens of the desert, living off the sparse growth of such "desolate wastelands."[22]

30:4 More rare words occur in this verse, but there is general agree-

---

[18] Some examples of despicable "dogs" are the dumb dogs and greedy dogs of Isa 56:10-11, the snarling dogs of Ps 59:6[7],14[15], the carrion eating dogs of 1 Kgs 14:11; 16:4; 21:19,23-24; 22:38, and the vomit-eating dog of Prov 26:11 (cf. 2 Pet 2:22). Gordis says, "There is probably nowhere in literature a more powerful expression of scorn than in this verse" (*Job,* 330).

[19] כֶּלַח occurs only here and in 5:26.

[20] Caleb, the only man other than Joshua to leave Egypt and enter Canaan, has a name that means "dog."

[21] All three of these words as well as the verb in the middle stich and the three words in the last stich are rare and therefore open to alternate translations. חֶסֶר, "want," is else-where only in Prov 28:22, "poverty," but well-represented cognate adjectives and verbs establish the meaning. כָּפָן, "hunger" is elsewhere only in 5:22, but its meaning is established as an Aramaic word that appears in the Targum of Ruth 1:1; Gen 12:10 (see M. Jastrow, *Dictionary of Talmud Babli, Yerushalmi, Midrashic Literature and Targumim* [New York: Pardes, 1950], 1:660). גַּלְמוּד, "haggard," was in 3:7; 15:34; and elsewhere only Isa 49:21. The verb in line *b*, עָרַק, "roamed/gnawed" (see NIV footnote) is elsewhere only in v. 17 (see Hartley, *Job,* 396 for a discussion of this root).

[22] אֶמֶשׁ, "at night," occurs in four other places with the meaning "yesterday/last night." Duhm (*Buch of Hiob,* 141) emended this to a form of the verb מוּשׁ, "depart/wander," which fits nicely with the verb in the second line (so too Gordis, *Job,* 330-31). E. Dhorme emended it to אִמָּם, "their mother" (*A Commentary on the Book of Job,* trans. H. Knight [London: Nelson, 1967], 431-32). שׁוֹאָה וּמְשֹׁאָה are from the same root and the alliteration (cf. the English words "flotsam and jetsam" or "riffraff"), especially with אֶמֶשׁ that precedes them, intensifies the meaning. The two words could be translated "desolate desolation." The combination, and the only occurrences of the latter form, are elsewhere only in 38:27 and in Zeph 1:15, where the NIV has "trouble and ruin."

ment on the meaning. These worthless gangsters were like animals foraging for food[23] among unappetizing desert plants—"salt herbs"[24] and "broom roots."[25]

30:5 The opposite of an esteemed elder sitting at the city gate would be a undesirable criminal banished from the community.[26] Job had been the honored patriarch, but now he was plagued by these "banished" outcasts.

30:6 "Beds" occurs only here, and "rocks" is rare, but most agree in general with the NIV.[27] It speaks of the destitution of those expelled from the community. They holed up in the limestone caves that line the sides of ravines in the desert country east and south of Palestine proper.

30:7 "The bushes" is the same word as "the brush" in v. 4. "Undergrowth" is a vague translation of a kind of scrub brush.[28] Even a bush can provide some shelter from the torrid sun or the blistering wind (cf. Jonah 4:6-8). The verb "bray," though it occurs only twice, is certain because of the other context (6:5).

30:8 The "base and nameless brood" are literally "sons of a fool and sons of a no name." The GNB makes the insult stronger, "A worthless bunch of nameless nobodies!"[29] These are the ones who took delight in

---

[23] Not all agree that לַחְמָם means "their food." The ASV margin, RSV, AB, AAT, REB, have "to warm them" or the like, reading an inf. of חמם (cf. 39:14). So also Hartley, Gordis, H. H. Rowley, *Job,* NCB (Grand Rapids: Eerdmans, 1978), and Tur-Sinai. The NIV has "fuel" in a footnote, but that is some distance semantically from "heat."

[24] The "*Atriplex halimus,* which grows abundantly around the shores of the Dead Sea and in the regions east of Sinai . . . is related to spinach, not to the common mallow. A bushy shrub with oval leaves, it grows up to 1 m tall" (*Fauna and Flora of the Bible* [London: UBS, 1972], 136).

[25] For identifications and a discussion of the problem with eating the poisonous roots of the broom tree, see *Fauna and Flora,* 100-101.

[26] "Fellow men" translates גֵו, usually "back/body" but here in its Aramaic sense of "midst/interior." See S. R. Driver and G. B. Gray, *Job,* ICC (New York: Scribners, 1921), II:209-10.

[27] עָרוּץ is not from the verb ערץ, "frightful" (ASV, NASB, BDB, 792), but is a noun of uncertain etymology related to Arabic ʿarḍ, ʿirḍ, ʿurḍ, "side of a mountain/cave." It is often translated "gully." See A. Guillaume, *Studies in the Book of Job* (Leiden: Brill, 1968), 113; Gordis, *Job,* 331. It is in construct with נְחָלִים, "wadi/torrent," so Dhorme (*Job,* 434) translates them "beside torrents." כֵּפִים, "rocks," is Aramaic and appears in Jer 4:29.

[28] BDB (355) suggest the "chick-pea." It is "nettles" according to Habel, Hartley, Gordis, Tur-Sinai, KJV, NASB, NRSV; but R. K. Harrison says that "would scarcely suit the conditions in the text. . . . The most probable is some species of *Acanthus*" ("Nettles," *ISBE* 3:526).

[29] The gentle British have "vile base-born wretches" in NEB. The expression "no name" means "without honor or station," though it might also mean "illegitimate."

dishonoring the afflicted Job, the most honorable man in their midst.

THEIR HOSTILE DEEDS (30:9-15).   Job actually spent more time describing the worthlessness of his assailants than he did in these verses spelling out their actions. Many graphic and violent verbs characterize them—"detest" and "spit" in v. 10, "attacks" and "lay snares" in v. 12, "break up" in v. 13, "advance" in v. 14, and "is driven away" in v. 15. Job was the innocent victim of the Satan and as a result became the victim of diabolical detractors.

30:9   The section opens with the same Hebrew word as in v. 1, where it is translated "but now." Job was picking up where he had started, returning from the sidetrack of venting his anger on their spiritual penury. The NIV added "their sons." Otherwise the verse simply reads, "I have become their song; I have become their byword."[30] Job was the object of their sarcastic, satirical ditties (cf. 17:6).

30:10   It may be that they kept their "distance" for fear of contracting Job's dreaded skin disease. Just as Job would have them expelled from the community (v. 8), so they shunned him as an outcast. Then, as now, to "spit" was a way of showing strong disapproval formally (Num 12:14; Deut 25:9) and informally (Job 17:6; Isa 50:6).[31] It was almost the ultimate insult (cf. Matt 26:67; 27:30 and parallels).

30:11   "God" has been added by the translators to provide a subject for the verbs.[32] The figure of "unstringing my bow" (lit. "loosed my string") is foreign to us (cf. 29:20).[33] The "restraint" they "throw off" is elsewhere "halter/bridle" (41:13[5]; Ps 32:9; Isa 30:28). Regardless of the details of these figures, the point is that the rabble relentlessly, ruthlessly, and unconscionably abused our hero.

30:12   The translation of v. 12 is uncertain because of one rare word, unequal lines, and the juxtaposition of words that can be fitted together only by adding to or deleting from the Hebrew text. The rare word is translated "tribe" and is from the root *prḥ*, "bud/blossom," hence "brood" or "tribe" in the sense of offspring.[34] The verb translated "attack" often

---

[30] The AB has a balanced and adequately caustic pair in "jest" and "gibe."

[31] This noun רֹק, "spit," occurs only here, 7:19, and Isa 50:6. The verb is only in Lev 15:8.

[32] Some make the verb plural with "they," i.e., Job's antagonists, as the subject. So Moffatt, AB, NAB, NEB, AAT.

[33] "String/cord" could be the bow string or the tent cord. There is also a textual problem. The Masoretic Text has יִתְרוֹ, indicating "his string" with the consonants (the *kethib*) and "my string" with the vowels (the *qere*). The Syriac and Targum have first person.

[34] See U. Adini, "A Biblical Hapax Legomenon in Modern Hebrew," *Hebrew Studies* 20/21 (1979-80): 12-17.

means "arise" (cf. KJV). The middle line says only, "they throw my feet," which the NIV alone has taken as "cast a net" or "lay snares" in order to trap something.[35] A literal translation of the third line is, "They build their paths of destruction against me." The same verb, *sll*, was in a similar context in 19:12.[36] Whatever the details, a mob of mockers set out to undo Job, using military means, although Job was speaking metaphorically.

30:13 The destruction of a road was a task for the army.[37] It helped render the enemy immobile. Job used the figure to describe how the thieving mob thwarted and even destroyed without outside help.[38] It is no great victory to destroy a man who is already crushed by grief, condemned by friends, and pining for death on an ash pile.

30:14 One major goal of an attacking army was to destroy part of the wall in order to gain access to the interior of the defending city. Job described his wall as vulnerable with "a gaping breach." One thinks of the walls of Jericho, with more holes than standing portions, so that their enemies likewise came rolling in (Josh 6:20; cf. Amos 4:3). The scene is not one of armored troop carriers or tanks assaulting the wall but of wave upon wave of enemy forces flooding through the now useless defenses.[39]

30:15 Verse 15 concludes the section recounting how the "base and nameless brood" mistreated Job, and it serves as a transition to the next section in which Job charged God with similar abuses.[40] This verse portrays a man with no "dignity,"[41] no hope of "safety," "prosperity" (RSV,

---

[35] The ways to render this are legion. The AB has "trip my feet." The KJV has "push away my feet." The JB has somehow come up with "stones are their weapons." AAT has "they set me free to run." The NJPS has "they put me to flight." The NRSV has "they send me sprawling." Others, e.g., NAB, NEB, simply omit the middle stich.

[36] For more discussion and more options see Dhorme, *Job*, 437-38.

[37] The verb נָתַס is a hapax, but most consider it an alternate spelling of the well-established נָתַץ, which appeared in 19:10, "tear down." Five manuscripts support this. Gordis (*Job,* 326, 333-34), however, connects it to an Arabic word meaning "thorns" to read, "They hedge my path with thorns."

[38] Note the alternate reading in the NIV footnote, "'No one can help him,' [they say]." This changes the sense only a little but requires an addition.

[39] The images of waves and floods may be behind the verb, וֹהִתְגַּלְגָּלוּ, a *hithpael* of גָּלַל, which as a noun can mean "wave." The NAB and REB have, "They come in waves." The NJPS has, "They roll in like raging billows."

[40] Note the change from third person plural subjects in the preceding verses to first singular here, then to third singular in v. 18.

[41] נָדִיב, an unusual derivative of נָדַב, occurs three more times, all in Isa 32:8 and translated "noble."

AB, GNB, NASB), "victory" (NEB), or "deliverance" (REB).[42] Job has not come very far since the end of chap. 3.

(2) Abuse from God (30:16-19)

> [16]"And now my life ebbs away;
>   days of suffering grip me.
> [17]Night pierces my bones;
>   my gnawing pains never rest.
> [18]In his great power [God] becomes like clothing to me;
>   he binds me like the neck of my garment.
> [19]He throws me into the mud,
>   and I am reduced to dust and ashes.

As the brackets indicate, the word "God" is not in the Hebrew text.[43] He must be the subject because of the context. So God, as well as Job's fellow citizens, turned on him and abused him in various ways.

30:16 From here to the end of the chapter appear several allusions to death. Job thought he was dying, that he would not live to see his vindication. "Life" (*nepeš*) is another word for "breath," that which makes a difference between the living and the dead (Gen 2:7; Matt 27:50).[44]

30:17 In poetry it would not be unusual for "night" to be the subject of a verb, but some read "by night he." In addition there is some question about "gnawing pains." The only other occurrence of the word is in v. 3 translated "roamed." The KJV has "sinews"; Gordis and Hartley both have "veins"; the AB has "torturers."

30:18 The translation of v. 18 is even less certain, as attested by the choices offered just in the English versions. To illustrate the variety, here are three renderings: "By the great force *of my disease* is my garment changed: it bindeth me about as the collar of my coat" (KJV); "My garments are all bespattered with my phlegm, which chokes me like the collar of a shirt" (NEB); "With great effort I change clothing; The neck of my tunic fits my waist" (NJPS).[45] Clearly the problems are with the meaning

---

[42] The NJPS and Habel (*Job,* 420) apparently follow Gordis (*Job,* 334) in reading יִשְׁעָתִי as from the same root as שׁוֹעַ, "noble" (elsewhere only in 34:19 and parallel to נָדִיב in Isa 32:5) rather than יֵשַׁע, thus making a better parallel to line *a*. Dhorme, however (*Job,* 440), notes the parallel in Ps 51:12[14] between יֵשַׁע, "salvation," and נְדִיבָה, "willingness/nobleness."

[43] It is not in vv. 11 or 20 either, but the NIV does not so indicate.

[44] The verb is a *hithpael* (with sibilant shift) of שָׁפַךְ, "pour out."

[45] The commentators are similarly divided. M. Jastrow (*Job,* 291) has, "With great force it clutches at my garment, / And grasps me at the hem of my undergarment." Tur-Sinai (*Job,* 428) has "In my cloth he disguiseth himself as an attorney; as 'my mouth' he clotheth himself in my coat."

of the verb in line *a* and whether the subject is "God" (NIV) or "I" (NJPS) or the clothing as in the other translations. In addition, the meaning of the verb in line *a,* usually "disguise," is uncertain in this context.

30:19 The straightforwardness of v. 19 is welcome after the irresolution of the preceding two verses. Both the verbs are known and not debated. Likewise the three elements, "mud," "dust," and "ashes." This last combination anticipates Job's repentance (42:6), where the combinations occurs again. In a figurative sense, all who come to God for pardon must grovel at his feet and submit to the humiliation that exposed sin and confession require.

(3) Address to God (30:20-23)

> ²⁰"I cry out to you, O God, but you do not answer;
> I stand up, but you merely look at me.
> ²¹You turn on me ruthlessly;
> with the might of your hand you attack me.
> ²²You snatch me up and drive me before the wind;
> you toss me about in the storm.
> ²³I know you will bring me down to death,
> to the place appointed for all the living.

Job is the only speaker in the book who addresses God, but it has been some time since he did that. While there have been complaints about God, speaking of him in the third person, 17:3-5 was the last section that could be labeled "address to God." Job's final prayer before "the words of Job are ended" (31:40) is here. He will, of course, respond briefly to God's revelation out of the whirlwind, but that is in a different category and in response to a different set of circumstances. These verses are like those earlier addresses, mainly complaint and seemingly devoid of hope.

30:20 Because of line *a,* one expects a negative predicate in the second line, so some commentators and translations supply it.[46] The NIV

---

[46] The KJV ("and thou regardest me not"), AT, RSV, MLB, JB, GNB, NJPS. The Vulgate has *non respicis me*. The line is lacking in the LXX, along with vv. 1c,2,3,4a,7a,11b,12,13a,16a,18a,22b,27. Among those reading in the negative are Dhorme, Rowley, Gordis, and Habel. F. Andersen says that the "not" of line *a* can do double duty providing a negation of the second line as well (*Job,* TOTC [Downers Grove: InterVarsity, 1976], 237). But this old solution was refuted by F. Delitzsch who translates the verb "lookest fixedly" (*The Book of Job* [Grand Rapids: Eerdmans, 1949], II:160). J. T. Marshall was on target with his "Thou lookest at me searchingly" (*The Book of Job,* An American Commentary [Philadelphia: American Baptist Publishing Society, 1904], 100).

and NRSV do it in a sense by supplying the word "merely."[47] Since the verb translated "look" can also mean "diligently look/examine/scrutinize," it is best to understand here that God "studied" or "inspected" Job with a view to discovering hidden sin.[48] This was Job's complaint in 7:17-20; 14:3-6. This interpretation fits better with the following line than with the preceding.

30:21 Job perceived God as an enemy rather than a friend, as a "ruthless" one rather than a merciful one.[49] This complaint too has been on his lips several times before (10:3; 16:9,14; 19:22). Instead of using "the might of your hand" to help, God used it to "attack" him.[50]

30:22 Two adjustments are necessary to make good sense of this verse. The verb, which ordinarily means "melt/dissolve/soften" (cf. KJV, NASB, NJPS) must be understood metaphorically and translated as the NIV and most others, "toss." Second, "storm" comes from noting the Masoretic suggestion in the margin and reading not "wisdom" but "noise/storm."[51] Again, this may look forward to the theophany by referring to the storm, the vehicle through which God eventually spoke to Job (cf. 9:17; 38:1).

30:23 At this point Job was certain that God would let him die. The prayer ends on a note as depressing as any in the book. Elsewhere he spoke of death as the land of no return (10:21; 16:22); here it is "the place appointed for all the living."

(4) Lamentation (30:24-31)

> [24]"Surely no one lays a hand on a broken man
>   when he cries for help in his distress.
> [25]Have I not wept for those in trouble?
>   Has not my soul grieved for the poor?
> [26]Yet when I hoped for good, evil came;

---

[47] The NIV similarly adds "only" to a negative clause in 32:9. The NASB has a felicitous compromise in reading the preposition בְּ differently, "Thou dost turn Thy attention against me." The ICB and NCV have "just" instead of "merely."

[48] The verb בִּין in the *hithpolel* is so used in 1 Kgs 3:21; Job 31:1; Ps 119:95; and Jer 2:10.

[49] The first line of this verse has a parallel in Isa 63:10.

[50] The verb "attack" is translated "assails" in 16:9, "held a grudge" in Gen 27:41, and "revile" in Ps 55:3[4]. BDB suggests that שָׂטַם may be related to שָׂטַן, "Satan."

[51] The text has תֻּשִׁיָּה. The Masoretic reading is תֻּשִׁיָּה, "wisdom." G. Gerleman, the *BHS* editor, suggests, and most follow, repointing the *Kethib* to read תְּשֻׁאָה, a defective writing of תְּשֻׁאָה, "noise/commotion/storm" (cf. 36:29; 39:7). Since it lacks a preposition, R. Gordis calls this an "accusative of place" (*Job*, 336).

when I looked for light, then came darkness.
²⁷The churning inside me never stops;
    days of suffering confront me.
²⁸I go about blackened, but not by the sun;
    I stand up in the assembly and cry for help.
²⁹I have become a brother of jackals,
    a companion of owls.
³⁰My skin grows black and peels;
    my body burns with fever.
³¹My harp is tuned to mourning,
    and my flute to the sound of wailing.

An eight-verse lamentation closes this dreary recitation by Job of his shabby treatment by the town's most disreputable outcasts and by God. Here he moaned his fate, wistfully thought of how undeserving he was of such misfortune, and vividly described his wretched condition.

30:24 Because of the difficulties of this verse, versions differ in their wording and interpretation.[52] The first line is literally, "Surely not in ruin does he stretch out a hand." With the addition of one letter, "in ruin" becomes "on the needy." RSV has "heap of ruins," but NRSV has "the needy."[53] The second line is literally, "If in his distress/disaster to them [feminine] a cry for help."[54] As it stands in the NIV, Job was the "broken man"; he cried "for help in his distress," but God was not answering, as Job said in v. 20.

30:25 The Hebrew idiom for "in trouble" is "for the hard of day."[55]

---

[52] Gordis (*Job,* 336) calls it "one of the most difficult in the book." The NEB margin indicates that the Hebrew is "unintelligible." LXX appears to read a text quite different from the MT (see Dhorme, *Job,* 445), resulting in what appears to be Job's contemplation of suicide. One difference, followed by some, is the first person אשלח rather than third person ישלח in the first line, and לי rather than להן in the second, providing a sense that fits well with v. 25. Thus, Dhorme (followed by Habel, *Job,* 414, 416-17) translates, "Yet I did not strike the poor man with my hand / if in his distress he cried out for my help."

[53] *BHS* has בְּעִי. "On the needy" is בְּעָנִי. The phrase שלח יד, "stretch out a hand," followed by בְּ, elsewhere is used of causing harm (1 Sam 24:6,10; 26:9,11,23; Ps 55:20[21]; Dan 11:42). The same sense is provided by the more common expression that uses the verb נטה and the preposition עַל (e.g., Isa 5:25; Jer 6:12; Ezek 6:14). Similar are expressions with יצא (Ruth 1:13), נשא (2 Sam 18:28), רום (1 Kgs 11:26-27), and שוב (Isa 1:25; Ps 81:14[15]).

[54] Some would read "death" and "the place/house" in v. 23 and "hand" in v. 24a as the antecedents of "them." In place of לְהֶן שׁוּעַ Hartley (*Job,* 404) would read לה יְשַׁוֵּעַ "one cries to him," removing the נ as a scribal error. Dhorme (*Job,* 446) thinks that this נ was displaced from its original place in בְעָנִי in line *a.*

[55] See margin of the KJV, NASB. The expression "hard of spirit," translated "deeply troubled," is in 1 Sam 1:15 in the NIV.

"Grieved" occurs only here but possibly is connected to a similar word in Isa 19:10, "dejected."[56] Job's recitation of his deeds of kindness is reminiscent of Ps 35:13-14, where David found he was repaid evil for good and malice for charity. Though he lived centuries earlier, Job's sympathy with suffering followed Paul's admonition in Rom 12:15, "Mourn with those who mourn" (cf. 29:12-17).

30:26 Job's problem was not complicated. Whatever he wished for, he received the opposite—"evil" instead of "good" and "darkness" rather than "light." Formerly he led the good life, but now his life was filled with trouble: no wealth, no health, no respect. He had lived in the "light," as it were, but now "darkness," symbolizing death and the grave, was all he saw.

30:27 "The churning inside me" is more delicate than the KJV's "my bowels boiled," although the latter is more literal.[57] Not only was Job afflicted with a grievous skin disorder, but the attendant troubles had an almost predictable psychosomatic effect on his digestion. Line *b* hints that he sensed no improvement in his condition, but rather a worsening. Ahead was only more suffering.

30:28 There is a division between those translations like NIV that read "black"[58] and those that read the color figuratively as "gloom/mourning."[59] If "black" is correct, it might refer either to mourning clothes, that is, sackcloth, or to the effects of the skin disease, which no one has diagnosed satisfactorily.[60] Even if v. 28 does not speak of Job's condition, v. 30 does, where a different term for "black" modifies "skin."[61] "Cry for help" echoes the beginning of v. 20, and the scene of Job searching for a sympathetic audience is frequent in the book (19:7; 31:35).

30:29 Most agree on the "jackals," but on the specie of bird in the second line there are two contenders: "owls" (KJV, NEB, NIV) and "ostriches" (RV, ASV, Moffatt, AT, RSV, MLB, NKJV).[62] In either case

---

[56] The root in Job is עֹצֵב; the one in Isaiah is אָגַם. See also possible support from Ugaritic in A. R. Ceresko, *Job 29–31 in Light of Northwest Semitic* (Rome: Biblical Institute Press, 1980), 91.

[57] The RV was like the KJV, but its American counterpart, the ASV, has "my heart is troubled." רָתַח is elsewhere only in Job 41:31[23] and Ezek 24:5. Cf. Lam 2:11, "I am sick to my stomach" (author's translation).

[58] RSV, MLB, Hartley, Gordis, Rowley, Duhm, etc.

[59] KJV, AB, JB, NAB, NEB, NASB, AAT, NJPS, NRSV, Habel, Jastrow, etc.

[60] Delitzsch called it leprosy (*Job*, II:169-70).

[61] Cf. Lam 4:8; Cant 1:5-6.

[62] The same pair occurs in Isa 13:21-22; 34:13; Mic 1:8. The "ostrich" of Lam 4:3 translates a slightly different Hebrew word. As in the seven other places where "owl" occurs, it is בְּנוֹת יַעֲנָה or בַּת יַעֲנָה, "daughter[s] of owl," which may be "daughter[s] of desert" if from Arabic or "daughter[s] of greed" if from Aramaic. See *Fauna and Flora of the Bible*, 60-61.

these are desert animals whose solitary habits illustrated for Job his condition of abandonment. Another analogy might be the moaning sounds that the jackals and owls make, which is the point of Mic 1:8. Forsaken by friends and family and driven to solitude, Job felt like a "brother" and "companion" to these reclusive creatures.

30:30 Verse 30 unquestionably describes Job's diseased skin. It was "black" and "peeled," or literally, "My skin grows black from off me." In the second line it was literally his "bones" that burned with fever. "Skin" and "bones" both are metonymies for "body." These last symptoms of Job's malady must be taken with others to complete the picture of his intense physical discomfort. He had scabs and festering sores over his entire body (7:5), malnutrition (17:7; 19:20), a repulsive appearance (19:19), bad breath (19:17), and pain day and night (30:17). Neither his condition nor his attitude toward God had improved.

30:31 Job ended his lament with a melancholic picture of musical instruments playing dirges. Both were simple instruments, unlike a modern "harp" and even more dissimilar to the KJV's "organ." Ordinarily music was for celebration, but occasionally the "harp" was used for mourning (Isa 16:11). The "flute" characteristically produces a plaintive sound. Job had nothing more to say by way of lament; he could only moan.

3. His Self-malediction (31:1-40)

Curses were taken very seriously by ancient Near Eastern peoples. Words, spoken or written, had real power, and to call down curses on oneself was a grave and daring thing to do. But so convinced was Job of his integrity and freedom from sin that he listed here about seven categories of crimes, whose consequences he would be glad to suffer.[63] The chapter seems almost a concession to his three friends, who accused him of the crimes cataloged here. By this means he took the ultimate risk to prove his innocence to them because he fully believed that God would act on these maledictions.

---

[63] By dividing up many that I have lumped together, Hartley (*Job*, 408-9) is able to list fourteen sins. Lust (vv. 1-4), falsehood (vv. 5-6), covetousness (vv. 7-8), adultery (vv. 9-12), mistreatment of one's servants (vv. 3-15), lack of concern for the poor (vv. 16-18), failure to clothe the poor (vv. 19-20), perversion of justice against the weak (vv. 21-23), trust in wealth (vv. 24-25), worship of the heavenly bodies (vv. 26-28), satisfaction at a foe's misfortune (vv. 29-30), failure to extend hospitality to a sojourner (vv. 31-32), concealment of a sin without confession (vv. 33-34), and abuse of the land (vv. 38-40b). Others assemble longer or shorter lists. E. M. Good, e.g., finds fifteen curses (*In Turns of Tempest: A Reading of Job* [Stanford: Stanford University Press, 1990], 309).

(1) Introduction (31:1-4)

[1]"I made a covenant with my eyes
    not to look lustfully at a girl.
[2]For what is man's lot from God above,
    his heritage from the Almighty on high?
[3]Is it not ruin for the wicked,
    disaster for those who do wrong?
[4]Does he not see my ways
    and count my every step?

The introduction begins with a repudiation of even an incipient sexual sin and moves on to speak in terms of retribution such as the friends have been propounding all along. It seems that Job agreed to submit to their terms if only temporarily and put himself under divine scrutiny. He averred that if he were wicked, he should deserve ruin; but by disavowing the sorts of sins they had in mind, he would clear himself of their charges and prove to them that God is indeed arbitrary and sends trouble to the innocent.

31:1 As in all the Old Testament's references to making "a covenant," the expression is "cut a covenant," alluding either to inscribing such solemn words on stone or to the cutting of a sacrificial animal to accompany the ceremony (Gen 15:10,18). The second stich is grammatically a question, "How could I look at a girl [bĕtûlâ, "virgin"]?" The effect, however, is that of a negative sentence.[64] Why is this one sin at the head of this chapter? Some would move it closer to v. 9, which addresses adultery.[65] Some say it is such a cardinal sin and avoidance of it bespeaks such a high level of purity that it comes first and ties in with God, who "sees my ways" (v. 4).[66] Others suggest that "virgin" refers to Venus or Anat, the virgin consort of Baal, and by this means Job swore that he would not so much as look at an idol (cf. vv. 26-28).[67] Still others emend the text to read "folly."[68] The NIV has added "lustfully" to the translation of the verb "look," which I wished to translate in 30:20 as "scrutinize/examine." The subject matter brings to mind Jesus' warning in Matt 5:28, "Anyone who looks at a woman lustfully has already committed adultery with her in his heart." Ben Sira had similar advice, "Entertain no thoughts against a vir-

---

[64] See GBH §144h.

[65] E.g., Jastrow, Job, 304; Moffatt; NAB. The NEB has v. 1 between vv. 5 and 6.

[66] See discussion in Habel, Job, 431-32; Andersen, Job, 240-41; Gordis, Job, 344-45.

[67] G. Jeshurun, "A Note on Job XXX:1 (sic)," JSOR 12 (1928): 153-54. He is followed by Ceresko, Job 29–31, 105-8; Smick, "Job," 992-93; and others.

[68] Pope (Job, 228) reads נְבָלָה for בְּתוּלָה.

gin, lest you be enmeshed in damages for her" (Sir 9:5, NAB). If such temptations existed in biblical times, how much more should Christians today heed these warnings and emulate Job.

31:2 The answer to these two perfectly parallel questions is in v. 3. Since the Hebrew specifies only the source ("God/the Almighty") of the "lot" and "heritage," the NIV added "man's" and "his." But others make it first person, "my" (RSV), "I" (MLB, AAT), or "us" (GNB).

31:3 The answer is one-sided because it only mentions the "ruin" and "disaster"[69] that befall "the wicked" and wrongdoers, not the positive rewards for the righteous (cf. 20:29). This is understandable in view of the fact that the chapter is about avoiding sin rather than about doing righteousness. Fear of punishment is a better motivator than promise of reward.

31:4 The answer to these questions is affirmative. The omniscient one watches and takes note of everything his subjects do, whether good or evil (Eccl 12:14). The two other contexts with a similar figure were both positive and hopeful (14:16; 21:10), whereas this one has an ominous tone to it.

(2) Disavowal of Falsehood (31:5-8)

⁵"If I have walked in falsehood
    or my foot has hurried after deceit—
⁶let God weigh me in honest scales
    and he will know that I am blameless—
⁷if my steps have turned from the path,
    if my heart has been led by my eyes,
    or if my hands have been defiled,
⁸then may others eat what I have sown,
    and may my crops be uprooted.

This section consists of two conditional verses alternating with two verses of result, but the topic is essentially the same throughout, namely, falsehood. None of the offenses in vv. 5,7 is very specific, nor is the malediction of v. 6. Only v. 8 provides a clue about what transgression Job disavowed in this opening section.

31:5 The two evils are "falsehood" (*šāwĕʾ*, translated "futility" in 7:3, "deceitful" in 11:11, and "worthless" and "nothing" in 15:31) and "deceit" (*mirmâ*), which appeared in 15:35 with the same meaning. Nei-

---

[69] The root נכר means "strange," but here and in Obad 12-13 it is parallel to איד, "ruin/destruction."

ther word suggests any specific area, but the malediction of v. 6 points to cheating with scales. The KJV, RV, and AB have "vanity" for the first word, which is a kind of self-deceit. Folks ancient and modern cheat and lie to themselves by pursuing what is hollow, fruitless, and lacking any redeeming value.

31:6 The reference to "weighing with honest scales" does not necessarily identify the sin Job had in mind. In this negative confession he asked that God verify his "blamelessness" through "right balances." The opposite, "balances of deceit" or "dishonest scales," are in Hos 12:7[8]; Amos 8:5; Mic 6:11. Daniel 5:27 (Aramaic) used "scales" metaphorically as here. The rider on the black horse in Rev 6:5 had a "pair of scales," obviously a symbol of judgment. In Islamic tradition the arches on the west side of Jerusalem's Dome of the Rock are the scales on which the deeds of all humanity will be weighed in the last days.

31:7 The "if" at the beginning does triple duty in this tricolon. The three subjects are "feet" ("steps"), "heart," and "hands." "The path" frequently refers to life lived under the law of God (Pss 1:6; 25:4, etc.). "The heart" following the "eyes" harks back to v. 1 and the lust that often accompanies the look (Prov 27:20; 1 John 2:16). Numbers 15:39 puts all three concepts together: lusts, hearts, and eyes. The third line is literally "[if] to my hands should cling defilement." The defilement of the hands is rather general,[70] but used with this verb (*dābaq*) it may allude to a penchant toward avarice. One might even discern a progression in these three lines, from inquisitiveness to covetousness to the act of sin.

31:8 The penalty Job called down on himself was the loss of his labor in the fields. The figure of eating what you have not sown or of others eating what you have sown is also recorded in Lev 26:16; Job 20:18; Mic 6:15. It is one of those arrangements in which the penalty corresponds to the crime. If v. 7c refers to gluttony and greed, then the loss of food and wealth is a fitting punishment.

(3) Disavowal of Adultery (31:9-12)

⁹**"If my heart has been enticed by a woman,**
    or if I have lurked at my neighbor's door,

---

[70] "Defiled" is a noun, מְאוּם, a variant spelling of מוּם, "blemish," that occurs with this spelling only here and Dan 1:4 (cf. Lev 24:19; 2 Sam 14:25; Prov 9:7). What looks like a fem. form of the same noun, מְאוּמָה, means "anything" (cf. Gen 30:31; Deut 13:18; 1 Sam 12:5; 1 Kgs 10:21; 2 Kgs 5:20; Jer 39:20), which would fit this context. Its negation would be "nothing." "To my hand nothing has stuck" would refer to freedom from greed or materialism.

¹⁰then may my wife grind another man's grain,
   and may other men sleep with her.
¹¹For that would have been shameful,
   a sin to be judged.
¹²It is a fire that burns to Destruction,
   it would have uprooted my harvest.

None of the friends suggested that Job was guilty of adultery, but the patriarch included it in his list of sins he did not commit because it was and still is so widespread. Technically Job spoke of lust or covetousness, not adultery itself, as he disavowed even the first step that leads to marital infidelity. The apodosis speaks in more graphic, but still not explicit, language of sexual union between partners not married to each other.

31:9 "Enticed" is the best translation of the verb (*petâ*) because it lies between "deceived," the most common meaning, and "simple," a meaning on the edge of its semantic sphere (so 5:2). Other choices are "tempted," "lured" (AB), "seduced" (AAT, Dhorme, Habel), and "ravished" (NJPS). This Hebrew word translated "woman" also means "wife," (i.e., married), the "girl" (usually unmarried) of v. 1. He certainly was not referring to lurking for his "neighbor" but for his neighbor's wife (Prov 5:8). The word "door" (*petaḥ*) may have been chosen for its similarity to the verb in line *a*.

31:10 "Grind" may be merely a euphemism (like "lie with" in English) or have a double meaning—the literal work of a slave[71] and the act of intercourse.[72] "Sleep with" is the dynamic equivalent translation of a verb meaning "bend over/bow down over," which, though still a euphemism, draws a clearer picture of the violation of Job's wife.[73]

31:11 Verses 11-12 constitute an expansion or commentary on the sin of adultery. Such an act is "shameful" and a matter for the courts (Lev 20:10; Deut 22:22-24).[74]

31:12 Proverbs 6:27-29 also connected sexual sins with "fire." "Fire" just spreads and consumes until all is "Destruction" (*Abaddon* in Hebrew as the NIV footnote indicates), a personification of death and the

---

[71] Exod 11:5; Isa 47:2 connect grinding and women slaves.

[72] Gordis (*Job*, 346-47) finds medieval rabbinic support for this.

[73] The verb כרע occurs here with a final paragogic *nun* (see *GBH* § 44e, which notes twenty-three occurrences of this grammatical feature in Job). The most explicit Hebrew term for sex is בוא, "enter into."

[74] "To be judged" here is פְּלִילִים and פְּלִילִי in v. 28, one a plural masc. noun, the other an adjective. These words appear elsewhere only in Exod 21:22; Deut 32:31; Isa 16:3; 28:7.

grave (cf. 26:6; 28:22; Prov 5:5; 6:32; 7:27). "Harvest" could well refer to children, not crops.[75] If so, it underscores the fact that children are innocent victims when a home is broken by adulterous unions. Such unions eventuated in death in ancient Israel and usually end in divorce in our society.

(4) Disavowal of Injustice (31:13-15)

> [13]"If I have denied justice to my menservants and maidservants
>   when they had a grievance against me,
> [14]what will I do when God confronts me?
>   What will I answer when called to account?
> [15]Did not he who made me in the womb make them?
>   Did not the same one form us both within our mothers?

As in the preceding paragraph we have here a protasis, an apodosis, and a commentary. The subject is the fair treatment of servants. Job reminded himself and us that all were created equal.

31:13 The Masoretes have divided the verse into the two unequal halves that the NIV reflects. From a poetic standpoint it would balance better if "maidservants" were in the second stich (cf. AB, JB, NAB, NEB). The point is still the same—Job denied that he had been indifferent toward those who worked for him. In modern terms his office door was always open and employees always received fair treatment.

31:14 In this chiastically arranged verse,[76] Job asked himself how he would respond if God charged him with neglecting the concerns of those in his employ. As a rhetorical question, there is no answer; but the understood one is that he would be ashamed, guilty, and deserving of the same treatment from God himself.

31:15 The commentary also consists of two negative rhetorical questions that anticipate affirmative answers. Yes, "my maker made him" (author's translation), but only figuratively did "he form us in one

---

[75] Some would emend שרש to שרף, "burn," to fit better with line *a*. So Duhm, *Buch Hiob*, 147; G. Fohrer, *Das Buch Hiob* (Götersloh: Mohn, 1963), 425; RSV, MLB, etc. The burning of crops seems a mild consequence compared with the death penalty or loss of children.

[76] The Hebrew order is:

  A   What will I do
  B   when God arises
  B'   when God visits
  A'   what will I respond?

womb."[77] He may have been alluding to the first parents of the entire race. Coming, as he did, from a culture where slaves were held, Job exhibited remarkably enlightened thinking.

(5) Disavowal of Uncharitableness (31:16-23)

> [16]"If I have denied the desires of the poor
>   or let the eyes of the widow grow weary,
> [17]if I have kept my bread to myself,
>   not sharing it with the fatherless—
> [18]but from my youth I reared him as would a father,
>   and from my birth I guided the widow—
> [19]if I have seen anyone perishing for lack of clothing,
>   or a needy man without a garment,
> [20]and his heart did not bless me
>   for warming him with the fleece from my sheep,
> [21]if I have raised my hand against the fatherless,
>   knowing that I had influence in court,
> [22]then let my arm fall from the shoulder,
>   let it be broken off at the joint.
> [23]For I dreaded destruction from God,
>   and for fear of his splendor I could not do such things.

In this pericope six verses constitute the protases, v. 22 is the apodosis, and v. 23 is the commentary. Those who produce longer lists of topics in this chapter do so by breaking this section into three. This commentary follows the NIV paragraphing, which, in turn, counts the result or "then" verses, not just the condition or "if" verses. All the subjects of this section touch on social concerns and matters of charity.

31:16 By this formula Job denied that he had failed to aid "the poor" and "the widow," who along with "the fatherless" of v. 17 were objects of special charity. Because those in dire straits ordinarily depended on their families for support and the governments had no arrangements for their care, it fell to individual members of the community to care for the indigent. Jesus said, "The poor you will always have with you" (Matt 26:11; cf. Deut 15:11). A thirteenth century Jewish sage said, "Poverty was created to give the rich an opportunity for charity."[78]

31:17 Grammatically the sentence continues, and the "if" (*'im*) of

---

[77] Line *b* is literally "and form him in one womb." "Womb" is בֶּטֶן in line *a* and רֶחֶם in line *b*.

[78] Jehiel ben Jekuthiel Anav, *Maalot ha-Midot*, cited in *Leo Rosten's Treasury of Jewish Quotations* (New York: McGraw-Hill, 1972), 406.

v. 16 introduces this verse as well. Eliphaz accused Job of this very sin in 22:7-9. Job already claimed he was generous to the needy (29:12-16), but here he reinforces that claim by this negative confession and self-maledictory oath.

31:18 Here is a digression or expansion on Job's care for "the fatherless." Job maintained that from his own birth he had "raised"[79] and supported those without a man in the house.[80] It may be hyperbole, but it speaks of Job's lifelong concern for the helpless.

31:19 Now the "If I have seen" does double duty, that is, has two objects, "anyone perishing" and "a needy one." The charity consisted of "bread," a generic term for food and maybe even money in v. 17. His gifts of benevolence included "clothing." Eliphaz had indicted Job for "stripping men of their clothing, leaving them naked" in 22:6. Not so, Job said; the opposite was true.

31:20 The NIV, NKJV, and JB read "heart" for the "loins" that "blessed" Job. The NAB has "limbs," and the NEB has "body." There is an "if" ('im) left untranslated at the beginning of this line, thus carrying the format of conditional sentences forward. Positively Job said that those recipients of his largess "blessed" him. A man with seven thousand sheep surely could have spared a few fleeces for the cold and poorly clothed of what probably was a relatively small community.

31:21 No one knows exactly what gesture the verse refers to, but the judges might have voted with upraised hands, or it might have been a way to signal bystanders to side against the defendant. In any event, Job denied using this tactic in court against the powerless. "Influence" translates, 'ezrātî, "my help," a word chosen for its similarity to 'ezrōʻ, "my arm" in the next verse. The same word was in Eliphaz's accusation in 22:9, "the strength/arm of the fatherless."

31:22 As in the pericope about adultery (vv. 9-10), here the punish-

---

[79] The verb גָּדְלַ֫נִי appears to be a third person singular *qal* perfect from the intransitive verb גָּדֵל, "be/become great/strong," plus a first singular suffix (unusual with an intransitive verb). The context, however, leads the reader to expect a first person subject, a transitive verb, and a third person object, parallel to אַנְחֶ֫נָּה, "I guided her," in line *b*. The suffix נִי may be understood as third person, a not uncommon occurrence in Hebrew and frequent in Ugaritic. The NIV, however, appears to have emended the verb to אֲגַדְּלֶ֫נּוּ, a *piel*. Others read the verb as transitive and assume God is the subject and Job the object, "He raised me," but then the two stichs are not coordinate. Gordis (*Job,* 349) reads the verb as intransitive and the suffix as "indirect" (see "datival accusative" in *IBHS* §16.4f, 10.2.1i; *GBH* §125ba), translating "he grew up with me" (RV, ASV, NASB). This makes the most sense but requires the preposition בְּ to be understood in the following word, "as (with) a father."

[80] "The widow" translates a third fem. sing. pronominal suffix on the verb "guided."

ment fits the crime. Job prayed that the very "arm" he raised against the defenseless "fall from the shoulder" and "be broken off at the joint."[81]

31:23 The verse focuses on the horror of God's judgment and how fear of it prompted good behavior. Two of the key words, "dread" and "splendor," were used in 13:11, where Job warned his friends to live in the light of these divine characteristics. These two dimensions of "the fear of the Lord" ought to motivate all of his people to fulfill his law, honor his name, and be kind to the poor.

(6) Disavowal of Materialism and Paganism (31:24-28)

> [24] "If I have put my trust in gold
>   or said to pure gold, 'You are my security,'
> [25] if I have rejoiced over my great wealth,
>   the fortune my hands had gained,
> [26] if I have regarded the sun in its radiance
>   or the moon moving in splendor,
> [27] so that my heart was secretly enticed
>   and my hand offered them a kiss of homage,
> [28] then these also would be sins to be judged,
>   for I would have been unfaithful to God on high.

Combined in this pericope are Job's disavowals of love of wealth (vv. 24-25) and of worshiping celestial bodies (vv. 26-27), a combination that suggests the seriousness with which materialism should be viewed. The result clause or apodosis is v. 28, but it does not explicitly include a curse that he called down on himself. Rather, it is a general confession that such deeds merit condemnation and represent disloyalty to God.

31:24 Here in this uncomplicated statement and by means of a conditional sentence, Job professed that he did not put his trust[82] in gold.[83] In Eliphaz's little evangelistic sermon he promised Job that if he abandoned his gold, God would become his "gold" (22:24-25). Job

---

[81] The first line is made difficult by two words for "shoulder," כָּתֵף and שְׁכֶם, although the first can be rendered "shoulder-blade" (ASV, REB, NRSV). The NIV moved "arm" to the first line and translated "it" in the second, thus leaving out one "shoulder" (also NCV). On the forms with feminine suffixes see *GBH* § 94h. "Joint" is קָנֶה, normally "reed/cane/stalk," but here it refers to the bones of the upper arm (KB).

[82] This relatively rare word, כֶּסֶל, which also means "foolish" and "loins," occurs in parallel with מִבְטַח again in 8:14. In that passage Bildad indirectly charged Job with trusting in what amounts to "a spider's web."

[83] The two kinds of gold mentioned here are the common זָהָב, and the infrequent כֶּתֶם. See comments at 28:16,19.

maintained that it was never otherwise (Prov 18:11).

31:25   Since Job was the richest man in the East, he had the greatest reason to celebrate his prosperity. That he did not is testimony to his modesty, piety, and generosity. He practiced the advice of Ps 62:10b[11b], though that counsel was written much later: "Though your riches increase, do not set your heart on them." This is a sage warning for all who live in a materialistic culture.

31:26   The heavenly bodies[84] were often deified by ancient peoples, who believed that their movements directly affected one's fortunes. To a limited extent agricultural societies in particular are dependent on the vicissitudes of weather, but to grant them personalities or presume them worthy of worship was and is a cardinal sin, the sin of worshiping the created instead of the Creator (cf. Deut 4:19; 17:3; 2 Kgs 23:5; Ezek 8:16; Rom 1:25).

31:27   "Enticed" is the same word as in v. 9, where the temptation to adultery was the subject. Just as not looking at the sun or moon removes the temptation to venerate them, so not looking at one's neighbor's wife also makes the possibility of sinning more remote. The second stich reads literally, "My hands kisses (to) my mouth," which most, along with the NIV, understand as throwing a kiss.[85]

31:28   Verse 28a is almost the same as v. 11b, another interesting connection between lust for women and the allure of sun and moon worship. "Unfaithful" further follows the analogy of marital infidelity, although this moderately uncommon verb is usually "lie" or "disown" as in 8:18. The "on high" might be considered an inconsequential detail or mere ballast, but in this context it reminded Job and reminds us that God is "up," up above the heavenly bodies that people are tempted to worship because they are visible and he is not.

(7) Disavowal of Meanness and Secret Sin (31:29-34)

> [29]"If I have rejoiced at my enemy's misfortune
>   or gloated over the trouble that came to him—
> [30]I have not allowed my mouth to sin
>   by invoking a curse against his life—
> [31]if the men of my household have never said,
>   'Who has not had his fill of Job's meat?—

---

[84] "Sun" here is not the usual שֶׁמֶשׁ but אוֹר, "light." Gen 1:16 speaks of the sun as "the greater light," מָאוֹר.

[85] So Dhorme, Gordis, Habel, Hartley, Moffatt, MLB footnote, JB, NAB, NASB, AAT, NCV.

³²but no stranger had to spend the night in the street,
    for my door was always open to the traveler—
³³if I have concealed my sin as men do,
    by hiding my guilt in my heart
³⁴because I so feared the crowd
    and so dreaded the contempt of the clans
    that I kept silent and would not go outside

Several unusual features of this section make it difficult to follow. First, it mixes declarative statements with the succession of conditions. There is also no "then" clause until v. 40, the condition-consequence structure being interrupted by the parenthetical requests in vv. 35-37 (note the absence of punctuation ending v. 34). Furthermore, the subject of the negative confession moves from an ill spirit of retaliation, to stinginess toward domestic help and travelers, to concealing sin.

31:29 Job denied that he harbored a vengeful spirit toward his enemies when they fell. The Edomites illustrated this mean attitude in Obad 12. Proverbs 24:17-18 warns against it. It takes a very generous spirit and a high degree of godliness not to "rejoice" at an "enemy's misfortune." The tendency is to praise God for his justice rather than offer a cup of cold water to the suffering.

31:30 The ASV put vv. 30 and 32 in parentheses because they are outright denials of despicable behavior rather than conditional sentences ("if" clauses) like vv. 29,31,33. The NIV has done the same with dashes. Apart from this irregularity v. 30 expands on v. 29. Job denied that he sinned with his mouth by cursing his enemy. Paul extended the beatitude about blessing enemies when he wrote in Rom 12:14, "Bless those who persecute you; bless and do not curse." Such was Job's way of life.

31:31 The negative in each line of v. 31 may confuse some readers. Paraphrased, and with the negatives removed, this confession says, "The men of my house have always said, 'Everyone has eaten all he wants of Job's food'" (ICB, NCV).⁸⁶ In 22:7 Eliphaz had accused Job of denying "water to the weary" and withholding "food from the hungry."

31:32 Like v. 30, this couplet is set off by dashes in the NIV because the format differs from that of the context. The two major dimensions of hospitality are food and shelter. In v. 31 Job insisted that he had been generous with his "meat." Now he swore that he always had an open door to traveling strangers. Job followed another admonition that Paul much later gave to Christians, "Practice hospitality" (Rom 12:13).

---

⁸⁶ Gordis (*Job*, 352) solves the problem by eliminating לֹא as dittography from v. 30.

31:33 Generosity toward enemies, employees, and strangers has been the subject matter of this section so far. Here Job turned to a disavowal of duplicity.[87] The NIV footnote gives the option of reading *'ādām* as the name of the first man, Adam, rather than the generic term "men" in the text. A case can be made for either because Adam did "conceal" his sin (Gen 3:8-12), but people in general are also loath to confess their transgressions (Ps 32:3-5; Prov 28:13; 1 John 1:8-10).

31:34 A tricolon concludes this section. Nevertheless, the long sentence that began in v. 29 does not end even with v. 34 but continues after the parenthesized "conclusion," with a period coming only after the apodosis at the end of the chapter. In the first two lines of v. 34, which are parallel, Job gave reasons why a secret sinner might "keep silent" and "not go outside." Today it is called peer pressure or social stigma. In those ancient, tightly knit societies such community pressure contributed to the good behavior of all. In cultures where neighbors do not know one another and it is easy to hide under the cloak of anonymity, sin exacts less public scorn. People feel freer to commit scandalous acts knowing there is no familial or clan reprisal.

(8) Conclusion (31:35-37)

> [35]("Oh, that I had someone to hear me!
>   I sign now my defense—let the Almighty answer me;
>   let my accuser put his indictment in writing.
> [36]Surely I would wear it on my shoulder,
>   I would put it on like a crown.
> [37]I would give him an account of my every step;
>   like a prince I would approach him.)—

The location of this pericope within the chapter is a problem because it seems like the conclusion; yet there was no resolution of the "if-then" verses that preceded, and there follow three more verses like those in the rest of the chapter. Moffatt moved vv. 38-40 ahead of v. 35. The NEB has them ahead of v. 29. The JB has them ahead of v. 16. The NAB puts them

---

[87] "Heart" is not the usual לֵב but חֹב, "bosom," a hapax legomenon related to the verb חָבַב, "love" (Deut 33:3), and to Aramaic חֻבָּא, which translates the Hebrew חֵיק, "bosom." KB explains it as the "pocket at the inside of the slit of a beduin's shirt." See Dhorme (*Job*, 467). But Tur-Sinai (*Job*) connects it with חָבָא, "hide," as in Gen 3:8, hence "hiding-place."

between vv. 8 and 9.[88] I agree with Smick's conclusion: "These verses are clearly anticlimactic, but that does not mean they belong in another place in this chapter. In several places before Job has shown his penchant for anticlimax (e.g., 3:23-26; 14:18-22)."[89] In vv. 35-37 Job unhesitatingly and unabashedly declared how proudly he would go to trial, just to have his name cleared and his reputation restored. He gladly welcomed the most detailed examination of his life, knowing full well he would pass and be exonerated. But, as in the earlier chapters, this opportunity was denied him, and he was left merely wishing for and imagining such a public acquittal. The human-God relationship cannot be contained within the framework of legal justice.[90]

31:35 The verse opens with the last of several such requests, "Oh that I."[91] Supposedly Eliphaz, Bildad, and Zophar have been listening, but in reality they have not been persuaded by any of Job's words and might as well never have heard what he said. "I sign now my defense" translates two little Hebrew words, "Look, my X."[92] Job probably was literate, however, because in the last line he asked for a written "indictment"[93] from his "accuser."

31:36 Job indicated that he would proudly and publicly display his signed affidavit as a "crown"[94] and as a sash, stole, or badge of office (cf. Isa 9:6[5]; 22:22).[95] Rather than hiding his sin and dreading the crowds (vv. 33-34), he gladly would proclaim his innocence.

31:37 The antecedent of "him" is the "accuser" of v. 37, which still might be construed as God, but more likely as one of the three friends or the unnamed antagonists of chap. 30. Without misgivings or doubts Job was happy to open his books, knowing full well that he had nothing to hide. In fact, such an investigation would demonstrate his impeccability.

---

[88] The commentators have a similar variety of solutions. Hartley, Gordis, Fohrer, and Gray put vv. 38-40b before v. 35. Duhm, E. J. Kissane (*The Book of Job* [New York: Sheed & Ward, 1946], and Dhorme have them follow v. 32. Pope (*Job*) and Driver (*Job*) put them after v. 8. Jastrow has them between vv. 12-13. M. Buttenwieser, in addition to many other transfers, puts vv. 38-40b in the middle of v. 12 (*The Book of Job* [New York: Macmillan, 1922], 135).

[89] Smick, "Job," EBC 4:996.

[90] M. B. Dick, "The Legal Metaphor in Job 31," *CBQ* 41 (1979): 50.

[91] See *GBH* §163d.

[92] The last letter of the alphabet, תָּו, was early on written + or x and served as a signature for illiterate people.

[93] Simple סֵפֶר, "book/writing."

[94] "Crown" is plural, perhaps pointing to a multitiered headpiece. But see Ceresko, *Job 29–31*, 184, and cf. Zech 6:11,14, where the unexpected plural also occurs.

[95] See Dhorme, *Job*, 470.

Then, like a victor in a court case or a newly elected public official, he would strut up to the one who had tried so hard to confound him.

(9) Disavowal of Tenant Farmer Abuse (31:38-40)

³⁸"if my land cries out against me
   and all its furrows are wet with tears,
³⁹if I have devoured its yield without payment
   or broken the spirit of its tenants,
⁴⁰then let briers come up instead of wheat
   and weeds instead of barley."

The words of Job are ended.

The last category of crimes that Job disavowed dealt with his treatment of the land and of those who worked it for him (cf. Jas 5:4). Symbolically the curse he invoked if he were guilty related directly to the land, that is, that instead of producing edible or marketable food it should yield him briers and weeds. Though this seems anticlimactic, the offense ties together several of the categories he already had addressed—injustice (vv. 13-15), uncharitableness (vv. 16-23,31), and materialism (vv. 24-25).

31:38 "Wet with tears" translates a simple "weep," but certainly the personified "land" and "furrows"[96] can hardly make a noise but might evidence their broken spirit in this way. A characteristic "if" (*'im*) begins this and the next verse. These conditions will find their resolution in the self-imprecation of v. 40.

31:39 From an ecological point of view, one might sin against the land, but even in v. 38 Job was thinking of malevolence toward the "husbandmen/tenants,"[97] whose responsibility it was to make the land profitable. "Broken the spirit" captures the sense of the Hebrew, which means something like "snuff out/blow away" the "soul/spirit/breath" (*nepeš*).[98]

31:40 The NIV has captured something of the alliteration of the Hebrew with its choice of "wheat" and "weeds" and "briers" and "barley."[99] Job prayed down on himself the curse of unprofitable and nuisance pro-

---

[96] Only four other times does תֶלֶם occur, including 39:10.

[97] The NJPS has "[rightful] owners." The NEB has "creditors." Cf. the use of בְּעָלִים in Prov 3:27, "those who deserve it" (NIV).

[98] The AB has "snuffed out the life."

[99] Four of the first five words in Hebrew have ח in them, and the last two both have a שׂ, a ח, and a guttural. Verse 40a,b reads: תַּחַת חִטָּה יֵצֵא חוֹחַ וְתַחַת שְׂעֹרָה בָאְשָׁה. Isaiah 5:7c on a similar theme also uses paranomasia, but it is not evident in English.

duce in the place of wholesome, salable grains. Let the punishment fit the crime.

The last three Hebrew words announce that we will hear no more from Job, except for his brief response to the divine challenges of chap. 38–41. The reader can judge whether "Job did not sin in what he said" (1:10). This writer tilts toward his acquittal even after twenty-eight chapters of debate, anger, frustration, charges, and countercharges. Neither his grievous circumstances nor his unsympathetic friends with their tightly knit orthodox theology of retribution could persuade the man from Uz that he was anything other than a righteous man.

VI. A YOUNG MAN MAKES HIS CONTRIBUTION TO THE
DISCUSSION (32:1–37:24)
  1. Elihu Contradicts the Friends and Job (32:1–33:33)
     (1) His Entrance (32:1-5)
        Anger with Job (32:1-2)
        Anger with the Friends (32:3-5)
     (2) His Pompous Self-introduction (32:6–33:7)
        Youth Versus Age (32:6-9)
        Inadequacy of the Three Friends (32:10-16)
        His Compulsion to Speak (32:17-22)
        Job's Requirement to Listen (33:1-7)
     (3) His Statement of Job's Argument (33:8-11)
     (4) His Answers to Job's Argument (33:12-30)
        How God Deals with People (33:12-22)
          Introduction (33:12-14)
          He Speaks through Dreams (33:15-18)
          He Speaks through Suffering (33:19-22)
        Exception One: An Angel (33:23-25)
        Exception Two: Repentance (33:26-28)
        God's Purposes (33:29-30)
     (5) Challenge to Job (33:31-33)
  2. Elihu Proclaims God's Justice (34:1-37)
     (1) Introduction (34:1-4)
     (2) His Statement of Job's Argument (34:5-9)
     (3) His Answers to Job's Argument (34:10-30)
        God's Unchanging Ways (34:10-15)
        God's Sovereign Justice (34:16-20)
        God's Punishment (34:21-30)
     (4) His Challenge to Job to Repent (34:31-33)
     (5) He Condemns Job for not Repenting (34:34-37)
  3. Elihu Condemns Self-righteousness (35:1-16)
     (1) His Statement of Job's Argument (35:1-3)
     (2) His Answers to Job's Argument (35:4-15)
        God and Human Good Behavior (35:4-8)
          God is Detached from Human Woe (35:9-15)
     (3) His Insult to Job (35:16)

4. Elihu Declares God's Goodness and Power (36:1–37:24)
    (1) Introduction of a New Tack (36:1-4)
    (2) God's Retribution to the Good and the Bad (36:5-15)
    (3) God's Discipline to Job (36:16-21)
    (4) Introduction to Anticipated Theophany (36:22-26)
    (5) Anticipated Theophany (36:27–37:13)
    (6) Application to Job (37:14-18)

——— VI. A YOUNG MAN MAKES HIS CONTRIBUTION ———
TO THE DISCUSSION (32:1–37:27)

The four speeches of the last major human participant fill the next six chapters. After a prose introduction that corresponds to 2:11-13, Elihu himself spouted an inordinately long introduction of himself, his frustrations, and his plan that he expected would put an end to the debate by satisfying both Job and his friends. In the long run he made little difference. Though he was somewhat kinkier than the others and did put greater emphasis on seeing life and its troubles from a divine perspective, he ultimately also subscribed to the theology of retribution, saw Job as guilty, and therefore blamed him for the grief he was experiencing.

Elihu had been on the scene for some time, but here for the first time he spoke. This young man held his tongue until it appeared that the four protagonists had spent their rhetorical energy. Then Elihu's four speeches, one right after another, constitute the book's longest uninterrupted monopoly of the floor.[1] No one answered him, and he is not included in the indictment of Eliphaz and the other two friends in chap. 42. Mainly for these reasons many consider these speeches a nonoriginal part of the book. But they are in the text, and in many ways they link to and echo other speeches.[2] The very fact that they are long, repetitive, and even boring points to the quandary human beings face when confronted by unresolvable propositions. The fact that no one answers Elihu points to the frustrating fact that there are no human answers to the dilemma Job and many subsequent sufferers have faced.

This commentary will treat Elihu's speeches just as it did the others,

---

[1] Elihu's speeches are longer than twelve other OT books and seventeen of the twenty-seven NT books.

[2] For support for their inclusion see J. B. Curtis, "Why Were the Elihu Speeches Added to the Book of Job?" *PEGLMBS* 8 (1988): 93-100.

ferreting out the meaning, seeking to grasp the larger picture, and addressing this young man's theological posture.[3]

1. Elihu Contradicts the Friends and Job (32:1–33:33)

Nearly half of Elihu's first speech is consumed with his elaborate introduction of himself. Long before he arrived at the substance of his message, he unburdened himself of frustration, partly with Job, but mainly with the other three protagonists. Unlike the others, Elihu appeared to have a plan that corresponded to a one-man debate. He stated Job's position, then proceeded to counter it. Reaching a guilty verdict for Job, repeating what he had said at the beginning, he challenged the patriarch to repent.

(1) His Entrance (32:1-5)

¹So these three men stopped answering Job, because he was righteous in his own eyes. ²But Elihu son of Barakel the Buzite, of the family of Ram, became very angry with Job for justifying himself rather than God. ³He was also angry with the three friends, because they had found no way to refute Job, and yet had condemned him. ⁴Now Elihu had waited before speaking to Job because they were older than he. ⁵But when he saw that the three men had nothing more to say, his anger was aroused.

An angry young man stepped from the sidelines to center stage. Three times his anger is mentioned (vv. 2-3,5).[4] He was frustrated because the debate had gone nowhere. Job insisted on his innocence; his three friends insisted on his guilt. As the four seemed confounded and silent, Elihu saw his chance to speak. Apart from the brief introductions to each speaker, this is the first prose section since the prologue (chaps. 1–2).

ANGER WITH JOB (32:1-2). Actually it was at the end of chap. 25 that "these three men stopped answering Job." But Job's three intervening speeches clearly indicated to them and to Elihu that Job was not in the least wavering from his stalwart defense of his own innocence.

32:1 The three friends rested their case.[5] Job was absolutely convinced of his own righteousness.

32:2 The newcomer is identified by four names: Elihu, Barakel, Buz,

---

[3] E. Dhorme has a brief but commendable essay on Elihu in the introduction to his commentary (*A Commentary on the Book of Job* [London: Nelson, 1967], liv-lvii).

[4] Actually four because the Hebrew has אַף חָרָה, "he burned with anger," twice in v. 2.

[5] "Stopped" is שָׁבַת, the root for "sabbath."

and Ram. Elihu means "he is my God."[6] He is the only character in the
book with a genealogy, which may point to his aristocratic heritage. His
father's name, Barakel (Barachel in KJV, RSV), means "God blesses."[7]
His tribe or home, Buz, is the name of two men (Gen 22:21; 1 Chr 5:14)
and one place. Jeremiah 25:23 listed together Buz, Dedan, and Tema, a
locale mentioned in Job 6:19. It indicates that Elihu, like the others, had
roots in the desert country east of Palestine proper. His clan name, Ram,
means "high one."[8] This Elihu "became very angry" (lit. "burned with
anger") with Job because he perceived that Job was "justifying himself"
and, by implication, charging God with wrong. Elihu heard and concluded correctly.

ANGER WITH THE FRIENDS (32:3-5).   Convinced that Job was wrong,
Elihu was immensely frustrated that the other three could not prove that
point. The fact that they were his seniors added to his impatience and anger.

32:3   Elihu must be credited with fairness because he saw the wrong
both in Job and in the friends. Their case seemed convincing on the surface, but they were unable to support their arguments and prove Job
wrong. It had turned into a shouting match rather than a formal debate,
so Elihu condemned all parties.

32:4   Elihu is commendable because of his respect for his elders. In
proper Semitic fashion the oldest speak first; the young must wait their
turn (cf. 1 Kgs 12:6,8).

32:5   We surmised that Job waited for Zophar to speak at 27:1, but
the Naamathite did not. Likewise at the beginning of chap. 29 Job had
waited for them to speak, but they did not. Finally, the words of Job ended at the close of chap. 31. Now Elihu saw his opportunity. "Elihu had
done his duty by listening; he will now do it by talking (32:16-17)."[9]

(2) His Pompous Self-introduction (32:6–33:7)

⁶So Elihu son of Barakel the Buzite said:

**"I am young in years,
    and you are old;**

---

⁶ Four other OT men have the same name, but none of them can be identified with this
Elihu. See 1 Sam 1:1; 1 Chr 12:20; 26:7; 27:18.
⁷ The name occurs only here, but there are seven men named Barachiah (Berechiah or
Berekiah), "Yahweh blesses."
⁸ For more on these names and the possible connection of "Elihu" with "Elijah," see R.
Gordis, *The Book of God and Man* (Chicago: University Press, 1965), 115-16.
⁹ Dhorme, *Job*, liv.

that is why I was fearful,
not daring to tell you what I know.
7 I thought, 'Age should speak;
advanced years should teach wisdom.'
8 But it is the spirit in a man,
the breath of the Almighty, that gives him understanding.
9 It is not only the old who are wise,
not only the aged who understand what is right.
10 "Therefore I say: Listen to me;
I too will tell you what I know.
11 I waited while you spoke,
I listened to your reasoning;
while you were searching for words;
12 I gave you my full attention.
But not one of you has proved Job wrong;
none of you has answered his arguments.
13 Do not say, 'We have found wisdom;
let God refute him, not man.'
14 But Job has not marshaled his words against me,
and I will not answer him with your arguments.

15 "They are dismayed and have no more to say;
words have failed them.
16 Must I wait now that they are silent,
now that they stand there with no reply?
17 I too will have my say;
I too will tell what I know.
18 For I am full of words,
and the spirit within me compels me;
19 inside I am like bottled-up wine,
like new wineskins ready to burst.
20 I must speak and find relief;
I must open my lips and reply.
21 I will show partiality to no one,
nor will I flatter any man;
22 for if I were skilled in flattery,
my Maker would soon take me away.

1 "But now, Job, listen to my words;
pay attention to everything I say.
2 I am about to open my mouth;
my words are on the tip of my tongue.
3 My words come from an upright heart;
my lips sincerely speak what I know.
4 The Spirit of God has made me;

the breath of the Almighty gives me life.
⁵Answer me then, if you can;
   prepare yourself and confront me.
⁶I am just like you before God;
   I too have been taken from clay.
⁷No fear of me should alarm you,
   nor should my hand be heavy upon you.

Elihu took a long while to get to his point. The brief, polite introduction of Eliphaz at 4:2 pales by comparison to this extended, windy, four-phase preamble of Elihu. His hearers and we readers are prepared for something much grander than what ensued. He might have been better off with a shortened, less stately opening. But he wanted all to know why he waited, what occasioned him now to speak, and the urgency and persuasion with which he lectured.

YOUTH VERSUS AGE (32:6-9).   These verses are an expansion on the simple statement of v. 4 that the other three were older and that Elihu deferred to them. But Elihu knew and we all know that age is no guarantee of wisdom, nor youth of ignorance.

32:6   Elihu's pedigree is abbreviated in the introductory line that corresponds in form to all those from 4:1 onward. In his own poetic way Elihu repeated what the narration in v. 3 had said, that is, that he was young and they were old.[10] Elihu's deference toward age had restrained him from giving his opinion.[11]

32:7   The substance of Elihu's quotation of himself sounds like an aphorism not original with him. It is something like our adage, "Children should be seen and not heard." Ibn Gabirol said: "In seeking wisdom, the first step is silence, the second listening, the third remembering, the fourth practicing, the fifth teaching others."[12]

32:8   Elihu came close to saying he was divinely inspired by alluding to "the breath of the Almighty," in parallel to "the spirit in a man" (cf. 33:4).[13] Such language brings back memories of Eliphaz's report of a

---

[10] "Old" in v. 4 was the usual זָקֵן, but here it is יָשִׁישׁ, a word unique to Job (12:12; 15:10; 29:8; 36:2).

[11] Both "was fearful" and "to tell" are also rare. זָחַל, "fear," is only twice more in the Bible, and חָוָה, "tell," has five of its six occurrences in Job (15:17; 32:10; 36:2,6). But the Aramaic cognate appears fourteen times in Daniel.

[12] Quoted in *Leo Rosten's Treasury of Jewish Quotations* (New York: McGraw-Hill, 1972), 543.

[13] The NIV footnote reports that a minority of the translation committee wanted to capitalize "spirit," thus making it a clear reference to the third member of the trinity. So too in v. 18.

(divine?) vision in his opening speech (4:12-16). But the Buzite stopped short of claiming his words were God's words.

32:9 The nub of Elihu's opening section of his introduction is that age[14] does not guarantee wisdom. It is possible that a youth is wise. By saying that the old are not the only wise ones, he indirectly said that the old may be foolish. Gray hair does not ensure understanding (cf. Eccl 4:13).[15]

INADEQUACY OF THE THREE FRIENDS (32:10-16). Having spoken in general terms about wisdom not being the exclusive domain of the elderly, Elihu now turned to the three friends and directly challenged their inadequacies. This section is an expansion of the simple statement of v. 3 that "they found no way to refute Job."

32:10 The verbose Elihu continued to multiply words that added little substance. "I say" is the same as "I thought" in v. 6. His order to them, "listen to me," will be repeated to Job in 33:1. "Tell you what I know" was also at the end of v. 6.[16] Despite all his talk, Elihu has yet to say very much.

32:11 No one can fault Elihu for being impatient while the debate rolled on for more than twenty chapters. Indeed, the three had "searched for words"[17] but failed to frame an argument that convinced Job of their position.[18]

32:12 Verse 12a almost repeats v. 11b with both "reasoning" and "attention" coming from the same root word.[19] Elihu's discontent was occasioned by the three friends' failure to "prove Job wrong" or "answer

---

[14] In the first stich "old" translates רַבִּים, "many," understood as elliptical for "many years" found in v. 7 parallel to "days" and translated "Age." The NIV footnote suggests that it might be read "great" (so KJV, RV, ASV), but the context argues against it. Cf. Gen 25:23 for רַב contrasted with "younger."

[15] Our proverb is, "There is no fool like an old fool."

[16] A similar expression is in v. 17b.

[17] *GBH* § 90c notes that מִלִּין with the Aramaic plural ending as here occurs thirteen times in Job, and the regular form מִלִּים ten times (cf. v. 18).

[18] While retaining the Hebrew verse division, the NIV has properly marked vv. 11-12 (by line indentation) as comprising three bicola, the second one spanning the division. Rather than having two verses of three lines each, the Masoretes (who divided the verses but did not number them) should have made three verses of two lines each. Other interconnections support this arrangement. In v. 11ab "I" is the subject. In v. 12b,c "you" is the subject." In what should be a separate verse, vv. 11c-12a, "you" is the first subject and "I" the second. The first and third couplets both begin with "behold," הֵן, in v. 11a and הִנֵּה in v. 12b. A more subtle poetic effect is the chiastic arrangement of prepositions: לְ in 11a, עַד in vv. 11b, 11c, and 12a, then לְ again in v. 12b. This is supported by the occurrence of the verb בִּין in vv. 11b and 12a.

[19] Verse 11b has the noun תְּבוּנֹת while v. 12b has the *hithpael* אֶתְבּוֹנָן.

him." Regardless of how convincing they sounded to one another and to themselves, they were failures unless their logic swayed Job. They were arguing from the textbook; Job was arguing from present experience. As F. Andersen says Zophar "detaches the words from the man." Zophar's wisdom is "a bloodless retreat into theory. It is very proper, theologically familiar and unobjectionable," but insipid compared with "Job's seismic sincerity."[20]

32:13 Nowhere did any of the three friends say that they had found wisdom, but certainly that was the gist of Eliphaz's statement in 15:10. Zophar's wish in 11:5-6 approximates the second line, that God would "refute him." Elihu's charge implied that they tacitly surrendered and admitted defeat by turning the case over to God.

32:14 With a touch of arrogance Elihu suggested that Job had yet to confront a formidable logician. He was persuaded that his arguments were different and better than those of the three friends. Elihu demonstrated a greater sensitivity, a better grasp of what Job was saying, and a perspective closer to God's, but in the final analysis he resorted to the same line of reasoning and so likewise failed to convince Job to abandon his claim to innocence.

32:15 The NIV and others make a stanza break at this point because Elihu now spoke of the friends in the third person instead of the second as in the preceding verses. I prefer to keep them together because the three friends are still the subjects of these four lines. It is as if Elihu turned from speaking *to* them to speaking *about* them to Job. Certainly he spoke to Job directly in 33:1. He indicted them for their silence that spoke of resignation and defeat, something he was not about to admit.

32:16 The answer to this rhetorical question is no. Elihu needed to wait no longer. It was more and more obvious that they had no comeback, no retort, no more reserves of words with which to refute the intractable Job.[21]

HIS COMPULSION TO SPEAK (32:17-22). As if we had not guessed what was coming, Elihu announced that now he was going to speak his

---

[20] F. I. Andersen, *Job*, TOTC (Downers Grove: InterVarsity, 1976), 156.
[21] "They answer no more," לֹא עָנוּ עוֹד, is in vv. 15a and 16b. This supports a discernible chiasmus for vv. 15-16.

  A   They are dismayed, they answer no more
    B words fail them
      C Must I wait?
    B' they do not speak
  A' they stand and answer no more.

mind and speak it without guile, duplicity, or compromise. Ready to explode like an unvented wineskin, he warned that he would release his frustration.

32:17 Twice the emphatic "even I" appears in this verse, which more literally reads: "I will answer, even I (will take) my turn. I will tell my knowledge, even I." Elihu felt that after all he had heard from them and the patience he had exercised, he deserved a hearing.

32:18 Elihu spoke no truer words than when he said he was "full of words."[22] The NIV has translated the expression "the spirit of my belly" with the more comprehensible "within me." Pope has "wind bloats my belly," an idea more likely to have come from Elihu's listeners.[23]

32:19 Wine was poured into a fresh animal skin with room for expansion (Matt 9:17). Filling it too full or using an old wineskin was courting a small disaster. Elihu compared himself to such a skin ready to explode. He must release the pressure or he would destroy himself.

32:20 His mouth was like a safety valve, giving vent to the stresses created by the unresolved case of the righteous Job who suffered as an unrighteous offender. At every turn in the debate the facts of the case contributed to a volatile condition in Elihu. If he did not release the pressure in a controlled manner, it might have been disastrous for all.

32:21 Elihu warned his listeners to expect a candid, unbiased, straightforward answer, one that would neither "lift up the face of a man" ("show partiality") nor "give a man any [undue] honor."[24]

32:22 The Hebrew of line *a* could be read, "For I do not know how to flatter/bestow honor."[25] The NIV makes it a conditional clause implying, "I do not know how to flatter, lest," which is more literal but less literary.[26] The point Elihu made is that out of fear of God he must speak the truth, the whole truth, and nothing but the truth.[27]

---

[22] This also was a pun, מָלֵתִי מִלִּים. This may be reflected in the NAB translation "full of matters to utter."

[23] M. Pope, *Job*, AB (Garden City: Doubleday, 1965), 211. He elaborates that "Elihu is flatulent with words" (p. 213).

[24] "Flatter" is כָּנָה, a word that occurs in the next verse and elsewhere only in Isa 44:5; 45:4.

[25] "How to bestow honor/flatter" is just the finite verb אֲכַנֶּה, "I will bestow honor" (see v. 21). It serves as a substantival clause, the object of the previous verb יָדַעְתִּי (*GBH* § 157b).

[26] Dhorme (*Job*, 485) expresses the conditional idea in the second line, "If I did so, my Maker would carry me off in a flash!" The line begins with כִּמְעַט, which can be translated "almost, quickly, easily, soon" (KB³; cf. Gen 26:10; Pss 2:12; 81:14[15]). Gordis (*Job*, 371) finds the condition expressed by emending לֹא to לֻא.

[27] The poet closed the chapter with one more pun on the words "my Maker take me away," יִשָּׂאֵנִי עֹשֵׂנִי.

JOB'S REQUIREMENT TO LISTEN (33:1-7).   With considerable verbosity Elihu ordered Job to listen (v. 1) and answer (v. 5). As much as possible Elihu puffed himself up so that Job would respond as if God himself were addressing him. Throughout these speeches Elihu did speak more of God than the others, and the closer he came to chap. 38, the more Elihu sounded like God speaking through the whirlwind. For now, however, Elihu tried both to intimidate Job (vv. 3-4) and to make him feel comfortable (vv. 6-7).

33:1   Corresponding to his command to the three friends in v. 10, Elihu now turned his attention directly to Job and preceded his order, "listen" with a strong disjunctive, "But now."[28]

33:2   "The tip of my tongue" (NEB, NIV) is a suitable paraphrase of the Hebrew that literally reads "my tongue in my mouth." The verse adds little except verbiage to Elihu's presentation.

33:3   Elihu assured Job that what he was about to hear was characterized by "uprightness," "sincerity/purity," and "knowledge." Was Elihu suggesting that the other three friends had spoken out of ignorance or with duplicity? Job himself had made similar claims to integrity (6:28; 27:4).

33:4   One expects a claim that "the Spirit of God" spoke through rather than made the speaker. It is true that God "breathed into his [Adam's] nostrils the breath of life, and the man became a living being" (Gen 2:7). Elihu was asserting his submission to God, his Creator, and at the same time affirming that he was a fellow human being and also accountable to the Almighty.

33:5   In addition to the two commands in v. 1, Elihu issued three more imperatives: "Answer me,"[29] "prepare yourself,"[30] and "confront me."[31] As it turns out, Job did not respond to Elihu. God interrupted the proceedings with similar challenges to Job (38:3) and posed questions to our hero, none of which Job did or could answer. Elihu asked many questions in the following four chapters, and his last questions are similar to the ones God asked (37:15-18).

33:6   In the preceding verses Elihu tried to impress Job with the gravity of his upcoming presentation. But here he apparently wanted to

---

[28] For the tenth and last time the strong adversative adverb (cf. *IBHS* § 39.3.5) אוּלָם, "nevertheless, on the other hand, but," appears in Job, usually with וֹ as here (cf. 1:11 with וֹ and 2:5 without). It is only nine other places in the Bible, always with וֹ (e.g., Gen 28:19).

[29] *Hiphil* of שׁוּב, "return (to me an answer)." The NASB has "refute."

[30] *Qal* imperative of עָרַךְ with paragogic ה, "set *thy words* in order" (KJV, ASV).

[31] *Hithpael* of יָצַב, "take your stand."

relax Job by reminding him that he was just another[32] mortal created[33] by God.

33:7   The two unusual words "fear" and "alarm" also occur in 9:34; 13:21, one of the indications that the same author is responsible for all parts of Job. "Hand" is based on an emendation. Others have "pressure," a word occurring only here.[34] By these words Elihu hoped to set Job at ease. Job would have welcomed any reduction in the psychological assault the other three had waged.

(3) His Statement of Job's Argument (33:8-11)

> [8]"But you have said in my hearing—
>   I heard the very words—
> [9]'I am pure and without sin;
>   I am clean and free from guilt.
> [10]Yet God has found fault with me;
>   he considers me his enemy.
> [11]He fastens my feet in shackles;
>   he keeps close watch on all my paths.'

In the first three of Elihu's speeches, he quoted Job at length, proving that he had been listening to the exchange between Job and his three friends (34:5-9; 35:2-3). Though not exactly Job's words, they certainly represent one of the major tenets of the protests from the patriarch of Uz.

33:8   Verse 8 is a brief introduction to the Job quotation. Elihu wanted Job to be certain that he was not fabricating this but rather quoting what he heard with his own ears.[35]

33:9   Two positive adjectives, "pure" and "clean," and two negated antonyms, "sin" and "guilt," plus two forms of "I" make up this well-

---

[32] "Just like you" translates כְּפִיךָ, literally "like your mouth," meaning, "I exist as a result of the same divine command as you." For further elaboration see R. Gordis, *The Book of Job* (New York: Jewish Theological Seminary, 1978), 362, 372. His translation is, "Behold, I am equal with you before God."

[33] This unusual verb, קֹרַץ, elsewhere means "wink" (the eye) as in Ps 35:19; Prov 6:13; 10:10, or "purse" (the lips) as in Prov 16:30. The fundamental meaning is "nip/pinch off," so here people are nothing more than bits of clay. See *BDB*, 902-3.

[34] The MT has אַכְפִּי. Removing the א leaves "hand" as in 13:21. A verb from the root אָכַף occurs in Prov 16:26, "drives." "Hand" is supported by the LXX; B. Duhm, *Das Buch Hiob* (Tübingen: Mohr, 1897); Dhorme, *Job*, 489; N. Habel, *The Book of Job* (Philadelphia: Westminster, 1985), 465. But H. H. Rowley argues, "It is a pity to get rid of a rare word which makes good sense here" (*The Book of Job*, NCB [Grand Rapids: Eerdmans, 1978], 211).

[35] "Hearing" is אָזְנָיִם, "ears."

balanced bicolon. In 16:17 Job said his prayer was "pure." "Clean" (*ḥap*) is unique to this verse, but its meaning is established by Akkadian and Syriac. Zophar also said Job claimed to be "pure" (11:4, using a common synonym). Job tacitly denied "sin" and "guilt" by his questions in 13:23 (cf. 10:7; 14:17). So Elihu was not wrong as he paraphrased what Job said.

33:10 In Hebrew "God" is not in the text but is supplied for the third singular masculine subject of the two verbs in v. 10. "Fault" appears only here and in Num 14:34, where the NIV translated it "what it is like to have me against you." The NIV joins most others in reading a variant root.[36] The second half of the verse is nearly identical with 13:24. Job indeed had said that God treated him as an enemy.

33:11 Elihu most certainly had 13:27a,b in mind when he selected this quotation from Job because the words are the same except for the change from "you" to "he."[37]

(4) His Answers to Job's Argument (33:12-30)

12"But I tell you, in this you are not right,
    for God is greater than man.
13Why do you complain to him
    that he answers none of man's words?
14For God does speak—now one way, now another—
    though man may not perceive it.
15In a dream, in a vision of the night,
    when deep sleep falls on men
    as they slumber in their beds,
16he may speak in their ears
    and terrify them with warnings,
17to turn man from wrongdoing
    and keep him from pride,
18to preserve his soul from the pit,
    his life from perishing by the sword.
19Or a man may be chastened on a bed of pain
    with constant distress in his bones,
20so that his very being finds food repulsive
    and his soul loathes the choicest meal.
21His flesh wastes away to nothing,

---

[36] Others follow Rashi and assume a metathesis and read it from the root אָנָה, "pretext/complaint," rather than נֵאת, "opposition." See N. Tur-Sinai, *The Book of Job* (Jerusalem: Kiryat-Sefer, 1967); Gordis, *Job*, 373; Rowley, etc. So too KJV, RSV, AB, JB, NAB, NASB.

[37] He even uses the anomalous jussive יָשֵׂם like וְתָשֶׂם in 13:27.

and his bones, once hidden, now stick out.
²²His soul draws near to the pit,
  and his life to the messengers of death.

²³"Yet if there is an angel on his side
  as a mediator, one out of a thousand,
  to tell a man what is right for him,
²⁴to be gracious to him and say,
  'Spare him from going down to the pit;
  I have found a ransom for him'—
²⁵then his flesh is renewed like a child's
  it is restored as in the days of his youth.
²⁶He prays to God and finds favor with him,
  he sees God's face and shouts for joy;
  he is restored by God to his righteous state.
²⁷Then he comes to men and says,
  'I sinned, and perverted what was right,
  but I did not get what I deserved.
²⁸He redeemed my soul from going down to the pit,
  and I will live to enjoy the light.'

²⁹"God does all these things to a man—
  twice, even three times—
³⁰to turn back his soul from the pit,
  that the light of life may shine on him.

Finally Elihu finished his prefatory remarks and arrived at the substance of his first speech. Essentially it is not a refutation of Job's claims to innocence but a discourse on how God deals with his people and something of an apologetic for the value of suffering. In that he did not simply counter Job, or insist that he must be a sinner, or charge him with duplicity, Elihu is to be commended more than the other three. Whether he has the ultimate answer and a satisfying solution for Job remains to be seen.

How God Deals with People (33:12-22).   Elihu's God is a sovereign whose ways are past finding out. He does, however speak through dreams or suffering to bring his subjects around to his will. Job had no dreams, but he certainly did experience what Elihu would call the chastening hand of God. By bringing up two categories, one that did not apply to Job and one that did, he tried gently to bring Job to see that he was not alone in receiving God's discipline.

Introduction (33:12-14).   Elihu made it clear at the outset that he disagreed with Job, but he did it in an inoffensive way. Quickly he focused attention on the greatness of God and his unquestionable ways.

33:12 "Right" in this context does not mean "correct" but "righteous." It is not proper to charge God with injustice or hostility. Rather than dwell on that point, however, Elihu in the second line moved to what will be a major theme in his speeches and eventually the prelude to the theophany, that is, the greatness of God and the gulf that exists between his ways and thoughts and human ways and thoughts.

33:13 The second half of the verse is almost another quotation from Job (cf. 13:23-26). Job certainly demanded answers from God for what happened to him. The Hebrew, however, has "his words/deeds," not specifying whose they are, man's or God's. Thus the NIV footnote offers as an alternative to line *b* "that he does not answer for any of his actions."[38] "Man" is the nearest antecedent, but "God" is not much further away. F. Delitzsch, NAB, and NASB agree with the footnote.[39] Whichever way it is read, the complaint is that God does not respond. Either he does not answer human beings, or he does not explain himself to them. Isaiah 55:8-9 is the response to this ancient and modern grievance.

33:14 Contrary to appearances, God does communicate. It may not be through the channels that people expect, but Elihu insisted that God does make his will known.[40]

He Speaks through Dreams (33:15-18). Few would challenge Elihu's premise that God speaks through dreams and visions. Both Old and New Testaments report valid revelations by this means: Abimelech (Gen 20:3), Jacob (Gen 31:11), Laban (Gen 31:24), Solomon (1 Kgs 3:5), Isaiah (6:1), Daniel (7:1), Joseph (Matt 1:20; 2:13), Ananias (Acts 9:10), Peter (Acts 10:9-16), and Paul (Acts 16:9-10). Despite scriptural examples, modern believers may not agree that dreams come from Go, because there is available to us now the inscripturated revelation, which was not the case with the biblical characters. The prophets (Deut 13:1-5; Jer 23:25-32; Zech 10:2) and Jude (8) warn of false and filthy dreamers (KJV).

33:15 Undistracted by the phenomenal world around, one is more receptive to the supernatural in the sleepy depths of night. Structurally

---

[38] By repointing דבריו from a plural noun with possessive suffix to a *qal* active participle with dative suffix, "who speaks to him," M. Dahood has a solution to this awkward expression ("The Dative Suffix in Job 33:13," *Bib* 63 [1982]: 258-59).

[39] F. Delitzsch, *The Book of Job* (Grand Rapids: Eerdmans, 1949), II:221. The RSV reads "my words." Cf. Habel, *Job*, 455. The AB has "your words." The NEB recasts line *b* to read, "No one can answer his arguments."

[40] "One way, now another" is an example of the x + 1 motif (cf. 5:19; 33:29; Ps 62:11[12]. The Masoretes divided the verse so that "one way" is in the first stich and "now another/two" in the second.

this verse is unusual. "Dream" and "vision" would ordinarily be in separate lines (e.g., Isa 29:7; Dan 4:5; Joel 2:28; Acts 2:17), but they are together in the first. Lines *b* and *c* then parallel each other with the key words "deep sleep" and "slumber."

33:16 The NIV has followed an emended Hebrew text to arrive at "terrify."[41] Others read "visions" instead of "warnings," but that involves changing consonants, a practice resisted by those with a high view of the text.[42] The reading "warnings" finds support in the simple fact that warnings follow. Earlier in this book Eliphaz spoke of a frightening vision (4:12-14).

33:17 Verses 17-19 give the purpose for such dreams and visions. "Wrongdoing" is literally "a deed,"[43] referring to a practice God wants people to stop, one which arises from "pride."[44] Line *b* reads literally, "And pride from a man he/it will hide," which Gordis,[45] followed by Hartley,[46] understands as amounting to separating people from their pride (cf. Neh 4:5[3:37], where the same verb is parallel to "blot out).

33:18 Freedom from "doing" (wrong) and "pride" will lead to deliverance from the "pit" or "grave"[47] and from death by "sword."[48] Elihu has not yet stated his theology explicitly, but this verse indicates that he is following the same line as the others, that is, that bad behavior leads to destruction.

He Speaks through Suffering (33:19-22). The second avenue of com-

---

[41] The MT has יַחְתֹּם, "he sealed," from the root חתם (so KJV, ASV, NASB, NJPS). By changing only vowels the NIV has read יְחִתֵּם, "terrify," from the root חתת with pronominal suffix, "them."

[42] Dhorme (*Job,* 494-95) with the support of the LXX's εἴδεσιν φόβου, changed מֹסָרָם, a defectively written plural, to מַרְאִים, "apparitions/visions."

[43] As much as one of the many synonyms for "sin" is expected and desired here, it is simply מַעֲשֶׂה, "a deed." BHS suggests via haplography that this came from an original מִמַּעֲשֵׂהוּ, "from his deeds."

[44] Not the usual word for "pride," גֵּוָה occurs only in Job 22:29; 33:17; Jer 13:17; and in Aramaic in Dan 4:37[34]. Hartley (*Job,* 443) believes God wants the deed stopped, but pride may follow "accomplishments," which in turn may lead to selfish acts.

[45] Gordis, *Job,* 375.

[46] Hartley, *Job,* 441.

[47] Cf. NIV footnote.

[48] Here and in 36:12 a quite different reading is possible. "From crossing the River" is in the NIV footnote and something like that in AB, JB, NEB, AAT, REB, and NRSV. For a defense of this, which is adopted by Dhorme and Hartley, see L. Grabbe, *Comparative Philology and the Text of Job* (Missoula, Mont.: Scholars Press, 1977), 103-4. Some, e.g., NAB and NASB, emend שֶׁלַח, "sword," to שְׁאוֹל in order to have a synonym for שַׁחַת ("pit") in line *a*. The Hebrew words that end each stich rhyme, and this may account for the unusual choice.

munication by which God bends people to his will is suffering. Pain is a firm teacher when other gentler means of discipline fail to bring the pupil around to acceptable deportment. Elihu seemed to break off this gruesome catalogue of physical terrors without the resolution that he came to in the preceding section. Was he focused on Job as he described this skinny, bony, wasted man on the brink of death?

33:19 This illustration struck nearer to home for Job. He had experienced the "chastening on a bed of pain" and "constant distress[49] in his bones." As elsewhere "bones" refers to the entire body or to the essence of physical life (7:15; 20:11; 30:17,30).

33:20 The verb "finds repulsive"[50] in line *a* does double duty since line *b* lacks a verb in Hebrew ("loathes" was supplied by the translators). In 6:6-7 Job referred to "tasteless food" he "refused to touch" because it made him "ill." Certainly sickness drives away the appetite, and most sufferers lose weight.

33:21 The poet played on the verb "see" in this verse although it is not very obvious in English. "To nothing" translates *mērō'î*, "from seeing," and "once hidden" translates *lō' ru'û*, "not seen." The point is that the subject is so emaciated that there appears to be no flesh, just skin and bones. The bones, on the other hand, that were more or less invisible because of muscle and fat are now exposed.[51] Job had confessed that this was his condition in 16:8 and 19:20.

33:22 Just as v. 18 concluded the previous section with a reference to death, so v. 22 concludes this section with the same word, "pit/grave." "Messengers of death" translates an unusual word that could be rendered "those who put to death" or simply "killers."[52] One may survive many

---

[49] The written text has רִיב, which the Masoretes read as רוֹב "abundance," similar to 4:14 ("all"). Nevertheless, the *kethib* רִיב "trial, agony" is accepted by most. Habel (*The Book of Job,* 469) translates the verb יכח in line *a* "indict" and explains that "according to Elihu, sickness may be evidence of a 'lawsuit' in the bones and suffering an 'indictment' in the body designed to provoke repentance."

[50] The line can be translated "and his life makes food loathsome to him." The verb זהם is a pure hapax legomenon without any noun cognates in Hebrew or biblical Aramaic. Its meaning is established from the Arabic *zahuma*, "stink," and later Aramaic זוהמא, "dirt/stench." See Delitzsch, *Job,* II:225-26.

[51] "Stick out," MT שֻׁפִּי, should be read as in the *qere*, שֻׁפּוּ, thus making a rhyme with the last word, רֻאוּ. It is from the root שׁפה, which occurs elsewhere only at Isa 13:2 where NIV translates "bare." The unpersuasive translation "transparent" is proposed by H. Rouillard, "Le sens de Job 33,21," *RB* 91 (1984): 30-50.

[52] The word is לַמְמִתִים, which most parse as a *hiphil* participle from the מות, "to die" plus the preposition. The NIV footnote has "to the dead," which comes by reading the first מ as part of the long form of the preposition לְמוֹ.

diseases, but the last illness always delivers the victim to the grave. Elihu's message was not a cheery one.

EXCEPTION ONE: AN ANGEL (33:23-25).   One avenue of deliverance is for an angel to intercede on behalf of the afflicted. Though this is rare, one case in a thousand, it is a possible means of preventing otherwise certain death.

33:23 "Mediator" is one of the words in the list of 16:19-20 that describe the person in whom Job hopes. Others were "witness," "advocate," and "friend." "Angel" is best pictured not as a feminine figure with gossamer wings but as a close friend or relative who agrees to do the duty of kinsman redeemer and stand by the plaintiff's side. The third line in most translations, including NIV, sounds like a rebuke. I prefer the NJPS or AB, "to tell of the man's uprightness," or the NEB, "to expound what he has done right."[53] The angel serves to defend, not condemn, his client. In the fullness of time Jesus, the son of God, came to stand up and represent his believing followers, and he is "much superior to the angels" (Heb 1:4).

33:24 The "gracious" intercessor pleads, presumably before the bar of divine justice on behalf of his friend. His last-minute discovery of a "ransom" saves the condemned from descent into the "grave/pit" (cf. vv. 18,22,24,28,30). "Ransom" is *kōper*, related to verb and noun "atone(ment)" whose even more basic meaning is "cover(ing)" (cf. Yom Kippur, Day of Atonement). Many of the words in these two verses become theologically freighted in the New Testament: angel, mediator, grace, ransom. For the Christian, Christ is the gracious mediator who ransoms the believer's soul from everlasting death.

33:25 The one so ransomed is born again, as it were, with the flesh of a child. The "flesh" that "wasted away to nothing" (v. 21) is somehow "renewed."[54] He himself or his flesh "is restored" so that he is young once more. This dimension of deliverance also has eschatological ramifications—Rev 21:4 encourages the faithful with the promise that "there will be no more death or mourning or crying or pain, for the old order of things has passed away." As Naaman (2 Kgs 5:14) and the ten lepers (Luke 17:12-14) found their flesh renewed, so "the perishable must clothe itself with the imperishable and the mortal with immortality (1 Cor 15:53).

---

[53] Moffatt was wrong by an even greater measure with his "he tells the man his faults." The REB alone has "to expound God's righteousness to man."

[54] This quadrilateral, רֻטֲפַשׁ, is found only here. For theories on the origin of this verb see BDB, 936; Gordis, *Job,* 378; or A. Guillaume, *Studies in the Book of Job* (Leiden: Brill, 1968), 119.

EXCEPTION TWO: REPENTANCE (33:26-28).   Prayer to God is the second possible means of escape from the pit. Since an interceding angel is only a remote possibility ("one out of a thousand"), a more viable option is the one Elihu, less directly than the other three, urged Job to take.

33:26   There is no "if" beginning this verse (as in v. 23), but a condition or subjunctive mood seems necessary in the context, "He may pray."[55] The verb in line *c* is active in Hebrew, with God as the understood subject (found only in line *a*) who "restores to the man his righteousness." The verse teaches, and Elihu intended to say, that prayer will produce divine favor. A vision of God, great joy, and restored right standing are by-products of a renewed relationship.

33:27   Some read "sings to men" rather than "comes to men," a change only of vowels, not consonants, in the original Hebrew.[56] The forgiveness the contrite sinner found prompts a confession before others and a happy declaration that justice was not carried out. The third line is open to alternate interpretations too because the verb can mean "be even/smooth/equal" (as in Prov 3:15; Isa 40:25), hence "what I deserved," or "profit/be worth" (as in Esth 3:8; 5:13).[57]

33:28   The last elements in this list of the good effects of prayer and reconciliation with God are "salvation/redemption" from the "grave" and ongoing "life" in "the light," that is, above ground on earth, as opposed to underground in some "pit." Neither Elihu nor Job were thinking much beyond physical death but, like their contemporaries, they unknowingly heralded important doctrines that would unfold as God progressively revealed his plan of the ages.

GOD'S PURPOSES (33:29-30).   By way of summary, Elihu reminded Job that these routes to redemption are God's provision. Such opportunities are rare but should be grasped.

33:29   "These things" refer back to the "dreams" and "visions" of v. 13 and to the "chastening" and "distress" of v. 19. Such are God's means to bring people to himself and to salvation.[58]

---

[55] Delitzsch has, "If he prayeth to Eloah, He showeth him favour" (*Job*, II:232).The NEB has, "If he entreats God to show him favour."

[56] If יָשֹׁר is from שׁוּר, it means "looks to" (KJV) or "comes" (שׁוּר II in KB), but if from שִׁיר it means "sing" (most translations and commentators).

[57] With NIV are AT, RSV, AB, JB, NAB, NASB, AAT, NJPS, E. Dhorme, N. Tur-Sinai, S. R. Driver and G. B. Gray, *The Book of Job*, ICC (New York: Scribner's, 1921); M. Jastrow, Jr. (*The Book of Job* [Philadelphia: Lippincott, 1920], and Delitzsch. The notion of "profit" is found in the KJV, RV, ASV, Hartley, *Job*, Habel, *Job*, and Gordis, *Job*.

[58] "Twice, even three times" is another x + 1 formula, which, together with the one in v. 14 forms an inclusio for this section where Elihu answered Job's argument (vv. 12-30).

33:30 Four of the key words in vv. 28 and 30 are the same: "soul," "pit," "light," "life." Verse 28 was part of the redeemed's confession; v. 30 is a purpose clause. Dreams and even suffering are gracious gifts from God because they eventuate in salvation from death and in longer (even eternal) life.

(5) Challenge to Job (33:31-33)

> ^{31}"Pay attention, Job, and listen to me;
>   be silent, and I will speak.
> ^{32}If you have anything to say, answer me;
>   speak up, for I want you to be cleared.
> ^{33}But if not, then listen to me;
>   be silent, and I will teach you wisdom."

Elihu's first speech concludes with an explicit command to Job either to be quiet or repent. Twice he said, "Listen to me." Twice he said, "Be silent." And he said, "I will speak" and "teach." Elihu did not leave the man from Uz many alternatives. Clearly Job chose silence because nothing comes between chaps. 33 and 34, the Buzite's second speech.

33:31 Three of the four verbs are imperatives, and the one declarative, "I will speak," is bolstered with an independent personal pronoun, "even I." "Job" in the vocative, taken with the tenor of the verse, serves with v. 1 to enclose the chapter as a unit. One wonders whether Job betrayed a wandering mind, so that Elihu had to demand his attention. Job had heard much of this before, so he can be pardoned for giving less than riveted attention to this young counselor.

33:32 The second stich evidences a tender spirit in Elihu, something that is hard to find in the other three. He really desired Job's vindication. He was hoping, of course, that Job would confess some transgression, thus clearing the way for reconciliation with God. But even to this gentler, less confrontational approach Job did not yield by compromising his own integrity.

33:33 It may be that Elihu waited after v. 32 for Job to respond. When he did not, Elihu simply repeated much of what he had said in v. 31. Near the beginning of this speech (32:7) Elihu nodded to the tradition that "wisdom" should be taught by those in "advanced years." Since it was not, he announced that he himself would "teach wisdom." This key word "wisdom" forms a bridge to the first verse of the next speech, where he addressed the "wise men." Where he presumed they failed, he presumed to speak.

2. Elihu's Second Speech (34:1-37)

Following the pattern set in the first speech, after the introduction Elihu quoted Job, answered his argument, and challenged him to repent. The large central part of the chapter, the substance of Elihu's speech, concentrates on God's attributes of justice, mercy, omniscience, and sovereignty.

(1) Introduction (34:1-4)

¹Then Elihu said:

²"Hear my words, you wise men;
  listen to me, you men of learning.
³For the ear tests words
  as the tongue tastes food.
⁴Let us discern for ourselves what is right
  let us learn together what is good.

Elihu addressed this chapter to "you wise men" (vv. 2,10,34), by which he most likely meant the three friends and Job. He could also have been speaking to a larger unspecified audience as is typical of wisdom literature (Prov 1:5; 8:4). There is a tinge of arrogance as he subtly suggested that, once tested, his advice would prove to be right.

34:1 See comments at 4:1.

34:2 This well-balanced synonymous parallel orders the wise and learned to "listen" and (lit.) "give ear." Similar commands from Elihu are in 32:10; 33:1,31,33; 34:10,16; 37:14.

34:3 Job used this proverb in its interrogative form in 12:11 (see comments there). By quoting it Elihu invited scrutiny of his logic and conclusion. It was his way of saying that he was very sure of himself.

34:4 Elihu invited the others to join him in a mutual search for "justice/right," *mišpāṭ*, and "good," *ṭôb*. It is a rhetorical device that God himself used in Isa 1:18, "Come, let us reason together."

(2) His Statement of Job's Argument (34:5-9)

⁵"Job says, 'I am innocent,
  but God denies me justice.
⁶Although I am right,
  I am considered a liar;
although I am guiltless,
  his arrow inflicts an incurable wound.'
⁷What man is like Job,

who drinks scorn like water?
⁸He keeps company with evildoers;
   he associates with wicked men.
⁹For he says, 'It profits a man nothing
   when he tries to please God.'

According to his pattern, Elihu indicted Job by quoting him and then added some interpretive remarks that further condemned him. As in the first speech (33:8-11) the quotes are not exact but certainly are not out of character with complaints Job made during the debate with the three friends.

34:5 The first quotation is like 33:9. Both of them have a basis in Job's extended apologia in 27:2-6. The verb "I am innocent" (from *ṣādaq*, "to be righteous") came from Job's lips in 9:15; 10:15, but both in conditional sentences. Job referred to his being denied "justice" in 14:3; 19:7. Certainly Job would not have quibbled about whether or not he said something like this.

34:6 The NIV has scanned v. 6 as four lines, but it is only of average length in Hebrew. The cryptic nature of the Hebrew requires all English translations to supply words (note the italics in KJV, ASV, NASB).[59] Literally the words are "against my justice I am (made) a liar, incurable my arrow without sin." "Justice/right" was in v. 5; 14:3; 19:7. "Lie" was in 6:28. In 6:4 Job complained that God's "arrows" were in him (cf. 16:13). He also maintained elsewhere that he was "without sin" (10:7; 13:23; 16:17).

34:7 Job certainly was subjected to "scorn," but it did not move him from his position. Like our expression "water off a duck's back," so he "drinks scorn like water" (cf. 15:16), that is, he is impermeable to criticism.

34:8 The certain words of the second stich help clinch the meaning of two rare ones in the first line, "keeps"[60] and "company."[61] "Associates" is the very common *hālak*, "walk/go," and brings to mind Ps 1:1. Elihu lumped Job in a general way with those who "do evil," with no specific people in mind.

34:9 One more quotation rounds out Elihu's statement of Job's posi-

---

[59] For more discussion of this verse's problems and more alternative readings, see Gordis, *Job*, 386; Dhorme, *Job*, 510-11; Tur-Sinai, *Job*, 476-77.

[60] The finite verb אָרַח, which occurs only here, is related to the well-known noun that means "way" (33:11; 34:11 and nine more times in Job).

[61] Though this spelling of the noun from the root חָבַר ("join") is unique, it is known from the verb and other nominal forms.

tion. Again, these words attributed to Job cannot be found, but the attitude from which they spring certainly evidenced itself in things Job did
say (9:29-31). The author of Ps 73:13 describes having felt the same way
when he said, "Surely in vain have I kept my heart pure; In vain have I
washed my hands in innocence." A few verses later the psalmist tells
what changed his mind. In the same way Job eventually changed his
mind, and so will all those who wonder if it is really worth it to fear God.

(3) His Answer to Job's Argument (34:10-30)

> [10]"So listen to me, you men of understanding.
>   Far be it from God to do evil,
>   from the Almighty to do wrong.
> [11]He repays a man for what he has done;
>   he brings upon him what his conduct deserves.
> [12]It is unthinkable that God would do wrong,
>   that the Almighty would pervert justice.
> [13]Who appointed him over the earth?
>   Who put him in charge of the whole world?
> [14]If it were his intention
>   and he withdrew his spirit and breath,
> [15]all mankind would perish together
>   and man would return to the dust.
>
> [16]"If you have understanding, hear this;
>   listen to what I say.
> [17]Can he who hates justice govern?
>   Will you condemn the just and mighty One?
> [18]Is he not the One who says to kings, 'You are worthless,'
>   and to nobles, 'You are wicked,'
> [19]who shows no partiality to princes
>   and does not favor the rich over the poor,
>   for they are all the work of his hands?
> [20]They die in an instant, in the middle of the night;
>   the people are shaken and they pass away;
>   the mighty are removed without human hand.
>
> [21]"His eyes are on the ways of men;
>   he sees their every step.
> [22]There is no dark place, no deep shadow,
>   where evildoers can hide.
> [23]God has no need to examine men further,
>   that they should come before him for judgment.
> [24]Without inquiry he shatters the mighty
>   and set up others in their place.

^{25}Because he takes note of their deeds,
  he overthrows them in the night and they are crushed.
^{26}He punishes them for their wickedness
  where everyone can see them,
^{27}because they turned from following him
  and had no regard for any of his ways.
^{28}They caused the cry of the poor to come before him,
  so that he heard the cry of the needy.
^{29}But if he remains silent, who can condemn him?
  If he hides his face, who can see him?
  Yet he is over man and nation alike,
^{30} to keep a godless man from ruling,
  from laying snares for the people.

The main part of Elihu's second speech concentrates on God, his immutability, his justice, and his just dealing with offenders. By and large, what Elihu said was good theology, but one wonders if all the references to the wicked, the evildoers, and the strong oppressors of the poor are not veiled allusions to Job. In that regard this fourth friend is little different from the other three who likewise lumped Job with various malefactors who are punished for their crimes on the basis of the inviolable system of divine retribution.

GOD'S UNCHANGING WAYS (34:10-15).   The first of three foci in this section is an undebatable precept. That, in fact, seems to be Elihu's pattern—move from generally accepted, incontestable, theological tenets to ones on which there might be disagreement. He hoped that his hearers would fall into a pattern of agreeing with him so that when he got to the controversial matters, they would concur on those points as well.

34:10   As Elihu frequently did, he urged his listeners to pay him attention (vv. 2,16,34). "Understanding," unlike the "understanding" of v. 16, is *lēbāb*, "heart," a broad term that refers not only to emotions, but also to intellect. Lines *b* and *c* are just five words in Hebrew, but it is impossible to make them into one line in English, so what looks like a tristich is not. The verse recalls v. 5, where Elihu quoted Job saying that God is not essentially just. Job had put it obliquely, not so directly as Elihu here phrased it (cf. Gen 18:25; Deut 32:4; Rom 9:14).

34:11   Here Elihu articulated the doctrine of retribution as clearly as it is done anywhere in the book. The problem is not with the truth of the principle because it is taught from the beginning to the end of the Bible. The problem is in the way these four friends applied it to Job, without exception, with no eye to eschatological retribution, and void of mercy and compassion.

34:12 This verse repeats the sense of v. 10 in a different form ("It is unthinkable" rather than "far be it"). Eliphaz also said the same thing in yet another form in 8:3. Since God is the essence of goodness and justice, he cannot act antithetically to those qualities. Such action, contradictory and unthinkable, would counter his very character.

34:13 This is the first of many verses that sound like God's speeches in chaps. 38–41. They are rhetorical questions, and they address the topic of the creation and governance of the world. Introducing this subject represents a slight turn from the question of God's justice to that of dominion.

34:14 This verse expresses the condition for which v. 15 is the result. Three physical dimensions speak of psychological ones, "heart/intention," "wind/spirit,"[62] and "breath."[63]

34:15 The disastrous result of God's withdrawing "air/wind/breath/spirit" would be instantaneous and universal death. From an ecological point of view, it is breathable air that sustains all life on earth. From a theological point of view, it is God's mercy that sustains the life of rebellious humanity. Imagine an uninhabited earth.

GOD'S SOVEREIGN JUSTICE (34:16-20). The singular verbs indicate that this section is addressed to Job in particular rather than to the friends and Job. It is an elaboration of vv. 10-12 with emphasis on the justice of God and his punishment of the wicked, a theme that the third subsection (vv. 21-30) augments even further.

34:16 Another command to listen opens this section. By qualifying the exhortation with "if you have understanding," Elihu inferred that since Job did not listen, he did not have understanding. It is a subtle way of aggrandizing oneself and belittling the opponent. "What I say" is literally "the sound of my words," a sound that Elihu loved to hear.

34:17 It was inconceivable that anyone "who hates justice" should "govern."[64] Elihu drove Job into an illogical corner by forcing on him the

---

[62] Some NIV translators wanted "spirit" capitalized to indicate the Holy Spirit (cf. Gen 2:7; Pss 51:11[13]; 104:29-30).

[63] Some question the presence of both רוּחַ and נְשָׁמָה together in the second stich and would adjust them so that one is in each line. Hartley (*Job*) does this and drops לֵב, producing a better parallel but treating lightly the Masoretic Text. Following the LXX and Syriac, he also changes the first verb from שִׂים to שׁוּב, *Job,* 453. See also Gordis, *Job,* 388; Rowley, *Job,* 218; Dhorme, *Job,* 515; RSV, JB, NAB, NEB, etc.

[64] The verb חָבַשׁ basically means "bind" with applications to binding wounds (5:18; Isa 30:26; 61:1), saddling donkeys (Num 22:21; 1 Kgs 13:13), and putting on clothes (Exod 29:9; Ezek 16:10). The first and third of these contribute to the meaning "govern," which unfortunately has no OT parallels. Tur-Sinai actually translates "heal" (*Job,* 480). See Gordis, *Job,* 388-89; Dhorme, *Job,* 516. From the idea of "saddling," the NEB has "holds the reins."

contradictory tenets—God rules, yet God is unjust. In ancient Semitic societies the monarch was the supreme court as well as head over the army and controller of the nation's wealth (Exod 18:13; 1 Kgs 3:28).

34:18 As judge in the last court of appeals, God censures and condemns those who themselves should be fair and honorable. "Belial" (the Hebrew word translated "worthless"; cf. 2 Cor 6:15) should not be king nor should a nobleman be "wicked." God, nevertheless, who is over all kings and nobles, may with his ultimate analytic authority so indict them.[65]

34:19 Verse 19 continues the thought of v. 18 and lists two more administrative actions that the sovereign does not do. He does not "lift the face of princes," a well-known Hebrew idiom for "show respect/partiality."[66] Neither is he prejudiced against the poor and in favor of the wealthy.[67] People who inherit or are elected to power are constantly tempted to oblige those who are most able financially to support them. The rich expect privileges from those whom they help into positions of authority. Since no one has put God in power, he is beholden to no one. All people, rich and poor alike, are children of Adam and Eve and the "work of God's hands" (Prov 22:2). God expects his people to emulate him (Lev 19:15).

34:20 The horror of the destruction of the wicked is made more intense by the fact that it happens without notice, "in an instant," and at a time when least expected, "in the middle of the night" (Matt 25:6; Luke 17:34; 1 Thess 5:3). Most understand "people" to be the "nobles," "princes," and "rich" of the preceding lines (cf. 12:2), where "people" is used in that sense). The word "hand" links vv. 19-20. All people are made by God's "hand"; and without a (human) "hand," that is, by God's hand, they perish. As sovereign he controls the beginning and the end of life. Our times also are in his hands (Ps 31:15a[16a]).

GOD'S PUNISHMENT (34:21-30).   God's justice and the execution of punishment on the wicked has been touched on already in this speech, but in this section in particular the focus is on the unpleasant rewards that fall to the unrighteous. First, the emphasis is on the searching eye of the

---

[65] Once past the first word, "Is he not the One who says," the verse is a chiasmus:

    A   to a king

      B   worthless

      B' wicked

    A' to nobles.

[66] The poet played on the word "face," with פְּנֵי שָׂרִים in the first stich and דָל לִפְנֵי in the second.

[67] This rare word (only here and Isa 32:5) is derived from יָשַׁע, "save." These are the "freedmen/freemen" who, in contradistinction to the "bonded/slave" class, are the wealthy.

omniscient God, and then on those whose particular sin was exploiting the poor.

34:21　To the all-seeing eye of God nothing and no one is hidden. In this simple synonymous parallel Elihu restated what Job himself said in 31:4. No human action goes unnoticed.

34:22　The two major words for "darkness"[68] appear here. Nothing interferes with God's ability to see those who would hide under its cover (cf. Ps 139:11-12; Dan 2:22).

34:23　The NIV stands with the NASB and NKJV in not emending "further/yet" to "date/time."[69] The gist of most of the others is that God does not forewarn people of impending judgment.[70] Verse 24a supports the NIV's choice. The point of the translation before us is that people are more than guilty. There is no need for a trial. It is an open-and-shut case. The mind of the divine Judge is made up. The godless are guilty.

34:24　Although "without inquiry" sounds strange, the phrase or one like it appears in 5:9; 9:10; 36:26. This verse, whose meaning is generally agreed on, complements the preceding one where there were questions, especially about the first line. Once more the sovereignty of God is the point. He is the one who sets up and deposes kings and governments (Dan 2:21). Mighty monarchs are like chess pieces to him who controls all.

34:25　A stronger verb is expected in the first line[71] because the two preceding verses have said that God does not need an inquiry, and here it says he "takes note[72] of their deeds."[73] The second line fits well with the "darkness" of v. 22 and the utter ruin the wicked experience in v. 24.

34:26　The godless may try to hide from the divine Judge, but he will discover them, "punish"[74] them, and do it in a place "where everyone can see."[75] This is the third verse in a row describing with different verbs what God will do to the wicked, "shatter," "overthrow," "crush," "punish."

---

[68] חֹשֶׁךְ and צַלְמָוֶת. See discussion at 3:5.

[69] The text had עוֹד, but many assume a מ dropped by haplography from an original מוֹעֵד, "appointed time" (RSV), "date" (AB), "writ" (JB), "appointed days" (NEB), "set times" (AAT).

[70] Gordis (*Job*, 382) followed by Hartley (*Job*, 455) makes "man" the subject of line *a*. Hence, "It is not for man to set a time." There is no word "God" in the text.

[71] Gordis would emend יַכִּיר to יַעֲכֹר, "destroy" (*Job*, 391).

[72] It is for this reason and because of the reference to "night" that some commentators, e.g., E. Kissane (*The Book of Job* [New York: Sheed & Ward, 1946]) and Dhorme (*Job*) and some translations (NAB, NEB, REB) put v. 25 between vv. 23 and 24.

[73] "Deeds" is מַעְבָּדִים, Aramaic for the expected Hebrew מַעֲשִׂים. Daniel 4:37[34] is the only other place it occurs.

[74] Coincidentally this infrequent verb appears again in v. 37 as "clap." Here סָפַק carries the idea of "slap down."

34:27   Up to this point the specific crimes of the wicked are not mentioned, and this verse addresses them only in a general way. Verse 28 is more specific. That "they turned from following him" suggests that they once were more faithful. Always there is less mercy for those who turn from the right road than for those who were never on it. "Have regard for" (*śākal*) includes in its semantic sphere ideas of "understanding/ wisdom/profit." To obey God is the intelligent course to follow as well as the profitable one.

34:28   The particular sin was some sort of oppression, exploitation, or abuse of the "poor" and "needy." This is the most common sin against other people in this book. Although specifics are lacking, the prophets Isaiah and Amos describe in greater detail the devious ways the rich made themselves richer at the expense of the poor who grew poorer (see Amos 2:6-8; 5:12; 8:5-6; Isa 5:22; 32:6-7).

34:29   Verses 29-33 are very difficult Hebrew and are missing from the LXX.[76] The NIV's translation of v. 29 is straightforward, except that it has created a conditional sentence where the Hebrew appears to be a simple declarative, "He remains silent." Lines *a* and *b* are coordinated and synonymous parallels. Job's complaint has been that God is "silent" and "hides his face." Elihu's contention was that that is God's prerogative. The NIV marked line *c* to be read as the first line of a triplet with v. 30, but it does not fit well with either the preceding or the following lines. Much of the interpretation hangs on the flexible preposition *'al*, "over/against/to/toward/on." There is no verb "he is." If the third stich goes with v. 29, then the meaning must be that God treats whole nations and individuals alike.

34:30   Verse 17 spoke to the impropriety of an unjust government, and v. 30 seems to address the same topic. One prerogative of God's oversight of the world is the appointment of kings and leaders, but this verse suggests he prevents the "godless man from ruling" and somehow thwarts those who would trap the common people. Insofar as the verse speaks of government, it connects with v. 29c. Has Elihu never seen or heard of a wicked king, an unjust judge, or a deceitful leader?

---

[75] The second line is quite short, רֹאִים בִּמְקוֹם, "in a place of ones who see." The verse is only partly preserved in the Qumran Targum, but it does begin with a verb, וּרְמָא, "and he will throw." M. Sokoloff, *The Targum to Job from Qumran Cave XI* (Ramat-Gan: Bar-Ilan University, 1974), 76-77.

[76] Gordis's counsel is worth following, "In view of the unconvincing and often un-Hebraic character of the emendations proposed, we prefer to interpret the MT, which is generally superior to the alternatives, in addition to possessing the basic advantage of being a datum and not merely a hypothesis" (*Job*, 392).

(4) His Challenge to Job to Repent (34:31-33)

[31]"Suppose a man says to God,
  'I am guilty but will offend no more.
[32]Teach me what I cannot see;
  if I have done wrong, I will not do so again.'
[33]Should God then reward you on your terms,
  when you refuse to repent?
You must decide, not I;
  so tell me what you know.

The difficulties of these verses lie not so much with rare or unknown words but with the way known words are strung together and the multiplicity of meanings that some of them allow. Whatever the specific translation is, the point of this section is a challenge from Elihu to Job to repent.[77] The invitation to speak what he "knows," though generous sounding, was rejected because Elihu said in v. 35 that Job spoke "without knowledge." The student of Job must use with caution the somewhat tentative translation and commentary on these verses.[78]

34:31 Since there is no apodosis to the clause that constitutes vv. 31-32, the translators have "suppose" rather than "if." The hypothetical case Elihu had in mind was, of course, Job. By this convoluted grammar Elihu suggested that Job say[79] the words, "I am guilty."[80]

34:32 The repeat-after-me clauses that Elihu indirectly suggested to Job continue through v. 32. In view of the way God "taught" Job in the theophany and the way Job repented with the words, "now my eyes have seen you" (42:5), Elihu's model prayer was answered. While the first part of this prayer could be prayed by Job, he gave no hint that he would confess any "wrong" or discontinue his complaint against God.

34:33 Elihu's ultimatum, again put indirectly, was that Job relinquish his position, abandon his adversarial posture toward God, and submit, as Eliphaz had suggested in 22:21-30. There are also some parallel

---

[77] It must be noted, however, that "to repent" was supplied by the NIV translators as an object for the verb "refuse."

[78] The surprising absence of footnotes in the NIV indicates no strongly supported alternatives in the final editorial committee.

[79] "Says," הֶאָמַר, looks like the *qal* perfect with interrogative prefix, "Does he say?" (Cf. NKJV.) Several commentators move the words around so that the problematic ה is on the end of God, אֱלוֹהַ, rather than the simple אֵל (Tur-Sinai, Dhorme, Gordis, Habel, Hartley; JB, NAB, NEB, NIV reflect this change as well).

[80] "I am guilty" translates נָשָׂאתִי, which, apart from this context, means "I will lift up" but often takes some synonym of "sin" as the object (BDB, 671).

key words between these two challenges to Job. Eliphaz's "accept instruction" (22:22) is the same word as Elihu's "teach" (v. 32). "What
you decide on" in 22:28 parallels "you must decide" here in v. 33. Elihu
put the heavy burden of making a decision on Job and then demanded an
answer. Obviously Job did not respond because Elihu simply turned his
attention to the others when he was met with silence by the man from
Uz.

(5) He Condemns Job for Not Repenting (34:34-37)

> ³⁴"Men of understanding declare,
>   wise men who hear me say to me,
> ³⁵'Job speaks without knowledge;
>   his words lack insight.'
> ³⁶Oh, that Job might be tested to the utmost
>   for answering like a wicked man!
> ³⁷To his sin he adds rebellion;
>   scornfully he claps his hands among us
>   and multiplies his words against God."

Elihu turned from the unrepentant Job to the three friends or to anyone
who would listen and asked them to affirm him in his guilty verdict. Then
before concluding this speech he leveled an imprecation on Job, reminding all once more of Job's arrogance toward them and God.

34:34 These words introduce the quotation of v. 35, which some
continue to the end of the chapter.[81] Elihu naturally assumed himself to
be among the "men of understanding" and a "wise man."

34:35 The judgment was that Job was not a wise man because "he
speaks without knowledge" and "insight."[82] A similar assessment closes
chap. 35 and opens chap. 38.

34:36 Two small problems affect this verse. First, the opening word,
'ābî, looks like "my father," which is unlikely but is treated as an inter-

---

[81] So AB, JB, NEB, NASB.

[82] Once past the name "Job," v. 35 is a well-balanced chiasmus:

A   Not with knowledge
  B   he speaks, יְדַבֵּר
  B'   his words, וּדְבָרָיו
A'   not with insight.

jection, "Oh that."[83] Second, "like" usually translates the preposition *kĕ*, but the majority of Hebrew manuscripts have *bĕ*, "in."[84] Despite these irregularities and uncertainties, nearly all agree on the central idea of the verse. It is a malediction pronounced on Job that he continue suffering as penalty for his failure to repent.

34:37 The two common words for "sin" illustrate how Elihu viewed Job's compounding of his godless condition. The second line in Hebrew is simply, "Between us he claps." The rest is interpolation by the translators. The last line of this tristich condemns Job because he "multiplies his words against God." As a matter of fact, Job has not spoken for some time, although he said enough earlier to justify this charge. It is Elihu who has been multiplying words and who will continue to do so uninterrupted for three more chapters. The courtesy with which Elihu began his speeches has worn thin, and he has become nearly as confrontational and cruel as the other three.

3. Elihu's Third Speech (35:1-16)

Typically, Elihu began his third speech with quotations from Job and then proceeded to answer his protests. The speech also closes with quotations from Job. The large middle section concentrates on God's lack of response to the needs of those who are prompted by impure motives.

(1) His Statement of Job's Argument (35:1-3)

¹**Then Elihu said:**

²**"Do you think this is just?**
 You say, 'I will be cleared by God.'
³**Yet you ask him, 'What profit is it to me,**
 and what do I gain by not sinning?'

Elihu chose two quotations that are contradictory. The first is typical of Job's protestations of innocence. The second is typical of his argument that God seems not to punish the wicked. To be "cleared by God" he must continue his good behavior. On the other hand he also was con-

---

[83] Suggestions to emend אָבִי include אִיּוֹב, "Job," אֲבוֹי, a synonym for אוֹי, "woe" in Prov 23:29, and בִּי, translated "please" in Num 12:11; 1 Kgs 3:26, and elsewhere. M. Dahood relates it to Ugaritic *ʾēbî*, "foe" ("Ugaritic-Phoenician Forms in Job 34,36," *Bib* 62 [1981]: 548-50). Gordis believes it is some form of the verb אָבָה, "want/wish/be willing" (*Job*, 395). The KJV has "my desire."

[84] The KJV has "because of *his* answers for wicked men."

vinced that God was not rewarding behavior good or bad.

35:1   See comments at 4:1.

35:2   Elihu began his speech with a question about the correctness or logic of two of Job's major contentions. In so many words Job said, "My righteousness is from God," paraphrased in the NIV as, "I will be cleared by God" (10:7; 13:19; 27:5).[85]

35:3   Job's statements in 7:20; 9:29-31; 34:9 are the background for these words put into his mouth by Elihu. He said that since God does not reward right or punish wrong, there is no point in being good (cf. Ps 73:13).[86]

(2) His Answers to Job's Argument (35:4-15)

[4]"I would like to reply to you
   and to your friends with you.
[5]Look up at the heavens and see;
   gaze at the clouds so high above you.
[6]If you sin, how does that affect him?
   If your sins are many, what does that do to him?
[7]If you are righteous, what do you give to him,
   or what does he receive from your hand?
[8]Your wickedness affects only a man like yourself,
   and your righteousness only the sons of men.

[9]"Men cry out under a load of oppression;
   they plead for relief from the arm of the powerful.
[10]But no one says, 'Where is God my Maker,
   who gives songs in the night,
[11]who teaches more to us than to the beasts of the earth
   and makes us wiser than the birds of the air?'
[12]He does not answer when men cry out
   because of the arrogance of the wicked.
[13]Indeed, God does not listen to their empty plea;
   the Almighty pays no attention to it.
[14]How much less, then, will he listen
   when you say that you do not see him,

---

[85] The phrase could also be "more righteous than God." See NIV footnote. But this Job never had claimed, although some might infer it for his criticisms of God's apathy. So KJV, ASV, NAB, NASB, NJPS.

[86] As the NIV footnote indicates, the preposition is followed by a second person suffix, "you," not "me." The easiest explanation of this irregularity is to take it as an editorial "you." Psalm 103:3b-5 has a similar problem. The 1978 edition of the NIV had "my" six times, but the 1984 edition has "your," following the Hebrew in those places.

> that your case is before him
>   and you must wait for him,
> ¹⁵and further, that his anger never punishes
>   and he does not take the least notice of wickedness.

In this reply to the quotations from Job, Elihu posited that God cares little about human behavior. He drew a picture of a dispassionate, distant deity who does not respond to the wicked even when they are in trouble and cry out to him. Since he put Job in that category, it was quite reasonable that Job received no satisfaction from God.

35:4 There is no question that Elihu addressed these words to Job, Eliphaz, Bildad, and Zophar. At the beginning of chap. 32 it was clear that Elihu thought all parties were mistaken.

35:5 Elihu bade all of them search the skies, as if to remind them that God is high above the earth but also invisible. In Gen 15:5 God directed Abram's attention skyward to impress him with the number of stars (cf. 22:12). The poet's choice of the less common word *šaḥaqîm*, "clouds," which God will use in 38:37, also points forward to those chapters that speak of God's grand and mysterious creation (36:28; 37:18,21).

35:6 Along with v. 7, Elihu asked rhetorically what difference it made to God whether people were bad or good. The two halves of this verse are synonymous parallels using two common words for "sin" and two common words for "do." The expected answer to such questions is negative, "Your sin does not affect God."

35:7 Likewise, good behavior does not involve "giving" anything to God or his "receiving" anything. The verse completes the merismus (see comment on 1:20) with "righteous" complementing "sin." These questions echo Eliphaz in 22:2-3 (cf. Rom 11:35).

35:8 In a sense Elihu answered his own questions by saying that "your wickedness" or "your righteousness" has an effect only on "yourself." It does not affect God, as v. 6a said in question form.[87] "Sons of men" (*ben 'ādām*) can simply be the synonym of "man" (*'îš*), but in this context Elihu said that Job's deportment affected Job himself and his community, but not his God.

GOD IS DETACHED FROM HUMAN WOE (35:9-15). The God Elihu described is not typically beneficent but one who responds only to his sincere devotees. His God has no time for those who call only when they are

---

[87] There are no verbs in this verse. All translations supply them as the italics in ASV, e.g., indicate. They have *may hurt* and *may profit*.

in trouble, who use their shallow faith only in emergencies, and who have no time for God when times are good. Elihu put Job in that category but castigated him even further for charging God with elusiveness and failure to exact justice.

35:9 Without giving any details, Elihu illustrated the point of this section by telling in a general way of people who oppress others. As poetry, the verse is a balanced parallelism, but the poet also incorporated a play on the root *rbb*, which forms the basis of "load" and "powerful," the first and last words of the verse in Hebrew.[88]

35:10 To whomever they "cry" and "plead," they do not think of him as "God my Maker." The second line begins a series of three clauses that describe what God does for his followers. First, he "gives songs in the night," an unusual epithet in this context, which suggests singing is what a true believer might do in times of trouble (cf. Pss 42:8[9]; 77:6; Acts 16:25).[89]

35:11 Second, he "teaches"[90] more to people than to animals.[91] Third, he "makes us wiser" than the birds. These two sentences are not very profound, but they are one more hint of the upcoming revelation of God, who will interrogate Job about the "beasts of the earth" and the "birds of the air" (38:39–39:27).

35:12 This verse is a classical statement of the traditional wisdom view of the prayer of the ungodly. Unless it is a cry of repentance, God does not listen. Until now in this section we have not read that those who cry out are wicked and arrogant. But these especially do not deserve to be heard, regardless of the hardship that has befallen them (Prov 1:28-30). A comma after the first line would make this interpretation clearer—people are not crying out because of the wicked; rather, because of the

---

[88] "Load" is רֹב, and "powerful" is רַבִּים.

[89] See L. Grabbe, *Comparative Philology and the Text of Job* (Missoula, MT: Scholars Press, 1977), 108-10, for a discussion of the זְמִרוֹת, which is also read as "strength" (AB, NJPS, NRSV), "succour" (Kissane), "protection" (NEB), or "hope" (GNB). For an eloquent defense and elaboration on "songs," see S. Terrien, *Job, Poet of Existence* (Indianapolis: Bobbs-Merrill, 1977), 205-7.

[90] This rare verb אָלַף occurs elsewhere only in 15:5; 33:33; Prov 22:25. Together with חכם it contributes to the chiastic structure of v. 11.

    A   He teaches us
        B   more than the beasts of the earth
        B' more than the birds of the air
    A' he makes us wise.

[91] Jastrow (*Job*) and Pope (*Job*, 264-65) read מִן in the sense of בְּ, thus producing "who teaches us through/by the beasts . . . through/by the birds." The NIV footnotes indicate that this interpretation was held by a minority of the translation committee.

arrogance of the wicked people, God does not answer them when they cry out.[92] The friends judged Job to be "arrogant" even if not "wicked."

35:13 The "plea" of the wicked is the Hebrew form for "vanity/noth-ingness/no count."[93] The word occurs twice in the Ten Commandments: "You shall not take the name of the LORD your God *in vain*, . . . you shall not bear *false* witness" (Deut 5:11,20, NASB). Such a prayer for help without the accompanying reverence and obedience is almost like break-ing the third Commandment.

35:14 Despite the four lines in the NIV, this verse is hardly more than average length in Hebrew. The first seven English words translate one Hebrew particle, 'ap, often rendered "surely" or left untranslated. What Elihu did here was rephrase three of Job's complaints that the friends would deem arrogant, grounds for God's refusal to respond. (1) In 9:11 Job said, "I cannot see him." (2) In several places Job claimed his legal right (10:2; 13:6,18; 23:4; 27:2; 31:35).[94] (3) In several places Job spoke of his hope[95] in God (6:8; 13:15; 14:14).[96]

35:15 Elihu added a fourth and fifth excerpt from Job's speeches to complete this list of reasons why God did not and will not respond to Job. In 9:24 and 21:17 Job had charged God with turning a blind eye to justice. In 12:6 and 21:17 he complained that God overlooked all manner of "wickedness."[97]

(3) His Insult to Job (35:16)

> [16]So Job opens his mouth with empty talk;
> without knowledge he multiplies words."

35:16 Such an insult recalls the way the other three friends opened some of their speeches to Job (8:2; 11:3; 15:2; 18:2). In 27:12 Job had accused his friends of "meaningless talk"—"empty" in this verse. It was

---

[92] See E. Smick, who makes this cogent suggestion to avoid ambiguity ("Job" *EBC* [Grand Rapids: Zondervan, 1988], 1016-1017).

[93] See note at 7:3, where this term first appeared.

[94] Here "case" is רִין, not מִשְׁפָּט or רִיב as in the verses cited.

[95] The unusual term here is תְּחֹלֵל, usually taken from חוּל, "travail/writhe/wait in an-guish." This form is a *polel*, but a *hithpolel* in Ps 37:7 has this meaning. Or it may be an anomalous form of יָהֵל, which always means "hope/wait." For an altogether different read-ing of the verse as an imperative, see Gordis, *Job*, 398, 402-3.

[96] In these last two references the verb is יָהֵל; in 6:8 the noun is תִּקְוָה.

[97] For the reading "wickedness" the NIV note points to the support of Symmachus and Theodotian who translated παραπτώματι and παραπτώματα, respectively, and the Vul-gate, which has *scelus*. This involves adding one letter to the unknown בַּפֶּשׁ to get בְּפֶשַׁע.

Elihu's chance to turn this phrase against Job, and he did, although Job has not said anything since Elihu began speaking one hundred verses ago. Thus Elihu showed himself to be of the same mold as the other three. He did not charge Job with social crimes, but he repeatedly indicted Job for attitudinal sins that caused his troubles.

4. Elihu Declares God's Goodness and Power (36:1–37:24)

The first third of this last speech of Elihu represents his last attempt to persuade Job that his losses and sickness are God's way of urging him to repent. It has no recorded effect. The last two-thirds of the speech prepare Job and us for the revelation of God in the whirlwind. By the time chap. 37 comes to an end, the so-far silent Almighty is waiting in the wings to silence all parties and make his own points, which are beyond dispute.

(1) Introduction of a New Tack (36:1-4)

¹Elihu continued:

²"Bear with me a little longer and I will show you
   that there is more to be said in God's behalf.
³I get my knowledge from afar;
   I will ascribe justice to my Maker.
⁴Be assured that my words are not false;
   one perfect in knowledge is with you.

The new tack that Elihu took was to claim the authority of God as he spoke. Eliphaz had done something similar when in his first speech he reported what had come to him in a (divine?) vision (4:12-16). The tone smacks of arrogance, a sin he indirectly accused Job of in 35:12. Insofar as he went on to speak of God's greatness, his veracity cannot be questioned, but scattered through the speech are innuendoes that indicate his assessment of Job's problem has not changed.

36:1 The introductory formula is similar (but not identical) to 27:1; 29:1, where Job resumed talking apparently after waiting for a response. Chapter 35 did not end with questions or challenges to Job, but perhaps Elihu thought what he said was adequate to provoke something from Job. If it did, it is not recorded.

36:2 "Bear with me a little longer" is the most popular reading of these words, but the verb ordinarily means "surround," which does not fit well here.[98] The "little" is another of Elihu's hyperboles because this is the longest of his four speeches!

36:3 The two lines are hardly parallel, although they do suit the context in a general way. "From afar" points to a heavenly source for his knowledge, and "justice" (*ṣedeq*) is a broad word that encompasses "right/righteousness/truth" as well as "justice (cf. RSV, AB, NAB, NASB). In a poetic way Elihu claimed that what he said was right because it came from God, who is right.

36:4 Elihu's presumption reached an apex with this verse in which he claimed freedom from falsehood and "perfect knowledge," a phrase he applied to God in 37:16. The singular object pronoun, "you," makes it clear that Elihu spoke directly to Job, the one who was called "blameless" by God in 1:8; 2:3, using the same verbal root, and who called himself "blameless" with the term spelled exactly as it is here (12:4).

(2) God's Retribution to the Good and the Bad (36:5-15)

⁵"God is mighty, but does not despise men;
   he is mighty, and firm in his purpose.
⁶He does not keep the wicked alive
   but gives the afflicted their rights.
⁷He does not take his eyes off the righteous;
   he enthrones them with kings
   and exalts them forever.
⁸But if men are bound in chains,
   held fast by cords of affliction,
⁹he tells them what they have done—
   that they have sinned arrogantly.
¹⁰He makes them listen to correction
   and commands them to repent of their evil.
¹¹If they obey and serve him,
   they will spend the rest of their days in prosperity
   and their years in contentment.
¹²But if they do not listen
   they will perish by the sword
   and die without knowledge.

¹³"The godless in heart harbor resentment;
   even when he fetters them, they do not cry for help.

---

[98] In Aramaic כתר means "wait." A. C. M. Blommerde offers with support the novel and viable, "Form a circle around me, a young man" (*Northwest Semitic Grammar and Job* [Rome: Pontifical Biblical Institute, 1969], 124). זְעֵיר ("little/young") occurs in this form only here and in Isa 28:10,13.

¹⁴**They die in their youth,**
  among male prostitutes of the shrines.
¹⁵**But those who suffer he delivers in their suffering;**
  he speaks to them in their affliction.

If this is the "more to be said on God's behalf" (v. 2), it is disappointing because essentially Elihu reiterated the tired, old theology of retribution—God will kill the wicked and preserve the righteous. In the middle
of this section (vv. 8-12) is a discourse on the opportunities that come to
the wicked by way of divine discipline, designed to turn them from the
broad road that leads to destruction to the narrow one that leads to life.
To ignore these lifesaving warnings means they will perish just as if they
had never been given a chance to repent. All these generalized statements
are, of course, aimed directly at Job. In Elihu's opinion he is that unrepentant, arrogant sinner whom God is judging and warning.

36:5 The lack of an object in Hebrew on the verb "despise" prompted the NIV translators to supply "men."[99] Others move the words around,
eliminating one of the occurrences of "mighty" to come up with "God is
mighty in strength [firm]; he does not despise the pure [the second
mighty] in heart [purpose].[100] As it stands, the meaning is that God is not
negatively predisposed. He is resolute, but not prejudiced.

36:6 In this antithetic parallelism Elihu restated a well worn maxim
about God's dealings with the evil and the good. The former are not
spared, while the latter receive legal protection. The verse epitomizes the
title of this section—"God's retribution to the good and the bad." These
points were made by the other friends from the beginning of the debate
(4:8-9; 5:15-16, etc.).

36:7 Verse 7 continues with three good things that God does for
good people. He continually watches over them (Deut 32:10; Ps 121:3-
8).[101] He sets them on royal thrones (Ps 113:8; 1 Pet 2:9). He "exalts
them forever" (1 Sam 2:7-8; Ps 41:12[13]). As true and proper as all this
sounds, we must not forget that Job's case is an exception to these generalizations. Through no fault of his own Job, who had been honored and

---

[99] D. A. Diewert maintains that the verb is מאס II, "melt," hence "he does not cower."
("Job xxxvi 5 and the Root *m's* II," *VT* 39 [1989]: 77).

[100] Dhorme (*Job*) proposed this emendation and rearrangement. It involves moving כֹּה
into the first line and emending the second כַּבִּיר to בַּר (539-40). He is followed by Pope,
Job, Hartley, *Job*, AAT, and others. For more variations, most of which simply shorten the
verse, see H. Rowley, *Job*, NCB (Grand Rapids: Eerdmans, 1976), 227-28.

[101] Contrary to the Masoretic placement of the *athnach*, the verb יֹשֵׁב, "seat," should go
with כִּסֵּא, "throne." The KJV, RSV, etc. preserve the Masoretic scansion.

exalted, was now despised and rejected. Rightly Job felt that God had re-moved his protective eye, but we who have read the beginning and end of the book know otherwise.

36:8   Verses 8-12 contain a series of conditions and results. Note "if" at the beginning of vv. 8,11,12 to mark the causes. The apodoses or ef-fects are in vv. 9-10,11b,12b (though the word "then" is only implied, not written). The first condition is "affliction" that binds and ties those need-ing divine discipline. It is like the foreign invaders God periodically sent during the Judges era to bring the people to repentance and back to the worship of Yahweh (Ps 107:10-16).

36:9   Afflictions are warnings or lessons, Elihu said, to teach people about sin (vv. 9-10a) and subsequently to move them to contrition (v. 10b). "Arrogantly" translates the simple verb "to be great" in the reflex-ive stem, hence, either "they outdo themselves in sinning" or "they exalt themselves with their sins." Either way it displays an attitude that is re-pugnant to God who alone is "great and greatly to be praised" (Ps 48:1[2], KJV).

36:10   "Correction" and "bound" (v. 8) and "fetters" (v. 13) are from similar roots, *ysr* and *'sr*,[102] evidencing an interesting process in the an-cient Semitic mind regarding the purpose of imprisonment. Incarceration is intended not merely to punish but to teach obedience and prompt re-morse. This is all similar to what Elihu said in 33:16-22 and is well illus-trated by the repentance of the wicked King Manasseh in the apocryphal prayer attributed to him (Pr Man 10-11, REB):

> Bowed with many an iron chain,
>
> .   .   .   .
> I have provoked your anger,
>
> .   .   .   .
> My heart submits to you,
> imploring your great goodness.

36:11   Both the conditions and the results are included in v. 11. Us-ing the imperative, Eliphaz preached a similar sermon in 22:21-28. Both represent the straightforward, uncomplicated message of the prophets and the apostles and every evangelist in the church—repent and be saved. The message is true. Elihu was orthodox. But Job was not an unregener-ate sinner who needed to hear this message. Like many a good gospel message, it was wasted, as it were, on the saved rather than being well invested and preached to the lost. A trained athlete does not need to be

---

[102] Cf. "chains" and "be warned" in Ps 2:3,10.

told the value of diet and exercise.

36:12 Verse 11 is the positive side of the preacher's message; v. 12 is the negative. Not only is there abundant life to gain both now and forever, but there is physical and spiritual death to avoid by submission to God. Verses 11 and 12 begin with the same words ("obey" and "listen" both translate šāmaʿ), but v. 12 has the particle "not." Instead of good days and contented years, the result of disobedience and refusal is ignorance (4:21) and a violent death.[103]

36:13 Verses 13-14 are an expansion on the last two lines of v. 12. While he was thinking of Job in particular, Elihu spoke in a general way of why the wicked perish. First, they are angry, and second, "they do not cry for help" because such crying is an evidence of weakness, the antithesis of the pride that otherwise characterizes their attitude toward others. They are slow learners, not realizing that the "fetters" are there to teach them lessons about the most important things in the world—God, sin, life, and death.

36:14 "They die in their youth" answers to "die without knowledge" (v. 12), since those two attributes often go together. The second line introduces a specific detail that seems out of order in this generalized alarm to the unconverted. Deuteronomy 23:17[18] and nine other places[104] have this term that the KJV translated "sodomite"[105] in the masculine and "whore" or "harlot" in the feminine.[106] RSV used "cult prostitute" in these places, but here, like most others, it paraphrased with "their life ends in shame."[107] The NIV left untranslated the word ḥayyātām, meaning "their life," and expanded the last word, baqqĕdēšîm, "among male prostitutes," with the addition "of the shrines." A prostitute could serve worshipers at the shrine of a fertility deity for only a limited number of years, and it is likely that sexually transmitted diseases claimed the lives

---

[103] The NIV footnote alternative, "will cross the River," points to a difficulty with the verb-noun combination found here and in 33:18. בְּשֶׁלַח יַעֲבֹרוּ is literally "by a weapon they pass (away)." The Qumran Targum supports the traditional reading with its יפלון בחרבא. But some (Dhorme, *Job*, 542; Pope, *Job*, 250, 269; J. Smith in AT; NEB; GNB; AAT) read שֶׁלַח as "channel/canal/river" or "Sheol." It still refers to the demise of the wicked, only the figure is one of crossing a river to the netherworld rather than death by violent means.

[104] First Kings 14:24; 15:12; 22:46[47]; 2 Kgs 23:7 (all masc.); Gen 38:21-22; Hos 4:14 (all fem.); Deut 23:17[18] has both masc. and fem.

[105] Pope translated "sodomite" in this verse. Habel *(Job)* has "perverts."

[106] See J. Oswalt, "Prostitution, 4" in *ZPEB* 4:911-12 (with bibliography).

[107] Some commentators believe Elihu made a connection between dying young and the profession of cult prostitution. So Duhm, J. T. Marshall, *The Book of Job*, AC (Philadelphia: American Baptist Publishing Society., 1904).

of many, then as now (Prov 6:26; 7:23).

36:15 Elihu brought this section to a close as he had v. 6 by referring to "those who suffer/are afflicted." "He speaks" translates the same
idiom as v. 10, "He makes them listen." Literally it is "he opens their
ears."[108] What he left out is the necessary response of the afflicted if they
expected to participate in God's benefactions. That is the place where he
put Job, that is, suffering, but not yet repenting.

(3) God's Discipline to Job (36:16-21)

> [16]"He is wooing you from the jaws of distress
>   to a spacious place free from restriction,
>   to the comfort of your table laden with choice food.
> [17]But now you are laden with the judgment due the wicked;
>   judgment and justice have taken hold of you.
> [18]Be careful that no one entices you by riches;
>   do not let a large bribe turn you aside.
> [19]Would your wealth
>   or even all your mighty efforts
>   sustain you so you would not be in distress?
> [20]Do not long for the night,
>   to drag people away from their homes.
> [21]Beware of turning to evil,
>   which you seem to prefer to affliction.

In one sense these are the last words of the four friends to Job because
with the next verse starts the introduction to the theophany. Even though
37:14 reads, "Listen to this, Job," it is here in 36:16-21 that Job received
his last rebuke and serious summons to repent. As usual, the words were
framed as if from God, who "is wooing you" (v. 16). As the speech went
on, Elihu was hard on Job, evaluating him as "laden with judgment" (v.
17), still in love with wealth (vv. 18-19), and prone to evil (vv. 20-21).
Some of the translation is so uncertain that the NAB completely skipped
vv. 16-20. The NIV footnote indicates that vv. 18-20 are uncertain.

36:16 The pronouns are singular; therefore the "he" is God and the
"you" is Job. Elihu wanted Job to interpret his troubles as God's nudg-
ing him toward repentance. It is a doctrine that comes logically right after that of theological retribution. Evil merits punishment. Good brings
blessing. But repentance can turn wrath into wealth, curse into grace,
and death into life, or, in the poetry of the middle line, from "restric-

---

[108] Within v. 15 the poet played with the words חלץ, "deliver," and לחץ, "affliction."

tion" to "a spacious place."[109]

36:17   The contrast and connection made by the verb "laden with" is immediately obvious. Job's current situation was like that of a condemned criminal at the bar of divine justice. A simple act of repentance would bring him to the "comfort" and plenty of v. 16c. Since Job refused to repent, however, Elihu saw his friend in the grip of the law, the inviolable law of a God who always gives people what they deserve.

36:18   Less obvious to the English reader is the connection between God's "wooing" (v. 16) and the "enticement" that comes from riches (v. 18), but the root words are the same. It is like the picture of the rich ruler who found himself having to choose between Christ and money (Luke 18:18-23). Elihu's admonition does not apply to Job. Though Job had been a very rich man, the text nowhere indicates that he thought that somehow wealth, his own or someone else's, was the solution to his problem. The NIV has emended the first word from "wrath" (KJV, ASV, NJPS) to "be careful."[110] The word, occurring only here, translated "riches" is defined by its well-established counterpart "bribe" in the second line.[111]

36:19   All versions must rearrange the seven Hebrew words and add English ones to produce a translation that makes sense. Word for word it reads, "Will he arrange your wealth (*or* cry)[112] not in distress[113] and all the powers of strength?" By adding "you" twice and "your" once and moving the clauses around, the NIV has produced a creditable translation.[114] The upshot of the verse then is the simple reminder to Job that he could not save himself, certainly not by riches and strength.

36:20   The second line of v. 20 is difficult. Its literal translation is, "To go up peoples under them *or* in their place." In a vague way it reminds of

---

[109] Both צָר, "distress" or "narrow place" (cf. Num 22:26), and מוּצָק, "restriction," are the opposite of רַחַב, "spacious place."

[110] A change of vowels, not consonants, is enough to change חֵמָה, "wrath," into חֲמֵה, a verb with Arabic cognates that means "be careful." See Dhorme, *Job*, 546-47. RSV and NASB include both the "wrath" and the "beware."

[111] The pausal form שָׁפֶק probably is an alternate spelling of שֶׂפֶק found in 20:22 as a noun and as a verb in 1 Kgs 20:10.

[112] The noun שׁוּעֲךָ may be related to שׁוֹעַ ("rich, noble") as in 34:19, but no emendation is required for the NIV translation. Hartley (*Job*, 472) read this word as יְשׁוּעָה, "deliverance," with the comment, "The meaning of v. 19 is virtually impossible to establish. Any suggestion is tentative." For a survey of other options see Rowley, *Job*, 231-32.

[113] The KJV read בְצָר not as "in distress" but as בֶּצֶר, "gold," as in 22:24-25.

[114] While literal translations (e.g., ASV) are nearly unintelligible, paraphrases (e.g., JB) are impossible to explain. The latter has for this verse:
Prosecute the rich, not merely the penniless;
strong-armed men as well as those who are powerless.

24:14-17, where Job complained that criminals operated at night. It is hard to imagine that Elihu suspected that Job would actually resort to nocturnal kidnapping, which is what the verse in the NIV seems to warn against. It is better to understand that Elihu cautioned Job about longing for the night as he did in 3:3-6 because it is a time when people disappear.[115]

36:21 The concluding verse is Elihu's final warning to Job. He cautioned him against "turning to evil," something he believed Job did by complaining to God. Elihu even thought that Job chose evil over "affliction," that is, that he would rather suffer and challenge God's justice than repent and find freedom, health, and restoration. Job's problem with this latter option was that it involved compromising his integrity. He would have to fabricate something to repent of, and such a fabrication would in itself be a sin.

(4) Introduction to the Anticipated Theophany (36:22-26)

> [22]"God is exalted in his power.
>   Who is a teacher like him?
> [23]Who has prescribed his ways for him,
>   or said to him, 'You have done wrong'?
> [24]Remember to extol his work,
>   which men have praised in song.
> [25]All mankind has seen it;
>   men gaze on it from afar.
> [26]How great is God—beyond our understanding!
>   The number of his years is past finding out.

Elihu's fourth speech makes an abrupt turn at this point. He moved from the subject of God's punishment of the wicked and rewarding of the righteous to a description of God the Creator, transcendent, mighty, and inexplicable. The one imperative, "remember," in v. 24 suggests that Elihu was still speaking to Job, but the essay seems intended for a wider audience, one that includes even us. It is the introduction to the prelude of the theophany.

36:22 The rhetorical question format of the second line of this verse and both halves of the next verse prepare Job and us for God's barrage of questions. "Exalted" (*śāgab*) is a verb found mostly in Psalms and Isaiah to describe God or the impregnable walls of a city (Ps 148:13; Isa 12:4). "Power" (*kōaḥ*) is a favorite word of the Joban poet who uses it more often than any other writer of the Bible (it is in vv. 5,19,22). Though this is

---

[115] So Delitzsch, Pope, Habel, Hartley, and most English versions.

the only time God is called "a teacher," Elihu indirectly suggested in 34:22 that Job ask God to "teach" him what he could not see. It also looks forward to chaps. 38-41, where God did "teach" Job about himself.

36:23 The answer to both these questions is no one. The sovereign takes orders from no one, and none can accuse him of "wrong." Again Elihu may have in mind Job's many complaints about God's apathy toward and tolerance of manifest crime. God's justice was a theme of the friends (4:17; 8:3; 34:12), while, on the contrary, Job contended that he overlooks evil in some (9:24; 21:17) and brings trouble to the righteous (12:17-21; 19:4-7). Elihu was definitely in the camp of Eliphaz, Bildad, and Zophar.

36:24 "His work," which translates the same word as "done" in v. 23, links these two verses together. Rather than having "done wrong," God is to be exalted for the "work" he has done. Those works will be the focus of 36:27–37:18. His people have sung[116] of them from the time of Job and will till the close of the age (Rev 15:3).

36:25 The specific work of God Elihu had in mind is not apparent at this point, but beginning with v. 27 he described a violent thunderstorm. It could be that he referred to the fact that such storms can be seen (and heard) from some distance. Nevertheless, Elihu probably spoke of general revelation in broad terms reminiscent of Ps 19:1-4[2-5]. As the psalmist went on to illustrate that revelation with the sun, so here Elihu described the storm as an example of God's mighty works.

36:26 Verses 26 and 24 are linked by the use of the root *śgʾ*, which occurs as the verb "extol" in v. 24 and the adjective "great" in v. 26. The inscrutability of God has been a theme on the lips of the friends as well as Job. The same expression translated here "past finding out" is in 5:9 (Eliphaz) and 9:10 (Job) as "cannot be fathomed." "Beyond our understanding" is used again in 37:5. All parties recognized that they were not dealing with another human being or a mortal king but with one who is "the King eternal, immortal, invisible, God only wise God, in light inaccessible hid from our eyes."[117]

(5) Anticipated Theophany (36:27–37:13)

27"He draws up the drops of water,

---

[116] For unknown reasons the KJV translated שׁוֹרֲרוּ as "behold." It is the only *polel* perfect of this verb, but *polel* participles abound. The two verbs for "see" in the next verse may have affected the translation in the KJV of v. 24b.

[117] Adapted from the hymn by Walter Chalmers Smith, "Immortal, Invisible, God only Wise" (Oxford: Oxford University Press, 1867).

which distill as rain to the streams;
²⁸the clouds pour down their moisture
  and abundant showers fall on mankind.
²⁹Who can understand how he spreads out the clouds,
  how he thunders from his pavilion?
³⁰See how he scatters his lightning about him,
  bathing the depths of the sea.
³¹This is the way he governs the nations
  and provides food in abundance.
³²He fills his hands with lightning
  and commands it to strike its mark.
³³His thunder announces the coming storm;
  even the cattle make known its approach.

¹"At this my heart pounds
  and leaps from its place.
²Listen! Listen to the roar of his voice,
  to the rumbling that comes from his mouth.
³He unleashes his lightning beneath the whole heaven
  and sends it to the ends of the earth.
⁴After that comes the sound of his roar;
  he thunders with his majestic voice.
When his voice resounds,
  he holds nothing back.
⁵God's voice thunders in marvelous ways;
  he does great things beyond our understanding.
⁶He says to the snow, 'Fall on the earth,'
  and to the rain shower, 'Be a mighty downpour.'
⁷So that all men he has made may know his work,
  he stops every man from his labor.
⁸The animals take cover;
  they remain in their dens.
⁹The tempest comes out from its chamber,
  the cold from the driving winds.
¹⁰The breath of God produces ice,
  and the broad waters become frozen.
¹¹He loads the clouds with moisture;
  he scatters his lightning through them.
¹²At his direction they swirl around
  over the face of the whole earth
  to do whatever he commands them.
¹³He brings the clouds to punish men,
  or to water his earth and show his love.

Except in v. 29 Elihu did not use the rhetorical question format that so characterizes God's speeches, but certainly this is a preamble to the "storm" out of which the Lord will shortly speak to Job (38:1). As in other nature hymns (Pss 18:7-15[8-16]; 19:1-6[2-7]; 29:3-9; 68:7-9[8-10]) the storm is evidence of divine power. Awesome in its power, it speaks to the difference between God's control over the elements and human inability to cope with them when they are stirred up. When the skies and seas are calm, people feel adequate, but storms remind them of the Creator's power and of their dependence on his mercy.

36:27   This is not a scientific treatise on meteorology, but it is interesting that Elihu began at the beginning of the cycle—water is drawn up.[118] Then he proceeded to the next step, precipitation. In contrast to the chance causation often presented on television and in textbooks, here God is the subject of the verbs because he is the ultimate cause behind all these phenomena.[119]

36:28   Along with "distill" of v. 27, here are two more relatively rare words that are in the same semantic sphere, "pour down" and "fall."[120] The verse elaborates on v. 27b and points to the concluding verse of this section (37:13; cf. 5:10).

36:29   Elihu paused to ask if anyone could explain how the weather works. Of course, no one could. The spreading of "the clouds" and the racket[121] from his dwelling in the skies was a mystery to them, and most people today cannot explain it either. Those loud noises "are but the outer fringe of his works; . . . the whisper we hear of him. Who then can understand the thunder of his power?" (26:14).

36:30   The first line is easy to understand because when one is in the midst of a thunderstorm, the lightning appears scattered in every direction. The second line is more problematic since the verb is the common word "to cover" (*kāsâ*). The translation "bathing," whatever that means, stretches the basic meaning.[122] R. Gordis's suggestion to read the polar

---

[118] The root נרע usually means "make small" (cf. KJV), but this is the sole occurrence of the *piel*. The meaning of the *qal* in 15:8, "limit/assume," points in the direction of its use here.

[119] As the footnote in NIV indicates, there is some question about the translation of "streams," which is preferred here. The word in question is עֵד, found only here and in Gen 2:6. For a discussion and bibliography see R. Alden, 'ed, *TWOT* I:17; M. Dahood, "Eblaite i-du and Hebrew 'ed, 'Rain Cloud,' " *CBQ* 43:4 (1981): 534-38.

[120] "Distill/refine," זקק, occurs seven times. "Drop/flow/pour down/distill," נזל, occurs sixteen times. "Fall/drop," רעף, occurs five times. None of them has any Hebrew cognates.

[121] "Thunder" is not the usual רעם (26:14; 39:19,25) or קול (of Ps 29:3-9), but תשאה, which occurs elsewhere only in 39:7; Isa 22:2; Zech 4:7.

[122] The same verb appears in v. 32 where NIV translated "fills," a meaning that would work in v. 30 if it could be justified.

meaning, "uncover," is equally difficult to picture.[123] Others change the "roots/depths" to "tops," which makes better sense but involves a radical emendation.[124] The poet probably intended a merismus (see comment on 1:20) with the opposites of sky and sea juxtaposed. If so, the verse points to the all-encompassing effect of the storm.

36:31 By controlling the weather God exercises his dominion over the world and its inhabitants. From the flood of Noah to the cataclysmic events of Revelation, God manipulates the rain or the heat to accomplish his purposes. To this day there is a certain mystery about the weather that makes people fear. Add to this the totally unannounced occurrences of earthquakes, and people realize that there are dimensions of this world quite removed from their control. "Governs" (*dîn*) could as well be "judge" as 37:13 brings out more clearly.

36:32 The verb *kissâ*, "fills," is a problem here as it was in v. 30, since the root meaning is "cover."[125] Perhaps the scene is of God's cupped hands releasing lightning bolts.[126] The storm gods of the ancient Near East were pictured with lightning bolts in their hands.[127] "Target/ mark" is what most translations (not KJV) have for the last word of the verse, but it requires a minor emendation (cf. 7:20).[128]

36:33 This verse is notoriously difficult. In 1905 A. S. Peake noted that more than thirty explanations had been offered.[129] "Thunder" is more literally "its sound," that is, the sound of the storm.[130] Indeed, most thunderstorms are short-lived, and their approach is usually preceded by

---

[123] Gordis, *Job*, 421-42. So too Hartley, *Job*, 476. Marshall (*Job*, 115) suggested reading כִּסֹּה as כִּסְאוֹ, "the roots of the sea are his throne." So too Pope, *Job*.

[124] Moffatt, AT, JB have apparently read רֹאשֵׁי, "heads," for שָׁרְשֵׁי, "roots." The NAB skipped v. 30. The NEB translates it "streamers"; the REB, "rays."

[125] Dhorme (*Job*, 556) emended כִּסָּה to נָסָה, an alternate of the widely used נָשָׂא, "lift up." So too G. Fohrer, *Das Buch Hiob* (Gütersloh: Mohn, 1963).

[126] "Lightning" was in v. 30, thus contributing to the chiastic structure of these verses.

 A He thunders (v. 29)

  B Lightning (v. 30)

   C He governs (v. 31)

  B' Lightning (v. 32)

 A' His thunder (v. 33).

[127] The Louvre has a stele from Ras Shamra called "Baal of the Lightning." Also from there is a statuette, likewise thought to be Baal, of a figure brandishing a thunderbolt.

[128] The MT has מַפְגִּיעַ, a *hiphil* participle from the root פֹגַע, "meet/encounter/reach," which BDB translates "assailant." As the *BHS* note indicates, the necessary מִפְגָּע is in 7:20, which is otherwise a hapax.

[129] A. S. Peake, *Job*, The Century Bible (Edinburgh: T. C. & E. C. Jack, 1905), 306.

[130] The thrice occurring noun comes from the more frequent verb רֵעַ, which occurs in this book at 30:5; 38:7 as "shout."

sounds of faraway thunder and distant flashes of lightning. Not all translate "cattle" as the subject of the second line because the Targum supports "anger."[131] Since Elihu mentioned animals in 35:11, and many more of them fill chap. 39, and "cattle" occurred in 1:3,10, it is not strange that an allusion to them should appear here. The last word of the second line, "its approach," is still more difficult. The options are plenty: KJV has "vapour"; ASV, RSV "that cometh up"; NJPS, NEB "iniquity"; GNB, "its coming."[132] The NIV captures the meaning as well as the ASV and the RSV.

37:1 At the coming storm both cattle and humans like Elihu responded spontaneously. In the unprotected deserts of the ancient Near East, the approach of an electric storm can be very frightening—something that makes the "heart pound" and "leap." All those who expose themselves to wild places know how natural dangers can quicken the pulse and tense the nerves. This is the first time Elihu spoke of himself since the beginning of chap. 36.

37:2 With rising drama Elihu bade Job listen to the approaching thunder, which he equated with the voice of God, as did the author of Ps 29. The first sound, "the roar," is what accompanies an earthquake (Ps 77:18[19]; Joel 2:10). The second sound is what accompanies deep thought and is elsewhere "moan" (Ps 90:9) and "mourning" (Ezek 2:10). Without becoming too analytical, might these be the rumbles that follow the initial, ear-splitting clap of thunder?

37:3 "Heaven" and "earth" constitute a merismus (see comment on 1:20). "Lightning" appears to come down from the sky, so Elihu, who speaks phenomenologically, described it that way. When the storm surrounds us, it seems to extend "to the ends of the earth." If one can abide the accompanying fear, lightning is an impressive sight.

37:4 The word *qôl* appears three times in this verse, once as "sound" and twice as "voice." All three speak of the thunder that follows the lightning, unless one is in the middle of the storm, at which time the sight and the sound are simultaneous. There are differences of opinion on the verb

---

[131] So Moffatt, RSV, AB, JB, NAB, NEB, AAT, NJPS, Kissane, Gordis, Hartley, etc. Delitzsch argues for "cattle," reminding the reader of the pastoral culture from which this book sprang (*Job*, II:292).

[132] The form in question may be pointed עַוְלָה (evil) or understood from the common verb עָלָה, "go up." Dhorme (*Job*) has suggested a combination of the preposition and this word to make the Aramaic עֲלְעוֹלָה. See M. Jastrow, *Dictionary of Talmud Babli, Yerushalmi, Midrashic Literature and Targumim* (New York: Pardes, 1950), II:1085. This may be the route the NIV translators took, although their "storm" is in the first line. More likely they supplied "storm" and "make known" and translated the word in question as "its approach."

translated "holds back," but the majority take it as the NIV has.[133]

37:5 Verse 5 concludes the description of the thunderstorm[134] and introduces observations on the natural world, with comments on the power and mysterious ways of the Creator. The first phrase is the same as v. 4b with the addition of "marvelous ways," which together with "he does great things" appeared in 5:9. "Beyond our understanding" repeats 36:26.

37:6 At v. 6 the poet moved to winter ("snow," "cold," v. 9, and "ice," v. 10). The NIV handled nicely what looks like dittography (copying something twice) in Hebrew (lit., "A shower of rain and a shower of rains his great."[135] Apparently the last word is read as a verb, "be great."[136] Thus it corresponds to the imperative of the verb "to be" in the first line.[137]

37:7 The NIV has reversed two lines and seems to have translated one word *maʿăśēhû* as both "he has made" and "his work." Taking a lead from the less ambiguous v. 8, many read something like, "He seals up men indoors."[138] Even the most resolute humans must capitulate to the whims of the weather. The point is the same whether they "stop their labor" or are "sealed indoors" for the duration of the storm.

37:8 Human beings are not the only ones to react to the storm and seek safety. The animals enter their "lairs" (NIV translates "take over") and "dens," two rare words also found in 38:40.[139]

37:9 "Wind" and "cold" are the unpleasant accouterments of a winter storm. "Chamber" is understood by some as "chamber of the south" as in 9:9.[140] That prompts the conjecture "north" for a word (*mĕzārîm*) in

---

[133] The root עקב, from which comes the name "Jacob," is in four OT verses, and this is the only *piel* (cf. Gen 27:36; Jer 9:4[3]; Hos 12:3[4]). In this context the question centers on who the subject is and what the implied object is. Habel (*Job*, 496), e.g., reads, "None can track it down." The AB has "men stay not." Delitzsch (*Job*, II:293) has, "He spareth not the lightnings." The NEB moves the phrase into v. 6.

[134] "Lightning" appears once more in v. 11.

[135] Many follow the Syriac and a few Hebrew manuscripts and solve the problem by eliminating one מָטָר. So RSV, AB, NEB, and numbers of commentators (e.g., Jastrow, Driver and Gray, Guillaume, and Gordis).

[136] This old emendation can be found in G. Hölscher, *Das Buch Hiob*, HAT (Tübingen: Mohr, 1952), 87, who credits it to J. Hoffmann, *Hiob* (Kiel: Häseler, 1891). In 1897 Duhm (*Job*, 176) offered a similar emendation, תָּעֹז, *werdet mächtig!*

[137] D. A. Baly says, "Snow falls on the high deserts of Transjordan almost every year, so it is not foreign for Elihu and the other speakers in the book to mention it" (6:16; 9:30; 24:19; 38:22; "Snow," *ISBE* 4:557).

[138] This means reading בְּיַד, which the NIV reads "from his labor," as a biform of the compound preposition בְּעַד. See Gordis, *Job*; Hartley, *Job*.

[139] אֶרֶב is from the verb meaning "lie in wait." מְעוֹנָה is the fem. form of the more common מָעוֹן, "habitation/dwelling."

[140] So KJV, ASV, JB, NASB, GNB.

the second line unique to this verse. The NIV's "driving winds" or "scattering winds" (RSV, AB) have more support, however, being derived from the well-established verb "disperse/winnow."[141]

37:10 The "cold" and the "wind," here identified as "the breath of God," in turn produce "ice."[142] "Broad waters," that is, puddles and ponds, freeze[143] sooner than water running in rivers. The poet used a different verb in 38:30, where the mystery of water turning rock hard because of the cold appears again.

37:11 The last three verses of this section rehearse some of the features touched on earlier. The phenomenon of water evaporating and turning into clouds recalls the beginning of this description of the storm (36:27-28). "Lightning" first appears in 36:30 and, with the thunder, crackles and reverberates through the passage (36:29-30,32-33; 37:2-5). Some uncertainty attaches to the first line, which has two unique words in it, "moisture"[144] and "loads."[145] Actually there are two words for "cloud" in this verse, but the second is rendered by the pronoun "them." The pair appears again in vv. 15-16.

37:12 While this section describes a winter storm and its effects, the point Elihu wished to make is that God is sovereign over the weather and, by implication, over everything and everyone on earth. The gist of v. 12 is certain, but any translation must unscramble the difficult Hebrew.[146]

---

[141] See Pope, *Job*, 281-82.

[142] Despite the similarity between קָרָה, "cold" (v. 9), and קֶרַח, "ice," they are from different roots. See BDB, 901, 903.

[143] The form is בְּמוּצָק, a preposition plus noun from צוּק I, "constrain/restrain," found elsewhere vocalized this way only in 36:16 ("restriction") and Isa 8:23 ("distress"). Frozen water is "restricted" or immobilized.

[144] One question is whether the ב on בְּרִי is a preposition or part of the root. The NIV follows Hölscher, *Das Buch Hiob*, and Gordis, *Job*, in understanding it from the verb רוה, "be watered/drunk." The Vulgate reads it as if בָּר, "grain." Others read it from בּרר, "choose" or "pure." Duhm emended it to בָּרָד, "hail." Driver, Gray, Dhorme, and Pope, emended it to בָּרָק, "lightning bolt." See Grabbe, *Comparative Philology*, 114-16.

[145] The root שרח appears elsewhere only as a noun in Deut 1:12 and Isa 1:14. But its meaning is further established by Aramaic and later Hebrew. Cf. Jastrow, *Dict.*, I:551.

[146] The impossible literal rendering is: "He/it/they turning around, turning upside down by his guidance over their doings, all that he commands them over the face of the world, to earth." There are three pairs of words as if this were an amplified Bible, "turns around" and "turns upside down"; "his guidance" and "he commands;" "world" and "earth." Rather than eliminate any of them as glosses (as Jastrow and others), the NIV has tried to represent them all with conflate phrases, "swirl around" and "whole earth" and by making the verse into a tricolon. The subject is "the clouds" according to NIV and most others, "the light" i.e., the sun according to Jastrow, or "the lightning" according to M. Buttenwieser, *The Book of Job* (New York: Macmillan, 1922) and S. R. Driver, *The Book of Job* (Oxford: Clarendon, 1908).

37:13 At the end of this section Elihu brought the hearer around to his main points, that is, the greatness and justice of God (cf. 33:12; 34:12,26; 36:5-7).[147] Weather can be a curse or a blessing. Out-of-season or very intense rain or hail have been God's vehicle to punish the wicked (Gen 6:17; Exod 9:18; Josh 10:11; 1 Sam 12:17). Likewise, he manipulates the weather to show his "love," *ḥesed*. Rain is a token of God's blessing (1 Kgs 8:36; 18:38,45; Jer 5:24; Hos 6:3; Zech 10:1; Acts 14:17).

(6) Application to Job (37:14-18)

14"Listen to this, Job;
  stop and consider God's wonders.
15Do you know how God controls the clouds
  and makes his lightning flash?
16Do you know how the clouds hang poised,
  those wonders of him who is perfect in knowledge?
17You who swelter in your clothes
  when the land lies hushed under the south wind,
18can you join him in spreading out the skies,
  hard as a mirror of cast bronze?

Elihu has been speaking to Job all along, but in a special way he directed these five verses at him in one last effort to move him to acknowledge the sovereignty of God. In this admonishment, which is largely made up of rhetorical questions, Elihu was correct because such a confession is required of all God's children, altogether apart from repentance. Elihu did not urge Job to confess sin as the others had done earlier but to grant God his place as suzerain and sovereign of all he has made, including earth's human inhabitants. The speech sounds very much like God's speech in the next chapter.

37:14 As at the beginning (32:10) and elsewhere (33:1,31, 34:10; 36:2) Elihu exhorted Job (and the others) to pay him attention. Did he notice how weary they were of listening to him and how uninterested they were in this long sermon? The second line of v. 14 is perhaps the most important statement that Elihu made and the one thing that Job was forced eventually to do. It was ultimately the solution to his problem and the cure for his ills, physical, emotional, and attitudinal. By heeding this advice people, even today, are converted, but most will not "stop," and even fewer "consider God's wonders."

---

[147] This verse also is very cryptic, and the NIV has added the words "clouds," "men," and "water" in order to give it meaning.

37:15 The first two questions deal with the "clouds" and "lightning." Neither Job nor anyone else would be able to explain how God "positions/controls" them.[148] While modern scientists can explain much about lightning, there remains a certain unpredictability about it, which shows that God has ultimate control.

37:16 Like v. 15, this verse begins with "do you know how?" "Hang poised" translates a word occurring only here.[149] Even if another verb proves to be correct, the issue remains the same—God is the author, architect, and administrator of the cosmos.[150] "Perfect in knowledge" is an epithet Elihu applied to himself in 36:4. Here and more properly it describes God.

37:17 In the previous section Elihu described a winter storm, complete with snow and ice. But apparently this scene occurred in the summer when the hot south wind made people "swelter" in their "clothes." The miserable, sand-laden sirocco generally came from the east, but it could also come from the south (cf. 15:2; 27:21; Luke 12:55).

37:18 Elihu's final query to Job once more challenged his ability to effect change in the weather. Having reminded him of the agony that the heat had brought, he asked if he could do anything about those brazen skies,[151] spread out like a mirror,[152] intensifying the torrid rays of a blazing summer sun.

(7) His Inconclusive Conclusion (37:19-24)

19"Tell us what we should say to him;

---

[148] The verb is an inf. const. of שִׂים. "Clouds" are in the second line; a simple "them" is in the first.

[149] Most, like the NIV, understand מִפְלְשֵׂי from the root פלס, usually "ponder" or "weigh" in a figurative sense. Here it would be more literal. In 36:29 the similar מִפְרְשֵׂי also appears with עָב, suggesting they are the same word with a *lamed-resh* exchange, perhaps occasioned by alliteration with the nearby מִפְלָאוֹת. "Hang" in 26:7 translates תָּלָה, not either of these words. In 36:29 the root פָרַשׂ, "spread out," fits nicely and would do so here as well.

[150] Instead of a verb, the AB has "banks"; NASB, "layers"; NJPS, "expanse."

[151] "Clouds" is the usual translation of שְׁחָקִים, but about a fourth of the twenty other occurrences of it might be read "skies." Certainly the verb רקע, "hammer/beat out," works better with "skies" than with "clouds." From this verb comes רָקִיעַ, the "expanse/firmament" of Gen 1:6-8. "Clouds," however, was the choice of Tur-Sinai, Dhorme, Gordis, and Habel.

[152] "Mirror," רְאִי, is a hapax but derived from the common verb רָאָה, "look/see," hence "looking glass" in the KJV although "glass" was a much later development. The NKJV has "cast metal mirror." See "Mirror" with accompanying photo of two ancient Egyptian bronze examples in *ZPEB* 4:251.

we cannot draw up our case because of our darkness.
²⁰Should he be told that I want to speak?
  Would any man ask to be swallowed up?
²¹Now no one can look at the sun,
  bright as it is in the skies
  after the wind has swept them clean.
²²Out of the north he comes in golden splendor;
  God comes in awesome majesty.
²³The Almighty is beyond our reach and exalted in power;
  in his justice and great righteousness, he does not oppress.
²⁴Therefore, men revere him,
  for does he not have regard for all the wise in heart?

In this final strophe before God appeared, Elihu confessed his confusion and declined any opportunity to do what Job wanted to do, that is, confront God. Such a confrontation would be suicidal, because God is so brilliant, so splendid, so awesome, and so exalted. The only proper response to the Almighty is reverent fear, trusting him to respond graciously to the submissive piety of the truly wise.[153]

37:19 Because the imperative is singular and the object plural, Elihu asked Job to counsel him and the other friends since all parties had reached an impasse. The "him" is clearly God as the following verses indicate. "Darkness," a word used often in the book, occurs for the twenty-second time. Unlike most of the other times when it is a synonym for "death," here it means "ignorance" and points to the inability of any of the characters to solve Job's problem. Curiously the first question God asked Job (38:2) was, "Who is this that darkens my counsel?" Not only Job but the four friends as well, failed to dispel the darkness of ignorance that characterized their speeches to one degree or another.

37:20 The tangled character of the syntax of this verse betrays the unclear thinking and frustration of Elihu who, so confident at the beginning, was now running out of arguments and eloquence.[154] The point of the two questions is that it would be certain death to contest God.[155] The fear reflects the widespread concern that "no one may see me [God] and

---

[153] That this section is difficult is evidenced by the fact that Kissane put vv. 21-22a after v. 8, the JB skipped v. 19 altogether, and the AB placed v. 21 after v. 18.

[154] It is unusual for a verse of five major words to have two verbs in the *pual*, יְסֻפַּר and יְבֻלָּע. The voluntative mood on the two verbs for "speak/say/ask" is the choice of the translators, not anything patent in the Hebrew text. Other versions give the verse a different tenor by using combinations of "shall," "should," "does," "did," etc.

[155] Other instances of the verb בלע, "swallow," in connection with God are 2:3 and 10:8 ("ruin" and "destroy" in NIV).

live" (Exod 33:20; Deut 5:26; Judg 6:22-23).

37:21 Because of the possibility of mixed metaphors, v. 21 allows a variety of translations and interpretations. Does *ʾôr*, "light," mean the "sun" (as NIV) or "understanding" in contrast to the "darkness" of ignorance in v. 19? Does *šĕḥāqîm* in line two mean "skies" as in v. 18 or "clouds" as in 35:5; 36:28; 38:37, with the consequent meaning that the "light" is behind the "clouds" (as JB)? Is the verse speaking about confronting God or about another storm? The correct and most succinct answer is found in H. Rowley: "The meaning appears to be that when the wind has blown away the clouds the sky is too bright for the eyes. The point then is that if the clear sky is too bright for human eyes, the dazzling brightness of God's presence would be even more unbearable."[156]

37:22 Just a few verses later God will appear "in golden splendor" and "in awesome majesty"[157] and will humble Job and all humanity who cannot adorn themselves as God does "with glory and splendor, . . . honor and majesty" (40:10). In Ugaritic literature "Zaphon" or the "north" was the abode of the gods,[158] but that was not necessarily in the poet's mind when he spoke of the direction from which God comes. Rather than try to explain this as a reference to a glowing sunrise or the northern lights, it is best to understand it as exalted, hyperbolic language, characteristic of all descriptions of theophanies from the swirling clouds of Mount Sinai (Exod 19:16-18) to the dazzling streets of the celestial city (Rev 21:21).

37:23 Unable to reconcile their theology of retribution with the facts of Job's case and his accompanying, unshaken belief in his own integrity, Elihu, speaking for himself and the other three friends, confessed that God is transcendent and inscrutable. The second line consists of three fundamental affirmations about God: he is just, he is right, and "he does not oppress." They abandoned their search for a solution and surrendered to divine sovereignty as Abraham did when he prayed for Sodom, "Will not the Judge of all the earth do right?" (Gen 18:25).

---

[156] Rowley, *Job*, 239.

[157] For a discussion of the problematic preposition עַל before "God" see Blommerde, *Northwest Semitic and Job*, 132.

[158] By it they meant Mount Casius (Jebel el-'aqra') twenty-five mi. NNW of Ras Shamra (ancient Ugarit) in Syria. See J. Hartley, "Zaphon," *ISBE* 4:1173. Only in Isa 14:13 might the word refer to that mountain. Otherwise צָפוֹן simply means "north" in the 150 or so places it occurs in the OT. For a defense of the view that Elihu alluded to the sacred mountain of Baal and that "gold" refers not to the color of the sky but literal gold mined there, see Pope, *Job*, 286-87. For a conservative appraisal of these mythopoetic terms in Job see Smick, "Job," EBC 4:863-71, and for Zaphon in particular 4:868-70 (p. 966).

37:24 The last word of Job's friends is Elihu's typical wisdom admonition, which is similar to the "conclusion of the matter" at the end of Ecclesiastes, "Fear God and keep his commandments, for this is the whole duty of man" (cf. 28:28). Leaving the Hebrew untouched, line *b* can be read two or three ways—as a negative rhetorical question (NIV) expecting a positive answer,[159] or as a statement that God will not look with favor on those who are wise in their own opinion (KJV, RV, ASV, RSV, AB, NASB, GNB, NCV, NIV footnote). Still others reverse the subject and object of the second line reading "all who are wise look to him" (NEB) or the opposite, "Whom none of the wise can perceive" (NJPS; cf. NAB, N. Habel).[160] Because the expression "wise in heart" is elsewhere never pejorative,[161] it is best to understand this final sentence of Elihu as a positive statement that God will not reject a blameless man (8:20), but look with favor on those with integrity.

---

[159] Another way to handle the problematic לֹא is to understand it as an asseverative לוּא, which is what some of the versions have done that do not reflect the negative. See R. Gordis, *Book of Job*, 434; J. Hartley, *Job*, 483-84 note.

[160] Because the verbs "fear/revere" and "see/regard" in the imperfect are so similar, יִרְאוּ and יִרְאֶה, some read both verbs as "revere/fear" (Moffatt, JB, REB).

[161] Exod 31:6; 35:10, 25; 36:1-2, 8; Job 9:4; Prov 10:8; 11:29; 16:21. "Conceited" is expressed in Hebrew by חָכָם בְּעֵינָיו (Prov 3:7; 26:5, 12, 16; 28:11).

VII. THE LORD FINALLY SPEAKS TO JOB (38:1–42:6)
    1. The Lord's First Introductory Challenge (38:1-3)
    2. The Divine Interrogation (38:4–39:30)
        (1) Creation (38:4-7)
        (2) The Sea (38:8-11)
        (3) The Earth's Administration (38:12-15)
        (4) The Underworld (38:16-18)
        (5) Light and Darkness (38:19-21)
        (6) Storm (38:22-30)
        (7) Stars (38:31-33)
        (8) Clouds (38:34-38)
        (9) Lions and Ravens (38:39-41)
        (10) Mountain Goats (39:1-4)
        (11) Wild Donkeys (39:5-8)
        (12) Wild Oxen (39:9-12)
        (13) Ostriches (39:13-18)
        (14) Horses (39:19-25)
        (15) Hawks (39:26-30)
    3. Concluding Challenge (40:1-2)
    4. Job's First Repentance (40:3-5)
    5. The Lord's Second Introductory Challenge (40:6-7)
    6. The Second Interrogation (40:8–41:34)
        (1) Challenge to Job's Defense (40:8-14)
        (2) The "Behemoth" (40:15-24)
        (3) The "Leviathan" (41:1-34)
    7. Job's Second Repentance (42:1-6)

VII. THE LORD FINALLY SPEAKS TO JOB (38:1–42:6)

The earlier speeches by the characters and Elihu in particular hinted at and anticipated this point in the book when Yahweh spoke. The prologue and epilogue contain words of God, but these chapters are what many consider the high point of the book.[1] They constitute a magnificent reso-

---

[1] J. G. Williams, "Deciphering the Unspoken: The Theophany of Job," *HUCA* 49 (1978): 59-72.

lution to the book and to Job's problem. Throughout the book Job longed
for God to speak, and the others have tried to represent God's opinion on
Job's case. What God finally said was totally unexpected—by them or by
the readers of the book. Instead of discoursing on authority, justice, and
sovereignty and completely ignoring the case of Job, he blitzed the patriarch from Uz with a myriad of questions about the created order. Some
consider this to be avoiding the question, but God is not subject to human
timetables or procedures. In the end his response satisfied Job, and it
should satisfy every suffering saint, because the very fact that God finally
spoke to Job was ennobling as well as humbling. Apart from their role in
the drama of Job, the poems about the creation and the two grandest,
wildest, and least tamable of the animals are masterpieces in themselves.
The two repentances by Job indicate that he was satisfied. "Seeing God,
Job forgets all he wanted to say, all he thought he would say if he could
but see Him."[2] And we too will forget (cf. Rev 21:3-5).

1. The Lord's First Introductory Challenge (38:1-3)

¹Then the LORD answered Job out of the storm. He said:
²"Who is this that darkens my counsel
  with words without knowledge?
³Brace yourself like a man;
  I will question you,
  and you shall answer me.

From the storm the deity spoke, and his first sentence was a question
that in itself chastened and mortified Job. Then came a challenge to be
manly and take an examination on the creation and administration of the
universe and its many untamed creatures.

38:1   Almost as if the Elihu speeches did not intervene, God spoke to
Job, and not to the friends. His name is Yahweh, not the generic ʾēl or
ʾĕlôah of the other speakers. He is the God who exists, who reveals himself, who deals with his people through covenant, and who now came to
Job "out of the storm." The Hebrew word is different, but it harks back to
the "mighty wind" of 1:19 that took the lives of his ten children. Storms
may destroy, but in them God's people often hear his voice (Ps 29:9-11).

38:2   "Darken" is used as it was in 37:19 to speak of ignorance. Of
course, God was not asking for information but reminding his challenger

---

[2] G. MacDonald, *Creation in Christ* (Wheaton: Harold Shaw, 1976, from *Unspoken Sermons*, 1885), 220.

that the divine will had not been represented by what he said. We all speak "words without knowledge" unless they are the properly understood and interpreted words of the Bible. Since they had such limited revelation and were immersed in a pool of similarly benighted others, it is amazing that Job and the others spoke as much truth as they did. Nevertheless, as will become clear, all missed the mark and spoke out of their darkness.

38:3 As all the more literal versions indicate, the first line in Hebrew is, "Gird your loins like a man." This may refer simply to the gathering of a flowing garment into the belt in order to do work (cf. Exod 12:11; 1 Kgs 18:46; 2 Kgs 4:29; 9:1; Jer 1:17).[3] Until now Job had been asking and demanding answers from God. Now God reversed the procedure, as he became the inquisitor and Job the defendant.

2. The Divine Interrogation (38:4–39:30)

Yahweh's first speech consists of dozens of questions about the cosmos. They begin with creation and advance in a pattern that approximates the first chapter of Genesis. In the last pericope of chap 38, which should have been the first of chap. 39, the examination turns to wild animals, those creatures that Job did not have in his herds and flocks, those elusive, mysterious, powerful denizens of places where people are not. "Yet all are among God's pets."[4] Naturally, Job could not and did not try to answer any of the questions. Their point was not to seek information but to impress Job with the fact that God operates in realms well beyond the range of human beings. His power, creativity, and omniscience are something that neither Job nor we can grasp, but maybe the reading of these chapters will help.

(1) Creation (38:4-7)

> [4]"Where were you when I laid the earth's foundation?
>   Tell me, if you understand.
> [5]Who marked off its dimensions? Surely you know!
>   Who stretched a measuring line across it?
> [6]On what were its footings set,
>   or who laid its cornerstone—

---

[3] Less likely is the explanation that it alludes to the ancient sport of belt wrestling where the object of the duel was to remove the opponent's loincloth. See C. Gordon, "Belt Wrestling in the Bible World," *HUCA* 23 (1950-51): 131-36.

[4] F. I. Andersen, *Job*, TOTC (Downers Grove: InterVarsity, 1976), 273.

⁷while the morning stars sang together
and all the angels shouted for joy?

There was irony in the voice of God as he challenged Job on such elementary and factual matters as the origins of the planet. The details of v. 7 remind us that we are dealing with a nature poem and not a treatise on geology. Literalists who press the details of this and any of the other segments of these chapters will immediately discover irreconcilable difficulties. The best advice is be poetic as you read. Position yourself thousands of years ago in the steppes of Transjordan, standing in the maelstrom and listening to an awesome voice coming through the wind. It is musical; it is impressive; it is scary but wonderful.

38:4 Unlike personified Wisdom, who was present at the creation (Prov 8:22-31), Job was a creature of time. When God "laid the earth's foundation," Job simply was not yet born. Not even Adam and Eve, the first couple, were present at this inaugural event that marked our planet's birth. Job could not answer because he was not there and could not know.

38:5 Isaiah 40:12 indirectly answers these questions by implying that the Sovereign Lord himself acted totally alone in the design and generation of the world we know.[5] God himself determined, surveyed, and charted the globe without consultation or assistance of any kind. There were only celestial observers, the "morning stars" and "angels" of v. 7.

38:6 Scientifically oriented moderns might pick at this verse, writing off the ancient poet as an unenlightened pre-Copernican. But the writer must be granted the freedom to describe the world from his point of view and to paint imaginatively a scene that depicts God as a master builder with appropriate analogies to structures as we know them. The "footings" and the "cornerstone"[6] are those most fundamental and essential parts of a building, so, figuratively speaking, the earth has them too. The writer knew as we do that these foundations are not literal because "he suspends the earth over nothing" (26:7).

38:7 "The morning stars" probably included the planet Venus (called Hesperus), which makes a regular morning and evening appearance. The old translation "God of hosts" ("God Almighty" in NIV) points to that celestial army that does God's bidding and that was present at the creation and "sang together." "Angels" is more literally "sons of God" as in

---

[5] The כִּי is certainly an emphatic particle and not a causal one in this context, hence the NIV's "surely."

[6] The term also could refer to the capstone (Zeph 1:16; 3:6), thus creating a merismus with the lowest and the highest parts of a building.

1:6; 2:1, those superhuman but subdivine creatures who joined in the song at earth's advent.[7] Some see a parallelism here that would make "morning stars" synonymous with "angels" and thus figurative.

(2) The Sea (38:8-11)

8"Who shut up the sea behind doors
   when it burst forth from the womb,
9when I made the clouds its garment
   and wrapped it in thick darkness,
10when I fixed limits for it
   and set its doors and bars in place,
11when I said, 'This far you may come and no farther;
   here is where your proud waves halt'?

Genesis 1:9 records the gathering of the water to one place and the appearance of the dry land. In a general way the pericope after the creation itself deals with the confinement of the seas. In graphic but poetic terms, vv. 8-11 deal with oceans and all their power and mystery. For desert people who were not seafaring the limitless expanse of water was not inviting but fearful. Few Old Testament characters had anything to do with sailing, fishing, or swimming. The sea was something God held back from overflowing the land.

38:8 The NIV translators repeated "who" from v. 5 because otherwise v. 8 is just a continuation of the long sentence begun three verses earlier (cf. RSV). The language of "doors," "womb," and "bars (v. 10) does have parallels in the Akkadian account of creation,[8] but the bizarre antics of the polytheistic pantheon of ancient Mesopotamia are manifold times more different from than similar to the Genesis account of creation and biblical nature poems.

38:9 The sea is like a newborn child, conceived "behind doors" (v. 8), emerging "from the womb" (v. 8), and now "dressed" in a "garment" of "clouds" and "wrapped in the swaddling clothes"[9] of "darkness." The sea is not the hostile monster whom the supreme god must subdue but part of Yahweh's created dominion, submissive to his will.

38:10 It is tempting to press the analogy between the sea and the

---

[7] Some make a close connection between these figures and those in Ugaritic literature. See, e.g., M. Pope, *Job*, AB (Garden City: Doubleday, 1973), 292-93.

[8] *ANET*, 67, lines 98, 139-40.

[9] The KJV, ASV, RSV, NASB all translate the once-occurring noun חֲתֻלִּים as "swaddling band." The verb חתל is only in Ezek 16:4, and a related noun is in Ezek 30:21.

small child by picturing in v. 10 a playpen and assorted rules that babies must learn. The setting of "limits" is similar to what Job said in 26:10 about God marking the horizon. To apportion land or distribute privileges implies ownership, control, and the right to that land and those privileges. When Joshua assigned the tribes their territories, he acted as vice-regent to the God who himself had promised the land, fought with Israel's armies, and now, as its sovereign ruler, gave it to his people. As Creator he has the authority to delimit the sea and confine it to its place with figurative "doors" and "bars."

38:11 God quoted himself as he rehearsed for Job his orders to the sea and its "proud waves." The sand of the beach is an unlikely restraint for crashing waves, but Jeremiah said precisely that: "I made the sand a boundary for the sea, an everlasting barrier it cannot cross. The waves may roll, but they cannot prevail; they may roar, but they cannot cross it" (Jer 5:22). While a great storm or tidal wave may temporarily threaten the integrity of a beach, the shoreline eventually prevails and remains as the boundary between land and sea.

(3) The Earth's Administration (38:12-15)

> ¹²"Have you ever given orders to the morning,
>   or shown the dawn its place,
> ¹³that it might take the earth by the edges
>   and shake the wicked out of it?
> ¹⁴The earth takes shapes like clay under a seal;
>   its features stand out like those of a garment.
> ¹⁵The wicked are denied their light,
>   and their upraised arm is broken.

On the fourth day of creation God ordered into existence "two great lights—the greater light to govern the day and the lesser light to govern the night" (Gen 1:16). This segment of the theophany moves from the sun's responsibility to initiate a new day to the connection of light with the execution of justice and the punishment of the wicked.[10]

38:12 The interrogative particle indicates a new section and also identifies these as questions, not statements. Of course, Job never (lit.

---

[10] In ancient Babylonia the sun was the god of justice. He is pictured on the top of Hammurapi's law code handing down legislation to the king (*ANET*, 163; cf. reverse xxiv:85 on p. 178). Our expression "sunshine laws" reflect this connection between light and justice.

"from your days") commanded the sun to rise or "show[11] the dawn its place." Those are God's responsibilities and prerogatives. So far he has never failed.

38:13   The rising sun seems to grasp the eastern edges of the earth before it mounts higher in the sky. Verse 13 points to that phenomenon familiar to every watcher of a sunrise. As the day grows brighter, evil doers[12] who love darkness and practice their crimes under its cover find themselves looking for places to hide. As a bright light scatters cockroaches, so each new day presents a threat to the murderers, adulterers, and burglars that Job mentioned in 24:14-17.

38:14   While it is dark, one can see nothing of the texture of the earth, but with the dawn the valleys, mountains, and a thousand other features are visible. It is analogous to a "seal" being pressed onto otherwise flat "clay." In the dark the earth might as well be naked, but with the light it is clothed with colors and shapes.

38:15   The poet returned to the subject of the wicked (v. 13) and with a mixed metaphor said that the wicked will have "their light denied," the "light" that they despise because it exposes their wickedness. Remembering that "light" and "life" go together just as "dark" and "death" do, this verse is saying that the ungodly will be incarcerated in darkness or put to death (cf. 18:5-6,18). The "upraised arm," like the clenched fist or the high hand, represents arrogance and defiance, all of which are undone with the advent of dawn and its accompanying justice.

(4) The Underworld (38:16-18)

> [16]"Have you journeyed to the springs of the sea
>   or walked in the recesses of the deep?
> [17]Have the gates of death been shown to you?
>   Have you seen the gates of the shadow of death?
> [18]Have you comprehended the vast expanses of the earth?
>   Tell me, if you know all this.

The Lord reminded Job through these questions of all the areas about

---

[11] The unusual ending on יְדַעְתָּה is, as the MT *qere* indicates, the following word's article that was separated by an incorrect word division. See E. Tov, *Textual Criticism of the Hebrew Bible* (Minneapolis: Fortress, 1992), 252-53.

[12] Two of four suspended letters in the Masoretic text are found in 38:13,15, and in both instances the ע is raised. It is probably a very old spelling correction. The other instances are in Judg 18:30; Ps 80:14. See GKC § 5n; Tov, *Textual Criticism*, 57. The NEB and REB read "Dog Star" in both places. Pope explains this translation although does not adopt it in AB, 295.

which he had no knowledge. While modern science may have explored the "springs of the sea," there is no certain knowledge of what lies beyond the "gates of death" except in the Bible. Likewise, faraway places were mysterious and foreboding.

38:16 The two lines are closely parallel, and therefore the otherwise unknown word behind "springs" can be translated with some certainty.[13] For someone like Job who was a dweller in a land-locked country, even sailing on an ocean was a remote possibility, much less any kind of underwater exploration.

38:17 Death too is off-limits to ordinary living mortals. Even the viewing of its "gates" was something Job had not done.[14] The Genesis creation accounts do not refer to this realm, but this netherworldly abyss was imagined by the biblical writers from Moses to Matthew (Deut 32:22; Job 17:16; Matt 16:18). By mentioning it here, God told Job that this sphere was as much within his purview and dominion as were the observable heavens and earth (cf. Ps 139:8; Amos 9:2-3).

38:18 From God's celestial perspective, somewhat analogous to the astronauts' view from the moon, the entire globe can be seen at once. To the earthbound Job such a viewpoint was unimaginable. He may have traveled a hundred miles or more, but still he was far from "understanding/comprehending" what was beyond the last mountain range or desert he had seen at the most distant point of his travels. Line *b* is like v. 4b, a satirical challenge to the transient, myopic, mortal man from Uz.

(5) Light and Darkness (38:19-21)

> [19]"What is the way to the abode of light?
>   And where does darkness reside?
> [20]Can you take them to their places?
>   Do you know the paths to their dwellings?
> [21]Surely you know, for you were already born!
>   You have lived so many years!

Personifying "light" and "darkness," God next asked Job where they lived. Knowing Job could not answer, he concluded this series of five questions with another satirical observation on Job's "many years."

38:19 Structurally the verse is both a merismus ("light" and "dark-

---

[13] The מִבְכִי, "the sources of" of 28:11 may be the same as the נִבְכֵי of this verse.

[14] The JB has the curious translation "janitors of Shadowland" for line *b*. It comes from following the LXX, πυλωροί, and B. Duhm's suggestion to read the second "gates" as שׁוֹעֲרֵי; *Pfortner*, "gate keepers," *Das Buch Hiob* (Tübingen: Mohr, 1897), 185.

ness"; see comment on 1:20) and a chiasmus (*A B B' A'* arrangement of subjects and predicates), but the latter would only be obvious if the second line were translated, "And darkness, where does it reside?" The question may be asking, Where is heaven, and where is Sheol? Regardless of the interpretation, Job had no answer.

38:20 Like wisdom and folly, depicted in Prov 9 as women, whose houses can be reached by following certain roads, so "light" and "darkness" are personified and understood to have "places" and "dwellings."

38:21 Job may have been one of the oldest men in his community, perhaps 70, if we extrapolate from 42:16, but these limited years are minuscule compared with the centuries, millennia, and eons that preceded him. Job was many generations removed from the first man (15:7), and certainly must have smarted from this blow from the whirlwind.

(6) Storm (38:22-30)

²²"Have you entered the storehouses of the snow
   or seen the storehouses of the hail,
²³which I reserve for times of trouble,
   for days of war and battle?
²⁴What is the way to the place where the lightning is dispersed,
   or the place where the east winds are scattered over the earth?
²⁵Who cuts a channel for the torrents of rain,
   and a path for the thunderstorm,
²⁶to water a land where no man lives,
   a desert with no one in it,
²⁷to satisfy a desolate wasteland
   and make it sprout with grass?
²⁸Does the rain have a father?
   Who fathers the drops of dew?
²⁹From whose womb comes the ice?
   Who gives birth to the frost from the heavens
³⁰when the waters become hard as stone,
   when the surface of the deep is frozen?

The longest pericope in Yahweh's first speech takes as its subject a favorite of the author, the storm with all its power, unpredictability, and mystery. As recently as 37:1-13 Elihu discoursed on the effects of the storm with particular fascination with the thunder, lightning, snow, and ice (cf. 36:29-30,32-33). Job himself mentioned "snow" and "ice" in 6:16 (cf. 24:19), and "thunder" appeared in 28:26. For people who live outdoors most of the time and whose shelter is merely a tent, foul weather can be especially close and threatening. For those in temperate climates, the formation of snow and the hardening of water into ice were particularly fascinating.

38:22 Just as rain is stored in "the water jars of heaven" (v. 37), so "snow" and "hail" are stored in "treasuries" (KJV) or "arsenals" (as the word is translated in Jer 50:25) like so many weapons to deploy on behalf of God's people in terrestrial battles.

38:23 Hail in particular is a weapon God used to fight for his people. It was the seventh plague that fell on Egypt to help persuade the pharaoh to let Israel go free (Exod 9:22-26). "The LORD hurled large hailstones" on the fleeing Amorites in Josh 10:11. The prophets predicted that God would use these icy missiles to press home his lessons and punish the presumptuous (Isa 30:30; Ezek 13:11), and hundred pound hailstones are recorded in Rev 16:21 as part of the plague of the seventh angel.

38:24 The very long lines of the NIV could be read simply, "How is the lightning dispersed or the east winds?"[15] Because "light[ning]," *'ôr*, is not synonymous with "east winds," *qādîm*, emendations to make them parallel abound, which reflect in the variety of choices in English translations: "mists/water" (Moffatt), "flood/east [wind]" (AB),[16] "lightning/sparks" (JB),[17] "winds/east wind" (NAB),[18] "heat/east wind" (NEB), "west wind/east wind" (NJPS). Like the questions about the "snow" and "hail" (v. 22), these two weather-related ones had no answer from Job.

38:25 Some of the gorges slicing through the Transjordanian plateau to carry water to the Jordan Valley are meandering, very deep, and precipitous. For example, "canyons" is not an inappropriate word to describe the Wadi Mojib (the biblical Arnon). The poet may have had these in mind when he crafted v. 25a. The lightning and its accompanying thunder,[19] likewise, take an unpredictable route, striking where they will,

---

[15] דֶרֶךְ, "way," need not be taken literally, but in the English sense, "the way to do it" is equivalent to "how to do it." So Moffatt, AAT, and cf. R. Gordis, *The Book of Job* (New York: Jewish Theological Seminary, 1978), and NCV. דֶרֶךְ also carries the meaning "power" as translated by Pope, *Job*.

[16] Duhm, following J. G. E. Hoffmann, *Das Buch Hiob* (Kiel: Haeseler, 1891), and G. Bickell, *Das Buch Hiob* (Vienna: Gerold, 1894) changed אוֹר to אֵד, "mist/flood." Cf. Dhorme, *A Commentary on the Book of Job*, trans. H. Knight (London: Nelson, 1967); Pope, *Job*.

[17] JB's "correction" is uncertain; perhaps reading קדח, "kindle" for the text's קָדִים.

[18] "Wind" is achieved by emending אוֹר to רוּחַ with M. Jastrow, Jr., *The Book of Job* (Philadelphia: Lippincott, 1920), G. Hölscher, *Das Buch Hiob* (Tübingen: Mohr, 1952), etc. "Wind" can, however, be supported without recourse to emendation according to N. Tur-Sinai, *The Book of Job* (Jerusalem: Kiryat-Sefer, 1967), and Gordis, *Job*.

[19] "Thunderstorm" translates חֲזִיז קֹלְלוֹת, as it did in 28:26b, which is identical to this. See comments and footnote there.

with rains drenching some areas and leaving adjacent ones parched. Only God knows the path it takes.

38:26 It is one of the extravagances of God that he sends rain on the "desert" where it seems to benefit no one. The science of ecology teaches correctly that all natural phenomena are interconnected and that even the desert rain ends up in oases or springs that contribute to life. What appears as a waste is really part of the design of nature.

38:27 Verse 27 concludes the three-verse question begun in v. 25. There is a progression from the origin of the storm (v. 24), to the route of the storm (v. 25), to the storm itself (v. 26), and now its effects (v. 27). Though no one may profit from the rain, it nourishes the "desolate wasteland"[20] and graces the normally barren hills with a thin growth of weeds, turning their color from dusty grey-brown to hazy green (Pss 107:35; 147:8).

38:28 With vv. 28-29 the poet introduced a new metaphor, that of God, who fathers and mothers the moisture. In the long hot summers of the Middle East, people and plants must depend on the dew[21] to water their world since no rain falls between the equinoxes (mid-March to mid-September). The answer to the question about who begets the rain and dew is God, the Creator and Sustainer of the universe. "All things bright and beautiful, / All creatures great and small, / And all things wise and wonderful; / The Lord God made them all" (C. F. Alexander; cf. Jer 14:22).

38:29 The poet adopted female imagery to describe the source of ice and frost, two particularly puzzling forms that water takes. Verses 28-29 also connect in that "ice" is frozen water, and "frost" is frozen dew.

38:30 Though similar to 37:10, "frozen" and "become hard" translate different words from those in 37:10.[22] "Deep," *těhôm*, is one of the poetic terms for the sea, but it is here used in a more limited sense, alluding to frozen lakes and springs.

(7) Stars (38:31-33)

31"Can you bind the beautiful Pleiades?
   Can you loose the cords of Orion?
32Can you bring forth the constellations in their seasons

---

[20] See discussion and footnote on this phrase at 30:3.

[21] "Drops" translates אֵגֶל, a hapax on whose meaning all seem agreed. Tur-Sinai translates "drops" but says the word means "pools," based on a Arabic etymology.

[22] Both חבא and לכד are in the *hithpael* and carry the sense of "draw together/thicken/harden" and "seize up/compact" respectively.

or lead out the Bear with its cubs?
³³Do you know the laws of the heavens?
Can you set up [God's] dominion over the earth?

Also on the fourth day (Gen 1:16) God created the stars. With clear skies fully half the year, desert dwellers made a study of the stars and constellations. These verses serve both as an apologetic for the uniqueness of God, as opposed to multiple celestial deities, and as proof of his creative artistry and control of all things terrestrial and celestial.

38:31 "Pleiades" and "Orion" (cf. 9:9) were the best known of the constellations. "Pleiades" is modified with an uncertain word translated here "beautiful." The NIV footnotes indicate two more possibilities: "twinkling" or "chains," which makes a better parallel to "cords" in line b.[23] But "cords" also is an uncertain word.[24]

38:32 In this verse the translation and identification of the key words "constellations" and "Bear" are in question. Most translations from KJV through NRSV simply transliterate the first term as "Mazzaroth." Others read "signs of the Zodiac" (NEB), "constellations" (NASB), "morning star" (JB, NIV footnote), or simply "stars" (AAT, NCV)[25] or "planets."[26] "The Bear" is also uncertain although generally translated that way, understanding it to be the "Great Bear" and "her children"[27] the "Little Bear."[28] The NIV footnote offers "Leo," which is based on a similar-sounding Arabic cognate that means "lion."[29] Whatever the identification of these celestial bodies, the point is that Job did not control them.

---

[23] The word מַעֲדַנּוֹת (fem. pl.) is found as a masc. sing. in Gen 49:20 and Lam 4:5 ("delicacies"), Prov 29:17 ("delight"), 1 Sam 15:32 ("confidently" in NIV, but "haltingly/reluctantly/struggling" in others). "Twinkling" is just a variation on "beautiful," but "chains" represents the widely held understanding that it is a metathesis for מַעֲנַדּוֹת, which appears in 31:36a and Prov 6:21 parallel to קָשַׁר, the root of the verb "bind" in this verse. So the LXX, ASV, RSV, etc., Dhorme, *Job*, J. Hartley, *The Book of Job*, NICOT (Grand Rapids: Eerdmans, 1988), etc. For more discussion see S. R. Driver and G. B. Gray, *Job*, ICC (New York: Scribner's, 1921), II 306-7.

[24] Usually it is thought to come from מָשַׁךְ, "draw/pull." Cf. 41:1[40:25]; Hos 11:4.

[25] Vulgate has *luciferum* (i.e. "Lucifer"), literally "light bearer," a name for Venus, the morning star, assuming מַזָּרוֹת is related to זָהַר, "brightness" (Ezek 8:2; Dan 12:3). G. Ewald, *The Book of Job*, trans. J. F. Smith (London: Williams & Norgate, 1854), translated it "crown," and Dhorme, "Corona," connecting it with מִנְזָר, (cf. Nah 3:17, KJV).

[26] J. Hartley, *Job*.

[27] Instead of "her children" NASB has "her satellites"!

[28] Its spelling, עַיִשׁ, is a variant of the form in 9:9, עָשׁ. See comments there.

[29] For discussion see Pope, *Job*, 301. "Lion" is Jastrow's choice for line *b,* and "Dippers" for line *a.*

38:33 The Lord declared in Isa 55:9, "As the heavens are higher than the earth, so are my ways higher than your ways." Likewise no mortal knows "the laws of the heavens," either in the astronomical sense or in the theological sense. The NIV has chosen to add "God" in brackets, but the antecedent of "his/its/their" on "dominion" is uncertain. It is a matter of small consequence. The question confronted Job with the truth that he had nothing to do with the administration of the earth. It is under divine or heavenly jurisdiction.

(8) Clouds (38:34-38)

> ³⁴"Can you raise your voice to the clouds
>   and cover yourself with a flood of water?
> ³⁵Do you send the lightning bolts on their way?
>   Do they report to you, 'Here we are'?
> ³⁶Who endowed the heart with wisdom
>   or gave understanding to the mind?
> ³⁷Who has the wisdom to count the clouds?
>   Who can tip over the water jars of the heavens
> ³⁸when the dust becomes hard
>   and the clods of earth stick together?

The passage is not strictly about clouds but about controlling the weather, a theme encountered in Elihu's preamble to the theophany (37:15-16). Neither the clouds nor the rain nor the lightning were Job's responsibility. The implication of this section and of the entire speech is that God is in charge of the universe, not mortals like Job. From the remote constellations to the day-by-day changes in the weather, it is all God's doing. *How, why, when,* and *where* are questions subordinate to *who.* In dozens of ways God was saying, "I, Job, not you."

38:34 The first question asked whether Job commanded "the clouds," and not whether he had a strong voice. Line *b* is identical to 22:11b but in this context asked Job if he could call down the rain. The verse follows closely the sense of v. 33, which pointed to the fact that God rules in heaven and on earth.

38:35 In chap. 36 the author of the book had Elihu answer many of the questions in chap. 38. So the matter of ordering the clouds to release their rain was found in 36:28, and the charge to the lightning, in 36:32; 37:3.[30] Just a touch of humor graces the second line, which perhaps hint-

---

[30] For all the times "lightning" occurs (seven in chaps. 36–38), this is the only occurrence of the standard word for it, בָּרָק.

ed to Job that Yahweh was approaching him on friendly grounds, intending to put him in his place but to do it gently.

38:36 One crucial and unknown word in each line of v. 36 has occasioned three basic interpretations of the verse.[31] The NIV agrees with most in rendering them "heart" and "mind."[32] Since the context is about "clouds," some make guesses in that sphere.[33] The third view is that these are birds known for their wisdom or ability to predict coming storms, the "ibis" and the "rooster" (JB, GNB).[34] If correct, the introduction of animals provides a bridge between the two major parts of this speech, the inanimate (38:4-38) and the animate (38:39–40:30).

38:37 The word "wisdom" links vv. 36-37 as the poet returned to the main subject of the passage, the regulation of the weather. Because clouds are so undefined, now joining together, now splitting apart, there is no way to number them. The phrase to "tip over the water jars of the heavens" is picturesque like "the windows of the heavens were opened" in Gen 7:11 (KJV, RSV, etc.).

38:38 Rain was particularly welcome after a long period of drought when the soil had turned to hardpan.[35] The welcome moisture softened the earth and prepared it for plowing and sowing. God designs both the vagaries of the weather and the prevailing annual patterns.

(9) Lions and Ravens (38:39-41)

> [39]**"Do you hunt the prey for the lioness**
> **and satisfy the hunger of the lions**
> [40]**when they crouch in their dens**
> **or lie in wait in a thicket?**

---

[31] See NIV footnote.

[32] On this view the first word, טֻחוֹת, which is found elsewhere only in Ps 51:6[8] ("inner parts"), parallel to סָתֻם ("inmost place") is read as "heart." The second word, שֶׂכְוִי, is derived from שָׂכַךְ ("cover"), which occurs only in Exod 33:22, but a biform of the more frequent סָכַךְ.

[33] BDB suggested "cloud layers" for the former and merely reviewed choices for the latter, 376, 967. Moffatt has "feathery clouds" and "meteors." RV and ASV margins have "dark clouds" and "meteor." RSV has "clouds" and "mists." NRSV, however, changed to "inward parts" and "mind."

[34] NAB skipped v. 36. For support for the birds see J. Hartley, *Job*, 501, n. 9. The picture of a cock on an eighth century B.C. cylinder seal from Nimrud is mustered for support by O. Keel, "Zwei kleine Beiträge zum Verständnis der Gottesreden im Buch Hiob (xxxviii 36f., xl 25)," *VT* 31 (1981), 220-25. For reasons spelled out in M. Pope, *Job* 302, transliterated them as the names of two Egyptian deities, "Thoth" and "Sekwi."

[35] Two of the three words in the first stich are from יָצַק, "pour" as clay into a brick mold. מוּצָק was "frozen" in 37:10 because there the hardened substance was water.

^{41}Who provides food for the raven
   when its young cry out to God
   and wander about for lack of food?

Beginning with v. 39 God took Job on a guided tour of his menagerie, pointing out to him those species that were especially wild, rare, or remote. The questions continue, not to demean Job but to glorify God. The first stanza, unlike the others, deals with two animals whose search for food has occasioned this grouping.

38:39 Lions may do their own hunting, but there is a sense in which God provides for them, giving them the necessary skills of stealth and strength to "hunt the prey" and to "satisfy their hunger" or literally to "fill their life" (Ps 104:21). There are enough references to lions in the Old Testament to indicate that they were widespread. The several synonyms for "lion" (cf. 4:10-11) may indicate varieties akin to African and Persian subspecies.[36]

38:40 The two lines may be parallel and speak of the way lions catch their prey, or they may contrast life in the lair with that of prowling for victims. In neither place would any man or woman want to be because lions eat people as well as other animals.

38:41 Since it was obvious that Job did not feed the lions, God next asked him if he "provided food for the raven," another animal whose feeding habits are totally foreign to those of humans (Ps 147:34; Luke 12:24).[37] The "young cry out to God," not to Job. Most commentators ignore the third line that depicts the young wandering about. In most animal families it is the parents who search for food,[38] and if parents did not provide, the young would starve. This seems to be God's point. The young ravens are incapable of feeding themselves apart from God's provision of inherited behavioral traits in their parents.

---

[36] For a succinct discussion of these and each of the animals in the following chapters, see *Fauna and Flora of the Bible* (London: UBS, 1972). It also contains a large but dated bibliography.

[37] The root צוד is behind the verb "hunt" in v. 39 and the noun "food" in v. 40. It is also in the name of the Galilean village of Bethsaida, which might be translated "Huntsville" or "Fishtown."

[38] The NEB fits all the ideas into two lines, the second of which reads, "When its fledglings croak (*sic*) for lack of food?" Without adopting any of them, Gordis (*Job*, 454-55) discusses a variety of explanations. One of the most attractive is to eliminate "raven" altogether by repointing the consonants as "evening," עֶרֶב. Thus it is the young lions who "cry out to God and wander about" as in 4:11.

(10) Mountain Goats (39:1-4)

¹"Do you know when the mountain goats give birth?
  Do you watch when the doe bears her fawn?
²Do you count the months till they bear?
  Do you know the time they give birth?
³They crouch down and bring forth their young:
  their labor pains are ended.
⁴Their young thrive and grow strong in the wilds;
  they leave and do not return.

"Mountain goats" are the subject of the first stanza of chap. 39, with particular emphasis on birth of their offspring. These elusive animals that seem to float gracefully over the roughest of terrain kept themselves far from any human eyes as they brought forth their young. In those days, before the scientific investigation of fauna and the persistent and prying eyes of biologists' cameras, these intimate details of the natural order were off-limits and unknown to people.

39:1 Two terms identify this animal, "mountain goats" and "does."[39] This is the ibex, whose pictographs are found in desert caves and that still roams in small herds around En Gedi ("Spring of the Goats") on the western edge of the Dead Sea and in other desert places.[40] Of course, Job did not "know when they give birth" and had never "watched the does bear."[41] The second line of v. 2 is almost identical to the beginning of v. 1, which has prompted some to eliminate "time" and/or "give birth" from the first verse.[42]

39:2 Just as the place of birth was unknown to the man from Uz, so the time of gestation and delivery were concealed from him. All the verb forms in vv. 2-3 are feminine, indicating, as would be expected, that the

---

[39] The first, יַעֲלֵי, occurs twice more in the masc. (1 Sam 24:2[3]; Ps 104:18) both in the context of "rocks" or "mountains." A fem. form is in Prov 5:19. The second, אַיָּלוֹת, is the fem. pl. of the very common אַיִל, "ram" or domestic male goat (42:8). Our word is apparently the female of a number of species, domestic and wild. Surely shepherds had seen the goats and sheep of their own flocks give birth. The "ibex" and "mountain sheep" of Deut 14:5 translates דִּישֹׁן and זֶמֶר, respectively. Neither word occurs elsewhere.

[40] *Fauna and Flora* identify it as *Capra ibex nubiana* or Nubian ibex (p. 46). Cf. G. S. Cansdale, "Ibex," *ZPEB* 3:238. A. Danin, " 'Do You Know When the Ibexes Give Birth?' " *BARev* 5 (1979): 50-51.

[41] The mother goats are plural, and "fawn" is not in the text, just the verb חלל, "writhe in labor."

[42] So G. Hölscher, *Das Buch Hiob*, E. J. Kissane, *The Book of Job* (New York: Sheed & Ward, 1946), Driver and Gray, *Job*, Dhorme, etc. The LXX lacks all of 39:1a.

poet had mother goats in mind.[43]

39:3 The NIV is paraphrased because the first line consists of three verbs: they crouch; they bring forth; they open up. Some maintain that the second line should more closely parallel the first and read something like "they send out their young" (RSV, AB, NAB, NEB, GNB, NJPS).[44] Others move "in the wilds" from v. 4a into v. 3b (AB, JB, NAB) thus balancing out those lines with three major words in each.

39:4 The cycle of life is complete for all animals when the young are independent of the parents. The baby mountain goats born just in the preceding verse are now pictured grown and gone. Verses 3-4 are not questions but a commentary on the four questions of vv. 1-2.

(11) Wild Donkeys (39:5-8)

> [5]"Who let the wild donkey go free?
>   Who untied his ropes?
> [6]I gave him the wasteland as his home,
>   the salt flats as his habitat.
> [7]He laughs at the commotion in the town;
>   he does not hear a driver's shout.
> [8]He ranges the hills for his pasture
>   and searches for any green thing.

In this segment God asked two parallel questions about the wild donkey and then proceeded to answer them in the next verse. As in the verses dealing with the mountain goat, the latter two form a commentary. The questions of vv. 1-2 had to do with when; these have to do with where.

39:5 The "wild donkey" appears ten times in the Old Testament, four of them in Job (6:5; 11:12; 24:5; and here).[45] Most of the contexts include something about the lonely and desert life it leads.[46] This passage is the classic one that speaks of the wild donkey's freedom. Yahweh asked Job who "untied his ropes" and let him "go free," a ridiculous

---

[43] In v. 3 a number of Hebrew manuscripts have the expected fem. possessive pronoun on "their labor pains," but the Masoretic text has חֶבְלֵיהֶם.

[44] This involves reading חֶבֶל not as "cord" or "pain" but "firstborn," as a metathesized form in Gen 4:4. See Tur-Sinai, *Job*, 540; חבל II in KB, 272.

[45] The term in line *a* is פֶּרֶא, a masculine form as it is everywhere else. The synonym of line *b*, עָרוֹד, is a hapax in the Hebrew Bible, but known in Aramaic (Dan 5:21). Numbers 21:1 is a play on the place name "Arad" and its king "who lived in the Negev" where the *ʿārôd* lived. See M. Jastrow, *Dictionary of Talmud Babli, Yerushalmi, Midrashic Literature and Targumim* (New York: Pardes), II:1114.

[46] Gen 16:12; Ps 104:11; Isa 32:14; Jer 2:24; 14:6; Hos 8:9.

question, that is, one aimed to ridicule Job.

39:6 The answer is God—he is the one who assigns all animals and nations their lots.[47] The "house" and "home" of the wild donkey was the *'ărābâ*, a word still used for the depression that extends from the Dead Sea to the Gulf of Aqaba, and the root behind the name Arabia. "Salt flats" even more points to the Dead Sea, which in the Bible is always called "Salt Sea" (Gen 14:3 and at least eight other places).

39:7 Another touch of humor is found here, as Job was asked to imagine the wild donkey's freedom from urban bustle and independence from orders that teamsters shouted at his domestic counterparts.[48]

39:8 In contrast to "the town" (v. 7), the donkey lives off the pasturage of "the hills." The price to pay for freedom from field work is the tough task of constantly foraging for food. Some people have chosen this way of life.

(12) Wild Oxen (39:9-12)

> ⁹"Will the wild ox consent to serve you?
>   Will he stay by your manger at night?
> ¹⁰Can you hold him to the furrow with a harness?
>   Will he till the valleys behind you?
> ¹¹Will you rely on him for his great strength?
>   Will you leave your heavy work to him?
> ¹²Can you trust him to bring in your grain
>   and gather it to your threshing floor?

Unlike the other sections in this chapter, this one consists entirely of questions, seven in all, as the NIV has translated it. As in the preceding pericope, the Lord contrasts the wild animal with its domestic cousin, asking Job if he could tame, harness, and render profitable for service these elusive and unruly beasts. Again one senses a smile on God's face as he made these preposterous propositions.

39:9 The seven passages where the "wild ox" appears outside of vv. 9-10 allude in some way to the strength of this animal.[49] It is a very large

---

[47] Grammatically speaking the verse is a relative clause that begins with אֲשֶׁר, "whose/which/when." See KJV, RSV, NEB, NASB, NJPS.

[48] This verse, like some I have pointed out and many I have not, is chiastically arranged in Hebrew with the verbs in the first and last positions and the objects in the interior positions.

[49] Num 23:22; 24:8; Deut 33:17; Pss 22:21[22]; 29:6; 92:10[11]; Isa 34:7. Usually it is spelled רְאֵם but here רֵים.

bovine with large pointed horns.[50] This is the term the KJV rendered the mythical "unicorn," with "rhinoceros" in the margin.[51] It is ludicrous to think that it would renounce its freedom to spend the night confined in "your manger."

39:10 Equally unimaginable was the prospect that this mighty creature would submit to a harness to plow or harrow the lowland "valleys" where the best soil was deposited. "Behind you" makes sense when plowing was a two-person operation—one to lead the ox and one to lean on the plow. It would take great courage or foolhardy trust to walk in front of a wild horned bull even if it were pulling a plow.

39:11 The farmers of the ancient Middle East must have coveted the strength of the wild ox because all that power could do the hardest tasks if only it could be subdued and disciplined. Unfortunately it could not be trusted but with its ferocious strength probably would damage and even kill.

39:12 The verse starts just as v. 11 did, with a synonym for "rely," "trust."[52] Domestic donkeys carried their loads in saddlebags, and oxen drew sleds or wagons, but the thought of a wild ox doing these chores was incredible.

(13) Ostriches (39:13-18)

[13]"The wings of the ostrich flap joyfully,
   but they cannot compare with the pinions and feathers of the stork.
[14]She lays her eggs on the ground
   and lets them warm in the sand,
[15]unmindful that a foot may crush them,
   that some wild animal may trample them.
[16]She treats her young harshly, as if they were not hers;
   she cares not that her labor was in vain,
[17]for God did not endow her with wisdom
   or give her a share of good sense.
[18]Yet when she spreads her feathers to run,
   she laughs at horse and rider.

---

[50] B. Clark argues convincingly that this is the almost extinct oryx or *oryx leucoryx*, a 1300 B.C. pictograph of which is on a cliff in the Timna Valley ("The Biblical Oryx—A New Name for an Ancient Animal," *BARev* 10,5 [1984]: 66-70).

[51] It is "*Bos primigenius*, which in ancient times was hunted by Assyrian kings. The Akkadian word *rlmu* undoubtedly stands for the arochs, or wild ox" (*Fauna and Flora*, 63).

[52] "Your grain" is in the second line in Hebrew despite the Masoretes' *athnach* under it. As the NIV and most others have scanned the lines, this imbalance is not obvious.

The poet moved from one of the scariest of wild animals to one of the silliest, the ostrich.[53] "This comical account suggests that amid the profusion of creatures some were made to be useful to men, but some are just there for God's entertainment and ours."[54] There are no questions in this section, simply descriptions of this large, flightless bird that seems negligent in the raising of her young.[55] Perhaps Job once stumbled upon an abandoned ostrich egg.

39:13 Only one of the six major Hebrew words in this verse appears more than six times, which means that the translation is tentative. "Ostrich" translates rĕnānîm, which looks like "songs" or "singers" but is understood as "screechers," that is, "ostriches."[56] The flapping of its stubby wings with their dull and mottled feathers is the male's courting gesture. "Stork" is ḥăsîdâ, a feminine form of the well-known word meaning "love/faithfulness/mercy,"[57] but the meaning "stork" is established by the other five occurrences in the Old Testament.[58] Of all the other birds the poet could have chosen, he selected the one whose name means "the kindly one" to contrast with the ostrich, who is depicted in the following verses as unloving.[59]

39:14 These details and those that follow confirm the translation "ostrich" in v. 13. Though this huge bird no longer inhabits the steppe north of Arabia, it was much more prevalent in biblical times. Possibly they were bred, and certainly they were hunted.[60] They lay their camouflaged eggs in the sand.

39:15 The ostriches' enemies are other animals and human hunters. Since the eggs have thick shells, they usually survive their abandonment

---

[53] The entire six verses are missing from LXX. For a thorough discussion of the vocabulary and interpretations of this passage see H.-P. Müller, "Die sog. Straussenperikope in den Gottenreden des Hiobbuches," ZAW 100 (1988): 90-105.

[54] Andersen, Job, 281.

[55] Driver and Gray (Job) wish to prefix an interrogative ה in order to make this section correspond to the question format of the others. Hartley (Job) makes them questions without discussing the addition of the particle.

[56] "The male ostrich has a strange voice. It gives a deep roar like that of a lion, but with a strange hissing sound" (R. A. Paynter, Jr., "Ostrich," in The World Book Encyclopedia [Chicago: Field Enterprises Educational Corporation, 1976], 14:660).

[57] Hence ASV, "But are they the pinions and plumage of love?" The NKJV has "kindly stork."

[58] An altogether different rendering of this line eliminates any mention of other birds. So Pope (Job), followed by Hartley (Job), has, "her pinions lack feathers."

[59] For more treatments of the difficulties of this line, see Driver/Gray and Gordis.

[60] G. S. Cansdale has assembled many facts about this bird including that it was kept in Egyptian zoos prior to 2000 B.C. See "Ostrich," ZPEB 4:551-52, and his Animals in Bible Lands (Exeter: Paternoster, 1970), 190-93.

in the sand. Mostly the male does the incubating, sitting on them through the night and some of the day. The females of his harem share the same nest and take turns sitting on it during the day, but still there are times when the eggs are unattended. The verse may also refer to the fact that when danger approaches ostriches flee, hoping to lure predators away from their eggs.

39:16 Verse 16 expands on the preceding by noting again the lack of maternal concern that the ostrich has toward her young (cf. Lam 4:3). Several hens deposit eggs in the same nest, so most of them are "not hers." "She cares not" is one of two major ways to translate the phrase at the end of the verse. Many read "fear" rather than "concern," both within the range of meanings of *pāḥad*.[61]

39:17 The positive verb "made her forget" or "deprived her" is put negatively in the NIV, "did not endow," thus making it correspond better to the negative in the second line. Though the Lord is speaking, he refers to himself in the third person, a practice found throughout the Old Testament, particularly by the psalmists who alternate between "he" and "you" when referring to God. The ostrich was considered stupid because she apparently abandons her eggs and also because when cornered and unable to run away, she lowers her head,[62] though does not put it into the sand as is widely believed.

39:18 Before the section closes, the poet added one positive point about the ostrich, as if to the balance the several negative ones. This large (up to three hundred pounds), long-legged bird, who when running makes steps fifteen feet apart, and reaches speeds of forty miles per hour, can outrace a horse. The meaning of the expression "spread her feathers to run" is uncertain.[63] The running ostrich is the second of four animals in these chapters that "laughs." The others are the wild donkey (v. 7), the horse (v. 22), and the leviathan (41:29[21]). The mention of the horse prompted the next stanza, which deals with the only domesticated animal in the list.

(14) Horses (39:19-25)

[19]"Do you give the horse his strength

---

[61] So KJV, RV, ASV, RSV, NRSV. AT's "anxiety" is a good compromise.

[62] G. Wyper, "Ostrich" in *ISBE*, 3:620.

[63] This hapax (תַּמְרִיא) usually is interpreted in light of Arabic *mara'*. So Driver and Gray, *Job*; A. Guillaume, *Studies in the Book of Job* (Leiden: Brill, 1968), 134, but Gordis reads it as a metathesized form of אָמִיר, "go aloft," as in Isa 17: 6,9 (NIV "branches/undergrowth"!).

or clothe his neck with a flowing mane?
20Do you make him leap like a locust,
    striking terror with his proud snorting?
21He paws fiercely, rejoicing in his strength,
    and charges into the fray.
22He laughs at fear, afraid of nothing;
    he does not shy away from the sword.
23The quiver rattles against his side,
    along with the flashing spear and lance.
25At the blast of the trumpet he snorts, 'Aha!'
    He catches the scent of battle from afar,
    the shout of commanders and the battle cry.

The horse of this pericope is strong, fearless, and anxious to do battle, clearly a warhorse. Domestication of horses predates the second millennium B.C., so this reference does not preclude dating the book early. Genesis 47:17 is the earliest biblical reference to horses, in connection with Joseph's administration of Egypt's resources. Throughout the biblical period, horses were mainly the possessions of royalty and served in their armies. They were not used for farming and not listed among Job's holdings.

39:19   The rhetorical question format is resumed with the appropriate interrogative particles beginning vv. 19-20. The point is that God gives "the horse his strength." "Flowing mane" translates a word whose root, r'm, means "thunder" (so KJV). Most guess that it has to do with the shaking/quivering on the neck of a horse running or tossing its head.[64] In any case Job was not responsible for it.

39:20   To "leap like a locust" is hyperbole, but considering the size of a horse compared to a grasshopper, such leaping was impressive.[65] Horses and locusts are compared in Jer 51:27; Joel 2:4; Rev 9:7. "Snorting" occurs elsewhere only in Jer 8:16.

39:21   To translate "fiercely" rather than "in the valley" like most translations, the NIV read a different verb that coordinates better with "in his strength."[66] "In the valley" can be explained by the fact that armies

---

[64] AT has "power"; RSV, AB, "strength"; NAB, "splendor" but most simply "mane."

[65] "Leap," *hiphil* of רעשׁ, "shake/quake," is another term that harks back to the meteorological section (chap. 38) even though it does not appear there.

[66] Ugaritic has an עמק II meaning "strength," as pointed out with documentation by A. C. M. Blommerde, *Northwest Semitic Grammar and Job* (Rome: Pontifical Biblical Institute, 1069), 135. The AB, AAT, NJPS, NRSV, Gordis, N. Habel, *The Book of Job*, OTL (Philadelphia: Westminster, 1985) understand this meaning also, but the traditional "valley" is kept by G. Fohrer, *Das Buch Hiob* (Gütersloh: Mohn, 1963) 490, 494; L. L. Grabbe, *Comparative Philology and the Text of Job* (Missoula, Mont.: Scholars Press, 1977), 124-46; Hartley, *Job*, 511. Although the NIV followed the Masoretic scansion rather than that of *BHS*, putting בְּכֹהַ in the second stich helps to balance the verse.

generally camped in valleys (e.g., Judg 7:1; 1 Sam 17:2). This spirited horse is eager to confront the enemy (Jer 8:6).

39:22 The horse's attitude is one of courage, even recklessness. Here is a good example of where "sword" represents violence in general and warfare in particular. The mention of three more tools of war in the next verse supports the literal translation here.

39:23 The noises[67] and sights of battle do not disturb the war horse. It is not clear if these weapons are borne by his rider or refer to the clash and flash of the fray itself.[68]

39:24 "Excitement" translates the same root as "leap" in v. 20. "Frenzied" is also from a word whose basic meaning is "shake/quake." Like our expression "eat up the miles," so the charger "eats up the ground," as it races across the open plain to engage the foe. The most elementary meaning of the root *ʾāman* ("amen") is "be firm," hence "stand still" in NIV[69] rather than the derived sense of "believe" in the older versions.[70]

39:25 The "trumpet" links this with v. 24 as it prompts the horse to echo what in transliteration sounds much like the translation *heʾāḥ*. The *raʿam*, "thunder" (KJV) of the "commanders" forms an inclusio with the *raʿĕmâ*, "flowing mane" or "thunder" (v. 19, KJV). Sandwiched between the "trumpet blast" and the "commanders' shout" is the "scent of battle." All these stimuli excite the war horse to fulfill its calling and engage the enemy. Though it is not a wild animal, the horse described here is on the very edge of being out of control, so it is a suitable component in this list of creatures that should have elicited Job's wonder and respect.

(15) Hawks (39:26-30)

> ²⁶"Does the hawk take flight by your wisdom
>   and spread his wings toward the south?
> ²⁷Does the eagle soar at your command
>   and build his nest on high?
> ²⁸He dwells on a cliff and stays there at night;
>   a rocky crag is his stronghold.
> ²⁹From there he seeks out his food;

---

[67] The verb רָנָה occurs nowhere else, but most agree that it is related to the common רִנָּן, "ring/rejoice."

[68] For alternate solutions to the problems of this verse see R. Borger, "Hiob XXXIX 23 nach dem Qumran-Targum," *VT* 27 (1977): 102-5.

[69] So too Dhorme (*Job*), Hartley (*Job*), AT, RSV, MLB, NASB, GNB, NKJV, etc.

[70] KJV, RV, ASV, but also AAT, H. H. Rowley, *Job*, NCB (Grand Rapids: Eerdmans, 1976), Gordis, *Job*, and Habel, *Job* etc.

his eyes detect it from afar.
³⁰His young ones feast on blood,
and where the slain are, there is he."

The "hawk" and "eagle" are the subjects of this last segment in the catalog of animals about which Yahweh questioned Job. Because of their similarity and juxtaposition in the text, they are treated together. The "mountain goats," "wild donkeys," and "wild oxen" all had domestic counterparts. The "horse" was more or less tamed, but not exactly a part of a nomad's herd. Of the birds the "ostrich" is one of the least birdlike because it does not fly, it does not care for its young in the usual way, and it is far larger than most birds. Representing the epitome of avian animals are the "hawk" and "eagle," predators known for their keen eyesight, inaccessible nests, and marvelous flying technique. This last feature is something they do without any coaching or commanding from Job, which is the point of God's questions.

39:26 Just as "hawk" in English covers several species, so *nēṣ* in Hebrew includes falcons, true hawks, and harriers. Probably the Lesser Kestrel is indicated here because it is one of the most common migratory hawks. In the autumn it would "spread it wings toward the south," that is, to its winter home in Africa.[71]

39:27 The "eagle" is the most common bird in the Bible and includes several species.[72] Most references to it are figurative with points made about its strength (Exod 19:4; Isa 40:31), speed (2 Sam 1:23; Jer 4:13), grandeur in flight (Prov 30:19; Jer 48:40), or ability to take prey (Job 9:26; Hab 1:8) or find carrion (Prov 30:17; Matt 24:28). Here, as in Jer 49:16 and Obad 4, the point is the "soaring" and "nesting" in high, craggy, inaccessible places. Yahweh asked Job if these magnificent creatures did any of these superhuman feats at his "command," literally "mouth."

39:28 "Cliff" and "crag" translate the same word, *selāʿ*, occasionally a place name and possibly Petra in 2 Kgs 14:7.[73] "Rocky" represents *šen*, "tooth," an appropriate term for a pinnacle or pointed summit.[74] "Stronghold" is *mĕṣûdâ* in Hebrew, *maṣādun* in Arabic, and the name of Herod's bastion on a butte just east of the Dead Sea, "Masada." As the

---

[71] Cansdale, *Animals of Bible Lands*, 146-47. In modern Hebrew נץ is the name of the sparrow hawk (*accipiter nisus*) whereas the Kestrel is *falco tinnunculus*. So *Fauna and Flora*, 40.

[72] Ibid., 82-84.

[73] See P. C. Hammond, "Sela," *ISBE* 4:383.

[74] Colorado has a 14,159-foot peak named El Diente, "The Tooth."

"wild donkey" inhabited the "wastelands" and "salt flats," so the "eagle" lives where no people can go, on the "cliffs" and "crags."

39:29 Such lofty perches give the eagle a splendid view of all that is below, and in particular anything edible. The keen vision of birds in general and eagles in particular is legendary and gave rise to our terms "bird's eye" and "eagle eye." A Talmudic proverb says that a vulture in Babylon can see a carcass in Palestine.[75]

39:30 The last of the three-verse commentary following the questions completes the progression from the lofty lookout of the eagles, to their spotting food, to their feasting on the blood of the slain and feeding it to the young.[76] Both the hawk and the eagle hunt for prey and eat carrion ("road kill"),[77] which is what the last line of the chapter refers to. Jesus had this verse in mind when he said in Matt 24:28 and Luke 17:37, "Wherever there is a carcass, there the vultures will gather." The motif of birds hunting prey forms an interesting inclusio to the section on animals that began with the question, "Do you hunt the prey for the lioness?" (38:39). So ends the first interrogation, with questions that ranged from the creation of the cosmos to the coming of the early rains and from the kings of the beasts to the king of the birds. What could Job say? What can anyone say?

3. Concluding Challenge (40:1-2)

¹The LORD said to Job:

²"Will the one who contends with the Almighty correct him?
    Let him who accuses God answer him!"

40:1 Except for the phrase about the storm, this verse is identical to 38:1 and follows the formula used through the debate cycle. In those introductory verses, however, none of the friends "answered Job"; they just "replied."

40:2 Eliphaz said of Job in 4:3, "You have instructed many." Now, with the same verb, God asked Job if he intended to "correct" the Almighty.[78]

---

[75] From Cansdale, *Animals of Bible Lands*, 142.

[76] "Feast" translates the unusual hapax עָלַע, probably from לוּעַ, "swallow" (6:3, KJV) or "drink" (Obad 16).

[77] H. van Broekhoven, Jr., "Eagle," *ISBE* 2:1.

[78] The hapax יָסוֹר is best read as a verb as NIV does from the well-established root יסר. The two lines are then syntactically parallel—subject object verb; subject object verb.

4. Job's First Repentance (40:3-5)

³Then Job answered the LORD:

⁴"I am unworthy—how can I reply to you?
   I put my hand over my mouth.
⁵I spoke once, but I have no answer—
   twice, but I will say no more."

The speeches of Yahweh are in two large blocks—chaps. 38–39 and 40:6–41:34[41:26]. After each of them Job repented, here in just two verses and at the beginning of chap. 42 in five verses. Both are marked by contrition and regret that he said as much as he did, but the second and more expansive repentance contains the actual word "repent," which this one does not. Perhaps because it does not, the Lord continued the interrogation.

40:3 The formula is the same as elsewhere with the notable exception that the addressee is "the LORD."

40:4 "Unworthy" translates *qāl*, "light in weight," as opposed to *kābēd*, "heavy/worthy/honorable." With a rhetorical question of his own, Job replied that he could not answer any of the questions. In a gesture of submission and surrender he covered his mouth, the same thing the "chief men" did toward him in the good old days Job described in 29:9.

40:5 The x + 1 formula was an ancient Hebrew way of saying, "I have spoken once too many times already." The GNB reads, "I have already said more than I should." What Job had said in 9:9 came back to haunt him and confirm its truth, "Though one wished to dispute with him [God], he could not answer him one time out of a thousand." Job had outtalked Eliphaz, Bildad, and Zophar; but in the presence of God he was dumbfounded, that is, dumb and confounded.

5. The Lord's Second Introductory Challenge (40:6-7)

⁶Then the LORD spoke to Job out of the storm:
⁷"Brace yourself like a man;
   I will question you,
   and you shall answer me.

40:6 See the comments on 38:1, since it is almost the same, including, "He said," which the NIV has dropped.⁷⁹

---

⁷⁹ "Storm" has an article in 38:1 but is anarthrous in 40:6.

40:7 This verse is essentially the same as 38:3, so see the comments there.[80]

6. The Second Interrogation (40:8–41:34)

Unlike the first series of questions over creation, weather, and a variety of animals, the second interrogation opens with additional words of challenge to Job that seem to elaborate on v. 2. Then with v. 15 the Lord concentrated his discourse laced with impossible questions on two especially powerful and dangerous beasts, which have been most often identified with the hippopotamus and the crocodile.

(1) Challenge to Job's Defense (40:8-14)

> ⁸"Would you discredit my justice?
>   Would you condemn me to justify yourself?
> ⁹Do you have an arm like God's
>   and can your voice thunder like his?
> ¹⁰Then adorn yourself with glory and splendor,
>   and clothe yourself in honor and majesty.
> ¹¹Unleash the fury of your wrath,
>   look at every proud man and bring him low,
> ¹²look at every proud man and humble him,
>   crush the wicked where they stand.
> ¹³Bury them all in the dust together;
>   shroud their faces in the grave.
> ¹⁴Then I myself will admit to you
>   that your own right hand can save you.

Rather than ask more questions about nature, God now confronted Job about his not-so-veiled statements concerning divine justice and his innuendoes that God was apathetic and uninvolved in the administration of his world. After the initial questions God ordered Job to enforce the laws and punish the wicked. Only then would God relinquish to Job his role as Savior.

40:8 Phrased this way, Job surely would not have said God was unjust, but in places (e.g., 9:24) he came close to discrediting divine justice. It is also true that in oblique ways Job maintained his innocence, that is, he justified himself but never outrightly condemned God (6:29; 9:20; 13:18; 27:2). Elihu and the other three said that Job justified himself

---

[80] One minor difference not evident in the NIV is the presence of "and" before "I will question" in 38:3.

(22:3; 32:2; 35:2).

40:9 Reflecting on chap. 38, where God spoke of his creative might and control of the elements, he asked Job if there were any comparison between their "arms" and their "voices." As usual, without giving Job an opportunity to speak, Yahweh continued, not with questions but with commands.

40:10 Here begins a series of four verses containing ten imperatives,[81] commands to do things that a man might try to do, but only God can do with effectiveness. Two pairs of alliterated words make up the four attributes of God that he ordered Job to adopt for himself. "Glory and splendor" are *gā'ôn* and *gōbah*; "honor and majesty" are *hôd* and *hādār*.[82]

40:11 The book of Job has about a dozen references to the wrath of God, a feature that often precedes or accompanies punishment of the wicked. By his withering glance God can "bring low" the "proud" (2 Kgs 8:11; Isa 13:11). Now he asked Job to do the same.

40:12 Except for the synonym "humble," v. 12a is identical to v. 11b.[83] Job had complained that God did not see crime and therefore did nothing about it (12:6; 24:1-12). Now God summoned Job to look for "every proud man" and appropriately "humble him."[84]

40:13 The same root underlies the verb "bury" and the noun "grave" at the beginning and end of this verse. Having discovered, identified, and crushed the proud, Job's task was to "bury them" and "shroud their faces" with grave clothes, a strange command but suitable to the tenor of the theophany, which was to demonstrate to Job that he was not God and could not do what God does. Therefore Job should not presume on God or lay charges at his door.

40:14 The conclusion of this summons was God's willingness to terminate his role as savior and allow Job to save himself. Its intent also was to bring Job to the logical conclusion that the same God who created

---

[81] Only תִלְבָּשׁ, "clothe yourself," is not an imperative but an imperfect with imperatival force (cf. *IBHS* § 31.5).

[82] In addition to the alliteration the verse is also a chiasmus with the verbs in the first and last positions and the four attributes in the interior: A B^1 B^2 B^3 B^4 A^2.

[83] Some, following the Syriac, eliminate one or the other of these similar lines. So M. Buttenwieser, *The Book of Job* (New York: Macmillan, 1922), 151; NAB. Most understand it as intentional repetition for emphasis.

[84] This theme of God humbling the proud is very widespread in both Testaments, e.g., Ps 18:27[28]; Isa 2:11-12,17; Matt 23:12; Prov 3:34 quoted in Jas 4:6 and 1 Pet 5:5. "Crush" translates a word unique to this verse but whose meaning is established from Aramaic and Arabic. Job used דכא in 6:9; 19:2, but this "crush" is הדך. Cf. KB, 225, which gives it the meaning "tear down" based on an Arabic cognate.

and controls the universe is and must be the Savior and Lord. The prospect of having to save yourself ought to be frightening, since the possibility is nil according to other parts of the Bible (Pss 3:8; 62:2[3]; Acts 4:12; 1 Tim 2:5-6).

(2) The "Behemoth" (40:15-24)

¹⁵"Look at the behemoth,
  which I made along with you
  and which feeds on grass like an ox.
¹⁶What strength he has in his loins,
  what power in the muscles of his belly!
¹⁷His tail sways like a cedar;
  the sinews of his thighs are close-knit.
¹⁸His bones are tubes of bronze,
  his limbs like rods of iron.
¹⁹He ranks first among the works of God,
  yet his Maker can approach him with his sword.
²⁰The hills bring him their produce,
  and all the wild animals play nearby.
²¹Under the lotus plants he lies,
  hidden among the reeds in the marsh.
²²The lotuses conceal him in their shadow;
  the poplars by the stream surround him.
²³When the river rages, he is not alarmed;
  he is secure, though the Jordan should surge against his mouth.
²⁴Can anyone capture him by the eyes,
  or trap him and pierce his nose?

The hippopotamus has been the most popular identification for the "behemoth," with the elephant a distant second.[85] A few consider it an animal now extinct. Some view it as a totally mythical animal.[86] The details of vv. 17-18 do not very accurately describe the hippopotamus, but the rest of the verses do. This enormous animal lives most of its days submerged in rivers or lagoons but grazes at night, even climbing hills (v. 20) to do so. There is no doubt that hippopotami lived in the ancient Near

---

[85] B. Couroyer believes it to be a buffalo, "Qui est Béhémoth," *RB* 82 (1976): 418-45. He catalogs twenty-eight modern translations of these verses in "Le 'glaive' de Béhémoth: Job XL, 19-20," *RB* 84 (1977): 59-71.

[86] So Tur-Sinai, *Job*, 556-59; Pope, *Job*, 320-22. Rather than "mythical," E. B. Smick prefers "mythopoeic" ("Job," EBC 4:1050). For a full discussion of the history of the identification of "behemoth" and "leviathan," see Gordis, *Job*, 569-72, who contends strongly that real animals, not mythological ones, are in view.

East because in Egypt especially there are numbers of pictures and references to them.[87] The word itself is the feminine plural of a common term
for "animal" and "cattle" in particular. Even though it is feminine plural,
all the verbs describing it are masculine singular, so most presume the
form to be a plural to express intensity or excellence (v. 19). In the Hebrew Bible chap. 40 includes the first eight verses of chap. 41, which has
led some to assume the "leviathan" description begins at 40:16, leaving
only 40:15 for the "behemoth."[88]

The format does not utilize rhetorical questions as chaps. 38; 39; 41
do but is simply an invitation to observe this mighty beast that is far beyond human strength but still one of God's pets.

40:15 God invited Job to look at the "behemoth," a word merely
transliterated rather than translated into English.[89] He reminded Job it
too was a creation[90] but that it ate "grass like an ox"[91] as he did not.

40:16 The animal has remarkable strength as the poet described it in
nontechnical terms. Certainly the "loins" and "belly" of the hippopotamus
are strong.[92] "Muscles" translates a word found nowhere else in the Old
Testament, but its meaning is established from Aramaic and later Hebrew.

40:17 Those who favor the elephant would translate "trunk" rather
than "tail," as the NIV footnote indicates, because the "tail" of a hippopotamus is short and curly like a pig's, not like a "cedar" tree.[93] All the

---

[87] For a picture from the twenty-sixth dynasty from Karnak of a statue of a pregnant
hippopotamus standing on her hind legs representing Taueret, goddess of childbirth, see
F. Guirand, *Egyptian Mythology* (London: Paul Hamlyn, 1965), 110. B. Lang ("Job xl 18
and the 'Bones of Seth'" *VT* 30 [1980]: 360-61) says that Behemoth is an allusion to the
Egyptian hippopotamus god Seth because its bones too were "like rods of iron."

[88] Note the arrangement of the NEB and REV, which have 41:1-6 describing "the whale,"
their translation of לִוְיָתָן after 39:30, thus leaving 40:15–41:34 to describe "the crocodile,"
their translation of בְּהֵמוֹת. JB, NAB, NJPS preserve Hebrew verse numbering.

[89] Because it is the fem. pl. of the common בְּהֵמָה it could be translated "beasts" (Gen
2:20), "livestock" (Gen 1:24), "animals" (Gen 6:7), or "cattle" (Exod 11:5). If it is the plural of amplification, "super cow" is a suggestion. See GKC, § 124e.

[90] The phrase "which I made" militates against the view that "behemoth" is a mythical
creature.

[91] "Hippopotamus" means "horse of the river" in Greek, although that is not the LXX
translation. Actually the hippopotamus is more closely related to the pig than either the ox
or the horse. See Cansdale, *Animals of Bible Lands*, 101.

[92] Eleazar Maccabeus killed a Syrian war elephant by stabbing it from beneath the belly
(1 Macc 6:46; Josephus, *Antiquities* 12.9.4).

[93] The verb חָפֵץ usually means "desire," but its most basic sense is "extend," so possibly this verse, whose second line is also riddled with uncertain words, refers to mating.
Gordis translates the verb as "stiffen." The Syriac, Vulgate, and Targum support this view.
The Vulgate has *constringit*, "he makes erect," in line *a* and *testiculorum eius*, "his testi-
cles," פַּחְדָיו in line *b*. The KJV has "stones."

words of the second line are rare, but nearly all modern English versions agree with the NIV.

40:18 This verse too does not well describe the hippopotamus, whose bulbous and pudgy appearance hides its "bones" and "limbs." The poet intended to convey a picture of great strength. The meanings of the unknown Hebrew words of the second line are defined by the parallelism of the first and by noting Aramaic cognates.

40:19 "First" does not mean that chronologically the behemoth was the first to be created but that it is the chief or mightiest of the animals. That it is "among the works[94] of God" and has a "Maker" indicates again that this creature is not some mythological monster with whom God fought for mastery but a product of divine creation. To "approach him with his sword" is a further statement that behemoth is not stronger than God.

40:20 As with most, NIV reads the rare word *bûl* as the better known *yābûl*, "increase/produce."[95] The verse is a highly poetic way of saying that the behemoth feeds on the grassy hills. The second line adds a colorful detail to the pastoral scene.

40:21 During the day hippopotami spend much of the time submerged, except for their nostrils, eyes, and ears, which remain above the water in order to sense everything around them. They are good swimmers and prefer the sluggish swamps and marshes of the Nile and other African rivers.[96] The "lotus" occurs only here and in the next verse. R. K. Harrison explains that "the reference is to the *Zisyphus lotus* . . . a species of jujube. . . . A shrub about one and a half m. (five ft.) tall . . . It has no connection with the Egyptian lotus."[97]

40:22 This verse expands on the preceding one, adding to the "lotus"[98] and the "reed," the "poplars," a tree found near rivers throughout the Middle East.[99]

---

[94] Literally, "ways," as in KJV, ASV, NASB.

[95] Dhorme, *Job*, Gordis, *Job*, etc., read "tribute" because of a similar phrase in Akkadian and because בּוּל in 1 Kgs 6:38[37], "the month of Bul," comes in the fall when the harvest was gathered and tribute, i.e., tax, was paid. It makes little difference in the meaning of the verse.

[96] Today the greatest concentration of hippopotami are in that part of the Rutshuru River protected by the Virunga National Game Park of eastern Zaire. The sights, smells, and sounds of the adjacent lagoons filled with these mighty beasts assault the visitors' senses.

[97] R. K. Harrison, "Lotus," *ISBE* 3:173.

[98] The poet made a play on the rhyming pair, צֶאֱלִים צְלָלוֹ. The two verbs, though not adjacent, also rhyme, יְסֻכֻּהוּ . . . יְסַבּוּהוּ.

[99] W. Walker identifies this as *Salix alba*, (*All the Plants of the Bible* [New York: Harper, 1957], 234-35). Some translate it "willow."

40:23 So large and heavy is the behemoth that even when he moves away from the pools, the swift-moving current is no threat. It is hard to know if the NIV translators extended the usual meaning of the first verb from "oppress" to "rage" or emended the Hebrew.[100] Many believe that the Nile is in view here and that "the Jordan" is simply a generic word for river and the necessary parallel word in the second line. The writer might have only heard of the Nile, but he probably had seen the Jordan.[101]

40:24 Like the crocodile in 41:2, 7, 26, the behemoth eluded all measures to capture him.[102] Capturing an animal "by the eyes" is unusual, so many follow the LXX and read, "When he is on watch" (RV, NASB). Others read "eyes" as "hooks/fishhooks/rings" (RSV, NJPS, NRSV).[103] This notion of catching the behemoth leads to the next verse, which in Hebrew is not a new chapter. Hence the double set of verse numbers that follows.

(3) The "Leviathan" (41:1-34[Heb. 40:25–41:26])

¹"Can you pull in leviathan with a fishhook
  or tie down his tongue with a rope?
²Can you put a cord through his nose
  or pierce his jaw with a hook?
³Will he keep begging you for mercy?
  Will he speak to you with gentle words?
⁴Will he make an agreement with you
  for you to take him as your slave for life?
⁵Can you make a pet of him like a bird
  or put him on a leash for your girls?
⁶Will traders barter for him?

---

[100] G. Gerleman in *BHS* footnotes suggests יִפְעַשׁ, "overflows." G. Fohrer suggests a metathesis of that, יִשְׁפַע, "bedrückt/overflows; Duhm, *Buch of Hiob*, followed by Hartley, *Job*, suggests יָשֹׁק, "heranstürzt/gushes forth." The KJV made the animal the subject rather than the river with its "he drinketh up a river."

[101] For the existence of hippopotami in Palestine, Syria, and Egypt see G. J. Botterweck, "*běhēmāh*," in *TDOT* 2:17. For a picture of a five-thousand-year-old perforated hippopotamus tusk found in a cave above the Dead Sea, see B. Clark, "Animals of the Bible," *BAR*,VII:1 (1981): 34.

[102] The Egyptians did capture hippopotami, another argument to support the view that this is a literal creature.

[103] Line *a* seems a word short. "Eyes" corresponds to "nose" in line *b*, but there is no synonym for "trap." If "hooks," or the like, is read, then "nose" lacks a synonym. The word for "eye" is also the letter עַיִן, which in the oldest orthography was a circle, hence "ring" (Gordis, *Job*) or some kind of round trap or lasso.

Will they divide him up among the merchants?
7Can you fill his hide with harpoons
   or his head with fishing spears?
8If you lay a hand on him
   you will remember the struggle and never do it again!
9Any hope of subduing him is false;
   the mere sight of him is overpowering.
10No one is fierce enough to rouse him.
   Who then is able to stand against me?
11Who has a claim against me that I must pay?
   Everything under heaven belongs to me.
12"I will not fail to speak of his limbs,
   his strength and his graceful form.
13Who can strip off his outer coat?
   Who would approach him with a bridle?
14Who dares open the doors of his mouth,
   ringed about with his fearsome teeth?
15His back has rows of shields
   tightly sealed together;
16each is so close to the next
   that no air can pass between.
17They are joined fast to one another;
   they cling together and cannot be parted.
18His snorting throws out flashes of light;
   his eyes are like the rays of dawn.
19Firebrands stream from his mouth;
   sparks of fire shoot out.
20Smoke pours from his nostrils
   as from a boiling pot over a fire of reeds.
21His breath sets coals ablaze,
   and flames dart from his mouth.
22Strength resides in his neck;
   dismay goes before him.
23The folds of his flesh are tightly joined;
   they are firm and immovable.
24His chest is hard as rock,
   hard as a lower millstone.
25When he rises up, the mighty are terrified;
   they retreat before his thrashing.
26The sword that reaches him has no effect,
   nor does the spear or the dart or the javelin.
27Iron he treats like straw
   and bronze like rotten wood.
28Arrows do not make him flee;

slingstones are like chaff to him.
^{29}A club seems to him but a piece of straw;
   he laughs at the rattling of the lance.
^{30}His undersides are jagged potsherds,
   leaving a trail in the mud like a threshing sledge.
^{31}He makes the depths churn like a boiling caldron
   and stirs up the sea like a pot of ointment.
^{32}Behind him he leaves a glistening wake;
   one would think the deep had white hair.
^{33}Nothing on earth is his equal—
   a creature without fear.
^{34}He looks down on all that are haughty;
   he is king over all that are proud.

The "leviathan" is given three times as much space as the behemoth, with much more detail about its temperament and habits. Most interpreters see the crocodile[104] here although, after the discovery of Ugaritic literature with its mythical dragon called Lotan, many have assumed that a dragonlike creature is what the poet had in mind.[105] Though some of the statements are hyperbolic (vv. 18-20[10-12]), there are enough that accurately describe the features and behavior of a crocodile to make it probable that the poet had seen this creature (note the scaly skin in vv. 7, 15-17[40:31; 41:7-9]; the many sharp teeth in v. 14[6] and the fast swimming in v. 32[24]). In the middle of the chapter (vv. 10-11[2-3]) God spoke of himself in the first person as if to remind Job what this long description was about: to demonstrate that he rather than Job was master of the animals. As a mortal who could be killed by a crocodile, Job's only choice was to trust and obey Yahweh.

41:1[40:25]   Returning once again to the examination format, the first questions are on the same theme that closed chap. 40, the matter of

---

[104] Though similar, this is not the new world alligator but the *crocodylus niloticus* or Nile crocodile. That this reptile's range extended beyond the Nile is obvious from the fact that the Zerka, a stream debouching into the Mediterranean north of Caesarea, was called Crocodile River, and crocodile bones were found in the Mount Carmel caves dating from the Pleistocene period. Cansdale, *Animals of Bible Lands*, 196. "Creation research" proponents see the dinosaur when they read about leviathan. J. Morris, *Tracking Those Incredible Dinosaurs* (San Diego: CLP, 1980), 65.

[105] M. Pope, *Job*, is one of the strongest proponents of this view. Gordis (*Job*, 571-73) rejects such a view, listing five reasons and concluding the discussion with this pronouncement: "These hypotheses have the attraction of sensational novelty, but they cannot be pronounced convincing. On the contrary, there may be more genuine creativity in a reasonable exegesis that takes its departure from MT, emending sparingly and only when the grounds are decisive."

catching and subduing one of these monsters.[106] Fish are normally caught with "hook" and "line," but such a system would be totally inadequate for "pulling in the leviathan."[107]

41:2[40:26] The theme of capturing the leviathan continues with two more questions with synonyms for "hook" and "rope/cord" arranged chiastically. While "tying down his tongue" was difficult to picture in the previous verse, the figures here are reminiscent of the way fish are caught and strung together. Naturally, Job was unable and even unwilling to try to catch this creature.

41:3[40:27] God, speaking through the inspired poet, inserted humor here as he had done periodically in chaps. 38–39. It is laughable to think of a crocodile "begging for mercy" from Job or anyone else, or entreating him "with gentle words."

41:4[40:28] The silly questions continue through this and the next verse before resuming the motif of catching leviathan in v. 7[40:31]. Both halves of the verse reflect language elsewhere in the Old Testament. "Make a covenant" is, as in all other places, "cut a covenant," referring most probably to the sacrifice cut in half that accompanied such an agreement (Gen 15:10). One who agreed to be a "slave for life" (Exod 21:6) also agreed to have his ear pierced, which is perhaps the connection with this passage, since Job was asked about piercing leviathan's "jaw with a hook" (v. 2[40:26]).

41:5[40:29] Almost as if to assure us that these are not serious questions, this verse has the word "laugh/play" (*śāḥaq*), translated here "make a pet of." The same word was in 40:20. "Girls" is not the word for "daughters," so this is not a cruel reminder that Job's children are dead. A girl leading on a leash a crocodile that may weigh as much as a ton is a whimsical if not absurd scene. God was having a good time with Job.

41:6[40:30] The lines describe the scene at the fish market where buyers, sellers, and brokers came to exchange money for what others had caught. "Traders" (*ḥabārîm*) is ordinarily "bands/friends," but in this case its meaning is determined by the parallel "merchants." The first verb is also defined by the key word "merchants" at the end of the verse.[108]

41:7[40:31] Both weapons translate words found only here. The

---

[106] O. Keel points out that an Egyptian papyrus from ca. 1430 B.C. shows a crocodile with a rope to its jaw ("Zwei kleine Beiträge zum Verständnis der Gottesreden im Buch Hiob [xxxviii 36f., xl 25]," *VT* 31 [1981]: 220-25).

[107] "Leviathan" may be from the same root as Levi, לוה, and carries the basic meaning of "coil/wrap around/attach" (cf. Gen 29:34).

[108] This is כָּרָה II, not I that means "dig" or III that means "give a feast" (KJV). One of the other three occurrences of כָּרָה II is in Job 6:27, which the KJV read as "dig."

first, "harpoons," probably is related to the "barbs" of Num 33:55, which are parallel to "thorns."[109] The second is helpfully connected with the word "fish," but the word itself has no certain cognate.[110]

41:8[40:32]   The NIV exclamation point (a device unavailable in Hebrew) points to the humor of this prediction. We might add that if you "live to" remember the struggle, you will not do it again. A person single-handed and without weapons is sure to lose against a leviathan.

41:9[1]   The NIV has added "subduing" to make sense of the first line, which more literally is, "Behold, his hope is deceptive." The poet further described the invincibility of leviathan by noting its overwhelming appearance.[111] Other animals shriek or fluff their fur or feathers to frighten their attackers, but "the mere sight" of this beast makes its would-be conquerors cower.

41:10[2]   Some would change "me" to match "him" of the first line,[112] but the point of this chapter is that the God who created and controls even the wildest of animals is not one to be challenged by a mere mortal. So midway through this speech about one of the most fearsome animals, God indirectly asked whether Job really wanted to pursue his case all the way to the divine court (cf. 13:22).

41:11[3]   One of the strongest reasons for letting "me" stand in line *b* of v. 10[2] is that both halves of this verse have first person pronouns.[113] The first line only is a question, and by it God challenged Job to present his claim. Of course, now that Job had the opportunity, he did not do it. He eventually came to realize the truth of the second line, that God owns everything, including Job. He has the whole wide world in his hand, a biblical truth that reverberates from Sinai (Exod 19:5), through the Psalms (24:1; 50:12), and into the centers of Greek civilization (1 Cor 10:26).

41:12[4]   The speaker, "I," is either Yahweh or the inspired poet who announced that he "would not be silent" about the assorted excellencies

---

[109] The word here is שְׂכוֹת; the one in Num 33:55, שִׂכִּים.

[110] The other four occurrences of צְלָצַל are onomatopoeic, "locusts" (Deut 28:42; Isa 18:1), "cymbals" (2 Sam 6:5; Ps 150:5). N. Tur-Sinai (*Job*) reads the preposition as a radical letter and associates this with the Mishnaic בְּצַלְצַל, "small onions," so that his v. 31 reads, "Couldst thou stud his body with cloves, with fish-onions his head?" assuming cooks are preparing it for eating.

[111] Technically line *b* is a question as ASV, NASB, NKJV indicate.

[112] So the Targum, JB, NAB, NEB, NRSV, etc.

[113] With the change from first to third person, the first line of this verse may be quoted by Paul in Rom 11:35. This is in Paul's doxology in praise of God's scheme of salvation which he has richly provided by pure grace in Jesus Christ. As J. Murray wrote (*The Epistle to the Romans*, NICNT [Grand Rapids: Eerdmans, 1968], 107), "God is debtor to none, his favour is never compensation; merit places no constraints upon his mercy."

of the mighty leviathan.[114] They are "his limbs,"[115] "his strength,"[116] and "his graceful[117] form," subjects that fill the rest of the chapter.

41:13[5] Not addressed to Job as "can you" questions, these last three (vv. 13-14[5-6]) are the more general, "who can" variety of questions. "Bridle" translates a peculiar phrase, which literally is "with double his halter." NIV ignores the "double," whereas most others shuffle the letters of "halter" to come up with "armor/mail" and thus make it "double coat of mail."[118] Efforts to keep "double" and "halter/bridle/jaw" are in the KJV's "double bridle," the ASV's "jaws," and the NJPS' "the folds of his jowls." The point of the verse is that the leviathan has a tough hide and an untamable temper.

41:14[6] Not only is the crocodile well protected with the defensive weapon of a tough, scaly skin, but he also has offensive weapons in the form of many sharp teeth—"thirty-six in the upper jaw and thirty in the lower."[119] Students of this animal point out that the jaws can be held closed by a single human hand, but they have such enormous closing power that cattle can be dragged under water and torn apart by the reptile's numerous teeth.

41:15[7] As the NIV indicates, there is a difference of opinion on rendering the first word of the verse. Almost all commentators change "his pride" into "his back."[120] The KJV, NASB, and NJPS retain "pride." The hide of a crocodile is not really made of scales, but the texture resembles individual tiles, which the poet calls "shields."

41:16[8] This verse and the next expand on the preceding by noting that the segments of the leviathan's hide are "one to another" so that they are airtight and presumably watertight as well.

41:17[9] From the hunter's point of view the impenetrable hide of the crocodile is what keeps him from being vanquished. Those "shields"

---

[114] The Masoretes read לוֹ for לֹא, which would make the first line read, "I silenced him," or "Indeed I silenced." Then the object בַּדָּיו is read "his boastings" as in 11:3. So Pope; AAT; NCV.

[115] This unusual word occurs twice in 18:13, which helps to fix the meaning.

[116] To get this reading MT גְּבוּרוֹת must be emended to גְּבוּרָתוֹ, a change that involves only vowels, not consonants.

[117] The simplest solution to this hapax, חִין, is to understand it as a plene spelling of the common חֵן.

[118] E.g., RSV, NASB. The text has רִסְנוֹ, but סִרְיֹנוֹ is necessary for "his armor" (Jer 46:4; 51:3). The LXX supports this metathesis with its θώρακος αὐτοῦ.

[119] J. T. Marshall, *The Book of Job*, AC (Philadelphia: American Baptist Pub. Soc., 1904), 128.

[120] This involves changing גַּאֲוָה into גֵּוֹה, understanding the א as a vowel letter and not a consonant. The Greek and Latin versions support this change.

of v. 15[7] abut one another, and no weapon can find its way through the places where they join. Details like this bolster the view that an actual animal with which the ancient poet had experience is in mind, and not some mythological monster.

41:18[10]   On the other hand, this and the next verse either describe something quite fanciful or are hyperbole, to portray sunlight sparkling in the water vapor that the leviathan "snorts" or "sneezes"[121] out of his nostrils. "Rays of dawn" is a paraphrase for "eyelids of the dawn," an expression that was in 3:9. The reflection of the light in its reddish eyes makes them look like the rising sun.[122]

41:19[11]   Just as the poet saw "flashes of light" and "rays of dawn" in the preceding verse, so he saw "firebrands" and "sparks" in this verse. The lines elaborate on the "sneezing/snorting" of v. 18[10]. "Sparks" translates a unique word whose meaning is almost entirely dependent on the context.

41:20[12]   With even greater imagination, the author described the cloud of mist coming from this mighty reptile as "smoke pouring from his nostrils."[123] That, in turn, he compared to the steam from "a boiling pot." This sounds like the description of the dragon that is found in many ancient tales.

41:21[13]   As there were three verses to describe the leviathan's thick hide (vv. 15-17[7-9]), so this is the last of four verses describing the vapor expelled from his nose or mouth. As a kind of climax of exaggeration, the breath of the leviathan is not only fire itself, but it ignites "coals." According to Ps 18:8[9], "Smoke rose from Yahweh's nostrils; consuming fire came from his mouth, and burning coals blazed out of it." He is more than a match for this creature. "If the fire-breathing mouth of Leviathan can be quelled by Yahweh, the intense fulminations of Job are no threat."[124]

41:22[14]   The neck of a crocodile is short and thick giving the appearance of being very strong, which, in fact, it is. The second line of

---

[121] This word is a hapax, עֲטִישֹׁתָיו, but the root is known from the Mishna with the sense "sneeze," which Dhorme (*Job*, 636) says is onomatopoeic.

[122] So Hartley, *Job*, 532. See Rowley (*Job*, 262) for a short discussion about the crocodile's eyes representing the rising sun in Egyptian hieroglyphics and/or paintings. "Like all night animals, the crocodile has a metallic flash from the inner surface of the choroid of the eye and its eyes shimmer with a reddish appearance several feet beneath the surface of the water" (Marshall, *Job*, 128).

[123] "Nostrils" translates נְחִיר, another hapax legomenon but known from cognates in 39:20 and Jer 6:29; 8:16.

[124] Habel, *Job*, 572.

this verse is not as certain as the first, because both the subject and the verb are rare words. "Dismay"[125] literally is "dances before him."[126] The meaning must be that the crocodile exudes terror. It is dangerous, perhaps fatal, to approach him.

41:23[15] Apparently the first word describes the jowls or flabby chins of this animal.[127] Like the rest of its hide, they are "tightly joined, firm, and immovable," meaning that even in this ordinarily vulnerable spot he is well defended.

41:24[16] Though Hebrew has "heart" here, NIV and others read "chest," i.e., the area of the heart, although the verse might be an observation about the obstinate attitude of this smug creature.[128] Certainly the heart is the target all hunters aim for, but unfortunately for them, the leviathan's "heart" or "chest" is "millstone" hard.[129]

41:25[17] Where the Hebrew text is easy and the words well known, the number of interpretations is minimal, but where the original is difficult with rare words and strange grammar, the translations and explanations are maximal.[130] This latter situation prevails in this verse,[131] as a glance at a variety of English Bibles will prove. As the NIV reads the verse, it simply says that "mighty" (hunters?) are afraid when the crocodile surfaces or comes up on land. Similarly, if he splashes around in the water, they keep their distance.

41:26[18] None of the four weapons used against leviathan has any effect. "The sword" is the most common word and here is used literally.

---

[125] The only cognate of דְּאָבָה is דְּאָבוֹן in Deut 28:65. Many follow F. Cross, "Ugaritic DB'AT and Hebrew Cognates" *VT* II (1952): 163, and read דבאה, fem. of a once occurring word in Deut 33:25 that means "strength," a better parallel to the first line. The Qumran Targum, which is in good condition in this part of Job reads ילימוֹ, "his strength" (M. Sokoloff, *The Targum to Job from Qumran Cave XI* [Ramat-Gan: Bar-Ilan University, 1974], 98).

[126] דוּץ is also a hapax, but appears in Aramaic and Syrian. See Gordis (*Job*) for references. The LXX, Vulgate, and the Qumran Targum translated the similar looking רוּץ, "run." NIV "goes" follows the versions rather than the Hebrew.

[127] The once occurring noun מַפֵּל is from the verb נפל, "fall," hence those drooping parts of his flesh that are most obvious near the neck.

[128] The NIV, followed by ICB, NCV, are alone in reading "chest." Tur-Sinai, Gordis, Hartley have "breast."

[129] "Hard," יָצוּק, occurs three times in three lines, vv. 23b,24a,b[15b,16a,b].

[130] An expansion on a maxim that S. Sandmel often used in classes at Hebrew Union College is, "Where the evidence is minimal, the theories are maximal, but where the evidence is maximal, the theories are minimal."

[131] The number of emendations and translations is too great to review here. See Pope (*Job*). Throughout this section he sees the mythological Lotan of Ugaritic literature, so the "gods" (אֵלִים) of this verse are competing deities, not merely "mighty" hunters.

"The spear" is the next most common and the logical weapon to use against a dangerous animal. "The dart" and "javelin"[132] are unique to this passage, and their meanings are determined by the context.

41:27[19]   The poet alluded to the metals the weapons of the preceding verse were made from when he compared them to "straw" and "rotten wood."

41:28[20]   This is a long verse in Hebrew because "arrows" translates "son of a quiver," "slingstones" are "stones of a sling," and the predicate in the second line is "he turns into for himself." Line *a* supplements v. 26[18] with its list of offensive weapons. Line *b* supplements v. 27[19] with its comparisons to useless things—iron, bronze, and stone are merely straw, wood, and chaff to a crocodile.

41:29[21]   Yet one more analogy makes up the first line of v. 29[21]. The verb is the same as in v. 27[19], and "piece of straw" was translated "chaff" in v. 28[20]. The "club" is unknown, but "the lance" appears eight other places in the Old Testament. As pointed out earlier, this is the fourth animal to laugh at Job and all of us (cf. the wild donkey in 39:7; ostrich in 39:22; horse in 39:23).[133]

41:30[22]   No crocodile can cross the mud without "leaving a trail" because his heavy underbelly and tail with their knobby, crusty skin drag like "a threshing sledge."

41:31[23]   The NIV is a bit overtranslated because the first line reads more literally, "He boils the depths like a caldron." "Pot of ointment" translates a rare word that had cognates pertaining to the mixing of perfumes or salves. Just as such small quantities are thoroughly mixed in a pot by an apothecary (cf. 2 Chr 16:14 in KJV), so the leviathan agitates his entire pool or pond.[134]

41:32[24]   So fast does this reptile swim that the bubbles and foam left behind are like a shining path, or, in the graphic language of the NIV, "a glistening wake." His thrashing leaves the water's surface covered with froth. The English idiom "a head of foam" is similar to the "white hair" of line *b*.

41:33[25]   This and the next verse form the conclusion to this speech about the mighty leviathan. Using his favorite word for "earth" (*ʿāpār*, "dust"), the author declares the leviathan without "equal," an interesting

---

[132] The LXX has "mail" here as it did in v. 13[5]. The KJV followed that with "habergeon," an old word for a coat of mail.

[133] The verb שׂחק is also in 40:20; 41:5[40:29] translated "play" and "make a pet," respectively.

[134] ים is used of bodies of water far smaller than an ocean. The "Sea" of Galilee and the laver in Solomon's temple called "the sea" (2 Chr 4:2-6) are examples.

use of *māšāl* in its most basic meaning. Otherwise it means "proverb" (a comparison) or some other kind of speech (27:1; 29:1).[135]

41:34[26] His exalted strength of body gives the leviathan an exalted view of himself so that as he gazes on other proud creatures, he fancies himself their king.

So concludes the Lord's speeches to Job. He has said nothing about Job's case but instead discoursed on many animals over which Job had no control, especially the dragonlike leviathan, the fiercest, least domesticated, and most awesome of beasts. The overall message is that these are God's creations. They are under his control. He is the sovereign. The complementary lesson for Job was that he had no authority in these spheres. He too was a creature made by God to be submissive to his dominion. Job had more in common with leviathan, an angry creature stirring up his world, than he did with God, who effortlessly created and continues to control both Job's world and the entire cosmos.

7. Job's Second Repentance (42:1-6)

> [1]Then Job replied to the LORD:
> [2]"I know that you can do all things;
>   no plan of yours can be thwarted.
> [3]["You asked,]'Who is this that obscures my counsel without knowledge?'
>   Surely I spoke of things I did not understand,
>   things too wonderful for me to know.
> [4]["You said,] 'Listen now, and I will speak;
>   I will question you,
>   and you shall answer me.'
> [5]My ears had heard of you
>   but now my eyes have seen you.
> [6]Therefore I despise myself
>   and repent in dust and ashes."

The concluding words of Job are about half quotations of what God had said to him. This famous confession of Job has been the source of countless essays, monographs, sermons, and opinions. It is important to note that Job did not confess any overt sins such as those Eliphaz had accused him of (22:2-11) nor any covert sins as Bildad has implied (8:11-18). The text does not, in fact, specify what Job "repented" of. Most who

---

[135] The other meaning of the root מֹשֵׁל is "rule," and it is possible that, in light of "king" in the next verse, this idea was in the author's mind. The NJPS has, "There is no one on land who can dominate him."

have come this far in the book say that Job confessed a bad attitude, a touch of arrogance, or mild blasphemy. I prefer to say that he confessed that his God had been too small. He needed the theophany to remind him of the fact that the God of the universe and the Creator of all creatures is greater, grander, higher, and wiser than a mortal can imagine, much less challenge.

42:1 This verse is identical to 40:3.

42:2 Sometimes when Job said "I know" in the past, he was right (9:2; 13:18; 19:25; 21:27), and sometimes he was wrong (9:28; 10:13; 30:23). This "I know" was Job's first response to the amazing revelation of God out of the storm, his confession that God "can do all things" (Matt 19:26). Since God has done such things in the past, Job recognized in the second part of this confession that "no plan" of God in the future "can be thwarted." Job was learning the lesson Nebuchadnezzar learned centuries later (Dan 4:35):

> He does as he pleases
>   with the powers of heaven
>   and the people of the earth.
> No one can hold back his hand
>   or say to him: "What have you done?"

42:3 As the brackets indicate, the NIV understands the first line of v. 3 as a quotation of God.[136] It is very similar to 38:2, the first words of Yahweh out of the storm. Job agreed with God that he was guilty as charged. He had spoken out of ignorance of things that were beyond his ability to understand (Ps 131:1). It is a charge that would indict us all.

42:4 As in v. 3 we have another quotation of God, this time from 38:3 or 40:7.[137]

42:5 In 26:14 Job heard a faint whisper of God in the thunderstorm. Now he confessed that in addition to hearing he had also "seen" God. When Isaiah "saw the King, the LORD Almighty," he cried, "Woe to me!" Job's response in the next verse is less dramatic but equally sincere and profound.

42:6 This is one of the most important verses in the book, if not the most important. As a result of seeing God, Job "hated/despised" himself,

---

[136] So too GNB. Other English versions e.g., RSV, NASB, put in the quotation marks with no other indication of the speaker. Others eliminate the line as a misplaced duplication of 38:2. So Moffatt, NAB, NEB. The JB has a convenient solution, "I am the man who obscured," reading מִי as a relative pronoun rather than interrogative. Cf. AAT.

[137] This verse as well is skipped by Moffatt, NAB, and NEB and bracketed by AB and JB. AAT adds a "you said," but NJPS, like KJV, ASV does not even use quotation marks.

a much stronger reaction than the "unworthy" of 40:4. Then he "repented in dust and ashes," an outward demonstration of his inward contrition and the death of his own opinions.[138] He deeply regretted the presumption of his foolish words. "Repent" and "comfort" are both translations of the same word, but certainly this context expects repentance.[139] None of the arguments of his friends could elicit this response, largely because their accusations were off the mark and their logic flawed. It was not his sin that brought about the suffering as they had claimed. Nevertheless, his confrontation with the Lord did bring about a change of mind and an expansion and deepening of his knowledge of God. Most conversions come not by way of apologetics but as people see the Lord and hear him through his Word.

---

[138] A. Wolters would read the preposition עַל as עֻל, "child." "'A Child of Dust and Ashes' (Job 42,6b)," *ZAW* 102 (1990): 116-19. It is an unconvincing proposal.

[139] Usually the *niphal* is "repent," and the *piel* is "comfort." Cf. 2:11. D. J. O'Connor, however, argues for "I am consoled" even though he was still "in dust and ashes." "Job's Final Word—'I Am Consoled . . .' (42:6b)," *ITQ* 50 (1983/84): 181. W. Morrow believes that the word was chosen for its ambiguity ("Consolation, Rejection, and Repentance in Job 42:6," *JBL* 105 [1986]: 225).

VIII. EPILOGUE (42:7-17)
   1. The Lord's Response to the Friends (42:7-9)
   2. Job's Latter Prosperity (42:10-15)
   3. Job's Latter Days (42:16-17)

VIII. EPILOGUE (42:7-17)

As in the prologue, so in the epilogue many questions are unanswered. Why was Elihu not included in the indictment? What was the Satan's response to all this? Was Job's wife and mother of the first ten children also the mother of the second ten? Why is she not mentioned in v. 11? The best answer is that these details, though important to us, were not important to the author of the story. Even the particulars that are given, to some extent, turn the readers attention from the major points of the book. Just as the Book of Revelation tantalizes us with its sketchy descriptions of heaven, so this book, while answering the main question, leaves us with most of our ancillary concerns unresolved.

1. The Lord's Response to the Friends (42:7-9)

⁷After the LORD had said these things to Job, he said to Eliphaz the Temanite, "I am angry with you and your two friends, because you have not spoken of me what is right, as my servant Job has. ⁸So now take seven bulls and seven rams and go to my servant Job and sacrifice a burnt offering for yourselves. My servant Job will pray for you, and I will accept his prayer and not deal with you according to your folly. You have not spoken of me what is right, as my servant Job has." ⁹So Eliphaz the Temanite, Bildad the Shuhite and Zophar the Naamathite did what the LORD told them; and the LORD accepted Job's prayer.

42:7 The first thing the Lord did after his theophany had accomplished its intended goal was deal with Job's friends. Speaking only to Eliphaz, but including in the indictment Bildad and Zophar, he told them of his anger and charged them with misrepresenting him. Throughout the commentary we have noted things that they said that were true enough standing out of context, but as those statements pertained to the case of

Job and God, they were wrong. Then, as if to add insult to injury, God credited Job with saying what was "right" about God. The allegation against them and the commendation of Job is repeated at the end of v. 8. Most witnesses to the debate would have done the opposite, affirming the friends and charging Job. The divine judge, however, hears more than words and sees more than faces; he knows the thoughts and the intents of the heart.

42:8   As always, God made a provision so the three friends could atone for their "folly." The sacrificial animals and the number of them, seven each, represent standard procedure even though these events were prior to or outside the geographical parameters of the Mosaic law (cf. Num 23:1,29). They offered their own sacrifices, but it was Job who interceded in their behalf. How little did Eliphaz realize what a prophet he was when he spoke the words of 22:30, "He will deliver even one who is not innocent, . . . through the cleanness of your hands." If believers do not plead for sinners, who will (cf. Jas 5:15-16; 1 John 5:16)?

42:9   Now all three friends are the subject of the sentence that simply says they followed divine orders. After their acts of contrition, "the LORD accepted Job's prayer,"[1] indicating the two basic elements of conversion—turning *from* sin (illustrated by the death of the sacrificial animals) and turning *to* God (illustrated by Job's mediatory prayer).

2. Job's Latter Prosperity (42:10-15)

[10]After Job had prayed for his friends, the LORD made him prosperous again and gave him twice as much as he had before. [11]All his brothers and sisters and everyone who had known him before came and ate with him in his house. They comforted and consoled him over all the trouble the LORD had brought upon him, and each one gave him a piece of silver and a gold ring.
[12]The LORD blessed the latter part of Job's life more than the first. He had fourteen thousand sheep, six thousand camels, a thousand yoke of oxen and a thousand donkeys. [13]And he also had seven sons and three daughters.
[14]The first daughter he named Jemimah, the second Keziah and the third Keren-Happuch. [15]Nowhere in all the land were there found women as beautiful as Job's daughters, and their father granted them an inheritance along with their brothers.

The Book of Job has a happy ending. Some say it spoils the story because it proves in the end the correctness of the theology of retribution—

---

[1] Literally, "lifted up the face of Job." For comments on this idiom see 22:26.

the good man was rewarded. While that is worth considering, it is better to look at the same facts from another perspective. In the long run God really did not forsake his "servant Job," an expression used four times in the preceding paragraph. The Satan expected and hoped that he would. Even though the Satan is not mentioned in the epilogue because that was not the author's concern, the felicitous resolution of the story is also the final ignominy to him who would destroy God's servants by luring them into sin and urging them to deny their Lord. Except for the additional cattle, Job ended the book just where he had started. But in the intervening forty chapters he passed through an ordeal that changed his perspective on life and God forever. It would be a great gift if we could be in Job's position at the end of the book without going through what he did throughout the book—gain his knowledge without suffering. But it is doubtful that it can happen. It takes fire to refine gold (23:10).

42:10 Job did not pray for himself or for the restoration of his wealth; he "prayed for his friends." It was then that "the LORD made him prosperous again." Prosperity meant doubling his holdings as the arithmetic of v. 12 indicates. Job had "sown in tears" and now he "reaped with joy" (Ps 126:5).

42:11 The first to welcome Job to his restored state were his siblings and friends, presumably the ones who shunned him during the height of his trial (19:13-15). They did what the friends had originally come to do, "comfort and console/sympathize with him" (2:11). "Trouble" is rendered "evil" in the older translations, but the Hebrew word (*rāʿ*) is also the opposite of "prosperity/peace/well-being" (*šālôm*) as Isa 45:7 indicates. Either as a house warming gift or, and more likely, as a token of atonement, each "gave him a piece² of silver and a gold ring."

42:12 A comparison with 1:3 shows that the numbers of sheep, camels, oxen, and donkeys is exactly double (see comments there on the significance of these numbers).

42:13 These seven (additional) sons and three daughters "replaced" the ones who perished in the collapse of the oldest brother's house. One might ask why he did not have fourteen sons and six daughters to correspond with the doubling of his other assets. The answer is that he did: the first set, to be reunited with him when he died, and the second set, born after his tragedies and trials (cf. 2 Sam 12:23; 1 Thess 4:13; 1 Cor 15:54).

---

² Only in Gen 33:19 and Josh 24:32, books from the oldest periods, does קְשִׂיטָה, "coin/piece/weight" appear. "Silver" is not in Hebrew but is the usual complement to "gold," which is what the nose, ear, or finger "ring" was made of.

42:14   The first of two unusual features about Job's daughters appears here—their names are given, while the names of the sons are not.[3]

42:15   The second unusual feature about Job's daughters, not counting their outstanding beauty, is that they received "an inheritance along with their brothers." Ordinarily only sons shared in the father's wealth, and daughters inherited it only if they had no living brothers (Num 27:8). This is another indication that Job did not come from mainstream Israel after the time of Moses.

3. Job's Latter Days (42:16-17)

[16]**After this, Job lived a hundred and forty years; he saw his children and their children to the fourth generation. **[17]**And so he died, old and full of years.**

Contrary to all Job's wishes in chap. 3 and his subsequent fears, he lived to a ripe old age, approximating the patriarchs in longevity, and saw his great-great-grandchildren.

42:16   One hundred and forty is twice "the length of our days" that Moses mentioned in Ps 90:10. It is not clear whether Job lived 140 total, suggesting he was 70 at the time of the trial or whether he lived 70 + 140 for a total of 210. In either case the principle of doubling prevailed.

42:17   Another of Eliphaz's prophecies came to fulfillment (5:26) as Job, like Abraham, "died, old and full of years" (Gen 25:8). In accord with the hope Job had before the trial, he presumably died in his own house, his days as numerous as the proverbial grains of sand (29:18).

---

[3] The Bible makes no point of the meaning of the names, so neither should we; but Jemimah sounds like an Arabic word for "dove," Keziah comes into English as "cassia," a cinnamon-like spice made from tree bark (Ps 45:8[9]), and Keren-Happuch means "horn (i.e., bottle) of eye shadow" (2 Kgs 9:30; Jer 4:30).

Person Index

Abraham 49, 116, 198
Adam 166, 337
Adini, U. 290
Ahab 196
Ahithophel 78
Akiba, Rabbi 108
Alden, R. L. 40, 357
Alexander, C. F. 377
Alter, R. 37
Andersen, F. I. 41, 110, 124, 128, 159, 163, 168, 170, 189, 207, 208, 218, 223, 250, 257, 294, 298, 320, 369, 386

Balaam 74
Baly, D. A. 360
Barnes, A. 206
Barnes, W. E. 105
Ben Sira 299
Berlin, A. 37
Bickell, G. 376
Bishai, W. 236
Block, D. L. 140
Blommerde, A. 84, 89, 110, 128, 129, 154, 190, 222, 242, 244, 273, 347, 365, 389
Borger, R. 389
Botterweck, G. J. 398

Bowes, D. R. 271
Breneman, M. 264
Brinker, Hans 26
Brueggemann, W. 40
Bullard, R. 272, 275
Bullinger, E. W. 25
Bunyan, Paul 26
Buttenwieser, M. 309, 362, 394

Cansdale, G. 386, 390, 391, 396, 400
Casanowicz, I. M. 37
Ceresko, A. R. 296, 298, 309
Charlesworth, J. H. 67
Clark, B. 385, 398
Clark, D. J. 25
Clines, D. 71, 90, 100, 103, 105, 108, 120, 130, 132, 137, 145, 150, 154, 156, 158, 159, 163, 167, 168, 175, 189, 190, 197, 203, 204, 212, 216, 217
Coogan, M. 173
Coughenour, R. A. 271
Couroyer, B. 395
Cox, S. 166
Craigie, P. C. 122
Cross, F. M. 37
Curtis, J. B. 314

Subject Index

Selected Scripture Index